FOOD & WINE

2000

an entire year's recipes

from america's **favorite** food magazine

Roasted Asparagus with Sage and Lemon Butter (p. 275)

FOOD & WINE
2000

an entire year's recipes
from america's **favorite** food magazine

American Express Publishing Corporation
New York **FOOD & WINE** BOOKS

FOOD & WINE MAGAZINE
EDITOR IN CHIEF Dana Cowin
CREATIVE DIRECTOR Stephen Scoble
EXECUTIVE FOOD EDITOR Tina Ujlaki

FOOD & WINE BOOKS
EDITOR IN CHIEF Judith Hill
ART DIRECTOR Perri DeFino
MANAGING EDITOR Terri Mauro
DESIGNER Leslie Andersen
ASSISTANT EDITOR Dana Speers
COPY EDITOR Barbara Mateer
EDITORIAL ASSISTANT Colleen McKinney

SENIOR VICE PRESIDENT, PUBLISHER Mark V. Stanich
SENIOR MARKETING MANAGER Johanna Growney
PRODUCTION MANAGER Stuart Handelman
PRODUCTION COORDINATOR Catherine DeAngelis
OPERATIONS MANAGER Doreen Camardi
BUSINESS MANAGER Joanne Ragazzo

COVER PHOTO Beatriz Da Costa (Chipotle-Lime Broth with Chicken and Pumpkin, p. 100)
BACK PHOTOS TOP—Maura McEvoy (Oodles of Noodles with Cheese, p. 115);
BOTTOM—Amy Neunsinger (Gorgonzola Cheeseburgers with Pancetta, p. 225)

ISBN 0-916103-60-9 (hardcover)

Published by American Express Publishing Corporation
1120 Avenue of the Americas, New York, New York 10036

Manufactured in the United States of America

contents

chapters

63

117

19

Wood-Grilled Veal Chops with Tomato-Basil Salsa (p. 207)

foreword

1999

1999 was a year of millennium fever: you couldn't turn on the TV, pick up a magazine or log on-line without being bombarded by end-of-the-century predictions. What did FOOD & WINE forecast for the future?

We predicted that the most appreciated food will be the simplest and most familiar. Also, that new frontiers promise the greatest excitement. The balance of comforting classics and surprising new tastes is reflected in this collection of all the recipes published in the magazine in 1999.

Pot roast and macaroni and cheese, apple pie and devil's food cake always taste good to us. Yet many of our favorite recipes have come from far-flung places: those from Nancy Harmon Jenkins, inspired by the tenacious cooks of war-torn Beirut; the ingenious uses for black peppercorns brought to us by Maya Kaimal, direct from the spice plantations of India; dishes from winemaker dinners in France, Portugal and Argentina.

We love the experimentation going on, especially when it teaches us about ingredients that are new to us. Over the past year, we were excited by contributing editor Paula Wolfert's recipes for purslane (who knew an annoying weed could be so tasty!), FOOD & WINE test kitchen supervisor Marcia Kiesel's buffalo recipes and associate Grace Parisi's *farro* and fregola dishes.

Here's our wish for the new millennium: we hope we'll all continue to embrace the tried and true as well as the exotic and new.

Dana Cowin

EDITOR IN CHIEF
FOOD & WINE MAGAZINE

Judith Hill

EDITOR IN CHIEF
FOOD & WINE BOOKS

Apple Tarts with Candied Ginger (p. 347) with Late Harvest Riesling Ice Cream (p. 384).

Some special recipes have been marked with colorful symbols so that you can easily find the dishes that fall in the categories below. Complete lists of these recipes begin on page 400.

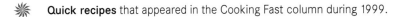

Quick recipes that appeared in the Cooking Fast column during 1999.

Health-conscious recipes that include nutritional breakdowns.

Recipes from this year's winners of the FOOD & WINE America's Best New Chefs awards.

Our annual FOOD & WINE collections are identified by the year in which each is released, rather than by the year in which the magazine issues were published. Hence this year's book, published in January of 2000, is titled 2000 FOOD & WINE and is a compilation of the recipes from the 1999 magazines.

chapter 1

hors d'oeuvres

Spicy Green Olives

Spicy Green Olives

MAKES 1½ PINTS

Bring a batch of these as a hostess gift instead of wine. The olives look beautiful in a simple mason jar with the bay leaves pressed against the glass and garlic, chiles and other seasonings scattered throughout.

- 2 teaspoons black peppercorns
- 2 teaspoons coriander seeds
- 2 teaspoons fennel seeds
- 2 teaspoons dried oregano
- 3 cups (1 pound) brine-cured green olives
- 6 garlic cloves, smashed
- 6 very small red or green chiles
- 4 bay leaves

About 2 cups extra-virgin olive oil

I. In a mortar, coarsely crush the peppercorns with the coriander and fennel seeds. Stir in the oregano.

2. Spoon half of the olives into a 1½- or 2-pint mason jar. Top the olives with half of the crushed seasonings and the garlic, chiles and bay leaves. Add the remaining olives and seasonings and pour in enough olive oil to cover. Let the olives stand for 2 hours and then add more olive oil if needed to keep the olives covered. Close the jar.

3. Let the olives marinate at room temperature for 5 days to allow the flavor to develop. —Lori De Mori

MAKE AHEAD The spicy marinated olives can be refrigerated in the jar for as long as 2 months. Let return to room temperature before serving.

Seasoned Radishes

MAKES 2 DOZEN HORS D'OEUVRES

Serve these with drinks at dinner parties. They're easy to make and don't ruin anyone's appetite.

- 12 large radishes, trimmed and halved
- 1 tablespoon plus 1 teaspoon soy sauce
- ½ teaspoon red wine vinegar

In a shallow bowl, combine the radishes with the soy sauce and vinegar and let stand at room temperature for 30 minutes, tossing occasionally. Drain the radishes and serve. —Madhur Jaffrey

Spicy Pickled Carrots and Asparagus

MAKES ABOUT 2½ CUPS PICKLED CARROTS AND 40 PICKLED ASPARAGUS

- 4 cups water
- 3 cups cider vinegar
- ½ cup sugar
- 10 thyme sprigs
- 4 garlic cloves, thinly sliced
- 1 tablespoon cracked black peppercorns
- 1 tablespoon crushed red pepper
- 1 tablespoon mustard seeds
- 1 tablespoon salt
- 1 pound large carrots, sliced diagonally ⅓ inch thick
- 2 pounds medium asparagus, trimmed

I. In a large saucepan, combine the water, cider vinegar, sugar, thyme, garlic, peppercorns, crushed red pepper, mustard seeds and salt and bring to a boil. Simmer over low heat for 10 minutes.

Remove from the heat and let cool for 5 minutes. In a wide heatproof bowl, cover the carrot slices with the pickling mixture. Let cool to room temperature.

2. In a large saucepan of boiling salted water, cook the asparagus until bright green, about 1 minute. Drain and refresh under cold water. Add the asparagus to the pickling mixture and refrigerate for 24 hours. Drain the pickles, transfer to a platter and serve. —John Currence

Chile-Honey Roasted Nuts

MAKES ABOUT 4 CUPS ✳

- ¼ cup sugar
- 1½ teaspoons salt
- ¼ cup honey
- ¾ teaspoon cayenne pepper
- 1 pound (about 4 cups) unsalted roasted mixed nuts

I. Preheat the oven to 325°. Line a rimmed baking sheet with parchment or wax paper. Lightly oil the parchment. In a bowl, combine the sugar with the salt.

2. In a large skillet, melt the honey with the cayenne. Add the nuts and stir to coat. Spread the nuts in a single layer on the baking sheet and bake for 10 minutes. Let the nuts cool slightly and then add them to the sugar-salt mixture; toss to coat. Discard the parchment and spread the nuts out on the baking sheet to cool completely. Transfer to a bowl and serve. —Grace Parisi

MAKE AHEAD The nuts can be kept in an airtight container for up to 4 days.

Pappadams

MAKES 8 PAPPADAMS

There are as many different variations of the crispy lentil bread called pappadam as there are ways to make them. South Indians pan fry them, while North Indians tend to cook them over a flame. You can also cook them in the microwave oven, but the simplest way is to put them under the broiler.

- 8 pappadams

Preheat the broiler and then arrange an oven rack as close to the heat as

Pappadams

possible. Set 1 pappadam in the center of a baking sheet. Keeping the oven door open, slide the baking sheet under the broiler. As soon as the pappadam begins to puff, after about 5 seconds, pull the baking sheet out of the oven and turn the pappadam 180 degrees. Return to the oven for about another 3 seconds, or until the pappadam is golden brown and puffed. Reserve on a wire rack and repeat with the remaining pappadams. —*Maya Kaimal*

Cracked Pepper–Nut Crackers

MAKES ABOUT 3 DOZEN
CRACKERS ✳

- 1 cup all-purpose flour
- ¾ cup salted macadamia nuts
- 1 teaspoon salt
- 1 teaspoon coarsely ground pepper
- 4 tablespoons cold unsalted butter
- 2 tablespoons water
- ¼ cup freshly grated Parmesan cheese
- 1 large egg yolk, lightly beaten with 1 tablespoon water

1. In a food processor, pulse the flour with ½ cup of the nuts, the salt and the pepper until the nuts are finely chopped. Add the butter and process until the mixture resembles fine meal. Add the water and process until the dough comes together. Shape the dough into an 8-inch log, wrap in plastic wrap and refrigerate until firm.
2. Preheat the oven to 375°. Line 2 baking sheets with parchment or wax paper. Finely chop the remaining ¼ cup of macadamia nuts and mix with the Parmesan. Cut the log into scant ¼-inch-thick slices and arrange them on the prepared baking sheets. Brush the slices with the egg wash and sprinkle with the Parmesan mixture. Bake the crackers for about 17 minutes, or until golden brown. Let cool on the baking sheets. Transfer the crackers to a large plate and serve. —*Grace Parisi*
MAKE AHEAD The crackers can be kept in an airtight container for 3 days or frozen for up to 1 month.

Easy Cheddar Wafers

MAKES ABOUT 4 DOZEN WAFERS

- ½ pound (about 2 cups) sharp Cheddar cheese, grated
- 4 tablespoons unsalted butter, softened
- ¾ teaspoon celery seeds
- ½ teaspoon Worcestershire sauce
- ¼ teaspoon dry mustard
- ¼ teaspoon Tabasco sauce
- ⅛ teaspoon cayenne pepper
- 1 cup all-purpose flour
- 1 teaspoon kosher salt

1. In a standing mixer or food processor, beat the Cheddar cheese, butter, celery seeds, Worcestershire, dry mustard, Tabasco and cayenne on medium speed or process until smooth. Add the flour and beat on low speed or process until combined. Gather the dough into a ball and knead a few times on a lightly

floured surface. Shape the dough into a 12-inch log, wrap in plastic and refrigerate until firm.
2. Preheat the oven to 350°. Sprinkle 2 baking sheets with the kosher salt. Slice the log ¼ inch thick and arrange the slices 1 inch apart on the baking sheets. Bake for about 20 minutes, or until the wafers are lightly browned on the bottom and around the edges. Transfer the wafers to a wire rack to cool before serving. —*Martha McGinnis*
MAKE AHEAD The wafers can be stored in an airtight container at room temperature for up to 1 week.

Soppressata Cheese Sticks

MAKES 5 TO 6 DOZEN
CHEESE STICKS ✳

- 4 ounces sliced soppressata or other spiced Italian salami, chopped
- ¼ cup freshly grated Pecorino cheese
- ½ tablespoon Dijon mustard
- 1½ teaspoons water
- 1 pound puff pastry, preferably all-butter, chilled
- 1 large egg yolk, lightly beaten with 1 tablespoon water
- ¼ cup sesame seeds (optional)

1. Line 2 large rimmed baking sheets with parchment or wax paper. In a food processor, work the soppressata with the Pecorino, mustard and water to a fine paste. Transfer the paste to a bowl.
2. On a lightly floured work surface, roll out the puff pastry ⅛ inch thick. Spread the soppressata paste evenly over the bottom half of the dough, leaving a ¼-inch border on the sides. Fold the top half of the dough over to cover the paste and press the edges to seal. Using a rolling pin, lightly press the top and bottom together. Slide the puff pastry onto one of the lined baking sheets and chill until firm.

CLOCKWISE FROM FRONT: Easy Cheddar Wafers, Chocolate Chip Macaroons (p. 353) and Raspberry-Almond Bars (p. 355).

3. Roll out the pastry a scant ⅛ inch thick and cut into 3 long 6-inch wide strips. Working with 1 strip at a time and keeping the others refrigerated, trim the pastry to a neat rectangle. Brush with the egg wash and sprinkle with one-third of the sesame seeds. Cut the dough crosswise into ¼-inch-wide sticks and arrange them ½ inch apart on the prepared baking sheets. Refrigerate until chilled.

4. Preheat the oven to 375°. Bake the cheese sticks for about 16 minutes, or until golden and crisp, shifting the pans halfway through baking. Serve warm or at room temperature. —*Grace Parisi*

MAKE AHEAD The baked sticks can be kept in an airtight container for up to 4 days or frozen for up to 2 weeks. Re-crisp the sticks in a 350° oven.

Soppressata Cheese Sticks

Grilled Bread

MAKES 4 TOASTS

This simple method for smoking thick slabs of peasant bread re-creates the satisfying flavor and the crisp texture of bread grilled over a wood fire. Serve the grilled bread, topped or not, as an hors d'oeuvre, or pair it with soups, stews or salads. It's also delicious topped with Gruyère, Cheddar or fresh mozzarella for a smoky grilled cheese sandwich. Add the cheese after you turn the slices halfway through toasting.

4 slices coarse peasant bread, cut
    ½ inch thick
1 tablespoon extra-virgin olive oil
½ tablespoon wood chips
1 garlic clove
Kosher salt

Brush the bread on both sides with the oil. Line a 10-inch cast-iron skillet with foil. Tear a ½-inch hole out of the center of the foil. Line the skillet lid with foil. Set the skillet over moderate heat until hot, about 5 minutes. Add wood chips (see How to Pan Smoke, p. 184) to the center of the skillet and set a round wire cake rack with 1-inch feet in the pan (see Note). When the chips begin to smoke, arrange the bread on the rack. Cover with the lid and toast until golden, 3 to 4 minutes per side. Rub the bread with the garlic, sprinkle with kosher salt and serve. —*Sally Schneider*

NOTE If you don't have a footed cake rack, roll foil into 5 tight 1-inch balls and place them under the edge of the rack.

ONE TOAST Calories 100 kcal, Total Fat 4.3 gm, Saturated Fat .7 gm

Grilled Zahtar Bread with Tomatoes

MAKES 4 TOASTS

Zahtar is a Middle Eastern spice mixture that includes summer savory, thyme, sesame seeds and a pinch of ground sumac.

4 large slices coarse peasant bread
Extra-virgin olive oil
4 teaspoons *zahtar* (see Note)
Salt and freshly ground black pepper
Crushed red pepper
Diced beefsteak tomatoes

Light a grill. Generously brush the bread with olive oil and sprinkle each slice with 1 teaspoon of the *zahtar*. Season with salt, black pepper and crushed red pepper. Grill the bread over a medium-hot fire, turning once, until the slices are nicely browned and crisp, 1 to 2 minutes per side. Top with diced tomatoes and serve. —*Steven Raichlen*

NOTE *Zahtar* is available at Middle Eastern markets and specialty food shops. You can order it by mail from Penzeys Spices (414-679-7207).

WINE These savory toasts need nothing more complicated than a glass of crisp white wine. Select a Washington State Chardonnay, such as the 1997 Columbia Crest or the 1997 Hogue.

Roasted Vegetable Bruschetta

8 SERVINGS

You won't be able to eat all the vegetables piled on the toasts in one bite. Some of them, such as the pieces of corn on the cob, will need to be removed from the bruschetta and eaten on their own.

8 large slices peasant bread, cut ½ inch thick from a round loaf
¼ cup plus 2 tablespoons olive oil, plus more for brushing
2 garlic cloves—1 whole, peeled, and 1 minced
2 teaspoons chopped rosemary
1 teaspoon sugar
2 large ears of corn, each cut crosswise into eight 1-inch rounds
1 large russet potato (¾ pound), peeled and cut crosswise into sixteen ¼-inch rounds
1 sweet potato (¾ pound), peeled and cut crosswise into sixteen ¼-inch rounds
1 yellow squash (½ pound), cut crosswise into sixteen ¼-inch rounds
1 red bell pepper, cut into 16 strips
1 yellow bell pepper, cut into 16 strips
4 large scallions, halved lengthwise and crosswise
Salt and freshly ground black pepper
½ ounce thinly shaved Parmesan cheese

1. Preheat the oven to 425°. Brush the bread on both sides with oil. Arrange the slices on a large baking sheet; toast in the oven until golden brown. Rub the toasts with the whole garlic clove.

2. In a very large bowl, combine the ¼ cup plus 2 tablespoons of olive oil with the rosemary, minced garlic and sugar. Add the corn, potatoes, squash, bell peppers and scallions to the bowl and toss well to coat. Season generously with salt and black pepper.

3. Spread the corn and potatoes on 1 large baking sheet and the squash, bell peppers and scallions on another. Bake the squash, peppers and scallions for about 20 minutes and the corn and potatoes for about 30 minutes. The vegetables are done when they are tender and lightly browned.

4. Arrange 2 piles of vegetables on each toast. Top with Parmesan shavings and serve the bruschetta hot or at room temperature. —*Pablo Massey*

WINE The black fruit aromas and tannins of the 1997 Catena Malbec Lunlunta Vineyard marry beautifully with the sweet roasted potatoes and bell peppers.

Chickpea Crostini

6 SERVINGS ✤

The tangy chickpea crostini at New York City's Babbo restaurant inspired this appetizer.

2 large shallots, finely chopped
½ teaspoon minced rosemary
¼ cup extra-virgin olive oil, plus more for drizzling
One 19-ounce can chickpeas, drained and rinsed
3 tablespoons water
Salt and freshly ground pepper
1½ teaspoons white balsamic vinegar or white wine vinegar
Twelve ½-inch-thick Italian bread slices
About ½ pound sliced soppressata or other coarse Italian salami
1 large fennel bulb, trimmed and cut into 12 thin wedges

1. Preheat the broiler. In a medium skillet, combine the shallots and rosemary with 2 tablespoons of the olive oil and cook over moderately low heat until the shallots soften, about 5 minutes. Add the chickpeas, water and a generous pinch each of salt and pepper. Cook over moderate heat, coarsely mashing the chickpeas, until heated through. Stir in the vinegar and keep warm.

2. Brush the bread slices on both sides with the remaining 2 tablespoons of olive oil. Arrange the slices on a baking sheet. Broil the bread about 4 inches from the heat for about 1 minute per side, or until the bread slices are golden and crisp.

LEFT: **Chickpea Crostini.** ABOVE: **Roasted Vegetable Bruschetta.**

3. Arrange the sliced soppressata and fennel wedges around the edge of a long serving platter. Spread the toasts with the warm mashed chickpeas and arrange them in the center of the platter. Drizzle with olive oil, sprinkle with pepper and serve. —*Michele Scicolone*
MAKE AHEAD The recipe can be prepared through Step 2 up to 4 hours ahead; keep the toasts and mashed chickpeas at room temperature. Rewarm the chickpeas before serving.

White Bean Crostini with Spicy Cucumbers
MAKES 40 CROSTINI

The navy beans need to soak overnight, so plan accordingly.
- ½ pound navy beans, soaked overnight and drained
- 3 large garlic cloves, 1 minced
- 2 thyme sprigs
- 1 bay leaf
- 3 tablespoons extra-virgin olive oil
- 1 teaspoon fresh lemon juice
- Table salt and freshly ground black pepper
- 1 European cucumber, very thinly sliced crosswise
- 2 tablespoons white wine vinegar
- 1 teaspoon sugar
- 1 teaspoon kosher salt
- ¾ teaspoon crushed red pepper
- 40 ½-inch-thick baguette slices, toasted

1. Put the beans in a medium saucepan and add enough water to cover by 2 inches. Add the 2 whole garlic cloves, the thyme sprigs and the bay leaf and bring to a simmer over moderate heat. Cover partially and simmer, stirring occasionally, until the beans are tender, about 1½ hours.
2. Discard the thyme and bay leaf. Transfer the beans, garlic and cooking liquid to a food processor and puree. Press the puree through a coarse strainer into a bowl. Stir in the olive oil and lemon juice and season with table salt and black pepper.

3. Spread the cucumber slices in a large glass baking dish. In a bowl, combine the minced garlic with the vinegar, sugar, kosher salt and crushed red pepper; stir to dissolve the sugar and salt. Pour the dressing over the cucumber and toss. Refrigerate for 1 to 2 hours, tossing occasionally.
4. Just before serving, spread each slice of the toast with white bean puree and top with cucumber slices. Arrange the white bean crostini on a platter and serve. —*Marcia Kiesel*
ONE SERVING Calories 112 kcal, Total Fat 1.9 gm, Saturated Fat 0.3 gm

Scallop Toasts with Wasabi Caviar
MAKES 2 DOZEN TOASTS

Pretty pale green wasabi caviar is a mixture of whitefish roe and wasabi powder; it's available at specialty food stores. You can also buy whitefish roe and wasabi powder and mix the two yourself.
- 6 thin slices sandwich bread
- 2 tablespoons unsalted butter, 1 tablespoon melted
- 3 large scallions, white and tender green parts minced, dark green part thinly sliced

White Bean Crostini with Spicy Cucumbers

1 tablespoon pickled ginger, minced, plus 1 tablespoon of the liquid from the jar

½ pound sea scallops

1 ounce (2 tablespoons) wasabi caviar

2 tablespoons sesame seeds, preferably black

1. Preheat the oven to 350°. Lightly brush the bread on both sides with the melted butter. Using a 1½-inch biscuit cutter, cut 4 rounds from each slice. Arrange on a baking sheet; toast 5 to 6 minutes, or until lightly golden. Let cool on the baking sheet. Leave the oven on.

2. Melt the remaining 1 tablespoon of butter in a small skillet. Add the minced scallions and cook over moderate heat, stirring, until softened, about 2 minutes. Scrape the cooked scallions into a food processor and let cool. Add the ginger and pulse until combined. Add the scallops and process to a paste.

3. Transfer the scallop mousse to a pastry bag fitted with a ½-inch round tip or a plastic bag with a corner snipped off. Pipe a rounded ½ teaspoon of the scallop mousse onto the toasts. Alternatively, spoon the mousse on the toasts.

4. Using your finger or a pastry brush, smooth the top of the mousse with the ginger pickling liquid. Bake the toasts for about 5 minutes or until the tops are firm but not rubbery. Let cool. Top half of each toast with the caviar; sprinkle the other half with the sesame seeds. Garnish with the sliced scallions. Serve at room temperature. —*Grace Parisi*

MAKE AHEAD The scallop mousse can be refrigerated for up to 1 day.

Scallop Toasts with Wasabi Caviar

King Crab Toasts

MAKES 45 TOASTS ✳

4 ounces cream cheese, softened

⅓ cup grated onion

2 tablespoons ketchup

2 tablespoons mayonnaise

2 tablespoons finely diced celery

½ pound king crabmeat, coarsely chopped

Tabasco sauce

Salt and freshly ground pepper

1 package (1 pound) sliced seeded cocktail rye, lightly toasted

1. Preheat the broiler. In a large bowl, combine the cream cheese with the onion, ketchup, mayonnaise and celery. Fold in the crabmeat and season with Tabasco, salt and pepper.

2. Spread a heaping teaspoon of the crab mixture on each toast to cover the surface. Broil in 2 batches for about 2 minutes, or until evenly browned. Serve hot. —*Marcia Kiesel*

Smoked Trout Toasts

MAKES 16 TOASTS ✳

If you're in a hurry, you can prepare this delectable recipe more quickly by omitting the goat cheese and baking the toasts just once.

8 thin slices sourdough or white bread

1 tablespoon extra-virgin olive oil

1 smoked trout (about 4 ounces), skin and pin bones removed, flesh flaked

3 tablespoons mayonnaise

1 ripe tomato—halved, seeded and finely chopped

2 tablespoons snipped chives

Salt and freshly ground pepper

¼ cup (about 2 ounces) crumbled fresh goat cheese

1. Preheat the oven to 375°. Brush the slices of sourdough or white bread on one side with the extra-virgin olive oil. Using a 2-inch round biscuit cutter, cut out 2 rounds from each of the slices of bread. Arrange the bread rounds on a lightly oiled baking sheet and then toast the rounds for about 10 minutes, or until they are golden. Leave the oven on.

2. Meanwhile, in a medium bowl, combine the flaked smoked trout with the mayonnaise, the chopped tomato and the snipped chives and season the mixture with salt and pepper. Spoon the trout mixture onto the toasts and top with the crumbled fresh goat cheese. Bake the smoked trout toasts until they are heated through and serve the toasts warm. —*Todd Slossberg*

Porcini and Black Olive Canapés

MAKES 3 DOZEN CANAPÉS

- 1 cup (about ¾ ounce) dried porcini mushrooms
- 5 tablespoons unsalted butter, 4 melted
- 1 garlic clove, minced
- ½ teaspoon minced thyme
- 1 cup (about 4 ounces) Calamata olives, pitted
- 1 tablespoon extra-virgin olive oil
- ¼ teaspoon truffle oil, or more to taste (optional)

Salt and freshly ground pepper
- 9 slices thinly sliced white sandwich bread
- ½ cup (2 ounces) grated Fontina cheese
- 2 tablespoons snipped chives

1. In a small bowl, soak the porcini in hot water until softened, about 30 minutes. Remove the mushrooms.

2. In a medium skillet, melt the 1 tablespoon of butter until foamy. Add the porcini and cook over moderately high heat, stirring occasionally, until lightly browned, about 5 minutes. Add the garlic and thyme and cook for 1 minute. Transfer to a plate and let cool.

3. In a food processor, pulse the olives and porcini until finely chopped. With the machine on, add the olive oil and truffle oil; process to a paste. Transfer to a bowl. Season with salt and pepper.

4. Preheat the oven to 350°. Lightly brush a baking sheet with melted butter. Brush the bread on 1 side with the remaining butter. Using a 1¼-inch round biscuit cutter, stamp 4 rounds from each slice; arrange, buttered side up, on the baking sheet. Sprinkle with the Fontina. Bake 6 to 8 minutes, or until the rounds are golden on the bottom and the cheese is bubbling.

5. Arrange the rounds on a platter; top each with 1 teaspoon of the tapenade. Garnish with the chives. —*Tim McKee*

MAKE AHEAD The recipe can be made through Step 4 and refrigerated up to 2 days. Recrisp in a 325° oven.

WINE Champagne, the ideal aperitif. Choose a crisp nonvintage brut, such as the Deutz Classic, or a Blanc de Blancs, such as the 1990 Taittinger Comtes de Champagne.

Creamy Crab Canapés with Lemon and Caviar

MAKES 32 CANAPÉS

Salmon and whitefish caviar make good, inexpensive alternatives to extravagant osetra and sevruga.

Eight ¼-inch slices of brioche or challah
- 2 tablespoons unsalted butter, melted
- ½ pound lump crabmeat, picked over
- 1 tablespoon chopped chives, plus 1-inch chive pieces for garnish
- 1 teaspoon minced shallot
- 1 teaspoon finely grated lemon zest

Pinch of salt
- ½ cup heavy cream
- 2 ounces caviar

1. Preheat the oven to 350°. Using a 1½-inch round biscuit cutter, cut out 4 rounds from each brioche slice. Brush both sides with the butter. Set on a baking sheet and bake for about 15 minutes, or until golden and crisp.

2. In a medium bowl, combine the crabmeat with the chopped chives, shallot, zest and salt. Whip the cream until firm. Gently fold the cream into the crab and spoon onto the croutons. Garnish with the caviar and 1-inch chive pieces and serve immediately. —*Grant Achatz*

MAKE AHEAD The croutons can be stored at room temperature in an airtight container for up to 3 days.

WINE Champagne, such as the 1985 Ployez-Jacquemart.

Smoked Salmon Cones with Green Herb Salsa

MAKES 18 CONES

Farm-raised salmon has become one of Chile's biggest exports. Here, smoked salmon wraps around a zesty salsa.

- ¼ cup finely chopped Vidalia onion
- ½ tablespoon sugar
- ¼ cup minced flat-leaf parsley
- ½ to 1 large jalapeño, seeded and finely chopped
- 2 medium radishes, finely chopped
- 2 tablespoons minced cilantro
- 2 tablespoons minced chives
- 3 tablespoons canola oil
- 3 tablespoons fresh lemon juice

Coarse sea salt
- 6 ounces thinly sliced smoked salmon, cut into 3-inch squares
- 9 thin slices whole wheat bread— crusts removed, bread cut into 18 triangles and toasted

1. In a small bowl, combine the onion and sugar, add cold water to cover and set aside for 15 minutes. Drain and then rinse the onion under cold water. Drain again, shaking to remove the excess water. Pat dry.

2. In a medium bowl, toss the onion with the parsley, jalapeño, radishes, cilantro and chives. Add the canola oil and lemon juice; season with sea salt.

3. Spoon 2 teaspoons of the salsa onto each piece of salmon and roll up into a cone. Set each cone on a piece of toast, arrange the cones on a platter and serve. —*Ruth Van Waerebeek-Gonzalez*

Smoked Salmon Cones with Green Herb Salsa

Escalivada and Serrano Ham Canapés

Escalivada and Serrano Ham Canapés

MAKES 32 CANAPÉS

Two of the favorite foods of Catalonia—raw cured ham and *escalivada,* a blend of eggplant and red peppers—top these crostini-like canapés. If Serrano ham is unavailable, use prosciutto instead.

One ½-pound eggplant
1 red bell pepper
1 baguette, cut into 32 slices about ¼ inch thick
1½ tablespoons extra-virgin olive oil, plus more for brushing
Salt and freshly ground black pepper
2 plum tomatoes
2 ounces thinly sliced Serrano ham, cut into 16 pieces
1 tablespoon minced chives
8 anchovy fillets, halved

I. Preheat the oven to 400°. Put the eggplant and the red bell pepper on a baking sheet. Roast the red bell pepper, turning it occasionally, for about 40 minutes, or until the pepper is blistered all over; roast the eggplant for about 1 hour, or until it has collapsed. Transfer the roasted eggplant and red bell pepper to a plate.

2. On a large baking sheet, lightly brush both sides of the baguette slices with olive oil. Bake in the oven for about 10 minutes, or until golden brown.

3. When the vegetables are cool enough to handle, remove the skins and stems. Remove the seeds from the pepper. If the seeds from the eggplant are in strips that are easy to lift out, remove these as well. Transfer the eggplant to a colander and let drain for 30 minutes. Finely chop the eggplant and transfer to a bowl. Cut the bell pepper into ¼-inch dice and add to the eggplant. Stir in the 1½ tablespoons of olive oil and season with salt and black pepper.

4. Cut 1 of the tomatoes in half crosswise. Rub 16 of the baguette toasts with the cut sides of the halved tomato. Top each toast with a piece of Serrano ham, folding it to fit neatly. Sprinkle with some of the chives.

5. Cut the other tomato crosswise into 8 slices and then cut each slice in half. Spread the eggplant mixture on the remaining 16 baguette toasts and top each with a half slice of tomato and half an anchovy. Serve the canapés at room temperature. —*Pilar Huguet*

MAKE AHEAD The *escalivada* can be refrigerated for up to 1 day.

FOUR CANAPÉS Calories 300 kcal, Total Fat 16 gm, Saturated Fat 2 gm

WINE 1994 Huguet Cava Gran Reserva Brut Nature.

Crab and Guacamole Tostaditos

MAKES 5 DOZEN TOSTADITOS

3 tablespoons mayonnaise
2 tablespoons heavy cream
1 teaspoon minced chipotle chile in *adobo* sauce
1 pound lump crabmeat, picked over
Salt and freshly ground pepper
2 large Hass avocados, cut into ½-inch dice
1 small onion, minced
1 large jalapeño, seeded and minced
2 tablespoons chopped cilantro, plus small leaves for garnish

3 tablespoons fresh lime juice
2 teaspoons pure olive oil
5 dozen round tortilla chips
1 large tomato, finely chopped

I. In a large bowl, combine the mayonnaise, cream and chipotle. Fold in the crabmeat. Season with salt and pepper and refrigerate.

2. In a large bowl, combine the avocados, onion, jalapeño, chopped cilantro, lime juice and oil. Season the guacamole with salt and pepper and refrigerate.

3. To serve, put a heaping teaspoon of the guacamole on each of the tortilla chips and then spoon a tablespoon of the crab salad on top. Garnish each tostadito with some chopped tomato and a cilantro leaf and serve the tostaditos on a platter. —*Robert Del Grande*

MAKE AHEAD The crab mixture can be refrigerated overnight.

WINE The floral notes of a nonvintage Iron Horse Brut from California will play up the avocado in the tostaditos. Another choice is the crisp 1997 Riffault Sancerre from France—or a margarita.

Beef and Fontina Tostaditos

MAKES 2 DOZEN TOSTADITOS

4 medium tomatillos, husked and finely chopped
2 tablespoons finely chopped red onion
2 tablespoons minced cilantro
1 teaspoon hot sauce
4 ounces thickly sliced roast beef, finely chopped
½ cup (2 ounces) shredded Fontina cheese, shredded
48 mini round corn tortilla chips
Salt

I. Preheat the oven to 350°. In a small bowl, combine the tomatillos, onion, cilantro and ½ teaspoon of the hot sauce.

2. In a medium bowl, combine the roast beef with the Fontina and the remaining ½ teaspoon hot sauce. Arrange half the tortilla chips on a large rimmed baking sheet. Spoon the roast beef filling on the chips; top with the remaining 24 chips.

3. Bake the tostaditos for 5 to 7 minutes, or until the filling is hot and bubbling. Transfer to a platter. Season the tomatillo relish with salt, spoon a little on top of each tostadito and serve immediately. —*Grace Parisi*

Sesame Crisps with Seared Sea Scallops

MAKES 16 HORS D'OEUVRES

These clever crisps are made of phyllo dough that has been sprinkled with sesame seeds, then cut into strips and folded into triangles.

- 8 sheets phyllo dough, plus extra in case of tearing (½ pound), thawed overnight in the refrigerator if frozen
- 5 tablespoons unsalted butter, melted
- 2 teaspoons white sesame seeds
- 2 teaspoons black sesame seeds
- ¼ cup sour cream
- ½ teaspoon fresh lime juice
- 16 medium sea scallops (¾ pound)
- Kosher salt and freshly ground pepper
- 2 tablespoons olive oil
- Zest of 1 lime, julienned

1. Preheat the oven to 400°. Lay 1 sheet of the phyllo dough on a work surface; brush with melted butter. Lightly sprinkle white and black sesame seeds over the phyllo. Make 2 more layers, brushing the phyllo with butter and sprinkling with seeds. Top with a fourth sheet of phyllo and brush with butter.

2. Cut the layered phyllo lengthwise into 4 strips and then cut each strip in half crosswise. Fold the top corner of a strip over to form a triangle and then continue folding the triangle like a flag. Repeat with the remaining 7 strips. Repeat the layering and folding with the remaining 4 sheets of phyllo, the butter and sesame seeds. Set the phyllo triangles on a cookie sheet and bake them for about 10 minutes, or until lightly browned. Transfer to a rack to cool.

3. In a small bowl, combine the sour cream with the lime juice. Season the scallops with kosher salt and pepper. Heat the oil in a nonstick skillet until very hot. Add the scallops; cook over high heat until lightly browned, about 2 minutes a side. Drain on paper towels.

4. Spoon ½ teaspoon of the sour cream mixture on each sesame crisp and top with a scallop. Spoon ¼ teaspoon of the sour cream mixture on each scallop and garnish with lime zest. Transfer to a platter; serve at once. —*Kimball Jones*

Basil Blini with Salmon Caviar

MAKES ABOUT 5 DOZEN BLINI

Serve these herbed blini topped with a combination of crème fraîche and salmon caviar or with a little dollop of the pesto that flavors them. You can substitute about eight ounces of store-bought pesto for the homemade version.

- ¾ cup milk
- 2 large eggs, separated
- 1 teaspoon salt
- Basil Pesto (recipe follows)
- ¾ cup all-purpose flour
- ¾ teaspoon baking powder
- ¼ teaspoon baking soda
- 1 tablespoon melted unsalted butter, plus more for brushing
- 1 tablespoon fresh lemon juice
- ¼ cup crème fraîche (optional)
- 3 ounces salmon caviar (optional)

1. In a blender, combine the milk with the egg yolks, the salt and ¼ cup of the pesto. Blend at high speed until combined, about 15 seconds.

2. In a large bowl, combine the flour with the baking powder and baking soda. Whisk in the milk mixture until smooth and then add the 1 tablespoon of melted butter and the lemon juice.

3. In another bowl, beat the egg whites until stiff peaks form. Using a rubber spatula, fold the egg whites into the batter just until no streaks remain.

4. Set a large nonstick skillet over moderately high heat and brush lightly with melted butter. Drop slightly heaping teaspoons of batter into the skillet and cook until golden on the bottom and just set on top, about 2 minutes. Flip the blini to brown the bottoms, about 30 seconds longer. Transfer the blini to a plate and cover loosely with foil. Repeat with the remaining batter, lightly buttering the skillet as needed.

5. Arrange the blini on a large platter. Spoon a small dollop of crème fraîche and a little salmon caviar on each blini; alternatively, dollop a little of the remaining pesto onto each. —*Tim McKee*

MAKE AHEAD The blini can be refrigerated overnight. Reheat, covered, on a large baking sheet, in a 325° oven.

BELOW: **Beef and Fontina Tostaditos.**
BOTTOM: **Sesame Crisps with Seared Sea Scallops.**

Warm Figs with Goat Cheese

BASIL PESTO

MAKES ABOUT ¾ CUP

¼ cup extra-virgin olive oil, plus
    more for brushing
¼ cup pine nuts
2 garlic cloves, smashed
¼ cup freshly grated Parmesan
    cheese
2 cups (lightly packed) basil leaves
½ teaspoon fresh lemon juice
Salt

1. Brush a small skillet with olive oil and heat. Add the pine nuts and toast over moderately high heat, stirring constantly, until golden, about 3 minutes. Transfer to a plate to cool.

2. In a food processor or blender, pulse the pine nuts with the garlic and Parmesan cheese until finely chopped. Add the basil leaves and pulse until minced, scraping down the side of the bowl. With the machine on, add the ¼ cup of olive oil in a thin stream and process until smooth. Add the fresh lemon juice and then season the basil pesto with salt. —*T.M.*

MAKE AHEAD The pesto can be refrigerated overnight; press a piece of plastic wrap directly on the surface to keep the pesto from discoloring.

Warm Figs with Goat Cheese

MAKES 4 DOZEN
HORS D'OEUVRES ✳

For an alternative to the goat cheese, try stuffing the figs with a slightly sharp, grated melting cheese, such as aged provolone or Manchego.

24 small fresh black figs, halved
    lengthwise
¾ cup (about 3 ounces) crumbled
    goat cheese
1½ tablespoons balsamic vinegar
Freshly ground black pepper

Preheat the oven to 350°. Arrange the figs on a baking sheet, cut sides up. Spoon a little goat cheese on each fig half. Lightly brush the figs with the vinegar and sprinkle the cheese with pepper. Bake for about 8 minutes, or until the figs are warmed through. Transfer the figs to a platter and serve immediately. —*Grace Parisi*

Broiled Garlic and Lime Shrimp

MAKES ABOUT 36 SHRIMP

You'll find that no one says "No thank you" to garlic-infused jumbo shrimp, and everybody licks the buttery, citrusy juices off their fingers.

2 pounds large shrimp in their
    shells
12 garlic cloves, peeled
1 stick (4 ounces) unsalted butter,
    melted and kept warm
2 serrano chiles, seeded and
    minced
¼ cup minced cilantro
1 tablespoon fresh lime juice
Kosher salt

1. Using a paring knife, slit each shrimp down the back through the shell and remove the dark intestinal vein. Spread the shrimp open and flatten them out. Arrange the butterflied shrimp in a single layer on a rimmed baking sheet, shell side down.

2. In a saucepan, cover the garlic with water and simmer until softened, about 20 minutes; add more water if necessary. Drain, let cool and finely chop.

3. In a bowl, combine the garlic, butter, serranos, cilantro and lime juice. Brush the shrimp with the butter mixture and season with kosher salt.

4. Preheat the broiler. Broil the shrimp for 3 to 4 minutes, or just until they are cooked through. Transfer the shrimp to a platter and then drizzle them with any remaining butter mixture. Serve the broiled shrimp with lots of paper napkins. —*Robert Del Grande*

MAKE AHEAD Prepare the shrimp through Step 3; refrigerate the shrimp and any remaining butter mixture overnight. Reheat the butter mixture before serving.

WINE Sparkling wine is an easy choice with these hors d'oeuvres. Nonvintage Iron Horse Brut from California brings out the sweetness of the shrimp.

Artichoke Leaves with Cumin Shrimp Salad

MAKES 50 HORS D'OEUVRES

3 large artichokes, stems discarded
Salt
¾ pound large shrimp, shelled and
    deveined
¾ teaspoon cumin seeds
2½ tablespoons extra-virgin olive oil
2 tablespoons fresh lemon juice
¼ cup minced red bell pepper
1 tablespoon minced parsley
Freshly ground black pepper

1. Put the artichokes in a steamer basket, stem ends down, and cook until the bottoms are tender when pierced, about 25 minutes. Transfer the artichokes to a plate and let cool.

2. Meanwhile, in a medium saucepan of boiling salted water, cook the shrimp until they are opaque throughout, about 2 minutes. Drain the shrimp and cut into ½-inch pieces.

3. Pull off and reserve 50 of the large outer leaves of the artichokes; reserve the remaining leaves for later use. Pull out the small pointed leaves in the centers and, with a spoon, scrape out the hairy chokes. Cut the bottoms of the

artichokes into ½-inch dice. In a large bowl, toss the diced artichokes with the shrimp pieces.

4. In a small skillet, toast the cumin seeds over moderate heat until they are fragrant, about 40 seconds. Transfer the toasted cumin seeds to a mortar or a spice grinder, let cool and then grind to a coarse powder. Empty the powder into a small bowl. Stir in the olive oil and lemon juice. Add the dressing to the artichokes and shrimp in the bowl along with the red bell pepper and parsley. Season with salt and black pepper and toss well.

5. Arrange the artichoke leaves on 2 platters. Spoon the shrimp salad onto the base of the artichoke leaves and serve the leaves chilled or at room temperature. —*Marcia Kiesel*

MAKE AHEAD The recipe can be prepared ahead through Step 4; refrigerate the artichoke leaves and shrimp salad separately overnight.

Salt-Baked Potatoes Stuffed with Goat Cheese and Hazelnuts

MAKES 2 DOZEN HORS D'OEUVRES

- 3 tablespoons hazelnuts
- 2 cups plus 1 tablespoon kosher salt
- 2 dozen small red bliss potatoes (about 2 pounds)
- 2 tablespoons canola oil
- 1 teaspoon freshly ground pepper
- ½ pound soft goat cheese, at room temperature
- 2 tablespoons minced chives
- 1 teaspoon minced thyme

1. Preheat the oven to 400°. Spread the hazelnuts in a pie plate and toast for about 8 minutes, or until the skins blister. Transfer the hazelnuts to a kitchen towel and rub to remove the skins. Finely chop the hazelnuts. Lower the oven temperature to 350°.

2. Spread the 2 cups of kosher salt on a rimmed baking sheet. In a large bowl, toss the potatoes with the canola oil, the remaining 1 tablespoon of salt and

the pepper. Spread the potatoes on the salt on the baking sheet and roast for about 35 minutes, or until tender when pierced. Let cool slightly and then rub off the excess salt.

3. Meanwhile, in a bowl, combine the goat cheese, the chives, the thyme and the hazelnuts.

4. Cut off the tops of the potatoes and scoop out half of the flesh; discard or reserve for another use. Fill the potatoes with the goat cheese mixture and serve warm. —*Kerry Sear*

WINE Try these stuffed baked potatoes with a full-bodied Chardonnay. The 1997 L'Ecole No. 41 Chardonnay has loads of minerals and oak that play off the salt and herbs, while the 1997 Woodward Canyon Columbia Valley Chardonnay enhances the richness of the goat cheese.

Tricolored Potato Cups with Caviar and Sour Cream

MAKES ABOUT 3 DOZEN CUPS

- 1½ pounds red, purple and yellow new potatoes, about 1 inch in diameter
- 1 tablespoon extra-virgin olive oil

Salt

- ¼ cup sour cream
- 2 ounces osetra caviar

Cut chives, for garnish

1. Steam the potatoes over boiling water until barely tender, about 5 minutes. Let cool slightly on a plate.

2. Cut each potato in half and use a small melon baller to scoop out an indentation, leaving a ¼-inch shell. Cut a thin slice from the bottom of each potato cup so that it won't wobble.

3. Preheat the oven to 400° and line a large baking sheet with foil. In a bowl,

Tricolored Potato Cups with Caviar and Sour Cream

toss the potatoes with the olive oil and season lightly with salt. Arrange the potatoes, scooped side down, on the baking sheet and bake in the lower third of the oven for about 25 minutes, or until the undersides are golden. Let the potatoes cool slightly.

4. Arrange the potatoes on a platter, mound each with sour cream and top with some of the caviar and chives. Serve immediately. —*Grace Parisi*

Smoked Ham Salad on Gruyère Potato Coins

MAKES ABOUT 3 DOZEN
HORS D'OEUVRES

- 2 long, thin Idaho potatoes, cut into ⅛-inch-thick slices
- 1 tablespoon olive oil

Salt and freshly ground pepper

- 1 cup (about 4 ounces) shredded Gruyère cheese
- ½ pound lean smoked ham, finely chopped
- 3 tablespoons mayonnaise
- 1 scallion, finely chopped
- 1 tablespoon finely chopped cornichons
- 1 tablespoon finely chopped capers
- 1 teaspoon finely chopped tarragon
- ½ teaspoon Dijon mustard

1. Preheat the oven to 350° and line a baking sheet with parchment paper or foil. Using a 2-inch round biscuit cutter, cut the potato slices into rounds. In a bowl, toss the potatoes with the olive oil and arrange them in a single layer on the baking sheet. Season lightly with salt and pepper and then sprinkle with the cheese. Bake the potato rounds for about 45 minutes, or until deep golden; let cool. Transfer the potato coins to paper towels.

2. In a small bowl, combine the smoked ham with the mayonnaise, scallion, cornichons, capers, tarragon and Dijon mustard. Season the ham salad with salt and pepper. Spoon the ham salad onto the Gruyère potato coins and serve. —*Grace Parisi*

Potato and Lamb Samosas

MAKES ABOUT 40 SAMOSAS

- 1 tablespoon extra-virgin olive oil
- ¼ pound lean lamb shoulder, cut into ½-inch dice
- 1 small onion, finely chopped
- 1 medium all-purpose potato, peeled and cut into ¼-inch dice
- 1½ teaspoons Madras curry powder
- ⅛ teaspoon ground cumin
- ⅛ teaspoon ground coriander

Pinch of cayenne pepper

- ½ cup canned low-sodium chicken broth
- ¼ cup thawed frozen baby peas

Salt

One 15-ounce package pie crusts

1. In a medium skillet, heat ½ tablespoon of the olive oil. Add the lamb and cook over moderately high heat until browned all over, 6 to 7 minutes. Using a slotted spoon, transfer the lamb to a plate. Add the onion to the skillet along with the remaining ½ tablespoon of olive oil and cook over moderately low heat, stirring, until the onion is softened, 3 to 4 minutes.

2. Return the lamb to the skillet, add the potato and cook until sizzling. Add the curry powder, cumin, coriander and cayenne and cook over low heat, stirring constantly, just until slightly darkened, about 4 minutes. Add the chicken broth and bring to a simmer, stirring, to scrape up any brown bits from the bottom. Cover the skillet and cook over low heat until the lamb and potato are tender, about 30 minutes. Remove the lid and cook until the liquid is absorbed. Stir in the peas and season with salt. Transfer the filling to a bowl and let cool completely.

3. Preheat the oven to 400°. On a lightly floured surface, roll out the pie crusts, one at a time, to a bare ⅛-inch thickness, and then cut out a total of 40 rounds with a 2-inch round biscuit cutter. Lightly brush the rounds with water, top each with a scant teaspoon of the filling and fold in half. Seal the edges

with a fork. Transfer the potato and lamb samosas to a large baking sheet.

4. Bake the samosas for 35 to 40 minutes, or until the crust is golden. Serve the samosas hot or at room temperature. —*Grace Parisi*

Rice Balls Rolled in Seaweed

MAKES 32 BALLS

- 2 cups Japanese sushi-style rice (see Note)
- 2½ cups water
- 1 tablespoon powdered sushi flavoring (see Note)
- 1 cup white vinegar mixed with 1 cup water
- 4 sheets nori (seaweed), cut into 4-by-1-inch strips (see Note)

Japanese sesame salt (see Note)

1. In a large bowl, rinse the rice in several changes of cold water until the water is thoroughly clear. In a medium saucepan, combine the rice with the 2½ cups of water and bring to a boil. Cover and cook over low heat until all of the water is absorbed, about 15 minutes. Remove the rice from the heat and let stand, covered, for 15 minutes.

2. Transfer the warm rice to a bowl and stir in the sushi flavoring. Let the rice cool to room temperature.

3. Moisten your hands in the vinegar mixture and roll rounded tablespoons of the rice into balls, moistening with the vinegar mixture as you roll. Mash a few grains of rice onto one short edge of a nori strip; wrap the nori around a rice ball, using the mashed rice to seal the edges. Repeat to form the remaining balls. Sprinkle the balls with the sesame salt and serve. —*Hisachika Takahashi*

NOTE Japanese sushi-style rice, powdered sushi flavoring, nori and Japanese sesame salt are available from Asian markets and specialty food shops or by mail order from Katagiri (212-755-3566) or The Oriental Pantry (800-828-0368).

MAKE AHEAD The rice balls can stand covered at room temperature for up to 3 hours.

Falafel

MAKES 2 DOZEN BALLS

Although falafel is made from chickpeas in this country, in Lebanon it is usually made from dried fava beans, sometimes with a handful of dried chickpeas thrown in. Favas have a wonderful flavor, but if you can't find them, dried white beans, such as cannellini or navy, can be substituted. Street vendors usually tuck falafel into pita bread with chopped lettuce and tomato and plenty of tahini sauce. At home, the balls can be served as an hors d'oeuvre, with a bowl of Tahini Sauce for dipping. You'll need to allow time for the beans and chickpeas to soak overnight.

  1 cup (7 ounces) dried peeled fava beans, soaked overnight
  ¼ cup dried chickpeas, soaked overnight
  1 small onion, finely chopped
  ⅓ cup minced flat-leaf parsley
  2 tablespoons minced cilantro
  1 garlic clove, minced
  1 teaspoon baking powder
  1 teaspoon kosher salt
  ¾ teaspoon ground cumin
Pinch of crushed red pepper
  3 tablespoons water
Pure olive oil or canola oil, for frying
Tahini Sauce (recipe follows)

I. Drain and rinse the fava beans and the chickpeas and put them in a food processor. Add the onion, parsley, cilantro, garlic, baking powder, kosher salt, cumin and crushed red pepper. Pulse, scraping down the side of the bowl, to form a coarse paste. Add the water and process until the mixture is gritty but fine and a brilliant green. Scrape the paste into a bowl.

2. In a medium saucepan, heat 2 inches of oil to 350°. Scoop rounded tablespoons of the falafel mixture into the hot oil and fry in small batches until browned and crisp, about 2 minutes. Drain the falafel on paper towels set over a wire rack and serve hot, with Tahini Sauce. —*Nancy Harmon Jenkins*

TAHINI SAUCE

MAKES ABOUT 1¼ CUPS

  ½ teaspoon minced garlic
  1 cup tahini
Fresh lemon juice
Salt

In a bowl, stir the minced garlic into the tahini. Add water, 1 teaspoon at a time, until the tahini sauce has the consistency of thick cream. Add fresh lemon juice until the tahini sauce is pleasantly tangy and then season the sauce with salt. —*N. H. J.*

MAKE AHEAD The tahini sauce can be refrigerated for up to 3 days.

Turkey and Ham Croquettes

MAKES 3 DOZEN CROQUETTES

Divinely old-fashioned, these croquettes are crisp on the outside and soft on the inside. The mixture needs to be chilled for at least six hours before being fried.

  2 cups milk
  3 tablespoons unsalted butter
  ½ cup all-purpose flour, plus ½ cup for dredging
  1 cup (4 ounces) finely chopped cooked turkey
  3 ounces (½ cup) Serrano ham, trimmed and finely chopped
Freshly ground white pepper
  2 large eggs
  1 cup dry bread crumbs
Pure olive oil, for frying

I. In a small saucepan, heat the milk until bubbles appear around the edge. In a heavy medium saucepan, melt the unsalted butter. Add ½ cup of the flour and cook over moderate heat, whisking constantly, until golden, about 2 minutes. Add the hot milk, ⅓ cup at a time, whisking vigorously, until smooth. Cook over low heat for 5 minutes, stirring often. Stir in the turkey and ham and remove from the heat. Season the mixture with white pepper; the ham will provide enough saltiness.

2. Spread the turkey and ham mixture in an 8-inch-square baking dish and

Turkey and Ham Croquettes

press a piece of plastic wrap directly on the surface. Refrigerate the mixture until chilled and semifirm, at least 6 hours or overnight.

3. Pour the remaining ½ cup of flour into a bowl. In another bowl, lightly beat the eggs. Pour the bread crumbs into a third bowl. Remove the plastic wrap from the turkey mixture and cut it into 36 squares. Using floured hands, dip 1 square into the flour and roll into a soft ball. Coat the ball with beaten egg and then bread crumbs. Set the croquette on a tray lined with wax paper. Repeat with the remaining squares. Refrigerate the croquettes for at least 1 hour to firm them up.

4. In a medium saucepan, heat 1½ inches of pure olive oil to 350°. Fry the turkey and ham croquettes in batches without crowding until they are golden brown, about 3 minutes. Drain the croquettes on paper towels. Reheat the oil between batches of croquettes and remove any stray crumbs. Serve the croquettes warm. —*Pilar Huguet*

ONE SERVING Calories 240 kcal, Total Fat 20 gm, Saturated Fat 4 gm
WINE The 1994 Huguet Brut Nature has the character and complexity to complement the croquettes.

chapter 2
first courses

33

35

Grilled Endives with Serrano Ham

4 SERVINGS

This simple salad is all about harmony of flavors, not complicated technique: the nutty acidity of the reduced sherry vinegar balances the rich salty ham and pleasantly bitter endives.

- ¼ cup plus 2 tablespoons sherry vinegar
- 3 tablespoons extra-virgin olive oil, plus more for brushing
- ½ garlic clove, finely chopped
- ½ teaspoon thyme leaves

Salt and freshly ground pepper
- 2 large endives, halved lengthwise
- ½ pound Serrano ham or prosciutto di Parma, thinly sliced
- 1 tablespoon coarsely chopped flat-leaf parsley
- 4 lemon wedges

1. In a small saucepan, simmer the sherry vinegar over low heat until it is reduced to 1 tablespoon, about 5 minutes. Let cool. In a small glass or stainless steel bowl, whisk 3 tablespoons of the olive oil with the reduced sherry vinegar, the garlic and the thyme. Season the dressing with salt and pepper.

2. Light a grill or preheat a grill pan. Brush the endive halves lightly with olive oil and then grill them over low heat until lightly charred, about 3 minutes. Turn and grill until lightly charred on the other side, about 3 minutes more. Thinly slice each half lengthwise. Arrange the endive slices in a layer on 1 side of each plate. Arrange the slices of Serrano ham next to the endive slices and then drizzle the salad with the sherry-vinegar dressing. Sprinkle the chopped flat-leaf parsley on top and serve with the wedges of lemon. —*Sam Clark*

SERVE WITH Sourdough bread.

WINE A chilled glass of bone-dry fino sherry will cope nicely with the strong flavors of the ham and endive. Try the Hidalgo Manzanilla La Gitana or the Gonzalez Byass Tio Pepe.

Goat Cheese Soufflés with Watercress Salad

MAKES 6 SOUFFLÉS

The goat cheese soufflés are partially baked and then finished in the oven just before serving. This is a variation on a recipe created by Stephanie Alexander, a wonderful chef from Melbourne, Australia. You will need six half-cup ramekins for these soufflés.

- 4 tablespoons unsalted butter, plus more for brushing
- ¼ cup all-purpose flour
- 2 cups milk
- 3 ounces mild fresh goat cheese
- 2 tablespoons freshly grated Parmesan cheese
- 1 tablespoon finely chopped flat-leaf parsley
- 1 tablespoon snipped chives

Salt and freshly ground white pepper
- 3 large egg yolks
- 4 large egg whites

Boiling water
- 1½ cups heavy cream
- 2 bunches watercress (¾ pound), tough stems trimmed
- 2 plum tomatoes—peeled, seeded and finely diced

1. Preheat the oven to 350°. Butter six ½-cup ramekins and set them in a large roasting pan.

2. Melt the 4 tablespoons butter in a medium saucepan. Whisk in the flour; cook over moderate heat until lightly golden, 1 to 2 minutes. Gradually whisk in the milk and simmer over low heat, whisking constantly, until the sauce is thick and has lost its floury taste, about 4 minutes. Stir in the goat cheese, Parmesan, parsley and chives and season generously with salt and white pepper. Transfer the sauce to a large bowl and let cool slightly. Whisk in the egg yolks.

3. In another bowl, beat the egg whites at medium speed until firm peaks form. Stir one fourth of the egg whites into the white sauce to lighten it and then fold in the remaining whites until no streaks remain. Pour the soufflé mixture into the ramekins, filling them almost to the top. Pour enough boiling water into the roasting pan to reach halfway up the sides of the ramekins. Bake the soufflés for about 35 minutes, or until they are golden and firm. Remove the soufflés from the roasting pan using tongs and let cool.

4. Increase the oven temperature to 425°. Run a thin sharp knife around the rims of the ramekins and invert the soufflés into a 9-by-13-inch glass baking dish. Spoon the heavy cream over the soufflés and bake in the upper third of the oven for about 15 minutes, or until nicely puffed and golden on top. Remove from the oven and let stand for 10 minutes.

5. Using a spatula, carefully transfer the soufflés to plates. In a large bowl, toss the watercress and the tomatoes with the warm cream from the baking dish. Season the salad with salt and white pepper and serve it alongside the soufflés. —*John Ash*

MAKE AHEAD The soufflés can be prepared through Step 2 and refrigerated for up to 2 days.

Eggplant and Three Cheese Soufflé

6 SERVINGS

Smoky flavored and peppery, this soufflé is more rustic than most. Since it's also more dense, cook it in a large shallow dish; that will make the soufflé rise quickly and evenly and give it a large, crisp top.

- 2 tablespoons olive oil
- 3 pounds slender eggplant, peeled

Salt
- 2 tablespoons unsalted butter, cut into 2 pieces
- 3 large garlic cloves, unpeeled
- ¼ teaspoon cumin seeds
- 4 large eggs, separated
- 1 large egg yolk
- 1½ ounces (about ½ cup) grated Pecorino pepato cheese (see Note)

2 ounces Italian Fontina cheese, cut into ⅓-inch dice (about ⅓ cup)

2 tablespoons freshly grated Parmesan cheese

1. Preheat the oven to 425°. Heat 1 tablespoon of the olive oil in each of 2 large ovenproof skillets until almost smoking. Season the eggplants with salt and arrange them in the skillets. Add a piece of butter to each and shake the pans over high heat to glaze the eggplants. Transfer the skillets to the oven and roast for about 40 minutes, or until tender and browned.

2. Meanwhile, wrap the garlic in foil and roast for about 25 minutes, or until softened. Squeeze the garlic from the skins into a small dish. Leave the oven on.

3. Working in 2 batches, puree the roasted eggplant with the garlic in a food processor and then scrape the puree into a bowl.

4. In a small skillet, toast the cumin seeds over moderate heat until fragrant, about 40 seconds. Transfer to a mortar or spice grinder; let cool and then grind to a powder. Stir the cumin and ½ teaspoon salt into the eggplant puree and then add the egg yolks, the Pecorino and the Fontina.

5. Butter a shallow 9-by-13-inch glass or ceramic baking dish. Sprinkle with 1 tablespoon of the Parmesan cheese. In a large bowl, beat the egg whites with a pinch of salt until firm peaks form. Fold one third of the beaten egg whites into the eggplant mixture and then gently fold in the remaining egg whites just until combined. Scrape the mixture into the prepared baking dish, sprinkle with the remaining 1 tablespoon of Parmesan cheese and bake in the upper third of the oven for about 17 minutes, or until the soufflé is puffed and barely firm; serve. —*Marcia Kiesel*

NOTE If you can't find Pecorino pepato cheese, you can use plain Pecorino cheese and add 1 teaspoon of coarsely cracked pepper.

Poached Eggs in Red Wine Sauce with Pancetta

8 SERVINGS

No question that this is a lot of trouble for eggs. But what eggs! The soft yolks mix with the salty pancetta, slightly tangy wine sauce and crisp buttery toast. The recipe can serve four as a main course, if you prefer. The sauce would also be delicious served with sautéed salmon fillets, chicken breasts or beef tenderloin.

6 tablespoons unsalted butter

2 large onions, halved and thinly sliced

2 shallots, thinly sliced

Salt and freshly ground pepper

2 tablespoons all-purpose flour

2 bottles (750 ml) Pinot Noir

10 whole juniper berries

1 parsley sprig

1 thyme sprig

1 bay leaf

¼ pound thinly sliced pancetta, cut into ½-inch-wide strips

½ pound white mushrooms

¼ cup plus 2 tablespoons ruby port

1 tablespoon canola oil

4 slices firm white bread, crusts removed, cut into 8 triangles

2 tablespoons vinegar

8 large eggs

Chives, for garnish

1. Melt 1 tablespoon of the butter in a large saucepan. Add the onions and shallots and cook over moderate heat, stirring, until softened but not browned, about 8 minutes. Season with salt and pepper. Add the flour and cook, stirring, for 1 minute. Whisk in ½ cup of the wine until smooth and then gradually whisk in the remaining wine.

2. In a square of cheesecloth, combine the juniper, parsley, thyme and bay leaf and tie with string. Add the herb bundle to the pan and simmer over low heat, skimming, until the wine has reduced to 1½ cups, about 45 minutes. Pass the sauce through a coarse strainer.

3. Meanwhile, melt 2 tablespoons of the butter in a large skillet. Add the pancetta and cook over moderately low heat until lightly crisped, about 4 minutes. Add the mushrooms, season with salt and pepper and cook over high heat, stirring occasionally, until lightly browned, about 8 minutes. Add the port and boil until almost evaporated, about 2 minutes. Stir in the wine sauce and simmer for 1 to 2 minutes. Remove the skillet from the heat, swirl in 1 tablespoon of butter and then season with salt and pepper.

4. In a large skillet, melt the remaining 2 tablespoons of butter in the oil. Add the bread and cook over moderately high heat until browned, about 2 minutes per side. Drain on paper towels.

5. Fill a large skillet with enough water to reach two thirds of the way up the side. Add the vinegar and bring to a boil. One at a time, break the eggs into the bubbling water. Regulate the heat so the water barely simmers and poach the eggs until the whites are set but the yolks are still soft, 3 to 4 minutes. Using a slotted spoon, transfer the eggs to paper towels.

6. Gently reheat the sauce and spoon it into soup plates. Add 1 bread triangle to each plate and set an egg on top of each triangle. Garnish with chives and serve hot. —*Marie-Andrée Nauleau*

Tomato and Goat Cheese Gratin

12 SERVINGS

4 pounds plum tomatoes, halved lengthwise

¼ cup plus 2 tablespoons extra-virgin olive oil, plus more for brushing

6 garlic cloves, thinly sliced

Salt and freshly ground pepper

1 cup coarse white bread crumbs

1 pound fresh goat cheese, crumbled

2 tablespoons chopped flat-leaf parsley

½ teaspoon minced oregano, or
¼ teaspoon dried
1 cup (4 ounces) Calamata olives,
pitted

1. Preheat the oven to 450°. Toss the tomatoes with ¼ cup of the olive oil and arrange them, cut side down, on 2 rimmed baking sheets. Bake the tomatoes for about 30 minutes, or until they exude some of their liquid. Carefully pour the tomato juices into a glass measuring cup. Remove and discard the tomato skins.

2. Roast the tomatoes for 20 minutes longer. Scatter the garlic around the tomatoes, season with salt and pepper and roast for about 5 minutes longer, or until the garlic is tender. Lower the oven temperature to 375°.

3. In a small skillet, toast the bread crumbs over moderate heat, stirring often, until golden, 2 to 3 minutes. Stir in the remaining 2 tablespoons of oil.

4. Brush a 9-by-13-inch baking dish with olive oil. Arrange half of the tomatoes in the baking dish. Top with the goat cheese, garlic, parsley and oregano; cover with the remaining tomatoes. Sprinkle the olives on top. Drizzle with the reserved tomato juices and scatter the bread crumbs over all.

Asparagus Tart

5. Bake the tomato–goat cheese gratin for about 40 minutes, or until bubbling and golden on top. Serve warm or at room temperature. —Tim McKee

MAKE AHEAD The recipe can be prepared through Step 4 and refrigerated for up to 1 day. Return to room temperature before baking.

Asparagus Tart

MAKES ONE 11-INCH TART

Eggs in some form—in hollandaise sauce, for instance—are a delicious accompaniment to spring asparagus. Here they appear in a custard flavored with Parmigiano-Reggiano cheese.

TART SHELL

1½ cups all-purpose flour
Pinch of salt
1 stick (4 ounces) unsalted butter, cut into small pieces
1 large egg, beaten
3 tablespoons ice water

FILLING

½ pound medium asparagus, trimmed
4 large eggs
1 cup milk
2 tablespoons unsalted butter, melted
½ teaspoon salt
½ cup (1½ ounces) freshly grated Parmigiano-Reggiano cheese

1. MAKE THE TART SHELL: In a medium bowl, combine the flour with the salt. Using a pastry blender or 2 knives, cut in the butter until the mixture resembles coarse meal. Add the egg and water and mix with a fork until a dough forms. Turn the dough out onto a lightly floured work surface and pat into a disk. Wrap in plastic and refrigerate until firm, at least 1 hour or overnight.

2. On a lightly floured surface, roll out the dough to a 13-inch round. Fold the dough in half and carefully transfer it to an 11-inch tart pan with a removable bottom. Unfold the dough and gently press it into the pan without stretching. Trim the overhang. Wrap the tart shell in

plastic and refrigerate it until firm, about 1 hour or overnight.

3. Preheat the oven to 350°. Line the shell with foil and fill with pie weights, dried beans or rice. Bake for about 1 hour, or until lightly browned around the edge; remove the weights and foil. Bake the shell for 10 minutes, or until evenly browned and cooked through. Transfer to a rack to cool. Leave the oven on.

4. MAKE THE FILLING: In a medium saucepan of boiling salted water, cook the asparagus until tender, about 4 minutes. Drain and rinse under cold running water. Drain again and pat dry with paper towels. Arrange the asparagus in the tart shell with all the spears facing the same direction; trim to fit if necessary.

5. In a medium bowl, whisk the eggs until the whites and yolks are mixed. Beat in the milk, butter and salt. Pour the custard mixture over the asparagus and sprinkle the cheese over the top. Set the tart on a baking sheet and bake for about 45 minutes, or until the custard is just set. Transfer to a rack to cool for about 10 minutes. Cut the tart into 8 wedges and serve warm or at room temperature. —Maria José Cabral and Emília Augusta Magalháes

MAKE AHEAD The tart shell can be baked, cooled and kept well wrapped at room temperature for up to 1 day.

Parmesan Tartlets with Tomato Confit

MAKE EIGHT 4-INCH TARTS

These tartlets are like quiche with an Italian accent. Piquant Parmesan replaces the usual mild Swiss in the custard, and the confit adds a note of deep flavor. You will need eight four-inch tartlet pans with removable bottoms.

PASTRY

1¾ cups all-purpose flour
½ teaspoon sugar
½ teaspoon salt
1 stick (4 ounces) cold unsalted butter, cut into ½-inch pieces

1 large egg, lightly beaten

3 tablespoons cold water

FILLING

1 cup milk

¾ cup (4 ounces) freshly grated Parmigiano-Reggiano cheese

1 cup heavy cream

3 large eggs, lightly beaten

½ teaspoon salt

Tomato Confit (recipe follows)

I. MAKE THE PASTRY: In a food processor, combine the flour with the sugar and salt. Add the pieces of butter and pulse until the mixture resembles small peas. Beat the egg with the water and pour it into the food processor. Pulse several times until the pastry is just moistened but still slightly crumbly. Transfer the pastry to a work surface and gather it into a ball, kneading it once or twice. Divide the pastry dough into 8 equal pieces. Flatten each of the pieces of dough into a 3-inch disk, wrap each disk in plastic and refrigerate for at least 30 minutes or overnight.

2. Preheat the oven to 350°. On a lightly floured surface, roll out a pastry disk to a 6-inch round. Fit it into a 4-inch fluted tartlet pan with a removable bottom; cut off any overhang. Lightly prick the bottom with a fork. Repeat with the remaining pastry. Set the pans on a baking sheet and bake for 30 minutes, or until the pastry is golden and cooked through.

3. MAKE THE FILLING: In a blender or food processor, blend the milk with the Parmigiano-Reggiano cheese until smooth. Add the heavy cream, the eggs and the salt and pulse just until combined. Pour the cheese mixture into the tartlet shells and bake for 15 minutes, or until the custard is just set. Let the tartlets cool for 10 minutes and then unmold them. Serve the tartlets hot or at room temperature with the Tomato Confit. —*Grant Achatz*

MAKE AHEAD The cooled tartlet shells can be wrapped in foil and kept at room temperature overnight.

8 SERVINGS

Garlicky and intense, this condiment also complements eggs, broiled fish or chicken.

2 pounds plum tomatoes—peeled, quartered and seeded

24 small thyme sprigs

3 garlic cloves, thinly sliced

2 tablespoons extra-virgin olive oil

Salt and freshly ground pepper

Preheat the oven to 350° and line a rimmed baking sheet with parchment paper. Arrange the tomatoes on the sheet, rounded sides down, and top with the thyme, garlic and oil. Season with salt and pepper. Roast the tomatoes for 50 minutes to 1 hour, or until they are softened and the garlic is golden. —*G. A.*

MAKE AHEAD The Tomato Confit can be refrigerated for up to 4 days. Bring to room temperature before serving.

Creamed Wild Mushrooms on Toast with Thyme

8 SERVINGS

At Cascadia in Seattle, these creamy sautéed mushrooms come to the table in a skillet.

½ cup (½ ounce) dried morels

½ cup boiling water

½ pound white mushrooms, stems trimmed, caps coarsely chopped

4 tablespoons unsalted butter, plus more for brushing

2 large shallots, minced

4 large garlic cloves, minced

Salt and freshly ground pepper

½ cup brandy

1 cup heavy cream

1 pound shiitake mushrooms, stems discarded, caps thickly sliced

4 ounces chanterelle or hedgehog mushrooms, thickly sliced

4 ounces oyster mushrooms, thickly sliced

½ cup chicken stock or canned low-sodium broth

2 teaspoons minced thyme

Sixteen ½-inch-thick baguette slices, buttered and toasted

I. In a small heatproof bowl, cover the dried morels with the boiling water and let them stand until softened, about 20 minutes. Swish the morels in the soaking liquid to remove any grit and drain on paper towels; halve any large morels. Reserve the soaking liquid.

2. In a food processor, mince the white mushrooms. In a large skillet, melt 2 tablespoons of the butter. Add the shallots and cook over low heat until softened, about 3 minutes. Add the garlic and cook until fragrant, about 2 minutes. Add the minced white mushrooms and a pinch each of salt and pepper; cook over moderate heat, stirring, until any exuded liquid evaporates, about 3 minutes. Add the brandy and cook until reduced by half, about 4 minutes.

3. Add the morels and their reserved soaking liquid, stopping when you reach any grit on the bottom. Add ¾ cup of the cream and simmer over moderate heat until slightly thickened, about 5 minutes.

4. In another large skillet, melt the remaining 2 tablespoons butter. Add the shiitake, chanterelle and oyster mushrooms, season with salt and pepper and cook over moderately high heat, stirring, until lightly browned, about 5 minutes. Add ¼ cup of the stock, cover and cook over low heat, stirring occasionally, until the mushrooms are tender, about 8 minutes. Add the remaining ¼ cup each of cream and stock and simmer until slightly reduced, about 2 minutes. Add the morels and thyme and simmer for 3 minutes. Season with salt and pepper.

5. Arrange the baguette slices on 8 plates. Spoon the creamed mushrooms on top and serve at once. —*Kerry Sear*

MAKE AHEAD The mushrooms can be prepared through Step 4 and refrigerated overnight.

WINE The earthy mushrooms call for a fruity Sauvignon Blanc, such as the 1997 Chateau Ste. Michelle Horse Heaven from Washington State.

Florentine Ravioli

8 SERVINGS

More like gnocchi than ravioli, these delicate dumplings have no pasta covering whatsoever. The Florentines call them *ravioli nudi*—naked ravioli.

- 15 ounces (about 2 cups) fresh ricotta cheese
- 3 pounds spinach, large stems discarded

About 3 cups (¾ pound) freshly grated Parmesan cheese

- ½ teaspoon freshly grated nutmeg

Salt and freshly ground pepper

- 5 extra-large egg yolks
- 1 cup all-purpose flour
- 1 stick (4 ounces) unsalted butter

Fresh sage leaves, for garnish

1. Spoon the ricotta cheese into a large coffee filter set in a strainer and let it drain for 1 hour.

2. Bring a large pot of salted water to a boil. Add the spinach and cook for 10 minutes. Drain in a colander and cool under cold running water; drain thoroughly. Working with one handful at a time, squeeze the spinach until it is very dry. Finely chop the spinach.

3. In a large bowl, combine the drained ricotta with the spinach, 2 cups of the Parmesan and the nutmeg. Season the mixture generously with salt and pepper, add the egg yolks and stir until evenly combined.

4. Bring a large pot of salted water to a boil. Spread the flour on a plate. Form level tablespoons of the spinach-ricotta mixture into balls. Roll the balls lightly in the flour until coated. Arrange the balls on a lightly floured baking sheet.

5. Melt the butter in a medium skillet. Pour the butter into a large, warmed baking dish; keep warm near the stove.

6. Gently drop one third of the balls into the boiling water and cook just until they rise to the surface. Using a wire skimmer or slotted spoon, transfer the ravioli to the baking dish in a single layer. Return the water to a boil and cook the remaining balls in 2 batches.

Sprinkle the ravioli with as much of the remaining Parmesan as desired. Garnish the ravioli with sage leaves and serve immediately. —*Giuliano Bugialli*

Señora Juana's Chilaquiles in Green Sauce

4 SERVINGS

This recipe has been adapted from *My Mexico* (Clarkson Potter).

- ¾ pound tomatillos, husks removed
- 4 serrano chiles, stems discarded
- 1 garlic clove, chopped

Vegetable oil

Salt

Eight 5-inch corn tortillas, cut into ½-inch dice and left to dry overnight

- ½ cup minced white onion
- ⅔ cup chopped cilantro
- ¾ cup crumbled *queso fresco* or farmer cheese
- ⅓ cup crème fraîche or sour cream, thinned with a little milk

1. In a small saucepan, cover the tomatillos and chiles with water and cook over low heat until soft. Using a slotted spoon, transfer the tomatillos and chiles to a blender with ⅓ cup of the cooking water and the garlic. Blend until smooth.

2. In a large skillet, heat 1 tablespoon of vegetable oil. Add the tomatillo sauce, season with salt and cook over moderate heat, stirring occasionally, until slightly reduced and flavorful, about 5 minutes. Remove from the heat and keep warm.

3. In another large skillet, heat ¼ inch of vegetable oil until shimmering. Add half of the tortillas in an even layer; fry over moderately high heat until lightly browned, about 3 minutes. With a slotted spoon, transfer the tortillas to paper towels to drain while you fry the rest in the same way; add a bit more oil to the skillet and lower the heat if necessary.

4. Drain off all but ¼ cup of the vegetable oil and return all of the tortillas to the skillet. Stir in the onion, cover and cook over low heat, shaking the pan from time to time, until the onion is

Crab and Lemon-Thyme Soufflés

translucent, about 4 minutes. Add the tomatillo sauce to the pan and cook, stirring to blend well, about 3 minutes. Serve at once, topping each portion with some of the cilantro, cheese and crème fraîche. —*Diana Kennedy*

Crab and Lemon-Thyme Soufflés

6 SERVINGS

These soufflés remain moist thanks to the juicy crab. You'll need six six-ounce ramekins, or to serve the soufflés as a main course, divide it among four eight-ounce ramekins.

Fine dry bread crumbs, for the ramekins

- 3 tablespoons unsalted butter
- 3 tablespoons all-purpose flour
- 1 cup milk

Salt

- 3 large egg yolks
- 2 teaspoons minced lemon thyme
- ½ pound fresh crabmeat, picked over to remove cartilage

Freshly ground pepper

- 6 large egg whites, at room temperature

Chervil Butter Sauce (recipe follows)

1. Butter six 6-ounce ramekins and coat with bread crumbs, tapping out any excess. Set the prepared ramekins in a large shallow roasting pan.

2. Melt the butter in a medium saucepan. Add the flour and whisk over moderate heat until bubbling, about 1 minute. Add the milk and ¼ teaspoon of salt and whisk until the mixture boils and thickens. Remove the pan from the heat, whisk in the egg yolks and then whisk vigorously over moderate heat until the mixture boils again. Whisk in the lemon thyme. Transfer the soufflé base to a large bowl, press a piece of plastic wrap directly on the surface and let cool.

3. Preheat the oven to 375°. Whisk the soufflé base until smooth and then fold in the crabmeat. Season with salt and pepper.

4. Beat the egg whites until they hold firm peaks. Stir one third of the beaten whites into the base to lighten it and then fold in the remaining whites. Spoon the batter into the ramekins, filling them to within ½ inch of the rims. Wipe the rims clean.

5. Pour enough hot water into the roasting pan to reach halfway up the sides of the ramekins. Bake the soufflés for 30 minutes, or until lightly browned. Serve immediately with the Chervil Butter Sauce. —*Jerry Traunfeld*

MAKE AHEAD The soufflé base can be prepared through Step 2 and refrigerated for up to 2 days. Bring to room temperature before proceeding.

CHERVIL BUTTER SAUCE
MAKES ABOUT ½ CUP

- ¾ cup dry white wine
- 2 tablespoons minced shallots
- 1 tablespoon fresh lemon juice
- ¼ teaspoon salt
- 3 tablespoons cold unsalted butter, cut into tablespoons
- ½ cup chervil leaves or ¼ cup flat-leaf parsley leaves plus 2 teaspoons tarragon leaves

1. In a small saucepan, combine the wine with the shallots, lemon juice and salt and boil over moderately high heat until reduced by half. Turn the heat to low and whisk in the butter, 1 tablespoon at a time, until smooth.

2. Just before serving, put the chervil in a blender. Reheat the butter sauce gently over low heat; do not let it boil. Pour the sauce over the chervil. Blend until smooth; serve at once. —*J. T.*

Shrimp Fans
8 SERVINGS

You'll need jumbo shrimp and a sharp knife for this appetizer. The *wakame* called for is a type of seaweed that's available at health food stores and Asian markets.

- ½ cup sake
- ½ cup mirin (sweet rice wine)
- ½ cup soy sauce
- 3 tablespoons sugar
- 8 jumbo shrimp (about 1 pound)
- 24 medium asparagus
- 2 cups (about 3 ounces) dried *wakame*
- 2 tablespoons wasabi powder mixed with 2 tablespoons water
- ¼ cup Japanese mayonnaise or regular mayonnaise

1. In a small saucepan, combine the sake, mirin, soy sauce and sugar and boil over moderate heat until reduced to ½ cup, 15 to 20 minutes. Transfer the dressing to a bowl to cool.

2. Bring a large pot of lightly salted water to a boil. Add the shrimp and simmer until they are pink, curled and just cooked through, about 5 minutes. Using a slotted spoon, transfer the shrimp to a bowl of cold water to cool. Drain thoroughly and pat dry.

3. Return the water in the saucepan to a boil. Add the asparagus and cook until just tender, about 2 minutes. Refresh the asparagus under cold water, and then drain the asparagus and pat

Shrimp Fans

thoroughly dry. Cut the asparagus on the diagonal into 2-inch lengths.

4. Peel the shrimp, leaving the last section of the tail shell on. Using a thin sharp knife, slice each shrimp into thirds lengthwise, stopping when you reach the tail. Remove and discard the dark intestinal veins. Refrigerate the shrimp until chilled.

5. Soak the *wakame* in a large bowl of cold water until pliable and tender, about 5 minutes. Drain and rinse the *wakame,* squeezing out as much water as possible. Toss with all but 2 tablespoons of the dressing and mound on 8 salad plates. Fan out 1 shrimp on top of each and arrange some of the asparagus alongside. Drizzle with the remaining dressing. Garnish each plate with a small spoonful of wasabi and mayonnaise and serve. —*Hisachika Takahashi*

MAKE AHEAD The recipe can be prepared through Step 4 and refrigerated overnight.

WINE This understated shrimp dish calls for a white wine with delicate flavors, such as a nonvintage Brut Champagne—Nicolas Feuillatte or Deutz.

Citrus Scallop Ceviche

4 SERVINGS

- 1 pound large sea scallops, sliced crosswise into ¼-inch-thick rounds (see Note)
- 2 medium celery ribs, peeled and cut into ¼-inch dice
- 1 fresh kumquat, seeded and cut into ¼-inch dice
- ⅓ cup minced red onion
- ¼ cup fresh lime juice
- 2 tablespoons extra-virgin olive oil

Freshly ground pepper

- ¼ cup cilantro leaves
- 1 tablespoon minced chives

Fine sea salt

Toasted or grilled thinly sliced white bread, for serving

1. In a large shallow glass or ceramic dish, spread the scallop slices in a single layer. In a small bowl, combine the

Korean Seafood Pancakes

celery, kumquat, onion, lime juice and oil; season with pepper. Mix well and spoon over the scallops. Cover and refrigerate until the scallops start to turn opaque, at least 1 hour or up to 4 hours.

2. Add the cilantro and chives to the scallops and toss. Season with sea salt. Arrange the ceviche in a shallow bowl or platter and serve with the toasted bread. —*Raphael Lunetta*

NOTE Because ceviche isn't actually cooked, be sure to pick the very best quality scallops you can find.

Korean Seafood Pancakes

4 SERVINGS

- 1 cup all-purpose flour
- ½ cup cornstarch
- ½ teaspoon salt
- 1 large egg
- 1¾ cups water
- ¼ cup vegetable oil
- 4 large scallions, halved crosswise and cut into very thin strips
- 1 large red bell pepper, cut into thin strips

- 1 large jalapeño—halved, seeded and thinly sliced
- ½ pound medium shrimp— shelled, deveined and halved lengthwise
- ½ pound cleaned squid, bodies cut into ½-inch rings, large tentacles cut in half

Soy Dipping Sauce (recipe follows)

1. In a large bowl, sift together the flour, cornstarch and salt. Whisk the egg with the water and then whisk into the flour mixture until smooth.

2. In an 8-inch nonstick skillet, heat 1 tablespoon of the oil until shimmering. Add one quarter each of the scallions, red bell pepper and jalapeño and cook over high heat until barely softened, about 1 minute. Add one quarter each of the shrimp and squid, scattering them evenly in the pan. Pour in ⅓ cup of the batter, tilting the pan to spread it. Cook over high heat until the bottom of the pancake is crisp and browned, about 3 minutes. Using a spatula, carefully flip the pancake and cook on the other side until set, about 20 seconds. Slide the pancake onto a plate and make 3 more pancakes with the remaining ingredients. Cut the pancakes into quarters, or leave them whole; serve with Soy Dipping Sauce. —*Marcia Kiesel*

SOY DIPPING SAUCE

MAKES ABOUT ¾ CUP

- ½ cup soy sauce
- 2 tablespoons rice vinegar
- 2 scallions, minced
- 2 jalapeños, seeded and minced
- 1½ teaspoons Asian sesame oil

Combine all ingredients in a small bowl. Serve at room temperature. —*M. K.*

Kahan's Seared Sea Scallops with Fennel Broth and Orange

4 SERVINGS 👑

Paul Kahan is the chef of Blackbird in Chicago. He recommends avoiding buying scallops that are sitting in a pool of white liquid. The scallops should be a little sticky and have a sweet, briny smell. If there's no smell at all, they've probably been treated with chemicals.

- 1 tablespoon unsalted butter
- 1 large fennel bulb—cored and cut lengthwise into ¾-inch-long matchsticks, feathery tops reserved
- 1 cup thinly sliced yellow onion
- 1 garlic clove, smashed
- ¼ teaspoon fennel seeds
- 1 cup fish stock, or ½ cup clam juice diluted with ½ cup water
- ½ tablespoon Pernod

Salt and freshly ground pepper
- 1 small navel orange
- 1 inner celery rib, cut into ¾-inch-long matchsticks
- ¼ small red onion, cut into ¾-inch-long matchsticks
- ½ tablespoon extra-virgin olive oil
- ½ teaspoon cider vinegar
- 1 tablespoon canola oil
- 12 large sea scallops
- ½ tablespoon snipped chives

Kahan's Seared Sea Scallops with Fennel Broth and Orange

1. Melt the butter in a large saucepan. Add all but ½ cup of the fennel along with the yellow onion, the garlic and the fennel seeds. Cook over moderately low heat, stirring, until the fennel is crisp-tender, about 20 minutes. Add the fish stock and bring to a simmer. Cover and cook over low heat until the vegetables are softened, about 20 minutes. Let cool slightly and then puree in batches in a blender.

2. Strain the mixture through a fine sieve and discard the solids. Pour the fennel broth into a small saucepan, add the Pernod and season with salt and pepper; keep warm.

3. Using a sharp knife, peel the orange, removing all of the bitter white pith. Working over a bowl, cut in between the membranes to release the orange sections. Add the celery, red onion, olive oil, cider vinegar and the reserved ½ cup of fennel to the orange sections and toss. Season with salt and pepper. Spoon the mixture into 4 shallow soup plates and let stand for 15 minutes.

4. In a large skillet, heat the canola oil until shimmering. Pat the scallops dry and season with salt and pepper. Cook the scallops over high heat until browned and crusty, 2 to 3 minutes. Reduce the heat to moderately high, turn the scallops and cook until browned, about 2 minutes longer. Arrange 3 scallops in the center of each soup plate and spoon a little broth over the vegetables. Garnish with the chives and feathery fennel tops and serve. —*Paul Kahan*

Saffron Oysters with Leeks

3 TO 4 SERVINGS

Oysters that don't open during cooking should be removed from the saucepan and opened with an oyster knife. As long as they were tightly closed before cooking, they will be fine to eat.

- ½ **cup plus 2 tablespoons semidry white wine, preferably Sémillon**
- ½ **cup water**
- 1 **dozen Bluepoint or other good-sized oysters such as Cape Cod, scrubbed**

Saffron Oysters with Leeks

- 2 **tablespoons unsalted butter**
- 2 **small leeks, halved lengthwise and thinly sliced**
- ¼ **teaspoon (packed) saffron threads**
- ¼ **cup heavy cream**

Salt and freshly ground pepper

- 1 **large egg yolk**

1. In a large saucepan, combine ½ cup of the wine with the water and bring to a boil over high heat. Using tongs, add the oysters to the saucepan in a single layer, cover and steam until they start to open, about 3 minutes. Using tongs, transfer the oysters to a plate as they open. Reserve the cooking liquid; you should have about ½ cup. Remove the oysters from their shells, put them in a bowl and cover with a damp paper towel. Reserve 12 concave shells.

2. Melt 1 tablespoon of the butter in a medium saucepan. Add the leeks and crumble in the saffron; stir. Cook over low heat until the leeks soften, about 8 minutes. Slowly add the reserved oyster liquid, stopping before you reach the grit at the bottom, and cook over moderate heat until the liquid is almost evaporated, about 3 minutes. Add the cream and the remaining 2 tablespoons wine. Simmer until thickened, about 3 minutes. Season with salt and pepper.

3. Preheat the broiler. Arrange the 12 oyster shells on a rimmed baking sheet or in a shallow baking dish. Using a fork, divide the sautéed leeks among the shells. Set an oyster on the leeks in each shell and stir any accumulated oyster juices into the sauce.

4. Melt the remaining 1 tablespoon of butter. Whisk the egg yolk and the melted butter into the cream sauce and spoon the sauce over the oysters. Broil as close to the heat as possible for about 45 seconds, just until the sauce is bubbling and the oysters are lightly glazed. Serve at once. —*Marcia Kiesel*

MAKE AHEAD The recipe can be prepared through Step 3 up to 1 hour ahead; let stand at room temperature.

Mussels with Lemon-Fennel Butter

8 SERVINGS

If you want to serve these mussels in bowls as a quick shellfish stew, add the lemon-fennel butter to the cooking liquid after you have removed the mussels. Simmer until it thickens slightly and use it as a sauce. This recipe is from *Sharing the Vineyard Table* (Ten Speed Press) by Carolyn Wente and Kimball Jones.

- 1 **cup dry white wine**
- 2 **tablespoons minced shallots**
- 2 **pounds mussels, scrubbed and debearded**
- 2 **teaspoons olive oil**
- ¼ **teaspoon fennel seeds**
- 1 **tablespoon finely chopped fennel, plus feathery sprigs for garnish**
- 2 **tablespoons Pernod**
- 4 **tablespoons unsalted butter, at room temperature**
- ½ **teaspoon fresh lemon juice**
- ½ **teaspoon finely grated lemon zest**

Kosher salt and freshly ground pepper

1. In a large saucepan, combine the wine and shallots and bring to a boil. Add the mussels, cover and cook over high heat, shaking the pan occasionally, until the mussels open, about 5 minutes. Using a slotted spoon, remove the mussels to a bowl as they are done. Let cool slightly. Discard any mussels that do not open.

2. Remove the mussels from their shells and transfer to a bowl. Add 1 teaspoon of the olive oil to the mussels and toss to coat. Sort through the mussel shells and keep the nicest shell from each pair; discard the rest.

3. Grind the fennel seeds in a spice grinder or mortar. Heat the remaining 1 teaspoon of olive oil in a small saucepan. Add the chopped fennel and cook over high heat, stirring, for 1 minute. Stir in the Pernod, tilt the pan and carefully ignite the Pernod with a long match. When the flames die down, remove the pan from the heat. Transfer the mixture to a small bowl and let cool to room temperature. Gradually whisk in the butter, ground fennel seeds, lemon juice and lemon zest and season with kosher salt and pepper.

4. Preheat the broiler. Place 1 mussel in each shell and set the mussels on a rimmed baking sheet. Top each mussel with ½ teaspoon of the fennel butter. Broil about 6 inches from the heat for 1 minute, just until the mussels sizzle. Garnish each with a small fennel sprig; serve immediately. —*Kimball Jones*

MAKE AHEAD The mussels can be prepared through Step 2 and refrigerated for up to 4 hours.

WINE Try a stainless steel–fermented dry white, such as the 1997 Wente Estate Grown—a crisp, clean Chardonnay that won't overpower the mussels. Or drink a brut sparkling wine.

Mint Pesto–Stuffed Mussels
6 SERVINGS
You'll definitely want crusty bread on hand for mopping up the garlicky pesto.

- ¼ **cup pine nuts**
- 2 **small garlic cloves**

Salt

- 2 **cups mint leaves, plus mint sprigs for garnish**
- ½ **cup flat-leaf parsley**
- ¼ **cup extra-virgin olive oil**

Freshly ground pepper

- 2 **pounds mussels, scrubbed and debearded**
- ½ **cup dry white wine**

I. In a food processor, mince the pine nuts with the garlic cloves and ¾ teaspoon of salt. Add the 2 cups mint leaves and the parsley and pulse until the leaves are coarsely chopped, scraping down the side of the bowl once or twice. With the machine on, gradually add the olive oil and process until a coarse paste forms. Season with salt and pepper.

2. Preheat the oven to 375°. In a large pot, combine the mussels and wine. Cover tightly and cook over high heat; as the mussels open, use a slotted spoon to transfer them to a bowl. Let cool slightly. Discard any mussels that do not open.

3. Discard 1 shell from each mussel and loosen the meat in the remaining shell. Set the mussels on the half shell on a baking sheet. Lift each of the mussels, stuff ½ teaspoon of pesto under it and then lightly press the mussel back in place.

4. Bake the mussels for about 10 minutes, or until they're hot to the touch and the pesto begins to bubble. Serve the mussels on plates or on a platter lined with mint sprigs. —*Jerry Traunfeld*

MAKE AHEAD The mussels can be prepared through Step 3 and refrigerated for up to 4 hours.

WINE All that's needed to complement the strong flavors of this pesto is a palate-cleansing, lean dry white. Stick with an Italian Pinot Grigio, such as the 1997 Livio Felluga or the 1997 Peter Zemmer.

Asian Tuna Tartare
4 SERVINGS
Despite the name, this specialty of Le Bernardin in New York City isn't authentically Asian—not with jalapeños and potato chips among the ingredients. It's a 100 percent New York invention.

- ¼ **cup corn oil**
- 2 **teaspoons grated fresh ginger**
- 1 **pound sushi-grade tuna**
- ¼ **cup finely chopped cilantro**
- 1 **teaspoon minced jalapeño**
- 1½ **teaspoons wasabi powder**
- 1 **teaspoon toasted sesame seeds**
- 1 **tablespoon finely chopped scallion**
- 1½ **tablespoons lemon juice, plus half a lemon**

Sea salt and freshly ground pepper

- 1 **tomato—peeled, seeded and cut into ⅛-inch dice**
- 20 **best-quality potato chips**

I. In a bowl, combine the oil and ginger and let stand at room temperature for at least 2 hours. Strain the oil.

2. With a very sharp knife, cut the tuna into ⅛-inch dice. In a large bowl, combine the tuna with 3 tablespoons of the

Mint Pesto–Stuffed Mussels

ginger oil, 3 tablespoons of the cilantro, the jalapeño, wasabi, sesame seeds, scallion and lemon juice. Mix gently and season with sea salt and pepper.

3. Stand a 1½-inch-tall and 2¼-inch-round mold or a biscuit cutter in the center of a salad plate. Fill the mold with tuna tartare, pressing gently. Lift off the mold. Repeat with the remaining tuna tartare.

4. Drizzle the remaining ginger oil around each tartare and sprinkle with the tomato, the remaining tablespoon of cilantro and a squeeze of lemon juice. Stand 5 potato chips in a circular pattern in each tartare and serve immediately. —*Eric Ripert*

Seared Tuna Salad with Creamy Mustard Sauce
4 SERVINGS

- 4 **small tomatoes**

Fine sea salt

Piment d'Espelette (see Note) or mildly hot paprika

- ¼ **pound haricots verts or thin green beans, ¼ cut in half crosswise**
- 2 **carrots, cut into matchsticks**
- 2 **tablespoons fresh lemon juice**
- 1 **teaspoon Dijon mustard**
- ¼ **cup crème fraîche or heavy cream**

4 spring onions or scallions, white parts only, halved lengthwise and sliced crosswise

2 tablespoons chopped chives, plus 4-inch-long chives for garnish

Four 4-ounce sushi-quality yellowfin tuna steaks, ½ inch thick

1 tablespoon extra-virgin olive oil

Coarsely crushed black peppercorns

¼ pound mixed greens

4 lemon wedges, for garnish

1. Cut a slice off the stem end of each tomato. Using a spoon, hollow out the tomatoes. Season with salt and *piment d'Espelette*. Cook the haricots verts and then the carrots in a medium saucepan of boiling salted water until just tender, 3 to 5 minutes for each. Drain, rinse in cold water and drain on paper towels.

2. In a medium bowl, combine 1 tablespoon of lemon juice with the mustard. Season with salt and *piment d'Espelette* and whisk in the crème fraîche. Stir in the haricots verts, carrots, onions and chopped chives. Fill the tomatoes with the halved haricots verts and some of the spring onions and carrots.

3. Heat a large skillet. Brush the tuna steaks with the olive oil and the remaining 1 tablespoon of lemon juice; season with salt and crushed black peppercorns. Add the tuna to the skillet and sear over high heat until well browned, about 2 minutes per side.

4. Mound the remaining vegetables on one side of each plate. Lean the tuna steaks off center on the vegetables and then top with the greens. Set a stuffed tomato alongside each. Dust each of the plates with *piment d'Espelette*, garnish with chives and lemon wedges and serve. —*Philippe Renard*

NOTE *Piment d'Espelette,* a crushed red pepper from the Basque region of France, is available by mail from Igo Foods (888-IGO-9966).

WINE 1995 Taittinger Brut Millésime. The full body, fresh acidity and sparkle of this wine make a nice contrast to the rich tuna and creamy, mustardy sauce.

Seared Tuna Salad with Creamy Mustard Sauce

Terrine of Pickled Herring with Caviar Cream

8 SERVINGS

1 cup water

½ cup rice vinegar

⅓ cup plus 2 tablespoons sugar

2 tablespoons kosher salt

1 teaspoon mustard seeds

1 teaspoon whole black peppercorns

1 teaspoon minced fresh ginger

½ jalapeño, seeded and minced

1 whole clove

1 pound fresh herring fillets (about 9)

1 tablespoon powdered gelatin

1 cup fish stock

1 medium red onion, thinly sliced

30 medium asparagus spears, trimmed

¼ cup crème fraîche

2 ounces osetra caviar

Freshly ground pepper

2 tablespoons extra-virgin olive oil

Table salt

¼ cup chervil or flat-leaf parsley leaves

¼ cup chopped dill

1. In a small saucepan, combine the water with the rice vinegar, sugar, kosher salt, mustard seeds, peppercorns, ginger, jalapeño and clove and bring to a boil. Simmer the pickling liquid over low heat until the sugar and the salt are dissolved.

2. Arrange the herring fillets in a large, shallow heatproof glass baking dish. Pour 1½ cups of the hot pickling liquid over the fish; reserve the remaining pickling liquid. Let the herring fillets and pickling liquid cool to room temperature. Marinate the herring until it is almost opaque throughout, about 20 minutes, depending on the thickness of the fillets.

3. Meanwhile, in a small saucepan, sprinkle the powdered gelatin over the fish stock and set aside until the gelatin is evenly moistened, about 10 minutes. Warm the gelatin mixture over low heat, stirring gently, just until it is warm to the touch.

4. Put the red onion slices in a shallow bowl and then strain the pickling liquid from the herring over them; let the onion slices marinate for 10 minutes. Pat the herring fillets and the red onion slices dry and wipe off any marinade solids.

5. In a large saucepan of boiling water, cook the asparagus spears until they are just tender, about 4 minutes; drain and refresh the asparagus under cold running water. Cut the tips from the asparagus and set aside.

6. Line an 8-by-3½-by-2¼-inch loaf pan with plastic wrap. Dip 10 of the asparagus stems in the gelatin mixture and lay them side by side on the bottom of the terrine. Layer one third of the red onion slices over the asparagus stems and then spoon 2 tablespoons of the gelatin mixture on top. Dip 3 of the herring fillets in the gelatin mixture and arrange them over the red onion slices in an even layer. Repeat the layering process 2 more times. Cover the pickled herring terrine with plastic wrap and refrigerate until it is firm, at least 2 hours or overnight.

7. Before serving the terrine, strain all but 2 tablespoons of the reserved pickling liquid into a bowl. Add the asparagus tips and refrigerate for 20 minutes. In a small bowl, stir the crème fraîche and then fold in the caviar. Season with pepper and refrigerate. Strain the remaining 2 tablespoons of pickling liquid into a small bowl and whisk in the olive oil. Season the vinaigrette with table salt and pepper.

8. Unmold the terrine onto a work surface. Sawing gently through the plastic wrap with a serrated knife, cut the terrine into 1-inch slices. Support each slice of the terrine as you transfer it to a plate and then discard the plastic wrap. Spoon the caviar cream on the slices. Garnish the slices of terrine with the asparagus tips, the chervil and the dill, drizzle the vinaigrette over each slice and serve. —*Charlie Trotter*

Smoked Fish Cakes with Root-Vegetable Slaw

8 SERVINGS

At Cascadia in Seattle, all the ingredients used are either grown, gathered or made in the area after which the restaurant is named—a region that stretches north to Alaska, south to Oregon, west to the Pacific Ocean and east to the Cascade Mountains. Cod, which comes from Alaska and is widely available in the Pacific Northwest, is a likely choice for these fried cakes. Any kind of smoked fish works well, though; you could use whitefish, trout or salmon.

ROOT-VEGETABLE SLAW

- ½ cup julienned celery root
- ½ cup julienned carrot
- ½ cup julienned parsnip
- 2 tablespoons apple cider vinegar
- 1 teaspoon finely chopped flat-leaf parsley

Salt and freshly ground pepper

FISH CAKES

- 3 large baking potatoes
- 1 pound skinless, boneless smoked fish, flaked
- 2 large eggs, lightly beaten
- 4 tablespoons unsalted butter, melted
- ½ cup coarsely chopped chives
- ¼ cup finely chopped flat-leaf parsley
- ½ teaspoon salt
- ¼ teaspoon freshly ground pepper
- 1 cup fine fresh bread crumbs

Canola oil, for frying

Onion Mustard Sauce (recipe follows), for serving

1. MAKE THE ROOT-VEGETABLE SLAW: In a medium bowl, combine the celery root, carrot and parsnip. Add the apple cider vinegar and the parsley, season the slaw with salt and pepper and toss well.

2. MAKE THE FISH CAKES: Preheat the oven to 400°. Roast the baking potatoes for about 35 minutes, or until they are tender. Let them cool slightly and then peel the potatoes and pass them through a ricer or coarse sieve. In a bowl, combine the potatoes, smoked fish, eggs, butter, chives, parsley, salt and pepper. Shape the mixture into 16 patties.

3. Lower the oven temperature to 300°. Spread the bread crumbs on a plate. Dredge the fish cakes in the bread crumbs and tap off any excess.

4. In a large skillet, heat ¼ inch of canola oil until almost smoking. Fry the fish cakes in batches over moderately high heat until they are browned and crisp, about 3 minutes. Turn the fish cakes, lower the heat to moderate and cook until browned on the bottom, about 2 minutes longer. Transfer the fried fish cakes to a plate and keep them warm in the oven while you fry the rest of the cakes.

5. Spoon the Onion Mustard Sauce onto each of 8 plates. Set 2 of the fish cakes in the sauce on each plate, spoon the root-vegetable slaw on top and serve. —*Kerry Sear*

MAKE AHEAD The fish cakes can be prepared through Step 2 and refrigerated overnight.

WINE A restrained Washington State Sémillon would be the perfect way to match the smoky flavor of these fish cakes. Both the 1998 Matthews Cellars and the 1997 Chinook are bottles worth seeking out.

ONION MUSTARD SAUCE

MAKES ABOUT 1¼ CUPS

- 1 small onion, minced
- ½ cup dry white wine
- ½ cup heavy cream
- 2 tablespoons cold unsalted butter, cut into 4 pieces
- ¼ cup whole-grain mustard

Salt and freshly ground pepper

1. In a small saucepan, combine the onion and the white wine and simmer over moderate heat until the wine is reduced to 1 tablespoon, about 5 minutes. Add the heavy cream and bring to a boil. Transfer the mixture to a blender

Smoked Fish Cakes with Root-Vegetable Slaw

and puree. With the machine on low speed, add the butter, 1 piece at a time, until the sauce is smooth.

2. Scrape the onion sauce into a small saucepan and stir in the mustard. Season with salt and pepper. Rewarm the sauce over low heat, stirring constantly. Serve the onion mustard sauce warm with the Smoked Fish Cakes with Root-Vegetable Slaw. —*K. S.*

MAKE AHEAD The sauce can be refrigerated overnight. Gently reheat, whisking constantly.

Warm Potatoes with Smoked Salmon

4 SERVINGS

Torpedo onions are red tinged, oval shaped and sweet. They add a slight edge to these potatoes.

- 1 small Torpedo onion, thinly sliced, or 1 cup thinly sliced Vidalia onion
- 1½ tablespoons red wine vinegar
- 1 pound fingerling potatoes, cut into 1½-inch chunks
- 1 bay leaf

Kosher salt and freshly ground pepper

- 2 tablespoons extra-virgin olive oil
- ½ pound thinly sliced smoked salmon
- 1 tablespoon capers, drained
- 1 tablespoon fresh lemon juice
- ¼ cup crème fraîche
- 2 tablespoons chervil leaves
- 1 teaspoon minced chives

1. In a small bowl, toss the onion with the vinegar to coat. In a medium saucepan, combine the potatoes with the bay leaf and 1 tablespoon of kosher salt. Cover with 1 inch of cold water; bring to a boil. Cook over moderate heat until fork-tender, about 12 minutes. Drain the potatoes, return to the saucepan and toss with a generous pinch of pepper and 1 tablespoon of the olive oil.

2. Spoon the potatoes onto 4 plates and arrange the salmon over them. Drain the onion and return to the bowl. Add the capers, lemon juice and the

remaining 1 tablespoon oil and spoon over the salmon. Add the crème fraîche to the bowl, stir once or twice and drizzle over all. Scatter the chervil and chives on top and serve. —*Seen Lippert*

WINE The rich flavors of this dish would go perfectly with a ripe, round, mouth-filling Chardonnay. Consider the 1997 Burgess from California or the 1996 Leeuwin from Australia.

Lemongrass-Infused Snails with Spicy Soy Sauce

8 SERVINGS

Live snails are traditionally used in this Vietnamese recipe, but canned snails work very well. The snails are chopped and mixed with pork, chile, ginger and other flavorings and then stuffed into snail shells and steamed. A lemongrass handle makes removing the filling easy.

- 2 fresh lemongrass stalks
- ½ pound ground pork

One 7-ounce can large Burgundy snails—drained, rinsed and minced (see Note)

- 2 teaspoons finely grated fresh ginger
- 2 Thai chiles, halved and seeded, 1 minced and 1 julienned
- 1 teaspoon Asian sesame oil
- ¾ teaspoon kosher salt
- ½ teaspoon freshly ground pepper
- 24 snail shells

Lettuce or cabbage leaves, for steaming

- ¼ cup vegetable oil
- 1 scallion, white and light green parts only, thinly sliced on the diagonal
- ⅓ cup soy sauce, preferably Chinese thin

1. Trim the root ends of the lemongrass; remove a total of 8 long outer leaves from the stalks. Tear each of the leaves into three 3-inch-long strands. Trim off

Warm Potatoes with Smoked Salmon

Lemongrass-Infused Snails
with Spicy Soy Sauce

and discard all but the bottom 3 inches of the stalks and finely chop 1 of the tender bulbs. Thinly slice the remaining bulb on the diagonal. In a mini processor, puree the chopped lemongrass to a fine paste.

2. In a bowl, combine the ground pork with the snails, ginger, the minced Thai chile, the Asian sesame oil, kosher salt, pepper and lemongrass paste.

3. Gently bend a lemongrass strand in half and stick it inside a snail shell, bent side in, and with the 2 ends protruding. Stuff the shell with 2 teaspoons of the pork-and-snail filling, working it between the lemongrass ends. Wipe the rim of the shell. Repeat with the remaining lemongrass, shells and filling.

4. Line a steamer rack with lettuce leaves and set the stuffed shells on top. Steam the snails until hot to the touch and cooked through, about 8 minutes.

5. Meanwhile, heat the vegetable oil in a small saucepan. Add the sliced lemongrass, the julienned chile and the scallion and cook over moderate heat until fragrant, about 1 minute. Pour the soy sauce into a heatproof serving bowl. Stir in the scallion-and-chile oil and serve with the snails. —*Corinne Trang*

NOTE The two snail species most commonly eaten are the Burgundy, or vineyard, snail (which has a yellowish brown shell with spiral stripes) and the *petit-gris,* or garden, snail (which is slightly smaller and has a yellowish gray shell with purplish brown stripes). Because Burgundy snails are plumper and tastier, they are the first choice for this dish. Canned snails and snail shells are available in specialty shops or by mail order from Zabar's (800-697-6301).

MAKE AHEAD The recipe can be prepared through Step 3 and refrigerated for up to 2 days.

Little Pork Tamales with Red Chile Sauce

MAKES ABOUT 2 DOZEN TAMALES
These tender tamales with smoky, smooth ancho sauce are easy to make, but they do take some time. However, all the work can be done ahead, and at the last minute all you need to do is reheat them.

1½ **pounds pork shoulder or butt**
5 **cups water**
Salt
1 **medium onion, coarsely chopped**
6 **garlic cloves**
4 **ancho chiles, stemmed and seeded**
2 **plum tomatoes, quartered**
Two 8-inch white corn tortillas, **quartered**
½ **cup unsalted pumpkin seeds**
1 **cup coarse white grits (see Note)**
1 **cup** *masa harina*
5 **cups chicken stock or canned low-sodium broth**
1 **stick (4 ounces) cold unsalted butter, cut into pieces**
24 **large dried corn husks (see Note)**

I. In a saucepan, cover the pork with the water and add 1½ teaspoons of salt. Bring to a boil, cover partially and simmer over low heat until the pork is very tender, about 2 hours. Transfer the pork to a plate; cover with a damp cloth and let cool.

2. Strain the cooking liquid and return it to the saucepan; skim off the fat. Add the onion, garlic, anchos, tomatoes and tortillas. Bring to a boil; simmer for 30 minutes. Let cool to room temperature.

3. In a skillet, toast the pumpkin seeds over moderate heat until puffed, about 3 minutes. Puree the ancho mixture with the seeds in batches. Return to the saucepan and simmer over moderate heat, stirring, until slightly thickened, about 10 minutes. Season with salt.

4. In a bowl, combine the grits, *masa harina* and 1½ teaspoons salt. In a saucepan, bring the stock to a simmer. Slowly stir in the grits mixture. Cover and cook over low heat for 30 minutes, stirring. Add the butter, season with salt and let the dough cool slightly.

5. Meanwhile, soak the corn husks in water until pliable, about 20 minutes; drain. Shred the pork into a bowl and stir in ¾ cup of the ancho sauce; season with salt.

6. Spread a corn husk on a work surface. Spread 3 tablespoons of tamale dough over the wide end of the husk to form a ¼-inch-thick rectangle. Spoon 1 heaping tablespoon of the pork filling in the center of the dough. Using the husk, bring the dough up to enclose the meat. Fold the husk around the dough and fold the narrow end of the husk under the tamale. Repeat with the remaining husks, dough and filling; rewarm the dough in a microwave oven or on a plate in a steamer if it cools down.

7. Cook the tamales in a large steamer until they are heated through and firm to the touch, about 15 minutes. Transfer to a platter. Rewarm the remaining ancho sauce and serve it with the tamales. —*Robert Del Grande*

NOTE Coarse-textured Arrowhead Mills grits are widely available at health-food and specialty food stores. Dried corn husks are also available at specialty food stores, or use fresh husks.

MAKE AHEAD The uncooked tamales can be frozen for up to 1 week.

Little Pork Tamales with Red Chile Sauce, with Broiled Garlic and Lime Shrimp (p. 22) and Crab and Guacamole Tostaditos (p. 20).

chapter 3

salads

47

50

ABOVE: **Lettuce and Fennel Salad with Citrus Vinaigrette.** LEFT: **Mixed Greens with Olive Vinaigrette.**

Mixed Greens with Olive Vinaigrette

6 SERVINGS

- 2 tablespoons black olive paste or finely chopped black olives, such as Calamata
- 2 tablespoons minced shallots
- 1 tablespoon red wine vinegar
- ½ teaspoon Dijon mustard
- ⅓ cup extra-virgin olive oil

Salt and freshly ground pepper

- 1 large head radicchio, torn into bite-size pieces
- 1 large endive, cut into bite-size pieces
- 1 large bunch of watercress, tough stems discarded, the rest torn into bite-size pieces

In a large bowl, whisk the olive paste, shallots, vinegar and mustard. Whisk in the olive oil in a thin stream. Season with salt and pepper. Add the radicchio, endive and watercress and toss. Season the salad with salt and pepper and serve immediately. —*Michele Scicolone*

MAKE AHEAD The dressing can be refrigerated overnight in a jar.

WINE Salad doesn't usually pair well with wine, but a light crisp white would be good with this recipe. Try the 1997 Villa Matilde Falerno del Massico Bianco or the 1997 Ruffino Libaio.

Winter Greens with Warm Caesar Dressing

6 SERVINGS

- 5 tablespoons extra-virgin olive oil
- 3 oil-packed anchovies, minced
- 2 garlic cloves, minced
- 2½ tablespoons fresh lemon juice
- ½ teaspoon finely grated lemon zest

Three ½-inch-thick slices sourdough bread—crusts removed, bread cut into ¾-inch cubes and toasted

- ⅓ cup freshly grated Parmesan cheese
- 3 medium heads escarole, tender green and white leaves only, torn into 2-inch pieces

Freshly ground pepper

1. Heat the olive oil in a small skillet. Mash the anchovies and the garlic to a paste; add the paste to the pan and cook over moderately high heat for 1 minute. Stir in the fresh lemon juice and the lemon zest.

2. In a large salad bowl, toss the croutons with 1 tablespoon of the warm Caesar dressing and 1 tablespoon of the Parmesan cheese. Add the escarole, the remaining dressing and Parmesan and a generous pinch of freshly ground pepper. Toss the salad well and serve at once. —*Grace Parisi*

ONE SERVING Calories 177 kcal, Total Fat 13.7 gm, Saturated Fat 2.6 gm

Lettuce and Fennel Salad with Citrus Vinaigrette

4 TO 6 SERVINGS

Fresh tangerine juice makes a lovely dressing. You can add sections of the fruit, too.

- ¼ cup fresh tangerine or orange juice
- 3 tablespoons fresh lemon juice
- 2 tablespoons olive oil
- ¾ teaspoon salt
- ¼ teaspoon freshly ground pepper
- 1 large head of red oak leaf lettuce, torn into bite-size pieces
- 1 large bunch of arugula, torn into bite-size pieces
- 1 small head of frisée, leaves torn into bite-size pieces
- 1 large fennel bulb—trimmed, halved, cored and thinly sliced crosswise

In a small glass or stainless steel bowl, combine the tangerine and lemon juices, the olive oil, salt and pepper. In a large salad bowl, toss the red oak leaf lettuce, arugula, frisée and fennel. Add the dressing; toss well. Serve the salad at once. —Edwin Goto

Fennel and Arugula Salad

4 SERVINGS ✳

- ¼ cup plus 1 tablespoon extra-virgin olive oil
- 2 tablespoons fresh lemon juice
- ½ teaspoon Dijon mustard
- 1 small shallot, minced
- 1 small garlic clove, minced

Salt and freshly ground pepper

- ½ pound small mushrooms, stems trimmed, mushrooms halved
- ½ pound arugula, large stems discarded
- 1 large fennel bulb—halved lengthwise, trimmed and thinly sliced crosswise
- ½ cup crumbled fresh goat cheese

1. In a large salad bowl, mix ¼ cup of the olive oil with the lemon juice, Dijon mustard, shallot and garlic. Season the dressing with salt and pepper.

2. In a large skillet, heat the remaining 1 tablespoon of olive oil. Add the mushrooms, season with salt and pepper and cook over high heat, stirring, until any exuded liquid evaporates and the mushrooms are browned, about 8 minutes; keep warm.

3. Add the arugula and the fennel slices to the dressing in the bowl and toss well. Scatter the mushrooms over the salad, top with the goat cheese and serve at once. —Anthony Roselli

Spinach and Mushroom Salad with Cumin Dressing

8 SERVINGS

This is a far cry from a classic spinach salad. The tangy lemon dressing, with a slight hint of exotic spice, is light and very refreshing.

- 1½ teaspoons cumin seeds, lightly toasted
- ¼ cup fresh lemon juice
- 1 teaspoon finely grated lemon zest
- 2 garlic cloves, minced

Salt

- ½ teaspoon paprika
- ½ teaspoon ground coriander
- ½ cup olive oil
- 1¼ pounds firm white mushrooms, stems trimmed, caps quartered

Freshly ground pepper

- 2 pounds spinach, large stems discarded, leaves torn into large pieces
- 8 small scallions, white and tender green parts, thinly sliced
- ⅓ cup chopped cilantro

1. In a spice grinder or mortar, crush the cumin seeds to a powder. In a small glass or stainless steel bowl, combine the lemon juice, lemon zest and garlic with 1 teaspoon of salt. Whisk in the

Fennel and Arugula Salad

cumin, paprika and coriander and then whisk in the olive oil.

2. In a medium glass or stainless steel bowl, toss the mushrooms with ½ cup of the dressing and season with salt and pepper. In a large salad bowl, toss the spinach with the scallions, cilantro and the remaining dressing. Add the mushrooms to the salad and toss well. Season the salad with salt and pepper and serve. —*Deborah Madison*

Watercress Salad with Fried Morels

6 SERVINGS

For this delicious salad, the morels are simmered in cream and then rolled in cracker crumbs and fried.

- 1 cup (1 ounce) dried morels
- 1 cup boiling water
- ½ cup heavy cream
- Salt and freshly ground pepper
- 2 tablespoons ketchup
- 2 teaspoons rice vinegar
- 1 teaspoon minced fresh ginger
- 1 garlic clove, minced
- ½ teaspoon soy sauce
- All-purpose flour, for dredging

- 2 large eggs, beaten with 1 tablespoon water
- 1 cup finely crushed crackers or cracker meal
- Vegetable oil, for frying
- 4 large bunches watercress, tough stems discarded
- 1 small red onion, halved lengthwise and thinly sliced crosswise

1. In a heatproof bowl, soak the morels in the boiling water until softened, about 20 minutes. Rub to loosen any grit and then lift the morels out. Let the soaking liquid stand for 5 minutes so the grit falls to the bottom. Pour off the liquid, leaving any grit behind, and reserve.

2. In a small saucepan, simmer the morels in the heavy cream over low heat, stirring a few times, until they absorb the cream, about 8 minutes. Season with salt and pepper.

3. In a small glass or stainless steel bowl, combine 6 tablespoons of the reserved morel soaking liquid with the ketchup, rice vinegar, fresh ginger, garlic and soy sauce. Blend well and season with salt and freshly ground pepper. Set the dressing aside.

4. Put the flour, the egg mixture and the crushed crackers in separate shallow bowls. Dredge each morel in the flour, shaking off the excess; dip it in the egg mixture, coat with crushed crackers and then set aside on a floured platter.

5. In a medium saucepan, heat 1 inch of vegetable oil until shimmering. Add 4 or 5 morels at a time and fry over moderate heat until golden brown, about 1 minute. Using a slotted spoon, transfer the morels to a plate and keep warm.

6. In a large salad bowl, toss the watercress with the onion and the dressing. Scatter the morels on top and serve the salad at once. —*Marcia Kiesel*

MAKE AHEAD The morels can be prepared through Step 2 and refrigerated for up to 1 day. The dressing can be refrigerated for up to 2 days.

Watercress Salad with Fried Morels

WINE By itself, tangy watercress with a soy sauce dressing would be too sharp to be wine friendly, but the addition of fried morels adds enough fattiness to make a crisp, herbaceous California Sauvignon (or Fumé) Blanc a natural choice. Top picks? The 1997 Matanzas Creek or the 1997 Chateau St. Jean La Petite Etoile.

Grilled Portobello and Bosc Pear Salad

10 SERVINGS

- 8 large Portobello mushrooms, stems discarded
- ½ cup pure olive oil
- Salt and freshly ground pepper
- 2 tablespoons balsamic vinegar, preferably aged
- 1 garlic clove, minced
- 2 tablespoons extra-virgin olive oil
- 2 tablespoons fresh lemon juice
- 1 teaspoon chopped thyme
- 3 large Bosc pears—peeled, halved, cored and cut lengthwise into thin wedges
- 6 cups bite-size pieces of romaine lettuce
- ½ cup thin shavings of Manchego, Pecorino or Parmigiano-Reggiano cheese (see Note)

1. Light a grill or heat a grill pan. Coat each mushroom with 1 tablespoon of the pure olive oil. Season with salt and pepper. Grill the mushrooms over a medium low fire or in a grill pan until very crusty and lightly charred outside and cooked through, about 10 minutes per side. Transfer the mushrooms to a large rimmed baking sheet, gills up.

2. Preheat the oven to 400°. In a small glass or stainless steel bowl, combine the balsamic vinegar and garlic. Brush the mixture over the mushroom gills. Roast the mushrooms for about 5 minutes, or until hot. Slice ½ inch thick.

3. In a small glass or stainless steel bowl, whisk the extra-virgin olive oil with the lemon juice and thyme. Season with salt and pepper. Toss the pear wedges with 1 tablespoon of the dressing. In a large salad bowl, toss the romaine with the remaining dressing. Add the pear wedges and the mushrooms and toss. Top the salad with the cheese shavings and serve. —*Marcia Kiesel*

NOTE If you don't own a cheese slicer, use a swivel-bladed vegetable peeler to make the cheese shavings.

MAKE AHEAD The grilled Portobello mushrooms can stand at room temperature for up to 4 hours.

Citrus and Avocado Salad with Pickled Onions
8 SERVINGS

- 3 medium ruby grapefruit
- 4 blood oranges
- 4 navel oranges
- 1 pomegranate, halved crosswise
- ⅛ teaspoon orange flower water (optional)
- 2 tablespoons extra-virgin olive oil

Salt and freshly ground pepper

- 3 bunches watercress, large stems discarded
- ¾ cup Pickled Red Onions (recipe follows)
- 2 Hass avocados, peeled and cut into ½-inch wedges

I. Using a sharp stainless steel knife, peel the grapefruits and oranges; be sure to remove all of the bitter white pith. Cut each fruit crosswise into five ¼-inch slices. Squeeze enough of the remaining citrus to yield ⅓ cup of juice; set aside.

2. Using a citrus reamer, squeeze one half of the pomegranate until you have 2 tablespoons of juice. Remove and reserve ¼ cup seeds from the other half.

3. In a glass or stainless steel bowl, whisk the citrus and pomegranate juices with the orange flower water and olive oil. Season with salt and pepper.

4. In a large glass or stainless steel bowl, toss the watercress with ¼ cup of the dressing and half of the pickled

onions. Arrange the watercress on a platter. Add the avocados to the bowl and gently toss with 3 tablespoons of the dressing. Arrange the avocado and sliced oranges and grapefruit on the watercress; drizzle with the remaining dressing. Garnish with the remaining pickled onions and the pomegranate seeds and serve. —*Deborah Madison*

PICKLED RED ONIONS
MAKES ABOUT 2 CUPS
A great addition to salads, these onions are also wonderful on burgers or hot dogs or with grilled poultry or meats.

- 1½ cups white wine or cider vinegar
- 1½ cups cold water
- 1 teaspoon sugar
- ½ teaspoon salt
- 1 large, dark red onion, sliced into ⅛-inch rounds
- 3 cups boiling water

I. In a medium glass or stainless steel bowl, combine the vinegar and the cold water with the sugar and salt. Stir to dissolve the sugar and salt.

2. Put the onion slices in a colander and pour the boiling water over them. Rinse under cool water and drain. Add to the vinegar brine, cover with plastic wrap and refrigerate until chilled. —*D. M.*

MAKE AHEAD The onions can be refrigerated for up to 1 week.

Fattoush
6 TO 8 SERVINGS
Vary the ingredients in this tasty salad with the seasons. Use purslane in the summer; replace it with romaine lettuce in winter. Other vegetables you can add include radishes, blanched cauliflower, pickled cucumbers and bitter greens.

- 2 pita breads, split horizontally
- 1 small garlic clove, smashed
- 1 teaspoon salt
- 2 tablespoons fresh lemon juice
- 1½ teaspoons pomegranate molasses (see Note)
- ¼ cup extra-virgin olive oil
- 2 large tomatoes, cut into wedges

- 4 scallions, thinly sliced
- 1 large cucumber—peeled, seeded and cut into ½-inch dice
- 1 green bell pepper, cut into ½-inch dice
- 1 head romaine lettuce, cut crosswise into ½-inch ribbons
- ½ cup minced flat-leaf parsley
- ½ cup minced mint
- 1 tablespoon crushed sumac (see Note)

I. Toast the pitas until golden and crisp. When cool enough to handle, break the pitas into pieces.

2. In a mortar, pound the garlic with the salt to a smooth paste. Stir in the lemon juice and pomegranate molasses. Drizzle in the olive oil, stirring until blended.

3. In a large salad bowl, combine the tomatoes, scallions, cucumber, green bell pepper, lettuce, parsley and mint. Stir the dressing, pour it over the salad and toss well. Sprinkle the toasted pita pieces and the sumac on top and serve at once. —*Nancy Harmon Jenkins*

NOTE Sumac is a spice widely prized in the Middle East for its dark red color and tangy flavor. Both the sumac and the pomegranate molasses are available from specialty food stores.

Allegro Salad
8 SERVINGS

- 1 large head romaine lettuce, torn into bite-size pieces
- 1 large Belgian endive, cored and cut into bite-size pieces
- 1 fennel bulb—halved lengthwise, cored and thinly sliced crosswise
- 4 hearts of palm—drained, rinsed and thinly sliced diagonally
- 3 scallions, thinly sliced diagonally
- 2 tomatoes, seeded and coarsely chopped
- 1 red bell pepper, thinly sliced
- 1 green bell pepper, thinly sliced
- 1 carrot, halved lengthwise and thinly sliced
- 1 small red onion, thinly sliced
- ⅓ cup pine nuts

ABOVE: **Allegro Salad.** RIGHT: **Purslane Salad with Baby Greens and Cabbage.**

¼ cup plus 2 tablespoons olive oil
2 tablespoons red wine vinegar
1 teaspoon minced garlic
Salt and freshly ground black pepper
¼ cup crumbled blue cheese

I. In a large salad bowl, combine the romaine, endive, fennel, hearts of palm, scallions, tomatoes, bell peppers, carrot and onion; refrigerate until chilled.

2. In a small skillet, toast the pine nuts over moderate heat, stirring, until golden, about 6 minutes; let cool.

3. In a glass or stainless steel bowl, mix the olive oil, red wine vinegar and garlic and season with salt and black pepper. Add the blue cheese and pine nuts to the salad, toss with the dressing and serve. —*Michael Locascio*

Purslane Salad with Baby Greens and Cabbage

6 SERVINGS

Here's a refreshing salad that stretches a couple of cups of young leaves to feed six. Purslane is also wonderful on its own, simply dressed with garlic and olive oil.

½ **small green cabbage (¾ pound), cored and finely shredded**
¾ **pound young purslane**

2 **cups baby greens or mesclun**
4 **medium scallions, white part only, thinly sliced and separated into rings**
1 **large cucumber—peeled, seeded and cut into ½-inch dice**
2 **tablespoons extra-virgin olive oil**
1½ **tablespoons fresh lemon juice**
Salt and freshly ground pepper
¼ **cup small mint leaves**

I. Soak the cabbage in salted cold water for 30 minutes. Drain and spin dry in a salad spinner. Trim the purslane down, leaving only the small sprigs and leaves; you should have about 2 cups. Wash well and spin dry. Toss the cabbage and purslane with the baby greens, scallions and cucumber.

2. In a large salad bowl, whisk the olive oil with the lemon juice and season the dressing with salt and pepper. Add the salad and toss to coat. Garnish with the mint and serve. —*Paula Wolfert*

SERVE WITH Grilled fish or lamb kebabs and crusty bread.

Napa Cabbage and Tofu Salad with Sesame Dressing

8 SERVINGS

When formally arranged, with the elements placed in a minimalist style or in geometric rows, this salad is especially beautiful. You can also toss the cabbages with the spinach and some of the dressing and use the salad as a base for the remaining elements. However you decide to display the salad, do toss it before eating.

DRESSING

1 **tablespoon minced fresh ginger**
1 **large garlic clove, coarsely chopped**
½ **large jalapeño, seeded and chopped**
1 **tablespoon plus 1 teaspoon tahini (sesame paste)**
1 **tablespoon Asian sesame oil**
1 **tablespoon vegetable oil**
2 **tablespoons soy sauce**
2 **tablespoons rice vinegar**
½ **teaspoon light brown sugar**

3 tablespoons chopped cilantro

1 tablespoon chopped mint

Salt and freshly ground pepper

SALAD

Salt

1 pound soft tofu, drained and cut into 1-inch cubes

4 cups finely shredded Napa cabbage (about ½ large head)

2 cups spinach leaves, finely shredded (see Note)

1 cup finely shredded red cabbage

1 medium kohlrabi or small jicama, peeled and cut into matchsticks

5 large radishes, cut into matchsticks

1 large carrot, shaved into thin curls with a vegetable peeler

Freshly ground pepper

1 tablespoon black sesame seeds or toasted white sesame seeds, for garnish

I. MAKE THE DRESSING: Combine the ginger, garlic, jalapeño, tahini, sesame oil, vegetable oil, soy sauce, rice vinegar and brown sugar in a mini-processor and puree until smooth. Transfer to a glass or stainless steel bowl and stir in the cilantro and mint. Season with salt and pepper.

2. MAKE THE SALAD: Bring a medium saucepan of water to a gentle simmer.

Add salt. Put half of the tofu in a small strainer and ease it into the water. Simmer over moderate heat for 2 minutes and transfer to paper towels to drain. Repeat with the remaining tofu.

3. On a large platter or individual plates, arrange the Napa cabbage, shredded spinach, red cabbage, tofu, kohlrabi, radish matchsticks and carrot curls. Season with salt and pepper. Spoon the dressing over the tofu or pass it separately. Garnish with the sesame seeds and serve. —*Deborah Madison*

NOTE To finely shred spinach leaves (make a chiffonade), simply stack and roll the leaves and then cut them crosswise into thin strips with a sharp knife.

MAKE AHEAD The dressing can be refrigerated for up to 2 days. Bring to room temperature before serving.

WINE Serve a simple and straightforward white with this salad as a refreshing contrast to the greens. Try the 1997 Francis Coppola Bianco from California or a Chilean Chardonnay, such as the 1997 Canepa.

Cauliflower, Broccoflower and Frisée Salad with Olives

8 SERVINGS

2 garlic cloves, coarsely chopped

Salt

2 hard-cooked eggs, yolks separated from the whites

2 tablespoons sherry vinegar

2 teaspoons Dijon mustard

½ cup extra-virgin olive oil

Freshly ground black pepper

1 pound broccoflower or broccoli, cut into florets and very thinly sliced lengthwise

1 pound cauliflower, cut into florets and very thinly sliced lengthwise

4 cups frisée or yellow escarole

4 scallions, white and tender green parts, thinly sliced

2 cups thinly sliced celery hearts and leaves

1 European cucumber—halved, seeded and coarsely chopped

Napa Cabbage and Tofu Salad with Sesame Dressing

1 cup flat-leaf parsley leaves
½ green bell pepper, thinly sliced
½ cup (2 ounces) Spanish green
   olives, pitted, or pimiento-stuffed
   olives, halved crosswise
2 tablespoons salted capers, rinsed

1. In a mortar, puree the garlic with ¼ teaspoon salt. Add the egg yolks and pound until smooth. Stir in the sherry vinegar and the mustard and transfer to a small glass or stainless steel bowl. Slowly whisk in the olive oil and season with salt and black pepper.

2. In a large salad bowl, combine the broccoflower, cauliflower, frisée, scallions, celery, cucumber, parsley, green bell pepper, olives and capers. Add the dressing and toss well. Finely dice the

egg whites, scatter them over the salad and serve. —*Deborah Madison*

WINE Look for a wine that will provide a counterpoint to this crunchy salad. Try one of the new dry California rosés, such as the 1998 Iron Horse Rosato or the 1997 Swanson Rosato.

Artichoke Heart Salad with Warm Herb Dressing

4 TO 6 SERVINGS
Artichokes star in this herb-speckled salad from the Mauna Kea Beach Hotel, on Hawaii's Kohala coast.

4 medium artichokes, stems
   removed
6 tablespoons plus 2 teaspoons
   olive oil

Cauliflower, Broccoflower and Frisée Salad with Olives

1 small shallot, minced
½ cup dry white wine
3 tablespoons fresh lemon
   juice
Salt and freshly ground pepper
8 cups (packed) mixed baby
   greens, such as mizuna and
   arugula
2 medium tomatoes, cut into
   wedges
2 tablespoons minced chives
1 tablespoon minced tarragon
1 tablespoon minced flat-leaf
   parsley or chervil

1. Arrange the artichokes in a steamer basket, stem end down, and steam over a few inches of boiling water until the artichokes are tender when pierced through the bottom with a small knife, about 20 minutes. Transfer the artichokes to a plate and let them cool slightly. Pull off all the leaves from the artichokes and, using a small spoon or melon baller, scrape out and discard the hairy choke. Cut each artichoke bottom into 6 wedges. Reserve the artichoke leaves for another use.

2. Heat 6 tablespoons of the olive oil in a small saucepan. Add the shallot and cook over low heat, stirring often, until softened, about 3 minutes. Add the white wine and the lemon juice and simmer over moderately low heat until reduced by half, about 5 minutes. Transfer the herb dressing to a glass or stainless steel bowl and let it cool slightly. Season the dressing with salt and pepper.

3. Put the mixed baby greens in a large glass or stainless steel bowl. In a large frying pan, heat the remaining 2 teaspoons of olive oil. Add the artichoke bottoms and cook over moderate heat, stirring frequently, until they are lightly browned, about 4 minutes. Add the tomato and cook until just heated through, about 2 minutes. Remove the artichoke mixture from the heat and season with salt and pepper. Add the warm herb dressing and the minced

Golden Beet and Endive Salad with Goat Brie

chives, tarragon and parsley to the artichoke mixture and spoon over the mixed
baby greens. Toss well and serve the
salad at once. —*Göran Streng*

MAKE AHEAD The steamed artichoke hearts can be refrigerated overnight. Let return to room temperature
before proceeding with the recipe.

Beet and Green Bean Salad

6 SERVINGS

- 3 tablespoons fresh lemon juice
- 1 tablespoon Dijon mustard
- 1 garlic clove, minced
- ¼ cup plus 2 tablespoons
  vegetable oil

Salt and freshly ground black pepper

- 2 tablespoons minced parsley
- ¼ pound green beans
- 2 large red beets
- 3 cups mixed lettuces
- 1 medium cucumber—halved
  lengthwise, seeded and sliced
  crosswise
- 4 large scallions, minced
- ½ green bell pepper, cut into strips

1. In a small glass or stainless steel
bowl, combine the lemon juice with the
mustard and garlic. Whisk in the oil in
a thin stream. Season with salt and
black pepper and then add the parsley.
2. In a large saucepan of boiling salted
water, cook the green beans until just
tender, about 4 minutes. Using a slotted
spoon, transfer the beans to a colander
and refresh under cold running water.
Drain and pat dry. Cut the beans into 2-
inch lengths. Add the beets to the boiling water and simmer over moderate
heat until tender, about 40 minutes;
drain. Peel, cut them in half and slice
them ½-inch thick.
3. In a large salad bowl, toss the beets,
beans, lettuces, cucumber, scallions
and bell pepper. Add a few tablespoons
of the vinaigrette; toss to coat. Serve
with the remaining vinaigrette on the
side. —*Ruth Van Waerebeek-Gonzalez*

Golden Beet and Endive Salad with Goat Brie

8 SERVINGS

Red beets can easily be substituted for
their milder, golden siblings. Dress
them with balsamic vinegar instead of
rice vinegar to lend a sweet note to this
salad. The red endives called for are
similar in flavor to their pale yellow
cousins. If you prefer, the filled endive
spears can be used as an elegant hors
d'oeuvre all on their own.

- 6 medium golden beets (about
  1½ pounds)
- 1 tablespoon olive oil
- 2 medium shallots, finely chopped
- 2 tablespoons rice vinegar
- 1 tablespoon aged red wine vinegar
  or sherry vinegar

Salt and freshly ground pepper

- 4 large endives (about 1½ pounds),
  preferably red
- 2 tablespoons plus 2 teaspoons
  walnut oil
- 6 ounces Brie, preferably goat's
  milk, cut into ¼-inch slices
  (see Note)

1. Preheat the oven to 375°. Stand the
beets in a baking dish and rub them
with the olive oil. Cover with foil. Bake
for about 1 hour, or until the beets are
tender when pierced.
2. Meanwhile, in a medium bowl, toss
the shallots with the rice vinegar and

Chopped Vegetable Salad

the red wine vinegar. Add ¼ teaspoon salt and season with pepper.

3. Peel the beets and cut them into chunks. In a food processor, pulse the beets until finely chopped; do not puree. Add the beets to the shallot mixture and toss. Refrigerate until chilled.

4. Cut off the top 3 inches of the endives and reserve. Halve and core the rest of the endives and then thinly slice crosswise. Toss the sliced endives with the walnut oil; season with salt and pepper. Mound the sliced endives on plates and arrange the spears around them. Toss the beets and spoon them onto the endive spears. Garnish with the cheese and serve. —*Deborah Madison*
NOTE Slice the Brie while it is still cold but let the cheese come to room temperature before serving.

MAKE AHEAD The recipe can be prepared through Step 3 and refrigerated overnight.

WINE This salad requires a wine that can match its sharpness. Look for a Sancerre from France, such as the 1997 Domaine Cherrier or the 1997 Lucien Crochet Le Chêne.

Chopped Vegetable Salad

4 SERVINGS

At his eponymous Honolulu restaurant, superstar chef Alan Wong makes this version of the classic American salad with baby lettuces instead of the usual iceberg.

- 3 tablespoons canola oil
- 1 tablespoon black bean salsa
- 2 teaspoons minced serrano or jalapeño chile
- 1 garlic clove, minced
- 1 tablespoon sherry vinegar
- 1 tablespoon rice vinegar
- 1 tablespoon soy sauce
- 2 teaspoons fresh lemon juice
- ¼ teaspoon Asian sesame oil

Salt and freshly ground pepper
- 4 ounces sugar snap peas
- 4 ounces green beans
- 1 cup small broccoli florets

- 5 baby beets—trimmed, scrubbed and halved lengthwise
- 4 cups (packed) mixed baby greens, such as frisée and romaine
- 2 plum tomatoes, cut into eighths
- 4 ounces feta cheese, preferably French, cut into ½-inch cubes

1. In a glass or stainless steel bowl, combine the canola oil, salsa, chile, garlic, sherry and rice vinegars, soy sauce, lemon juice, sesame oil and ¼ teaspoon each of salt and pepper.

2. In a medium saucepan of boiling salted water, cook the sugar snap peas until just tender, about 3 minutes. Using a slotted spoon, transfer the sugar snaps to a colander and refresh under cold water; pat dry with paper towels and transfer to a large bowl. Repeat the process with the green beans, the broccoli and the beets, cooking each of the vegetables individually until just tender.

3. Add the greens, tomatoes and feta to the bowl. Pour the dressing over the salad, toss well and serve. —*Alan Wong*
MAKE AHEAD The recipe can be prepared through Step 2 up to 1 day ahead; refrigerate the vegetables and dressing separately and bring them to room temperature before assembling the salad.

Endive Salad with Lemon Mascarpone Dressing

6 SERVINGS

- 1½ tablespoons fresh lemon juice
- 1 tablespoon mascarpone
- 1½ teaspoons finely grated lemon zest
- ¼ cup extra-virgin olive oil

Salt and freshly ground pepper
- 4 medium endives, leaves separated
- 2 bunches watercress, stemmed
- 1 small red onion, thinly sliced
- 8 anchovy fillets
- 4 hard-cooked eggs, halved
- ¼ cup pine nuts, lightly toasted

In a large salad bowl, whisk the lemon juice with the mascarpone and lemon zest. Whisk in the olive oil and season

with salt and pepper. Add the endives, watercress and onion and toss with the dressing. Place an anchovy fillet on each egg half and arrange the eggs around the salad. Garnish with the pine nuts and serve. —*Erica De Mane*
WINE This aggressively flavored salad is best accompanied by an assertive California Sauvignon Blanc, such as the 1997 Cakebread or the 1997 Groth.

Thai-Style Shrimp Salad with Spicy Peanut Dressing

4 SERVINGS

Crisp vegetables and shrimp are tossed with a tropical coconut milk dressing for this Asian-flavored salad from Maui's Ritz-Carlton, Kapalua.

- ½ cup unsweetened coconut milk
- 1 tablespoon plus 2 teaspoons chunky peanut butter
- 2 teaspoons rice vinegar
- ½ teaspoon Thai red curry paste (see Note)

Salt and freshly ground black pepper
- 1 pound medium shrimp, shelled and deveined
- 8 cups (packed) mixed baby greens, such as arugula, frisée and spinach
- 1 pound jicama, peeled and cut into matchsticks
- 2 cups (about ½ pound) mung bean sprouts
- 2 large scallions, cut into matchsticks
- 1 large carrot, cut into matchsticks
- 1 large red bell pepper, cut into matchsticks
- ½ cup cilantro leaves

1. In a small glass or stainless steel bowl, whisk together the coconut milk, peanut butter, rice vinegar and curry paste until combined. Season with salt and black pepper.

2. In a medium saucepan of boiling water, blanch the shrimp until they start to curl, about 1 minute. Drain; set aside.

3. In a large glass or stainless steel bowl, toss the mixed greens, jicama, bean sprouts, scallions, carrot, red bell pepper and cilantro. Add the shrimp and the coconut dressing and toss well. Mound the salad on 4 large plates and serve at once. —*Patrick Callarec*

NOTE Thai curry pastes are available in supermarket ethnic-foods sections.

MAKE AHEAD The recipe can be prepared through Step 2 up to 1 day ahead. Refrigerate the shrimp and dressing separately and let them return to room temperature before finishing the salad.

WINE The spicy peanut dressing pairs well with an unfussy light Italian white, such as the 1997 Antinori Galestro or the 1997 Alois Lageder Pinot Grigio.

Lobster Salad

8 SERVINGS

The great thing about this simple yet luxurious dish is the lobster-infused olive oil used to make the vinaigrette.

Four 1½-pound lobsters
¾ cup olive oil
3 tablespoons red wine vinegar
Salt and freshly ground pepper
6 ounces mesclun (about 8 cups)
1 tablespoon minced chives

1. Bring a stockpot of water to a boil. Add the lobsters head first, cover and cook over high heat for 9 minutes. Using tongs, transfer the lobsters to a large bowl; let cool. Twist off the claws. With kitchen shears, snip the underside of the tails down the center and remove the meat in one piece. Crack the claws with a mallet and remove the meat.

2. Using a heavy knife, finely chop enough of the lobster legs and shells to make 4 packed cups. In a medium saucepan, combine the olive oil with the chopped lobster legs and shells and bring to a simmer over low heat. Cook, stirring occasionally, for 30 minutes.

Strain the oil and let cool. Whisk the red wine vinegar into the oil; season the vinaigrette with salt and pepper.

3. Slice each lobster tail crosswise into 8 pieces. In a medium glass or stainless steel bowl, combine the tail and claw meat with the vinaigrette. Toss to coat. Mound the mesclun on 8 plates; arrange the lobster alongside. Drizzle the mesclun with some of the remaining vinaigrette. Sprinkle with the chives and serve. —*Pilar Huguet*

ONE SERVING Calories 257 kcal, Total Fat 20.8 gm, Saturated Fat 2.8 gm

Lobster Caesar Salad

4 SERVINGS

For a richer salad, add an egg yolk to the dressing. If you prefer not to eat raw egg, the dressing will still taste delicious without it.

Two 1½-pound lobsters
5 garlic cloves, 2 minced and 3 smashed
3 tablespoons fresh lemon juice
2 anchovy fillets, minced
1 large egg yolk (optional)
1 teaspoon Worcestershire sauce
1 teaspoon Dijon mustard
¼ cup extra-virgin olive oil
¼ cup plus 2 tablespoons freshly grated Parmesan cheese
Salt and freshly ground pepper
2 tablespoons unsalted butter
1 cup ½-inch-square bread cubes
One 1-pound head romaine lettuce, large leaves torn into pieces, small leaves left whole
1 cup small frisée or chicory leaves in torn pieces
½ pound peeled celery root, cut into 2-inch matchsticks

1. In a large pot of boiling water, cook the lobsters until they are bright red all over, about 8 minutes. Drain the lobsters and when cool enough to handle, crack the claws and knuckles and remove the meat. Split the tails lengthwise, remove the meat and remove and discard the dark vein. Cut the tail meat

Lobster Salad

in half lengthwise. Refrigerate the lobster meat until ready to use.

2. In a small glass or stainless steel bowl, combine the minced garlic, lemon juice, anchovies, egg yolk, Worcestershire sauce and mustard. Whisk in the olive oil. Add 2 tablespoons of the Parmesan; season with salt and pepper.

3. Preheat the oven to 400°. In a small saucepan, combine the butter with the smashed garlic. Cook over low heat until the garlic has flavored the butter, about 2 minutes. Let cool slightly and then discard the garlic. In a cake pan, toss the bread cubes with the garlic butter. Spread in an even layer; bake until golden brown, about 5 minutes.

4. In a large salad bowl, combine the romaine, frisée and celery root. Pour the dressing over the lettuce mixture and toss well. Add the croutons and the remaining ¼ cup of Parmesan; toss well again. Mound on 4 plates. Garnish each salad with a lobster claw and half of a lobster tail. —*John Ash*

MAKE AHEAD The recipe can be prepared through Step 2 up to 2 days in advance.

Lobster Cobb Salad

Lobster Cobb Salad

8 SERVINGS

At the restaurant Vida in Los Angeles, the dressed salad is packed into small square dishes and then carefully unmolded. Alternatively, you can dress the lettuce, lobster, bacon and vegetables separately and layer them in a deep glass bowl.

Three 1½-pound lobsters
6 thick slices of bacon
4 ounces green beans
¼ cup buttermilk
¼ cup sour cream
3 tablespoons prepared horseradish
2 tablespoons mayonnaise
1 tablespoon fresh lemon juice
1 teaspoon Dijon mustard
Salt and freshly ground pepper
½ head iceberg lettuce, cored and
   coarsely chopped

3 hard-cooked eggs, coarsely
   grated
2 large tomatoes, coarsely chopped
2 medium carrots, cut into
   ½-inch dice
½ small red onion, coarsely
   chopped
1 medium cucumber—peeled,
   seeded and coarsely chopped

1. In a pot of boiling salted water, cook the lobsters until bright red all over, about 9 minutes. Drain and let cool slightly. Twist off the tails and claws. Crack the claws and remove the meat. With kitchen scissors, slit the tail shells lengthwise; remove the meat. Discard the vein that runs the length of the tail. Cut the meat into 1-inch pieces.

2. In a large skillet, cook the bacon over moderate heat until it is crisp, about 5

minutes. Drain well on paper towels and then coarsely chop the bacon.

3. In a small saucepan of boiling water, cook the green beans until just tender, about 3 minutes. Drain and refresh under cold running water. Pat dry with paper towels and cut into ½-inch pieces.

4. In a medium glass or stainless steel bowl, whisk together the buttermilk, sour cream, horseradish, mayonnaise, lemon juice and mustard. Season with salt and pepper.

5. In a large bowl, toss the lettuce with ¼ cup of the dressing; transfer to a shallow bowl. Add the lobster, bacon, eggs, beans, tomatoes, carrots, onion and cucumber to the small bowl and toss with the remaining dressing. Mound the salad on top of the lettuce and serve at once. —*Fred Eric*

Lobster and Lemon-Orange Salad

Lobster and Lemon-Orange Salad

6 SERVINGS

Lobsters are trapped off Italy's Amalfi Coast and brought fresh to the restaurant Don Alfonso 1890 in Sant'Agata sui Due Golfi. There they are cooked briefly and served with citrus fruits from the owners' garden. If you don't want to prepare fresh lobsters yourself, you can buy ones that are already boiled or use one pound of cooked lobster meat.

Two 1½-pound lobsters
2 navel oranges
1 small lemon
2 tablespoons extra-virgin olive oil
Salt and freshly ground pepper
4 cups arugula leaves, torn into bite-size pieces
6 chives, cut into 3-inch lengths
1 tablespoon flat-leaf parsley leaves

1. In a large pot of boiling water, cook the lobsters until they turn bright red all over, about 8 minutes. Drain; let cool slightly. Twist off the tails and claws. Crack the claws and remove the meat, keeping it whole. Using kitchen scissors, slit the tail shells lengthwise and remove the black veins. Remove and thinly slice the tail meat. Cover and refrigerate the lobster.

2. Using a small, sharp knife, peel the oranges and lemon; be sure to remove all of the bitter white pith. Working over a glass or stainless steel bowl, cut in between the membranes to release the orange and lemon sections into the bowl; transfer the sections to a plate. Squeeze the juice from the orange and lemon membranes into the bowl, measuring as you go. You should have 2 tablespoons of orange juice and 1 tablespoon of lemon juice. Add the olive oil to the citrus juices and season with salt and pepper.

3. Arrange the arugula on 6 salad plates. Top with the lobster and citrus sections. Scatter the chives and parsley over the salads, drizzle with the dressing and serve. —*Alfonso Iaccarino*

MAKE AHEAD The shelled lobster meat can be refrigerated overnight.

Seared Scallop Salad with Apple Wedges

4 SERVINGS

At Padovani's Bistro & Wine Bar in Honolulu, tender scallops join sautéed apples and potatoes for a luxurious salad.

2 tablespoons sherry vinegar
1 teaspoon Dijon mustard
3 tablespoons extra-virgin olive oil
Salt and freshly ground pepper
3 tablespoons unsalted butter
1 Golden Delicious apple—peeled, cored and cut into 12 wedges
1 large potato, peeled and sliced ¼ inch thick
16 large sea scallops (about 1 pound)
8 cups (packed) mixed baby greens, such as frisée and romaine

1. In a glass or stainless steel bowl, whisk the sherry vinegar with the mustard. Slowly whisk in the olive oil and season with salt and pepper.

2. In a large nonstick skillet, melt 1 tablespoon of the butter until foamy. Add the apple wedges and cook over moderately high heat until softened and golden, about 4 minutes; transfer to a plate. Melt 1 more tablespoon of the butter in the skillet. Add the potato slices and cook until tender, about 5 minutes; add to the apple wedges.

3. Melt the remaining 1 tablespoon of butter in the skillet. Season the scallops with salt and pepper and add them to the skillet in a single layer. Cook over moderately high heat, turning once, until golden, 5 to 6 minutes. Transfer the scallops to the plate with the apple wedges. Add half of the vinaigrette to the skillet and cook, scraping up any brown bits, just until heated through.

4. In a bowl, toss the greens with the remaining vinaigrette. Arrange on 4 plates. Top with the apples, potatoes and scallops; drizzle the pan juices all around. —*Philippe Padovani*

Seared Scallop Salad with Apple Wedges

Big Sky Niçoise Salad

Big Sky Niçoise Salad

8 SERVINGS

Trout is a specialty at Triple Creek Ranch in Montana's Bitterroot Valley. So using smoked trout for the classic tuna in this salad was a natural.

- 2 tablespoons fresh lemon juice
- 1 tablespoon white wine vinegar
- 1 tablespoon minced shallot
- 1 teaspoon Dijon mustard
- 1 small garlic clove, mashed
- ½ teaspoon finely grated lemon zest
- ½ cup extra-virgin olive oil
- 1 tablespoon drained capers

Salt and freshly ground pepper

- 1½ pounds small red potatoes
- 6 ounces haricots verts or thin green beans, stemmed
- 12 cups mixed salad greens
- 1 pound smoked trout, skin discarded and fish flaked
- 1 pint cherry tomatoes, halved
- 6 hard-cooked eggs, quartered
- ½ cup Niçoise olives, pitted

I. In a blender, combine the lemon juice with the white wine vinegar, shallot, mustard, garlic and lemon zest and pulse until finely chopped. With the machine on, add the olive oil in a thin stream and blend until emulsified. Add the capers and a pinch each of salt and pepper and pulse until the capers are coarsely chopped.

2. Put the potatoes in a large pot of cold water. Bring to a boil and cook until tender, about 18 minutes. Using a slotted spoon, transfer the potatoes to a colander and rinse under cold water until cool. Pat dry and cut into quarters.

3. Return the water to a boil. Add the haricots verts and cook until crisp-tender, about 5 minutes. Drain and refresh under cold water. Pat dry.

4. In a large glass or stainless steel bowl, toss the salad greens with ¼ cup of the lemon-caper dressing and transfer to large plates. Working with 1 ingredient at a time, toss the cooked potatoes and haricots verts, the trout and the tomatoes with the remaining dressing and

arrange over the salad greens. Garnish with the eggs and olives. Serve immediately, passing any remaining dressing separately. —*Martha McGinnis*

MAKE AHEAD The lemon-caper vinaigrette can be refrigerated for up to 3 days in a screw-top jar.

Smoked Chicken Salad with Baby Greens

4 TO 6 SERVINGS

At Chef Mavro in Honolulu, this extraordinarily simple salad is prepared with smoked duck, which you can use here instead of the chicken.

- 1 pound medium asparagus, trimmed
- 2 tablespoons extra-virgin olive oil
- 1 tablespoon sherry vinegar
- 1 tablespoon minced shallots
- ½ teaspoon Dijon mustard
- ¼ teaspoon five-spice powder
- ¼ teaspoon salt
- ¼ teaspoon freshly ground pepper
- 8 cups (packed) mixed baby greens, such as frisée and lolla rosa
- 1 pound smoked chicken breast, skin removed, thinly sliced
- 4 plum tomatoes, quartered, or 8 cherry tomatoes, halved

I. In a medium saucepan of boiling salted water, cook the asparagus until just tender, about 4 minutes. Drain, refresh the asparagus under cold water and pat dry with paper towels. Cut the asparagus into 2-inch pieces.

2. In a small glass or stainless steel bowl, combine the olive oil, sherry vinegar, shallots, mustard, five-spice powder, salt and pepper. In a large salad bowl, toss the mixed baby greens, the sliced smoked chicken breast, the tomatoes and the cooked asparagus. Add the dressing to the salad, toss well and serve. —*George Mavrothalassitis*

WINE A round, fruity California Chardonnay, such as the 1996 Geyser Peak Reserve or the 1997 Simi, will complement the smoky chicken.

Frisée Salad with Sautéed Chicken Livers and Croutons

Frisée Salad with Sautéed Chicken Livers and Croutons

8 SERVINGS

Chicken livers are cooked until pink, then tossed while warm with frisée, crisp bread rubbed with garlic, bacon, hard-cooked eggs and spicy radishes to make a totally satisfying salad.

Eight ½-inch-thick baguette slices, freshly toasted

- 1 garlic clove
- 2 tablespoons wine vinegar
- 2 tablespoons canola oil
- 1 tablespoon hazelnut or walnut oil

Salt and freshly ground pepper

- 7 ounces thinly sliced bacon, cut crosswise into 3-inch lengths
- ½ pound chicken livers, large livers halved
- 2 heads frisée (1 pound), torn into bite-size pieces
- 10 radishes, thinly sliced
- 4 hard-cooked eggs, quartered lengthwise

I. Rub the warm baguette toasts on both sides with the garlic clove. Stack the baguette slices and cut them into ½-inch dice.

2. In a salad bowl, combine the wine vinegar with the canola oil and the

Mazzio's Smoked Duck with Tangerine-Rosemary Salad

hazelnut oil. Season the dressing with salt and pepper.

3. In a large skillet, fry the bacon in 2 batches over moderate heat until crisp, about 5 minutes per batch. Drain the bacon on paper towels. Add the chicken livers to the skillet, season them with salt and pepper and cook over moderately high heat until the chicken livers are browned on the outside but still pink inside, about 4 minutes. Return the bacon to the skillet to rewarm it.

4. Add the frisée, the croutons and the radishes to the salad bowl and toss to coat them with the dressing. Top the salad with the bacon and the chicken livers, garnish with the hard-cooked eggs and serve. —*Josette Riondato*

WINE Look for the 1998 Domaine Tempier Bandol Rosé, which is full bodied and peppery enough to stand up to the bacon and the garlicky croutons in this salad.

Mazzio's Smoked Duck with Tangerine-Rosemary Salad

4 SERVINGS ♛

James Mazzio, formerly chef at 15 Degrees in Boulder, Colorado, recommends adding oil to the salad dressing as slowly as possible. If the emulsion breaks, gradually pour the dressing back into a running blender. You'll need to allow a day for marinating the duck; if you want to save time, buy smoked duck breasts at your local specialty food shop.

SMOKED DUCK

- 1 cup fresh tangerine or orange juice
- 5 tablespoons light brown sugar
- 2 tablespoons unsulphured molasses
- 1 tablespoon kosher salt
- 1 tablespoon coarsely chopped rosemary

Zest of 2 tangerines or oranges, cut into very thin strips

- ¼ teaspoon each freshly ground white pepper and black pepper

Four 5- to 6-ounce boneless duck breasts, with skin

- ½ cup long-grain white rice
- ¼ cup loose black tea, such as Ceylon

TANGERINE SALAD

- ½ cup fresh tangerine or orange juice
- ½ small shallot, finely chopped
- 2 tablespoons Champagne vinegar
- 2 teaspoons honey
- ½ teaspoon minced rosemary, plus 4 sprigs
- ¼ cup plus 2 tablespoons extra-virgin olive oil

Salt and freshly ground pepper

- 2 large tangerines or oranges
- 4 cups (packed) mixed tender greens, such as Boston lettuce and mâche

I. PREPARE THE SMOKED DUCK: In a shallow glass or ceramic baking dish, combine the tangerine juice with 3 tablespoons of the light brown sugar, the molasses, kosher salt, rosemary, tangerine zest and white and black peppers. Add the duck breasts and turn to coat. Cover and refrigerate overnight, turning occasionally.

2. Line a wok and its lid with heavy-duty foil, allowing a 6-inch overhang around both the wok and the lid. Add the white rice, the loose black tea and the remaining 2 tablespoons of light brown sugar to the wok and stir to mix. Set the wok over moderate heat and cook until wisps of smoke rise up from the sugar-and-tea mixture.

3. Pat the duck breasts dry with paper towels and arrange them on a 9-inch round cake rack. Carefully set the rack in the wok over the smoking mixture. Cover the wok with the lid and crimp the foil tightly all around. Smoke the duck breasts over moderate heat for about 18 minutes, or until the meat is medium rare. Transfer the duck breasts to a cutting board and let them rest for 5 minutes.

4. MAKE THE TANGERINE SALAD: In a blender, combine the tangerine juice, the shallot, the Champagne vinegar, the honey and the rosemary and blend until smooth. With the machine on, gradually drizzle in the olive oil until the dressing is smooth and slightly thickened. Transfer the tangerine dressing to a large glass or stainless steel bowl and season with salt and pepper. Using a small, sharp knife, peel the tangerines. Cut in between the membranes to release the sections.

5. Carefully remove the skin from the duck and thinly slice the meat diagonally across the grain. Add the greens to the large bowl and toss with the tangerine dressing. Mound the salad on plates and scatter the tangerine sections alongside. Arrange the sliced duck alongside the salad and garnish with the rosemary sprigs. —*James Mazzio*

MAKE AHEAD The smoked duck can be refrigerated overnight.

WINE Meaty duck breasts need a concentrated red; for this recipe, the wine also must have enough acerbic tannins to check the sweet notes of the molasses marinade. That's a Bordeaux. Choose a vigorous example, such as a 1995 Saint-Estèphe, particularly the Château Meyney or the Château les Ormes de Pez.

Smoked Duck Salad with Foie Gras and Walnuts

4 SERVINGS

Don't let the ingredients in this recipe scare you away. It's worth a trip to a specialty market—and it's simple to prepare.

- 12 walnut halves
- 1 tablespoon walnut oil
- 1 tablespoon extra-virgin olive oil
- 1 tablespoon canola oil
- ½ tablespoon walnut or red wine vinegar (see Note)
- ½ tablespoon sherry vinegar
- ½ shallot, finely chopped
- Salt and freshly ground pepper
- 4 cups packed mixed salad greens
- 16 cherry tomatoes, halved
- ¾ pound smoked duck breast (see Note), skin removed, sliced crosswise ¼ inch thick
- ¼ pound chilled foie gras terrine or mousse (see Note), chilled and sliced to match the duck breast
- Fine sea salt
- Chives, for garnish

1. Preheat the oven to 400°. Put the walnut halves on a pie plate and bake for 6 minutes, or until the nuts are fragrant and browned. Let the walnuts cool and then coarsely chop.

2. In a large bowl, whisk the walnut oil, olive oil and canola oil with the walnut vinegar and sherry vinegar. Add the shallot and season the dressing with salt and pepper. Add the salad greens, tomatoes and walnuts to the bowl with the dressing and toss to coat.

3. Mound the salad on plates and top with alternating slices of duck breast and foie gras. Sprinkle the foie gras with sea salt, garnish with the chives and serve. —*Marie-Andrée Nauleau*

NOTE Walnut vinegar is available by mail order from Sutton Place Gourmet (800-346-8763). Smoked duck breast and foie gras terrine and mousse are available in specialty-food stores and by mail order from D'Artagnan (800-327-8246; www.dartagnan.com).

Caesar Salad with Crisp Shredded Pork

4 SERVINGS

At the restaurant Alan Wong's in Honolulu, this version of the ubiquitous Caesar salad is topped with kalua pork—ultra-tender meat that's been pit-roasted with hot lava rocks.

- ½ loaf Italian bread, crusts removed, bread cut into 1-inch cubes
- ¼ cup plus 1 tablespoon extra-virgin olive oil
- 1 anchovy fillet, mashed
- ½ teaspoon minced garlic
- ¼ teaspoon Worcestershire sauce
- ¼ teaspoon Dijon mustard
- 1 teaspoon fresh lemon juice
- 1 teaspoon red wine vinegar
- Salt and freshly ground pepper
- ½ pound roast pork, coarsely shredded, or two 6-ounce pieces of duck confit, meat removed from the bone and shredded
- 1 large head of romaine lettuce, torn into bite-size pieces
- ⅓ cup freshly grated Parmesan cheese

1. Preheat the oven to 350°. Toss the bread with 1 tablespoon of the olive oil

Smoked Duck Salad with Fois Gras and Walnuts

ABOVE: **Caesar Salad with Crisp Shredded Pork.**
RIGHT: **Salad of Mixed Greens with Mushroom Vinaigrette.**

and spread the croutons on a baking sheet. Toast for about 10 minutes, or until they are golden and just crisp.

2. In a blender, combine the anchovy, garlic, Worcestershire, mustard, lemon juice and red wine vinegar and blend until smooth. With the machine on, add the remaining ¼ cup of olive oil in a slow stream until the dressing is emulsified. Season with salt and pepper.

3. Heat a medium skillet. Add the pork and cook over high heat until beginning to crisp, about 3 minutes.

4. In a large salad bowl, toss the lettuce and croutons with the dressing. Add the Parmesan; toss again. Top with the pork and serve immediately. —*Alan Wong*

MAKE AHEAD The recipe can be prepared through Step 2 up to 6 hours ahead; let the croutons and dressing stand separately at room temperature.

WINE A glass of crisp Sauvignon (Fumé) Blanc, such as the 1997 Villa Maria from New Zealand or the 1997 Murphy-Goode from California, would cut the richness of the shredded pork.

Salad of Mixed Greens with Mushroom Vinaigrette

12 SERVINGS

- 6 ounces shiitake mushrooms, stems discarded
- ¾ cup extra-virgin olive oil
- 1 garlic clove
- ¼ cup plus 1 tablespoon fresh lemon juice
- ½ teaspoon truffle oil, or more to taste (optional)

Salt and freshly ground pepper

- 2 cups vegetable oil
- 5 large shallots, thinly sliced and separated into rings
- ½ cup all-purpose flour
- 3 heads of frisée, torn into bite-size pieces
- 2 heads of radicchio, coarsely shredded
- 4 Belgian endives, separated into individual spears
- 12 thin slices of prosciutto

1. Preheat the oven to 350°. Toss the shiitakes with 1 tablespoon of the olive oil. Spread them on a baking sheet and

roast for about 20 minutes, turning once, until the shiitakes are tender and barely crisp. Let cool.

2. In a blender or food processor, pulse the mushrooms and garlic until finely chopped. Add the lemon juice and, with the machine on, pour in the remaining olive oil in a thin stream. Transfer to a bowl. Stir in the truffle oil and season with salt and pepper.

3. Heat the vegetable oil in a saucepan. In a bowl, toss the shallots with the flour, shaking off the excess. Working in 2 batches, fry the shallots over high heat, stirring, until golden and crisp, about 6 minutes. Transfer the shallots to paper towels to drain. Season lightly with salt.

4. In a large glass or stainless steel bowl, toss the frisée with the radicchio and endives. Add half of the dressing and toss well. Season with salt and pepper, add the remaining dressing and toss again. Transfer the salad to a platter, top with the prosciutto and fried shallots and serve. —*Tim McKee*

MAKE AHEAD The recipe can be prepared through Step 3 up to 1 day ahead. Refrigerate the mushroom vinaigrette and store the shallots at room temperature.

WINE The tart salad needs an acidic white with some body. Pick a French Sauvignon Blanc–based wine, such as the 1996 Château Carbonnieux Graves Blanc from Bordeaux or the 1997 Michel Redde Pouilly-Fumé La Moynerie from the Loire.

Besh's Fried Goat Cheese and Frisée Salad

6 SERVINGS

John Besh is chef at Artesia in Abita Springs, Louisiana. He recommends letting the goat cheese, or any food, firm up in the refrigerator for fifteen minutes before dredging it in flour. This makes for easier handling and a more even coating.

One 11- to 12-ounce log of goat cheese, chilled
1 teaspoon minced garlic
¾ teaspoon minced rosemary
Salt and freshly ground pepper
¼ cup all-purpose flour
1 large egg, beaten
½ cup fine dry bread crumbs
2 tablespoons red wine vinegar
½ teaspoon honey
1 tablespoon plus 1 teaspoon walnut oil
2½ tablespoons sugar
2 small plums, pitted and coarsely chopped
¼ cup plus 1 tablespoon extra-virgin olive oil
1 tablespoon water
1 small head frisée, large leaves torn into bite-size pieces
2 tablespoons minced oil-cured black olives
6 thin slices (about 4 ounces) country ham or prosciutto
1 tablespoon minced chives

Besh's Fried Goat Cheese and Frisée Salad

1. Cut the goat cheese into 6 equal rounds and gently press each piece into a 2½-inch round. In a small bowl, combine ½ teaspoon of the garlic with ½ teaspoon of the rosemary and season with salt and pepper. Sprinkle both sides of the goat cheese with the garlic mixture.

2. Put the flour, egg and bread crumbs into 3 separate shallow bowls. Dredge the goat-cheese rounds in the flour and then dip them in the egg and coat with the bread crumbs. Transfer the breaded goat-cheese rounds onto a platter lined with wax paper and refrigerate the goat-cheese rounds until chilled.

3. In a small bowl, whisk 2 teaspoons of the red wine vinegar with the honey until dissolved. Whisk in the walnut oil and then season the walnut vinaigrette with salt and pepper.

4. In a small saucepan, combine the remaining 1 tablespoon plus 1 teaspoon red wine vinegar with the remaining ½ teaspoon garlic and ¼ teaspoon rosemary. Add the sugar and stir over moderately high heat until it dissolves. Add the plums and cook, stirring occasionally, until softened, 5 to 8 minutes. Transfer the plum mixture to a blender along with 1 tablespoon of the olive oil and the water and blend until smooth. Return the plum sauce to the saucepan and keep warm.

5. In a medium nonstick skillet, heat the remaining ¼ cup of olive oil until shimmering. Add the breaded goat-cheese rounds and cook over moderately high

Warm Salad of Winter Fruits, Endives and Pancetta

heat until they are golden and crisp, about 2 minutes per side.

6. In a large glass or stainless steel bowl, toss the frisée with the walnut vinaigrette and olives and season with salt and pepper. Spoon the plum sauce onto 6 plates. Set a goat-cheese round in the center of each plate and arrange a slice of the country ham alongside with a little of the frisée. Sprinkle with the chives and serve the salads immediately. —*John Besh*

MAKE AHEAD The goat-cheese rounds can be prepared through Step 2 and refrigerated, covered, for up to 2 days.

WINE The goat cheese and olives suggest Sauvignon Blanc, and the plum sauce says fruity West Coast bottlings, rather than austere French ones. Try the 1998 Geyser Peak from California or the 1997 Chateau Ste. Michelle from Washington State.

Warm Salad of Winter Fruits, Endives and Pancetta

8 SERVINGS

You can embellish this hearty salad with other winter fruits, such as grapefruit (which we used) or persimmon.

- 1 pomegranate, halved crosswise
- 1 tablespoon red wine vinegar
- 3 tablespoons canola oil

Salt and freshly ground pepper

- 3 cups water
- 1 cup sugar
- 2 quinces—peeled, cored and cut into 8 wedges each
- 4 ounces thickly sliced pancetta, cut into 1-inch pieces
- 3 large endives, cored and cut into 1½-inch pieces
- 2 firm ripe Bartlett pears— peeled, cored and cut into thin wedges
- 1 teaspoon chopped tarragon

1. Using a large citrus reamer, squeeze ½ cup of juice from the pomegranate halves. Transfer the pomegranate juice to a small saucepan and boil until the juice is reduced to 3 tablespoons, about 10 minutes. Transfer the pomegranate syrup to a small glass or stainless steel bowl; whisk in the red wine vinegar and then the canola oil. Season the pomegranate dressing with salt and freshly ground pepper.

2. In a medium saucepan, combine the water and the sugar and bring to a boil, stirring until the sugar dissolves. Add the quinces and set a small lid or heat-proof saucer directly on top to keep the wedges submerged. Cook the quinces over moderate heat until they are just tender, about 10 minutes. Using a slotted spoon, transfer the quinces to a plate to cool. Cut the quinces into thin wedges.

3. In a large skillet, cook the pancetta pieces over moderate heat until crisp. Drain the pancetta and reserve 1 tablespoon of the fat in the skillet. Return the skillet to high heat, add the endives and cook, tossing, until just warmed through. Add the cooked quinces, the pears and the pancetta, season the salad with salt and pepper and toss gently. Transfer the salad to a platter. Drizzle the salad with some of the dressing, sprinkle with the tarragon and serve. Pass the remaining dressing separately. —*Grant Achatz*

WINE With its overtones of pears and peaches, the 1997 La Jota Viognier is a good match for the winter fruits in this salad.

Grilled Tomato, Onion and Fennel Salad

4 SERVINGS

The fennel and onion are cooked on the grill so they char slightly before they are braised in foil with the tomatoes and lemon vinaigrette.

- 1 large fennel bulb—halved, trimmed, cored and cut lengthwise into 8 wedges
- ¼ cup plus 1 tablespoon olive oil

Salt and freshly ground pepper

- 1 large sweet onion, such as Maui or Vidalia, sliced ½ inch thick
- 4 large red or yellow tomatoes or a mixture, quartered
- 2 tablespoons Champagne vinegar
- 1 tablespoon fresh lemon juice
- 1 garlic clove, minced
- ½ tablespoon Dijon mustard
- 1 tablespoon coarsely chopped basil, preferably Thai
- 1 teaspoon finely chopped mint

1. Light a grill or heat a lightly oiled grill pan. In a bowl, toss the fennel wedges with 2 tablespoons of the olive oil and season the fennel with salt and pepper. Brush the onion slices on both sides with 1 tablespoon of the olive oil and season with salt and pepper. Grill the fennel wedges and the onion slices over a medium-hot fire for about 4 minutes per side, or until they are lightly charred and just tender. Alternatively, cook the fennel wedges and onion slices in the grill pan over moderate heat for about 5 minutes per side.

2. Lay two 2-by-3-foot pieces of heavy-duty foil on top of each other and put the tomato quarters in the center. Add the grilled fennel wedges and onion slices and season the vegetables with salt and pepper.

3. In a small glass or stainless steel bowl, combine the Champagne vinegar, lemon juice, garlic and Dijon mustard and blend in the remaining 2 tablespoons of olive oil. Spoon the dressing over the vegetables and then seal the foil package.

4. Set the vegetable package over a medium-hot fire and grill for 5 to 7 minutes, or until bubbling inside. Alternatively, set the vegetable package in the grill pan and cook over moderate heat for 5 to 7 minutes. Remove the package from the heat and let it stand for 3 minutes. Carefully open the foil and sprinkle the vegetables with the basil and mint. Serve the grilled salad hot or warm. —*Raphael Lunetta*

Beet, Green Bean and Shallot Salad

8 SERVINGS

If you buy beets with the leaves still on, you'll be assured of their freshness and you can cook the leaves as you would spinach.

- 2 pounds small beets, leaves removed
- 2 pounds tender green beans
- ¼ cup plus 2 tablespoons extra-virgin olive oil
- ¼ cup red wine vinegar

Salt and freshly ground pepper

- 4 shallots, thinly sliced
- ¼ cup chopped basil
- 1 tablespoon chopped mint

1. In a large saucepan, cover the beets with cold water and bring to a boil. Simmer over moderate heat until tender when pierced, about 45 minutes. Drain in a colander and then rinse in cold water and slip off the skins. Thinly slice the beets crosswise and let cool.

2. In a large saucepan, steam the green beans until just tender, about 5 minutes. Rinse in cold water and drain well.

3. In a large salad bowl, whisk the olive oil with the red wine vinegar and season with salt and pepper. Add the beets, the green beans, the shallots, the basil and the mint to the bowl, toss to coat and then serve. —Lori De Mori

MAKE AHEAD The cooked beets can be refrigerated overnight. Bring to room temperature before proceeding.

Tomato and Sweet Onion Salad

6 SERVINGS

To eliminate the unpleasant sharpness of onions, Chilean cooks thinly slice them and then soak them in salted or sugared water.

- 1 medium Vidalia onion, halved and thinly sliced
- 1 tablespoon sugar
- 6 large tomatoes, sliced ½ inch thick

Salt

- 3 tablespoons extra-virgin olive oil
- 2 jalapeños, seeded and minced
- 2 tablespoons chopped cilantro

1. In a medium bowl, toss the onion slices with the sugar and cover with cold water. Let soak for 10 minutes. Drain, rinse the onion and then pat dry.

2. Layer the tomato slices and onion slices on a large platter or in a bowl; season generously with salt and drizzle with the olive oil. Sprinkle the salad with the jalapeños and the cilantro and serve. —Ruth Van Waerebeek-Gonzalez

Grilled Eggplant and Tomato Salad

4 SERVINGS

Alternating the eggplant and tomato slices in this salad produces an attractive zebra effect.

- 4 slender eggplants (½ pound each), sliced crosswise ½ inch thick
- 4 large firm tomatoes, sliced crosswise ½ inch thick
- ½ cup plus 2 tablespoons extra-virgin olive oil

Sea salt and freshly ground pepper

- 1 teaspoon dried oregano
- 1 tablespoon drained capers, plus 1 tablespoon juice from the jar
- ½ tablespoon sherry vinegar
- ¼ teaspoon finely grated lemon zest
- ½ cup basil leaves

1. Light a grill. Arrange the eggplant slices and the tomato slices on a rimmed baking sheet and brush on both sides with ½ cup of the olive oil. Season with salt and pepper and sprinkle with the oregano. Grill the tomato slices over a hot fire for about 1 minute per side, or until they are charred but still hold their shape. Transfer to a platter. Grill the eggplant slices over a medium-hot fire for about 5 minutes per side, or until lightly charred and tender.

2. In a glass or stainless steel bowl, combine the capers and the caper juice with the sherry vinegar, the lemon zest

and the remaining 2 tablespoons of olive oil. Season the dressing with salt and pepper.

3. To assemble the salad, overlap alternating grilled tomato slices and eggplant slices on a large platter. Tuck the basil leaves between the tomato and eggplant slices. Drizzle the dressing on top of the eggplant and tomato salad and serve. —Steven Raichlen

WINE Tomatoes and capers add bite to eggplant. A fruity, attractively herbal California Sauvignon Blanc, such as the 1997 Rodney Strong Charlotte's Home or the 1997 J. Fritz Jenner Vineyard, would balance these flavors best.

Beet Salad with Greens and Walnuts

4 SERVINGS ♔

- 2 large beets, preferably golden, tender greens trimmed and rinsed
- 10 small red beets, tender greens trimmed and rinsed
- ¼ cup extra-virgin olive oil, plus more for brushing

Salt

- ½ cup walnut halves
- 2 teaspoons walnut oil
- 2 tablespoons sherry vinegar
- 1 teaspoon balsamic vinegar
- 1 shallot, thinly sliced lengthwise

Four 1-ounce goat cheese rounds

1. Preheat the oven to 400°. Brush the beets with olive oil. Spread the large beets in one roasting pan and the small ones in another. Season the beets with salt and add ½ inch of water to each pan. Cover the pans with foil and roast until tender, about 25 minutes for the small beets and 35 for the large. Let cool and then peel the beets. Slice the golden beets about ¼ inch thick and quarter the red beets; keep them separate. Leave the oven on.

2. Toast the walnut halves on a small pie plate for about 5 minutes, or until fragrant. Break the toasted walnuts into pieces, toss them with 1 teaspoon of

the walnut oil and season the nuts with salt. Leave the oven on.

3. In a glass or stainless steel bowl, mix the sherry and balsamic vinegars and a pinch of salt. Whisk in the ¼ cup of olive oil and then whisk in the remaining 1 teaspoon of walnut oil.

4. In a large glass or stainless steel bowl, toss the sliced beets with half of the dressing. Arrange them on 4 plates and season lightly with salt.

5. Heat a large skillet. Add the beet greens with the water that clings to the leaves and cook over high heat, tossing, until wilted. Drain well and transfer to the large bowl. Add the quartered red beets, the shallot and the remaining dressing and toss well. Mound the wilted greens and beets on the plates.

6. Set the goat cheese rounds on a small pie plate and bake for about 2 minutes, or until the cheese is just beginning to melt. Using a spatula, transfer the cheese to the plates, scatter the walnuts on top and serve. —*Suzanne Goin*

MAKE AHEAD The recipe can be prepared through Step 3 up to 2 days ahead. Refrigerate the beets and dressing separately, and keep the walnuts at room temperature.

Grilled Escarole and White Bean Salad

8 SERVINGS

Combining grilled wedges of garlicky escarole with tender cannellini beans makes a simple first course that's also an excellent side dish. You'll need to allow time for the cannellini beans to soak overnight.

  2 **cups dried cannellini beans, rinsed and picked over**
  6 **cups water**
  4 **thyme sprigs**
  ¼ **cup plus 2 tablespoons extra-virgin olive oil**
  ¼ **cup thinly sliced garlic cloves**
  ¼ **cup fresh lemon juice**
  2 **large heads escarole, quartered lengthwise through the core**

Grilled Escarole and White Bean Salad

    Salt and freshly ground pepper
  ¼ **cup coarsely chopped flat-leaf parsley**

1. In a bowl, cover the beans with water and let soak overnight. Drain and transfer to a medium saucepan. Add the water and thyme and bring to a boil. Cook the beans over moderately low heat until tender, about 1 hour; drain. Transfer to a glass or stainless steel bowl and let cool. Discard the thyme.

2. In a small saucepan, combine ¼ cup of the olive oil with the garlic and cook over moderate heat until the garlic is golden, about 6 minutes. Transfer the garlic and the oil to a small glass or stainless steel bowl and stir in the lemon juice.

3. Heat a large grill pan or cast-iron skillet. Brush the escarole with the remaining 2 tablespoons of olive oil, season with salt and pepper and grill, turning once, until the leaves are wilted and slightly charred. Transfer to a platter.

4. Add the parsley and the dressing to the beans and season with salt and pepper. Spoon the beans over the escarole and serve warm or at room temperature. —*Trey Foshee*

MAKE AHEAD The recipe can be prepared through Step 2 one day ahead; refrigerate the beans and dressing separately. Serve at room temperature.

ONE SERVING Calories 261 kcal, Total Fat 11 gm, Saturated Fat 1.6 gm

WINE Garlic, lemons, earthy beans and bitter escarole need a dry but assertive white to act as a flavor foil. Try the 1997 Tiefenbrunner Pinot Grigio from Italy or the 1996 Adelsheim Pinot Gris from Oregon.

White Bean and Red Pepper Salad with Pine Nut Dressing

8 SERVINGS

The white beans need to soak overnight, so plan accordingly.

- ⅓ cup pine nuts
- 1½ cups (9 ounces) dried large white beans, such as white Aztec, gigantes or limas, soaked overnight in cold water and drained
- 2 garlic cloves

Salt

- 2 large red bell peppers—halved lengthwise, cored and seeded

Vegetable oil, for brushing

- ¼ cup water

One 4-inch square of crustless white bread

- 2 tablespoons fresh lemon juice
- 1 tablespoon extra-virgin olive oil
- 3 tablespoons finely chopped parsley

Freshly ground black pepper

- ¼ cup black olives, such as Niçoise

1. Preheat the oven to 375°. Spread the pine nuts in a small baking dish and bake for about 2 minutes, or until they are lightly toasted. Let the pine nuts cool. Finely chop 1 tablespoon of the

pine nuts and reserve the rest of the nuts for garnish.

2. In a large saucepan, cover the white beans generously with water. Add 1 garlic clove and bring to a boil. Cover partially and simmer over low heat until the beans are almost tender, about 1 hour and 45 minutes. Add 1½ teaspoons of salt and simmer until the beans are tender, about 20 minutes longer. Measure out and reserve ¼ cup of the bean cooking liquid.

3. Meanwhile, preheat the broiler. Flatten the red bell pepper halves with your hands and brush the skins with vegetable oil. Arrange the red bell peppers skin side up on a baking sheet and broil 5 inches from the heat for about 8 minutes, or until the skins are blistered and charred in places.

4. Transfer the red bell peppers to a plate and stack them to steam and cool. Remove the skins from the bell peppers and then slice the peppers lengthwise into 1-inch strips.

5. In a shallow bowl, pour the water over the bread and set aside for 5 minutes. Coarsely chop the remaining garlic clove. In a food processor, combine the bread with the garlic, pine nuts, lemon juice, olive oil and ¼ teaspoon salt. Add the reserved ¼ cup of warm bean cooking liquid and puree until smooth. Transfer to a salad bowl.

6. Drain the beans thoroughly. Add to the dressing along with 2 tablespoons of the parsley and fold into the dressing. Season with salt and black pepper. Garnish with the red bell peppers, olives and the remaining 1 tablespoon of parsley and serve. —*Deborah Madison*

MAKE AHEAD The salad can be prepared through Step 3 and refrigerated overnight. Chill the beans and bell peppers separately. Rewarm the beans before continuing and serve the salad at room temperature.

WINE White beans, red peppers and a nutty dressing give this salad plenty of substance. A flavorful white with some

acidity would work particularly well. Look for the 1997 Torres Viña Sol or the 1997 Marqués de Cáceres Blanco.

Chicken-Avocado Salad with Soybeans

6 SERVINGS

Fresh green soybeans are now showing up in American restaurants. They're available at Asian markets and some grocery stores.

- ¼ cup canola oil
- 2 tablespoons fresh lime juice
- ½ teaspoon minced fresh ginger

Pinch of sugar

Salt and freshly ground white pepper

- 1 pound fresh or thawed frozen soybeans in their pods
- 1 pound cooked skinless chicken breast meat, cut into ¾-inch dice (about 3 cups)

Two ½-pound Hass avocados, cut into ¾-inch dice

- 3 scallions, thinly sliced on the diagonal
- 1 small celery rib, thinly sliced on the diagonal
- ⅓ cup cilantro leaves

1. In a small glass or stainless steel bowl, combine the canola oil, fresh lime juice, minced fresh ginger and a pinch of sugar. Season the dressing with salt and white pepper and whisk until the dressing is blended.

2. Bring a large pot of salted water to a boil. Add the soybeans in their pods and cook until they are tender, about 5 minutes. Drain the soybean pods and cool under running water. Remove the soybeans from their pods and pat dry with paper towels.

3. In a large salad bowl, combine the cooked soybeans with the diced cooked chicken, the diced avocados, the sliced scallions and celery rib and all but 1 tablespoon of the cilantro leaves. Add the dressing and gently toss to combine all of the ingredients, being careful not to

White Bean and Red Pepper Salad with Pine Nut Dressing

mash the avocados. Mound the chicken-avocado salad on plates, sprinkle the salads with the remaining 1 tablespoon of cilantro and serve. —*Grace Parisi*

ONE SERVING Calories 486 kcal, Total Fat 31.3 gm, Saturated Fat 4.7 gm

WINE The acidity of the lime points to an equally tart Sauvignon Blanc as the best match. Look for the 1997 Mulderbosch from South Africa or the 1996 Matua Valley from New Zealand.

Warm Lentil Salad with Mint-Marinated Feta

8 SERVINGS

- 2 tablespoons pine nuts
- 2 tablespoons minced mint leaves
- 1 tablespoon minced flat-leaf parsley
- 6 garlic cloves, minced
- ¼ cup plus 3 tablespoons extra-virgin olive oil

Freshly ground pepper

- 4 ounces feta cheese, preferably French, cut into ½-inch pieces
- 2 cups (14 ounces) French green lentils, picked over
- 6 cups water
- 2 medium carrots, cut into ½-inch dice
- 2 medium leeks, white and tender green, cut into ½-inch dice
- 2 teaspoons ground cumin
- 1 teaspoon minced fresh ginger
- ½ teaspoon ground coriander
- ¼ cup red wine vinegar

Salt

1. Preheat the oven to 375°. Spread the pine nuts in a small baking dish and bake for about 2 minutes, or until they are lightly toasted; let cool. Finely chop 1 tablespoon of the pine nuts; reserve the rest for garnish.

2. In a bowl, combine the chopped pine nuts with the mint, parsley, ½ teaspoon of the garlic and 2 tablespoons of the olive oil; season with freshly ground pepper. Add the diced feta and let marinate in the refrigerator for at least 1 hour or overnight.

3. In a medium saucepan, cover the lentils with the water and bring to a boil. Simmer over moderately low heat until tender, about 30 minutes. Drain well.

4. In a small saucepan of boiling salted water, cook the carrots until they are just tender, about 5 minutes. Drain and let the carrots cool.

5. In a large heavy skillet, heat 1 tablespoon of the olive oil. Add the diced leeks, the cooked carrots and the remaining minced garlic and cook over moderately low heat until tender, about 10 minutes. Add the cumin, ginger and coriander and cook, stirring, for 3 minutes. Add the cooked lentils and stir until warmed through.

6. In a small glass or stainless steel bowl, whisk the red wine vinegar with the remaining ¼ cup of olive oil and pour it over the lentils. Season the salad generously with salt and pepper and transfer it to a salad bowl. Top the salad with the marinated feta and mint dressing and the toasted pine nuts and serve. —*Trey Foshee*

MAKE AHEAD The recipe can be prepared through Step 4 up to 1 day ahead; refrigerate the lentils, feta and carrots separately and let the nuts stand at room temperature.

ONE SERVING Calories 354 kcal, Total Fat 17.1 gm, Saturated Fat 4.1 gm

Bulgur and Lentil Salad with Chickpeas

8 SERVINGS

- ½ cup walnut halves
- 1 cup (½ pound) beluga or French green lentils, rinsed and picked over
- 1 bay leaf

Salt

- 3 cups warm water
- 1 cup (6 ounces) fine bulgur
- 3 medium shallots, finely chopped
- ¼ cup aged red wine vinegar
- 2 garlic cloves, coarsely chopped

- 1 tablespoon fresh lemon juice
- ½ cup extra-virgin olive oil
- 3 tablespoons walnut oil

Freshly ground pepper

- 1½ cups cooked chickpeas, or one 19-ounce can, rinsed
- 1 cup finely chopped parsley
- 3 tablespoons finely chopped tarragon

1. Preheat the oven to 400°. Put the walnut halves on a pie plate and bake for 6 minutes, or until the nuts are fragrant and browned. Let the walnuts cool and then coarsely chop.

2. In a medium saucepan, cover the lentils with water. Add the bay leaf and ½ teaspoon salt and bring to a boil. Reduce the heat and simmer until the lentils are tender, about 20 minutes. Drain well.

3. Meanwhile, in a medium bowl, pour the warm water over the bulgur and let soak until tender, about 30 minutes. Drain the bulgur and lightly squeeze it dry. Transfer the bulgur to a large salad bowl.

4. In a small glass or stainless steel bowl, combine the shallots with the red wine vinegar. In a mortar, puree the garlic with ½ teaspoon salt; add to the shallot mixture. Whisk in the lemon juice and the olive and walnut oils. Season with pepper.

5. Add the cooked lentils and the chickpeas, parsley and tarragon to the bulgur in the salad bowl. Add the dressing and stir the salad gently but thoroughly. Serve the salad warm or at room temperature, garnished with the toasted walnut halves. —*Deborah Madison*

MAKE AHEAD The salad can be refrigerated for up to 1 day. Bring to room temperature before serving.

WINE The chewy grains and chickpeas in this salad make a tart red wine a better choice than a white. Some good selections: the 1997 Hogue Cabernet Sauvignon-Merlot from Washington State or the 1998 Rosemount Diamond Grenache-Shiraz from Australia.

Chicken-Avocado Salad with Soybeans

Tabbouleh

6 TO 8 SERVINGS

Tabbouleh is classically served on a platter surrounded by crisp romaine lettuce leaves to use as scoops. Or you can serve it instead with toasted pita triangles.

- ⅓ cup medium bulgur
- 2 cups (1 pound) finely chopped ripe tomatoes
- 3 cups finely chopped parsley
- ½ cup finely chopped mint
- ½ cup minced onion
- 1 teaspoon salt
- ½ teaspoon freshly ground pepper
- ½ teaspoon allspice
- ½ cup extra-virgin olive oil

About ¾ cup fresh lemon juice

- 2 large scallions, thinly sliced

1. Put the bulgur in a large bowl and stir in enough water to cover. When the wheat dust and chaff rise to the surface, pour off the water. Rinse the bulgur 3 or 4 more times, until the water is clear. Cover the bulgur with fresh water and let it soak for 20 minutes.

2. Pour off the water and then squeeze the bulgur dry. Transfer the bulgur to a large salad bowl and add the tomatoes. Stir in the parsley, mint, onion, salt, pepper and allspice and then add the olive oil. Gradually add the lemon juice, tasting the Tabbouleh until it is balanced; it should be lemony but not unpleasantly tart. Cover and let stand for 20 minutes. Garnish with the scallions. —Nancy Harmon Jenkins

MAKE AHEAD The Tabbouleh can stand at room temperature for up to 4 hours. Don't add the tomatoes until 20 minutes before serving.

Shrimp and Soba Noodle Salad

4 SERVINGS

- ½ pound soba noodles
- 2 quarts water
- 2 bay leaves
- 1 tablespoon whole peppercorns

Salt

- 1 lemon, halved
- 1 pound large shrimp, shelled and deveined

Ice water

- ¼ cup rice vinegar
- 2 tablespoons light miso paste (see Note)
- 1½ teaspoons sugar
- 1 teaspoon Asian sesame oil
- ⅓ cup canola oil

Freshly ground black pepper

- 2 tablespoons chopped pickled ginger
- ½ cup chopped scallions
- 1 large unpeeled European cucumber—halved lengthwise, seeded and cut into matchsticks
- 1 red bell pepper, finely chopped

1. Bring a large saucepan of salted water to a boil. Add the soba noodles and cook over high heat, stirring occasionally, until al dente, about 5 minutes. Drain the soba noodles, let them cool under cold running water and then drain them again.

2. In the same saucepan, combine the 2 quarts of water with the bay leaves, peppercorns and 1 tablespoon of salt. Squeeze in the juice from the lemon, add the lemon halves and bring to a boil. Add the shrimp and cook over moderately high heat until pink throughout, 3 to 4 minutes. Drain the shrimp and plunge them into a bowl of ice water to cool. Drain the shrimp again and pat dry.

3. In a small glass or stainless steel bowl, combine the rice vinegar with the miso, sugar and sesame oil. Whisk in the canola oil and season with salt and black pepper. Stir in the pickled ginger. Toss the shrimp with ¼ cup of the dressing. In a large salad bowl, gently toss the noodles with the scallions, cucumber and red bell pepper. Add the remaining dressing and toss gently to coat. Transfer the soba salad to a platter and top with the shrimp. —Ming Tsai

NOTE Light miso paste is available from specialty food shops and health food stores.

MAKE AHEAD The recipe can be prepared up to 1 day ahead. Refrigerate the soba noodles, shrimp and dressing separately. Toss together and serve at room temperature.

Warm New Potato and Herb Salad

4 SERVINGS

- 1½ pounds new potatoes (about 2 inches in diameter), scrubbed but not peeled
- 1 dried red chile
- 1 teaspoon salt
- 2 tablespoons plus 2 teaspoons fresh lemon juice
- ¼ teaspoon sugar
- 2 tablespoons extra-virgin olive oil
- 1 garlic clove, smashed
- 3 ounces (4 packed cups) arugula leaves
- ¼ cup packed small basil leaves
- 1 tablespoon snipped chives
- 1 teaspoon thyme leaves
- 1 teaspoon chopped tarragon

Freshly ground pepper

1. In a medium saucepan, combine the potatoes and chile and add cold water to cover. Partially cover the pan and cook over moderately high heat until the potatoes are just tender when pierced, 25 to 30 minutes. Drain well and set aside to cool slightly.

2. Cut the potatoes into ⅓-inch dice. In a medium salad bowl, toss the potatoes with ¾ teaspoon of the salt. In a small glass or stainless steel bowl, combine the lemon juice, sugar and the remaining ¼ teaspoon salt. Whisk in the olive oil and the garlic.

3. Tear the arugula and the basil into small pieces; add to the potatoes along with the chives, thyme and tarragon. Discard the garlic from the dressing. Add the dressing to the salad and toss gently. Season the salad with pepper and serve. —Sally Schneider

ONE SERVING Calories 213 kcal, Total Fat 8 gm, Saturated Fat 1 gm

Potato Salad with
Roasted Shallot Dressing

4 SERVINGS

The idea of adding olives to this mustard-dressed salad comes from Trey Foshee, chef at George's at the Cove in La Jolla, California.

½ cup extra-virgin olive oil
4 thyme sprigs
2 shallots
2 garlic cloves
2 pounds small Yukon Gold potatoes, scrubbed
Salt
1 tablespoon Dijon mustard
1 tablespoon whole-grain mustard
1 tablespoon sherry vinegar
½ tablespoon fresh lemon juice
Large pinch of cayenne pepper
Freshly ground black pepper
1 cup (about 6 ounces) Niçoise olives, pitted and coarsely chopped
2 tablespoons minced chives

1. Preheat the oven to 400°. In a small baking dish, combine the olive oil, thyme, shallots and garlic. Cover the dish with foil and roast for about 15 minutes, or until the shallots and garlic are very tender. Discard the thyme sprigs. Strain the olive oil, reserving the shallots and garlic. Let cool.

2. In a large pot, cover the potatoes with cold water and bring to a boil. Add salt and cook until the potatoes are tender when pierced, about 20 minutes. Drain the potatoes, let them cool slightly and then quarter them and transfer to a large salad bowl.

3. Put the reserved shallots and garlic in a blender and puree with the Dijon mustard, the whole-grain mustard, the sherry vinegar, the lemon juice and the cayenne. With the machine on, slowly pour in the reserved olive oil until well blended. Scrape the dressing into a glass or stainless steel bowl and season the dressing with salt and black pepper. Pour the dressing over the potatoes,

add the olives and toss well. Sprinkle the chives on top of the salad and serve. —*Raphael Lunetta*

MAKE AHEAD The dressing can be refrigerated for up to 3 days.

Warm Potato and Grilled Sweet
Onion Salad

4 SERVINGS 🌸

1 pound new potatoes (about 2 inches in diameter)
1 cup French white vermouth, such as Boissiere
1 tablespoon minced shallots
½ teaspoon sugar
Salt
1 tablespoon Champagne vinegar or white wine vinegar
1 medium Vidalia or Bermuda onion (about 7 ounces), sliced crosswise ⅛ inch thick
1 teaspoon extra-virgin olive oil
5 teaspoons roasted walnut oil (see Note)
6 ounces (4 packed cups) frisée or chicory, torn into bite-size pieces
Freshly ground pepper
¼ cup (1 ounce) chopped walnuts

1. In a medium saucepan, cover the potatoes with cold water. Partially cover the saucepan and cook over moderately high heat until the potatoes are tender, 25 to 30 minutes. Drain the potatoes thoroughly and set them aside to cool slightly.

2. Preheat the broiler. In a small saucepan, combine the vermouth, shallots, sugar and ¼ teaspoon salt and bring to a boil. Carefully ignite the hot vermouth with a long kitchen match and boil until the flames die down and the vermouth is reduced by half, about 4 minutes. Stir in the Champagne vinegar.

3. Cut the warm potatoes into 1-inch slices or ½-inch wedges. In a medium bowl, toss the potatoes gently with half of the vermouth mixture.

4. Separate the onion into rings and spread on a lightly oiled baking sheet.

Brush the onion slices with the olive oil and season with salt. Broil the slices as close to the heat as possible for 3 to 5 minutes, or until the slices are soft and beginning to char.

5. Bring the remaining vermouth mixture to a boil and add the walnut oil. Boil for 1 minute. Add the frisée and the onion to the potatoes, pour the dressing on top and toss to coat. Sprinkle the salad with pepper and the walnuts and serve. —*Sally Schneider*

NOTE Roasted walnut oil is available from specialty food stores.

ONE SERVING Calories 277 kcal, Total Fat 12 gm, Saturated Fat 1 gm

Red Potato Salad
with Mustard Dressing

12 SERVINGS

6 pounds red potatoes, peeled
Salt
1 teaspoon fennel seeds
1 cup Creole or Dijon mustard
½ cup mayonnaise
1 tablespoon cider vinegar
½ tablespoon Worcestershire sauce
1 shallot, minced
1½ teaspoons minced garlic
Freshly ground pepper

1. In a large pot, cover the potatoes with water, add a large pinch of salt and boil until just tender, about 25 minutes. Drain and let cool slightly.

2. In a small skillet, toast the fennel seeds over moderate heat until lightly browned, about 40 seconds. Let cool and then crush the seeds to a coarse powder in a mortar. Transfer the fennel to a glass or stainless steel bowl and stir in the mustard, mayonnaise, cider vinegar, Worcestershire sauce, shallot and garlic.

3. Quarter the potatoes and transfer them to a large salad bowl. Add the mustard dressing to the potatoes and toss well. Season the potatoes with salt and pepper. Serve the salad warm or chilled. —*John Currence*

Warm Potato and Fontina Salad

Tarragon Potato Salad

8 SERVINGS

If you use small Yukon Gold potatoes rather than medium ones, you don't have to peel after cooking.

- 4 pounds medium Yukon Gold potatoes
- 1 tablespoon extra-virgin olive oil
- 3 medium leeks (about 1½ pounds), white and tender green parts, quartered lengthwise and thinly sliced
- 1½ cups mayonnaise
- 2 tablespoons whole-grain mustard
- 2 tablespoons cider vinegar
- 3 celery ribs, finely chopped
- ¼ cup finely chopped tarragon
- ¼ cup snipped chives

Salt and freshly ground pepper

1. Put the potatoes in a large pot of cold water. Bring to a boil and cook over moderate heat until tender, 20 to 25 minutes. Drain and let cool under running water. Peel the potatoes and cut them into ½-inch chunks.

2. In a large skillet, heat the oil until shimmering. Add the leeks and cook over moderate heat, stirring occasionally, until tender but not browned, about 5 minutes. Let cool completely.

3. In a large salad bowl, whisk the mayonnaise with the mustard and cider vinegar until smooth. Add the sautéed leeks, the celery, the tarragon and the chives and season with salt and pepper. Gently fold in the potatoes until coated. Serve the potato salad chilled or at room temperature. —Martha McGinnis

MAKE AHEAD The potato salad can be refrigerated overnight.

Warm Potato and Fontina Salad

4 SERVINGS ♛

For this luxurious salad, imported Fontina cheese is melted over sautéed potatoes, which are served on watercress.

- 2 tablespoons red wine vinegar
- 4 whole black peppercorns
- 2 whole allspice berries
- 2 juniper berries
- 1 bay leaf
- 1 whole clove
- 1 shallot, thinly sliced
- 2 teaspoons whole-grain mustard
- ¼ cup plus 1 tablespoon extra-virgin olive oil

Salt and freshly ground pepper

- 1 pound small Yukon Gold potatoes
- 4 ounces imported Fontina cheese, sliced
- 2 bunches watercress, tough stems discarded

1. In a small skillet, bring the vinegar, peppercorns, allspice berries, juniper berries, bay leaf and clove to a boil. Remove from the heat, add the shallot and let cool. Strain; reserve the shallot and 1 tablespoon plus 1 teaspoon of the vinegar. In a small glass or stainless steel bowl, whisk the reserved vinegar with the mustard and 3 tablespoons of the olive oil. Season with salt and pepper.

2. Steam the potatoes over boiling water until still slightly firm, about 10 minutes. Let cool; cut each into 6 wedges.

3. Heat the remaining 2 tablespoons of oil in a large cast-iron skillet. Add the potatoes; cook over moderate heat, turning once, until golden and cooked through, about 10 minutes. Remove from the heat. Top with the Fontina and let melt. Add 2 tablespoons of the vinaigrette to the skillet and swirl to coat.

4. In a large salad bowl, toss the reserved shallot with the watercress and remaining vinaigrette. Transfer to a platter, top with the potatoes and cheese and serve at once. —Suzanne Goin

Warm Potato, Oven-Roasted Tomato and Parmesan Salad

8 SERVINGS

- 2 pounds tiny yellow potatoes

Oven-Roasted Tomatoes (recipe follows), coarsely chopped

- 2 tablespoons chopped mixed herbs, such as dill, chives and tarragon
- ¼ cup plus 1 tablespoon extra-virgin olive oil
- 1 tablespoon plus 2 teaspoons white wine vinegar

Sea salt and freshly ground white pepper

Chunk of Parmigiano-Reggiano cheese, shaved with a vegetable peeler

1. Steam the potatoes over simmering water until tender, 20 to 30 minutes. When the potatoes are just cool enough to handle, peel and thinly slice them. In a glass or stainless steel bowl, toss the potatoes with the tomatoes and herbs.

2. In a small glass or stainless steel bowl, whisk ¼ cup of the oil with the vinegar. Season with sea salt and white pepper. Pour the dressing over the potatoes and tomatoes and toss gently to coat. Garnish with the cheese shavings and the remaining 1 tablespoon of olive oil. Serve immediately. —Eric Lecerf

WINE A sturdy Côtes-du-Rhône white goes well with this salad—for example, a Château de Beaucastel Coudoulet Blanc from Châteauneuf-du-Pape.

OVEN-ROASTED TOMATOES

MAKES ABOUT 2 CUPS

- 2 pounds fresh plum tomatoes— peeled, quartered lengthwise and seeded

Fine sea salt and freshly ground white pepper

Confectioners' sugar, for dusting

- 2 teaspoons thyme leaves
- 1 tablespoon extra-virgin olive oil

Preheat the oven to 200°. Arrange the tomatoes in a single layer on a rimmed baking sheet. Sprinkle lightly with sea salt, white pepper and confectioners' sugar. Scatter the thyme over the tomatoes; drizzle with the oil. Bake for about 1 hour, or until very soft. Turn the tomatoes; baste with their juices. Bake about 1 hour longer, or until meltingly tender. They should remain moist and soft. Remove from the oven; let cool. —E. L.

MAKE AHEAD The cooled tomatoes can be refrigerated in their juices for up to 2 days.

Russian Tuna and Potato Salad

4 SERVINGS

High-quality ingredients make all the difference in this simple salad. Imported Italian canned tuna adds extra flavor, as does a freshly roasted pepper, and you can even make your own mayonnaise if you prefer.

- 1 red bell pepper
- 3 medium Yukon Gold potatoes
- 1 large carrot, halved
- 2 large hard-cooked eggs, cut into 1-inch chunks

One 6-ounce can Italian tuna packed in olive oil, drained

- ⅓ cup green olives, pitted and quartered
- ¾ cup mayonnaise

Salt and freshly ground black pepper

1. Roast the red bell pepper over a gas flame or under the broiler until charred all over. Transfer the bell pepper to a bowl, cover with plastic wrap and let steam for 20 minutes. Peel the bell pepper, discarding the seeds and core. Finely chop the bell pepper.

2. Meanwhile, put the potatoes and carrot in a saucepan of cold water and bring to a boil. Cook over moderately low heat until tender, about 20 minutes. Drain and let cool.

3. Peel the potatoes. Cut the potatoes and the carrot into 1-inch chunks; transfer to a bowl. Add the roasted bell pepper, eggs, tuna and olives. Fold in the mayonnaise and season with salt and black pepper. Serve at room temperature or chilled. —*Teresa Barrenechea*

MAKE AHEAD The salad can be refrigerated overnight.

Asian Sweet Potato Salad

6 SERVINGS

- 3 pounds sweet potatoes
- ½ cup plus 1 tablespoon canola oil
- 1 tablespoon minced garlic
- 1 tablespoon rinsed and minced fermented black beans, or 1½ tablespoons soy sauce
- 1 tablespoon minced fresh ginger
- 2 tablespoons rice vinegar
- 1 tablespoon Dijon mustard
- 3 scallions, thinly sliced

Salt and freshly ground pepper

1. Preheat the oven to 350°. Wrap the sweet potatoes in foil and roast for about 35 minutes, or until tender. Let the potatoes cool slightly and then peel and cut them into 1-inch chunks.

2. Heat 1 tablespoon of the oil in a small skillet. Add the garlic, black beans and ginger and cook over moderate

BELOW: **Niçoise-Style Orzo Salad.**
RIGHT: **Savory Cantaloupe Salad.**

heat, stirring, until very fragrant, 2 to 3 minutes. Remove from the heat and whisk in the vinegar and mustard. Transfer to a bowl and whisk in the remaining ½ cup of oil. Stir in the scallions and season with salt and pepper. Gently fold in the potatoes. Serve warm or at room temperature. —*Ming Tsai*

MAKE AHEAD The sweet potato salad can be refrigerated overnight.

Niçoise-Style Orzo Salad

4 SERVINGS ✳

- ½ **pound orzo**
- ½ **cup Niçoise olives, pitted**
- ½ **cup pear or cherry tomatoes, halved lengthwise**
- ½ **small red onion, finely chopped**
- ¼ **cup finely chopped flat-leaf parsley**
- 1½ **tablespoons drained capers**
- 1 **tablespoon balsamic vinegar**
- 1 **garlic clove, minced**

Kosher salt and freshly ground pepper

- ¼ **cup extra-virgin olive oil**

I. Bring a medium pot of salted water to a boil. Add the orzo and cook until al dente. Drain, rinse under running water and then drain again. Transfer the orzo to a salad bowl and add the olives, tomatoes, onion, parsley and capers.

2. In a small glass or stainless steel bowl, combine the balsamic vinegar, the garlic and a pinch each of kosher salt and pepper. Whisk in the olive oil and stir the dressing into the pasta salad. —*Todd Slossberg*

Savory Cantaloupe Salad

6 SERVINGS ✳

Black pepper and vinegar bring out the cantaloupe's sweetness, making it a good foil for creamy fresh goat cheese. The cheese is served on slices of crusty bread alongside the melon salad.

One 3-pound ripe cantaloupe, cut into 1-inch cubes (see Note)

Salt and freshly ground pepper

- 2 **teaspoons extra-virgin olive oil**
- 2 **teaspoons white wine vinegar**

- 2 **slices soppressata salami, cut into thin strips**
- 1 **tablespoon snipped chives**
- ½ **pound fresh goat cheese**
- 6 **slices country bread**

Put the melon cubes in a salad bowl and season with salt and pepper. Add the olive oil, toss gently and then add the white wine vinegar. Garnish with the soppressata and chives. Spread the cheese on the bread and serve it alongside. —*Lynne Rossetto Kasper*

NOTE Here's the fastest way to cut a melon into cubes. Cut a thin slice from both ends of the melon. Halve the melon crosswise and scoop out the seeds. Lay the halves on a work surface, cut side down, and slice off the skin in lengthwise strips with a small sharp knife. Slice the melon 1-inch thick with a large knife and then cut across to make 1-inch cubes.

Honey Pumpkin Salad with Sage Croutons

8 SERVINGS

- 1 **sugar pumpkin or butternut squash (1½ pounds)—peeled, seeded and cut into 1-inch dice**
- ¼ **cup honey**
- 2 **tablespoons unsalted butter, melted**

Eight ½-inch-thick slices of country bread

Roasted pumpkin seed oil, for brushing (see Note)

- 5 **sage leaves**
- ¼ **cup pumpkin seeds**
- 1 **Granny Smith apple—halved, cored and thinly sliced**
- 2 **tablespoons apple cider vinegar**

Salt and freshly ground pepper

- 1 **Fuyu persimmon, peeled and finely chopped (optional)**

I. Preheat the oven to 375°. In a bowl, toss the pumpkin with the honey and the melted butter. Spread the pumpkin on a rimmed baking sheet and roast for about 35 minutes, or just until tender; let cool.

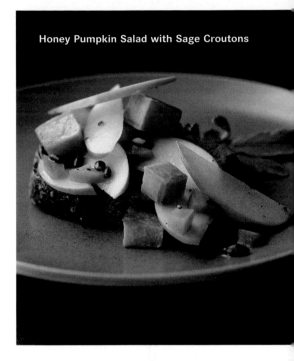

Honey Pumpkin Salad with Sage Croutons

2. Arrange the bread on a cookie sheet and bake in the oven with the pumpkin for about 5 minutes, or until lightly toasted. Brush the toasts generously with pumpkin seed oil and rub with the sage leaves. Spread the pumpkin seeds in a pie plate; toast in the oven for about 3 minutes, or until fragrant.

3. In a glass or stainless steel bowl, toss the apple slices with ½ tablespoon of the cider vinegar. In another glass or stainless steel bowl, toss the pumpkin with the remaining 1½ tablespoons of cider vinegar. Season both with salt and pepper.

4. Set a crouton on each plate and top with the apple slices. Spoon the pumpkin salad and the chopped persimmon over the apple slices. Garnish the salads with the toasted pumpkin seeds and serve. —*Kerry Sear*

NOTE Roasted pumpkin seed oil is available from specialty food stores.

WINE This subtle salad with roasted pumpkin pairs well with a bright white, such as the 1997 Cristom Pinot Gris or the 1997 WillaKenzie Pinot Blanc, both from Oregon.

chapter 4

soups

85

101

Homemade Broth with Egg Noodles

Homemade Broth with Egg Noodles

8 SERVINGS

Note that the flavor of the soup depends entirely on the quality of the broth. Canned really won't do here.

  2 **quarts beef broth from Pot-au-Feu (p. 230) or a flavorful homemade stock**
Salt
  ¼ **pound fine egg noodles**
Freshly ground pepper

Strain the broth into a saucepan and bring to a boil. Season with salt. Add the noodles and cook, stirring occasionally, until tender, about 4 minutes. Season with pepper, ladle into soup plates and serve. —*Josette Riondato*

Lettuce and Tarragon Soup

6 SERVINGS

  4 **tablespoons unsalted butter**
  2 **medium leeks (about 1 pound), white and tender green parts only, halved lengthwise and thinly sliced crosswise**

  1 **garlic clove, finely chopped**
  4 **cups chicken or vegetable stock or canned low-sodium broth**
Salt
  1 **head romaine lettuce (1½ pounds), cored and cut crosswise 1 inch thick**
  ¼ **cup (packed) tarragon leaves**
Freshly ground pepper

I. Melt the butter in a medium saucepan. Add the leeks and garlic and cook over moderate heat, stirring often, until lightly browned, about 10 minutes. Add the stock; season with salt. Cover and simmer over low heat for 15 minutes.

2. Stir in the lettuce. Cook over moderate heat for 5 minutes; stir in the tarragon. Puree half of the soup at a time in a blender until smooth. Transfer to a medium saucepan and gently reheat. Season with salt and pepper. Serve in warmed bowls. —*Jerry Traunfeld*

WINE The tarragon and leeks in this soup have a distinct affinity for Chardonnay. Try one from California, such as the 1997 Toad Hollow or the 1997 Qupé Bien Nacido Vineyard.

Chilled English Pea Soup with Extra-Virgin Olive Oil

4 SERVINGS

All the flavor in this soup comes from the peas. If you can't find really sweet fresh ones, use frozen baby peas.

  3 **quarts water**
Salt
  4 **pounds fresh peas, shelled (4 cups shelled)**
  ¼ **cup extra-virgin olive oil, plus more for drizzling**
Freshly ground pepper
  2 **tablespoons unsalted butter**
  1 **tablespoon vegetable oil**
  ¾ **cup diced crustless day-old country bread (⅜-inch dice)**

I. Bring the water to a boil in a large saucepan. Salt the water, add the peas and bring the water back to a boil. Cook over moderate heat until the peas are very tender, about 20 minutes. Drain

fresh herbs 101

1. If you have your own garden, gather herbs just before using them.

2. Cut herbs with a sharp chef's knife so as not to bruise the leaves.

3. Add herbs with tough leaves (thyme, rosemary, oregano, sage) at any point during cooking; flavors will be mellower when herbs are added at the beginning, brighter when they are added at the end.

4. Add herbs with soft leaves (cilantro, mint, tarragon, parsley, basil, chervil) toward the end of cooking.

5. Be generous; the flavors of fresh herbs are not as concentrated as those of dried, so more is usually better.

the peas, reserving the cooking liquid. Set aside ¼ cup of peas.

2. In a food processor, combine the remaining peas with ¼ cup of the olive oil and ¼ cup of the reserved cooking liquid and puree until smooth. Work the puree through a fine sieve into a large bowl. Discard the contents of the sieve. Stir in about 4 cups of the cooking liquid and season with salt and pepper; add more cooking liquid if necessary to make a nice, creamy soup. Refrigerate the soup until cold, at least 2 hours.

3. In a large skillet, melt the butter in the vegetable oil. Add the diced bread and brown the cubes on all sides over moderately high heat, 3 to 5 minutes. Drain the croutons on paper towels.

4. Ladle the cold soup into bowls and garnish each serving with a few of the croutons and reserved peas. Drizzle with olive oil, sprinkle with pepper and serve. —*Philippe Renard*

MAKE AHEAD The soup can be prepared through Step 2 and refrigerated up to 1 day. The croutons can be stored in an airtight container for up to 3 days.

WINE Try the 1993 Taittinger Comtes de Champagne Blanc de Blancs. This elegant wine, made from 100 percent Chardonnay grapes, harmonizes beautifully with the delicate taste of the peas.

Chilled English Pea Soup with Extra-Virgin Olive Oil

Trio of Fresh Peas and Scallion Soup

4 SERVINGS

The flavor of the chicken stock for this soup is boosted by cooking it with the empty pea pods and scallion greens.

- 2 cups chicken stock or canned low-sodium broth
- 2 cups water
- 1 pound English peas, shelled and pods reserved
- 6 small scallions, whites thinly sliced and greens coarsely chopped

One ¼-inch-thick slice fresh ginger, peeled

Salt

- ¼ pound sugar snap peas, cut on the diagonal into 1-inch pieces (1 cup)
- ¼ pound snow peas, cut into matchsticks (1 cup)
- 2 ounces soft tofu, cut into ¼-inch dice (½ cup)
- ¼ cup cilantro leaves
- 1½ teaspoons rice vinegar

Freshly ground pepper

I. In a large saucepan, combine the chicken stock with the water, pea pods, scallion greens and ginger. Cover and simmer over low heat until flavorful, about 10 minutes. Strain, pressing on the solids to extract as much liquid as possible. Discard the solids.

2. Return the stock to the pan, season with salt and bring to a simmer. Add the English peas and cook over moderately high heat until tender, about 7 minutes. Add the sugar snaps and snow peas; cook until crisp-tender and bright green, about 1 minute. Add the tofu and cook just until heated through, about 30 seconds. Remove from the heat; stir in the sliced scallions, cilantro and vinegar. Season with salt and pepper, ladle into bowls and serve. —*Grace Parisi*

WINE Match the attractive "green" flavors of this soup with an herbal California Sauvignon Blanc, such as the 1997 Markham or the 1997 St. Supéry.

Trio of Fresh Peas and Scallion Soup

Cream of Artichoke Soup and Mushroom Toasts

6 SERVINGS

This cool, sophisticated soup comes from Restaurant L'Ermitage in Clarens, Switzerland. The wild mushroom toasts are a lovely foil for the soup's silkiness.

- 1 lemon, halved
- 4 large, firm artichokes
- 2 cups chicken stock or canned low-sodium broth
- 2 tablespoons olive oil
- ¼ cup dry white wine
- 2 thyme sprigs
- 1 shallot, chopped
- 1 garlic clove, chopped

Salt and freshly ground pepper

- 1 cup milk
- ¼ cup heavy cream

Mushroom Toasts (recipe follows)

I. Squeeze the lemon into a bowl of cold water; add the halves to the bowl. Trim 1 inch off the stem ends of the artichokes. Using a sharp stainless steel knife, halve the artichokes crosswise.

Pull off all of the green outer leaves until you reach the yellow leaves. Peel the tough skin off the bottoms and stems. With a teaspoon, scrape out the hairy chokes. Add the artichokes to the bowl of lemon water as they are trimmed.

2. In a medium saucepan, combine the stock, oil, wine, thyme, shallot and garlic. Add the artichokes; season lightly with salt and pepper. Bring to a simmer and cook over low heat until the artichokes are very tender, about 40 minutes. Remove and discard the thyme.

3. Working in batches, transfer the contents of the saucepan to a blender and puree until completely smooth. Transfer the soup to a bowl, let cool and then refrigerate until thoroughly chilled.

4. Just before serving, stir in the milk and cream; season with salt and pepper. Ladle into shallow bowls. Serve the toasts on the side. —*Restaurant L'Ermitage*

MAKE AHEAD The soup can be prepared through Step 3 and refrigerated, covered, for up to 2 days.

MUSHROOM TOASTS

MAKES 6 TOASTS

1½ teaspoons olive oil

¾ pound mixed fresh wild mushrooms, thinly sliced

4½ teaspoons minced shallots

2 teaspoons minced garlic

¼ cup plus 2 tablespoons chicken stock or canned low-sodium broth

Salt and freshly ground pepper

4 tablespoons unsalted butter, softened

6 large slices white peasant bread, cut ½ inch thick

I. In a large skillet, heat the olive oil. Add the wild mushrooms and cook over moderate heat, stirring, until softened, about 3 minutes. Add the shallots and the garlic and cook, stirring, for 2 minutes. Add the chicken stock, season with salt and pepper and simmer until the stock has evaporated, about 3 minutes. Let the mushrooms cool to room temperature.

2. Transfer the mushrooms to a blender and puree. Blend in the butter.

3. Toast the bread and spread with the mushroom butter. Serve the mushroom toasts warm. —*Restaurant L'Ermitage*

Red Curry Carrot Soup

4 SERVINGS

The spiciness of this Thai-inspired soup comes from red curry paste, a mixture of red chiles, herbs and spices.

1 tablespoon canola oil

6 large carrots, peeled—4 thickly sliced and 2 cut into fine matchsticks

2 thin slices peeled fresh ginger

1 medium white onion, finely chopped

4 cups chicken stock or canned low-sodium broth

2 cups water

⅓ cup unsweetened coconut milk

¾ teaspoon red curry paste (see Note)

Salt and freshly ground pepper

1 scallion, cut into matchsticks

1 tablespoon cilantro leaves

1 tablespoon finely chopped basil

I. Heat the canola oil in a large saucepan. Add the sliced carrots and the ginger and cook over moderately high heat, stirring, until the carrots are crisp-tender and lightly browned, 6 to 7 minutes. Add the white onion and cook until softened but not browned, about 2 minutes.

2. Add the stock, water, coconut milk and curry paste to the saucepan and bring to a boil. Simmer over moderate heat until the carrots are tender, about 25 minutes. Strain the cooking liquid into another saucepan, reserving the solids; discard the ginger. Transfer the carrots to a blender and puree with 1 cup of the cooking liquid until very smooth. Return the puree to the cooking liquid, add the carrot matchsticks and cook until tender, about 3 minutes. Season the soup with salt and pepper. Ladle the soup into bowls, sprinkle with the scallion, cilantro and basil and serve. —*Grace Parisi*

NOTE Red curry paste is available at Asian groceries and by mail order from The CMC Company (800-CMC-2780).

MAKE AHEAD The soup can be refrigerated for up to 1 day.

WINE To contrast with the coconut milk, ginger and red curry paste in this soup, try an aromatic, fruity California white, such as the 1997 Trefethen Dry Riesling or the 1997 Pine Ridge Chenin Blanc.

Red Curry Carrot Soup

Curried Cauliflower Soup

6 SERVINGS ✳

One of Nell Newman's recipes in *Newman's Own Cookbook* was the inspiration for this soup. Part of the book's profits help fund Paul Newman's Hole in the Wall Gang camps for critically ill children.

½ cup millet
1 cup water
Salt
1 tablespoon olive oil
1 medium onion, coarsely chopped
3 garlic cloves, minced
1 teaspoon ground cumin
1 teaspoon ground coriander
1 teaspoon turmeric
½ teaspoon cayenne pepper
One 2-pound head of cauliflower, cut into 1-inch florets
6 cups chicken stock or canned low-sodium broth
2 cups fresh peas or thawed frozen peas

1. In a medium saucepan, combine the millet with the water and ¼ teaspoon of salt and bring to a boil. Cover and simmer over moderately low heat until the millet is tender, about 25 minutes.

2. Meanwhile, heat the olive oil in a large saucepan. Add the onion and cook over moderate heat, stirring occasionally, until softened, about 5 minutes. Add the garlic, cumin, coriander, turmeric, cayenne and ½ teaspoon of salt and cook, stirring, until fragrant, about 1 minute. Add the cauliflower and 2 cups of the chicken stock and bring to a boil. Cover, reduce the heat to moderately low and simmer the soup until the cauliflower is very tender, about 15 minutes.

3. Working in batches, puree the soup in a blender or food processor. Return the soup to the saucepan and then stir in the remaining 4 cups of chicken stock, the cooked millet and the peas. Rewarm the soup gently over moderate heat. Season the soup with salt and serve. —*Jan Newberry*

Caramelized Vidalia Onion Soup

8 SERVINGS

Herbes de Provence—an aromatic mixture of herbs from southern France, including basil, lavender and thyme—enhances this smooth, slightly sweet soup. Cheese croutons add crunch.

6 tablespoons unsalted butter
5 pounds Vidalia or other sweet onions, such as Walla Walla, thinly sliced
2 thyme sprigs
Salt and freshly ground pepper
1 tablespoon sugar
2 large celery ribs, cut into ½-inch dice
1 tablespoon minced garlic
1 tablespoon *herbes de Provence*
1 cup fino sherry
2 quarts chicken stock or canned low-sodium broth
4 cups cubed white country bread
¼ cup freshly grated Parmesan cheese
1 cup heavy cream

1. Melt 3 tablespoons of the butter in a large enameled cast-iron casserole. Add the onions, thyme and a pinch each of salt and pepper and cook over moderate heat, stirring occasionally, until the onions soften and release their liquid, about 20 minutes. Add the sugar and cook, stirring often, until the exuded liquid evaporates and the onions are caramelized, about 30 minutes longer. Transfer the onions to a medium bowl and discard the thyme sprigs.

2. Melt 1 tablespoon of the butter in the casserole. Add the celery, garlic and *herbes de Provence* and cook over moderate heat, stirring, until fragrant, about 3 minutes. Raise the heat to high and add the sherry. Cook, stirring up the brown bits from the bottom of the casserole, until the sherry has reduced by half, about 3 minutes. Return the onions to the casserole; add the stock. Simmer over low heat for 30 minutes.

3. Preheat the oven to 400°. Melt the remaining 2 tablespoons of butter in a small pan. Spread the bread cubes on a rimmed baking sheet and toss with the melted butter. Sprinkle with the Parmesan and toss again. Bake the croutons for about 8 minutes, or until golden brown and crisp.

4. Add the cream to the soup and simmer over low heat for 10 minutes. Working in batches, puree the soup in a food processor or blender until smooth. Return the soup to the casserole and reheat gently. Season the soup with salt and pepper. Ladle the soup into bowls, garnish with the cheese croutons and serve. —*John Currence*

MAKE AHEAD The recipe can be prepared through Step 3 up to 1 day ahead. Refrigerate the soup and store the croutons separately in an airtight container.

French Onion Soup

6 SERVINGS

At The Woodside Restaurant in Los Angeles, the onion soup has everything traditional Parisian onion soups have: a rich broth, lots of onion flavor, a delicious crouton and just the right amount of cheese. The chef adds a splash of balsamic vinegar for an extra edge.

4 tablespoons unsalted butter
3 large white onions (about 2½ pounds), thinly sliced
½ cup plus 2 tablespoons Madeira
4 cups chicken stock or canned low-sodium broth
4 cups beef stock or canned low-sodium broth
Salt and freshly ground pepper
2 tablespoons balsamic vinegar (optional)
6 thick slices stale sourdough bread
2 cups (about 6½ ounces) grated Gruyère cheese

1. Melt the butter in a large saucepan. Add the sliced white onions and cook over moderately high heat, stirring frequently, until the onions are softened

French Onion Soup

and starting to brown, about 15 minutes. Add 2 tablespoons of the Madeira, reduce the heat to moderate and cook until the Madeira has evaporated. Continue until a total of ½ cup of the Madeira has been added to the soup 2 tablespoons at a time. Stir often and cook until the Madeira has evaporated before adding more, about 15 minutes. Continue cooking the onions, stirring, until they are deep brown, about 10 minutes more.

2. Add the chicken and beef stocks to the saucepan and bring to a rolling boil. Reduce the heat to low and simmer until the soup is flavorful and the onions are tender, about 1 hour. Season the soup with salt and pepper and stir in the balsamic vinegar and the remaining 2 tablespoons of Madeira.

3. Preheat the broiler. Arrange 6 oven-proof bowls on a baking sheet. Divide the soup among the bowls, top each with a bread slice and cover the bread with the cheese. Broil for 1 to 2 minutes, until the cheese is golden and bubbling. —*The Woodside Restaurant*

MAKE AHEAD The onion soup recipe can be prepared through Step 2 and refrigerated for up to 2 days.

Rustic Gazpacho

Rustic Gazpacho

4 SERVINGS

If you prefer a smoother gazpacho than this chunky version, just leave the food processor or blender on a little longer to make a silky puree.

- 6 ripe tomatoes, cut into chunks
- ½ large cucumber—peeled, halved, seeded and cut into chunks
- 1 green bell pepper, cut into chunks
- 2 garlic cloves, smashed
- 1 cup water
- ⅓ cup extra-virgin olive oil
- 2 tablespoons sherry vinegar
- Salt
- Hot sauce, for serving

In a blender or food processor, combine the tomatoes, cucumber, bell pepper, garlic, water, oil and vinegar and process until coarsely pureed. Season with salt and refrigerate until chilled. Serve with hot sauce. —*Teresa Barrenechea*

MAKE AHEAD The gazpacho can be refrigerated overnight.

Summery Hot-and-Sour Soup

4 TO 6 SERVINGS

- 1 tablespoon vegetable oil
- 1 tablespoon minced fresh ginger
- 1 large garlic clove, minced
- 1 small red bell pepper, cut into 1-inch dice
- 6 cups vegetable stock, preferably homemade
- 4 dried shiitake mushrooms
- 1 cup small cauliflower florets
- 1 zucchini, cut into 1-inch cubes
- 1 cup vegetables from Jamaican Jardinière Pickles (recipe, p. 326), cut into ½-inch dice, plus ½ to 1 Scotch bonnet chile pickle, minced, plus 1 to 2 tablespoons pickling liquid from the jar
- 2 teaspoons tomato paste
- 10 cherry tomatoes, halved
- 3 tablespoons soy sauce
- 1 tablespoon cornstarch dissolved in 3 tablespoons water

- ½ pound firm tofu, cut into 1-inch cubes
- Salt and freshly ground black pepper
- Asian sesame oil and cilantro leaves, for garnish

1. Heat the vegetable oil in a large saucepan. Add the ginger, garlic and red bell pepper and cook over moderate heat, stirring, until fragrant, about 2 minutes. Add the vegetable stock; bring to a boil. Add the shiitakes, cover and simmer over low heat until tender and the stock is flavorful, about 25 minutes.

2. Remove the shiitakes from the soup. Discard the stems and thinly slice the caps. Return the caps to the soup. Add the cauliflower, zucchini and pickled vegetables, but not the Scotch bonnet. Simmer the soup over moderate heat until the cauliflower is al dente and the zucchini is just tender, about 4 minutes.

3. Whisk the tomato paste into the soup and then add the cherry tomatoes and soy sauce. Raise the heat to moderately high and stir in the dissolved cornstarch. Simmer, stirring, until the soup thickens, about 1 minute. Add the tofu, Scotch bonnet and pickling liquid; season with salt and black pepper. Ladle into bowls. Garnish each serving with a few drops of sesame oil and some cilantro leaves; serve hot. —*Marcia Kiesel*

Provençal Pistou

4 TO 6 SERVINGS

Using a food processor and a blender for the potent basil puree gives it an ultrasmooth consistency that helps it blend easily into the vegetable soup.

- 4 ounces (about 1 cup) fresh shelled beans, such as cranberry beans, or ½ cup dried black-eyed peas, soaked overnight in cold water and drained
- 1 bay leaf
- 2 cups plus 3 tablespoons water
- ½ cup plus 2 tablespoons extra-virgin olive oil
- 1 medium leek, thinly sliced
- 1 large shallot, thinly sliced

Provençal Pistou

Delicata Squash Soup

2 small celery ribs, cut
   into ½-inch dice
2 medium carrots, cut into
   ½-inch dice
1 red bell pepper, cut into
   ½-inch dice
2 thyme sprigs
4 cups chicken stock or canned
   low-sodium broth
Salt and freshly ground black pepper
4 ounces green beans, cut into
   1-inch pieces
½ cup fresh or frozen corn kernels
2 cups coarsely chopped basil
3 medium garlic cloves, quartered
1 medium zucchini, quartered
   lengthwise and cut crosswise
   into ½-inch pieces

1. In a small saucepan, combine the beans with the bay leaf and 2 cups of the water. Cover partially and simmer over low heat until tender, about 20 minutes for fresh beans and 45 minutes for dried. Discard the bay leaf.
2. Heat 2 tablespoons of the olive oil in a large saucepan. Add the leek, shallot, celery, carrots, red bell pepper, thyme and the remaining 3 tablespoons of water and cook over moderate heat until the water has evaporated and the vegetables soften, about 10 minutes.

3. Add the stock and a large pinch each of salt and black pepper; bring to a simmer. Add the green beans, the corn and the cooked shelled beans along with any remaining cooking liquid. Cover and simmer over low heat until the corn is tender, about 5 minutes.
4. Meanwhile, in a food processor, combine the basil and garlic and process to a paste. With the machine on, slowly pour in the remaining ½ cup of olive oil. Transfer the puree to a blender and blend until very smooth. Scrape the puree into a bowl and season with salt.
5. Add the zucchini to the soup and simmer just until tender, about 4 minutes. Discard the thyme sprigs and then season the soup with salt and black pepper. Remove the soup from the heat, stir in the basil puree and serve at once. —*Marcia Kiesel*

Delicata Squash Soup

8 SERVINGS
Delicata is a cream-colored oblong squash with green stripes; its sweet flesh is deep orange-yellow.

Three 1-pound delicata squashes,
   halved lengthwise and seeded
3 tablespoons unsalted butter
Salt and freshly ground pepper
1 small onion, chopped
1 small thyme sprig
3 cups vegetable stock, chicken
   stock or canned low-sodium
   broth
1⅓ cups heavy cream
¼ cup crème fraîche (optional)
1 small black truffle, shaved
   (optional)

1. Preheat the oven to 300°. Set the squashes, cut sides up, on a rimmed baking sheet lined with foil. Add ½ teaspoon of the butter to each of the squash halves and season with salt and pepper. Add ⅛ inch of water to the baking sheet. Roast the squashes for 45 minutes, or until tender.
2. In a large saucepan, melt the remaining 2 tablespoons of butter. Add the

onion and thyme and cook over low heat, stirring occasionally, until the onion is softened but not browned, about 5 minutes. Scrape the flesh out of the squashes and add it to the saucepan along with the stock and cream. Cook over moderate heat, stirring occasionally, until the liquid has reduced by one-fourth, about 20 minutes.
3. Puree the squash soup in batches in a blender or food processor. Strain the soup into a clean saucepan and season with salt and pepper. Ladle into soup plates and garnish with a dollop of the crème fraîche and a fresh truffle shaving if desired. —*Grant Achatz*
MAKE AHEAD The strained soup can be refrigerated for up to 1 day.

Velvety Leek Soup

8 SERVINGS
An easy way to remove the grit from leeks is to chop or slice them and then soak them in a large bowl of cold water. When you lift the leeks out of the water, the grit stays behind.

4 teaspoons unsalted butter
4 teaspoons extra-virgin olive oil
11 medium leeks (white and light
   green parts only), 9 chopped
   and 2 thinly sliced crosswise for
   garnish
4 medium white onions, chopped
1 quart water
3 medium red potatoes, peeled and
   chopped
½ cup milk
½ cup heavy cream
Salt and freshly ground white pepper
1 tablespoon minced chives
8 small parsley sprigs
8 slivers of fresh tomato (optional)

1. In a large heavy saucepan, melt the butter in 2 teaspoons of the olive oil. Add the chopped leeks and the onions and cook over moderate heat, stirring occasionally, until softened, about 10 minutes. Add the water and bring to a simmer. Cover and cook for 10 minutes. Add the potatoes, cover and cook until

Velvety Leek Soup

tender, about 15 minutes. Working in batches, puree the soup in a blender.

2. Return the soup to the saucepan. Stir in the milk and heavy cream and cook, stirring occasionally, until bubbles appear around the edge, about 6 minutes. Season with salt and white pepper.

3. In a small skillet, heat the remaining 2 teaspoons olive oil. Add the sliced leeks and cook over moderate heat, stirring, until tender, about 4 minutes. Ladle the soup into bowls, garnish with the leeks, chives, parsley and tomato and serve. —*Pilar Huguet*

ONE SERVING Calories 210 kcal, Total Fat 11 gm, Saturated Fat 5 gm
WINE 1997 Can Feixes Blanc Selleccío.

Early Summer Vichyssoise with Sorrel and Asparagus

4 SERVINGS

Sorrel adds a tanginess to this classic soup. If you can't find any in your market, fresh baby spinach and a dash of lemon juice would make a good substitute. Don't be tempted to save a few minutes by pureeing the soup in a food processor or blender, as the texture will turn gluey.

- 4 cups chicken stock or canned low-sodium broth
- 1 pound tender young leeks, white and tender greens thinly sliced and dark green tops reserved
- 1 tablespoon vegetable oil
- 1 pound small white new potatoes, thinly sliced
- 1 large bunch sorrel (¼ pound), stemmed and cut into thin ribbons
- ¼ pound (about 10) pencil-thin asparagus, cut into 1-inch lengths
- ¼ cup half-and-half

Salt and freshly ground pepper

I. In a large saucepan, combine the stock and the leek tops. Cover; simmer over low heat until the stock is flavorful, about 10 minutes. Strain, pressing on the leeks to extract as much liquid as possible. Discard the solids.

2. In another large saucepan, heat ½ tablespoon of the vegetable oil. Add the sliced leeks and the potatoes and cook over moderate heat, stirring, until the leeks are softened but not browned, 9 to 10 minutes. Add the enhanced stock, cover and simmer until the vegetables are tender, about 10 minutes. Stir in the sorrel and cook until wilted, about 2 minutes.

3. Puree the soup in a food mill or work it through a fine sieve, discarding the fibers and potato skins. Refrigerate until chilled, about 2 hours.

4. Meanwhile, in a small skillet, heat the remaining ½ tablespoon vegetable oil. Add the asparagus; cook over moderately high heat until slightly browned, about 5 minutes. Transfer to a plate to cool.

5. Stir the half-and-half and the asparagus into the soup and season with salt and pepper. Ladle the soup into bowls and serve. —*Grace Parisi*

MAKE AHEAD The soup can be made through Step 3 and refrigerated for up to 1 day.

WINE The rich texture of this soup suggests Chardonnay, but the sorrel and asparagus add a tartness that makes a savory California Sauvignon Blanc a better partner. Two choices are the 1996 Chalk Hill or the 1996 Simi.

Rasam

4 SERVINGS

Sometimes called pepper water, this tasty and soothing Indian broth is made with small yellow lentils. Extra pepper goes in when it's prepared for the sick, because of pepper's warming qualities. Think of this as a kind of vegetarian chicken soup.

- 1 cup (7 ounces) *thoor dhal*
- 8¼ cups cold water
- ⅛ teaspoon turmeric
- 1 tablespoon seedless tamarind pulp (see Note)
- 1 cup hot water
- 2 tablespoons vegetable oil
- 1 teaspoon mustard seeds

- 1 teaspoon cumin seeds
- 1 teaspoon coarsely cracked black peppercorns
- ¼ teaspoon fenugreek seeds
- 1 sprig fresh curry leaves (optional)
- 2 dried red chiles
- ¼ teaspoon asafetida
- 1 cup chopped tomato
- ½ cup sliced onion
- 2 teaspoons salt

I. In a medium saucepan, cover the *thoor dhal* with 2¼ cups of the cold water and stir in the turmeric. Bring to a boil and then cover and simmer over low heat until the *dhal* is tender, about 30 minutes. Using a potato masher, puree the *dhal* and then transfer the puree to a bowl.

2. Meanwhile, in a heatproof bowl, soak the tamarind pulp in the hot water until it is thoroughly dissolved, about 10 minutes. Strain the tamarind liquid through a coarse sieve and set aside. Discard the tamarind solids.

3. In a medium saucepan, heat the vegetable oil. Add the mustard seeds, the cumin seeds, the black peppercorns and the fenugreek seeds and cook over moderate heat until the mustard seeds start to pop. Stir in the curry leaves, the dried chiles and the asafetida. Add the *dhal* to the pan along with the tomato, the onion, the salt, the tamarind liquid and the remaining 6 cups of cold water. Bring to a boil over high heat. Cover the saucepan and simmer the mixture over low heat for 30 minutes. Stir and then allow the solids to settle. Using a ladle, skim off the hot broth and serve in large bowls or mugs. —*Maya Kaimal*

NOTE *Thoor dhal* and seedless tamarind pulp are both available at Indian groceries as well as from the following mail-order sources: Kalustyan's (212-685-3451) and Patel Brothers (562-402-2953).

MAKE AHEAD The pepper broth can be refrigerated for up to 1 day. Reheat before serving.

Reitzer's Sweet Corn Soup with Shiitake Crab Cakes

6 SERVINGS ♔

Dale Reitzer, chef at Acacia in Richmond, Virginia, recommends adding a pinch of salt first when sautéing onions or shallots; it helps release their juices and prevents burning.

CORN SOUP

6 ears of corn, shucked
2 tablespoons unsalted butter
1 tablespoon canola oil
2 shallots, thinly sliced
¾ teaspoon cumin seeds
6 cups vegetable stock or canned low-sodium chicken broth
¼ cup heavy cream
Salt and freshly ground white pepper

CRAB CAKES

¼ cup olive oil
6 ounces fresh shiitake mushrooms, stemmed and finely chopped
1 shallot, minced
1 garlic clove, minced
Salt and freshly ground pepper
½ cup vegetable stock or canned low-sodium chicken broth
¼ cup mayonnaise
1 large egg, lightly beaten
1 teaspoon Dijon mustard
Pinch of cayenne pepper
2 teaspoons snipped chives
½ pound jumbo lump crabmeat, picked over
¾ cup coarse dry bread crumbs
All-purpose flour, for dusting
4 tablespoons unsalted butter

I. MAKE THE CORN SOUP: Using a thin sharp knife, cut the corn kernels from the cobs and transfer them to a bowl. Working over the bowl to catch the liquid, scrape the corn milk from the cobs with the back of a knife.

2. In a large soup pot, melt the butter in the oil. Add the shallots and cumin seeds and cook over moderate heat, stirring occasionally, until the shallots are translucent, about 5 minutes. Add the corn and cook for 1 minute. Add the stock and cook for 25 minutes.

3. Working in batches, puree the soup in a blender until smooth. Pass the soup through a fine sieve, pressing to extract as much pulp as possible. Rinse out the soup pot and return the soup to it. Add the cream and season with salt and white pepper.

4. MAKE THE CRAB CAKES: In a large skillet, heat the olive oil until shimmering. Add the shiitakes and cook over moderately high heat until softened, about 4 minutes. Add the shallot and garlic, season with salt and pepper and cook for 1 minute. Stir in the stock and cook until evaporated, about 3 minutes. Transfer to a plate to cool.

5. In a bowl, combine the mayonnaise, egg, Dijon mustard, cayenne and 1 teaspoon of the chives. Fold in the cooked shiitakes and the crabmeat and then the bread crumbs. Shape rounded tablespoons of the mixture into 18 small crab cakes and transfer to a baking sheet lined with lightly floured wax paper; refrigerate until firm.

6. Reheat the soup. Meanwhile, dust the crab cakes with flour, tapping off any excess. Melt the butter in a large nonstick skillet. Add the crab cakes and cook over moderately high heat until browned and crisp, about 2 minutes per side. Transfer the cakes to a paper-towel-lined plate and season with salt.

7. Ladle the soup into shallow soup plates and arrange 3 crab cakes in each plate. Sprinkle with the remaining 1 teaspoon chives and serve. —Dale Reitzer

MAKE AHEAD The recipe can be prepared through Step 3 and refrigerated overnight.

WINE The sweet corn soup calls for a tart, not-too-dry white. Try the 1997 Jekel Johannisberg Riesling from California or 1997 Kerpen Wehlener Sonnenuhr Riesling Kabinett from Germany.

Reitzer's Sweet Corn Soup with Shiitake Crab Cakes

Crab and Asparagus Soup

Steamed Oysters and Oyster Broth

Crab and Asparagus Soup

8 SERVINGS

Asparagus (or Western bamboo, as the Vietnamese call it) was introduced to Southeast Asia by the French. Because asparagus does not grow in tropical climates, the French imported it in cans, which the Vietnamese continue to use to make this delicate soup. In the United States, where asparagus grows easily, you can use fresh spears.

- 3 pounds chicken wings
- 4 quarts plus 3 tablespoons water
- One 2-inch piece of fresh ginger, peeled, thickly sliced and lightly smashed
- 3 scallions, white parts only, lightly smashed
- 3 tablespoons Asian fish sauce
- 1 pound asparagus, sliced crosswise ½ inch thick
- 1 pound fresh lump crabmeat
- 3 large egg whites, lightly beaten
- 1½ tablespoons cornstarch

Kosher salt and freshly ground pepper

- ½ cup cilantro leaves

1. In a large pot, combine the chicken wings with 4 quarts of the water and the ginger, the scallions and 2 tablespoons of the fish sauce. Bring to a boil over high heat and skim. Cover partially and simmer over low heat until the stock has reduced by half, about 3 hours. Skim occasionally during cooking. Strain into a large saucepan; discard the solids.

2. Add the asparagus and the crabmeat to the stock and bring to a boil over high heat. Cover partially and then simmer over low heat until the asparagus is tender and the flavors come together, about 5 minutes.

3. Pour the egg whites into the soup in a slow steady stream and blend a few times so the whites cook into strands. In a small bowl, stir the cornstarch with the remaining 3 tablespoons of water until smooth and then stir into the soup. Simmer until the soup thickens, about 1 minute. Season with the remaining 1 tablespoon fish sauce and kosher salt and pepper. Ladle the soup into bowls, garnish generously with cilantro and serve hot. —Corinne Trang

MAKE AHEAD The soup can be prepared through Step 1 and refrigerated for up to 3 days.

Steamed Oysters and Oyster Broth

8 SERVINGS

This recipe is actually served in two parts—first come the slightly steamed oysters and then the light, aromatic broth. If you are using canned chicken broth, refrigerate the cans for an hour or two and remove the congealed fat from the surface.

- 4 cups chicken stock or canned low-sodium broth
- 2 cups dry white wine
- 2 fish bouillon cubes dissolved in 6 cups water
- 1 bunch of celery, tops trimmed, separated into ribs
- 2 bunches scallions, 2 julienned, the remaining trimmed
- ½ cup finely julienned peeled fresh ginger
- 1 lemon, thinly sliced, ends reserved
- 3 dozen oysters, scrubbed clean
- 1 teaspoon each of finely chopped parsley, cilantro, ginger and shallots (optional)

1. In a large, deep flameproof roasting pan, combine the chicken stock, the white wine and the dissolved fish bouillon cubes. Arrange the celery in the pan with all of the ribs facing the same direction. Arrange the scallions perpendicular to the celery ribs. Scatter the ginger and the reserved ends of the sliced lemon over the celery ribs and scallions. Cover the roasting pan with foil, set it over 2 burners and bring the liquid to a boil.

2. Arrange the oysters on the floating vegetable mat. Cover the roasting pan with foil and simmer until the oysters just begin to open, 3 to 5 minutes. Using tongs, carefully transfer the oysters to a platter. With a knife tip or a small spoon, open the oysters and tip some of their juices into the broth. Serve the oysters warm or at room temperature.

3. Continue to simmer the oyster broth until it has been reduced by half, 35 to

Chilean Seafood Soup

40 minutes. Strain the oyster broth into a medium saucepan and ladle it into small bowls or rimmed soup plates. Put a lemon slice on the side of each plate and top the soup with the scallion julienne and optional parsley, cilantro, ginger and shallots. —*Hisachika Takahashi*

Creamy Lentil Soup with Mussels

4 SERVINGS

- 3 tablespoons unsalted butter
- 2 shallots, minced
- 1 cup dry white wine
- 2 thyme sprigs
- 1 pound mussels, scrubbed and bearded
- 1 tablespoon olive oil
- 2 carrots, minced
- 4 cups water
- 2 cups bottled clam juice
- 1½ cups green lentils

Snipped chives

1. Melt 1 tablespoon of the butter in a medium saucepan. Add half of the shallots and cook over low heat for 2 minutes. Add the wine and thyme and bring to a boil. Add the mussels, cover and cook for 3 to 5 minutes; remove them to a bowl as they open. Strain and reserve the cooking liquid. Remove the mussels from their shells. Discard the shells and any mussels that have not opened.

2. Heat the olive oil in a medium saucepan. Add the carrots and the remaining shallot and cook over low heat until softened but not browned, about 5 minutes. Add the water, clam juice, reserved cooking liquid and lentils. Cover and simmer over low heat until tender, about 1 hour.

3. Puree the lentil soup in a food processor or blender. Pass it through a fine sieve set over the saucepan and whisk in the remaining 2 tablespoons of butter. Arrange the mussels in soup plates and then ladle the lentil soup over them. Sprinkle the soup with the chives and serve. —*Didier Banyols*

Chilean Seafood Soup

6 SERVINGS

An adaptation of the popular *caldillo de congrio,* the soup is traditionally made with eel.

- 3 tablespoons olive oil
- 3 leeks, white and tender green parts only, thinly sliced
- 1 large onion, halved and thinly sliced
- 1 carrot, thinly sliced lengthwise
- 2 garlic cloves, minced
- 3 tomatoes—peeled, seeded and coarsely chopped
- 1 red bell pepper, thinly sliced
- ½ teaspoon dried oregano
- ½ teaspoon paprika
- 1 bay leaf
- 3 cups bottled clam juice diluted with 2 cups water
- 1 cup Chilean Sauvignon Blanc

Salt and freshly ground black pepper

- 6 medium Yukon Gold potatoes, peeled and quartered
- 1 pound skinless Chilean sea bass fillet, about 1 inch thick, cut into 6 chunks
- 24 mussels, scrubbed and debearded
- 12 littleneck clams, scrubbed
- 12 medium shrimp, shelled and deveined
- ¼ cup minced cilantro or parsley
- ¼ cup thinly sliced scallion greens

1. Heat the oil in a large enameled cast-iron casserole. Add the leeks, onion, carrot and garlic and cook over moderately low heat until softened but not browned, about 10 minutes. Add the tomatoes, red bell pepper, oregano, paprika and bay leaf and cook, stirring, for another 3 minutes. Pour in the diluted clam juice and wine and season with salt and black pepper. Cover and simmer over low heat for 20 minutes.

2. Meanwhile, in a medium saucepan, boil the potatoes in salted water until tender, about 15 minutes; drain.

3. Bring the soup to a boil. Add the cooked potatoes, sea bass, mussels, clams and shrimp. Cover and simmer over moderate heat until the clams and mussels open; remove them with tongs as they are done. Discard any clams and mussels that do not open. Continue cooking until all of the fish is cooked through, about 8 minutes total. Return the clams and mussels to the casserole. Discard the bay leaf. Sprinkle with the minced cilantro and scallions and serve. —*Ruth Van Waerebeek-Gonzalez*

MAKE AHEAD The recipe can be made through Step 1 and refrigerated overnight. Reheat before proceeding.

Grouper Chowder

12 SERVINGS

If you can't find grouper, substitute tilefish or cod fillets.

- 1 large baguette, thinly sliced
- ¼ cup plus 2 tablespoons olive oil
- 10 garlic cloves, 9 thinly sliced and 1 halved
- 2 large onions, thinly sliced
- 1 large pinch of saffron threads
- 1½ teaspoons ground cumin
- 1 teaspoon sweet paprika
- ¼ teaspoon cinnamon
- ¼ teaspoon cayenne pepper
- 1 tablespoon honey
- 2 tablespoons tomato paste
- 4 cups bottled clam juice
- 2 cups dry white wine
- 3 cups water
- 3 pounds Yellow Finn or white new potatoes, peeled and cut into ¾-inch chunks

Salt and freshly ground black pepper

- 4 pounds skinless grouper fillets, cut into 2-inch chunks
- ¼ cup chopped parsley

Rouille (recipe follows)

1. Preheat the oven to 350°. Spread the baguette slices on a baking sheet and brush with ¼ cup of the olive oil. Bake for 10 to 12 minutes, or until golden. Rub the croutons on 1 side with the halved garlic.

2. Heat the remaining 2 tablespoons of olive oil in a large pot. Add the sliced

Grouper Chowder

garlic, the onions and the saffron and cook over moderately high heat, stirring, until the onions soften, about 6 minutes. Add the cumin, the paprika, the cinnamon and the cayenne; cook for 2 minutes. Stir in the honey and tomato paste and cook until lightly caramelized, about 4 minutes. Add the clam juice, wine and water; bring to a boil.

3. Add the potatoes and cook over moderate heat until tender, about 20 minutes. Transfer 3 cups of the potatoes and onions to a blender along with a little of the broth and puree until smooth. Stir the puree into the soup and bring to a boil. Season with salt and black pepper.

4. Just before serving, add the grouper to the soup and simmer just until it flakes easily. Ladle the chowder into bowls and sprinkle with the parsley. Pass the croutons and the rouille separately. —*Tim McKee*

MAKE AHEAD The chowder can be prepared through Step 3 and refrigerated for up to 2 days. Bring to a simmer before adding the fish.

ROUILLE

MAKES ABOUT 1 CUP

- 1 garlic clove, smashed
- Salt
- ¼ teaspoon saffron threads, crumbled
- 1 tablespoon fresh lemon juice
- ½ teaspoon cayenne pepper
- ½ cup mayonnaise
- ½ cup extra-virgin olive oil

On a work surface, mince the garlic clove with a pinch of salt. In a mini-processor, combine the garlic with the saffron, lemon juice and cayenne and pulse until blended. Add the mayonnaise and pulse until smooth. With the machine on, add the extra-virgin olive oil in a thin stream and blend until emulsified. Transfer the rouille to a bowl and season with salt. —*T. M.*

MAKE AHEAD The rouille can be refrigerated for up to 3 days.

Chipotle-Lime Broth with Chicken and Pumpkin

6 SERVINGS

Chipotle chiles give the broth a smoky, spicy taste here. A hefty squeeze of fresh lime juice just before serving is essential to brighten the flavor.

- 1 small sugar pumpkin or butternut squash (about 1¼ pounds)— halved, seeded and sliced 1¼ inches thick
- 1 tablespoon vegetable oil
- 1 medium onion, chopped
- 2 garlic cloves, finely chopped
- 2 quarts chicken stock
- 2 canned chipotle chiles in *adobo*— rinsed, seeded and thinly sliced
- 1½ cups fresh or frozen corn
- 1½ cups cooked black or pink beans (optional)
- 2 cups shredded roasted chicken breast meat
- 3 tablespoons fresh lime juice, plus 1 lime, cut into wedges
- ½ cup chopped cilantro
- Salt
- 1 ripe Hass avocado, thinly sliced

1. Preheat the oven to 400°. Brush the pumpkin slices with ½ teaspoon of the vegetable oil and bake on a nonstick baking sheet for about 20 minutes, or until just tender. Let the pumpkin slices cool and then remove and discard the skin. Cut the pumpkin slices into ½-inch dice.

2. Heat the remaining 2½ teaspoons of vegetable oil in a large nonstick skillet. Add the onion, cover and cook over moderately low heat until softened, about 5 minutes. Uncover, increase the heat and cook, stirring, until golden. Add the garlic and cook until fragrant, about 2 minutes.

3. In a large saucepan, bring the chicken stock to a simmer. Add the chipotle chiles and cook for 2 minutes. Add the cooked pumpkin and onion, the corn and the beans, if using, and simmer over moderate heat for 10 minutes. Stir in the roasted chicken meat and cook just until warmed through. Add the lime juice and cilantro and season with salt. Serve the soup in large bowls and pass the avocado and lime wedges alongside. —*Sally Schneider*

ONE SERVING Calories 341 kcal, Total Fat 11.1 gm, Saturated Fat 2.4 gm

WINE This piquant and spicy soup has a sweet edge from the corn and a sharp edge from the lime juice. Best bet for a match? An aromatic dry white, such as a Viognier, with fruity, tart flavors of its own. Try the 1996 Réserve St-Martin from France or the 1997 Rabbit Ridge from California.

Vietnamese Chicken Noodle Soup

4 SERVINGS

Vietnamese noodle soups—light broths with various garnishes, fresh herbs, crunchy sprouts and hot chiles—warm the body, clear the head and soothe the soul. This version of *moc,* as the dumpling soup is known in Vietnam, is served at Truc Orient Express in Hartford, Connecticut. The chewy chicken dumplings are accompanied by rice noodles, snow peas and cilantro. Each serving should be put together individually; the rice noodles will stick together if you cook too many at once.

- One 3½-pound chicken
- One 2-inch piece of ginger, peeled and thickly sliced
- 6 whole peppercorns
- 3½ quarts water
- Salt
- ¼ cup plus 1 tablespoon Asian fish sauce (*nuoc mam*)
- 2 teaspoons cornstarch
- 1½ teaspoons vegetable oil
- Pinch of sugar
- 2 white mushrooms, finely chopped
- 1 large scallion, finely chopped
- 1 pound dried thin rice noodles, such as vermicelli or rice sticks
- Freshly ground pepper

Chipotle-Lime Broth with Chicken and Pumpkin

½ pound snow peas, trimmed

1 cup cilantro sprigs

Asian sesame oil, for serving

Chinese chili oil, for serving

2 cups mung bean sprouts,
    for serving

1. Using a sharp knife, remove the breast meat from the chicken. Put the rest of the chicken in a large pot and add the sliced ginger, the peppercorns and the water. Bring to a boil over moderately high heat, skimming. Add 1 tablespoon of salt, reduce the heat to low and simmer for 1½ hours, skimming occasionally.

2. Meanwhile, bring a large saucepan of salted water to a boil. Skin the chicken breasts and cut the meat into 1-inch pieces. Put the meat in a food processor, add 1 tablespoon of fish sauce, the cornstarch, vegetable oil and sugar and process to a fine paste. Scrape the paste into a large bowl and stir in the mushrooms and scallion.

3. Using 2 teaspoons, shape the chicken mixture into 24 dumplings. Add the dumplings to the boiling water and simmer over moderate heat until firm and springy, about 5 minutes. Using a slotted spoon, transfer the dumplings to a bowl and cover with a kitchen towel. Reserve the cooking liquid.

4. Put the rice noodles in a large bowl, cover with cold water and let soak until pliable, about 25 minutes. Drain and return to the bowl.

5. Strain the chicken stock. Remove the meat from the chicken, discarding the skin. Tear the chicken meat into large pieces. Return the chicken stock to the pot, add the remaining ¼ cup of fish sauce and season with salt and pepper. Bring to a gentle simmer and keep warm.

6. Bring the dumpling cooking liquid back to a boil. For each serving, put one quarter of the rice noodles in a small strainer and cook them in the boiling liquid, stirring occasionally, until al dente, about 40 seconds. Lift out the strainer, shaking the noodles to drain them, and turn them out into a soup bowl. Add one quarter of the chicken meat and dumplings to the strainer, rewarm in the cooking liquid and then add to the rice noodles. Ladle about 3 cups of the chicken broth on top and garnish with snow peas, cilantro and a few drops each of sesame oil and chili oil. Top with bean sprouts and serve at once. Repeat with the remaining ingredients. —*Binh Duong*

MAKE AHEAD The soup can be prepared through Step 1 and refrigerated for up to 2 days.

Curried Turkey Soup

8 SERVINGS

Make this curried soup any time you roast a big bird. Adding cooked rice, pasta or potato chunks turns the soup into a hearty main dish.

3 tablespoons unsalted butter

2 tablespoons curry powder

1 pound onions, cut into ¼-inch dice

¼ pound white mushrooms, cut into ¼-inch dice

8 cups turkey stock (p. 192)

1¾ pounds sweet potatoes, peeled and cut into ¼-inch dice

¾ pound carrots, half cut into ¼-inch dice, the other half sliced crosswise ¼-inch thick

3 large celery ribs, cut into ¼-inch dice

1 pound zucchini, halved lengthwise and cut crosswise into ¼-inch-thick slices

2 cups cooked turkey, cut into ¼-inch dice

½ cup small pieces of broccoli

3 tablespoons fresh lime juice

Kosher salt and freshly ground pepper

Crusty bread, for serving

1. In a large, heavy enameled cast-iron casserole or stockpot, melt the unsalted butter over moderate heat and then

Curried Turkey Soup

add the curry powder. Cook, stirring, until very fragrant, about 1 minute. Add the diced onions and cook, stirring occasionally, until the onions are softened, about 10 minutes. Stir in the diced white mushrooms and cook for 5 minutes longer.

2. Add the turkey stock and bring to a boil over moderately high heat. Add the sweet potatoes and the carrots, reduce the heat to moderate and simmer for 10 minutes. Add the celery and zucchini and cook for 10 minutes longer. Stir in the turkey and bring the soup just to a simmer. Add the broccoli and lime juice and season with kosher salt and pepper. Serve the soup hot, with crusty bread. —*Barbara Kafka*

MAKE AHEAD The soup can be made a day ahead. Add the broccoli and lime once it's reheated.

WINE This curried soup calls for a light, moderately fruity wine to play off the savory flavors. Try the 1998 Trefethen Dry Riesling or the 1998 Dry Creek Clarksburg Dry Chenin Blanc, both from California.

chapter 5

pasta

Longevity Noodles

4 SERVINGS

Long noodles represent long life in Chinese culture. At feasts that relate to longevity—birthdays, New Year's, anniversaries—noodles are always served, and great care is taken not to cut them.

- 2 quarts water
- 5 ounces (2 cups) mung bean or soybean sprouts
- 1½ teaspoons salt
- ½ pound fresh Chinese egg noodles
- ¼ cup chicken stock or canned low-sodium broth
- 1 tablespoon plus ½ teaspoon light soy sauce
- ½ teaspoon Asian sesame oil
- 1 tablespoon peanut oil

One ¼-inch-thick slice of fresh ginger, peeled and lightly smashed
- ¼ pound snow peas
- 3 large fresh water chestnuts, peeled and sliced ⅛ inch thick (see Note)

1. Bring the water to a boil in a large saucepan. Put the bean sprouts in a strainer, lower it into the boiling water and blanch the bean sprouts for 10 seconds. Remove the strainer and rinse the sprouts in cold water; drain well.

2. Add the salt to the water in the saucepan and bring it back to a boil. Add the Chinese egg noodles and cook, stirring, for 1 minute. Drain the noodles thoroughly in a colander and rinse them in cold water; drain. Rinse again and then drain, lifting the noodles to separate and dry the strands.

3. In a small bowl, combine the stock with the soy sauce and sesame oil to make the sauce.

4. Warm a wok over high heat for 45 seconds. Add the peanut oil and swirl to coat the wok. Stir in the fresh ginger and cook for 10 seconds. Add the snow peas and stir-fry until they are bright green, about 1 minute. Add the water chestnuts and stir-fry for 30 seconds. Add the blanched bean sprouts and stir-fry for 1 minute.

5. Stir the sauce, add it to the wok and bring to a boil. Add the noodles and stir-fry until they absorb the sauce, about 1½ minutes. Transfer to a platter and serve at once. —*Eileen Yin-Fei Lo*

NOTE Fresh water chestnuts are truly wonderful, but if they are unavailable, substitute one quarter of a peeled jicama, thinly sliced.

ONE SERVING Calories 150 kcal, Total Fat 5 gm, Saturated Fat 1 gm

Sizzling-Herb Fedelini

4 SERVINGS

Fedelini is a very thin spaghetti that is ideal to toss with this spicy garlic-infused sauce. The pasta cooks while you prepare the rest of the dish. You can use any combination of fresh herbs, including a little finely chopped thyme, rosemary and sage, as long as you have a total of three quarters of a cup.

- 1 pound fedelini or capellini pasta
- ½ cup extra-virgin olive oil
- 2 large garlic cloves, minced
- ½ teaspoon crushed red pepper
- ¼ cup minced flat-leaf parsley
- ¼ cup finely chopped basil
- ¼ cup finely chopped chives

Kosher salt and freshly ground black pepper
- 1 cup (about 4 ounces) freshly grated Pecorino-Romano cheese

1. Bring a large pot of salted water to a boil. Add the pasta and cook until al dente. Transfer to a colander and drain.

2. Meanwhile, in a large, deep skillet, combine the olive oil with the garlic and the crushed red pepper and cook over moderate heat until the garlic is fragrant but not colored, about 1 minute. Add the parsley, basil and chives and cook just until they begin to sizzle, about 30 seconds. Remove from the heat, add the pasta and toss to evenly coat with the herbs. Season with kosher salt and pepper. Transfer the pasta to a

Longevity Noodles

Sizzling-Herb Fedelini

ABOVE: **Fregola with Blood Oranges and Sicilian Olives.** RIGHT: **Warm Fusilli with Tomatoes and Watercress.**

large bowl, toss with the cheese and serve immediately. —*Seen Lippert*
WINE A Zinfandel will match the spiciness of this dish and deliver some pepperiness of its own. Among various California contenders, opt for the 1997 Cline Cellars or the 1997 Hendry Ranch.

Fregola with Blood Oranges and Sicilian Olives

6 SERVINGS

Fregola, sometimes called *friulli*, is a flour product from Sardinia that is similar to pasta. It resembles lumpy golden pebbles and comes in small, medium and large.

- 1¼ cups (½ pound) medium *fregola*
- ½ cup (4 ounces) green Sicilian olives, pitted and cut into slivers
- ⅓ cup finely chopped red onion
- 2 tablespoons drained small capers
- 2 tablespoons fresh lemon juice
- 1 tablespoon extra-virgin olive oil
- 3 small blood oranges

Salt and freshly ground white pepper
Shredded orange zest, for garnish

1. Cook the *fregola* in a medium saucepan of boiling salted water until al dente, 8 to 9 minutes. Drain well in a colander, shaking off the excess water. Let stand for 15 minutes, shaking the colander occasionally to dry the grains.

2. In a large glass or stainless steel bowl, toss the olives with the onion, capers, lemon juice and olive oil. Add the *fregola* and toss to coat.

3. Using a sharp knife, peel the oranges, removing all of the bitter white pith. Working over the bowl, cut in between the membranes to release the sections. Squeeze the juice from the membranes into the salad, season with salt and white pepper and let stand for 10 minutes to blend the flavors. Scatter the orange zest over the top of the salad and serve. —*Grace Parisi*

MAKE AHEAD The noodles can be prepared through Step 2 and refrigerated for up to 4 hours. Bring to room temperature before serving.

Udon Noodles with Citrus Vinaigrette

4 SERVINGS

- 1 cup boiling water
- 1 large ancho chile
- ¾ pound dried thin Japanese udon noodles (see Note)
- 1 cup fresh orange juice
- ¼ cup mirin (sweet rice wine)
- ½ teaspoon finely grated orange zest
- ¼ teaspoon Asian sesame oil

Salt

- 1 medium cucumber—peeled, halved lengthwise, seeded and sliced crosswise ¼ inch thick
- 1 cup mung bean sprouts
- 2 scallions, thinly sliced

1. In a heatproof medium bowl, pour the boiling water over the ancho. Cover; let stand until softened, about 20 minutes.

2. Meanwhile, in a large pot of boiling water, cook the udon, stirring often, until just tender, about 8 minutes. Drain the udon in a colander; rinse well with cold water. Let drain, lifting the noodles occasionally to keep them separate.

3. Remove and discard the stem and seeds from the ancho and finely chop the chile. Transfer to a blender, add the orange juice, mirin and orange zest and blend to a smooth sauce. Add the oil and season the vinaigrette with salt.

4. In a large glass or stainless steel bowl, toss the udon with the cucumber, the bean sprouts and the scallions. Add the orange vinaigrette, toss well and serve immediately. —*Marcia Kiesel*

NOTE Dried thin Japanese udon noodles are available at Asian markets and specialty food shops.

Warm Fusilli with Tomatoes and Watercress

6 SERVINGS

This summery pasta plays opposites off each other—cool sauce and warm pasta, sweet tomatoes and snappy lemon, hot chile and cool mint. The sauce is delicious when served at room temperature (it can stand for an hour), so resist the urge to refrigerate it.

- 1 Italian frying pepper or ½ red bell pepper, finely chopped
- ½ red onion, finely chopped
- ½ jalapeño—halved, seeded and minced
- 1 large garlic clove, minced
- 2 tablespoons fresh lemon juice

Pinch of dried oregano

Salt and freshly ground black pepper

- 1½ pounds of mixed red and yellow cherry tomatoes, such as pear tomatoes and red currant tomatoes, halved

Heaping ¼ cup Calamata olives, pitted and coarsely chopped

- 1 tablespoon (tightly packed) torn mint leaves
- 1 tablespoon (tightly packed) torn basil leaves
- 2 tablespoons extra-virgin olive oil
- 1 pound fusilli
- ½ cup shredded Asiago cheese, plus more for serving

- 1 large bunch watercress, large stems discarded

1. In a large glass or ceramic serving bowl, combine the frying pepper, red onion, jalapeño, garlic, lemon juice and oregano. Season with salt and black pepper; let stand for 10 minutes. Add the tomatoes, olives, mint, basil and oil.

2. Bring a large pot of water to a boil. Add salt and then add the fusilli. Cook until al dente and then drain. Add the fusilli to the tomato sauce along with the Asiago cheese and the watercress. Toss the pasta with the sauce and serve. —*Lynne Rossetto Kasper*

WINE The sauce gives this pasta dish a tartness that is best complemented by a bright, zesty red wine: Sangiovese. Try a Chianti Classico (the 1993 Castello di Gabbiano Riserva Oro) or a California bottling (the 1996 Forest Glen).

Penne with Charred Green Beans

4 SERVINGS

Letting the green beans blacken in spots adds a light smoky flavor.

- ¼ cup coarsely chopped walnuts
- 2 tablespoons walnut oil
- 1 pound young green beans, cut into 1½-inch lengths

perfect-pasta tip

One key to making a great-tasting pasta dish with an uncooked tomato sauce has nothing to do with adding extra-virgin olive oil, butter or cheese. The secret is to use the liquid that almost all tomato sauces give off as they sit. Undercook the pasta slightly, drain it, return the pot to the stove and spoon in the liquid. Add the pasta and stir over moderately high heat until it's just tender and nicely coated. Not only will the pasta be perfectly cooked, it will be infused with flavor.

- 2 shallots, minced
- 1 large garlic clove, minced
- 1 tablespoon finely chopped summer savory or flat-leaf parsley
- 2 tablespoons fresh lemon juice

Salt and freshly ground pepper

- 1 pound penne rigate
- 4 ounces (about 1 cup) ricotta salata, crumbled

1. Bring a large pot of salted water to a boil. Meanwhile, in a large deep skillet, toast the walnuts over high heat, stirring constantly, until fragrant, about 5 minutes. Transfer to a plate to cool.

2. Add 1 teaspoon of the oil to the skillet along with the green beans and cook over high heat, stirring, until tender and blackened in spots, about 8 minutes. Add 1 tablespoon of the oil, the shallots, garlic and summer savory. Cook until fragrant, about 2 minutes. Add the lemon juice; season with salt and pepper.

3. Cook the penne in the boiling water until al dente. Drain the pasta, reserving 1 cup of the cooking water. Add the pasta to the skillet and toss with the green beans; stir in some cooking water if the pasta seems dry. Add the ricotta salata, toasted walnuts and the remaining 2 teaspoons of walnut oil. Toss well and serve. —*Seen Lippert*

Fusilli with Broccoli Rabe

4 TO 6 SERVINGS

Fusilli (corkscrews) and farfalle (butterflies) are perfect for sauces with chunks of vegetables and meat—the folds and cavities in the pasta hold the pieces.

- 1½ pounds broccoli rabe, thick stems trimmed and peeled
- 3 tablespoons extra-virgin olive oil
- 6 large garlic cloves, minced
- 3 anchovy fillets, mashed
- ½ teaspoon crushed red pepper

Salt and freshly ground black pepper

- 1 pound fusilli
- 1 tablespoon unsalted butter

Freshly grated Pecorino Romano cheese, for serving

1. Steam the broccoli rabe until just tender, about 3 minutes. Coarsely chop.
2. Heat the oil in a large skillet. Add the garlic and cook over low heat until golden, about 3 minutes. Add the anchovies and crushed red pepper and cook for 1 minute. Add the broccoli rabe and cook, stirring, until the flavors are well blended, about 4 minutes. Season with salt and black pepper and keep warm.

3. Cook the fusilli in a large pot of boiling salted water, stirring occasionally, until al dente. Reserve 3 tablespoons of the pasta cooking liquid. Drain the fusilli and return to the pot. Add the butter and toss well. Add the broccoli rabe and reserved liquid and toss again. Season with salt and black pepper; transfer to a warmed bowl. Serve at once, passing the cheese separately. —*Marcia Kiesel*

Fusilli with Broccoli Rabe

Orzo Risotto with Swiss Chard and Fontina

4 SERVINGS

This faux risotto made with orzo, earthy Swiss chard and melted cheese is an easy vegetarian dish. Adding a salad makes it into a meal.

- 2½ **cups chicken or vegetable stock or canned low-sodium broth**
- 2½ **cups water**
- 1 **tablespoon unsalted butter**
- 1¾ **cups (¾ pound) orzo**
- 1 **tablespoon olive oil**
- 1 **large shallot, thinly sliced**
- 1 **pound red Swiss chard, stems trimmed and finely chopped, leaves torn into large pieces**
- 2 **teaspoons sherry vinegar**
- 5 **ounces imported Fontina cheese, cut into ¼-inch dice (1 cup)**
- ¾ **cup (3 ounces) freshly grated Parmesan cheese**

Salt and freshly ground pepper

1. Bring the chicken stock and water to a simmer in a saucepan and keep warm over low heat. Melt the butter in a medium nonstick saucepan. Add the orzo to the butter and cook over moderately high heat, stirring often, until the orzo is golden, about 8 minutes. Add 1 cup of the warm stock mixture and cook, stirring gently, until nearly all of the stock has been absorbed. Gradually add more of the stock mixture, 1 cup at a time, and cook, stirring frequently, until the orzo is al dente and creamy but not soupy, about 20 minutes.

2. Meanwhile, heat the olive oil in a large nonstick skillet. Add the shallot and Swiss chard stems and cook over moderately high heat, stirring occasionally, until the stems are tender and lightly browned, about 7 minutes. Add the chard leaves and cook over moderately high heat, tossing, until the leaves are wilted, about 2 minutes. Add the sherry vinegar. Stir the Swiss chard and the Fontina and Parmesan cheeses into the risotto, season with salt and pepper and serve. —*Grace Parisi*

Savory Swiss chard and nutty Fontina will pair successfully with a crisp, lean Soave from Italy, such as the 1998 Bolla Tufaie Castellaro or the 1998 Anselmi San Vincenzo.

Perciatelli with Ricotta Salata

4 TO 6 SERVINGS

Perciatelli are long round noodles similar to spaghetti, but thick and hollow.

- 1 tablespoon extra-virgin olive oil
- 2 slices (1½ ounces) pancetta, finely chopped
- 1 medium onion, finely chopped
- 1 small carrot, finely chopped
- 1 small celery rib, finely chopped
- ½ cup dry white wine
- One 14-ounce can peeled Italian tomatoes, chopped, liquid reserved
- 1 teaspoon tomato paste
- Salt and freshly ground pepper
- 1 pound perciatelli or bucatini
- ¼ pound ricotta salata, crumbled, or fresh ricotta
- 2 tablespoons chopped basil
- 1 tablespoon chopped parsley
- 1 small garlic clove, minced

1. Heat the oil in a large skillet. Add the pancetta, onion, carrot and celery and cook over low heat until the onion is soft but not browned, about 5 minutes. Add the white wine and simmer over moderate heat until reduced by half, about 3 minutes. Add the canned tomatoes with their liquid and the tomato paste and bring to a simmer. Cover and cook over low heat until thickened, about 20 minutes. Season with salt and pepper and keep warm.

2. Cook the perciatelli in a large pot of boiling salted water, stirring occasionally, until al dente. Reserve ½ cup of the pasta cooking water. Drain the perciatelli and return it to the pot. Add the tomato sauce, the reserved pasta cooking water, the ricotta salata, basil, parsley and garlic and toss to coat. Transfer the pasta to a warmed bowl and serve at once. —*Anna Teresa Callen*

Pasta with Provençal Wine Sauce

4 SERVINGS

Traditionally, this Provençal sauce would be made with a wine from the southern Rhône, but you can use whatever you have open. Serve any leftovers with fish or chicken.

- ¼ cup plus 2 tablespoons olive oil
- 1 medium onion, finely chopped
- Salt
- One 35-ounce can Italian plum tomatoes, drained and chopped
- 2 cups red or dry white wine
- 1 whole clove
- 1 bay leaf
- 3 garlic cloves, finely chopped
- ⅔ cup oil-cured black olives, pitted and halved
- 1 tablespoon capers, drained
- ½ cup coarsely chopped mixed herbs, such as basil, parsley and thyme
- Freshly ground pepper
- 1 pound penne rigate or rigatoni

1. Heat 2 tablespoons of the olive oil in a medium saucepan. Add the onion, season lightly with salt and cook over moderate heat, stirring, until softened but not browned, about 5 minutes. Add the tomatoes, wine, clove and bay leaf and cook over moderate heat, stirring occasionally, until the sauce is thick and very little liquid remains, about 1 hour. Discard the bay leaf and the clove (if you can find it). Pass the wine sauce through a food mill or puree it in a food processor and then transfer the sauce to a clean saucepan.

2. Heat the remaining ¼ cup of olive oil in a small saucepan. Add the garlic and cook over moderately low heat, stirring, until golden, about 5 minutes. Add the olives and the capers and cook until heated through, 3 to 5 minutes. Add the mixture to the tomato sauce along with the chopped herbs. Season the sauce with pepper.

3. Cook the pasta in a large pot of boiling salted water until al dente. Drain

Orzo Risotto with Swiss Chard and Fontina

picks of the pans

Nonstick cookware is more rugged than ever, with scratch-resistant surfaces that incorporate ceramic or metal flecks for extra protection. And, though the surfaces of the old grill pans flaked away when exposed to high heat, the new ones can get hot enough to sear food properly. As an extra advantage, some of the new nonstick cookware is actually pretty, with surfaces in bright colors like yellow and blue. Our favorites:

• **ProLine** and **Wearever** 3-quart saucepans. The scratch-resistant surface works especially well for foods that require constant stirring or whisking, such as risotto, polenta and oatmeal.

• **Circulon** 12-inch round grill pan and **ProLine** 10-inch square grill pan. Good for delicate foods such as skinless chicken breasts and fish fillets, which tend to stick even to nonstick surfaces treated with oil.

• **Cybernox** all-metal 10-inch skillet. (Needs to be heated thoroughly before adding ingredients, or the food will stick.)

• **Le Creuset** 12-inch enameled cast-iron skillet. Great for potato cakes and other foods that call for serious browning.

and transfer the pasta to a serving dish. Add the wine sauce and toss to coat. Serve at once. —*Jane Sigal*

MAKE AHEAD The Provençal wine sauce can be refrigerated for up to 2 days.

WINE All this rustic pasta dish requires for accompaniment is a bright-flavored red, like a Côtes-du-Rhône.

Penne with Yellow Peppers and Tomatoes

4 TO 6 SERVINGS

2½ tablespoons extra-virgin olive oil
2 large garlic cloves, minced
2 large yellow bell peppers— quartered, peeled and thinly sliced lengthwise
One 35-ounce can Italian peeled tomatoes, drained and chopped
Salt and freshly ground black pepper
1 pound penne
Freshly grated Parmigiano-Reggiano cheese, for serving

1. In a large skillet, heat 2 tablespoons of the olive oil. Add the garlic and cook over low heat until golden, about 2 minutes. Add the yellow bell peppers and cook until tender, about 10 minutes. Add the tomatoes and cook over moderate heat until thickened, about 5 minutes. Season with salt and black pepper and keep warm.

2. Cook the penne in a large pot of boiling salted water, stirring occasionally, until al dente. Drain the penne and return it to the pot. Add the sauce to the pasta along with the remaining ½ tablespoon of olive oil and toss to coat. Season the pasta with salt and black pepper and transfer to a warmed bowl. Serve at once, passing the cheese separately. —*Marcia Kiesel*

WINE The sweet yellow peppers and the tart tomato sauce in this simple pasta dish need the contrast of a crisp white wine with some herbal character. Consider a California Sauvignon Blanc, such as the 1997 Groth or the 1997 Silverado.

Pasta with Provençal Wine Sauce

Rigatoni alla Panna

4 TO 6 SERVINGS

1 pound rigatoni
½ cup heavy cream
2 tablespoons unsalted butter, at room temperature
¾ cup (3 ounces) freshly grated Parmigiano-Reggiano cheese
Salt and freshly ground pepper

1. Cook the rigatoni in a large pot of boiling salted water, stirring occasionally, until al dente. Drain the pasta and return to the pot.

2. Meanwhile, warm the heavy cream in a small saucepan over low heat. Add the butter to the rigatoni and toss well. Add the cream and cheese; toss to coat. Season with salt and pepper, transfer to a warmed bowl and serve. —*Marcia Kiesel*

Fusilli with Four Cheeses and Balsamic Vinegar

4 SERVINGS

Boiling the balsamic vinegar concentrates its flavor; just a drizzle is all that's needed to balance the rich sauce.

1 pound fusilli
1 cup heavy cream
¾ cup (3 ounces) freshly grated Parmesan cheese
½ cup (2 ounces) freshly grated Fontina Val d'Asta cheese
2 ounces Gorgonzola or other creamy blue cheese, cut into ½-inch dice (½ cup)
2 ounces Taleggio, Brie or Camembert, rind discarded, cheese cut into ½-inch dice (½ cup)

Rigatoni alla Panna

Salt and freshly ground pepper

¼ cup balsamic vinegar

1 tablespoon finely chopped flat-leaf parsley

1. Preheat the oven to 350°. Cook the fusilli in a large pot of boiling salted water, stirring occasionally, until al dente. Drain the fusilli, reserving ¼ cup of the cooking water, and then return the pasta to the pot.

2. Meanwhile, in a medium saucepan, bring the heavy cream to a simmer. Reduce the heat to low and stir in ½ cup of the Parmesan and the Fontina. Remove from the heat and stir in the Gorgonzola and Taleggio. Let the sauce stand until all the cheese is melted, about 5 minutes.

3. Toss the pasta with the cheese sauce along with the reserved pasta cooking water. Season the pasta with salt and pepper. Transfer the pasta to a 9-by-13-inch baking dish and sprinkle with the remaining ¼ cup of Parmesan. Bake for 15 minutes, or until the top is lightly browned.

4. Meanwhile, in a small skillet, boil the balsamic vinegar until it is reduced to 1½ tablespoons, about 8 minutes. Drizzle the balsamic vinegar over the pasta, sprinkle with the parsley and serve at once. —*Mark Strausman*

WINE The strong, sharp flavors of the vinegar call for a wine with similar intensity. Stick with a Barbera d'Asti, like the 1997 Michele Chiarlo.

Fusilli Carbonara with Herbs

4 TO 6 SERVINGS

The abundance of fresh tarragon, chervil, chives and parsley—a mixture called *fines herbes*—is balanced here by the addition of cream and egg yolks. Note that the yolks are cooked only by the heat of the pasta, which thickens them enough to make a sauce.

1 pound long fusilli

½ cup heavy cream

5 large egg yolks

¼ cup chopped chervil

¼ cup chopped chives

¼ cup chopped parsley

2 tablespoons finely chopped tarragon

Salt and freshly ground pepper

¼ cup plus 2 tablespoons (1½ ounces) freshly grated Parmesan cheese

1. Cook the fusilli in a large pot of boiling salted water until al dente. Meanwhile, in a large stainless steel bowl, whisk the heavy cream with the egg yolks. Stir in the chervil, chives, parsley and tarragon and season with salt and pepper. Heat the herb sauce to lukewarm by briefly setting the bowl on top of the boiling pasta water and whisking rapidly.

2. Drain the fusilli and add it to the bowl with the herb sauce. Sprinkle the fusilli with the Parmesan cheese and toss to coat the pasta thoroughly. Serve the fusilli carbonara immediately in warmed bowls. —*Jerry Traunfeld*

WINE The herbal notes in this pasta dish are dominant, pointing directly to an herbaceous Sauvignon Blanc. Try the 1997 Michel Lynch from Bordeaux or the J. Fritz Jenner Vineyard from California.

Baked Rigatoni with Zucchini and Eggplant

4 SERVINGS

You can substitute any pasta with twists or ridges, such as fusilli or farfalle, for the rigatoni called for here.

1 pound rigatoni

One 28-ounce can peeled Italian tomatoes

½ cup vegetable oil

1 large eggplant, cut into ⅓-inch dice

¼ cup extra-virgin olive oil

1 garlic clove, finely chopped

2 large zucchini, halved lengthwise and sliced crosswise ⅓ inch thick

1 medium onion, thinly sliced

¼ cup torn basil leaves

1 teaspoon dried oregano

Salt and freshly ground pepper

½ pound mozzarella, shredded

½ cup (2 ounces) freshly grated Parmesan cheese

1. Preheat the oven to 350°. Cook the rigatoni in a large pot of boiling salted water, stirring occasionally, until the pasta is al dente. Drain the pasta, reserving ¼ cup of the cooking water. Return the pasta to the pot while preparing the sauce.

2. Puree the canned Italian tomatoes with their juices in a blender or food processor. Pass the tomato puree through a fine sieve set over a bowl to remove the seeds.

3. Heat ¼ cup of the vegetable oil in a large nonstick skillet. Line a large plate with paper towels. Add half of the eggplant to the skillet and cook over moderately high heat, stirring occasionally, until the eggplant is golden brown, about 6 minutes. Using a slotted spoon, transfer the eggplant to the plate to drain. Repeat with the remaining eggplant and vegetable oil and add to the first batch of eggplant. Discard the oil in the skillet.

4. Heat the olive oil in the same skillet used to cook the eggplant. Add the chopped garlic clove and cook over moderate heat, stirring occasionally, until fragrant, about 30 seconds. Add the zucchini and onion slices and cook over high heat, stirring often, until the vegetables are slightly softened, about 6 minutes. Add the tomato puree, the basil and the oregano and simmer over moderate heat until the sauce is reduced by one third, about 15 minutes. Stir in the eggplant and season the sauce with salt and pepper.

5. Fold the eggplant and zucchini sauce into the rigatoni along with the shredded mozzarella cheese and the reserved pasta cooking water. Transfer the rigatoni to a 9-by-13-inch baking dish and sprinkle the Parmesan cheese

Fusilli Carbonara with Herbs

evenly over the top. Bake the rigatoni for 15 minutes, or until it is heated through. Serve the baked rigatoni piping hot. *—Mark Strausman*

MAKE AHEAD The rigatoni and the zucchini and eggplant sauce can be prepared through Step 4 and kept at room temperature for up to 2 hours. Add about 10 minutes to the baking time in Step 5.

WINE Chianti is a classic pairing with satisfying dishes like Baked Rigatoni with Zucchini and Eggplant. Pick either a young 1997 Chianti, such as the Castello di Gabbiano, or a deeper 1995 Riserva, such as the Nozzole.

Macaroni Gratin

8 SERVINGS

Deliciously moist, this gratin is a far cry from American macaroni and cheese. Cooking the pasta in milk and then cooling the cooking liquid down with ice cubes keeps the macaroni from drying out. The dish can serve as an accompaniment to roasted meats or poultry.

- 3 **quarts milk**
- 4 **garlic cloves, lightly crushed**
- 1 **tablespoon unsalted butter**
- 1 **tablespoon all-purpose flour**

Fine sea salt

Freshly ground white pepper

Freshly grated nutmeg

- ¾ **cup heavy cream**
- ¾ **pound ridged penne pasta**
- 2 **trays of ice cubes**
- 1 **cup (3½ ounces) freshly grated imported Gruyère cheese**
- 2 **tablespoons minced chives**

1. In a large saucepan, combine the milk and garlic. Warm the milk over high heat until bubbles appear around the edge. Remove from the heat, cover and let steep for 10 minutes. Remove and discard the garlic. Measure out 1 cup of milk and reserve; set aside the rest.

2. In a small saucepan, melt the butter over moderate heat. Whisk in the flour. Cook, stirring constantly, without browning, for 1 minute. Remove the saucepan from the heat and gradually whisk in the reserved 1 cup of milk, stirring constantly, until the sauce is completely smooth. Season with a large pinch of sea salt and generous gratings of white pepper and nutmeg. Return the pan to low heat. Cook the sauce, whisking constantly, until thick, about 5 minutes. Remove from the heat. Let cool slightly; stir in the cream. Season with sea salt.

3. Preheat the oven to 500°. Add 2 tablespoons of salt to the remaining milk and bring back to a simmer. Add the pasta; cook, stirring, over moderately high heat so the milk is just simmering, until al dente, about 10 minutes. Remove the saucepan from the heat and add the ice cubes to stop the cooking. Once all the ice has melted, drain the pasta in a colander and transfer to a large bowl.

4. Add the sauce to the pasta and toss to coat. Transfer the mixture to a buttered 9-by-13-inch gratin dish. Sprinkle the Gruyère all over the top and bake for about 10 minutes, or until bubbling around the edges. Turn on the broiler and broil, rotating the dish, until the cheese is golden, 2 to 3 minutes. Let stand for 5 minutes. Season generously with white pepper, garnish with the chives and serve. *—Benoît Guichard*

Baked Rigatoni with Zucchini and Eggplant

Oodles of Noodles with Cheese

4 SERVINGS

Because most people go to Seattle's Dahlia Lounge for the innovative northwestern food and the groovy scene, a lot of them miss this excellent take on macaroni and cheese. It's not one of those Cheddar-heavy versions. Instead it has the slight tang of goat cheese, a spicy bread crumb and bacon topping and a healthy dose of grated Parmesan.

- 4 slices of bacon
- 3 tablespoons unsalted butter
- 1 tablespoon olive oil
- 1 cup coarse dried bread crumbs
- 2 tablespoons finely chopped flat-leaf parsley
- 1 teaspoon finely grated lemon zest
- 1 teaspoon crushed red pepper
- 1 teaspoon minced shallot
- 1 teaspoon minced garlic
- 1¼ cups heavy cream
- ¾ cup (about 3 ounces) freshly grated Parmesan cheese
- ⅓ cup soft goat cheese
- 1 tablespoon minced chives

Salt and freshly ground black pepper

- 1 pound penne pasta

1. Bring a large pot of salted water to a boil. In a small skillet, cook the bacon over moderate heat until crisp, about 8 minutes. Transfer to paper towels to drain; let cool. Crumble the bacon.

2. In a small saucepan, melt 1 tablespoon of the butter in the olive oil until foamy. In a bowl, toss the bacon with the bread crumbs, parsley, lemon zest and crushed red pepper. Stir in the butter mixture until incorporated.

3. Melt the remaining 2 tablespoons of butter in a saucepan. Add the shallot and cook over moderate heat until lightly browned, about 3 minutes. Add the garlic and cook, stirring, until fragrant, about 30 seconds. Add the cream and simmer, stirring, until reduced by one third, about 5 minutes. Remove from the heat and stir in the Parmesan, goat cheese and chives. Season with salt and black pepper.

4. Add the penne to the boiling water; cook until al dente. Drain and transfer to a serving bowl. Add the cheese sauce and toss. Sprinkle the bread crumbs on top and serve. —*Dahlia Lounge*

WINE The red pepper can be balanced by acidity, fruit and a touch of sweetness. Try the 1997 Chateau Ste. Michelle Vineyard Select Riesling, from Washington State, or the 1997 Livio Felluga Tocai Friulano, from Italy.

Oodles of Noodles with Cheese

Pasta Frittata with Mushrooms

4 SERVINGS

Have leftover pasta? Here's a great way to use it up. It's so good you'll find yourself making extra spaghetti one night just to enjoy this dish the next.

- 1 tablespoon unsalted butter
- ¼ cup extra-virgin olive oil
- 1 garlic clove, finely chopped
- ¼ pound white mushrooms, thinly sliced

1 small onion, minced

2 cups leftover spaghetti in tomato sauce

2 ounces thinly sliced prosciutto, finely chopped

½ cup heavy cream

½ cup (2 ounces) freshly grated Parmesan cheese

Salt and freshly ground pepper

8 large eggs, lightly beaten

1. Preheat the oven to 350°. In a medium skillet, melt the butter in 2 tablespoons of the oil. Add the garlic; cook over moderately high heat until fragrant, about 30 seconds. Add the mushrooms and cook, stirring often, until softened, about 2 minutes. Add the onion and cook until softened, about 5 minutes.

2. Transfer the mixture to a large bowl and add the spaghetti in tomato sauce, the prosciutto, the cream and ¼ cup of the Parmesan. Season with salt and pepper. Add the eggs and stir to combine.

3. Heat the remaining 2 tablespoons of oil in a large ovenproof skillet until shimmering. Swirl the pan to coat the side with oil and then pour in the pasta frittata mixture, spreading it evenly. Cook over moderately high heat until the frittata is barely set on the bottom, about 3 minutes. Sprinkle the remaining ¼ cup of Parmesan evenly over the top of the frittata.

4. Transfer the skillet to the oven and bake the frittata for about 30 minutes, or until firm in the center and cooked through. Run a knife around the edge to loosen the frittata. Using 2 oven mitts, invert a large round platter over the frittata and flip the skillet and platter to unmold. Serve the pasta frittata cut into wedges, either hot or at room temperature. —*Mark Strausman*

MAKE AHEAD The pasta frittata can stand at room temperature for up to 3 hours before serving.

WINE Mushrooms and prosciutto add earthy flavors to this baked omelet that are best matched with a dry Tuscan white, such as Vernaccia di San Gimignano. Try the 1996 San Quirico or the 1997 Teruzzi & Puthold.

Pasta with Garlic Shrimp and Zucchini

4 SERVINGS ✻

3 tablespoons olive oil, plus more for drizzling

1 medium onion, finely chopped

3 medium zucchini, halved lengthwise and sliced crosswise

Salt and freshly ground pepper

2 tablespoons unsalted butter

1 pound medium shrimp, shelled and deveined, tails left on

3 garlic cloves, minced

3 ripe plum tomatoes, seeded and finely chopped

½ cup basil

1 pound fresh or dried fettuccine

1. Bring a large pot of water to a boil. Meanwhile, heat the oil in a large skillet. Add the onion and zucchini; season with salt and pepper. Sauté over moderate heat until tender and starting to brown around the edges, about 8 minutes.

2. In another large skillet, melt the butter. Add the shrimp and garlic; season with salt and pepper. Sauté over high heat until the shrimp are just tender, about 3 minutes. Add the tomatoes and the basil and sauté for 1 more minute.

3. Cook the fettuccine in the boiling water until tender; drain well and transfer to a bowl. Add the zucchini and the shrimp mixture, drizzle with olive oil and toss well. Season with salt and pepper and serve. —*Howard Miller*

WINE Pair this dish with a dry, lightly spicy wine. Consider the 1998 Hogue Pinot Gris from Washington State or the 1998 Bonny Doon Ca' del Solo Malvasia Bianca from California.

Pasta Frittata with Mushrooms

Spaghetti with Mussels, Clams and Shrimp

6 SERVINGS

- ¼ cup dry white wine
- 2 dozen mussels, scrubbed
- 2 dozen littleneck clams, scrubbed
- 3 tablespoons extra-virgin olive oil
- 8 garlic cloves, minced
- ½ teaspoon crushed red pepper
- 1½ pints cherry tomatoes (1½ pounds), halved
- 1 pound spaghetti
- ¾ pound medium shrimp— shelled, deveined and halved crosswise

Salt and freshly ground black pepper

- 2 tablespoons chopped parsley

1. Bring the white wine to a boil in a medium saucepan. Add the mussels, cover and cook over high heat until they open, about 2 minutes. Using tongs, transfer the mussels to a bowl. Discard any that do not open. Add the clams to the saucepan, cover and cook until they open. Transfer the clams to the bowl with the mussels. Discard any clams that do not open. Pour the cooking liquid into a small glass measure, leaving behind any grit. Shell the mussels and clams and return them to the bowl.

2. Heat the olive oil in a medium saucepan. Add the garlic and cook over low heat until golden, about 3 minutes. Add the crushed red pepper and half of the cherry tomatoes and cook over moderate heat, crushing the tomatoes with a wooden spoon, until the juices thicken, about 4 minutes. Add the reserved shellfish cooking liquid and simmer over moderate heat until slightly reduced, about 3 minutes.

3. Cook the spaghetti in a large pot of boiling salted water, stirring occasionally, until al dente. Meanwhile, bring the sauce to a simmer over moderate heat. Add the shrimp and cook for 1 minute. Add the remaining cherry tomatoes and the reserved mussels and clams and simmer briefly to heat through.

4. Drain the spaghetti and return it to the pot. Add the seafood sauce and toss to coat. Season with salt and black pepper and transfer to a warmed bowl. Sprinkle with the parsley and serve at once. —*Marcia Kiesel*

WINE A citrusy, sharp dry white wine would offer a welcome contrast to the briny mussels and clams in this pasta dish. Look for an Italian Pinot Grigio, such as the 1996 Pighin or the 1996 Formentini.

Penne with Tuna, Olives and Capers

4 SERVINGS

A classic Sicilian pasta is the inspiration for this dish. In both the original and baked versions, crisp homemade bread crumbs mixed with Parmesan cheese give the topping lots of flavor. To make the crumbs, whir stale white bread with its crust in a food processor.

- 1 pound penne rigate
- ¾ cup bread crumbs
- 2 tablespoons freshly grated Parmesan cheese
- ¼ cup plus 2 tablespoons extra-virgin olive oil
- 1 garlic clove, thinly sliced

Two 6-ounce cans imported tuna packed in olive oil

- 3 scallions, finely chopped
- ⅓ cup brine-cured black olives, pitted and coarsely chopped
- 1 tablespoon capers, drained
- 1 tablespoon fresh lemon juice
- ½ teaspoon dried oregano
- ½ teaspoon crushed red pepper

Salt and freshly ground black pepper

- 1 tablespoon finely chopped flat-leaf parsley

1. Preheat the oven to 350°. Cook the penne in a large pot of boiling salted water, stirring occasionally, until al dente. Drain, reserving ½ cup of the pasta cooking water, and then return the pasta to the pot.

2. In a small bowl, toss the bread crumbs with the Parmesan and 2 tablespoons of the olive oil. In a large skillet, heat the remaining ¼ cup of olive oil, add the garlic and cook over moderately low heat until golden, about 4 minutes. Stir in the tuna and scallions and remove from the heat. Add the

TOP: **Pasta with Garlic Shrimp and Zucchini.** BOTTOM: **Spaghetti with Mussels, Clams and Shrimp.**

Spaghetti with Tuna and Basil

olives, capers, lemon juice, oregano and crushed red pepper. Season with salt and black pepper.

3. Toss the penne with the tuna sauce, adding a few tablespoons of the pasta cooking water to moisten the pasta. Transfer to a 9-by-13-inch baking dish and sprinkle with the bread crumbs. Bake for 8 minutes, or until heated through. Sprinkle with the parsley and serve. —*Mark Strausman*

WINE This rustic dish needs a hearty wine to match its style and provide a cleansing contrast. Sicily has the answer in the 1997 Regaleali Bianco or the 1997 Corvo Bianco.

Spaghetti with Tuna and Basil

4 TO 6 SERVINGS

Spaghetti and linguine go particularly well with light tomato sauces and seafood sauces, which cling to the long strands.

- 3 tablespoons extra-virgin olive oil
- 8 garlic cloves, minced
- ½ teaspoon crushed red pepper (optional)

One 35-ounce can Italian peeled tomatoes, chopped, ½ cup liquid reserved

Two 6-ounce cans imported tuna in olive oil, drained and lightly flaked

Salt and freshly ground black pepper

- 1 pound spaghetti
- 1 tablespoon unsalted butter
- ½ cup thinly sliced basil

1. Heat the olive oil in a large skillet. Add the garlic and crushed red pepper and cook over low heat until the garlic is golden, about 3 minutes. Add the tomatoes and the reserved liquid and simmer over moderate heat, stirring occasionally, until slightly thickened, about 7 minutes. Add the tuna and simmer briefly to heat through; stir gently to keep the tuna in large pieces. Season with salt and black pepper and keep warm.

2. Cook the spaghetti in a large pot of boiling salted water, stirring occasionally, until al dente. Reserve ¼ cup of the pasta cooking water. Drain the spaghetti and return it to the pot. Add the butter and toss well. Add the tuna sauce, the reserved pasta cooking water and the basil and toss again. Season the spaghetti with salt and black pepper, transfer to a warmed bowl and serve at once. —*Marcia Kiesel*

WINE Garlicky sauce, meaty tuna and fresh basil all point to a tart but assertive white, such as a Tocai Friulano from Italy, as a perfect flavor foil. Top choices include the 1996 Ronco del Gnemiz or the 1996 Schiopetto.

Spaghettini with Veal and Porcini Meatballs

8 SERVINGS

To satisfy a craving for spaghetti and meatballs, turn to lean ground veal and intensely flavorful porcini mushrooms for a lighter version of a classic dish. Don't be put off by the hefty amount of pure olive oil in the ingredient list; almost all of it is drained off after sautéing the meatballs.

- ⅔ cup (about 1 ounce) dried porcini mushrooms
- 1½ cups hot water
- ⅓ cup extra-virgin olive oil
- 1 large shallot, minced
- 1¾ teaspoons finely chopped rosemary
- ¼ cup skim milk
- 3 slices firm-textured bread, crusts removed
- 1½ pounds lean ground veal
- 1 large egg, lightly beaten
- 1½ tablespoons finely chopped flat-leaf parsley

Salt and freshly ground pepper

- ¾ cup pure olive oil, for frying

About ½ cup all-purpose flour, for dusting

- 1 medium onion, finely chopped
- 2 medium garlic cloves, minced
- 2 teaspoons finely chopped thyme
- ¼ cup tomato paste
- 1 cup chicken stock or canned low-sodium broth

Two 28-ounce cans peeled Italian tomatoes—juices reserved, tomatoes seeded and chopped

Pinch of sugar

- 1½ pounds spaghettini
- 2 ounces shaved Parmigiano-Reggiano cheese, for serving

1. In a small bowl, soak the porcini in the hot water until softened, about 20 minutes. Drain the mushrooms, reserving the soaking liquid; squeeze the excess liquid from the mushrooms and finely chop them. Slowly pour the porcini soaking liquid into a large cup, stopping when you reach the grit at the bottom.

2. Heat 1 teaspoon of the extra-virgin olive oil in a small skillet. Add the shallot; cook over moderate heat until softened, about 3 minutes. Add the finely chopped porcini and cook for 2 minutes. Add ¾ teaspoon of the rosemary and 2 teaspoons of the reserved porcini liquid and cook until the liquid has evaporated. Transfer to a plate to cool.

3. In a large bowl, combine the skim milk with ¼ cup of the reserved porcini liquid. Add the bread and let stand until the liquid is absorbed. Add the veal, egg, parsley, 1¼ teaspoons of salt, a scant ½ teaspoon of pepper and the mushroom mixture and knead gently until evenly combined.

4. With lightly moistened hands, roll the veal mixture into thirty-two 1½-inch meatballs. Set them on a wax paper-lined tray and chill until firm, about 15 minutes.

5. Heat the pure olive oil in a large cast-iron skillet until shimmering. Dust the meatballs lightly with the flour, shaking off the excess. Add half of the meatballs to the skillet and cook over moderate heat until golden all over, about 8 minutes. Transfer the meatballs to a rack set in a baking dish and cook the remaining meatballs; discard the oil.

6. Combine the remaining ¼ cup plus 1 tablespoon of extra-virgin olive oil and the onion in a large enameled cast-iron

casserole. Cook over moderate heat until the onion is softened and just beginning to brown, about 6 minutes. Add the garlic, thyme and the remaining 1 teaspoon of rosemary and cook for 30 seconds. Add the tomato paste and cook, stirring, for 2 minutes. Add the chicken stock and the remaining porcini liquid and bring to a boil over high heat. Add the tomatoes and their juices, season with salt, pepper and the sugar and bring to a boil. Reduce the heat to moderately low and cook, stirring occasionally, until thickened, about 1 hour.

7. Add the meatballs to the sauce and simmer just until heated through, about 15 minutes. Meanwhile, cook the spaghettini in a large pot of boiling salted water until al dente. Drain the spaghettini well, transfer to 8 bowls and toss with a little of the tomato sauce. Top each serving with meatballs, some of the remaining sauce, and a cheese shaving. —*Grace Parisi*

MAKE AHEAD The recipe can be prepared through Step 6 up to 3 days ahead; refrigerate the sauce and meatballs separately. Warm the meatballs in the sauce before serving.

ONE SERVING Calories 656 kcal, Total Fat 20.7 gm, Saturated Fat 4.7 gm

WINE A California Merlot, such as the 1996 St. Supéry or the 1996 Geyser Peak, has just the right earthy richness to underscore the flavor of the porcini as well as enough bite to tolerate the acidic tomato sauce.

Penne with Sausage and Fennel

4 SERVINGS

- 2 tablespoons extra-virgin olive oil
- 1 medium onion, finely chopped
- 1 small carrot, finely chopped
- 1 small celery rib, finely chopped
- 1 tablespoon chopped sage

One 35-ounce can peeled Italian tomatoes, chopped
- 1 teaspoon tomato paste
- 2 tablespoons chopped basil

Salt and freshly ground pepper

- ½ pound Italian sweet sausage, pricked with a fork
- 1 large fennel bulb (1½ pounds)— halved lengthwise, cored and sliced crosswise, fronds chopped
- 1 pound penne
- 1 tablespoon chopped parsley
- 2 tablespoons freshly grated Pecorino Romano cheese, plus more for serving

1. Heat the oil in a medium saucepan. Add the onion, carrot, celery and sage. Cook over low heat until the onion is softened but not browned, about 10 minutes. Add the tomatoes, tomato paste and 1 tablespoon basil. Season with salt and pepper. Cover; cook for 30 minutes.

2. In a medium saucepan of water, simmer the sausage over moderate heat until cooked through, about 8 minutes. Drain, cut into ¼-inch rounds and add to the tomato sauce.

3. Cook the fennel slices in a large pot of boiling salted water until just tender, about 3 minutes. Using a slotted spoon, transfer them to the tomato sauce. Add the penne to the boiling water and cook, stirring occasionally, until al dente; drain and return to the pot. Add the sauce, parsley and fennel fronds and toss. Add the 2 tablespoons of cheese and the remaining 1 tablespoon of basil and toss again. Transfer the pasta to a warmed bowl and serve with the additional cheese. —*Anna Teresa Callen*

Baked Shells with Sweet Sausage, Tomatoes and Peas

4 SERVINGS

The pasta shells in this hearty dish don't get stuffed; instead, they are tossed with the sauce and hold the small pieces of meat and vegetables.

- 1 pound medium pasta shells

One 28-ounce can peeled Italian tomatoes
- 2 tablespoons extra-virgin olive oil
- ½ pound sweet Italian sausage, casings removed
- 1 garlic clove, smashed

- 1 onion, finely chopped
- 1 cup heavy cream

Pinch of dried oregano

Salt and freshly ground pepper
- ½ pound baked ham, cut into ⅓-inch dice
- ½ cup frozen baby peas
- ½ cup (2 ounces) freshly grated Parmesan cheese

1. Preheat the oven to 350°. Cook the pasta in a large pot of boiling salted water, stirring occasionally, until al dente. Drain and return to the pot.

2. Puree the tomatoes in a blender or food processor. Pass the puree through a fine sieve to remove the seeds.

3. Heat 1 tablespoon of the oil in a large skillet. Add the sausage; cook over moderately high heat, stirring the meat and breaking it up with the side of a wooden spoon, until browned and cooked through, 8 to 10 minutes. Transfer to a plate and set aside. Wipe out the skillet.

4. In the same skillet, heat the remaining 1 tablespoon of olive oil. Add the garlic and cook over moderate heat until golden, about 1½ minutes. Add the onion and cook until softened but not browned, about 5 minutes. Stir in the tomato puree, cream and oregano and season lightly with salt and pepper. Simmer the sauce over moderately low heat for 10 minutes. Add the sausage and ham and simmer for 10 minutes longer.

5. Stir the sauce into the pasta along with the peas; season with salt and pepper. Transfer to a 9-by-13-inch baking dish and sprinkle with the Parmesan. Bake for 10 minutes, or until the pasta is heated through and the Parmesan is melted. Serve hot. —*Mark Strausman*

MAKE AHEAD The pasta can be prepared through Step 4 and refrigerated overnight. Add about 10 minutes to the baking time.

WINE This dish can showcase a round, deep-flavored, spicy red wine. A California Zinfandel, such as the 1996 St. Francis Old Vines or the 1997 Geyser Peak Cucamonga, would be perfect.

Lasagnette Ricce with Cotechino Braising Sauce

6 SERVINGS

Lasagnette ricce is a long, thin pasta with curly edges. If the lightly cured *cotechino* sausages called for below are unavailable, fresh Italian pork sausages can be substituted—but their cooking time should be shortened.

- 2 tablespoons pure olive oil
- 2½ pounds *cotechino* sausages
- 3 thin slices pancetta, chopped
- 1 medium onion, finely chopped
- 1 medium carrot, finely chopped
- 2 garlic cloves, finely chopped
- ½ cinnamon stick

Scant ⅛ teaspoon ground cloves

- 1 bay leaf
- ½ cup dry white wine
- 1½ cups homemade meat broth or canned low-sodium chicken broth

One 28-ounce can Italian plum tomatoes, drained and coarsely chopped

- 3 tablespoons chopped flat-leaf parsley
- ½ teaspoon chopped rosemary

Salt and freshly ground pepper

- 1 pound dried lasagnette ricce
- 1 cup (about 4 ounces) freshly grated pecorino Toscano cheese

1. Heat the oil in a medium enameled cast-iron casserole. Prick the sausages several times with a fork and brown them in the casserole over moderately high heat. Transfer the sausages to a plate and set aside.

2. Add the pancetta to the casserole and cook until most of the fat has been rendered, 3 to 4 minutes. Add the onion and the carrot and cook until lightly browned, about 5 minutes. Add the garlic, cinnamon, cloves and bay leaf to the casserole and cook until the garlic is beginning to color. Add the white wine and simmer until almost evaporated, about 5 minutes.

3. Return the sausages to the casserole. Add the broth and tomatoes and bring to a boil; the liquid should almost cover the sausages. Reduce the heat to low and simmer the sausages, turning them several times, until they are tender, about 35 minutes. Remove the sausages, cover with foil and set aside for later use. Skim the sauce; if it seems very brothy, boil it down for about 5 minutes. Discard the cinnamon stick and bay leaf. Add the parsley and rosemary and season the sauce with salt and pepper.

4. In a large pot of boiling salted water, cook the pasta just until al dente. Drain well and transfer to a serving bowl. Add ½ cup of the pecorino Toscano cheese and toss briefly. Add the sauce and toss again. Pass the remaining cheese at the table. —*Erica De Mane*

WINE Tomatoes add an acidic note that's best matched by a tart red, such as an Italian Barbera. Try the 1997 Michele Chiarlo Barbera d'Asti or the 1996 Coppo Barbera d'Asti Camp du Rouss.

Ziti with Lamb and Saffron

4 SERVINGS

With its *ragù* of lamb and saffron, this dish offers a true taste of the Abruzzo region in central Italy.

- 1 cup beef or lamb stock or canned low-sodium beef broth
- ½ teaspoon packed saffron threads
- 3 tablespoons extra-virgin olive oil
- ½ pound lean boneless lamb shoulder or leg, cut into ¼-inch dice

Salt and freshly ground pepper

- 1 medium onion, chopped
- 1 garlic clove, minced
- ½ cup dry white wine

Lasagnette Ricce with Cotechino Braising Sauce

1 sage leaf, minced

1 small dried red chile

1 pound ziti

Freshly grated Pecorino Romano
cheese, for serving

1. In a small saucepan, gently warm the beef stock. Add the saffron threads and let them infuse. In a large skillet, heat the extra-virgin olive oil. Add the diced lamb, season with salt and pepper and cook over high heat, stirring once, until the lamb is browned, about 5 minutes total.

2. Add the onion and garlic to the skillet and cook over low heat until softened but not browned, about 5 minutes. Add the wine and simmer over moderately high heat until almost evaporated. Add the saffron-infused stock, sage and chile, cover and simmer gently for 30 minutes; remove the chile.

3. Cook the ziti in a large pot of boiling salted water, stirring occasionally, until al dente; drain and return to the pot. Add the lamb sauce and toss well. Season with salt and freshly ground pepper, transfer to a warmed bowl and serve, passing the grated Pecorino Romano separately. —*Anna Teresa Callen*

bake and switch

Tips for turning tossed pasta into baked:

1. **Use any dried pasta other than capellini.** These ultrathin strands blot up the sauce and dry out when baked.

2. **Boil the pasta until it's al dente.** There's no need to undercook the pasta before baking because it's in the oven for only a short time and won't turn mushy.

3. **Avoid tossed pastas with egg sauces.** The raw eggs in carbonara and similar sauces will scramble when baked. Add more eggs to make a frittata.

4. **Stay away from seafood pastas.** Canned tuna is fine but cooked fresh seafood like shrimp will dry out in the oven.

5. **Save some of the pasta cooking water.** Stir it into the sauced pasta before baking to add moisture without fat.

Vetri's Almond-Ricotta Tortellini with Truffle Butter

4 TO 6 SERVINGS ♛

Marc Vetri is chef and owner of Vetri in Philadelphia. His tortellini combines subtle toasted almonds and sweet ricotta. When making the pasta dough, Vetri advises, it must be kept moist. It should be pliable not sticky. If it seems dry after you've rolled it out, brushing it very lightly with water will make it easier to shape. Start the recipe a day ahead to allow time for the ricotta to drain and the pasta dough to rest.

PASTA DOUGH

1½ cups all-purpose flour, plus
more for dusting

⅔ cup semolina

3 large eggs

3 large egg yolks

1 tablespoon extra-virgin olive oil

FILLING

1 cup (½ pound) fresh ricotta

¾ cup (about 4 ounces) whole
blanched almonds

½ cup (2 ounces) freshly grated
Parmesan cheese

Salt and freshly ground white
pepper

About 1 teaspoon white truffle
puree (see Note)

1 large egg, lightly beaten

3 tablespoons unsalted butter

Thyme sprigs, for garnish

1. MAKE THE PASTA DOUGH: Combine the flour and semolina in a food processor and pulse to mix. With the machine on, add the eggs, the egg yolks and the olive oil and process until moist crumbs form. Turn the dough out onto a lightly floured work surface and knead until silky and smooth; knead in more flour if the dough is too sticky. Wrap the dough in plastic and refrigerate overnight.

2. MAKE THE FILLING: Line a strainer with a coffee filter and spoon in the ricotta. Set the strainer in a bowl, cover and let the ricotta drain overnight in the refrigerator.

3. Preheat the oven to 350°. Spread the almonds on a pie plate and toast for about 8 minutes, or until golden and fragrant. Let the nuts cool completely, finely grind them in a food processor and then transfer to a bowl.

4. Puree the ricotta in a food processor until creamy. Add to the ground almonds along with the Parmesan and season with salt and white pepper. Stir in 1 teaspoon of truffle puree and then the beaten egg. Transfer the filling to a pastry bag fitted with a ¼-inch-round tip or to a sturdy plastic bag with a corner snipped off. Refrigerate the filling.

5. Cut the pasta dough into 6 pieces and let it return to room temperature. Using a hand-cranked pasta machine, roll 1 piece of dough through successively narrower settings to the thinnest setting. Lay the pasta sheet on a lightly floured work surface, sprinkle with flour and cover with a piece of wax paper. Repeat the process with the remaining pasta dough, dusting the sheets with flour and layering them between wax paper. Using a 2¼-inch round biscuit cutter, cut out rounds from each pasta sheet and cover with plastic wrap.

6. Pipe a scant ½ teaspoon of the filling in the center of a dough round. Fold the dough over the filling to form a half moon and press the edges to seal; lightly brush the dough with water if it becomes dry. Bring the corners of the half moon together around a finger, overlapping them slightly and pressing together to secure. Fill and shape the remaining tortellini, transferring them to a tray lined with floured wax paper as they're shaped.

7. Bring a large pot of salted water to a boil. Add the tortellini and cook, stirring occasionally, until they rise to the surface and the pasta is cooked through, 7 to 8 minutes. Drain the tortellini and transfer to a large bowl.

8. In a saucepan, bring 2 tablespoons of water to a boil and add the butter, shaking the saucepan to combine. Add

a few dabs of truffle puree and season with salt. Add the sauce and transfer the almond-ricotta tortellini to warmed bowls. Garnish with thyme sprigs and serve. —*Marc Vetri*

NOTE The intensity of flavor in truffle puree depends on the brand, so make sure to adjust the amount of puree according to taste. As an alternative to the truffle puree, you can use truffle oil, which also varies in intensity. Truffle puree is available from Buon Italia (212-633-9090).

MAKE AHEAD The uncooked tortellini can be frozen in a single layer on a baking sheet lined with wax paper and then transferred to an airtight container between layers of paper and frozen for up to 2 weeks. Do not thaw the frozen tortellini before boiling them.

WINE This rich and creamy tortellini dish would be showcased by a round, ripe California Chardonnay. Look for the 1996 Belvedere Russian River Valley or the 1996 Rodney Strong Chalk Hill.

Spinach and Ricotta Gnocchi

6 SERVINGS

Mark your calendar: it's a popular tradition in Argentina, from which this dish hails, that gnocchi should be eaten on the 29th day of each month.

Vetri's Almond-Ricotta Tortellini with Truffle Butter

2 pounds fresh spinach—large stems discarded, leaves rinsed but not dried
3 large eggs
3 large egg yolks
1 cup whole milk ricotta cheese
½ cup freshly grated Parmesan cheese, plus ¾ cup shavings
Kosher salt and freshly ground pepper
¼ teaspoon freshly grated nutmeg
2 cups all-purpose flour
2 cups heavy cream
1 tablespoon minced sage, plus 6 large leaves for garnish

1. Heat a skillet. Add the spinach leaves by handfuls and cook over high heat, stirring, until they are just wilted. Transfer the spinach to a colander and press out the excess water. Finely chop the spinach.

2. In a large bowl, combine the spinach with the eggs, egg yolks, ricotta, grated Parmesan, 2 teaspoons kosher salt, ¼ teaspoon freshly ground pepper and the nutmeg and stir well. Add the flour and stir just until combined; the dough will be soft and sticky.

3. Scoop out rounded teaspoons of the gnocchi dough onto a well-floured work surface, and roll each piece into a ball. On lightly floured baking sheets, arrange the balls of dough so that they aren't touching.

4. Bring a large saucepan of salted water to a boil. In a medium saucepan, simmer the heavy cream and the minced sage over low heat, stirring, until slightly thickened, about 12 minutes. Season with kosher salt and freshly ground pepper and keep warm.

5. Cook the gnocchi in the boiling water until they rise to the surface, about 5 minutes. Transfer the gnocchi to a shallow bowl and pour the sage sauce over. Garnish the gnocchi with the sage leaves and the Parmesan shavings and serve. —*Francis Mallmann*

MAKE AHEAD The uncooked gnocchi can be refrigerated overnight, covered.

Butternut Squash Gnocchi with Sage Butter

8 SERVINGS

1   tablespoon mixed black and white sesame seeds
One 2½-pound butternut squash, halved lengthwise and seeded
Olive oil
Salt and freshly ground pepper
1¼   cups semolina flour, plus more for dusting
⅓   cup cornstarch
4   tablespoons unsalted butter
16   sage leaves
¼   teaspoon freshly grated nutmeg

I. Preheat the oven to 375°. Spread the black and white sesame seeds in a pie pan and bake for about 2 minutes, or until lightly browned. Transfer the seeds to a plate to cool.

2. Rub the cut sides of the squash with olive oil and season with salt and pepper. Set the squash, cut side down, on a baking sheet and roast for about 25 minutes, or until tender. Scoop the flesh into a large bowl and mash into a chunky puree with a potato masher. Transfer the puree to a fine sieve set over a bowl and let drain for at least 4 hours or overnight in the refrigerator.

3. Return the puree to the large bowl and use a wooden spoon to gradually stir in the semolina and cornstarch. Add ¾ teaspoon of salt and continue stirring until a soft dough forms. Divide the dough into 12 pieces. Generously dust a work surface with semolina and roll each piece of dough into a ½-inch-thick rope. Cut the ropes crosswise into ½-inch pieces. Sprinkle the gnocchi with semolina and lightly press each piece against the tines of a fork to make a ridged pattern. Dust a baking sheet with semolina and arrange the gnocchi on it in a single layer. Refrigerate for up to 4 hours.

4. Bring a large pot of salted water to a boil. Meanwhile, melt the butter in a large skillet. Add the sage and cook over moderate heat until crisp, about 3 minutes. Using a slotted spoon, transfer the sage to a plate. Remove the skillet from the heat.

5. Add the gnocchi to the boiling water and cook, stirring occasionally, until all the gnocchi float to the surface, about 4 minutes. Remove 2 tablespoons of the cooking water and reserve. Drain the gnocchi in a colander and immediately transfer them to the skillet with the butter. Season with the nutmeg and add the reserved cooking water. Cook the gnocchi until bubbling hot. Add the sage and season with salt and pepper. Divide the gnocchi among 8 soup plates. Sprinkle with the sesame seeds and serve. —Pablo Massey

WINE   The fruity, golden 1997 Catena Alta Chardonnay Luca Vineyard nicely complements the slightly sweet gnocchi.

Butternut Squash Gnocchi with Sage Butter

Lebanese Couscous

6 TO 8 SERVINGS

This dish is entirely unlike North African couscous. In the first place, the grains of the couscous are quite large, more like small peas than the tiny fluffy grains of Tunisian or Moroccan couscous. In the second, the fiery flavors of North African couscous are missing from this preparation, which relies on warm, rounded Middle Eastern aromatics, like cinnamon and cumin, offset by cooling cilantro. The dried chickpeas need to soak overnight, so plan accordingly.

1   cup (7 ounces) dried chickpeas, soaked overnight
5   tablespoons extra-virgin olive oil
4   tablespoons unsalted butter
One 4-pound chicken
Two 1-pound lamb shanks
1½   pounds pearl onions, peeled
6   cups water
3   small cinnamon sticks
3   bay leaves
Kosher salt
1   pound *maghrabiyeh* couscous (see Note)
Boiling water
2   teaspoons cinnamon
2   teaspoons cumin
⅓   cup minced cilantro plus 2 tablespoons coarsely chopped
Lemon wedges and toasted pita triangles, for serving

I. Drain and rinse the chickpeas. In a medium saucepan, cover the chickpeas with 1 inch of fresh water and bring to a boil. Reduce the heat to low and simmer, stirring occasionally, until the chickpeas are tender, about 1 hour. Drain, cover and set aside.

2. Meanwhile, in a large enameled cast-iron casserole, heat 3 tablespoons of the olive oil until shimmering. Add 3 tablespoons of the butter and, once it melts, add the chicken and brown well on all sides over moderately high heat. Transfer the chicken to a platter and add the lamb shanks to the casserole. Brown the lamb shanks on all sides and add them to the chicken. Add the pearl onions to the casserole and cook over moderately low heat, stirring occasionally, until golden brown, about 20 minutes. Transfer to a bowl. Pour the fat from the casserole.

3. Add the water to the casserole along with the cinnamon sticks, bay leaves and 1 tablespoon of kosher salt. Return

Lebanese Couscous

the chicken and lamb shanks to the pot and bring to a boil. Cover and simmer over low heat, skimming as necessary, until the chicken is cooked through, about 1 hour. Transfer the chicken to a plate and pull off all the meat in as large pieces as possible. Cover the chicken with foil. Continue to simmer the lamb shanks until tender, about 40 minutes longer.

4. Meanwhile, put the couscous in a large heatproof bowl and toss with 1 tablespoon of the olive oil. Pour in enough boiling water to cover the couscous by 1 inch. Cover and set aside for 45 minutes.

5. When the lamb is done, strain the cooking liquid and skim the fat from the surface; you should have about 6 cups. Remove the meat from the shanks and cut it into 1-inch pieces.

6. In a medium saucepan, combine the lamb with the pearl onions, chickpeas, 1 teaspoon each of cinnamon and cumin, a large pinch of salt and 2 cups of the reserved cooking liquid. Cover and simmer over moderately low heat until the onions are tender and the liquid is flavorful, about 25 minutes. Stir in the ⅓ cup cilantro.

7. Drain the couscous. In a large saucepan, melt the remaining 1 tablespoon of butter in the remaining 1 tablespoon of oil. Add the couscous, the remaining 1 teaspoon each of cinnamon and cumin and a pinch of salt. Cook over moderate heat, stirring, until most of the butter has been absorbed, about 3 minutes. Stir in the remaining 4 cups of the reserved cooking liquid and bring to a boil. Cover and simmer over low heat until the couscous is very tender and most of the liquid has been absorbed, about 30 minutes.

8. Meanwhile, preheat the oven to 350°. Put the chicken in a baking dish and add a little water. Cover and bake just until warmed through, about 10 minutes. Reheat the lamb stew. Mound the couscous on a large platter and arrange the chicken on top. Spoon the lamb stew over all and sprinkle with the remaining 2 tablespoons of cilantro. Serve at once with lemon wedges and pita triangles. —*Nancy Harmon Jenkins*

NOTE *Maghrabiyeh* couscous is available from Middle Eastern groceries.

MAKE AHEAD The recipe can be prepared through Step 5 up to 2 days ahead, but don't soak the couscous until the day you will be serving it. Refrigerate all of the components separately.

Toasted Israeli Couscous with Shrimp and Almonds

4 SERVINGS

Serve this pretty salad on Boston lettuce leaves for lunch.

- ¼ **cup extra-virgin olive oil**
- ⅓ **cup (1 ounce) sliced almonds**

Salt

- 1 **pound large shrimp, shelled and deveined, each cut crosswise into thirds**
- ½ **pound small sugar snap peas**
- 1 **cup (7 ounces) Israeli couscous**

Three 3-by-1-inch strips of lemon zest

- 3 **cups water**
- 3 **scallions, white and tender green parts only, cut into 2-inch matchsticks**
- 1½ **tablespoons sherry vinegar or white wine vinegar**

Freshly ground pepper

- ½ **cup quartered cherry tomatoes**

I. Heat 2 tablespoons of the olive oil in a large deep skillet. Add the almonds and cook over moderate heat, stirring, until golden, about 2 minutes. Using a slotted spoon, transfer the almonds to a plate and season with salt. Add the shrimp to the skillet and cook over high heat, turning once, until pink, about 3 minutes. Transfer to another plate. Add the sugar snap peas to the skillet and cook until lightly browned, about 3 minutes.

2. Add another tablespoon of the olive oil to the skillet. Add the couscous and lemon zest; cook over moderate heat, stirring constantly, until the couscous is

Toasted Israeli Couscous with Shrimp and Almonds

deep golden, about 5 minutes. Add the water, bring to a boil and cook until barely tender, 10 to 15 minutes. Remove from the heat, cover the pan and let the couscous stand until all of the liquid has been absorbed, about 30 minutes. Discard the lemon zest.

3. In a large bowl, toss the couscous with the shrimp, sugar snap peas, scallions, sherry vinegar and the remaining 1 tablespoon of olive oil. Season with salt and pepper. Gently fold in the quartered cherry tomatoes, sprinkle with the almonds and serve warm or at room temperature. —*Grace Parisi*

MAKE AHEAD The recipe can be prepared through Step 2 and refrigerated overnight.

chapter 6
fish shellfish

149

133

Provençal-Style Lemon Sole

Provençal-Style Lemon Sole

4 SERVINGS

It takes less than 25 minutes to make this dish from start to finish. Any mild white fish, such as halibut or flounder, or even scallops, can replace the sole.

- 2 navel oranges
- 2 tablespoons extra-virgin olive oil
- 1 large red onion, thinly sliced
- 1 tablespoon thinly sliced garlic
- ¾ cup drained, seeded and coarsely chopped canned tomatoes
- ¾ cup dry white wine

Salt and freshly ground pepper

- 5 Calamata olives, pitted and cut into thin slivers

Four 6-ounce lemon sole fillets

Chives, cut into 1-inch lengths, for garnish

1. Using a sharp knife, peel the oranges, removing all of the white pith. Cut in between the membranes to release the orange sections into a medium glass or stainless steel bowl.

2. Heat the olive oil in a large, deep skillet. Add the onion and garlic and cook over moderate heat until lightly browned, about 5 minutes. Stir in the tomatoes and wine; season with salt and pepper. Cook until the liquid is slightly reduced, about 4 minutes. Add the olives and set the fish on top in a single layer. Season with salt and pepper, cover and cook until the fish flakes easily, about 7 minutes. Using a long spatula, carefully transfer the fish to a platter and keep warm.

3. Stir the oranges into the sauce and spoon the sauce onto plates. Set the fish fillets on top. Garnish with chives; serve at once. —*John Ash*

SERVE WITH Steamed rice mixed with chopped fresh cilantro.

WINE A New Zealand Sauvignon Blanc, with its herbal overtones, is an obvious choice with delicate fish and the sharp flavors of citrus, tomatoes and olives; the 1998 Seresin or the 1997 Cloudy Bay would be ideal. A light red, such as the 1997 Coldstream Hills Pinot Noir from Australia, is a more daring pairing.

Perch Fillets with Herbs and Brown Butter

4 SERVINGS

Small perch abound in Switzerland's Lake Geneva, and they are served at many local restaurants in towns all along the lakeshore. This recipe comes from Auberge de L'Onde in St. Saphorin.

- 2 tablespoons vegetable oil
- 1½ pounds small, skinless perch fillets or gray sole fillets, cut into 4-inch pieces

Salt and freshly ground pepper

- ¼ cup all-purpose flour
- 1 tablespoon chopped parsley
- 4 tablespoons unsalted butter
- 1 tablespoon fresh lemon juice

1. Heat the oil in a large nonstick skillet until shimmering. Season the fish with salt and pepper and dredge in the flour, shaking off any excess. Add half of the fillets to the skillet and sauté over moderately high heat until lightly browned and cooked through, about 2 minutes per side. Transfer the fish to a warmed platter and repeat with the remaining fillets. Season with salt and pepper and sprinkle with the parsley; keep warm.

2. In a small skillet, cook the butter over moderate heat until it is fragrant and nut brown, about 3 minutes. Remove the skillet from the heat and add the fresh lemon juice, shaking the skillet to blend. Pour the butter over the fish and serve. —*Auberge de L'Onde*

Poached Striped Bass

4 SERVINGS

For the Chinese, fish is the second most important source of protein (the soybean in all its forms is the premier source). Fish is also valued because it is easy to digest, and the Chinese believe that this ease keeps the body's strength from being sapped.

- 10 cups cold water
- 1 large onion, cut into wedges
- One ½-inch piece of fresh ginger, peeled and lightly smashed
- 10 cilantro sprigs
- 1 tablespoon kosher salt

One 2-pound sea bass, cleaned

- 2½ tablespoons soy sauce
- 2 tablespoons chicken stock or canned low-sodium broth
- 1 tablespoon Asian sesame oil
- 1 teaspoon white vinegar
- 1 teaspoon sugar

Pinch of freshly ground white pepper

- ¼ cup finely shredded red cabbage

1. In a large enameled cast-iron casserole, combine the water with the onion, ginger, cilantro and kosher salt. Cover and bring to a boil. Reduce the heat to low and simmer, covered, for 15 minutes. Increase the heat to high and add the fish. Cover and bring back to a boil. Remove from the heat; let the fish poach in the aromatic liquid for 10 minutes.

2. Meanwhile, in a small bowl, combine the soy sauce with the stock, sesame oil, vinegar, sugar and white pepper.

3. Using 2 large spatulas, transfer the fish to a platter. Pour the sauce over the fish, sprinkle with the red cabbage and serve. —*Eileen Yin-Fei Lo*

ONE SERVING Calories 128 kcal, Total Fat 5.2 gm, Saturated Fat 1 gm

Roasted Bass with Potatoes, Onions and Fennel

8 SERVINGS

- ¼ cup plus 2 tablespoons extra-virgin olive oil
- 4 large white onions, thinly sliced
- 2 red bell peppers, thinly sliced
- ¼ cup water

Salt and freshly ground black pepper

Pure olive oil, for frying

- 4 large Idaho potatoes, scrubbed but not peeled, sliced crosswise ⅓ inch thick

Eight 6- to 7-ounce skinless striped bass fillets, 1½ inches thick

One 1½-pound fennel bulb—halved lengthwise, cored and very thinly sliced crosswise

- 2 tablespoons fresh lemon juice
- 1 teaspoon sesame seeds, preferably unhulled

1. Heat ¼ cup of the extra-virgin olive oil in a large saucepan. Add the onions, cover and cook over low heat, stirring occasionally, until softened but not browned, about 20 minutes. Add the red bell peppers and water, cover and cook, stirring occasionally, until the vegetables are very tender, about 20 minutes. Season with salt and black pepper.

2. In a large skillet, heat ⅛ inch of pure olive oil. Add half of the potato slices in a single layer and cook them over moderately high heat until the slices are nicely browned on the bottom, about 5 minutes. Turn and cook until the slices are golden on the second side, about 3 minutes. Transfer the potato slices to a baking sheet lined with paper towels to drain. Repeat with the remaining potato slices, reducing the heat to moderately low if the oil gets too hot. Wipe out the skillet.

3. Preheat the oven to 450°. Add ⅛ inch of pure olive oil to the skillet and heat. Season the bass fillets with salt and black pepper. Add 4 of the bass fillets to the skillet and brown on 1 side over moderately high heat, about 3 minutes. Turn and cook until the bass fillets are firm on the second side, about 1 minute; transfer the fillets to a large baking sheet. Repeat with the remaining bass fillets.

4. Grease a large roasting pan with pure olive oil. Remove the paper towels from the baking sheet and bake the potato slices for about 5 minutes or until they are heated through. Season the potato slices with salt and black pepper and then arrange them, overlapping, around the edge of the roasting pan.

5. Reheat the onions and red bell peppers and then spread the mixture in a neat square inside the potato border in the roasting pan. Set the bass fillets on

Roasted Bass with Potatoes, Onions and Fennel

the onion mixture, browned side up, and bake for about 20 minutes, or until the fish is just cooked through, the potatoes are crisp and the onion mixture is bubbling.

6. Meanwhile, in a medium bowl, toss the fennel with the remaining 2 tablespoons of extra-virgin olive oil and the lemon juice. Season with salt and black pepper and stir in the sesame seeds.

7. Using a metal spatula, transfer the bass fillets and vegetables to plates. Top the fish with a spoonful of fennel salad and serve. —*Pilar Huguet*

ONE SERVING Calories 481 kcal, Total Fat 22 gm, Saturated Fat 3.4 gm

WINE 1997 Can Feixes Chardonnay.

Pan-Fried Striped Bass with Stir-Fried Tomatoes and Dill

8 SERVINGS

The use of fish sauce in the stir-fried tomatoes that accompany the bass is typically Vietnamese.

- 8 medium plum tomatoes, quartered lengthwise

  Kosher salt
- 3 tablespoons safflower oil
- 1 large garlic clove, thinly sliced
- 2 tablespoons Asian fish sauce

  Eight 6-ounce striped bass fillets with skin

  Freshly ground pepper
- 20 dill sprigs, tough stems discarded
- 20 cilantro sprigs
- 20 large basil leaves, preferably Holy basil (see Note)

1. Preheat the oven to 300°. In a bowl, toss the tomato quarters with a large pinch of kosher salt and set aside. Heat 2 tablespoons of the safflower oil in a large skillet. Add the garlic and cook over low heat until golden, about 2 minutes. Add the tomatoes and the fish sauce and stir-fry over moderate heat until soft, about 10 minutes. Remove from the heat and cover to keep warm.

2. Heat 1 teaspoon of the oil in a large nonstick skillet. Season the fish with

Pan-Fried Striped Bass with Stir-Fried Tomatoes and Dill

kosher salt and pepper. Add 4 of the bass fillets to the skillet, skin side down, and cook over moderately high heat until the skin is browned and crisp, about 4 minutes. Turn and cook until the fillets are opaque all the way through, about 1 minute. Transfer the bass fillets, skin side up, to a baking sheet and keep warm in the oven. Add 1 teaspoon of the safflower oil to the skillet and repeat with the remaining bass fillets.

3. In the same skillet, heat the remaining 1 teaspoon safflower oil. Add the dill sprigs, the cilantro sprigs and the basil leaves and stir-fry over high heat until they are barely wilted, about 1 minute.

Mound the stir-fried tomatoes on plates and set the pan-fried bass fillets on top. Garnish with the herbs and serve at once. —*Corinne Trang*

NOTE Holy basil can be found at Asian groceries.

MAKE AHEAD The cooked tomatoes can be refrigerated for up to 2 days. Reheat gently before serving.

WINE Mild white fish pairs well with a light white wine, but the tomatoes accompanying the fish here require a bottling with richness. The 1995 Domaine Laroche Chablis Saint Martin, which is mildly fruity and has a delicate floral scent, is a good choice.

Poached Sea Bass with Lemon Butter

8 SERVINGS

A simple lemon butter makes a tangy sauce for the delicate sea bass.

- 1 quart water
- 2 cups Vinho Verde or other dry white wine
- 1 large leek, split lengthwise and thinly sliced crosswise
- 1 large carrot, thinly sliced
- 1 bay leaf

Salt and freshly ground pepper

Eight 4-ounce sea bass or cod fillets with skin

- 4 tablespoons unsalted butter
- 3 tablespoons fresh lemon juice
- 2 hard-cooked eggs, chopped
- 2 tablespoons chopped parsley
- 2 tablespoons chopped chives

I. In a stainless steel roasting pan set over 2 burners, combine the water, white wine, leek, carrot and bay leaf and bring to a boil over high heat. Reduce the heat to low and simmer for 10 minutes. Season the poaching liquid with salt and pepper and add the fish fillets, skin side up. Simmer gently until the fish fillets are just cooked through, 3 to 4 minutes.

2. Meanwhile, melt the butter in a small saucepan. Add the lemon juice, season with salt and freshly ground pepper and keep warm. Drain the fish fillets on paper towels and then transfer to warmed dinner plates. Drizzle the lemon butter over the fish, sprinkle with the chopped eggs, parsley and chives and serve at once. —*Maria José Cabral and Emília Augusta Magalháes*

Poached Sea Bass with Lemon Butter, with steamed broccoli and new potatoes.

Ginger-Chile Sea Bass with Grilled Tomatoes

4 SERVINGS

While this recipe calls for a nonstick grill pan, an outdoor grill will work fine, too.

- 2 tablespoons finely chopped peeled fresh ginger
- 2 large serrano chiles, stemmed and finely chopped

Kosher salt

- 2 tablespoons canola oil, plus more for brushing

Eight 4-ounce skinless Chilean sea bass fillets

- 2 pounds firm tomatoes, thickly sliced

Lime wedges, for serving

I. In a mortar, combine the ginger, chiles and a pinch of kosher salt; pound to a paste. Stir in 2 tablespoons oil and transfer to a small bowl. Lay the fish fillets on a work surface, skinned side down. Using a sharp knife, make 3 long, shallow slashes across the grain in each. Rub all over with half the chile paste, working some into the slashes. Transfer to a platter, cover and refrigerate 1 hour or overnight. Refrigerate the remaining paste.

2. Arrange the tomatoes on paper towels to drain briefly; pat dry. Lightly brush a nonstick grill pan with oil and set over moderately high heat. Season the fish with kosher salt; add to the pan, skinned side up. Grill over moderately high heat until golden and crusty on the bottom, about 5 minutes. Turn the fish; reduce the heat to moderate. Cook until cooked through and the flesh begins to flake, 4 to 5 minutes more. Transfer to a platter. Cover loosely with foil and keep warm.

3. Wipe out the grill pan. Brush the tomatoes with the remaining chile paste, season with kosher salt and cook in the grill pan over moderately high heat until browned, about 2 minutes per side. Serve the fish with the tomatoes and lime wedges. —*Grace Parisi*

WINE This dish has a bite best matched with a tart Bordeaux Blanc, such as the 1998 Château Bonnet Entre-Deux-Mers.

McDevitt's Miso-Marinated Sea Bass

McDevitt's Miso-Marinated Sea Bass

4 SERVINGS

James McDevitt is chef at Hapa in Scottsdale, Arizona. He recommends using a spoon to peel ginger; it will scrape away only the outermost skin and leave the juiciest part behind.

RELISH

- 4 medium artichokes
- 1 lemon, halved
- 4 cups water
- 1 cup white wine
- 2 quarter-size slices of fresh ginger, peeled
- 1 tablespoon curry powder
- 1 teaspoon turmeric
- ½ pound (½ cup) fresh or frozen soybeans, shelled (see Note)
- 2 scallions, thinly sliced
- ½ small red onion, finely chopped
- 1 plum tomato, finely chopped

GINGER MAYONNAISE

- ¼ cup mayonnaise
- 1 garlic clove, minced
- 1 teaspoon minced fresh ginger
- 1 tablespoon fresh lime juice
- 1½ teaspoons Dijon mustard
- 1½ teaspoons rice vinegar
- ¼ teaspoon hot sauce, preferably Sriracha
- Pinch of salt and freshly ground pepper

SEA BASS

- One 4-inch piece of fresh ginger
- 1 cup sake
- ¼ cup mirin (sweet rice wine)
- 2 tablespoons soy sauce
- 2 tablespoons yellow miso paste (see Note)
- Four 6-ounce sea bass fillets, about 1 inch thick, with skin
- Salt and freshly ground pepper
- 2 tablespoons olive oil
- 2 tablespoons fresh lime juice
- 2 tablespoons minced chives

1. MAKE THE RELISH: Using a sharp knife, trim the artichoke stems. Cut off the top third of each artichoke; pull off the outer leaves. Trim the artichoke bottoms, cutting off any tough green skin. Rub the artichokes with the lemon.

2. In a saucepan, bring the water, white wine, ginger, curry and turmeric to a boil; simmer for 2 minutes. Add the artichoke bottoms and simmer until tender, about 15 minutes. Transfer to a plate to cool. Scrape out the hairy chokes and cut the artichokes into ½-inch dice.

3. Return the broth to a boil, add the soybeans and cook until just tender, about 2 minutes. Drain and transfer to a bowl. Add the scallions, the onion, the tomato and the artichokes; refrigerate until chilled.

4. MAKE THE GINGER MAYONNAISE: Combine the mayonnaise, garlic, fresh ginger, lime juice, mustard, rice vinegar, hot sauce, salt and pepper in a small bowl; refrigerate until chilled.

5. PREPARE THE SEA BASS: Peel and finely grate the ginger and put it in a small strainer set over a bowl. Press on the ginger to extract as much juice as possible; you should have 2 tablespoons. In a baking dish, whisk the ginger juice with the sake, mirin, soy sauce and miso. Add the sea bass fillets and turn to coat with the marinade. Refrigerate for up to 2 hours, turning the sea bass fillets once or twice.

6. Preheat the oven to 500°. Pat the sea bass dry with paper towels and season with salt and pepper. In an ovenproof skillet, heat the olive oil until almost smoking. Add the sea bass, skin side down, and cook over high heat until well browned, about 2 minutes. Turn the fillets, transfer to the oven and roast for about 5 minutes, or until just cooked through.

7. Stir the lime juice into the relish and season with salt and pepper. Spoon the relish onto 4 plates. Set a sea bass fillet on top of each and add a dollop of ginger mayonnaise. Sprinkle with chives and serve. —*James McDevitt*

NOTE Soybeans and yellow miso paste are available at Asian groceries.

WINE Sea bass pairs with most light whites, but ginger suggests aromatic bottlings. Try the 1997 Bonterra Roussanne (California) or the 1997 Vignoble Boudinaud Marsanne-Viognier (France).

Fish with Squash and Indian Seed Pop

4 SERVINGS

The side dish called *pop* is based on *raita*, a cooling Indian condiment. This version is a colorful salad of juicy cucumbers and crisp squash with a spicy yogurt dressing. The black onion seeds are available at Indian markets.

- 2 medium cucumbers—peeled, seeded and finely diced
- 2 medium summer squash— halved, seeded and finely diced

Kosher salt

- 6 scallions, white and tender green parts only, thinly sliced
- 1 large jalapeño, seeded and minced
- 2 tablespoons minced cilantro
- 2 tablespoons minced mint
- 2 tablespoons fresh lime juice
- 1 teaspoon finely grated lime zest
- 1 cup plain yogurt
- ½ teaspoon minced garlic
- 2 tablespoons extra-virgin olive oil, plus more for grilling
- 1 teaspoon cumin seeds
- 1 teaspoon mustard seeds
- 1 teaspoon black onion seeds (*nigella*; optional)

Freshly ground pepper

Four 6-ounce skinless grouper or sea bass fillets

1. Light the grill if using. In a colander, toss the cucumbers and squash with 1 teaspoon of kosher salt and let drain for 10 minutes. Transfer to a kitchen towel and gently squeeze dry. In a large bowl, combine the vegetables with the scallions, jalapeño, cilantro, mint, lime juice, lime zest and yogurt; stir well.

2. In a small skillet, cook the garlic in the 2 tablespoons of extra-virgin olive oil over moderate heat until fragrant and lightly golden, about 1 minute. Add the cumin, mustard and black onion seeds and shake the pan until the seeds begin to sputter and pop. Stir into the vegetable mixture; season with kosher salt and pepper.

3. Rub the fish lightly with olive oil and season with salt and pepper. Heat a grill pan, if using, over moderately high heat. Grill the fish or sear it in the grill pan, turning once, until golden and cooked through, 6 to 7 minutes. Transfer the fillets to plates, spoon the vegetables alongside and serve. —*Seen Lippert*

WINE A refreshing Italian Pinot Grigio, such as the 1998 Pighin or the 1998 Zenato, would make a fine match.

Crisp Paupiettes of Sea Bass in Barolo Sauce

4 SERVINGS

You can either grill the sea bass or cook it in a grill pan on top of the stove.

Four 4-ounce skinless sea bass fillets
Salt and freshly ground pepper

- 1 teaspoon chopped thyme, plus 4 small sprigs for garnish
- 2 very large baking potatoes
- 5 tablespoons unsalted butter, 1 melted
- 3 large leeks, white part only, thinly sliced

Barolo Sauce (recipe follows)

- 1 tablespoon minced chives

1. Trim each of the sea bass fillets into a 5-by-1½-inch rectangle. Season with salt, pepper and the chopped thyme.

2. Using a knife, slice each of the potatoes lengthwise to remove the rounded portions and make a block shape; do not cut off the tips of the potatoes, but do peel them. Using a mandoline, slice the potatoes lengthwise into very thin slices. Brush the slices on both sides with the melted butter and season with salt.

3. For each *paupiette*, on a 10-inch sheet of wax paper, arrange 8 slightly overlapping potato slices to form a 5-inch wide rectangle. Center a fish fillet horizontally in the rectangle and wrap the potatoes over and around the fillet to enclose it completely. Use the wax paper to help seal the potato wrap around the fish; remove the paper. Repeat to form the remaining *paupiettes*. Cover and refrigerate for up to 2 hours.

4. In a medium skillet, melt 2 tablespoons of the butter over moderate heat. Add the sliced leeks and cook, stirring, until softened, about 5 minutes. Season the leeks with salt and pepper and keep warm.

5. In a large nonstick skillet, melt the remaining 2 tablespoons of butter over moderately high heat. Add the *paupiettes* and cook until the potatoes are tender and golden, turning once with a large spatula, 8 to 10 minutes per side.

6. Spoon the leeks onto 4 warmed serving plates; ladle the sauce around them. Set the *paupiettes* on the leeks and top each with a thyme sprig. Garnish with the chives and serve. —*Daniel Boulud*

WINE The leeks and the red wine sauce find their match in a light red. A California Pinot Noir would be perfect; try the 1997 Robert Sinskey Aries or the 1996 Robert Mondavi.

BAROLO SAUCE

MAKES ABOUT ½ CUP

- 1 tablespoon olive oil
- ½ cup chopped shallots
- ½ cup sliced white mushroom caps
- 1 small thyme sprig
- 1 cup chicken stock or clam juice
- 1 bottle (750 ml) Barolo or other full-bodied red wine
- 1 tablespoon heavy cream
- 1 stick (4 ounces) cold unsalted butter, cut into tablespoons

Pinch of sugar
Salt and freshly ground pepper

Heat the olive oil in a medium saucepan. Add the shallots, mushrooms and thyme and cook over high heat for 10 minutes, stirring frequently. Add the chicken stock and boil until the mushrooms are almost dry. Stir in the wine and boil until reduced to 2 tablespoons, about 30 minutes. Stir in the heavy cream and bring to a boil over low heat. Whisk in the butter and sugar and season with salt and pepper. Strain the sauce through a fine sieve, pressing on the solids, and keep warm. —*D. B.*

Salt-Baked Sea Bass

4 SERVINGS

Two 2-pound whole sea bass or red
    snappers, cleaned and scaled
Freshly ground pepper
8 sprigs each thyme, parsley
    and basil, plus ¼ cup shredded
    basil
4 garlic cloves, crushed
1 cup (3 ounces) each fennel seeds,
    dill seeds and coriander seeds,
    toasted
9 cups (about 3 pounds) kosher
    salt
2 cups water
1 tomato—peeled, seeded and
    minced
¼ cup extra-virgin olive oil
2 tablespoons fresh lemon juice
Table salt

1. Preheat the oven to 475°. Season the fish inside and out with pepper. Divide the thyme, parsley and basil sprigs and the garlic between the fish cavities; close the cavities with bamboo skewers. In a bowl, combine the fennel, dill and coriander seeds with the kosher salt and the water. On a very large rimmed baking sheet, make 2 shallow piles with half of the salt mixture. Set each fish on a pile of the salt mixture and cover completely with the remaining salt mixture, pressing to adhere.

2. Bake the fish for about 30 minutes, or until an instant-read thermometer inserted into the thickest part of the fish registers 130°.

3. Meanwhile, in a glass or stainless steel bowl, combine the tomato, olive oil, lemon juice and the shredded basil; season the tomato sauce with table salt and pepper.

4. Using a small hammer or the back of a heavy knife, break the salt crust and brush off any salt on the fish. Make a cut just above the backbone of each fish and then lift the fish fillet from the bones. Turn over and repeat on the other side. Serve the fish fillets with the tomato sauce. —*Terrance Brennan*

Snapper with Cucumber Vinaigrette, with Braised Endives (p. 270).

Snapper with Cucumber Vinaigrette

4 SERVINGS

1 large lemon
4 plum tomatoes—halved, seeded
    and cut into ¼-inch dice
1 European cucumber—halved
    lengthwise, seeded and thinly
    sliced
1 large shallot, thinly sliced
1 tablespoon minced thyme
¼ cup minced chives
¼ cup extra-virgin olive oil, plus
    more for brushing
Salt and freshly ground pepper
Four 6-ounce skinless red snapper
    fillets (about 1 inch thick)

1. Light a grill or preheat the oven to 500°. Using a small, sharp knife, peel the lemon, removing all the bitter white pith. Cut the lemon into ¼-inch dice, discarding the seeds. Transfer the diced lemon to a medium glass or stainless steel bowl and add the tomatoes, cucumber, shallot, thyme and chives. Stir in the ¼ cup of olive oil and season with salt and pepper.

2. Lay two 20-inch-square sheets of heavy-duty foil on top of each other and then fold them in half to form a rectangle. Fold up 2 inches on each side, neatly folding in the corners to form a low-sided box. Brush the foil with olive oil and set the red snapper fillets on the foil. Season the fillets with salt and pepper and spoon ⅓ cup of the vinaigrette on each. Using 2 long spatulas, set the foil package on a medium-hot grill and cook for about 15 minutes, or until the snapper fillets are just cooked through. Alternatively, roast the foil package on a cookie sheet in the oven for about 20 minutes. Transfer the fillets to a platter and serve. —*Raphael Lunetta*

Red Snapper en Papillote with Sherry, Pancetta and Grapes

2 SERVINGS

This dish is particularly good in early fall, when fragrant Muscat grapes are available. If you do use Muscats, peel them first. You can use firm, white-fleshed fish fillets, such as tilefish or cod, in place of the whole fish, if you prefer. Select one-inch-thick fillets and reduce the cooking time to 20 minutes. If you want to prepare the recipe here for four people, assemble two packages.

One 1½-pound red snapper, rinsed and patted dry

Kosher salt and freshly ground pepper

3 thin slices pancetta (2 ounces), cut into ½-inch pieces

1 large shallot, minced

2 thyme sprigs

16 large green grapes, halved lengthwise

¼ cup dry sherry

2 tablespoons finely chopped flat-leaf parsley

I. Preheat the oven to 400°. Make three ¼-inch-deep diagonal cuts on each side of the fish, about 1 inch apart. Season the fish inside and out with kosher salt and pepper.

2. In a small nonstick skillet, cook the pancetta over low heat, covered, until the fat is rendered and the meat is crisp. Transfer the pancetta to a small bowl and spoon 1 teaspoon of the rendered fat from the pan.

3. Place a 26-by-14-inch sheet of parchment paper or foil on a work surface. Brush with the reserved pancetta fat, leaving a 2-inch border uncoated. Turn up the edges of the paper slightly.

4. Add the shallot to the remaining fat in the skillet. Cover and cook over low heat until softened, about 5 minutes. Scatter the shallot in the center of one half of the paper and set the seasoned fish on top. Stuff the cavity of the fish with half of the crisp pancetta, the thyme sprigs and half of the grapes. Scatter the remaining pancetta and grapes over and around the fish and drizzle the sherry on top.

5. Seal the *papillotes* by folding the parchment paper or foil in half over the fish. Starting at one folded corner, fold the edges of the paper over in neat pleats; be sure to fold each successive pleat so it slightly overlaps the previous one to make a tight seal. Continue folding all around in this manner until the package is sealed. Set the package on a baking sheet and bake for 25 minutes. Remove from the oven and let stand for 3 minutes.

6. With scissors, carefully cut along the pleats; take care to avoid the escaping steam. Make a cut just above the backbone and lift the fillet from the bones. Turn over and repeat with the other side. Spoon the pancetta, grapes and cooking juices over the fillets, garnish with parsley and serve. —*Sally Schneider*

ONE SERVING Calories 327 kcal, Total Fat 19.2 gm, Saturated Fat 6.8 gm

Grilled Halibut with Herb Salad and Chive Oil

6 SERVINGS

The dressing for the herb salad is flavored with shallots, which lose some of their pungency and turn sweet when marinated in vinegar.

3 shallots, thinly sliced

3 tablespoons sherry or tarragon vinegar

Finely grated zest of 1 lemon

Six 6-ounce skinless halibut fillets

¼ cup plus 2 tablespoons Chive Oil (recipe follows)

Salt and freshly ground pepper

½ cup flat-leaf parsley leaves

½ cup torn basil leaves

½ cup watercress leaves

¼ cup small mint leaves

¼ cup tarragon leaves

18 nasturtiums (optional)

I. In a medium glass or stainless steel bowl, combine the shallots with the vinegar and lemon zest; let marinate at room temperature for about 30 minutes.

2. Light a grill or preheat a grill pan and oil it lightly. In a glass baking dish, coat the fish with 2 tablespoons of the Chive Oil and season with salt and pepper.

3. Stir 2 tablespoons of the Chive Oil into the shallots. Add the parsley, basil, watercress, mint, tarragon and nasturtiums, season with salt and pepper and toss gently to coat.

4. Grill the fish until cooked through, 3 to 5 minutes per side. Transfer the fish to plates and mound the herb salad alongside. Drizzle the remaining 2 tablespoons of Chive Oil around the plates and serve at once. —*Jerry Traunfeld*

WINE Mild white fish pairs well with a light white wine, but the sharp greens require a bottling with acidity. Look for a tart French Sauvignon Blanc, like the 1997 Hervé Seguin Pouilly-Fumé or 1997 Jean-Claude Châtelain Pouilly-Fumé.

● CHIVE OIL

MAKES ABOUT ¾ CUP

Use this oil as a sauce for basting grilled fish—it makes a nice crust—and as a sauce for serving.

1 cup snipped chives

¾ cup extra-virgin olive oil

Put the chives and olive oil in a blender and blend on high until the oil begins to warm, 2 to 3 minutes. Pour through a very fine strainer set over a bowl and let drip for at least 1 hour. Discard the contents of the strainer. —*J. T.*

MAKE AHEAD The Chive Oil can be refrigerated for up to 1 day. Bring to room temperature before serving.

Coconut-Baked Halibut

4 SERVINGS

This dish from The Sugar Club in London is wonderful for serving to guests; it can be assembled early in the day and then baked briefly at the last minute.

½ cup finely shredded unsweetened coconut

1 bunch cilantro (2 ounces), stems and leaves finely chopped separately

1 medium onion, coarsely chopped

3 garlic cloves

2 serrano or Thai chiles—halved, seeded and coarsely chopped

1 stalk fresh lemongrass, white inner bulb only

2 tablespoons finely chopped fresh ginger

1 lime, zest finely grated, then juiced

Pinch of freshly grated nutmeg

Vegetable oil

2 cups unsweetened coconut milk

1 tablespoon Asian fish sauce or soy sauce

1 pound bok choy, coarsely chopped

Four ½-pound halibut steaks, 1 inch thick

Salt

4 large scallions, thinly sliced

I. Preheat the oven to 400°. Spread the shredded unsweetened coconut in a pie plate and toast for 5 minutes, or until lightly browned. Increase the oven temperature to 450°.

2. In a food processor, combine the cilantro stems with the onion, garlic, 1 chile, the lemongrass, ginger, lime zest and nutmeg and process.

3. In a medium saucepan, heat 1 tablespoon of oil. Add the cilantro paste and cook over low heat, stirring occasionally, until very aromatic, about 10 minutes. Add the coconut milk and fish sauce; simmer for 10 minutes longer.

4. In a saucepan of boiling salted water, blanch the bok choy for 2 minutes. Drain in a colander and then rinse in cold running water; pat dry. Spread the bok choy in a 9-by-12-inch gratin dish.

5. In a large skillet, heat ⅛ inch of oil. Season the halibut steaks with salt and add 2 of them to the skillet. Cook over high heat, turning once, until golden, about 2 minutes per side. Set the fish steaks on the bok choy and repeat with the remaining halibut.

6. Add the lime juice to the sauce and season it with salt. Strain the sauce over the fish and top with the scallions. Cover with foil and bake for 8 minutes, or until the fish is opaque throughout.

7. In a bowl, combine the remaining chopped chile with the cilantro leaves and toasted coconut. Transfer the halibut steaks to plates and spoon the sauce from the gratin dish over the top. Sprinkle the cilantro-coconut salad over the fish; serve at once. —David Selex

MAKE AHEAD The recipe can be prepared through Step 4 up to 1 day ahead. Store the toasted coconut in an airtight container. Refrigerate the bok choy and the cilantro-coconut sauce separately; reheat before proceeding.

SERVE WITH Steamed jasmine rice.

WINE Try an aromatic but dry white that can provide some contrasting crispness to this dish but play off the hints of sweetness. An ideal choice is Viognier, especially a full-flavored California bottling. Consider the 1997 Smith & Hook or the 1997 Calera Mt. Harlan.

Roasted Cod with Italian Peppers

4 SERVINGS ✳

4 mild medium red or green Italian frying peppers (about 1 pound)

4 anchovies, coarsely chopped

1 garlic clove, smashed

½ teaspoon cracked black peppercorns

¼ teaspoon salt

¼ cup extra-virgin olive oil

2 tablespoons capers, drained and coarsely chopped

Four ½-pound cod fillets

2 tablespoons finely chopped flat-leaf parsley

Lemon wedges, for serving

I. Preheat the broiler. Roast the peppers as close to the heat as possible for about 10 minutes, turning, until charred and blistered all over. Transfer the peppers to a bowl, cover and let cool. Lower the oven temperature to 400°.

2. Peel the peppers and cut them into thin strips; discard the cores and seeds.

In a mortar, crush the anchovies to a coarse paste with the garlic, peppercorns and salt. Transfer to a bowl and stir in the olive oil, capers and roasted peppers.

3. Arrange the cod on a baking sheet and spread the pepper mixture evenly over each fillet. Roast for about 10 minutes, or until the flesh flakes easily. Sprinkle the roasted cod with the parsley and serve with the lemon wedges on the side. —Jan Newberry

WINE The fish is mild, but the peppers, anchovies and capers are not. Pair the dish with a round, ripe California Chardonnay, such as the 1997 Franciscan or the 1997 Au Bon Climat.

Caponata-Style Escarole and Cod

4 SERVINGS

½ cup extra-virgin olive oil

All-purpose flour

1½ pounds fresh cod or other firm white fish fillets

Salt and freshly ground pepper

6 garlic cloves

2 large heads of escarole (about 1½ pounds), cored and coarsely chopped (about 10 cups)

20 anchovies (about 6 ounces), drained and coarsely chopped

20 oil-cured black olives, halved and pitted

¼ cup capers, well rinsed

3 pounds tomatoes—peeled, halved, seeded and coarsely chopped

Flat-leaf parsley leaves, for garnish

I. Heat 3 tablespoons of the olive oil in a large enameled cast-iron casserole. Lightly flour the fish and season with salt and pepper. Cook over moderate heat until lightly browned and cooked through, about 3 minutes per side, depending on the thickness of the fish. Transfer the fish to a platter.

2. Add the garlic to the oil and cook over moderate heat until deep golden, about 2 minutes; discard the garlic. Add the

escarole to the casserole along with the anchovies, olives and capers. Cook, stirring constantly, until the escarole turns bright green and wilts, about 3 minutes. Transfer the escarole to a bowl.

3. Heat the remaining 1 tablespoon olive oil in the casserole. Add the tomatoes

and cook over moderately high heat, stirring, until thickened, about 5 minutes. Add the tomato sauce to the escarole and season with salt and pepper. Garnish with parsley and serve with the fish. —*Alfonso Iaccarino*

MAKE AHEAD The escarole and cod can stand at room temperature, covered, for up to 2 hours before serving.

Seared Cod with Fig Tapenade
4 SERVINGS

- 1 cup (¼ pound) Calamata olives, pitted and finely chopped
- 8 dried figs, finely chopped
- 2 tablespoons capers, finely chopped
- 2 tablespoons finely chopped basil, plus 4 leaves for garnish
- ¼ cup plus 2 tablespoons extra-virgin olive oil
- Freshly ground pepper
- Four 6-ounce cod fillets, ½ inch thick
- Salt

1. In a bowl, combine the olives with the figs, capers, chopped basil and ¼ cup of the olive oil. Season with pepper.

2. Preheat the oven to 300°. In a heavy skillet, heat 1 tablespoon of the olive oil. Season the fish with salt and pepper and add 2 of the fillets to the skillet. Cook over high heat until browned on the bottom, about 3 minutes. Turn and cook just until opaque throughout, about 2 minutes. Remove the fish and keep it warm in the oven. Repeat with the remaining 1 tablespoon of olive oil and 2 cod fillets. Transfer the fish to dinner plates and spoon the tapenade over the top. Garnish with the basil leaves and serve. —*Stephen Kalt*

MAKE AHEAD The tapenade can be refrigerated for up to 2 days.

WINE The sweet-salty notes in the tapenade need the balance of a wine with ripe fruit. Try a dry rosé from Provence, an unoaked Viognier from Italy or a Long Island Merlot with soft tannins.

Batter-Fried Cod with Minted Pea Puree
4 SERVINGS

The yeast in the batter makes the fried fish especially light and crisp.

- 1⅓ cup milk
- 1 package (¼ ounce) active dry yeast
- ⅔ cup all-purpose flour, plus more for dredging
- ½ cup cornstarch
- ½ teaspoon soy sauce
- ⅛ teaspoon baking powder
- Pinch of cayenne pepper
- Salt
- Vegetable oil, for frying
- Four 6-ounce cod fillets
- Freshly ground black pepper
- Minted Pea Puree, for serving (recipe follows)

1. In a small saucepan, heat the milk until bubbles appear around the edge. Remove from the heat; add the yeast. Let stand until foamy, about 5 minutes.

2. In a large bowl, combine ⅔ cup of the flour, the cornstarch, soy sauce, baking powder, cayenne and ½ teaspoon salt. Stir in the yeast mixture and cover; let stand in a warm place for 1½ to 2 hours.

3. In a large skillet, heat 2 inches of oil to 350°. Season the cod with salt and black pepper. Dredge 1 fillet at a time in flour, tapping off the excess. Coat the fish in the batter and fry in batches until golden, about 4 minutes per side. Drain on paper towels and serve at once. Pass the Minted Pea Puree separately. —*J. Sheekey, London*

MINTED PEA PUREE
4 SERVINGS

- 2½ tablespoons unsalted butter
- ½ small onion, finely chopped
- Two 10-ounce packages frozen peas
- ½ cup chicken stock or canned low-sodium broth
- Salt and freshly ground pepper
- 2 tablespoons finely chopped mint

LEFT: **Seared Cod with Fig Tapenade.** ABOVE: **Caponata-Style Escarole and Cod.**

Melt ½ tablespoon of the butter in a medium saucepan. Add the onion and cook over moderate heat, stirring occasionally, until softened but not browned, about 3 minutes. Add the peas and stock and season with salt and pepper. Simmer over low heat for 15 minutes. Transfer to a food processor and puree until smooth. Return to the pan and beat in the remaining 2 tablespoons of butter and the mint. —*J. Sheekey*

MAKE AHEAD The puree can be made while the batter for the fried cod is fermenting. Reheat it and then stir in the butter and mint before serving.

Salted Codfish Faro

4 SERVINGS

The salt cod needs to soak for 12 hours before cooking, so plan accordingly. And be sure to warn your guests about the unpitted olives in the garlicky sauce.

- 1 **pound skinless, boneless salt cod fillets**
- 16 **cups cold water**
- 6 **cups water**
- 1 **pound medium red potatoes**
- 3 **tablespoons extra-virgin olive oil**
- 1 **green bell pepper, cut into ¼-Inch pieces**
- 6 **scallions, finely chopped**
- 1 **small onion, chopped**
- 5 **garlic cloves, thinly sliced**
- ½ **cup dry white wine**
- ½ **cup chicken stock or canned low-sodium broth**
- 1 **cup (5 ounces) mixed olives**

Salt and freshly ground pepper

- 2 **tablespoons chopped parsley**

1. In a large bowl, soak the salt cod in 8 cups of cold water for 2 to 3 hours. Drain off the water, add the 8 cups of fresh cold water to the bowl and soak the cod in the refrigerator for 9 to 10 hours longer, for a total of 12 hours. Taste the salt cod; it should be pleasantly tasty but not salty. Drain the fish.
2. In a medium saucepan, bring the 6 cups of water to a boil. Add the salt cod and bring back to a boil. Reduce the

Salted Codfish Faro

heat to moderate and simmer very gently until the fish is tender and beginning to flake apart, about 5 minutes. Drain the fish thoroughly and pat dry.

3. When the fish is cool enough to handle, use your fingers to separate the flesh into large flakes. Remove and discard any bones or stray bits of skin; you should have 2 cups of flaked fish.

4. In a medium saucepan, cover the potatoes with 2 inches of cold water; bring to a boil over high heat. Reduce the heat and simmer until tender, about 20 minutes. Drain, let cool slightly and then peel and cut into ¾-inch slices. Cover loosely with foil and keep warm.

5. Heat the oil in a large heavy saucepan. Add the green bell pepper, scallions, onion and garlic. Cover and cook over low heat for 5 minutes, stirring occasionally. Add the wine and simmer over moderate heat until reduced by half, about 3 minutes. Add the stock and simmer until reduced by half, about 3 minutes. Add the flaked salt cod and the olives and season with salt and pepper. Cover the stew and simmer over low heat until warmed through and the flavors are blended, about 4 minutes.

6. Arrange the potatoes on 4 warmed dinner plates and spoon the stew on top. Sprinkle with the parsley and serve immediately. —*Jacques Pépin*

WINE A simple, aromatic, fruity dry white wine will complement the stew's savory flavors. Try the 1996 King Estate Pinot Gris from Oregon or the 1997 Landskroon Steen from South Africa.

Potato Cakes Stuffed with Trout

4 SERVINGS

Trout is a staple in Patagonia, and it's often served with potatoes. To remove the tiny pin bones, arrange a trout fillet, skinned side down, on an upside-down bowl; the bones will stick out. Remove them with tweezers or small pliers.

2 pounds medium all-purpose potatoes, scrubbed

Salt and freshly ground pepper

4 skinless rainbow trout fillets, cut crosswise into 3 pieces

About 1 stick (4 ounces) unsalted butter

About ½ cup canola oil

12 spinach leaves, stems removed

1. In a large saucepan, cover the potatoes with cold water and bring to a boil. Cook over moderate heat until the outsides of the potatoes are tender but the centers are still hard, about 15 minutes. Drain the potatoes and cool under running water. Peel the potatoes and then coarsely grate them. Season the grated potatoes with salt and pepper and toss to combine.

2. Season the rainbow trout fillets with salt and pepper. On a cast-iron griddle or skillet, melt ½ tablespoon of the butter in ½ tablespoon of the canola oil. Spoon a scant ½ cup of grated potatoes onto the griddle and flatten it into a rough circle. Set a piece of trout in the center, cover with a spinach leaf and top with a scant ½ cup of grated potatoes, flattening them. Cook the potato cake over moderately low heat until crispy and golden on the bottom, 5 to 7 minutes. Carefully turn the cake and cook until the potatoes are crisp and golden and the trout is cooked through, about 5 minutes longer; add more butter and oil as necessary. Transfer the potato-trout cake to paper towels to drain and then serve hot. Repeat with the remaining grated potatoes, trout and spinach, serving the potato-trout cakes hot. *—Francis Mallmann*

WINE Pick a Sauvignon Blanc–based wine to provide a foil for these potato and trout cakes. Try the 1997 Murphy-Goode Fumé Blanc (California) or the 1997 Villa Maria Sauvignon Blanc (New Zealand).

Skate with Brown Butter and Capers

4 SERVINGS

In the classic skate *grenobloise,* the fish is pan-fried and served with a vinegar and brown butter sauce. In this lower fat rendition, you boil the brown butter with vinegar and stock to achieve a similar effect with just one third of the fat. A combination of balsamic and aged sherry vinegars produces a rich-tasting sauce that has a nutty, sweet-tart flavor. The sauce is also delicious on pasta, beans, grains and most cooked vegetables, especially leeks, potatoes, beets and sweet potatoes.

4 skinless, boneless skate wings (about 6 ounces each)

Salt and freshly ground pepper

All-purpose flour, for dredging

3 tablespoons unsalted butter

2 tablespoons balsamic vinegar

1 tablespoon aged sherry vinegar

2 tablespoons canned low-sodium chicken or fish broth

2 tablespoons small capers, rinsed twice

¼ cup finely chopped flat-leaf parsley

Pinch of sugar

1. Pat the skate wings dry and season them with salt and pepper. Dredge the skate wings in flour, shaking off the excess.

2. Heat 2 large nonstick skillets. Add 1 teaspoon of the butter to each and swirl to coat the skillets. When the butter stops bubbling, add 2 skate wings to each pan and cook over moderate heat until the fish is golden on the bottom, about 3 minutes. Carefully lift 1 skate wing with a flat spatula, drop ¼ teaspoon of butter into the skillet and flip the skate over onto the butter. Repeat with the remaining skate wings. Continue cooking until the fish is golden on the bottom and opaque throughout, about 3 minutes longer. Remove the skate to a warmed platter and cover loosely with foil.

3. In a small saucepan, combine the balsamic vinegar and the sherry vinegar and boil together until the mixture is reduced by half, about 2 minutes. Meanwhile, in another saucepan, cook the remaining 2 tablespoons of butter over moderate heat until the butter is golden brown and smells like roasted hazelnuts. Carefully pour the reduced vinegars into the browned butter; when the sputtering stops, add the broth and the capers. Boil the sauce until it becomes creamy, about 30 seconds. Add the parsley and season with salt, pepper and sugar, if needed. Spoon the brown butter sauce over the skate wings and serve at once. *—Sally Schneider*

ONE SERVING Calories 263 kcal, Total Fat 9.9 gm, Saturated Fat 5.4 gm

WINE Serve a crisp, herby California Sauvignon Blanc with this fish. Good choices include the 1998 Morgan and the 1997 Bernardus.

Potato Cakes Stuffed with Trout

Catfish Cakes

6 SERVINGS

Catfish is hugely popular at River Run in Plainfield, Vermont—mixed into jambalaya, fried with horseradish or transformed into these savory little cakes. Using cracker crumbs instead of bread is an American tradition that is popular both in the South and in New England; the crackers add crispness and a toasty flavor.

1½ pounds catfish fillets
¼ cup all-purpose flour, plus more for dusting
4 tablespoons unsalted butter
¾ cup cracker crumbs
1 large egg
¼ cup plus 2 tablespoons mayonnaise
1 tablespoon Dijon mustard
1 tablespoon milk
2 teaspoons Worcestershire sauce
1 teaspoon Old Bay seasoning
½ teaspoon hot sauce
½ teaspoon freshly ground pepper
3 tablespoons vegetable oil

I. Dust the catfish fillets with flour, tapping off any excess. In a large skillet, melt 1 tablespoon of the butter. Add the catfish and sauté over moderately high heat until golden and cooked through, about 3 minutes per side. Transfer to a plate, break into large pieces and let cool.

2. In a large bowl, combine the cracker crumbs, egg, mayonnaise, mustard, milk, Worcestershire, Old Bay seasoning, hot sauce and pepper. Gently fold in the catfish. Shape the mixture into twelve 3-inch patties and arrange them on wax paper. Refrigerate until firm, about 20 minutes.

3. Dredge the catfish patties in the ¼ cup of flour, tapping off any excess. In a large cast-iron skillet, melt the remaining 3 tablespoons of butter in the vegetable oil. Add the catfish cakes and cook over moderately high heat until golden and cooked through, about 2 minutes per side. Drain on paper towels and serve. —*Jimmy Kennedy*

Poached Salmon with Sour Cream Sauce

6 SERVINGS

A warm sour cream–dressed cucumber salad serves as a sauce for the fish in this take on poached salmon.

1 bottle (750 ml) dry white wine
3 cups water
2 medium carrots, thinly sliced
1 medium onion, thinly sliced
1 celery rib, thinly sliced
1 garlic clove, smashed
5 parsley sprigs
4 thyme sprigs
1 small rosemary sprig
1 bay leaf
Salt
6 center-cut skinless salmon fillets (about 6 ounces each)
About 2 cups boiling water
1 teaspoon unsalted butter
1 cup sour cream
1 European cucumber—peeled, halved lengthwise, seeded and thinly sliced crosswise
2 tablespoons capers, rinsed and drained
2 tablespoons finely chopped dill
Freshly ground pepper

I. In a large deep skillet, combine the white wine with the 3 cups water, the carrots, onion, celery, garlic, parsley, thyme, rosemary and bay leaf and bring to a boil. Cook over moderate heat until the liquid has reduced by half, 10 to 12 minutes. Strain the liquid, return it to the skillet and bring to a simmer; season with salt.

2. Add the salmon to the skillet so the fish is immersed in liquid; if necessary, add boiling water. Turn off the heat and let the salmon stand uncovered in the hot liquid until slightly rare in the center, about 10 minutes. Carefully transfer the fillets to a platter to cool somewhat and then pat dry with paper towels.

3. Melt the butter in a saucepan. Add the sour cream, cucumber and capers and cook over moderate heat, stirring, just until warmed through. Stir in the dill

and season with salt and pepper. Serve the poached salmon warm or at room temperature with the warm cucumber salad. —*Bob Farrish*

WINE The rich salmon and creamy salad are a perfect showcase for a round Chardonnay. Try the 1996 Fetzer Reserve from California or the 1997 Evans & Tate Margaret River from Australia.

DiSpirito's Seared Salmon with Onions and Rhubarb

4 SERVINGS ♔

Rocco DiSpirito is the chef at Union Pacific in New York City. To ensure crispness in these seared salmon fillets, he recommends starting the fish skin side down, pressing the fillet with a spatula. The skin will stick at first; when it releases, flip the fish over. In early summer, when it's in season, lean, wild Alaskan Copper River Salmon is DiSpirito's favorite fish. But any wild salmon would be delicious for this complexly flavored main course.

1½ cups dry fino sherry
¼ cup turbinado sugar or palm sugar (see Note)
½ pound rhubarb, trimmed and sliced diagonally ⅓ inch thick
3 tablespoons unsalted butter
1 pound bulb onions or sweet white onions, thinly sliced (see Note)
½ cup chicken stock or canned low-sodium broth
1 thyme sprig
Salt and freshly ground pepper
1 pound fava beans, shelled
Four 6-ounce salmon fillets, skin on
Vegetable oil
1 teaspoon fresh lemon juice

I. In a medium saucepan, combine the sherry with the sugar and cook over high heat, stirring occasionally, until the sugar is dissolved. Add the rhubarb and cook until just tender, about 1 minute. Strain the rhubarb in a colander set over a bowl to catch the cooking liquid. Return the liquid to the saucepan and boil over high heat until reduced to ½ cup, about 8 minutes.

2. Melt the butter in a medium saucepan. Add the onions and cook over low heat, stirring, until softened, about 1 minute. Add the stock and thyme and a pinch each of salt and pepper. Cover and simmer over low heat until the onions are tender, about 8 minutes.

3. In a medium saucepan of boiling salted water, cook the fava beans for 2 minutes. Using a slotted spoon, transfer the beans to a bowl and refresh under cool running water. Peel off the tough bean skins and add the favas to the onions.

4. Heat a cast-iron skillet. Lightly coat the salmon fillets with some oil and season with salt and pepper. Cook the salmon, skin side down, over moder-

ately high heat until the skin is very crisp, about 4 minutes. Turn the salmon fillets and cook over moderate heat until they are barely cooked through, about 4 minutes more, depending on the thickness of the fillets.

5. To serve, discard the thyme sprig and rewarm the onion mixture; add the lemon juice and season with salt and pepper. Bring the sherry-rhubarb liquid to a boil and add the cooked rhubarb. Spoon the rhubarb onto 4 large plates and set the onion mixture alongside. Top with the salmon fillets and serve at once. —*Rocco DiSpirito*

NOTE Turbinado sugar is available at most supermarkets, and palm sugar is available at Asian groceries. Bulb onions, which are immature onions harvested early in the season, are available

in the produce department of some supermarkets and in most specialty food stores.

WINE Salmon is meaty enough to match with light red wines or big white wines, but the tangy rhubarb, sweet spring onions and earthy fava beans in this dish make a big, fruity, opulent California Chardonnay the best bet. Consider the 1997 Byron Santa Maria Valley Estate or the 1997 Au Bon Climat Santa Barbara County.

Salt-Baked Salmon with Fennel, Capers and Orange

4 SERVINGS

The salt crust that coats the salmon during baking acts like a clay oven, keeping the fish fillets succulent and flavorful.

> 2 center-cut salmon fillets
>   (¾ pound each), with skin
> Freshly ground white pepper
> 3 large strips of orange zest
> 1 large fennel bulb—halved, cored
>   and very thinly sliced, 1 cup
>   feathery tops reserved
> 6 cups kosher salt
> ¼ cup fresh orange juice
> 1 tablespoon fresh lemon juice
> 2 tablespoons pure olive oil
> Table salt
> 1 tablespoon capers, rinsed

I. Preheat the oven to 500°. Set 1 salmon fillet, skin side down, on a work surface and season with white pepper. Arrange the orange zest on the salmon and top with half of the fennel tops. Cover with the second salmon fillet, skin side up. Pack the remaining fennel tops on the sides of the salmon so that there's no exposed flesh. Tie the fillets together with kitchen string.

2. Spread the kosher salt in a large roasting pan in an even layer and bake for 15 minutes. Carefully spread 1 cup of the hot salt in the bottom of a large loaf pan that is at least 5 inches wide. Set the salmon in the loaf pan and then pour the remaining salt over and

DiSpirito's Seared Salmon with Onions and Rhubarb

Salt-Baked Salmon with Fennel, Capers and Orange

Sesame Salmon with Soba Noodles

around. Gently pack the salt and bake the salmon for 45 minutes.

3. Meanwhile, in a shallow glass or stainless steel bowl, combine the citrus juices with the oil. Season lightly with table salt and white pepper. Add the sliced fennel and the capers, toss and let stand at room temperature for 30 minutes.

4. Scrape the salt off the top of the salmon. Using the string, gently lift the salmon from the pan and set it on a work surface. Scrape the salt from the sides and remove the string. Using a spatula, lift the top fillet and transfer it to a plate, skin side down. Discard the fennel tops and orange zest and cut each fish fillet in half. Lift the salmon from the skin, leaving behind the salt, and transfer to plates. Spoon the fennel salad on top and serve. —*Grace Parisi*

ONE SERVING Calories 399 kcal, Total Fat 25.4 gm, Saturated Fat 4.6 gm
WINE The meatiness of salmon calls for a full-flavored Chardonnay. Look for a rich, round California example, such as the 1997 Peju Province H. B. or the 1996 Rodney Strong Chalk Hill.

Glazed Salmon with Brussels Sprout Hash

8 SERVINGS

Brussels sprouts torn apart into individual leaves are an elegant addition to the potato and bacon hash that accompanies the cider glazed salmon.

- ¾ **pound medium Yukon Gold potatoes, scrubbed**
- 1 **pound brussels sprouts**
- 4 **thick slices of smoky bacon**
- 1 **large onion, minced**

Salt and freshly ground pepper

- 2 **cups apple cider**
- ¼ **cup applejack or other brandy**
- 1 **tablespoon unsalted butter**

Eight ½-pound salmon steaks

1. In a medium saucepan of boiling salted water, cook the potatoes until they are just tender, about 15 minutes. Using a slotted spoon, transfer the potatoes to a plate and let them cool slightly. Separate the brussels sprouts into individual leaves. Add the leaves to the boiling water, cook until they turn bright green, about 2 minutes, and then drain. Peel the potatoes and cut them into ½-inch dice.

2. In a large skillet, cook the smoky bacon over moderate heat, turning once, until the bacon is crisp, about 5 minutes. Drain the bacon and coarsely chop. Pour off all but 2 tablespoons of the bacon fat from the skillet. Add the diced potatoes and cook over moderate heat until they are browned on the bottom, about 4 minutes. Stir the potatoes and cook until they are browned all over, about 3 minutes.

3. Add the minced onion to the skillet and cook over moderate heat, stirring, until the onion is softened and starting to brown, about 4 minutes. Add the brussels sprout leaves and the chopped bacon and cook, stirring, until the hash is heated through, about 1 minute. Season the hash with salt and freshly ground pepper.

4. Meanwhile, in a medium saucepan, boil the cider with the applejack and the unsalted butter until the cider glaze is reduced to ⅔ cup, about 25 minutes.

5. Preheat the broiler. Season the salmon with salt and freshly ground pepper and brush on both sides with the glaze. Arrange the salmon steaks in a broiler pan or on a rack set in a rimmed baking sheet. Broil, brushing occasionally with the glaze, for about 8 minutes, or until crisp and just cooked through.

6. Reheat the brussels sprout hash. Brush the salmon steaks with any remaining cider glaze and then transfer the salmon steaks to plates and serve with the hash. —*Kerry Sear*

WINE The applejack glaze, with its hint of creaminess, requires a medium-bodied, slightly tannic Pinot Noir, such as the 1996 Domaine Drouhin Laurène from Oregon or the 1997 Ici/La-Bas La Detente from California.

Sesame Salmon with Soba Noodles

4 SERVINGS ✻

- 6 **ounces soba noodles**
- ¼ **cup soy sauce**
- 1 **tablespoon fresh lemon juice**
- 2 **tablespoons minced fresh ginger**

Four 6-ounce skinless salmon fillets

- ¼ **cup sesame seeds**
- 1 **teaspoon vegetable oil**
- 2 **teaspoons Asian sesame oil**
- 3 **scallions, coarsely chopped**

1. Bring a large pot of salted water to a boil. Add the noodles and cook until al dente, about 5 minutes. Drain, transfer to a medium bowl and keep warm.

2. Meanwhile, in a small bowl, combine the soy sauce, lemon juice and 1 tablespoon of the ginger. Lightly brush the salmon fillets on both sides with a little of the soy-ginger mixture and dredge in the sesame seeds.

3. Heat the vegetable oil in a large nonstick skillet. Add the salmon fillets to

Glazed Salmon with Brussels Sprout Hash

the pan and cook over moderately high heat until the sesame seeds are golden and the fish is just cooked through, about 5 minutes per side.

4. Add the sesame oil, scallions, the remaining 1 tablespoon of ginger and the remaining soy-ginger mixture to the soba noodles and toss to combine. Transfer the soba noodles to serving bowls, top with the salmon fillets and serve. —*Nell Newman*

Pancetta-Wrapped Salmon with Red Wine Butter
4 SERVINGS

- 2 tablespoons plus 1 teaspoon unsalted butter, softened
- 1 tablespoon minced shallots
- ½ cup red wine
- ½ teaspoon finely chopped flat-leaf parsley, plus 1 tablespoon whole leaves
- Salt and freshly ground pepper
- Four 6-ounce center-cut salmon fillets
- 1 teaspoon thyme leaves
- 8 thin slices of pancetta

- 20 pearl onions, unpeeled
- 2 tablespoons extra-virgin olive oil
- 1 head escarole, large leaves torn
- ¼ cup chicken stock or canned low-sodium broth
- 1 tablespoon fresh lemon juice
- Lemon wedges, for serving

1. Preheat the oven to 400°. Melt 1 teaspoon of the butter in a small saucepan. Add the shallots and cook over moderate heat until softened, about 2 minutes. Add the wine and boil over high heat until reduced to a thick, syrupy glaze, 5 to 7 minutes. Transfer to a small bowl and let cool. Stir in the remaining 2 tablespoons of butter until thoroughly blended, add the chopped parsley and season with salt and pepper.

2. Lay the salmon on a work surface and press the whole parsley and thyme leaves on the fillets. Season with salt and pepper. Wrap 2 slices of pancetta around each piece of salmon.

3. In a pie plate, toss the onions with 1 teaspoon oil. Cover with foil and bake for about 20 minutes, or until softened and slightly caramelized. Let cool slightly, trim the root ends and peel the onions.

4. In a large skillet, heat 1 tablespoon oil until shimmering. Add the escarole; season with salt and pepper. Cook over moderately high heat, tossing, until tender, about 5 minutes. Add the onions, stock and lemon juice. Cover and keep warm.

5. Heat the remaining 2 teaspoons oil in a large nonstick skillet. Add the salmon; cook over high heat, turning, until the pancetta is browned all over and the fish is medium rare, about 7 minutes. Carefully transfer to paper towels to drain.

6. Transfer the escarole mixture to 4 warmed plates and set the salmon on the greens. Top each fillet with a little of the red wine butter and serve at once with lemon wedges. —*Suzanne Goin*

MAKE AHEAD The recipe can be prepared through Step 3 and refrigerated for up to 1 day.

WINE A rich, deep, oak-aged California Chardonnay, such as the 1996 Morgan Reserve or the 1996 Shafer Red Shoulder Ranch, would balance the strong flavors of the salty pancetta and the sharp escarole. If you'd prefer a red, try a flavorful light Pinot Noir, such as the 1996 Carneros Creek from California or the 1996 Panther Creek from Oregon.

Yellowfin Tuna with Scallions and Ginger
4 SERVINGS

- 1½ cups extra-virgin olive oil
- 1½ pounds fresh yellowfin tuna steaks (at least 1 inch thick), cut into 8 equal pieces
- Salt and freshly ground pepper
- 10 large scallions, thinly sliced
- 1½ teaspoons minced fresh ginger
- 3 tablespoons balsamic vinegar
- 2 tablespoons soy sauce
- 1 tablespoon ketchup
- ½ tablespoon cold unsalted butter

1. In a medium saucepan, heat the oil until a piece of scallion sizzles in it. Season the tuna pieces with salt and pepper and carefully add to the saucepan; they should be completely immersed. Cook over low heat at a bare simmer until the tuna is just cooked through and a fork inserted in the fish comes out easily, about 7 minutes. Transfer to a plate; cover with foil to keep warm.

2. In a small saucepan, heat 3 tablespoons of the tuna cooking oil. Add the scallions and ginger and sauté over low heat until the scallions are tender, about 10 minutes. Add the balsamic vinegar and simmer for 1 minute. Stir in the soy sauce and ketchup and simmer gently for 1 minute. Remove from the heat and stir in the butter until smooth. Season the sauce with salt and pepper.

3. Set 2 tuna pieces on each of 4 plates. Using a slotted spoon, spread a layer of the scallions on top. Spoon the sauce on the fish and serve. —*Marcia Kiesel*

Pancetta-Wrapped Salmon with Red Wine Butter

Yellowfin Tuna with Scallions and Ginger

Grilled Tuna with Pepper Sauce

8 SERVINGS

The yellow bell peppers, roughly pureed with potato, look like cooked polenta. They complement the tuna nicely.

- 2 tablespoons extra-virgin olive oil, plus more for brushing
- 1 small onion, coarsely chopped
- 2 yellow bell peppers, coarsely chopped
- 1 medium Yukon Gold potato—peeled, halved lengthwise and sliced crosswise paper-thin
- 1 cup water

Salt

- 1 tablespoon fresh lemon juice

Freshly ground black pepper

Eight 6-ounce tuna steaks, 1 inch thick

Sage leaves, for garnish

I. Light a grill or preheat the broiler.

2. In a saucepan, heat 2 tablespoons of the oil. Add the onion; cook over low heat until softened but not browned, about 5 minutes. Add the yellow bell peppers, potato, water and a large pinch of salt. Cover and cook until the bell peppers and potatoes are tender, about 12 minutes. Transfer the vegetables and their liquid to a food processor and process until roughly pureed. Scrape the sauce into a bowl, add the lemon juice and season with salt and black pepper.

3. Brush the tuna steaks with olive oil and season with salt and black pepper. Grill or broil for 2 minutes on each side, or until lightly charred on the outside and medium rare in the center. Spoon the sauce onto large plates and set the tuna steaks on top. Garnish with sage leaves and serve. —*Lori De Mori*

MAKE AHEAD The sauce can be refrigerated for up to 2 days. Bring to room temperature before serving.

WINE The meaty flavors of the grilled tuna and sweet peppers point away from white wine to a soft, smooth Pinot Noir, such as the 1995 Fess Parker Pinot Noir Reserve from Santa Barbara.

Seared Tuna with Anchovy-Roasted Vegetables

8 SERVINGS

- 6 anchovy fillets, rinsed
- 6 garlic cloves, smashed
- 1 dried red chile, seeded and chopped
- $\frac{1}{3}$ cup chicken stock or canned low-sodium broth
- 2 tablespoons fresh lemon juice
- $\frac{1}{4}$ cup coarsely chopped flat-leaf parsley
- 1 tablespoon rosemary leaves
- $\frac{1}{4}$ cup extra-virgin olive oil
- 8 medium Yukon Gold potatoes (about 2 pounds), cut into $\frac{3}{4}$-inch wedges
- 8 cipollini onions, trimmed, or 4 small yellow onions, halved
- 2 fennel bulbs (about 1 pound each)—halved, cored and cut lengthwise into 1-inch wedges

Salt and freshly ground pepper

Eight 7-ounce tuna steaks (1 inch thick)

I. Preheat the oven to 400°. In a blender, puree the anchovies, garlic, chile, stock, lemon juice, parsley, rosemary and 3 tablespoons of the olive oil until smooth. In a large roasting pan, preferably nonstick, toss the potatoes, onions and fennel with the anchovy puree. Season with salt and pepper and spread in an even layer. Roast for about 35 minutes, stirring twice, or until just tender.

2. Divide the remaining 1 tablespoon of oil between 2 large nonstick skillets. Season the tuna with salt and pepper, add 4 steaks to each pan and cook over high heat until nicely browned, about 6 minutes. Turn and cook for 1 minute.

3. Set the tuna steaks, browned side up, on top of the vegetables and roast for about 6 minutes, or until the tuna is cooked through. Arrange the tuna steaks and vegetables on a large platter and serve. —*Trey Foshee*

ONE SERVING Calories 447 kcal, Total Fat 16.5 gm, Saturated Fat 3.4 gm

WINE Pair the rustic, hearty taste of this dish with an intense dry white, such as a Vernaccia di San Gimignano from Italy. Look for the 1996 Teruzzi & Puthod Terre di Tufi or the 1996 San Quirico.

Fresh Sardines with Two-Olive Bread Crumb Crust

4 SERVINGS

If omega-3-rich fresh sardines are hard to find, small bluefish or mackerel fillets can be used instead.

- 12 fresh whole sardines (about 2$\frac{1}{2}$ pounds), heads and bones removed
- 1$\frac{1}{2}$ cups coarse fresh bread crumbs
- $\frac{1}{3}$ cup Sicilian green olives, pitted and chopped
- $\frac{1}{4}$ cup oil-cured black olives, pitted and chopped
- 2 tablespoons extra-virgin olive oil
- 1$\frac{1}{4}$ teaspoons minced rosemary

Salt and freshly ground pepper

Lemon wedges, for serving

Grilled Tuna with Pepper Sauce

1. Preheat the broiler. Spread the sardines open on a large baking sheet, skin side down. In a medium bowl, combine the bread crumbs, green and black olives, 1½ tablespoons of the olive oil and the rosemary and season with salt and pepper. Top each sardine with 2 heaping tablespoons of the bread crumbs, pressing them to adhere.

2. Divide the remaining ½ tablespoon of olive oil between 2 large nonstick ovenproof skillets. Arrange 6 sardines in each skillet, skin side down, and cook over moderately high heat until browned on the bottom and cooked through, 3 to 4 minutes.

3. Set the skillets under the broiler, 1 at a time if necessary, and broil the sardines for 1 to 2 minutes, or until the bread crumbs are golden and crisp. Serve the sardines immediately with lemon wedges. —*Grace Parisi*

ONE SERVING Calories 380 kcal, Total Fat 25.4 gm, Saturated Fat 4.6 gm

WINE The assertive flavors of sardines and olives need a clean, pleasantly sharp white wine for contrast. Look for a Sauvignon Blanc–based French wine, such as the 1996 Comte Lafond Sancerre or the 1997 Michel Lynch Sauvignon Blanc from Bordeaux.

Seafood Bisteeya

6 SERVINGS

Classic *bisteeya*—made with spiced pigeons, lemony eggs, tangy onion sauce and toasted sweetened almonds—is one of the world's great dishes, but it's too rich for many occasions. Moroccan cooks have developed a lighter seafood version that is so good it has become a favorite even in traditional Moroccan homes, which proves that cuisines are always in transition. The fish fillets and shrimp are seasoned with *charmoula*, the Moroccan marinade typically used for fish, vegetables and chicken. It's best to use large shrimp and thick chunks of skinless cod, sea bass, halibut, monkfish or swordfish here. Large

pieces of preserved lemon peel are baked right into the *bisteeya*, but they're not meant to be eaten.

CHARMOULA

½ cup plus 1 tablespoon olive oil
3 large tomatoes—peeled, seeded and finely chopped
¾ cup (packed) cilantro leaves
¾ cup flat-leaf parsley leaves
3 tablespoons fresh lemon juice
1 tablespoon minced garlic
1½ teaspoons sweet paprika
1 teaspoon ground cumin
1 teaspoon salt
Scant ½ teaspoon mildly hot red pepper or cayenne

BISTEEYA

5 ounces vermicelli or angel hair pasta, broken into 1-inch pieces (2 cups)
1 pound skinless firm-fleshed white fish fillets, thinly sliced
1 pound fresh spinach, tough stems removed, leaves washed but not dried
About ½ cup olive oil
½ pound phyllo dough (about 15 sheets)
1 preserved lemon, cut into quarters, pulp discarded (optional; see Note)
½ pound large shrimp, shelled and deveined
About ¼ cup soda water

1. MAKE THE CHARMOULA: In a medium saucepan, heat 1 tablespoon of the olive oil. Add the tomatoes and cook over moderately high heat, stirring, until reduced to ½ cup, about 10 minutes. Transfer the tomato sauce to a blender. Add the cilantro, parsley, lemon juice, garlic, paprika, cumin, salt, mildly hot red pepper and the remaining ½ cup of olive oil and blend until the *charmoula* is smooth.

2. MAKE THE BISTEEYA: Bring a medium saucepan of water to a boil. Add the vermicelli; cook until barely al dente, about 2 minutes. Drain well, shaking off any excess water. Transfer to a bowl and

stir in ¾ cup of the *charmoula*. Refrigerate until chilled and almost all of the sauce has been absorbed by the vermicelli, about 1 hour. In another bowl, toss the fish with the remaining *charmoula* and refrigerate.

3. Heat a large skillet. Add the spinach leaves by the handful and cook over high heat, turning with tongs, until thoroughly wilted. Transfer the spinach to a colander and let cool. Squeeze the spinach dry and then finely shred it.

4. Preheat the oven to 375°. Brush a 10- or 12-inch pizza or paella pan with olive oil. Unroll the phyllo sheets and cover them with plastic wrap and a damp kitchen towel to keep them from drying out. Lightly brush 10 sheets of the phyllo with olive oil and lay them across the pizza pan in every direction to completely cover the bottom of the pan with some overhang. Spread half of the vermicelli evenly over the phyllo and cover with the marinated fish fillets in an even layer, separating any slices of fish that stick together. Arrange the preserved lemon rind quarters on the fish and top with the shrimp and spinach. Spread the remaining vermicelli over the spinach.

5. Brush the remaining sheets of phyllo dough with olive oil and then layer them over the *bisteeya*. Fold all of the overhanging edges under the *bisteeya*, as if tucking in sheets. Using a sharp knife, make a 2-inch slit in the top. Brush the top with olive oil. Sprinkle lightly with soda water and bake for about half an hour, or until golden and crisp. Carefully transfer the *bisteeya* to a large round platter and cut it into wedges. Serve hot or warm. —*Paula Wolfert*

NOTE Preserved lemons are available at Middle Eastern groceries.

MAKE AHEAD The recipe can be prepared through Step 2 and refrigerated for up to 3 hours.

WINE A dry and aromatic white wine will play off the sweet spiciness of the *bisteeya*. Consider a Châteauneuf-du-

Pape Blanc from France, like the 1996 Château Mont-Redon, or the 1997 King Estate Pinot Gris Reserve from Oregon.

Hot and Spicy Shrimp Posole with Tomatillos

4 SERVINGS 🌟

- 1 pound tomatillos, husked and rinsed
- Salt
- 2 canned chipotle chiles in *adobo,* stemmed
- 1 tablespoon olive oil
- 1 onion, finely chopped
- 3 garlic cloves, minced
- ½ teaspoon ground cumin
- ½ teaspoon ground coriander
- ½ teaspoon dried oregano
- One 28-ounce can white hominy, drained and rinsed
- 2 cups chicken stock or canned low-sodium broth
- 1 cup fresh or frozen corn
- 1 pound medium shrimp, shelled and deveined
- ¼ cup coarsely chopped cilantro
- 1 small avocado, coarsely chopped
- 1 fresh lime, sliced

I. In a medium saucepan, cover the tomatillos with water, add salt and bring to a boil. Simmer over moderate heat until the tomatillos soften, about 10 minutes. Drain and transfer to a blender or food processor. Add the chipotles and puree until smooth.

2. Meanwhile, heat the olive oil in a large saucepan. Add the onion; cook over moderately high heat, stirring occasionally, until softened, about 5 minutes. Stir in the garlic, cumin, coriander, oregano and 1 teaspoon salt. Cook until the garlic is fragrant, about 1 minute.

3. Add the tomatillo puree, hominy and stock and simmer for 15 minutes. Stir in the corn and shrimp and simmer until the shrimp are pink and just cooked through, about 5 minutes. Ladle the stew into shallow bowls, garnish with the cilantro, avocado and lime and serve. —*Nell Newman*

Shrimp in Fragrant Green Sauce

4 SERVINGS 🌟

At Jimmy's Bronx Café in New York City, cilantro pesto is stirred into the reduced pan sauce for this delicious shrimp.

- 2 cups (packed) cilantro sprigs
- 2 small garlic cloves, minced
- 1 tablespoon fresh lemon juice
- ¼ cup plus 1 tablespoon extra-virgin olive oil
- Salt and freshly ground pepper
- 1½ pounds large shrimp, shelled and deveined
- 3 large scallions, thinly sliced
- 1 small jalapeño, minced
- ¼ cup dry white wine
- 1 cup fish stock or bottled clam juice
- 1 tablespoon unsalted butter

I. In a food processor, combine the cilantro sprigs, the minced garlic and the lemon juice and process to a paste. With the machine on, pour in 2 tablespoons of the extra-virgin olive oil. Scrape the cilantro pesto into a small

Seafood Bisteeya

Spicy Shrimp with Basil

1. In a small dry skillet, toast the peppercorns over moderate heat just until fragrant, about 1 minute. Transfer the peppercorns to a mortar and coarsely crush. Add the garlic, cilantro, ginger, chiles, lime zest and salt and pound to a coarse paste.

2. Heat the vegetable oil in a large skillet. Add the peppercorn paste and stir-fry over high heat for 30 seconds. Add the shrimp and stir-fry until they are opaque throughout, about 2 minutes. Stir in the soy sauce. Transfer the spicy shrimp to a bowl, add the basil and serve. —*Su-Mei Yu*

NOTE Holy basil can be found at Asian groceries.

SERVE WITH Steamed jasmine rice.

Shrimp Stir-Fried with Napa Cabbage

4 SERVINGS

If served with other dishes as part of a traditional Chinese meal, this dish feeds four. Double the recipe if you will be using it as a main course.

- 2 quarts water
- 1 pound Napa cabbage, leaves and ribs sliced separately ½ inch thick
- 4½ tablespoons chicken stock or canned low-sodium broth
- 1 tablespoon cornstarch
- 1 tablespoon dark soy sauce
- ¾ teaspoon Asian sesame oil
- Pinch of freshly ground white pepper
- 2 teaspoons peanut oil
- 2 teaspoons minced fresh ginger
- 1½ teaspoons minced garlic
- ½ pound medium shrimp, shelled and deveined, tails left on
- ¼ cup thinly sliced red bell pepper

1. Bring the water to a boil in a large saucepan. Add the Napa cabbage ribs and cook them for 10 seconds. Add the Napa cabbage leaves and cook them for 20 seconds. Drain the cabbage and rinse under cold water; drain well.

2. In a small bowl, combine the chicken stock with the cornstarch, soy sauce,

bowl and season with salt and freshly ground pepper.

2. In a large skillet, heat the remaining 3 tablespoons of olive oil. Add half of the shrimp and cook over moderate heat, stirring, until barely cooked through, about 4 minutes. Transfer to a plate and repeat with the remaining shrimp.

3. Add the scallions and jalapeño to the skillet and cook over moderate heat, stirring, for 1 minute. Add the wine and simmer until reduced by half, about 3 minutes. Add the stock and simmer over moderately high heat until reduced by half, about 4 minutes. Return the shrimp to the skillet with any accumulated juices. Stir in the cilantro pesto and bring just to a simmer. Season with salt and pepper and remove from the heat. Stir in the butter and serve. —*Luis Rivera*

Spicy Shrimp with Basil

4 SERVINGS

- 1 teaspoon white peppercorns
- 2 garlic cloves, finely chopped
- 1½ tablespoons coarsely chopped cilantro
- 1 tablespoon minced fresh ginger
- 1 or 2 fresh Thai or serrano chiles, cut into thin strips
- 1½ teaspoons finely grated lime zest
- 1 teaspoon salt
- 2 tablespoons vegetable oil
- 1 pound medium or large shrimp, shelled and deveined
- 2 tablespoons soy sauce
- 1 cup holy basil leaves (see Note), or ½ cup torn Italian basil leaves plus ½ cup torn mint leaves

Shrimp Stir-Fried with Napa Cabbage

sesame oil and white pepper to make the sauce.

3. Warm a wok over high heat for 45 seconds. Add the peanut oil and swirl to coat the wok. Add the ginger and cook for 10 seconds. Stir in the garlic and cook for 10 seconds. Add the shrimp in a single layer and cook, turning once, until they begin to turn pink and curl up, about 15 seconds per side. Add the Napa cabbage ribs and leaves and stir-fry for 2½ minutes. Make a well in the center of the shrimp and cabbage mixture, pushing the mixture to the side of the wok. Stir the sauce and pour it into the well. Bring to a simmer, stir-frying to blend. Transfer the stir-fry to a platter, sprinkle with the red bell pepper and serve. —*Eileen Yin-Fei Lo*

ONE SERVING Calories 130 kcal, Total Fat 4.5 gm, Saturated Fat 1 gm

Coconut Curried Shrimp

8 SERVINGS

This simple shrimp curry can be made as fiery as you like. It is particularly good served with Saffron Rice (p. 306).

1¾ **cups chicken stock or canned low-sodium broth**
1 **tablespoon Thai red curry paste (see Note)**
1 **can (14 ounces) unsweetened coconut milk**
2 **tablespoons Asian fish sauce**
2 **tablespoons peanut oil**
4 **pounds medium shrimp, shelled and deveined, tails left on (see Note)**
Salt
1 **cup shaved fresh coconut**
1 **cup (4 ounces) roasted unsalted peanuts**
1 **cup cilantro leaves**

1. In a large saucepan, bring the chicken stock to a boil with the curry paste. Simmer over moderate heat until reduced by half, about 7 minutes. Stir in the coconut milk and Asian fish sauce and cook until reduced by half again, about 10 minutes.

2. Heat a wok or a large heavy skillet. Add ½ tablespoon of the oil and swirl over high heat until smoking. Season the shrimp with salt and add one fourth of them to the wok. Stir-fry until the shrimp are opaque, 2 to 3 minutes. Transfer the shrimp to a platter. Repeat with the remaining oil and shrimp; be sure to heat the oil in the wok between batches.

3. Return the shrimp to the wok. Add the curry sauce; bring just to a simmer. Put the fresh coconut, peanuts and cilantro in separate bowls. Spoon the shrimp onto warmed plates. Serve with the accompaniments. —*Rori Spinelli*

NOTE Thai curry pastes are available in supermarket ethnic-foods sections. Freeze the shrimp shells for making a quick shellfish stock at a later time.

Grilled Shrimp with Basil Emulsion

4 SERVINGS

¼ **cup unsalted pistachios**
¾ **cup coarsely chopped basil**
¼ **cup coarsely chopped mint**
1 **tablespoon fresh lime juice**
1 **tablespoon rice vinegar**
¼ **teaspoon dry mustard**
Large pinch of cayenne pepper
½ **cup extra-virgin olive oil**
Four 1-inch ice cubes
Salt and freshly ground black pepper
2 **pounds large shrimp, shelled and deveined, tails left on**
Vegetable oil, for brushing

1. Preheat the oven to 400°. Spread the pistachios in a pie plate and toast them for about 5 minutes, or until the nuts

Coconut Curried Shrimp, with Saffron Rice (p. 306).

are lightly browned. Let the toasted pistachios cool completely and then coarsely chop them.

2. In a blender, combine the pistachios with the basil, mint, lime juice, rice vinegar, mustard, cayenne and olive oil. Blend at low speed until pureed. Add the ice cubes and blend at high speed until the sauce is very smooth. Scrape the basil emulsion into a small glass or stainless steel bowl and season with salt and black pepper.

3. Light a grill or heat a lightly oiled grill pan. Brush the shrimp with vegetable oil and season with salt and black pepper. Grill over a hot fire for 1 minute per side, or until lightly charred and just cooked through. Alternatively, cook the shrimp in the grill pan over high heat for 1 to 2 minutes per side. Serve the hot shrimp with the basil emulsion alongside for dipping. —*Raphael Lunetta*

MAKE AHEAD The basil emulsion can be refrigerated overnight. Whisk well before serving.

Shrimp with Thai Lemongrass Marinade

4 SERVINGS

Variations on this marinade are used throughout Southeast Asia, especially with seafood, pork and beef.

- 3 garlic cloves, thinly sliced
- 3 Thai chiles, thinly sliced
- 2 stalks of fresh lemongrass, bottom third only, thinly sliced
- 1 shallot, thinly sliced
- 1 tablespoon chopped fresh ginger
- ½ cup Asian fish sauce
- ¼ cup sugar
- ¼ cup fresh lime juice
- ¼ cup chopped cilantro
- 2 teaspoons ground coriander
- ½ teaspoon freshly ground pepper
- 1½ pounds large shrimp, shelled and deveined

Grilled Shrimp with Basil Emulsion

1. In a food processor, combine the garlic, Thai chiles, lemongrass, shallot and ginger and process to a paste. Scrape the paste into a bowl and then stir in the fish sauce, sugar, lime juice, cilantro, coriander and pepper.

2. Light a grill. Coat the shrimp with ⅔ cup of the lemongrass marinade and let sit for 15 minutes. Thread the shrimp onto skewers and cook them over a hot fire for about 2 minutes per side, using the remaining lemongrass marinade for basting. —*Steven Raichlen*

WINE The briny shrimp would benefit from the accent of a crisp white wine, but the zing of the marinade narrows the choice to a white with assertiveness as well. Top pick? An Oregon Pinot Gris, such as the 1996 Eyrie or the 1996 King Estate.

Shrimp with Chickpea Pancakes and Mango Relish

4 SERVINGS

These pancakes are a takeoff on *socca,* the classic Niçoise chickpea pancake. The original *socca* is a three-foot-wide pancake that's baked in an oven and then cut into single servings. The individual pancakes here are only a few inches wide and are cooked in a skillet.

SHRIMP

- 24 medium shrimp, shelled and deveined
- ¼ cup olive oil
- 2 garlic cloves, finely chopped
- 2 small shallots, finely chopped
- Salt and freshly ground pepper

MANGO RELISH

- 1 ripe mango, peeled and finely chopped (about 1 cup)
- 2 scallions, white and tender green parts only, finely chopped
- 2 oil-packed sun-dried tomatoes, drained and finely chopped
- ¼ cup fresh lime juice
- ¼ cup olive oil
- Salt and freshly ground pepper

PANCAKES

- ½ cup canned chickpeas, 2 tablespoons of the liquid reserved
- 1 cup milk
- 1 cup all-purpose flour
- ½ cup olive oil, plus more for frying
- 1 large egg
- 1 tablespoon chopped parsley
- 1 teaspoon ground cumin
- 1 teaspoon salt
- ¼ teaspoon freshly ground pepper
- ¼ cup dried currants
- Coriander sprigs, for garnish

1. PREPARE THE SHRIMP: In a medium bowl, toss the shrimp with the olive oil, the garlic and the shallots. Season with salt and pepper and refrigerate for 1 hour.

2. MAKE THE MANGO RELISH: In a bowl, combine the mango with the scallions, the sun-dried tomatoes, the lime juice and the olive oil. Season the mango relish with salt and pepper.

3. MAKE THE PANCAKES: In a food processor, puree the chickpeas along with the reserved chickpea liquid until smooth. Transfer the puree to a medium bowl and gradually whisk in the milk, flour, ½ cup of olive oil, egg, parsley, cumin, salt and pepper.

4. Heat 2 tablespoons of olive oil in a large, heavy skillet. Add ¼ cup of the pancake batter and sprinkle with 1 teaspoon of the currants. Cook the pancake over moderate heat, turning once, until it is golden brown on both sides, 2 to 3 minutes; transfer the pancake to a plate, cover with foil and keep warm. Repeat with the remaining pancake batter and currants to make 11 more pancakes; add more olive oil to the skillet as needed.

5. Light a grill or preheat the broiler. Skewer the shrimp, sprinkle with salt and pepper and grill over a hot fire or broil for about 1 minute per side. Overlap 3 of the pancakes on each plate and top with 6 of the shrimp. Garnish with the mango relish and coriander sprigs and serve. —*Stephen Kalt*

MAKE AHEAD The shrimp can be prepared through Step 1 and refrigerated overnight. The mango relish can also be refrigerated overnight.

WINE Mild shrimp suggests a lean, crisp white Pigato from Liguria. The grilled flavor also points to a medium-bodied Sauvignon Blanc from New Zealand or an easy-to-drink Chilean Merlot.

Scattered California Roll with Lobster

4 SERVINGS

This dish was inspired by failed attempts at eating a piece of sushi in two bites. Instead of preparing a live lobster, you can also buy a cooked one.

- ¼ cup rice vinegar
- 1 teaspoon sugar
- 1½ cups (10 ounces) Japanese or sushi rice
- 2 cups water
- One 1½-pound lobster
- 1 tablespoon sesame seeds
- 4 teaspoons vegetable oil
- 1 tablespoon finely chopped pickled ginger
- 2 teaspoons powdered wasabi mixed with 2 tablespoons water
- 2 teaspoons soy sauce
- ⅛ teaspoon sea salt
- 4 radishes, cut into 1-inch matchsticks
- 2 scallions, cut into 1-inch matchsticks
- 1 cucumber—peeled, seeded and cut into 1-inch matchsticks
- 1 ripe Hass avocado, cut into 1-inch matchsticks
- One 8-by-7½-inch sheet of nori (Japanese seaweed), finely shredded

1. In a small glass or stainless steel bowl, combine 2 tablespoons of the rice vinegar with the sugar, stirring until dissolved. In a medium saucepan, combine the rice with the water and bring to a boil. Stir, cover and cook over low heat until the liquid is absorbed, about 15 minutes. Remove from the heat and let stand, covered, for 10 minutes. Spread the rice on a large platter and toss with the sweetened vinegar. Refrigerate briefly until cool.

2. Bring a large pot of water to a boil. Add the lobster and cook for 8 minutes. Remove the meat from the lobster tail and claws. Discard the intestine in the tail. Coarsely chop the lobster meat and let cool.

Lobster Eggs Benedict

3. Toast the sesame seeds in a small dry skillet over moderate heat, stirring constantly, until golden, about 3 minutes. Transfer to a plate to cool.

4. In a large glass or stainless steel bowl, combine the remaining 2 tablespoons of rice vinegar with the vegetable oil, pickled ginger, wasabi paste and soy sauce. Season with the sea salt. Add the rice, radishes, scallions, cucumber and lobster meat and toss gently to combine; let stand for 15 minutes to blend the flavors. Fold in the avocado, sesame seeds and nori just before serving. —*Grace Parisi*

MAKE AHEAD The lobster, sesame seeds and dressing can all be prepared up to 1 day ahead.

WINE Toasted sesame seeds, sweet sushi rice and mild lobster make this dish a good match for a crisp, aromatic Australian Riesling, such as the 1997 Pikes or the 1998 Grosset Polish Hill.

Lobster Eggs Benedict

4 SERVINGS

This is superdecadent brunch food. To save time, you can use cooked lobster meat—you'll need about three quarters of a pound.

Two 1-pound live lobsters
  8 large eggs
Four ¾-inch-thick slices of peasant bread, toasted
  3 large egg yolks
  2 tablespoons boiling water
  2 sticks (½ pound) unsalted butter, melted and hot
  2 tablespoons fresh lemon juice
Pinch of cayenne pepper

1. In a large pot of boiling water, cook the lobsters until bright red all over, about 12 minutes. Let cool slightly under cold running water and then twist off the tails and claws. Crack the claws and remove the meat. Using kitchen scissors, slit the tail shells lengthwise and then remove the meat. Remove the dark intestinal veins and cut the tail meat crosswise into thin slices.

2. Half fill 2 large deep skillets with water and bring to a simmer. Crack 4 of the eggs into each skillet and poach the eggs over moderate heat just until set, about 3 minutes. Using a slotted spoon, remove the poached eggs from the skillets and pat them dry with paper towels. Arrange the lobster meat on the toast. Top each serving with 2 poached eggs and keep warm.

3. Meanwhile, in a blender, briefly pulse the egg yolks to break them up. With the machine on, add the boiling water in a thin stream and then add the hot butter in a thin stream, stopping when you reach the milky liquid at the bottom; blend just until the butter is incorporated and the sauce is thick and pale. Add the lemon juice and cayenne. Spoon the hollandaise sauce onto the eggs and serve immediately. —*Jonathan King*

Sea Scallops with Pepper-Lemon Relish

4 SERVINGS

Gypsy peppers—which are long, pointy and mild and come in a variety of colors—are popular on the West Coast. If you can't find them, use red bell peppers. Cook the scallops on a grill or in a grill pan.

1½ tablespoons red wine vinegar
  1 tablespoon minced shallots
  2 lemon quarters
  1 gypsy pepper or 1 small red bell pepper, finely chopped
  1 tablespoon capers, rinsed and coarsely chopped
  ¼ cup extra-virgin olive oil, plus more for brushing
Kosher salt and freshly ground black pepper
  1 head of frisée, torn into pieces
1½ pounds large sea scallops

1. Light the grill if using. In a small glass or stainless steel bowl, combine the red wine vinegar and the shallots and let stand for 5 minutes. Cut one of the lemon quarters into paper-thin slices. Finely chop the slices, including the rind, and add to the shallots along with the gypsy pepper, the capers and the ¼ cup olive oil. Squeeze the juice from the remaining lemon quarter into the lemon relish and season the relish with kosher salt and black pepper. Arrange the frisée on 4 plates and top with half of the lemon relish.

2. Brush the scallops with olive oil and season with kosher salt and black pepper. Heat a grill pan, if using, over moderately high heat. Grill or sear in a grill pan, turning once, until the scallops are charred and cooked through, about 6 minutes. Arrange the scallops on the frisée, garnish with the remaining lemon relish and serve. —*Seen Lippert*

chapter 7

chicken other birds

178

183

191

180

chicken other birds

ABOVE: **Basil-Stuffed Chicken Breasts.**

RIGHT: **Sautéed Chicken with Ancho-Orange Sauce.**

Basil-Stuffed Chicken Breasts

4 SERVINGS

- 6 slices bacon
- 2 cups coarsely chopped basil
- 1 small garlic clove
- ¼ cup extra-virgin olive oil
- ½ teaspoon fresh lemon juice

Salt

- 4 skinless, boneless chicken breast halves, halved diagonally (about 5 ounces each)

Freshly ground pepper

- 1 cup all-purpose flour
- 2 large eggs, lightly beaten
- 1 cup fine fresh bread crumbs
- 2 tablespoons unsalted butter
- 2 tablespoons pure olive oil

1. In a large skillet, cook the bacon over moderate heat until crisp, about 5 minutes. Drain and then coarsely chop the bacon. In a food processor, puree the bacon, basil and garlic to a paste. With the machine on, add the extra-virgin olive oil in a thin stream. Transfer the basil stuffing to a bowl. Stir in the fresh lemon juice and then season the stuffing with salt.

2. Make a 1-inch horizontal incision in each piece of chicken to form a pocket. Spoon 1 tablespoon of the basil stuffing into each pocket and press gently to close. Season the chicken breasts on both sides with salt and pepper.

3. Put the flour, eggs and bread crumbs in separate shallow bowls. Lightly flour the chicken breasts, shaking off any excess, and then dip them in the eggs and coat with the bread crumbs.

4. In a large skillet, melt 1 tablespoon of the butter in 1 tablespoon of the pure olive oil. Add half of the chicken. Cook the chicken over moderately high heat until browned and just cooked through, about 3 minutes per side; lower the heat if the chicken browns too quickly. Repeat with the remaining butter, pure olive oil and chicken. Transfer the chicken to plates and serve. —*Marcia Kiesel*

Sautéed Chicken with Ancho-Orange Sauce

4 SERVINGS ✳

To double this dish, multiply all of the ingredients by two, except the flour—you will only need one or two more tablespoons.

- 1 dried ancho chile
- ¼ cup all-purpose flour

Salt and freshly ground pepper

- 4 boneless chicken breasts, skin on (about 5 ounces each)
- 3 tablespoons unsalted butter
- 5 scallions, white and tender green only, thinly sliced
- 1 tablespoon fresh lemon juice
- ½ cup fresh orange juice
- 2 tablespoons chopped cilantro

1. In a bowl, cover the ancho with warm water and let soak until softened, about 20 minutes. Drain the chile and discard the stem and seeds; mince the chile.

2. Meanwhile, spread the flour on a plate and season well with salt and freshly ground pepper. Pat the chicken breasts dry and dredge them in the flour; shake off any excess flour.

3. Melt the butter in a large, heavy-bottomed skillet. Add the chicken breasts, skin side down. Sauté over moderate heat until the chicken breasts are well browned and crisp, about 5 minutes. Turn and continue cooking until the chicken breasts are browned and just cooked through, about 5 more minutes; lower the heat, if necessary. Transfer the chicken breasts to a large plate.

4. Pour off any excess fat from the skillet. Add the scallions and cook over moderate heat, stirring, just until softened, about 1 minute. Add the lemon juice and cook until almost completely evaporated. Add the chopped ancho chile and sauté for 1 minute. Add the orange juice, season with a pinch of salt and cook until reduced by half. Return the chicken breasts to the skillet and warm through, turning them in the sauce. Add the chopped cilantro and transfer the chicken breasts to plates. Spoon the ancho-orange sauce on top and serve. —*Howard Miller*

WINE Serve these lightly spicy chicken breasts with an authentic Texas beer, such as Shiner Bock.

Jamaican Chicken Stir-Fry

2 SERVINGS

- 2 large egg whites
- 2 teaspoons cornstarch
- 2 tablespoons plus 2 teaspoons soy sauce
- 1 pound skinless, boneless chicken breast halves, cut crosswise into ½-inch-thick slices

Salt and freshly ground pepper

Mixture of Jamaican Jardinière Pickles (p. 326)—2 garlic cloves, 2 ginger slices, 1 to 2 Scotch bonnet chile halves, 8 cauliflower florets, 2 carrot sticks, 2 red bell pepper strips, plus ¼ cup pickling liquid from the jar

- 1 tablespoon vegetable oil

- 2 small tomatoes, coarsely chopped
- ½ teaspoon Asian sesame oil

1. In a shallow bowl, combine the egg whites, cornstarch and 2 teaspoons of the soy sauce. Add the chicken breasts and a pinch each of salt and pepper and turn to coat. Refrigerate the chicken for 30 minutes.

2. Cut the pickled garlic and ginger into slivers. Seed the Scotch bonnet chile pickle and finely chop. Cut the remaining pickles into bite-size pieces.

3. Set a wok over high heat. Add the vegetable oil and heat until smoking. Add the pickled garlic and ginger and stir-fry for 10 seconds. Add the chicken and stir-fry until almost cooked through, about 3 minutes. Add the tomatoes and stir-fry for 1 minute. Add the pickled chiles and vegetables, the pickling liquid and the remaining 2 tablespoons of soy sauce and stir-fry for 10 seconds to blend. Season the stir-fry with salt and pepper and stir in the sesame oil. Serve at once. —*Marcia Kiesel*

SERVE WITH Steamed rice.

Lime-Coconut Chicken

4 SERVINGS

Tangy watercress balances sweet coconut milk in this quick skillet dish.

- 1 tablespoon plus 1 teaspoon canola oil
- 1 tablespoon hot sauce
- 1 teaspoon soy sauce
- 1 teaspoon sugar
- 1 pound skinless, boneless chicken breasts, cut into 1-inch pieces

Salt and freshly ground pepper

- 3 large scallions, thinly sliced
- ¾ pound watercress, stems trimmed, finely chopped and reserved

One 14-ounce can unsweetened coconut milk

- 1 tablespoon fresh lime juice, plus lime wedges for serving
- 3 tablespoons coarsely chopped cilantro

1. In a medium bowl, combine 1 tablespoon of the oil, 1 teaspoon of the hot sauce, the soy sauce and ½ teaspoon of the sugar. Add the chicken; toss to coat. Refrigerate 1 hour or overnight.

2. Heat a large nonstick skillet over moderately high heat. Add the chicken, season with salt and pepper and cook, shaking the pan occasionally, until browned and just cooked through, 4 to 5 minutes. Transfer to a plate.

3. Heat the remaining 1 teaspoon of oil in the skillet. Add the scallions and the watercress stems and cook until crisp-tender and lightly browned, 2 to 3 minutes. Add the watercress leaves; cook, stirring, until wilted, 1 to 2 minutes. Transfer the watercress and scallions to the plate with the chicken.

4. Add the coconut milk, lime juice and the remaining 2 teaspoons of hot sauce and ½ teaspoon of sugar to the skillet. Bring to a simmer and cook until reduced by one third, about 5 minutes. Stir the chicken and watercress into the sauce, season with salt and pepper and warm through. Add the cilantro; serve immediately with lime wedges. —*Grace Parisi*

SERVE WITH Steamed rice.

WINE The lime-coconut sauce calls for a wine with a citrusy acidity of its own. Pick an Australian Riesling, such as the 1998 Grosset Polish Hill or 1998 Pikes.

Chilean Chicken Stew with Squash and Wild Rice

8 SERVINGS

- 2 tablespoons extra-virgin olive oil
- 8 carrots, cut into ½-inch pieces
- 6 celery ribs, cut into ½-inch pieces
- 2 large white onions, 1 coarsely chopped and 1 minced
- 20 medium garlic cloves, minced
- 1 tablespoon cumin seeds
- 1 tablespoon dried oregano
- 8 large chicken legs (about 3 pounds), skin removed
- 8 chicken breast halves (about 3 pounds) on the bone, wings and skin removed

Chilean Chicken Stew
with Squash and Wild Rice

1 large butternut squash, peeled,
  halved lengthwise, seeded and
  cut crosswise into 1-inch slices
16 small fingerling potatoes
2 cups wild rice (about ¾ pound)
4 quarts chicken stock or canned
  low-sodium broth
Salt and freshly ground pepper
½ cup finely chopped cilantro

1. Heat the olive oil in a large pot. Add the carrots, the celery and the coarsely chopped onion and cook over moderate heat, stirring often, until the vegetables are softened but not browned, about 10 minutes. Add the garlic, cumin and oregano and cook, stirring, until fragrant, about 4 minutes.

2. Spoon half of the vegetables into another large pot. Divide the chicken legs and breasts, the squash, potatoes and wild rice between the pots and then pour 2 quarts of the stock into each pot. Season well with salt and pepper. Add enough water to just cover the chicken and vegetables and bring to a boil. Simmer over moderately low heat until the vegetables and rice are tender and the chicken is cooked through, about 1¼ hours. Season the stew with salt and pepper.

3. In a small strainer, rinse the minced onion. Transfer the onion to a kitchen towel and squeeze dry. In a small bowl, combine the onion with the cilantro.

4. Ladle the chicken stew into deep bowls. Sprinkle with the onion-cilantro mixture and serve. —*Trey Foshee*

MAKE AHEAD The stew can be refrigerated for up to 2 days. Prepare the cilantro garnish just before serving.

ONE SERVING Calories 683 kcal, Total Fat 13.6 gm, Saturated Fat 3.7 gm

WINE This hearty stew calls for a full-bodied white—why not make it a Chilean Chardonnay? Try the 1997 Casa Lapostolle or the 1997 Los Vascos.

Asian Chicken Casserole

4 SERVINGS ✺

If you can't find cellophane, or glass, noodles (also known as bean threads) at your supermarket, substitute three cups of cooked jasmine rice.

½ pound skinless, boneless chicken
  breast halves, thinly sliced
  crosswise into strips
1 tablespoon soy sauce
1 teaspoon minced fresh ginger
½ teaspoon dry sherry
½ teaspoon unsulphured molasses
¼ teaspoon Asian sesame oil
2 ounces cellophane noodles
4 ounces Chinese sweet pork
  sausages or Italian pork sausages
3 fresh Thai or serrano chiles,
  thinly sliced
3 tablespoons fish sauce *(nam pla)*
1 tablespoon fresh lime juice
2 tablespoons vegetable oil
2 garlic cloves, lightly crushed
4 ounces shiitake mushrooms,
  stemmed and sliced
4 ounces snow peas (about 1 cup)
½ tablespoon oyster sauce
  (optional)
1 cup chicken stock or canned
  low-sodium broth
1 teaspoon cornstarch dissolved in
  2 tablespoons water
3 tablespoons chopped cilantro

1. In a glass or stainless steel bowl, toss the chicken with the soy sauce, ginger, sherry, molasses and sesame oil; let stand for 15 minutes.

2. Preheat the broiler. Cover the cellophane noodles with hot water and let stand until softened, about 10 minutes. Drain the noodles and cut them into 3-inch lengths.

3. Prick the sausages several times and broil, turning once, for about 5 minutes, or until the Chinese sausages are crisp or the Italian sausages are cooked through. Let the sausages cool slightly and then thinly slice them on the diagonal. In a small bowl, combine the chiles, fish sauce and lime juice.

4. Preheat the oven to 375°. Lightly oil a 3-quart baking dish. Heat the vegetable oil in a large nonstick skillet. Add the garlic and cook over high heat until golden. Add the chicken and stir-fry until opaque. Add the shiitakes, snow peas and oyster sauce and cook until the snow peas turn bright green, about 5 minutes. Add the stock and bring to a boil. Stir the dissolved cornstarch, add it to the skillet and stir-fry until the sauce thickens slightly.

5. Spread the noodles in the prepared baking dish and spoon the chicken mixture and then the sausages on top. Cover with foil and bake for about 8 minutes, or until heated through. Top with the cilantro and serve with the chile sauce. —*Su-Mei Yu*

Curried Chicken Kebabs

4 SERVINGS

1 teaspoon coriander seeds
¾ teaspoon cumin seeds
2 teaspoons Madras curry powder
1 teaspoon turmeric
1 cup unsweetened coconut milk
1 tablespoon olive oil
½ tablespoon rice vinegar
½ tablespoon mirin (sweet rice
  wine)
½ tablespoon honey
Salt and freshly ground pepper

Curried Chicken Kebabs

Hannah's Barbecued Chicken

1½ pounds skinless, boneless chicken breasts, cut into 2-inch chunks

I. In a small skillet, toast the coriander and cumin seeds over moderate heat until fragrant, about 45 seconds. Transfer the seeds to a plate to cool and then grind to a powder in a spice grinder. Meanwhile, soak eight 6-inch wooden skewers in water for at least 1 hour.

2. Put the curry powder and turmeric in the skillet and toast over low heat, stirring, until fragrant, about 20 seconds. In a large bowl, whisk all the spices with the coconut milk, olive oil, vinegar, mirin, honey and a large pinch each of salt and pepper. Add the chicken; toss to coat well. Refrigerate for 1 to 2 hours.

3. Light a grill or heat a lightly oiled grill pan. Loosely thread the chicken onto the skewers and season with salt and pepper. Grill the chicken over a medium-hot fire for about 4 minutes per side, or until nicely browned and just cooked through. Alternatively, cook the chicken in the grill pan over moderate heat for about 4 minutes per side. Serve hot. —*Raphael Lunetta*

BEER These spicy kebabs would best be paired with an easy-to-drink ale, such as Bass or Sierra Nevada.

Hannah's Barbecued Chicken

6 SERVINGS

1 cup light brown sugar
½ cup cider vinegar
¼ cup olive oil
¼ cup fresh lemon juice
6 garlic cloves, smashed
3 tablespoons grainy mustard
2 tablespoons fresh lime juice
2 teaspoons Worcestershire sauce
½ teaspoon finely grated lime zest
12 skinless boneless chicken breast halves (about 6 ounces each), lightly pounded
Salt and freshly ground pepper

I. In a blender, combine the brown sugar, cider vinegar, olive oil, lemon juice, garlic, mustard, lime juice, Worcestershire sauce and lime zest; blend until smooth. Arrange the chicken breasts in a large glass or stainless steel dish and pour the marinade on top. Let stand at room temperature up to 1 hour, turning occasionally.

2. Light a grill or heat a grill pan. Remove the chicken breasts from the marinade. Season the chicken breasts with salt and pepper and grill until they are browned and cooked through, about 3 minutes per side. Serve the barbecued chicken breasts hot or at room temperature. —*Larry Mufson*

Mexican Chicken Breasts with Scotch Bonnet Sauce

8 SERVINGS

Yellow tomatoes add bright juiciness to a potently spicy Scotch bonnet sauce. Use boneless chicken breasts if you can't find boneless breasts with the wing joints attached.

MARINATED CHICKEN

3 dried pasilla chiles (see Note)
2 dried guajillo chiles (see Note)
1 cup boiling water
4 large garlic cloves, halved
1 medium onion, coarsely chopped
3 tablespoons fresh lime juice
2 tablespoons olive oil
Salt

Eight ½-pound boneless chicken breast halves with wing drumettes attached
Freshly ground black pepper

SCOTCH BONNET SAUCE

1 yellow bell pepper
1 large yellow tomato
1 Scotch bonnet or habanero chile, seeded and coarsely chopped
¼ cup vegetable or chicken stock or canned low-sodium chicken broth
2 tablespoons pure olive oil
Salt

I. **MARINATE THE CHICKEN:** In a large bowl, cover the pasilla and guajillo chiles with the boiling water and let stand until softened, about 20 minutes. Stem and seed the chiles and then coarsely chop them. Put the chiles in a blender with the garlic, onion, lime juice, olive oil and ½ teaspoon of salt and blend until smooth.

2. In a large pan, pour the chile marinade over the chicken breasts. Turn to coat completely, and let marinate in the refrigerator for 2 to 4 hours.

3. **MAKE THE SCOTCH BONNET SAUCE:** Light a grill or preheat the broiler. Grill or broil the yellow bell pepper and the tomato, turning, until the skins are charred all over. Transfer the bell pepper and tomato to a bowl, cover

---

menu

Spinach and Serrano Dip (p. 320) with crudites

———

Lobster Cobb Salad (p. 57)

———

Mexican Chicken Breasts with Scotch Bonnet Sauce

Grilled Ratatouille (p. 284)

Chunky Fried Potato Cakes (p. 300)

———

Peach Spice Cake with Caramel Sauce (p. 333)

Mexican Chicken Breasts with Scotch Bonnet Sauce, with Grilled Ratatouille (p. 284) and Chunky Fried Potato Cakes (p. 300).

with plastic wrap and let steam for 5 minutes. Discard the charred skins, stems and seeds and coarsely chop the bell pepper and tomato. Transfer to a blender and add the Scotch bonnet chile, vegetable or chicken stock and olive oil. Blend until smooth and season with salt.

4. Remove the chicken from the marinade and season the breasts with salt and black pepper. Grill or broil over a medium-hot fire for about 8 minutes per side, or until the chicken is lightly charred and just cooked through. Transfer the chicken breasts to plates and serve them with the Scotch bonnet sauce. —*Fred Eric*

NOTE Spicy pasilla chiles and fruity guajillo chiles are available at many supermarkets and by mail order from the Coyote Cafe General Store (800-866-HOWL).

MAKE AHEAD The marinade can be refrigerated for up to 3 days.

Grilled Chicken with Lemon-Herb Sauce

6 SERVINGS

1⅓ cups olive oil
⅓ cup red wine vinegar
3 garlic cloves, smashed
Grated zest of 1 lemon

1 tablespoon crushed red pepper
Six 7-ounce skinless boneless chicken breast halves, scored in a crosshatch pattern
2 tablespoons oregano leaves
2 tablespoons thyme leaves
Kosher salt
⅓ cup fresh lemon juice
Freshly ground black pepper
4 large Idaho potatoes, peeled and cut into 1-inch dice
1 medium onion, coarsely chopped
2 medium tomatoes, chopped

I. In a glass or stainless steel bowl, combine ½ cup of the olive oil with the vinegar, garlic, lemon zest and crushed red pepper. Add the chicken breasts and turn to coat evenly with the marinade. Refrigerate for 1 hour, turning the chicken breasts.

2. In a mortar, crush the oregano, thyme and ½ teaspoon of kosher salt. Stir in the lemon juice and ⅓ cup of the olive oil and season with kosher salt and black pepper.

3. In a large cast-iron skillet, heat the remaining ½ cup of olive oil until shimmering. Add the diced potatoes in an even layer and cook them over moderate heat until browned on the bottom, about 15 minutes; lower the heat halfway through cooking. Stir the potatoes and cook until they are browned all over, about 10 minutes longer. Add the onion and cook over moderate heat, stirring, until beginning to brown. Season the potatoes with kosher salt and black pepper.

4. Light a grill or heat a grill pan. Remove the chicken breasts from the marinade and season with kosher salt and black pepper. Grill the chicken over a moderately hot fire until charred and cooked through, about 5 minutes per side. Transfer to a platter.

5. Warm the potatoes over high heat, stirring, until sizzling. Add the tomatoes

and cook, stirring, for 1 minute. Spoon the lemon-herb sauce over the chicken breasts and serve at once with the potatoes. —*Francis Mallmann*

Grilled Chicken Salad with Buttermilk Dressing

At River Run in Plainfield, Vermont, this dill-infused salad is sometimes prepared with fried chicken instead of grilled. The creamy dressing gets a dash of homemade hot sauce; if you're in Plainfield, you'll want to buy a bottle or two to take with you. Or use Tabasco instead.

6 SERVINGS

⅓ cup mayonnaise
¼ cup buttermilk
2 tablespoons finely chopped dill
2 tablespoons minced yellow onion
1 teaspoon minced garlic
Dash of hot sauce
Salt and freshly ground black pepper
6 boneless, skinless chicken breast halves
Olive oil, for brushing
12 cups mixed torn lettuces, such as red leaf, green leaf, romaine and Bibb
1 red bell pepper, finely chopped
½ medium sweet onion, such as Vidalia or Walla Walla, finely chopped

I. In a small bowl, combine the mayonnaise and the buttermilk until smooth. Add the dill, yellow onion, garlic and hot sauce and season with salt and black pepper.

2. Light a grill or heat a grill pan. Brush the chicken breasts with the olive oil and then season with salt and freshly ground black pepper. Grill the chicken breasts until they are slightly charred and just cooked through, about 4 minutes per side.

3. In a large bowl, combine the mixed lettuces, the red bell pepper and the

Grilled Chicken Salad with Buttermilk Dressing

sweet onion. Toss the salad with all but 2 tablespoons of the buttermilk dressing and transfer to large plates. Slice the chicken breasts and arrange the slices alongside the salad. Drizzle the chicken-breast slices with the remaining buttermilk dressing and serve the salad. —*Jimmy Kennedy*

Flattened Lemon Chicken

4 SERVINGS

Partially freeze the chicken breasts before cutting them into thin slices for this recipe. The job will be much easier than it is with soft meat.

- 3 large skinless, boneless chicken breast halves (about 1½ pounds), partially frozen
- ¼ cup canola oil
- 2 cups dry white wine
- Juice of 1 lemon
- Salt and freshly ground pepper
- 1 bunch watercress, large stems discarded
- 1 large head radicchio, leaves separated
- 2 lemons, thinly sliced crosswise, for garnish

1. Using a sharp knife, thinly slice each chicken-breast half on the diagonal ½ inch thick. Pound the chicken slices between sheets of wax paper until they are ¼ inch thick.

2. Heat 2 tablespoons of the canola oil in a large skillet. Add half of the chicken slices and cook over high heat until barely done, about 1 minute per side; the slices will still be opaque in places. Transfer the cooked chicken slices to a plate and repeat with the rest of the chicken slices, adding more oil to the pan as necessary.

3. Add any remaining oil to the skillet, along with the white wine and the lemon juice. Season the mixture with salt and pepper and bring to a boil over high heat. Return the chicken slices to the skillet and cook, stirring constantly, until the chicken is white throughout, 2 to 3 minutes.

4. Line a platter with the watercress and radicchio. Arrange the chicken-breast slices on top of the watercress and radicchio. Garnish the chicken with the lemon slices and serve immediately. —*Hisachika Takahashi*

WINE The floral fruitiness of a Viognier will frame the flavors of this tangy lemon chicken. Try the 1997 Duboeuf from France or the 1997 Calera Mt. Harlan from California.

Thai Chicken and Jicama Salad

4 SERVINGS ❋

Thai cooking is quick cooking. Once the ingredients are chopped, most of the work is done. To make this salad even easier, use leftover cooked chicken and skip Step 1. Just shred enough of the cooked chicken to make 3 cups.

- 1 tablespoon vegetable oil
- 1½ pounds skinless, boneless chicken breast halves, pounded ½ inch thick
- Salt and freshly ground pepper
- 2 tablespoons fish sauce *(nam pla)*
- 1½ tablespoons light brown sugar
- 1 teaspoon granulated sugar
- ¼ cup fresh lime juice
- 2 fresh Thai or serrano chiles, minced
- 1 garlic clove, minced
- 1 small jicama (about 1 pound), peeled and cut into matchsticks
- 2 large carrots, shredded
- 2 shallots, thinly sliced and separated into rings
- 3 tablespoons chopped cilantro
- 2 tablespoons mint leaves, torn
- ¼ cup roasted unsalted peanuts, coarsely ground

1. Heat the oil in a large skillet. Season the chicken breasts with salt and pepper and cook over high heat until the chicken is golden on both sides and cooked through, about 8 minutes. Let cool and then tear the chicken breasts into thin shreds.

2. Meanwhile, in a saucepan, combine the fish sauce with the brown sugar and

the granulated sugar and cook over low heat, stirring, until dissolved. Let cool; add the lime juice, chiles and garlic.

3. In a medium bowl, combine the chicken, jicama, carrots, shallots, cilantro and mint. Add the dressing and peanuts. Toss gently; serve. —*Su-Mei Yu*

Crisp Chicken with Fennel-Mushroom Salad

4 SERVINGS

A mandoline makes the job of thinly slicing the fennel and mushrooms for this salad much easier. Inexpensive plastic models are available at most kitchenware stores.

- 2 fennel bulbs—halved, cored and sliced paper-thin crosswise, feathery tops finely chopped
- ½ pound cremini mushrooms, sliced paper-thin lengthwise
- ½ cup (tightly packed) flat-leaf parsley leaves
- 2 tablespoons snipped chives
- 3 tablespoons fresh lemon juice
- ¼ cup extra-virgin olive oil
- Kosher salt and freshly ground pepper
- 4 medium boneless chicken breast halves
- 1 tablespoon fennel seeds, coarsely ground
- 1 cup shaved Parmesan cheese (from a 2-ounce chunk)

1. In a large bowl, toss the fennel with the mushrooms, parsley, chives, lemon juice and 3 tablespoons of the olive oil. Season the fennel salad with kosher salt and freshly ground pepper.

2. Heat the remaining 1 tablespoon of oil in a large cast-iron skillet. Season the chicken breasts on both sides with the fennel seeds and kosher salt and pepper and add them to the skillet, skin side down. Cook the chicken over moderate heat, turning once, until golden, crisp and cooked through, about 15 minutes.

3. Transfer the cooked chicken breasts to plates and then mound the fennel

Crisp Chicken with Fennel-Mushroom Salad

salad alongside. Scatter the Parmesan shavings over the salad and serve immediately. —*Seen Lippert*

WINE The mushrooms and the fennel in this recipe point to a wine that also has earthy flavors and hints of licorice: Chianti Classico. Two great choices are the 1997 Isole e Olena and the 1997 Lilliano.

Burn-Your-Fingers Chicken Wings

12 SERVINGS

The wings need to marinate overnight before roasting, so plan accordingly.

- 14 scallions, coarsely chopped
- 14 garlic cloves, coarsely chopped
- ¾ cup chopped, peeled fresh ginger
- 10 anchovy fillets, coarsely chopped
- 3 tablespoons crushed red pepper
- ¾ cup light brown sugar
- ¼ cup plus 2 tablespoons soy sauce
- 1 tablespoon vegetable oil
- 2 teaspoons freshly ground black pepper
- 2 teaspoons kosher salt
- 1 cup pineapple juice
- 14 pounds chicken wings

1. In a food processor, blend the scallions with the garlic, ginger, anchovies and crushed red pepper. Add the brown sugar, soy sauce, oil, black pepper and salt; blend. Add the pineapple juice.

pepper lexicon

Ground and whole peppercorns come in various colors, and all but the pink type are from the same perennial plant, *Piper nigrum*.

Green peppercorns are the unripe berries, which are sold pickled or freeze-dried but rarely fresh.

Black peppercorns are the dried form of the green, unripe berries.

White peppercorns are made by soaking ripened (red) peppercorns until the skin peels off.

Pink peppercorns are the dried and only slightly spicy berries of the *Schinus molle* plant.

2. Make small slashes on the meaty parts of the chicken wings. Spread the wings in 2 very large roasting pans and pour the marinade on top. Rub the marinade into the wings. Cover and refrigerate overnight. Bring to room temperature before roasting.

3. Preheat the oven to 500°. Arrange the wings in a single layer on large, oiled, rimmed baking sheets; pour any remaining marinade on top. Roast the wings on as many shelves as possible, rotating the pans, for 1 hour, or until the wings are deeply browned and crisp. Serve piping hot. —*Marcia Kiesel*

WINE Try a light, fruity Viognier, such as the 1997 McDowell from California or the 1997 Georges Duboeuf Vin de Pays de l'Ardèche from France, for a refreshing contrast to the zing of these wings.

Black Pepper Chicken Curry

4 SERVINGS

In this rich South Indian curry, the sweetness of the fried cashews complements the heat of the pepper.

- 2 teaspoons ground coriander
- 2 teaspoons ground cumin
- 1½ teaspoons coarsely crushed black peppercorns

Burn-Your-Fingers Chicken Wings

Black Pepper Chicken Curry

½ teaspoon turmeric

1 teaspoon salt

1¾ pounds skinless, boneless
chicken thighs, cut into 1½-inch
pieces

¼ cup plus 2 tablespoons
vegetable oil

2 medium onions, thinly sliced

1 large garlic clove, minced

1½ teaspoons minced fresh ginger

1 teaspoon minced serrano or
Thai chile

¾ cup canned unsweetened
coconut milk

¼ cup water

½ cup broken raw cashews

1 teaspoon fresh lemon juice

I. In a bowl, combine the coriander
with the cumin, peppercorns, turmeric
and ¼ teaspoon of the salt. Add the
chicken and rub with the spices to coat.
Cover with plastic wrap and let stand at
room temperature for 20 to 30 minutes.

2. In a large deep nonstick skillet, heat
¼ cup of the oil. Add the onions and
cook over moderately high heat, stirring
occasionally, until golden, about 8 minutes. Add the chicken, garlic, ginger,
serrano chile and the remaining ¾ teaspoon of salt and cook, stirring occasionally, until the chicken is golden
brown and just cooked through, about
10 minutes. Stir in ¼ cup of the coconut
milk and the water and then cover and
cook over low heat for 20 minutes.

3. Meanwhile, in a small skillet, heat the
remaining 2 tablespoons of oil. Add the
cashews and cook over moderate heat,
stirring constantly, until golden brown,
4 to 5 minutes. Drain on paper towels.

4. Add the remaining ½ cup of coconut
milk and the lemon juice to the chick-
en and simmer, stirring. Transfer to a
bowl, sprinkle with the cashews and
serve hot. —Maya Kaimal

SERVE WITH Steamed rice

WINE Choose an aromatic, fruity (but
not sugary) white—perhaps a Riesling,
such as the 1997 Chateau Ste. Michelle
Vineyard Select from Washington State.

Enchilada Stacks with Chicken-and-White-Bean Stew

6 SERVINGS

Allow time for the beans to soak overnight for this hearty stew.

STEW

½ pound dried white beans (about
1 cup), such as Great Northern

1½ cups chicken stock or canned
low-sodium broth

1½ cups water

½ cup chopped sweet onion

½ tablespoon minced garlic, plus
7 unpeeled whole cloves

1 bay leaf

¾ teaspoon dried oregano,
crumbled

½ teaspoon dried thyme

½ teaspoon cumin seeds

1 ancho chile, stemmed and
seeded

Salt

2 cups shredded roasted chicken
(about ¾ pound)

Freshly ground pepper

ENCHILADAS

1 large poblano chile

¼ cup plus 1 tablespoon
vegetable oil

1 cup coarsely chopped sweet
onion

12 corn tortillas

About ½ pound shredded sharp
Cheddar cheese (2½ cups)

I. MAKE THE STEW: In a bowl, soak
the beans in cold water overnight. Drain
the beans and put them in a saucepan.
Add the stock, water, onion, minced
garlic, bay leaf, oregano and thyme.

2. Heat a small skillet. Add the cumin
seeds and toast over low heat just until
fragrant, about 2 minutes. Transfer to
a spice grinder or mortar and crush to a
coarse powder; add to the beans. Add
the ancho to the skillet and toast until
softened and fragrant, about 30 seconds per side. Cut the chile into 4-inch
pieces and add to the beans. Cover partially and simmer until the beans are
tender but not mushy, about 1½ hours.

Season with salt about 10 minutes before the beans are done. Pick out and
discard the bay leaf and chile pieces.

3. Toast the unpeeled garlic in the skillet over moderate heat, turning, until
softened and blackened in spots, about
12 minutes. Peel and mince the garlic
and then stir it into the beans. Stir in
the shredded chicken; season with salt
and pepper. Cook until heated through;
keep warm.

4. MAKE THE ENCHILADAS: Roast
the poblano over a gas flame or under
the broiler until charred all over. Transfer the chile to a bowl, cover and let
cool. Peel, seed and chop the chile.

5. Preheat the oven to 350°. Heat 1
tablespoon of the oil in a skillet. Add the
onion and poblano and cook over high
heat until the onion is translucent,
about 2 minutes. Transfer to a bowl.
Heat the remaining ¼ cup of oil in the
skillet until shimmering. Using tongs,
dip both sides of a tortilla into the hot
oil just until softened, about 10 seconds. Pat dry with paper towels and set

Enchilada Stacks with
Chicken-and-White-Bean Stew

the tortilla on a work surface. Repeat with the remaining tortillas.

6. Arrange 6 of the tortillas on a large baking sheet and top with the onion mixture and half of the cheese. Cover with the remaining 6 tortillas and sprinkle with the remaining cheese. Bake for about 10 minutes, or until the cheese is melted. Transfer the enchiladas to large plates, top them with the hot stew and serve. —*Lisa Ahier*

BEER A chilled Texas beer, such as Lone Star, is all that's required in the supporting role here.

Skillet Paella

4 SERVINGS ✳

A specialty at Jimmy's Bronx Café in New York City, this excellent classic pasta with chicken, clams and chorizo is surprisingly quick to make.

8 chicken drumsticks
Kosher salt and freshly ground black
**   pepper**
2 tablespoons pure olive oil
1 small onion, coarsely chopped
1 red bell pepper, coarsely chopped
2 garlic cloves, minced
Large pinch of saffron threads
Large pinch of cayenne pepper
1¼ cups Valencia or other medium-
**   grain rice (about 9 ounces)**
4 ounces chorizo sausage, sliced
**   crosswise ½ inch thick**
½ cup drained chopped canned
**   tomatoes**
2½ cups chicken stock or canned
**   low-sodium broth**
½ cup frozen peas
16 littleneck clams, scrubbed
1 large scallion, thinly sliced

I. Preheat the oven to 350°. Season the chicken with kosher salt and black pepper. Heat the oil in a large ovenproof skillet. Add the drumsticks; cook over moderately high heat until browned all over, about 8 minutes. Transfer to a plate.
2. Add the onion and the red bell pepper to the skillet and cook over moderately low heat until softened, about 5 minutes.

Add the garlic, saffron and cayenne and cook, stirring, until fragrant, about 2 minutes. Add the rice and stir until lightly toasted, about 3 minutes. Add the chorizo and tomatoes and cook, stirring, for 2 minutes. Stir in the stock and simmer over moderately high heat until the liquid has slightly reduced, about 4 minutes. Stir in 1 teaspoon kosher salt and season with black pepper.
3. Nestle the chicken in the rice and cover tightly with foil. Bake in the center of the oven for 30 minutes. Turn the oven up to 450°. Scatter the peas over the paella and arrange the clams, hinge down, on top. Cover with foil and bake for about 8 minutes, or until the clams are open and the chicken is cooked through. Loosen the foil and let the paella stand for a few minutes. Garnish with the scallion and serve. —*Luis Rivera*

Chicken with Spiced Yogurt Marinade

8 SERVINGS

The tangy marinade contrasts the perfume of saffron with the piquancy of lemon juice and garlic. Popular in Central Asia (especially Iran and Afghanistan), it works particularly well with lamb and chicken.

2 cups plain whole milk yogurt
2 tablespoons fresh lemon juice
4 garlic cloves, minced
1 medium onion, minced
2 teaspoons ground coriander
1 teaspoon ground cumin
2 teaspoons kosher salt
1 teaspoon freshly ground pepper
½ teaspoon (lightly packed)
**   saffron threads, crumbled**
½ teaspoon cinnamon
Two 3½-pound chickens, each cut
**   into 8 pieces**

I. In a bowl, combine the yogurt, lemon juice, garlic, onion, coriander, cumin, kosher salt, pepper, saffron and cinnamon. Stir well to blend.
2. Place the chicken pieces in a large glass or ceramic dish; pour the yogurt

marinade on top and let the chicken pieces marinate for at least 4 hours or overnight.
3. Light a grill. Cook the chicken pieces over a medium-hot fire, turning often, until lightly charred on both sides and just cooked through, about 10 minutes per side. —*Steven Raichlen*

VARIATION To use this marinade for lamb, simply substitute 1 whole butterflied leg of lamb (4 pounds) for the chicken pieces.

WINE The yogurt marinade adds tang to the grilled chicken. Showcase the flavors with a round, ripe California Chardonnay, such as the 1997 Groth or the 1997 Cakebread.

Parmesan Chicken with Balsamic Butter Sauce

4 SERVINGS ✳

Grated Parmesan cheese gives roasted chicken a lovely crisp crust without the trouble of frying.

One 3-pound chicken, cut into
**   8 pieces**
¼ cup extra-virgin olive oil
¼ cup freshly grated Parmesan
**   cheese**
2 tablespoons minced oregano
2 garlic cloves, minced
Salt and freshly ground pepper
1 cup chicken stock or canned
**   low-sodium broth**
½ cup balsamic vinegar
2 tablespoons cold unsalted butter

I. Preheat the oven to 400°. In a large bowl, toss the chicken pieces with the olive oil, Parmesan, oregano and garlic. Arrange the chicken pieces, skin side up, on a large rimmed baking sheet and season with salt and pepper. Bake the chicken pieces for about 45 minutes, or until they are lightly browned and just cooked through.
2. Meanwhile, in a small saucepan, combine the chicken stock and balsamic vinegar and boil over high heat until reduced to ⅓ cup, about 10 minutes. Remove from the heat. Whisk in

the butter, 1 tablespoon at a time, until smooth. Season the sauce with salt and pepper. Transfer the chicken pieces to plates, spoon the sauce on top and serve. —*Anthony Roselli*

SERVE WITH Sautéed spinach or steamed broccoli and roasted potatoes.

New Orleans Fried Chicken

4 SERVINGS

In New Orleans, a place where frying is a fetish, Jacques-Imo's can't be beat—although only locals seem to know about it. A few doors down from the city's coolest music venue, the Maple Leaf, this three-year-old restaurant is packed every night, but no one minds the squeeze. Credit the crispy, tender fried chicken, which comes with juicy bits of dill pickle on top that add a fabulous kick to each bite.

- 1½ cups peanut oil, for frying
- One 12-ounce can evaporated milk
- 1 cup water
- 1 large egg, lightly beaten
- Salt and freshly ground white pepper
- One 3- to 3½-pound chicken—rinsed, patted dry and cut into 8 pieces
- ½ cup all-purpose flour
- ½ cup chopped dill pickles
- ¼ cup chopped flat-leaf parsley

1. In a large, heavy skillet, heat the oil to 350°. In a bowl, whisk together the evaporated milk, water and egg and season the mixture generously with salt and white pepper.

2. Season the chicken pieces with salt and white pepper and dip each piece in the milk mixture and then in the flour. Add the chicken pieces to the skillet and cook over moderate heat, turning often, until they are golden and cooked through, about 25 minutes; lower the heat so that the chicken doesn't brown too quickly. Transfer the chicken pieces to a rack to drain and then arrange on a platter. Sprinkle with the pickles and parsley and serve. —*Jacques-Imo's*

Almond-Sesame Fried Chicken

4 SERVINGS

A brown-sugar marinade makes this sesame-coated chicken slightly sweet. You'll need to plan ahead; the chicken needs to marinate overnight.

- ¼ cup fresh lime juice
- ¼ cup light brown sugar
- 2 tablespoons white wine vinegar
- 2 tablespoons soy sauce
- 2 garlic cloves, minced
- 1 tablespoon mashed chipotle chile in *adobo* sauce
- ½ teaspoon dry mustard
- Salt and freshly ground black pepper
- One 4-pound chicken, cut into 8 pieces
- 1½ cups blanched almonds (about 5 ounces)
- 1½ cups all-purpose flour
- 1 cup fine dry bread crumbs
- ⅓ cup sesame seeds
- ½ teaspoon cayenne pepper
- 4 large eggs
- 4 tablespoons unsalted butter
- 1 cup vegetable oil

1. In a glass or ceramic baking dish, combine the lime juice, brown sugar, white wine vinegar, soy sauce, garlic, chipotle chile and dry mustard and season with ¾ teaspoon of salt and ½ teaspoon of black pepper. Add the chicken pieces to the marinade and turn to coat. Cover the chicken and refrigerate overnight.

2. In a food processor, pulse the almonds until finely ground. Transfer to a large paper bag and add 1 cup of the flour, the bread crumbs, sesame seeds and cayenne; shake well. Put the remaining ½ cup of flour in a separate paper bag. In a shallow bowl, beat the eggs with 1 teaspoon salt.

3. Drain the chicken pieces and pat dry. Working in batches, put the chicken pieces in the bag with the flour and shake. Dip the floured chicken pieces in the beaten eggs and add them to the bag with the almond crumb coating; shake to coat.

Parmesan Chicken with Balsamic Butter Sauce

4. In each of 2 medium cast-iron skillets, melt 2 tablespoons of the butter in ½ cup of the vegetable oil. Add the chicken pieces and cook over moderately low heat, turning once or twice, until the chicken is golden brown and cooked through, about 10 minutes. Transfer the fried chicken to paper towels to drain. Serve hot. —*Lisa Ahier*

Grilled Chicken with Sweet Mustard Barbecue Sauce

8 SERVINGS

A sweet mustard glaze gives this grilled chicken from City Grocery in Oxford, Mississippi, a crisp coating—but the juicy marinated birds are also delicious without the glaze. The chickens need to marinate overnight so plan accordingly.

- ¾ cup unsulphured molasses
- ½ cup pure olive oil
- ½ cup ruby port
- 2 tablespoons Dijon mustard
- 2 tablespoons soy sauce
- 2 tablespoons freshly ground pepper
- 1 tablespoon Worcestershire sauce

Grilled Chicken with Sweet Mustard Barbecue Sauce

1 shallot, minced
Four 3-pound chickens, backbones
removed and chickens cut into
quarters
Sweet Mustard Barbecue Sauce
(recipe follows)

I. In a large bowl, stir together the molasses, olive oil, port, mustard, soy sauce, pepper, Worcestershire sauce and shallot. Let the marinade stand at room temperature for 30 minutes. Add the chicken quarters to the marinade and turn to coat. Refrigerate the chicken overnight.

2. Light a grill or preheat the broiler. Remove the chicken quarters from the marinade and arrange the pieces on large rimmed baking sheets. Brush the chicken quarters with the Sweet Mustard Barbecue Sauce and grill them over a medium-hot fire or broil them 12 inches from the heat, turning often and rotating to cook evenly, until the chicken is cooked through and nicely glazed, 8 to 10 minutes per side. Serve the grilled chicken quarters hot or at room temperature. —*John Currence*

SWEET MUSTARD BARBECUE SAUCE

MAKES ABOUT 2 CUPS

Sweet and pungent, this mustard sauce is also perfect on pork chops.

2 cups yellow mustard
¾ cup light brown sugar
¼ cup strong brewed coffee
2 tablespoons honey
1 tablespoon unsulphured
   molasses
1 tablespoon liquid smoke
   (optional)
2 teaspoons Worcestershire sauce
2 teaspoons Tabasco sauce

In a medium saucepan, combine all of the ingredients and bring to a simmer over moderate heat. Stir well and remove from the heat. Let the sauce cool to room temperature and then spoon into a glass jar and refrigerate until ready to use. —*J. C.*

MAKE AHEAD The sauce can be refrigerated for up to 1 month.

Devil's Chicken with Mustard and Bread Crumbs

4 SERVINGS ♔

This organic chicken dish is a one-pot meal. You can ask your butcher to split the chickens, remove the backbones, trim the wings to the second joint and debone the breasts and thighs. But don't waste the bones; take them home and use them to make stock.

½ cup extra-virgin olive oil
½ cup dry vermouth
½ small yellow onion, thinly sliced,
   plus 2 medium yellow onions
3 thyme sprigs plus 1 tablespoon
   thyme leaves
2 small dried red chiles, crushed
Two 3-pound organic chickens,
   split and semi-boned (see above)
2 medium red onions
2 medium leeks, white and tender
   green parts only
1 pound large Yukon Gold potatoes
Salt and freshly ground pepper
3 tablespoons unsalted butter
2 tablespoons minced shallots
¼ cup Dijon mustard
1 teaspoon finely chopped tarragon
1 cup coarse fresh bread crumbs
1 tablespoon minced parsley
½ cup chicken stock or canned
   low-sodium broth

I. In a large glass dish, combine ¼ cup of the olive oil with ¼ cup of the vermouth, the sliced onion, thyme sprigs and chiles. Add the chicken halves and turn to coat. Cover the chicken and refrigerate for 5 hours.

2. Trim and peel the 2 yellow and 2 red onions, keeping the root ends intact. Cut each onion into 8 wedges. Trim the leeks, keeping the root ends intact, and cut each one lengthwise into sixths.

3. Steam the potatoes over boiling water until still slightly firm, about 10 minutes. Let cool slightly and then peel and cut each one lengthwise into 6 wedges.

4. Preheat the oven to 450°. Heat 2 tablespoons of olive oil in each of 2 large skillets. Add the potatoes to 1 skillet and the onions and leeks to the other; cook over moderately high heat, turning, until golden, 6 to 8 minutes. Transfer the vegetables to a roasting pan. Sprinkle with salt, pepper and 2½ teaspoons of thyme.

5. Return the skillets to moderately high heat and scrape the marinade off the chickens. Add them to the skillets, skin side down, and cook over moderately high heat until the skin is deep golden and crisp, about 5 minutes. Set the chickens on the vegetables, skin side up, and season with salt and pepper.

6. Melt 1 tablespoon of the butter in a small skillet. Add the shallots and cook over moderately high heat until translucent. Add the remaining ¼ cup of vermouth and cook until reduced by half. Remove from the heat and stir in the mustard, tarragon and the remaining ½ teaspoon of thyme. Slather the chickens with this mixture.

7. In a small skillet, melt the remaining 2 tablespoons of butter. Add the bread crumbs and parsley. Season with salt

Devil's Chicken with Mustard and Bread Crumbs

Double-Boiled Chicken

4 soup bowls. Pour the juices on top of the chicken along with the dates. Serve with small bowls of soy sauce, for dipping. —*Eileen Yin-Fei Lo*

ONE SERVING Calories 320 kcal, Total Fat 15 gm, Saturated Fat 4 gm

Roasted Chicken with Bay Leaves

4 SERVINGS

Bruising fresh bay leaves by holding both ends of each leaf and twisting in opposite directions brings out their full flavor. If fresh bay leaves are unavailable, use sprigs of thyme or marjoram.

Two 3-pound chickens, preferably free range

24 fresh bay leaves, bruised, plus bay branches, for garnish

4 garlic cloves, thinly sliced

3 tablespoons olive oil

Salt and freshly ground pepper

1. Preheat the oven to 450°. Bend back the chicken wing tips and tuck them under their first joints. Using your fingertips, carefully loosen the chicken skin: begin at the bottom of the breast and, without tearing the skin, work your hand under it all the way up the breast and down into the thighs on each side of the chicken.

2. Insert 2 bay leaves in the cavity of each bird. Tuck the remaining leaves under the loosened skin, 2 on each thigh and 3 on each side of each breast. Distribute the garlic slices evenly under the skin. Tie the legs of each chicken together with string.

3. Set the chickens in a large shallow roasting pan. Rub them all over with the olive oil and season generously with salt and freshly ground pepper. Roast the chickens for 55 to 65 minutes, rotating the pan halfway through, until the chickens are browned and the juices run clear.

4. Remove the roasted chickens from the oven and let them stand in a warm place for 10 minutes. Transfer the chickens to a platter and garnish with the bay

and pepper; toss to combine. Spoon the crumbs over the chicken and add the stock to the roasting pan. Roast the chicken in the oven for about 25 minutes, or until the crumbs are golden and the chicken is cooked through. Serve at once. —*Suzanne Goin*

MAKE AHEAD The recipe can be prepared through Step 2 up to 1 day ahead. Refrigerate the chicken and the topping mixture separately.

WINE The onions, shallots and leeks in this hearty chicken dish find a flavor echo in a fruity, low-tannin Pinot Noir. Try a California bottling, such as the 1996 Wild Horse Central Coast or the 1996 Charles Krug Carneros.

Double-Boiled Chicken

4 SERVINGS

In China this dish is made with black chicken, a special breed. The chicken is steamed in its own juices for about four hours, until it's falling-off-the-bone tender. Boxthorn seeds—small, red mini-oval berries—add a lovely red color.

One 3½-pound free-range chicken— visible fat removed, gizzard and neck reserved

¼ cup salt

8 dates

2 tablespoons boxthorn seeds (optional)

Soy sauce, for dipping

1. Set a cake rack in a large stockpot, add 3 inches of water and bring to a boil. Rub the chicken all over with the salt and then rinse well. Put the chicken, breast side up, in a large heatproof bowl and add the gizzard, neck, dates and boxthorn seeds. Set a heatproof plate on top of the bowl to seal it, and then carefully set the bowl on the cake rack in the stockpot. Cover the stockpot and boil over high heat until the chicken is very tender, about 4 hours; replenish the stockpot as necessary with boiling water.

2. Carefully remove the bowl with the chicken from the stockpot. Using a fork, pull the chicken from the bones and remove the skin; place the chicken in

Roasted Chicken with Bay Leaves

Chicken and Duck Potpie

branches. Remove and discard the bay leaves from under the skin before carving the chickens. —*Jerry Traunfeld*

WINE A medium-bodied red, like Chianti, is the best match for this aromatic chicken. Consider the 1995 Antinori Pèppoli Chianti Classico or the 1995 Frescobaldi Nipozzano Chianti Rufina Riserva.

Chicken Baked in Wild Grasses
8 SERVINGS

Wild grasses mixed with herbs flavor the chicken and keep it moist. You can use parsley and chives instead.

One 8-pound roasting chicken
Salt and freshly ground pepper
- 2 cups (loosely packed) rye grass or clover
- 2 cups mixed herbs, such as mint, sage and thyme, preferably wild
- 4 large romaine lettuce leaves
- 2 carrots, coarsely chopped
- 2 parsnips, coarsely chopped
- 2 celery ribs, coarsely chopped
- 1 medium onion, coarsely chopped
- 1 tablespoon canola oil
- ½ cup dried sour cherries (about 2 ounces)
- 1 cup unsweetened cherry juice or apple cider
- 1 cup chicken stock or canned low-sodium broth
- ½ cup bourbon

1. Preheat the oven to 350°. Season the chicken inside and out with salt and pepper. Fold the wing tips under the chicken. Pack the grass and herbs over the breast and drumsticks of the chicken and cover with the lettuce leaves. Starting behind the wings, crisscross cotton kitchen string over the lettuce and around the legs of the chicken to secure the aromatics.

2. In a flameproof roasting pan, combine the carrots, parsnips, celery and onion. Add the oil and toss well. Set the chicken, breast side up, on the vegetables and roast for about 3½ hours, or until the inner thigh juices run clear.

Transfer the chicken to a carving board and let rest for 10 minutes.

3. Meanwhile, in a medium saucepan, combine the cherries and cherry juice and boil until almost all of the liquid has evaporated, about 10 minutes. In a small saucepan, boil the stock over high heat until reduced by half, about 5 minutes. Add the reduced stock to the dried cherries.

4. Strain the chicken pan juices into a glass measuring cup. Set the roasting pan over 2 burners. Add the bourbon and simmer over moderately low heat, scraping up the brown bits, until the bourbon has reduced to 2 tablespoons, about 3 minutes. Skim the fat from the chicken pan juices and add the juices to the cherry sauce. Simmer for 5 minutes and season with salt and pepper.

5. Cut the string from the chicken and discard the lettuce, grass and herbs; leave any herbs that stick to the skin. Carve the chicken and arrange on a platter. Pass the cherry sauce at the table. —*Kerry Sear*

WINE The infusion of herbs and grass into the meat makes this a perfect candidate for a Washington State Syrah. Try the 1997 McCrea Cellars Boushey Vineyard or the 1996 Columbia Red Willow.

Five-Spice Roasted Chicken
4 SERVINGS

- 2 tablespoons canola oil
- 1 tablespoon minced garlic
- 1½ teaspoons five-spice powder
One 4-pound chicken, rinsed and dried
Salt and freshly ground pepper

1. Preheat the oven to 550°. In a small bowl, combine the oil with the garlic and five-spice powder; rub all over the chicken. Set the bird in a roasting pan and season with salt and pepper.

2. Bake the chicken for about 15 minutes, or until the skin is browned. Reduce the oven temperature to 325°, cover the chicken loosely with foil and cook until the juices run clear when the thigh of the chicken is pierced with a

fork, about 1 hour. Let the chicken cool slightly and then carve it into 8 pieces and serve. —*Ming Tsai*

MAKE AHEAD The roasted chicken can be refrigerated overnight. Return to room temperature before serving.

Chicken and Duck Potpie
8 SERVINGS

The small college town of Oxford, in the hills of north Mississippi, is one of the capitals of southern literature. It's also home to the popular City Grocery restaurant, where this sumptuous potpie, made with both chicken and duck, epitomizes comfort.

- 8 medium carrots, cut into ½-inch pieces
- 3 medium onions, coarsely chopped
- 1 pound small red potatoes, quartered
- 1 pound assorted mushrooms, such as cremini and stemmed shiitakes, sliced ½ inch thick
- 12 garlic cloves, thinly sliced
- 1 tablespoon dried thyme
- ¼ cup olive oil
- 7 cups chicken stock or canned low-sodium broth
Two 3½-pound chickens
One 5-pound duck
Salt and freshly ground pepper
- 4 tablespoons unsalted butter
- ½ cup plus 2 tablespoons all-purpose flour
- 1 pound all-butter puff pastry dough, chilled
- 1 large egg, beaten with 1 tablespoon of water

1. Preheat the oven to 375°. In a large flameproof roasting pan, combine the carrots, onions, potatoes, mushrooms, garlic, thyme and olive oil and toss well. Spread the vegetables in an even layer and add 4 cups of the stock. Set the pan over 2 burners and bring to a boil over moderately high heat.

2. Meanwhile, season the chickens and the duck inside and out with salt and

pepper. Set the chickens, breast side up, on the vegetables. Set the duck on a rack in another roasting pan. Roast for about 2 hours, or until the chickens and duck are just cooked through and the vegetables are tender. Transfer the chickens and duck to a carving board and let cool slightly.

3. Discard the skin from the chickens and duck, remove the meat and cut it into 2-inch pieces. Strain the chicken pan juices, reserving the vegetables. Skim the fat from the juices.

4. Melt the butter in a medium saucepan. Stir in the flour and cook over moderate heat until bubbling, about 1 minute. Gradually whisk in 1 cup of the pan juices and then whisk in the remaining pan juices and 3 cups of stock. Bring to a boil and simmer over moderately low heat, whisking often, until no floury taste remains, about 12 minutes. Transfer the sauce to a large saucepan and add the reserved vegetables and the chicken and duck meat.

5. Preheat the oven to 450°. On a lightly floured surface, roll out half of the puff pastry ⅛ inch thick. Using a 7-inch bowl, cut out 4 rounds. Repeat with the remaining puff pastry. Spoon the chicken and duck stew into eight 2- to 3-cup ovenproof bowls, about 6 inches wide. Set a puff pastry round on each bowl and press the pastry around the rim to seal. Brush the pastry with the beaten egg and arrange the bowls on a large baking sheet. Bake the potpies for about 25 minutes, or until the pastry is puffed and deeply browned. Serve the potpies at once. —*John Currence*

MAKE AHEAD The potpie recipe can be prepared through Step 4 and refrigerated for up to 3 days.

WINE The duck and the mushrooms call for a wine of equal finesse—one that's aromatic, with medium body and a great deal of flavor, like the 1997 Eyrie Vineyards Pinot Noir and the 1996 Domaine Robert Arnoux Bourgogne Rouge Pinot Noir.

Duck Breasts with Artichoke Hearts and Balsamic Syrup

4 SERVINGS

The use of sweet balsamic vinegar and earthy artichokes in this dish recalls the traditional Jewish cooking of Spain, Morocco and the republic of Georgia.

- 1 cup balsamic vinegar
- 4 large artichokes
- 1 lemon, halved
- 1 quart water
- 2 tablespoons all-purpose flour

Salt

- ¼ cup extra-virgin olive oil, plus more for drizzling
- 1 tablespoon finely chopped shallot
- 1 tablespoon finely chopped garlic

Four 6-ounce boneless duck breast halves, skin trimmed

Freshly ground pepper

1. In a medium saucepan, boil the balsamic vinegar over moderate heat until reduced to ¼ cup, about 12 minutes. Remove from the heat and let cool.

2. Working with 1 of the artichokes at a time, snap off the outer leaves. Using a sharp knife, cut off the leaves flush with the base and trim the base and stem. Using a spoon or a melon baller, scoop out the furry choke. Rub the artichoke bottom all over with 1 lemon half and add it to a bowl of water.

3. In a medium saucepan, combine the quart of water with the flour and 1 teaspoon of salt. Squeeze in the juice from

Duck Breasts with Artichoke Hearts and Balsamic Syrup

the remaining lemon half and bring to a boil. Drain the artichokes. Add them to the saucepan and simmer over moderate heat until just tender, about 12 minutes. Transfer the artichokes to a plate, let cool slightly and then cut each one into 6 wedges.

4. In a large skillet, heat the ¼ cup of olive oil. Add the artichokes; cook over moderate heat until browned, about 3 minutes. Turn the artichokes, add the shallot and garlic and season with salt. Cook until browned on the other side, stir well and transfer to a plate.

5. Wipe out the skillet and set it over moderate heat. Season the duck with salt and pepper and add to the skillet, skin side down. Cook until the skin is deep brown and crisp, about 5 minutes. Turn and cook until browned on the bottom and medium rare, about 3 minutes longer. Transfer the duck to a cutting board and let rest for 5 minutes.

6. Slice the duck breasts crosswise 1 inch thick; arrange on plates. Mound the artichokes alongside. Drizzle some balsamic syrup and olive oil around the plates and serve. —*Stephen Kalt*

MAKE AHEAD The artichokes can be prepared through Step 3 and refrigerated for up to 1 day.

WINE Meaty duck breasts pair well with full-bodied wines that have some tannin, such as a Tempranillo from Spain, a spicy California Zinfandel or a rosé made from Cabernet Franc.

Duck Breasts with Thyme-Infused Honey

4 SERVINGS

This recipe showcases duck's affinity for sweet, pungent sauces. The duck breasts are lightly cured with salt and sugar before being seared. A quick pan sauce made with thyme-infused honey and balsamic vinegar enhances the meaty flavor of the duck.

1¼ **teaspoons kosher salt**
½ **teaspoon black peppercorns**
¼ **teaspoon sugar**

Four ½-pound boneless Pekin duck
  breast halves, skinned (see Note)
3 **tablespoons lime blossom, thyme**
  or wildflower honey
1 **tablespoon thyme leaves and**
  flowers, plus sprigs for garnish
1 **teaspoon duck fat or olive oil**
¼ **cup veal demiglace or very**
  concentrated chicken broth
  (see Note)
3 **tablespoons balsamic vinegar**
2 **teaspoons cold unsalted butter**

1. In a mortar or spice grinder, combine the kosher salt, peppercorns and sugar and grind to a coarse powder. Rub the spice mixture evenly over the duck breasts and transfer to a plate. Cover with plastic wrap and refrigerate for at least 4 hours or overnight. Bring the duck to room temperature and pat dry with paper towels before cooking.

2. In a small saucepan, combine the honey and thyme leaves and flowers. Bring just to a simmer over low heat, crushing the leaves with the back of a spoon. Set aside 5 minutes to infuse.

3. Heat the duck fat in a large heavy skillet until shimmering. Add the duck breasts and cook over high heat until nicely browned, 2 to 3 minutes per side. Brush each duck breast with some of the thyme-infused honey and cook until lightly caramelized, about 10 seconds per side. Transfer the breasts to a work surface and let rest for 5 minutes.

4. Add the demiglace, vinegar and the remaining infused honey to the skillet; bring to a boil, scraping up any brown bits from the bottom of the pan. Simmer over moderate heat until slightly thickened, about 2 minutes. Stir in the butter. Strain the sauce into a bowl and add any accumulated duck juices. Thinly slice the duck breasts and arrange on warmed plates. Drizzle the sauce over the duck, top with the thyme sprigs and serve. —*Sally Schneider*

NOTE Boneless Pekin duck breasts are available at some supermarkets and specialty food shops, or they can

how to pan-smoke

Line a ten-inch cast-iron skillet with foil. Tear a one-and-a-half-inch hole out of the center of the foil so that the tinder will lie directly on the pan bottom. Line the skillet lid with foil to facilitate cleanup. Heat the pan until it is very hot.

Add the tinder to the skillet. Try aromatic wood chips; alder, apple and cherry make sweet, mellow smoke, as do grapevines. Buy unsprayed grapevine wreaths for a few dollars at a florist or garden shop and break off pieces as you need them. Pliable ancho chiles, surprisingly, also create smoke that imparts a sweet, subtle flavor.

Smoke foods on a round wire cake rack with one-inch feet; if you don't have a footed rack, roll foil into five tight one-inch balls and place them under the edge of the rack. Cover tightly and smoke.

be mail ordered from Culver Duck Farms (800-825-9225). Veal demiglace, a concentrated veal stock, is available frozen at fine supermarkets and specialty food shops. It keeps indefinitely and is great to have on hand to give instant body and richness to quick pan sauces.

WINE Duck meat definitely calls for red wine, but when the duck is given a sweet, spicy rub and served with an intense and aromatic sauce, an equally inky, concentrated bottle of wine is required. Go for a mouth-filling Australian Shiraz, such as the 1996 Wynns Coonawarra Estate or the 1995 Mitchelton Print.

Smoked Duck Breasts

4 SERVINGS

Curing the duck breasts first with salt, pepper and sugar tenderizes them. The breasts are then lightly seared and smoked over smoldering thyme sprigs. You can also prepare broiled or pan-seared lamb chops, steaks, pork chops and boneless chicken breasts in this way, if you like, but it isn't necessary to cure them first.

2 teaspoons kosher salt
¾ teaspoon coarsely ground pepper
½ teaspoon sugar
Four 6-ounce skinless Long Island or Pekin duck breast halves
1 teaspoon olive oil
1 small bunch of thyme, soaked in water for ½ hour and drained

I. In a small bowl, combine the kosher salt, coarsely ground pepper and sugar. Rub the mixture on the duck breasts and then cover and refrigerate them for at least 4 hours or overnight. Bring the duck breasts to room temperature before cooking.

2. Pat the duck breasts dry and then brush them all over with the olive oil. Prepare a 10-inch cast-iron skillet (see box, left). Set the skillet over high heat for 5 minutes.

3. Meanwhile, heat a large nonstick skillet until hot. Add the duck breasts and sear until they are crusty but very rare within, about 4 minutes total. One minute before the duck breasts are done, add the thyme to the center of the cast-iron skillet and set a round wire cake rack in the pan.

4. Arrange the seared duck breasts on the rack and, when the thyme begins to smoke, cover the skillet with the prepared lid. Reduce the heat to moderate and cook the duck breasts until springy to the touch for rare, about 3 minutes. Transfer the duck breasts to a cutting board and let stand for 5 minutes. Thinly slice the duck breasts on the diagonal and serve. —*Sally Schneider*

ONE SERVING Calories 200 kcal, Total Fat 2.5 gm, Saturated Fat .4 gm

WINE Duck is traditionally a red wine dish, but an Alsace Gewürztraminer could also work here. Look for the 1996 Domaine Weinbach Cuvée Laurence or the 1995 Domaine André Ostertag Vin de Pierre.

Roasted Cornish Hens with Date and Orange Compote

4 SERVINGS

The cuisine of Islamic Spain was the inspiration for this dish. Arab farmers planted exotic fruits, such as oranges, in their gardens, while Arab traders brought spices, such as cumin and cinnamon, from the East and dates from North Africa.

½ cup hazelnuts (¼ pound)
½ cup water
Zest of 2 oranges, slivered
2 tablespoons sugar
8 large dates, pitted and chopped
⅓ cup plus 2 tablespoons olive oil
1 teaspoon granulated garlic
1 teaspoon granulated onion
¼ teaspoon cumin
¼ teaspoon cinnamon
Salt and freshly ground pepper
Four 1-pound cornish hens
2 tablespoons unsalted butter
2 tablespoons dry white wine
½ cup chicken stock or canned low-sodium broth

I. Preheat the oven to 400°. Put the hazelnuts in a pie plate and bake for about 10 minutes, or until fragrant and browned. Transfer the nuts to a kitchen towel and rub well to remove as much of their skin as possible. Coarsely chop the hazelnuts. Leave the oven on.

2. In a small saucepan, combine the water, orange zest and sugar. Simmer over low heat until the zest is tender, about 10 minutes. Transfer the zest and its syrup to a bowl and let cool to room temperature. In a mini-processor, combine the hazelnuts with the dates, zest and syrup and chop coarsely.

3. In a small bowl, blend ⅓ cup of the olive oil with the granulated garlic and onion. Add the cumin, cinnamon, 1 teaspoon of salt and ¼ teaspoon of pepper and then rub the oil all over the hens, working it under the skin. Put 2 tablespoons of the orange compote in the cavity of each hen and truss the birds with kitchen string.

4. Heat the remaining 2 tablespoons of oil in a large ovenproof skillet. Add 2 of the hens and brown them well on all sides over moderate heat, about 4 minutes per side. Transfer to a plate and repeat with the remaining 2 hens. Pour off the oil and melt the butter in the skillet. Return all of the hens to the pan, breast up, and roast in the oven until the juices run clear, about 30 minutes. Transfer the hens to a cutting board and discard the trussing strings.

5. Set the skillet over high heat, add the remaining orange compote and cook, stirring, until the zest starts to caramelize, about 1 minute. Add the wine and bring to a boil, stirring. Add the stock and boil for 4 minutes. Season the sauce with salt and pepper. Set one hen on each plate and pass the sauce separately. —*Stephen Kalt*

MAKE AHEAD The orange zest mixture can be prepared through Step 2 and refrigerated overnight.

WINE Opt for a medium-bodied wine that won't overwhelm the mild hens, such as a fruity white from Rueda, Spain, a Saumur with some oak from France or an Australian Pinot Noir.

Roasted Capon with Mushroom Cream Sauce

6 TO 8 SERVINGS

One 8-pound capon, rinsed and dried
Salt and freshly ground pepper
1 teaspoon *herbes de Provence*
1 cup dry white wine
2 tablespoons unsalted butter
1½ pounds shiitake mushrooms or a mixture of creminis, Portobellos and chanterelles, tough stems discarded, caps thinly sliced
2 tablespoons Cognac
1 cup heavy cream
1 tablespoon chopped tarragon

I. Preheat the oven to 400°. Season the capon inside and out with 1 teaspoon each of salt and pepper and the *herbes de Provence*. Tie the legs of the capon together with cotton kitchen

Roasted Capon with Mushroom Cream Sauce

and pepper. Cover and cook over low heat until the mushrooms soften, about 5 minutes. Uncover; cook over moderately high heat, stirring occasionally, until any mushroom liquid in the pan has evaporated and the mushrooms start to brown, about 5 minutes.

6. Add the Cognac to the skillet and carefully ignite it with a long match; stand back until the flames die down. Add the heavy cream, cover and simmer over moderately low heat until the cream reduces slightly, about 5 minutes. Add the reserved pan sauce and simmer for 2 minutes to blend the flavors. Stir in the tarragon and season the sauce with salt and pepper. Transfer to a warmed gravy boat.

7. Remove the strings from the capon and carve it at the table. Pass the sauce on the side. —*Jacques Pépin*

MAKE AHEAD The mushroom cream sauce base can be refrigerated for up to 2 days. Reheat the cream sauce gently and then add the pan sauce and the tarragon. Season the mushroom cream sauce carefully and serve.

SERVE WITH Sautéed potatoes or rice with chopped parsley, glazed carrots and a wintery green, such as Swiss chard or spinach.

WINE The capon's rich sauce makes Pinot Noir a perfect match for this dish. Consider a California bottling, such as the 1997 Villa Mt. Eden Bien Nacido Vineyard Grand Reserve or the 1997 Robert Mondavi Carneros.

Tuscan-Style Turkey Breast with Sage Gravy

10 SERVINGS

STUFFING

10	ounces pancetta, finely chopped
2	medium onions, finely chopped
1	tablespoon minced garlic
1½	teaspoons finely chopped thyme
1½	teaspoons finely chopped sage
1¼	cups coarse toasted bread crumbs

Salt and freshly ground pepper

string. Set the capon, breast up, in a flameproof roasting pan and roast for 30 minutes.

2. Carefully turn the capon over onto its breast and roast it for 1 hour. Turn the capon breast side up once again and roast it for about 10 minutes longer, or until an instant-read thermometer inserted in the inner thigh registers 160°.

3. Transfer the capon to a warmed platter or a carving board. Cover the capon loosely with foil and let stand in a warm place for at least 10 minutes.

4. While the capon is resting, pour the juices from the roasting pan into a glass measuring cup and skim the fat off the surface. Set the roasting pan on 2 burners. Add the wine and the reserved pan juices and bring to a simmer over low heat, scraping up the brown bits from the bottom of the roasting pan. Cook until reduced to ½ cup, about 5 minutes. Strain the pan sauce into a bowl.

5. In a large skillet, melt the butter over high heat. When the foam subsides, add the mushrooms and season with salt

TURKEY AND GRAVY

One 6-pound boneless whole turkey
    breast with skin

Salt and freshly ground pepper

½ pound pancetta, sliced ⅛ inch
    thick, 2 ounces finely chopped

1 large onion, thickly sliced

2 carrots, cut into 1-inch pieces

16 fresh sage leaves, plus
    1 tablespoon finely chopped sage

10 thyme sprigs

2 tablespoons unsalted butter,
    softened

1 cup water, more if necessary

2 tablespoons all-purpose flour

½ cup dry white wine

5 cups turkey stock (p. 192)

1. MAKE THE STUFFING: In a large
skillet, cook the chopped pancetta over
moderate heat until softened, about 6
minutes. Add the onions and cook, stirring, until the pancetta and onions are
browned, 6 to 7 minutes. Add the garlic, thyme and sage and cook for 1
minute. Stir in the bread crumbs and
season with salt and pepper. Transfer to
a bowl to cool.

2. PREPARE THE TURKEY AND
GRAVY: Preheat the oven to 400°. Set
the turkey breast on a work surface,

Tuscan-Style Turkey Breast with Sage Gravy

skin side down. Carefully remove the cartilage at the center; be careful not to cut through the skin. Fold the tenders outward, keeping them attached. Cover the turkey with plastic wrap and flatten it to an even 1¼-inch thickness with a meat pounder. Season the turkey with salt and pepper and evenly spread the stuffing over the meat. Beginning at one side, roll the turkey breast into a compact roast. Tie the roast in 5 places with kitchen string.

3. Line a 13-by-9-inch flameproof roasting pan with the pancetta slices and scatter the onion, carrots, whole sage leaves and thyme sprigs in the pan. Set the turkey on top. Rub 1 tablespoon of the butter over the turkey and season with salt and pepper.

4. Roast the turkey in the middle of the oven for 30 minutes. Add 1 cup of water to the pan and brush the turkey with the remaining 1 tablespoon of butter. Roast for 45 minutes longer, or until an instant-read thermometer inserted in the thickest part registers 140°; add more water to the pan if necessary. Transfer the turkey to a carving board.

5. Pour the juices from the roasting pan into a bowl. Spoon off the fat, reserving 2 tablespoons in a small bowl. Stir the flour into the fat to make a paste.

6. Set the roasting pan over moderately high heat. When it begins to sizzle, add the wine and cook until evaporated, scraping the pan. Transfer the contents of the pan to a large saucepan. Add the stock and any accumulated juices from the turkey and bring to a boil. Simmer until reduced to 3 cups, about 25 minutes. Strain the liquid, pressing hard on the solids, and return it to the saucepan. Bring to a simmer, whisk in the flour paste and cook for 5 minutes.

7. Meanwhile, in a small skillet, cook the chopped pancetta over moderate heat until browned, about 4 minutes. Add the chopped sage and cook until fragrant. Add the pancetta to the gravy and season with salt and pepper.

8. Discard the strings and carve the turkey into ⅓-inch slices. Arrange the slices on a platter and pass the gravy separately. —*Grace Parisi*

MAKE AHEAD The turkey and gravy can be prepared up to 4 hours ahead and kept at room temperature. Rewarm before serving.

Roasted Turkey Breast with Spiced Cranberry Glaze

10 SERVINGS

The turkey breast has to marinate overnight, so plan accordingly.

- ½ **cup pure maple syrup**
- 6 **garlic cloves, thinly sliced**
- ½ **teaspoon cinnamon**
- ½ **teaspoon cayenne pepper**
- 12 **ounces cranberries**
- ½ **cup fresh orange juice**

Salt and freshly ground black pepper

One 8-pound turkey breast on the bone, preferably with wings

Vegetable oil

- 1 **medium red onion, thickly sliced**
- 6 **cups turkey stock (p. 192)**

1. In a medium saucepan, heat the maple syrup. Add the garlic and cook over moderate heat for 3 minutes. Add the cinnamon and cayenne and cook for 1 minute. Add the cranberries and simmer for 5 minutes. Add the orange juice and simmer for 5 minutes longer. Transfer the hot mixture to a blender and puree. Pass the puree through a coarse strainer into a bowl and season with salt and black pepper. Let the puree cool completely.

2. Loosen the turkey breast skin. Fold the wing tips under the breast to stabilize it. Put half of the spiced cranberry puree in a large resealable plastic bag and close. Cut off a corner of the bag and pipe the cranberry puree under the turkey breast skin; press the skin all over to evenly distribute the puree. Put the turkey breast on a plate, cover with plastic wrap and refrigerate overnight. Bring the turkey breast to room temperature before roasting.

3. Preheat the oven to 400°. Rub vegetable oil over the turkey breast and season with salt and freshly ground black pepper. Stand the turkey breast in a large roasting pan. Scatter the onion slices in the pan, pour in 2 cups of the turkey stock and roast for 30 minutes. Turn the oven down to 325° and add the remaining 4 cups of stock to the pan. Cover the turkey breast with foil and roast for 1½ hours longer.

4. Remove the turkey breast from the oven and discard the foil. Increase the oven temperature to 350°. Brush the turkey breast with ¼ cup of the remaining cranberry puree and roast for 20 minutes, or until glazed. Brush another ¼ cup of the cranberry puree over the turkey breast and roast for 15 minutes longer, or until the turkey is a deeply glazed crimson-brown and an instant-read thermometer inserted in the thickest part of the meat registers 145°. Transfer the turkey breast to a carving board and allow it to rest for at least 15 minutes.

5. Strain the juices from the roasting pan through a coarse strainer set over a bowl; press on the onion to extract as much liquid as possible. Set a fine strainer over a medium saucepan and pour in the pan juices. Skim off the fat from the juices and then boil the juices until reduced to 3½ cups, about 15 minutes. Stir in the remaining ½ cup of the cranberry puree and season the mixture with salt and black pepper. Pour this cranberry jus into a warmed gravy boat.

6. Cut down on either side of the breast bone and remove each turkey-breast half in 1 piece. Thickly slice the turkey-breast halves crosswise and arrange the slices on a platter. Pass the cranberry jus at the table. —*Marcia Kiesel*

MAKE AHEAD The cranberry puree can be refrigerated for up to 3 days.

ONE SERVING WITH SKIN Calories 510 kcal, Total Fat 18.1 gm, Saturated Fat 5.2 gm

Wine-Braised Turkey with Porcini

4 SERVINGS

- ½ cup dried porcini mushrooms (½ ounce)
- 1 cup boiling water
- ¼ cup olive oil
- 4 turkey drumsticks (about 3 pounds)

Salt
- 2 carrots, finely chopped
- 1 onion, finely chopped
- 2 cups red or dry white wine
- 3 thyme sprigs
- 2 bay leaves
- 3 bunches scallions, trimmed to 5 inches
- ½ pound Portobello mushrooms, stems discarded, caps halved and sliced crosswise ¼ inch thick

Freshly ground pepper

1. In a heatproof bowl, soak the porcini mushrooms in the boiling water until softened, about 20 minutes. Rub the mushrooms to loosen any grit and then coarsely chop. Let the soaking liquid stand for 5 minutes and then pour it into a bowl, leaving any grit behind.

2. Heat 2 tablespoons of the oil in an enameled cast-iron casserole. Add the turkey drumsticks, season with salt and brown on all sides over moderately high heat, about 10 minutes. Transfer the drumsticks to a plate. Add the carrots and onion to the casserole, season with salt and cook, stirring, until they are lightly browned, 8 to 10 minutes.

3. Return the drumsticks to the pan. Add the wine, the porcinis and their soaking liquid, the thyme sprigs and the bay leaves; bring to a boil. Cover and simmer over low heat until the turkey is falling off the bones, about 3 hours; turn the drumsticks 2 or 3 times during cooking. Discard the thyme and bay leaves.

4. Heat the remaining 2 tablespoons of oil in a medium skillet. Add the scallions; season with salt. Cook over moderately high heat until the scallions are softened and lightly browned, 3 to 5 minutes. Transfer the scallions to a plate. Add the Portobellos to the skillet, season with salt and cook over high heat, turning once, until softened and golden, 5 to 8 minutes.

5. Cut the turkey meat off the bone into large pieces and discard the sticklike tendons. Boil the cooking liquid until it lightly coats a spoon, 10 to 15 minutes. Add the cooked Portobellos and season with pepper.

6. Put the turkey into soup plates and spoon the Portobellos and sauce on top. Arrange the scallions alongside and serve. —*Jane Sigal*

SERVE WITH Steamed rice.

WINE The richness of this dish points to a full-flavored red of equal intensity, like a Merlot.

Roasted Turkey with Asian Flavors and Sticky Rice

10 SERVINGS

The rice has to soak overnight in cold water, so plan accordingly.

STUFFING
- 3 cups long-grain Asian sweet, or sticky, rice (21 ounces)
- ½ cup whole blanched almonds
- 2 tablespoons vegetable oil
- 8 scallions, coarsely chopped
- 1 tablespoon minced fresh ginger
- 2 garlic cloves, minced
- 4 Chinese sausages, sliced ½ inch thick, or ¼ pound honey-cured ham, diced
- 3 tablespoons dry white wine
- 3 cups turkey stock (p. 192)
- 3 tablespoons soy sauce

Salt and freshly ground pepper
- ½ teaspoon Asian sesame oil

TURKEY AND GRAVY

One 12-pound turkey

Salt and freshly ground pepper

Vegetable oil
- 5½ cups turkey stock (p. 192)
- ½ cup dry white wine
- 1 small onion, quartered
- 1 celery rib, quartered, plus 2 cups celery leaves
- 10 large garlic cloves, 4 peeled and 6 thinly sliced
- 4 teaspoons soy sauce
- 2 tablespoons Asian oyster sauce
- 3 tablespoons all-purpose flour
- ¼ teaspoon Sriracha chile sauce or other hot sauce

1. MAKE THE STUFFING: In a large bowl, soak the rice overnight in water to cover by 2 inches; drain.

2. Preheat the oven to 400°. Put the almonds in a pie plate and bake them until they are browned, about 8 minutes. Let the almonds cool. Turn the oven down to 325°.

3. Heat the vegetable oil in a large saucepan. Add the scallions and the minced ginger and garlic and cook over moderately high heat, stirring, until fragrant, about 3 minutes. Add the sausages or ham, cook for 1 minute and then stir in the rice. Add the white wine and simmer for 1 minute. Stir in the turkey stock, soy sauce and a large pinch of salt and freshly ground pepper. Cover, reduce the heat to low and cook until the liquid is absorbed, about 10

Wine-Braised Turkey with Porcini

minutes. Stir the rice well and then stir in the almonds and the sesame oil; season with salt and pepper. Spread the rice on a large rimmed baking sheet and let it cool to room temperature.

4. PREPARE THE TURKEY AND GRAVY: Season the turkey inside and out with salt and freshly ground pepper. Fill the cavity of the turkey with 5 cups of the rice stuffing and secure the skin with toothpicks. Put 1 cup of the rice stuffing in the turkey's neck cavity and secure with toothpicks. Put the remaining rice stuffing in an oiled glass baking dish and cover with foil.

5. Set the turkey in a large flameproof roasting pan and rub the skin all over with vegetable oil. Pour 2 cups of the stock and the wine into the roasting pan. Add the onion, celery rib and 4 whole garlic cloves. Roast the turkey for 1¾ hours. Add 1 cup of the stock to the pan and cover the turkey loosely with foil. Continue roasting the turkey for about 2½ hours longer, or until an instant-read thermometer inserted in the thickest part of the inner thigh registers 160°.

6. Remove the turkey from the oven and discard the foil. Increase the oven temperature to 400°. Brush the turkey with 1 tablespoon each of the soy and oyster sauces and roast for 10 minutes, or until glazed. Transfer the turkey to a carving board and let rest for at least 30 minutes. Bake the reserved rice stuffing for 20 minutes.

7. Strain the pan juices into a bowl. Using a ladle, skim the fat from the pan juices; return 2 tablespoons of the fat to the roasting pan. Set the pan over low heat, stir in the flour and cook for 1 minute. Slowly whisk in the remaining 2½ cups of stock until smooth, scraping up the brown bits from the bottom of the pan. Stir in the strained pan juices and bring the gravy to a boil, whisking constantly. Simmer the gravy over low heat for 10 minutes.

8. Meanwhile, in a medium saucepan, heat 1 tablespoon of vegetable oil. Add the 6 sliced garlic cloves and cook over low heat until golden, about 3 minutes. Add the celery leaves and cook until the leaves are wilted, about 1 minute. Pour in the gravy from the roasting pan and simmer for 2 minutes. Add the chile sauce and the remaining 1 tablespoon of oyster sauce and 1 teaspoon of soy sauce to the gravy and season with salt and pepper. Scoop the rice stuffing from the turkey cavities into the dish with the rest of the stuffing. Carve the turkey at the table and pass the rice stuffing and the celery leaf gravy alongside. —*Marcia Kiesel*

menu

**Broiled Garlic and
Lime Shrimp (p. 22)**

**Little Pork Tamales with
Red Chile Sauce (p. 42)**

**Crab and Guacamole
Tostaditos (p. 20)**

NONVINTAGE IRON HORSE BRUT
1997 RIFFAULT SANCERRE

MARGARITAS

––––––––

Mole-Inspired Roasted Turkey

Creamy Anchos and Onions (p. 285)

**Country Corn Bread
Stuffing (p. 255)**

Creamed Corn (p. 288)

**Sweet Potatoes with
Poblano Chile Rajas (p. 304)**

Green Beans with Sea Salt (p. 271)

1997 ETUDE PINOT NOIR
1996 LONG CHARDONNAY

––––––––

Deep Dish Pecan Pie (p. 350)

**Mexican Chocolate
Pots de Crème (p. 377)**

Mole-Inspired Roasted Turkey

8 TO 10 SERVINGS

The cinnamon, cocoa and chile-powder paste flavors the turkey here and also produces a wonderful aroma as the bird roasts.

¼   **cup unsweetened cocoa
     powder**
1   **tablespoon ancho chile powder
     (see Note)**
1   **tablespoon cinnamon**
1   **tablespoon light brown sugar**
Salt and freshly ground pepper
3   **tablespoons extra-virgin olive oil**
1   **teaspoon balsamic vinegar**
**One 10- to 12-pound turkey, rinsed
     and patted dry**
4   **tablespoons unsalted butter,
     melted**
2   **cups turkey stock (p. 192),
     chicken stock or canned
     low-sodium broth**
1½ **tablespoons all-purpose flour,
     mixed with ¼ cup water**

1. Preheat the oven to 450°. In a bowl, combine the cocoa powder, chile powder, cinnamon, light brown sugar, 1 teaspoon salt and ¼ teaspoon pepper. Stir in the olive oil and balsamic vinegar. Rub half of the paste all over the turkey and then spoon the remaining paste into the cavity.

2. Set the turkey on a rack in a large flameproof roasting pan and cook for 5 minutes. Baste the turkey with some of the melted butter and add 3 to 4 tablespoons of the turkey stock to the roasting pan.

3. Lower the oven temperature to 350° and roast the turkey for 1½ hours. Lower the oven temperature to 250° and add a little more stock to the pan. Baste the turkey with the remaining butter and roast for about 1½ hours longer, or until an instant-read thermometer inserted in the thickest part of the thigh registers 170°. Transfer the turkey to a

**Mole-Inspired Roasted Turkey, Green Beans with Sea Salt (p. 271), Country Corn
Bread Stuffing (p. 255) and Sweet Potatoes with Poblano Chile Rajas (p. 304).**

cutting board, cover loosely with foil and let rest for at least 30 minutes.

4. Pour the pan juices into a saucepan and skim off the fat. Set the roasting pan on a burner over moderately high heat. Add the remaining stock to the roasting pan and bring to a boil, scraping up any brown bits.

5. Strain the stock into the saucepan and bring it to a boil. Spoon the paste from the turkey cavity into the stock. Boil the stock until reduced to about 1½ cups, about 10 minutes. Whisk in the flour mixture and simmer over moderate heat until the gravy is thickened. Season the gravy with salt and pepper. Carve the turkey and serve it hot or at room temperature along with the gravy. —*Robert Del Grande*

NOTE Ancho chile powder adds sweet heat to the turkey. If you can't find the powder, you can grind a stemmed whole ancho in a spice grinder and use that instead.

WINE The 1997 Etude Pinot Noir is a favorite; the turkey's cocoa and cinnamon flavors enhance the wine's perfume and fruit beautifully. A full, rich Chardonnay, such as the 1996 Long, works equally well.

Roasted Turkey with Bacon-Cider Gravy
10 SERVINGS ✳

One 11-pound turkey
2 medium onions, quartered
2 Granny Smith apples—peeled, quartered and cored
2 large sage sprigs
2 large thyme sprigs
2 large rosemary sprigs
2 small oregano sprigs
Salt and freshly ground pepper
8 garlic cloves
½ pound sliced meaty bacon
1¼ cups apple cider
2 cups turkey stock (see box, right)
1½ tablespoons all-purpose flour
1 teaspoon cider vinegar
Herb sprigs, for garnish

1. Preheat the oven to 425°. Cut along both sides of the wishbone and remove it. Tuck 1 wedge of onion and 1 wedge of apple in the neck cavity of the turkey along with 1 sprig each of sage, thyme, rosemary and oregano. Fold the skin under the turkey. Season the turkey's main cavity with salt and pepper and then stuff it with 3 onion wedges, 3 apple wedges, 2 garlic cloves and the remaining sage, thyme, rosemary and oregano sprigs. Tie the legs together.

2. Set the turkey in a large flameproof roasting pan and season with pepper. Arrange the bacon strips over the turkey breast and legs and roast for 1 hour. Remove the bacon and spoon off some of the fat from the roasting pan. Add the remaining onion wedges, apple wedges and garlic cloves to the roasting pan and turn to coat them with fat. Roast the turkey for 45 minutes longer or until an instant-read thermometer inserted in the thickest part of the thigh registers 160°; baste the turkey occasionally. Transfer the turkey to a platter, cover loosely with foil and let rest for at least 30 minutes.

3. Transfer the onion wedges, apple wedges and garlic in the roasting pan to a food processor and puree. Set the roasting pan over 2 burners on moderately high heat; when the juices begin to sizzle, stir in 1 cup of the apple cider and cook, scraping up the brown bits, until reduced by half, about 5 minutes. Strain the pan juices into a medium saucepan. Add the stock to the saucepan and boil until reduced to 2 cups. Skim off the fat.

4. In a bowl, stir the flour into the remaining ¼ cup of apple cider and then whisk the paste into the gravy. Bring the gravy to a boil; simmer until it is slightly thickened, about 5 minutes. Stir in the apple and onion puree and the cider vinegar and season the gravy with salt and pepper. Garnish the roasted turkey with herb sprigs and serve with the bacon-cider gravy. —*Grace Parisi.*

Roasted Turkey with Foie Gras and Prune Gravy
10 SERVINGS

1½ sticks (6 ounces) plus 1 tablespoon unsalted butter, softened
1 ounce dried morels or porcini, ground to a powder (⅓ cup)
1 shallot, minced
2 tablespoons minced parsley
2 teaspoons fresh lemon juice
Salt and freshly ground pepper
One 14-pound fresh turkey, wing tips reserved, neck cut into 3 pieces
15 pitted prunes
4 thyme sprigs
1½ cups dry white wine
1 cup water
¼ cup Cognac or brandy
1 small onion, quartered
1 small celery rib, quartered
5 tablespoons all-purpose flour
5 cups turkey stock (see box, below)
3 ounces foie gras mousse, cut into 1-inch pieces and chilled

1. In a medium bowl, blend 1½ sticks of the butter with the mushroom powder, shallot, parsley and lemon juice. Season with salt and pepper.

2. Preheat the oven to 400°. Carefully loosen the skin from the turkey breast,

F&W's Favorite Turkey Stock
MAKES 2 QUARTS

6 pounds turkey wings and drumsticks • 11 cups water • 1 large onion, sliced • 1 carrot • 1 celery rib • 2 garlic cloves, sliced • Handful of parsley • 1 bay leaf

Preheat the oven to 400°. In a flameproof roasting pan, roast the turkey parts until browned, about 1 hour. Transfer to a pot; add 10 cups water and the remaining ingredients. Add the remaining 1 cup water. Bring to a boil over high heat, scraping up the brown bits. Add to the pot, bring to a boil, cover partially and simmer gently for 2½ hours. Strain and refrigerate until chilled. Scrape off the fat and freeze.

Roasted Turkey with Bacon-Cider Gravy

legs and thighs. Season the turkey inside and out with salt and pepper. Spread a thick layer of the mushroom butter under the skin and press the skin to distribute the butter evenly. Put the prunes and thyme sprigs in the cavity; tie the legs together with kitchen string.

3. Set the turkey in a large roasting pan. Pour 1 cup of the wine, the water and the Cognac into the pan and roast the turkey for 20 minutes. Turn the oven down to 325°, cover loosely with foil and roast for 2 hours. Remove the foil and continue to roast for about 1 hour and 15 minutes longer, turning the pan halfway through. The turkey is done when it is nicely browned all over and an instant-read thermometer inserted in the inner thigh registers 160°.

4. While the turkey is roasting, melt the remaining 1 tablespoon of butter in a medium saucepan. Add the wing tips and neck pieces, season with salt and pepper and cook over moderate heat until browned, about 10 minutes. Add the onion and celery and cook until lightly browned. Sprinkle in 2 tablespoons of the flour and cook, stirring, for 1 minute. Slowly pour in the remaining ½ cup of wine and stir until smooth. Gradually stir in the stock and bring to a boil. Cover and simmer over low heat until reduced to 3½ cups, about 2 hours. Strain and set aside.

5. When the turkey is done, transfer it to a carving board and let rest for at least 30 minutes. Discard the string. Remove the prunes from the cavity and coarsely chop. Pour the pan drippings

FIVE MENUS FOR A HOLIDAY DINNER

	luxurious	healthy	make ahead	quick & easy	modern
starters	CREAM OF CELERY ROOT WITH SHRIMP BUTTER P. 287	WHITE BEAN CROSTINI WITH SPICY CUCUMBERS P. 17	ARTICHOKE LEAVES WITH CUMIN SHRIMP SALAD P. 22	KING CRAB TOASTS P. 18	GRILLED PORTOBELLO AND BOSC PEAR SALAD P. 48
turkey	ROASTED TURKEY WITH FOIE GRAS AND PRUNE GRAVY P. 192	ROASTED TURKEY BREAST WITH SPICED CRANBERRY GLAZE P. 188	TUSCAN-STYLE TURKEY BREAST WITH SAGE GRAVY P. 186	ROASTED TURKEY WITH BACON-CIDER GRAVY P. 192	ROASTED TURKEY WITH ASIAN FLAVORS AND STICKY RICE P. 189
sides	TURNIPS AND TURNIP GREENS WITH MUSTARD BUTTER P. 286	WILD RICE WITH ESCAROLE P. 307	BREAD PUDDING WITH LEEKS AND GARLIC P. 285	CREAMED PARSLEY AND HOMINY P. 314	CARAMELIZED BRUSSELS SPROUTS WITH PISTACHIOS P. 278
potatoes	GOLDEN MASHED POTATOES WITH TRUFFLE BUTTER P. 298	PAN-ROASTED SWEET POTATOES WITH FENNEL P. 304	CRISP POTATO-PARSNIP CAKE P. 300	SWEET POTATO OVEN-FRIES WITH LEMON-MINT GREMOLATA P. 303	WHIPPED SWEET POTATOES WITH CRISPY SHALLOTS P. 303
desserts	FROZEN CHOCOLATE SOUFFLES WITH BERRY COMPOTE P. 384	SPICED ANGEL FOOD CAKE WITH BUTTERSCOTCH GLAZE P. 330	CRANBERRY-WALNUT TART P. 346	ALMOND CAKES WITH BANANAS AND WARM CARAMEL SAUCE P. 331	MOCHA PANNA COTTA WITH CHERRY COULIS P. 380
wines	1995 CHATEAU LA GAFFELIERE SAINT-EMILLION	1995 PEPPOLI CHIANTI CLASSICO	1997 CARMENET RESERVE SAUVIGNON BLANC-SEMILLON	1995 EYRIE RESERVE PINOT NOIR	1995 CAKEBREAD RESERVE CHARDONNAY

through a coarse strainer set over a bowl. Use a ladle to skim off the fat, reserving 2 tablespoons.

6. In a medium saucepan, combine the reserved fat with the remaining 3 table-spoons of flour and stir over moderate heat for 1 minute. Gradually whisk in the pan drippings and strained stock. Simmer over moderately low heat for 10 minutes, whisking frequently. Remove from the heat. Whisk in the foie gras mousse, 2 pieces at a time. Stir in the prunes and season with salt and pep-per. Carve the turkey at the table; pass the gravy separately. —*Marcia Kiesel*

MAKE AHEAD The wild mushroom butter can be refrigerated for 1 week. Soften before using. The finished gravy can stand off the heat for up to 1 hour. Bring to a simmer over low heat, whisk-ing constantly; do not let it boil.

Maple-Chile Grilled Quail

4 SERVINGS

These incredibly simple quail are also delicious glazed with honey. To get the best level of spiciness, use a mixture of mild and fiery chile powders, such as ancho and chipotle; you can also use sweet and hot paprika.

½ **cup pure maple syrup**
2 **tablespoons pure chile powder**
8 **semi-boneless quail**
2 **tablespoons vegetable oil**
Salt and freshly ground pepper

Light a grill or preheat the broiler. In a small bowl, combine the maple syrup and chile powder. Brush the quail with the oil and season with salt and pepper. Grill or broil on a rimmed baking sheet until browned, about 1 minute per side. Brush the quail all over with the maple glaze and grill or broil them, breast side toward the heat, for about 2 minutes, or until the quail are well browned and just pink at the bone; serve. —*Lisa Ahier*

WINE Delicate, sweet-flavored quail is best with a light and elegant red, such as an Oregon Pinot Noir. Try the 1996 Domaine Drouhin or the 1996 Ponzi.

pork veal

Pork with Sweet-Sour Peppers and Onions

4 SERVINGS

¼ cup extra-virgin olive oil

1 red bell pepper, cut into ½-inch strips

1 yellow bell pepper, cut into ½-inch strips

2 red onions, halved and sliced crosswise ½ inch thick

¼ cup dried currants

1½ tablespoons sherry vinegar

1½ teaspoons minced rosemary

1½ teaspoons finely chopped mint

2 tablespoons water

Salt and freshly ground black pepper

2 medium Yukon Gold potatoes, cut into ¾-inch dice

Eight 4-ounce boneless pork loin chops, about ½ inch thick

2 tablespoons flat-leaf parsley leaves

1. In a large skillet, heat 2 tablespoons of olive oil until shimmering. Add the red and yellow bell peppers and the onions and cook over moderate heat, stirring often, until they are softened and charred in spots, about 10 minutes. Add the dried currants, sherry vinegar, rosemary, mint and water and cook, stirring, until the liquid is evaporated. Season with salt and black pepper, cover and keep warm.

2. Meanwhile, in another large skillet, heat the remaining 2 tablespoons of oil until shimmering. Add the potatoes and cook over moderate heat, stirring occasionally, until golden and cooked through, 10 to 12 minutes. Using a slotted spoon, add the potatoes to the bell peppers and onions and stir to combine.

3. Set the empty skillet over moderate heat. When the oil shimmers, season the pork chops with salt and black pepper, add them to the skillet and cook over high heat until browned and just cooked through, 2 to 3 minutes per side. Arrange the vegetables on a platter or on plates and top with the pork chops. Garnish with the parsley leaves and serve. —*Seen Lippert*

Pork Chops with Mustard and Sour Cream Sauce

4 SERVINGS

Two mustards—grainy and smooth— add layers of flavor to the creamy sauce that tops these pork chops.

¼ cup chicken stock or canned low-sodium broth

¼ cup low-fat sour cream

2 teaspoons Dijon mustard

2 teaspoons stone-ground mustard

½ teaspoon cornstarch

1 tablespoon finely chopped flat-leaf parsley

4 boneless pork loin chops (about 5 ounces each)

Salt and freshly ground pepper

1. In a blender, process the stock, sour cream, mustards and cornstarch until smooth. Transfer the sauce to a small saucepan and simmer over moderate heat until thickened, about 3 minutes. Stir in the parsley and keep warm.

2. Heat a large skillet. Season the pork chops with salt and pepper and cook over moderately high heat until well browned, about 5 minutes. Turn the pork chops and cook until browned and just cooked through, about 3 minutes

Pork Chops with Mustard and Sour Cream Sauce, with Buttermilk Mashed Potatoes with Tarragon (p. 298).

longer. Transfer the pork chops to warm dinner plates, spoon the mustard and sour cream sauce on top and serve at once. —*Sue Chapman*

ONE SERVING Calories 301 kcal, Total Fat 17.5 gm, Saturated Fat 6.8 gm

WINE The mustardy, moist pork chops point to a big white wine—a Chardonnay—or a light red, ideally a California Pinot Noir, which would underscore the tangy flavors here. Try the 1997 Echelon or the 1996 Buena Vista Carneros.

Pork Chops on Creamy Hominy

4 SERVINGS

At the Magnolia Grill in Durham, North Carolina, there's always some sort of delectable hominy on the menu. Here it's served with braised pork chops and an excellent bourbon sauce.

CREAMY HOMINY

One 15-ounce can white hominy, drained and rinsed
1 cup heavy cream
2 tablespoons peanut oil
1 medium onion, finely chopped
1 small green bell pepper, finely chopped
2 celery ribs, finely chopped
6 garlic cloves, minced
1 cup canned tomatoes, coarsely chopped
1 jalapeño, seeded and minced
2 tablespoons chopped oregano
1 tablespoon thyme leaves
1 bay leaf
2 cups chicken stock or canned low-sodium broth
2 tablespoons cider vinegar
Salt and freshly ground black pepper
Tabasco sauce

PORK CHOPS

Peanut oil, for frying
¼ cup all-purpose flour
1 teaspoon hot paprika
1 teaspoon dried oregano
½ teaspoon cayenne pepper
Salt and freshly ground black pepper
Four 8-ounce pork loin chops, about 1 inch thick

1 cup dry white wine
¼ cup bourbon
¼ cup cider vinegar
6 scallions, green tops only, thinly sliced

I. PREPARE THE HOMINY: In a small saucepan, combine the hominy and the cream. Simmer over moderate heat until slightly thickened, about 5 minutes. Remove from the heat.

2. Heat the oil in a medium saucepan. Add the onion, green bell pepper and celery and cook over moderate heat, stirring, until the vegetables are softened, about 10 minutes. Add the garlic, tomatoes, jalapeño, oregano, thyme and bay leaf and simmer for 2 minutes. Stir in the chicken stock and cider vinegar; bring to a boil and then lower the heat and simmer for 15 minutes. Stir in the hominy and bring just to a simmer. Discard the bay leaf. Season with salt, black pepper and Tabasco and keep warm.

3. PREPARE THE PORK CHOPS: Heat ¼ inch of peanut oil in a heavy skillet. On a shallow plate, combine the flour, paprika, dried oregano, cayenne, 1 teaspoon of salt and 1 tablespoon of black pepper. Dredge the pork chops in the seasoned flour, shaking off the excess. Cook the chops over moderately high heat until well browned, about 3 minutes per side. Transfer to a plate and pour out the oil in the skillet.

4. Add the white wine, bourbon and cider vinegar to the skillet and cook over moderately high heat for 3 minutes, scraping up any brown bits. Add the pork chops and bring to a simmer. Reduce the heat to low, cover and simmer gently until the pork chops are just cooked through, about 8 minutes more. Transfer the chops to a plate. Boil the pan juices over high heat until reduced to 1 cup, about 5 minutes. Season with salt and pepper.

5. Spoon the hominy into 4 shallow bowls and top each with a pork chop. Spoon the pan juices and scallions over the chops and serve. —*Ben Barker*

MAKE AHEAD The creamy hominy can be prepared through Step 2 and refrigerated overnight.

BEER If ever a dish was suited to beer, this is it. Good choices include India Pale Ale, Negra Modelo and Dos Equis.

Indian-Spiced Ribs

4 SERVINGS

1 tablespoon plus 1 teaspoon coriander seeds
1 tablespoon plus 1 teaspoon cumin seeds
2 teaspoons yellow mustard seeds
2 cardamom pods, seeds removed
1 cinnamon stick
1 teaspoon turmeric
1 teaspoon cayenne pepper
4 racks of baby back pork ribs (about 1 pound each)
1 tablespoon plus 1 teaspoon vegetable oil
Salt and freshly ground black pepper
6 large garlic cloves, minced
½ cup minced onion

I. Preheat the oven to 350°. In a medium skillet, combine the coriander, cumin, mustard, cardamom and cinnamon; toast over low heat until fragrant and starting to brown, about 1 minute. Transfer to a plate, let cool and then grind to a powder in a mortar or spice mill. Put the powder in a small bowl and stir in the turmeric and cayenne.

2. Put the rib racks on 2 large rimmed baking sheets, meaty side up. Rub the top of each rack with 1 teaspoon of the oil and season with salt and pepper. Spread the garlic and then the onion evenly on top of the racks. Sprinkle the racks with all but 2 teaspoons of the spice mixture. Roast the racks for about 30 minutes, or until they start to brown.

3. Raise the oven temperature to 400° and sprinkle the racks with the reserved 2 teaspoons of spice mixture. Roast the ribs for about 30 minutes longer, or until the meat is tender. Cut the racks in between the ribs and serve hot or at room temperature. —*Marcia Kiesel*

Guava-Glazed Ribs, with Fried Plantains (p. 287).

Guava-Glazed Ribs

4 SERVINGS ✷

Juicy pork ribs with a fruity guava-garlic glaze are hugely popular at Jimmy's Bronx Café in New York City. Guava paste is available at Latin American markets and many supermarkets.

- 4 racks of baby back pork ribs (about 1 pound each)
- 1 tablespoon vegetable oil
- 2 large garlic cloves, minced

Cayenne pepper

Salt and freshly ground black pepper

- 1 cup (about 10 ounces) guava paste
- ⅓ cup water
- 2 tablespoons soy sauce
- 2 tablespoons fresh lime juice

1. Preheat the oven to 400°. Bring a large pot of water to a boil. Add the racks of pork ribs, cover and simmer over low heat for 10 minutes. Using tongs, transfer the pork rib racks to 2 rimmed baking sheets, meaty side up.

Rub the rib racks with the vegetable oil and garlic and season with cayenne, salt and black pepper. Bake the rib racks for 30 minutes.

2. Meanwhile, in a small saucepan, cook the guava paste and water over low heat, mashing with a fork, until melted and smooth, about 5 minutes. Add the soy sauce and simmer for 2 minutes, stirring. Remove from the heat, stir in the lime juice and season with salt and freshly ground pepper.

3. Raise the oven temperature to 500°. Brush the ribs with the guava glaze, spreading it all over the top. Bake 2 racks at a time on the top shelf of the oven for about 10 minutes, or until the ribs are browned and cooked through. Cut in between the ribs and arrange them on a platter or on plates. Serve hot. —*Luis Rivera*

BEER A hearty ale—Bass, for example—is all that's needed for these tasty glazed ribs.

Pork Tenderloin with Mexican Chipotle Marinade

4 SERVINGS

This marinade owes its firepower to chipotle chiles, which are smoked jalapeños. Use canned chipotles in *adobo,* so you can add some of the sauce from the can to the mixture. This marinade also goes well with chicken and pork.

- 6 canned chipotle chiles in *adobo,* stemmed, plus 2 tablespoons of sauce from the can
- 5 garlic cloves, thinly sliced

One 3-inch strip of orange zest

- ¾ cup fresh orange juice
- ¼ cup fresh lime juice
- 2 tablespoons red wine vinegar
- 1 tablespoon tomato paste
- 1 teaspoon dried oregano
- 1 teaspoon ground cumin
- ½ teaspoon freshly ground pepper

One 1½-pound whole pork tenderloin

1. In a small saucepan, combine the chipotles and their sauce with the garlic, orange zest, orange juice, lime juice, vinegar, tomato paste, oregano, cumin and pepper. Simmer over high heat until reduced by one third, about 3 minutes. Transfer to a food processor and puree until smooth. Let cool before using.

2. Coat the pork with ¼ cup of the marinade and refrigerate for 2 hours.

3. Light the grill. Grill the pork over a hot fire, turning, until cooked through, about 15 minutes. Let stand for 3 minutes, slice and serve. —*Steven Raichlen*

WINE The spicy, smoky marinade is full of flavor. Try a full buttery Chardonnay for balance. Among California bottlings, look for the 1997 Long Vineyards or the 1997 Au Bon Climat.

Soy-Marinated Pork Tenderloin with Cilantro

8 SERVINGS

Served with steamed jasmine rice, two pounds of pork tenderloin is enough for eight people.

- ⅓ cup Chinese mushroom soy sauce (see Note)

Soy-Marinated Pork Tenderloin with Cilantro, with Stir-Fried
Baby Bok Choy and Shiitake Mushrooms (p. 270).

4 medium garlic cloves, minced
2 tablespoons finely grated fresh ginger
2 tablespoons vegetable oil
1½ tablespoons honey
1 tablespoon freshly ground pepper
Two 1-pound whole pork tenderloins
1 cup water
¼ cup cilantro leaves
Steamed jasmine rice, for serving

I. In a large shallow baking dish, whisk the soy sauce with the garlic, ginger, oil, honey and pepper. Add the pork and turn to coat. Marinate the meat in the the refrigerator for 2 hours, turning every 30 minutes. Bring to room temperature before roasting.

2. Preheat the oven to 375°. Pour the water into a roasting pan. Set the pork tenderloins on a rack over the water and roast for 40 minutes, turning the meat once and basting with the marinade every 10 minutes. Remove the tenderloins from the oven and let them stand for 15 minutes. Thinly slice the tenderloins and arrange on a platter.

menu

Litchi Champagne Cocktail (p. 392)

Lemongrass-Infused Snails
with Spicy Soy Sauce (p. 41)

Crab and Asparagus Soup (p. 95)

Pan-Fried Striped Bass with
Stir-Fried Tomatoes and Dill (p. 133)

1995 DOMAINE LAROCHE
CHABLIS SAINT MARTIN

———

Soy-Marinated Pork Tenderloin
with Cilantro (p. 200)

Stir-Fried Baby Bok Choy and
Shiitake Mushrooms (p. 270)

1997 M. CHAPOUTIER
COTES-DU-RHONE BELLERUCHE

———

Coconut and Fresh Mint
Ice Cream (p. 385)

Garnish the tenderloins with the cilantro leaves and serve. Pass the rice separately. —*Corinne Trang*

NOTE Chinese mushroom soy sauce is available at Asian groceries.

WINE The kick of ginger and pepper calls for a robust wine with some spiciness, such as the 1997 M. Chapoutier Côtes-du-Rhône Belleruche.

Roasted Pork Tenderloin with Indian Spice Crust

4 SERVINGS

Combining crushed peppercorns and other Indian spices with browned bread crumbs for the crust gives an Indian flavor to a Western roast.

2 teaspoons white vinegar
Two ¾-pound whole pork tenderloins, trimmed
1 tablespoon plus 1 teaspoon ground coriander
1 teaspoon coarsely crushed black peppercorns
1 teaspoon salt
½ teaspoon coarsely crushed fennel seeds
⅛ teaspoon cayenne pepper
3 tablespoons vegetable oil
1 medium onion, finely chopped
¼ cup unflavored dry bread crumbs
2 garlic cloves, minced

I. In a shallow glass or ceramic baking dish, rub the vinegar over the tenderloins. In a small bowl, combine the coriander with the peppercorns, salt, fennel seeds and cayenne. Rub half of the spice mixture on each tenderloin. Cover the tenderloins and refrigerate for at least 4 hours or overnight.

2. Preheat the oven to 400°. In a large skillet, heat the oil. Add the onion and cook over low heat, stirring occasionally, until softened but not browned, about 5 minutes. Add the bread crumbs and garlic and stir over moderately high heat until the crumbs are toasted and fragrant, about 3 minutes. Transfer the crumb mixture to a plate and let cool completely.

3. In a food processor, pulse the crumb mixture until even textured. Transfer the mixture to a large plate and toss it with a fork to break up any lumps; spread the crumbs in an even layer.

4. Roll the spiced pork tenderloins in the crumb mixture, pressing firmly to help the crumbs adhere all around. Transfer the tenderloins to a rack set on a rimmed baking sheet and bake for about 25 minutes, or until the crumb coating is crisp and browned on the outside and the meat is juicy and slightly pink on the inside. Let the pork stand for 5 minutes and then carve into thick slices and serve. —*Maya Kaimal*

WINE Tender, moist pork tenderloin and Indian spices are perfect complements to a dry, spicy Alsace Gewürztraminer. Top choices include the 1995 Zind-Humbrecht Wintzenheim and the 1994 Trimbach.

Hoisin Pork Sandwiches

4 SERVINGS

Tender glazed roasted pork and a tangy cabbage slaw come together in this delicious sandwich. Be sure to allow time for the pork tenderloin to marinate overnight.

½ cup hoisin sauce
1 tablespoon *sambal oelek* (ground chili paste) or Asian chili sauce
1 tablespoon minced ginger
1 tablespoon minced garlic
¼ cup red wine
¼ cup plus 2 tablespoons finely chopped scallions
1 pork tenderloin (10 to 12 ounces)
Salt
¼ cup plus 1 tablespoon canola oil
2 tablespoons fresh lemon juice
½ teaspoon sugar
¼ teaspoon crushed red pepper
1½ cups shredded Napa cabbage (from ½ small head)
2 medium carrots, shredded
½ cup torn basil leaves
Freshly ground black pepper
4 large sandwich rolls, split

1. In a small shallow glass or stainless steel bowl, combine the hoisin sauce, *sambal oelek,* ginger, garlic, wine and 2 tablespoons of the scallions. Add the pork tenderloin; turn to coat with the marinade. Cover and refrigerate overnight, turning occasionally.

2. Preheat the oven to 350°. Drain the pork and season all over with salt. Heat 1 tablespoon of the oil in a large ovenproof skillet until shimmering. Add the pork; cook over high heat until browned, about 5 minutes. Transfer the skillet to the oven and roast the tenderloin for about 10 minutes for medium doneness. Let the pork rest for 15 minutes and then slice thinly.

3. In a large glass or stainless steel bowl, stir the remaining ¼ cup of oil with the lemon juice, sugar and crushed red pepper until the sugar is dissolved. Add the cabbage, carrots, basil and the remaining ¼ cup of scallions. Season with salt and black pepper and toss.

4. Assemble the sandwiches on the rolls with the pork slices on the bottom and the slaw mounded on top and serve. —*Ming Tsai*

MAKE AHEAD The recipe can be prepared through Step 2 and refrigerated overnight. Slice the pork tenderloin before serving.

BEER The tang of these pork sandwiches suggests the hoppiness of a cold lager beer—say, Pilsner Urquell.

Molasses-Cured Pork Loin with Apples

8 SERVINGS

This juicy pork is delicious served with watercress tossed with a lemony olive oil dressing. Allow the meat to marinate in the brine overnight.

  2 **quarts water**
  ½ **cup unsulphured molasses**
  ½ **cup sugar**
  2 **garlic cloves, smashed**
  ⅓ **cup coarse salt**
  1¼ **teaspoons cracked black pepper**
  ½ **cinnamon stick**

Hoisin Pork Sandwiches

  1½ **teaspoons coriander seeds**
  2 **whole cloves**
One 4-pound pork loin, trimmed of fat
Table salt and finely ground pepper
  2 **tablespoons unsalted butter**
  4 **tart crisp unwaxed apples, cored and cut into 16 wedges each**
  ½ **cup cider vinegar**

1. In a large saucepan, combine the water with ¼ cup of the unsulphured molasses and the sugar, garlic cloves, coarse salt, cracked pepper, cinnamon stick, coriander seeds and cloves and bring to a boil. Let the brine cool completely and then refrigerate until completely chilled.

2. Put the pork loin in a medium bowl and add the brine so that the meat is submerged. Cover and refrigerate for 24 hours.

3. Preheat the oven to 400°. Remove the pork loin from the brine and pat dry. Season the pork loin generously with table salt and finely ground pepper. Set the pork loin on a rack in a roasting pan and roast for about 50 minutes, or until an instant-read thermometer inserted in the center registers 145°. Transfer the pork loin to a platter and cover loosely with foil. Let the pork loin rest for 10 minutes.

4. Meanwhile, melt the butter in a large skillet. Add the apple wedges and cook over moderately high heat, tossing, until they are just tender, about 10 minutes. Using a slotted spoon, transfer the apple wedges to a bowl. Add the cider vinegar and the remaining ¼ cup of unsulphured molasses to the skillet and boil to a syrupy glaze, about 3 minutes. Pour the glaze over the apple wedges and toss to coat.

5. Carve the pork loin ⅓ inch thick and arrange on a platter. Add the pork juices to the skillet and boil for about 1 minute. Pour the juices over the pork, spoon the glazed apples around the meat and serve. —*Trey Foshee*

ONE SERVING Calories 461 kcal, Total Fat 19.5 gm, Saturated Fat 7.8 gm

WINE The off-dry flavors of a West Coast Gewürztraminer will echo the mildness of the pork and the sweetness of the molasses and apples. Try the 1997 Henry Estate from Oregon or 1996 Belvedere Floodgate from California.

Marinated Pork Roast with Prunes and Apricots

8 SERVINGS

Stuffing a roast is an easy way to make a plain cut of meat instantly elegant. You'll need a good knife to cut open the meat and cotton kitchen string to hold it together once it is stuffed.

One 4-pound boneless pork loin
Salt and freshly ground pepper

1 cup Vinho Verde or other dry white wine
4 garlic cloves, finely chopped
16 pitted prunes (5 ounces), 8 whole, 8 quartered
16 dried apricots (5 ounces), 8 whole, 8 quartered
2 tablespoons all-purpose flour
1½ cups chicken stock or canned low-sodium broth
1 teaspoon Dijon mustard

1. Set the pork on a work surface, fat side down. To butterfly the meat, make a lengthwise cut in the pork from end to end, cutting two-thirds of the way through the meat. Make a ½-inch-deep lengthwise cut in each side of the first cut, so the roast lies flat. Season the pork all over with salt and pepper.

2. In a large shallow baking dish, combine the wine, garlic and pork, turning to coat. Let marinate at room temperature for 1 hour, turning the meat once.

3. Preheat the oven to 450°. Remove the pork loin from the dish and scrape off the garlic. Strain the wine and reserve ½ cup. Lay the pork on a work surface, cut side up, and season with salt and pepper. Arrange the whole prunes down the length of 1 of the side cuts. Repeat with the whole apricots along the other side cut. Roll up the roast to reshape it and tie at even intervals with cotton string.

4. Set the pork in a small flameproof roasting pan and season with salt and pepper. Roast in the upper third of the oven for 15 minutes. Baste with the pan juices, reduce the oven temperature to 400° and roast for about 30 minutes, or until an instant-read thermometer registers 150° for rosy meat. Transfer the roast to a cutting board, cover loosely

Molasses-Cured Pork Loin with Apples

menu

Asparagus Tart (p. 30)

1998 QUINTA DA AVELEDA
VINHO VERDE BRANCO SECO

———

Poached Sea Bass with Lemon Butter (p. 134)

Steamed broccoli and new potatoes

1998 AVELEDA VINHO VERDE

———

Marinated Pork Roast with Prunes and Apricots

Carrot Pudding (p. 273)

1996 CHARAMBA DOURO RED

———

Orange Delicia (p. 360)

1994 TAYLOR PORT

with foil and let stand for 10 minutes.

5. Meanwhile, whisk the flour into the pan juices to form a smooth paste. Gradually whisk in the reserved ½ cup of wine until smooth. Set the roasting pan over 2 burners on low heat; whisk in the stock. Add the quartered prunes and apricots. Simmer, stirring often, until the sauce is flavorful, about 10 minutes. **6.** Add any accumulated juices from the roast to the sauce and whisk in the mustard. Season the sauce with salt and pepper and pour into a warmed gravy boat. Carve the pork into ⅓-inch-thick slices and serve at once with the sauce. —*Maria José Cabral and Emília Augusta Magalhães*

Three-Hour Thyme-Braised Pork

8 SERVINGS

In the past several years, braised meats have become increasingly popular among Parisian chefs. Rare lamb, rosy pork, and duck with a touch of pink all have their place, but the homey, wholesome flavors of meat and poultry cooked until meltingly tender and falling off the bone are once again in vogue.

- 3 tablespoons unsalted butter
- 6 garlic cloves, minced
- 2 carrots, finely chopped
- 2 medium onions, finely chopped
- 2 celery ribs, finely chopped

Sea salt and freshly ground pepper

One 5-pound untrimmed pork loin, pork shoulder or fresh ham on the bone

- 2 teaspoons thyme leaves, plus 2 bunches of thyme sprigs
- ¼ cup extra-virgin olive oil
- 2 cups chicken stock or canned low-sodium broth

1. Preheat the oven to 275°. In a large skillet, melt the butter. Add the garlic, carrots, onions and celery; season with sea salt and pepper. Cover and cook over low heat, stirring occasionally, until the vegetables are softened but not browned, about 10 minutes.

2. Season the pork all over with salt, pepper and the thyme leaves. In a medium enameled cast-iron casserole, heat the oil. Add the pork, sear over moderate heat until browned on all sides and transfer to a platter. Discard the fat from the casserole, wipe it clean and return the pork, meaty side up.

3. Spoon the vegetables around the meat and add the stock and bunches of thyme sprigs. Cover with a sheet of buttered wax paper and a lid and bring to a boil on the stove. Transfer the casserole to the oven and braise the pork, basting every 30 minutes, for about 3 hours, or until the pork is very tender.

4. Remove the casserole from the oven. Carefully transfer the meat to a carving board and season generously with salt and pepper. Cover loosely with foil and let stand for about 15 minutes. Strain the cooking juices through a fine sieve into a gravy boat. Thickly slice the pork; serve with the juices. —*Frédéric Anton*

MAKE AHEAD The pork can be prepared up to 1 day ahead through Step 3. Cool and refrigerate the meat in its cooking liquid. Before serving, skim off the fat and reheat gently.

SERVE WITH Brussels sprouts, wilted spinach and rice.

WINE A fairly light red or a rich white would be good here. Try a Beaujolais, a selection from the Médoc or a white Roussanne-Marsanne blend from the Coteaux du Languedoc Faugères house of Domaine Gilbert Alquier.

Cuban Sandwiches

MAKES 6 SANDWICHES

Chipotle mayonnaise gives this Cuban classic a Mexican twist. You can use a loaf of soft Italian bread instead of rolls.

- ½ cup mayonnaise
- 4 canned chipotle chiles in adobo
- 6 long sandwich rolls, split in half
- 6 thin slices Black Forest ham
- 12 thin slices imported Swiss cheese
- 2 kosher dill pickles, thinly sliced lengthwise

Cuban Sandwiches

1½ pounds Mexican Roast Pork (recipe follows), thinly sliced or shredded (about 3 cups), plus reserved pan juices

Salt

1. In a mini-processor, combine the mayonnaise and chipotles and process until smooth. Spread the cut sides of the rolls with the chipotle mayonnaise. Assemble sandwiches with the ham, cheese, pickles and pork. Top the meat with a spoonful of the pork pan juices and season with salt. Close the sandwiches; tuck in any overhanging filling.

2. Preheat the oven to 325°. Set a large griddle over moderately low heat. Arrange the sandwiches on the griddle; cover with a large baking sheet weighted down with several heavy skillets. Cook the sandwiches, turning once, until crisp outside, about 6 minutes.

3. Transfer the sandwiches to a cookie sheet and bake until the cheese is melted, about 8 minutes. Cut the baked sandwiches in half and serve immediately, passing the remaining pan juices separately. —*Richard Ampudia*

BEER Any good microbrew would be great with this flavorful pork, ham and cheese sandwich. A Dos Equis or a Red Stripe would be an easy match.

Mexican Roast Pork

6 TO 8 SERVINGS

This highly seasoned, richly flavored meat that's cooked until it's falling off the bone is delicious in Cuban Sandwiches (p. 205), wrapped in warm tortillas or served with rice and beans. Allow time for the pork to marinate overnight.

One 8-pound whole fresh pork
    shoulder, boned
1½ tablespoons minced garlic
  1 cup plus 2 tablespoons white
    vinegar
  ¾ cup fresh lime juice
  ¼ cup fresh grapefruit juice
  ¼ cup fresh orange juice
  2 tablespoons dried oregano,
    crumbled
  1 tablespoon freshly ground pepper
  1 teaspoon Goya *adobo* seasoning
  1 teaspoon Goya Sazón with
    Coriander and Annato
  1 large green bell pepper, coarsely
    chopped
  1 medium onion, coarsely chopped

1. Set the pork shoulder on a work surface. Using a small, sharp knife, make 1-inch-long slashes in the skin, about 2 inches apart. Rub the garlic into the slashes and along the underside of the pork shoulder.

2. In a large glass or ceramic bowl, combine the vinegar with the lime juice, grapefruit juice, orange juice, oregano, pepper, *adobo* seasoning and Sazón. Stir in the green bell pepper and onion and then add the pork, skin side up. Refrigerate overnight, turning the meat once or twice. Bring to room temperature before cooking.

3. Preheat the oven to 400°. Transfer the pork shoulder and its marinade to a roasting pan. Cover with foil and roast for about 3 hours, or until the meat is very tender. Let the pork cool in the liquid. Transfer the pork to a cutting board and discard the skin and fat. Strain the pan juices into a glass measure and skim off the fat. Slice or shred the pork meat before serving. Pass the pan juices separately. —*Richard Ampudia*

MAKE AHEAD The roast pork and its pan juices can be refrigerated for up to 3 days.

Porchetta

12 SERVINGS

You will need to season the fresh ham the day before you plan to cook it. The total roasting time is six hours.

One 12-pound fresh ham roast from
    the leg, bone in
 10 garlic cloves, halved
  1 tablespoon chopped rosemary
Kosher salt
  ½ teaspoon fennel seeds
  2 teaspoons olive oil
Freshly ground pepper

1. Remove the skin from the ham, leaving a thick layer of fat. Using a 4-inch paring knife, make incisions all over the ham about 1 inch apart and as deep as the blade will go.

2. In a mortar, pound the garlic to a paste. Add the rosemary, 2 teaspoons of kosher salt and the fennel seeds and pound until finely crushed. Stir in the olive oil and ½ teaspoon of pepper.

3. Using a chopstick, push ½ teaspoon of the garlic paste deep into each of the incisions. Rub any remaining garlic paste all over the ham. Set the ham fat side up and, using a knife, score the fat ½ inch deep in a crosshatch pattern. Wrap the ham in plastic and refrigerate overnight.

Porchetta

4. Preheat the oven to 300°. Set the ham in a roasting pan in which it fits snugly and bring to room temperature. Rub the ham with generous amounts of kosher salt and pepper. Roast the ham in the oven for 3 hours. Drain the pan juices and fat into a small saucepan; skim off the fat. Return the ham to the oven and roast for 3 hours longer, or until it is deeply browned and the meat is very tender.

5. Remove the roasting pan from the oven. Spoon any pan juices and fat into the small saucepan and skim again. Let the roast stand for 15 minutes. Heat the juices, adding a little water if the flavor is too strong. Cut the crisp fat from the top of the ham and then carve. Serve the ham with the crisp fat and pan juices. —*Marcia Kiesel*

WINE This fresh ham demands a red with enough tannin to cut the meat's fattiness and some earthiness to echo the fennel and garlic. That's Barolo. Consider the 1993 Michele Chiarlo Cerequio or the 1993 Ceretto Bricco Rocche Brunate.

Lentils with Leeks and Cotechino Sausage

6 SERVINGS

Cotechino are the traditional spicy pork sausages of Emilia-Romagna. They're available at Italian groceries and specialty food stores.

  1 pound French green lentils
  2 bay leaves
  ¼ cup balsamic vinegar
Salt
  ⅓ cup plus 2 tablespoons fruity extra-virgin olive oil
  1 tablespoon Dijon mustard
Freshly ground pepper
  2 thin slices pancetta, chopped
  5 medium leeks, white part only, finely chopped
  ¼ cup chopped flat-leaf parsley, plus extra sprigs for garnish
  1 teaspoon chopped thyme
  5 winter savory leaves, chopped

  2½ pounds cooked *cotechino* sausages, thickly sliced on the diagonal and warmed through

1. In a large saucepan, cover the lentils with 3 inches of cold water, add the bay leaves and bring to a boil. Reduce the heat and simmer for 15 minutes. Add 1 tablespoon of the balsamic vinegar and a generous pinch of salt and cook until the lentils are tender, about 5 minutes longer. Drain the lentils and discard the bay leaves.

2. In a small bowl, whisk ⅓ cup of the olive oil with the Dijon mustard and the remaining 3 tablespoons of balsamic vinegar. Season the vinaigrette with salt and pepper.

3. In a large skillet, heat the remaining 2 tablespoons of olive oil. Add the pancetta and cook over moderately high heat until lightly browned, 3 to 4 minutes. Add the leeks and cook until they begin to soften, 3 to 4 minutes. Add the lentils and cook, stirring, for 1 minute. Stir in the vinaigrette and the chopped parsley, thyme and savory. Season with salt and pepper.

4. Transfer the lentils to a wide bowl and arrange the sausage slices on top. Garnish with the parsley sprigs and serve. —*Erica De Mane*

WINE Sangiovese-based Tuscan reds, with their fruity, tart taste, are a natural choice for this dish. Consider the 1995 Costanti Rosso di Montalcino, or try a Chianti, such as the 1994 Nozzole Chianti Classico Riserva.

Veal Sauté Zurichoise

4 SERVINGS

Although the title of this recipe refers to Zurich, you'll find this rich and creamy veal dish on restaurant menus throughout Switzerland's Lake Geneva region. This version comes from L'Auberge de L'Onde in the wine village of St. Saphorin, where the dish is served with *rösti* potatoes. For maximum tenderness, make sure that the veal is sliced across the grain.

  1¼ pounds thinly sliced veal scaloppine, cut into 2-by-⅓-inch strips
Salt and freshly ground pepper
  3 tablespoons all-purpose flour
  2 tablespoons vegetable oil
  ½ pound white mushrooms, thinly sliced
  ⅓ cup minced shallots
  ⅓ cup dry white wine
  1¼ cups heavy cream
  1 teaspoon fresh lemon juice

1. Season the strips of veal with salt and pepper. Put the flour in a small bag, add the veal strips and shake to coat. Shake off any excess.

2. Heat the oil in a large skillet. Add half of the veal and cook over moderately high heat until barely cooked through, about 2 minutes. Transfer to a plate and repeat with the remaining meat.

3. Add the mushrooms and shallots to the skillet. Cook over moderate heat, stirring occasionally, until softened, about 5 minutes. Add the wine and simmer briefly until almost evaporated.

4. Add the heavy cream and simmer over moderate heat until slightly reduced and the mushrooms are tender, about 5 minutes. Return the veal to the skillet and bring to a simmer. Add the lemon juice, season with salt and pepper and serve. —*L'Auberge de L'Onde*

Wood-Grilled Veal Chops with Tomato-Basil Salsa

4 SERVINGS

Oak is the best wood for grilling these chops. It is readily available, burns hot and imparts a lovely flavor.

VEAL

Four ¾-pound veal rib chops
  2 tablespoons extra-virgin olive oil
  2 tablespoons fresh lemon juice
  1 tablespoon chopped oregano
Kosher salt and freshly ground pepper
SAUCE
  2 tomatoes—peeled, seeded and diced
 20 basil leaves, slivered

Wood-Grilled Veal Chops with Tomato-Basil Salsa

2 garlic cloves, minced

½ cup extra-virgin olive oil

2 tablespoons fresh lemon juice

2 teaspoons red wine vinegar

Table salt and freshly ground pepper

1. PREPARE THE VEAL: Set the veal chops in a large glass baking dish and add the olive oil, lemon juice and oregano. Season with kosher salt and pepper and turn to coat. Let marinate at room temperature for 30 minutes.

2. PREPARE THE SAUCE: In a glass or ceramic bowl, toss the tomatoes with the basil and garlic. Add the olive oil, lemon juice and vinegar and toss gently. Season generously with table salt and pepper.

3. Light a grill, preferably using oak for fuel. Grill the veal chops over a medium-hot fire for 6 to 7 minutes per side for medium; rotate the chops 90 degrees after 3 minutes on each side for attractive grill marks. Transfer the chops to a platter and let stand for 2 minutes before spooning the sauce on top and serving. —*Steven Raichlen*

WINE An elegant California Cabernet Sauvignon would have enough tannic edge to take on the salsa but plenty of fruity flavor to complement the chops. Look for the 1995 Joseph Phelps or the 1995 Laurel Glen.

Osso Buco with Red Wine

6 SERVINGS ✳

Have your butcher tie the pieces of veal shank around the middle with cotton kitchen string like a belt; this will help the meat keep its shape as it cooks. You can also tie the veal yourself. Serve the osso buco with small spoons so guests can scoop out the luscious marrow.

2 tablespoons extra-virgin olive oil

Six 2-inch-thick meaty veal shanks, each tied with string (¾ to 1 pound each)

Salt and freshly ground pepper

2 large carrots, cut into ½-inch dice

1 medium onion, cut into ½-inch dice

1 celery rib, cut into ½-inch dice

2 garlic cloves, minced

1 cup dry red wine, such as Barbera or Chianti

1 cup drained canned Italian tomatoes, coarsely chopped

1 cup chicken stock or canned low-sodium broth

1. Preheat the oven to 325°. Heat the olive oil in a large enameled cast-iron casserole. Season the veal shanks with salt and pepper and cook over moderate heat until they are browned, about 8 minutes per side. Transfer the veal shanks to a plate.

2. Add the diced carrots, onion and celery and the garlic cloves to the casserole. Reduce the heat to moderately low and cook, stirring, until the vegetables are tender, about 7 minutes. Add the red wine and cook, scraping up any brown bits, until slightly reduced, about 5 minutes. Add the canned tomatoes and chicken stock and bring to a simmer over high heat.

3. Return the veal shanks to the casserole, nestling them into the vegetables; add any accumulated juices. Cover the casserole and braise the veal shanks in the oven for 1 hour. Turn the shanks, cover and cook for about 1 hour longer, until the meat is very tender. Transfer the veal shanks to a rimmed platter and cover them loosely with foil. Measure the sauce; you should have 2 cups. If necessary, reduce the sauce over high heat. Season the sauce with salt and pepper.

4. Cut the strings off the veal shanks. Spoon the sauce on top of the shanks and serve. —*Michele Scicolone*

MAKE AHEAD The osso buco can be refrigerated overnight and reheated, covered, in a 325° oven.

WINE Serve a red that echoes the wine in the osso buco and can stand up to the tomatoes. A good choice would be the 1997 Michele Chiarlo Barbera d'Asti Superiore or the 1997 Jacopo Biondi Santi Sassoalloro.

Osso Buco with Red Wine, with Mushroom Orzotto (p. 315).

Braised Veal
with Wild Mushrooms

8 SERVINGS

Use this recipe as a blueprint for any cut of meat that benefits from slow cooking: shank, shoulder, short ribs, butt. The braising time may vary; what you're aiming for, whatever the cut, is extremely tender meat.

2 tablespoons canola oil

Four meaty 1-pound pieces of veal shank

Salt and freshly ground pepper

1 onion, chopped

1 carrot, chopped

1 celery rib, chopped

6 cups chicken stock or canned low-sodium broth

Bouquet garni made with 5 parsley sprigs, 5 thyme sprigs, 2 bay leaves and 10 peppercorns tied in cheesecloth

2 tablespoons unsalted butter

2 tablespoons extra-virgin olive oil

2½ pounds wild mushrooms, such as chanterelle, cremini and oyster, thinly sliced

1 tablespoon minced garlic

1 tablespoon finely chopped thyme

I. In a large enameled cast-iron casserole, heat the canola oil. Season the veal shanks with salt and pepper and brown them in the oil over moderate heat, about 7 minutes per side. Transfer to a plate. Add the onion, carrot and celery to the casserole and cook, stirring, until softened but not browned, about 5 minutes. Add the stock and bring to a boil, scraping up any brown bits from the bottom of the casserole.

2. Return the veal shanks to the casserole and add the bouquet garni. Cover and cook over low heat until the meat is very tender, about 1½ hours.

3. Meanwhile, in a large skillet, melt the butter in the olive oil. Add the wild mushrooms and season with salt and pepper. Cook the mushrooms over moderately high heat until they are dry and just beginning to brown, about 10 minutes. Add the garlic and thyme to the mushrooms and cook until fragrant, about 2 minutes longer.

4. Transfer the veal shanks to a platter; when cool enough to handle, discard the bones and gristle. Strain the cooking liquid, pressing hard on the solids. Return the liquid to the casserole and boil until reduced to 2 cups, about 20 minutes. Return the veal to the sauce, add the mushrooms and cook over low heat just until warmed through. Serve hot. —*Grant Achatz*

MAKE AHEAD The finished dish can be refrigerated in the sauce for up to 3 days.

SERVE WITH Sautéed Swiss chard.

WINE La Jota's 1996 Cabernet Franc is hearty and rich, mirroring the flavors of these braised shanks.

Najwa's Okra Stew

6 SERVINGS

Najwa Rawda is a Lebanese home cook of wonderful elegance and sophistication. She is superbly gifted in the kitchen, as her family readily attests. This stew and her Fried Potatoes with Cilantro (p. 298) are surprisingly simple family favorites.

¼ cup extra-virgin olive oil

1 pound very lean veal shank meat, cut into ½-inch cubes

Salt and freshly ground pepper

2 medium onions, halved and thinly sliced

4 garlic cloves, 2 chopped and 2 minced

1 cup drained canned tomatoes, chopped

1½ cups water, plus more as needed

1½ pounds okra, sliced on the diagonal ½ inch thick

¼ cup finely chopped cilantro

⅓ cup fresh lemon juice

I. Heat the oil in a large enameled cast-iron casserole. Season the veal shank meat with salt and pepper and add half of the meat to the casserole. Cook the veal over moderately high heat until nicely browned all over. Transfer the browned veal to a plate and repeat with the remaining meat.

2. Add the onions and the chopped garlic to the casserole, reduce the heat to low and cook until the onions are softened, about 8 minutes. Return the veal shank meat to the casserole and add the tomatoes and water. Cover partially and simmer until the veal is tender, about 25 minutes.

3. Stir in the sliced okra and enough water to just cover the meat. Cover and simmer for 20 minutes and then uncover and cook until the liquid reduces slightly, about 10 minutes. Stir in the minced garlic and the cilantro and simmer for 2 minutes. Stir in the lemon juice and season the stew with salt and pepper. Remove the stew from the heat and let it stand for 10 minutes before serving. —*Nancy Harmon Jenkins*

SERVE WITH Steamed rice.

menu

Creamy Crab Canapés with Lemon and Caviar (p. 19)

Parmesan Tartlets with Tomato Confit (p. 30)

1985 PLOYEZ-JACQUEMART CHAMPAGNE

Warm Salad of Winter Fruits, Endives and Pancetta (p. 67)

1997 LA JOTA VIOGNIER

Delicata Squash Soup (p. 90)

Braised Veal with Wild Mushrooms

Quinoa with Caramelized Onions (p. 315)

1996 LA JOTA CABERNET FRANC

Chocolate-Chestnut Semifreddo Pops with Candied Cranberries (p. 383)

Braised Veal with Wild Mushrooms

chapter 9
beef lamb buffalo

239

225

231

243

Rosen's Lemon Charred Beef with Crisp Herbed Spaetzle

Rosen's Lemon Charred Beef with Crisp Herbed Spaetzle

4 SERVINGS

Steve Rosen, the chef at Salts in Cambridge, Massachusetts, likes to use a little sugar in meat marinades; it caramelizes and yields a delicious crust. But the sugar should always be balanced with something acidic—in this case, lemon juice.

¼ cup fresh lemon juice
1 teaspoon finely grated lemon zest
½ cup light brown sugar
Freshly ground black pepper
2 tablespoons olive oil
4 center-cut filet mignon steaks (about 6 ounces each), tied
1 tablespoon sweet paprika
1 cup rich beef stock or canned beef broth
¼ cup sour cream
1 small yellow onion, minced
1 red onion, cut into thick slices
1 red bell pepper
1 yellow bell pepper
½ pound pencil-thin asparagus, cut into 2-inch lengths
1 tablespoon canola oil
Salt
2 tablespoons unsalted butter
Herbed Spaetzle (recipe follows)

1. In a blender, process the fresh lemon juice, lemon zest, brown sugar, ½ teaspoon black pepper and the olive oil until smooth. Put the steaks in a shallow bowl and add all but 2 tablespoons of the marinade; turn to coat. Cover and refrigerate for 1 hour.

2. Meanwhile, toast the paprika in a small dry skillet over moderate heat, shaking the pan, until brick colored, 3 to 4 minutes. Transfer to a plate to cool.

3. In a small saucepan, boil the beef stock until reduced to ⅔ cup. Add the toasted paprika, the sour cream and the yellow onion and cook over moderate heat until the sauce is slightly thickened, 6 to 7 minutes.

4. Preheat the broiler. Brush the red onion slices with the reserved 2 tablespoons of marinade and arrange them on a broiling pan along with the red and yellow bell peppers. Broil the red onion slices and the bell peppers for about 15 minutes, turning occasionally, until they are charred all over. Transfer the bell peppers to a bowl, cover and let steam for 15 minutes. Coarsely chop the red onion. Peel, core and seed the bell peppers and cut them into ½-inch pieces.

5. Bring a medium saucepan of salted water to a boil. Add the asparagus and cook until crisp-tender, 3 to 4 minutes. Drain the asparagus and cool under running water.

6. Preheat the oven to 450°. Heat the canola oil in an ovenproof skillet until shimmering. Drain the steaks and season with salt and black pepper. Cook over moderate heat until browned, about 7 minutes per side. Transfer the skillet to the oven and cook the steaks for 4 to 5 minutes for medium rare. Transfer the steaks to a cutting board and let rest for 10 minutes.

7. Rewarm the sauce. Melt the butter in a large nonstick skillet. Add the Herbed Spaetzle and cook over high heat, stirring occasionally, until crisp and golden, 8 to 10 minutes. Add the cooked bell peppers, asparagus and red onion, season with salt and black pepper and cook until warmed through. Mound the spaetzle and vegetables on 4 large plates and set the steaks on top with some spoonfuls of the sauce. Serve at once. —*Steve Rosen*

WINE To highlight the tender filet mignon, consider a plummy California Merlot, such as the 1995 Rosenblum Russian River Valley or the 1996 Flora Springs Napa Valley.

HERBED SPAETZLE

4 SERVINGS

- 1 medium baking potato (½ pound), peeled and cut into large chunks
- 1 cup milk
- 2 large eggs, lightly beaten
- 1 tablespoon minced dill
- 1 tablespoon minced flat-leaf parsley
- 1 teaspoon kosher salt
- 2¼ cups all-purpose flour

Pinch of freshly grated nutmeg

1. In a medium saucepan of boiling water, cook the potato until tender, about 8 minutes; drain. Let cool slightly and transfer to a large bowl. Mash the potato and then mash with the milk, eggs, dill, parsley, kosher salt, flour and nutmeg to form a sticky dough.

2. Bring a large pot of salted water to a boil. Pat one quarter of the dough into a 3-inch square on a small cutting board with a handle or on the back of a square cake pan. Using a moistened chef's knife, cut off ¼-inch-thick strips of the dough and scrape them into the boiling water; moisten the knife if it sticks to the dough. Boil for 30 seconds without stirring and then gently stir to separate the strips. Cook just until the strips rise to the surface. Using a small strainer or a wire skimmer, transfer to a bowl of ice water. Return the water in the saucepan to a boil and cook the remaining spaetzle. Drain well, shaking off the excess water. —*S. R.*

MAKE AHEAD The spaetzle can be refrigerated for up to 3 days; toss with a little olive oil before storing.

Beef Tenderloin and Mushrooms in Golden Puff Pastry

4 SERVINGS

The meat and the surrounding layer of chopped mushrooms are wrapped in rice-paper rounds before being swaddled in pastry. This keeps the crust from becoming overly soggy when baked.

- 1 tablespoon canola oil
- 2 pounds beef tenderloin

Salt and freshly ground pepper

- 1 stick plus 3 tablespoons unsalted butter
- 1 pound white mushrooms, stems trimmed, thinly sliced
- 2 tablespoons crème fraîche

Two 12-inch rice-paper rounds (see Note)

- 14 ounces all-butter puff pastry dough, chilled
- 1 large egg yolk beaten with 1 tablespoon water
- 1 medium leek, white part only, thinly sliced crosswise
- 1 medium carrot, thinly sliced
- 1 shallot, finely chopped
- 1⅔ cups Pinot Noir
- ¼ cup plus 2 tablespoons ruby port

1. Preheat the oven to 425°. Heat the canola oil in a large skillet until it is almost smoking. Add the beef tenderloin and brown it well on all 4 sides over moderately high heat, about 4 minutes per side. Transfer the beef to a plate and season with salt and pepper. Reserve the skillet for later use.

2. In another large skillet, melt 3 tablespoons of the butter. Add the mushrooms and cook over high heat, stirring, until they are lightly browned, about 15 minutes. Season the mushrooms with salt and pepper. Finely chop the mushrooms in a food processor. Add the crème fraîche and process until combined. Season the mushroom mixture with salt and pepper.

3. Moisten the rice paper rounds under cool water and lay them on a cutting board until softened. Pat the rounds dry with paper towels. On a lightly floured work surface, roll out the puff pastry to a 14-by-12-inch rectangle about ⅛ inch thick. Slightly overlap the rice paper rounds in the center of the puff pastry. Set the beef tenderloin on the rice paper rounds and then pat the mushroom

mixture all over the meat. Wrap the rice papers around the meat to hold the mushrooms in place.

4. Bring the long sides of the puff pastry up and over the beef tenderloin, brush the seam with the egg wash and then press to seal. Trim off any excess puff pastry from the short sides and brush with the egg wash. Fold the ends to enclose the beef tenderloin and then set the bundle on a lightly greased baking sheet, seam side down. Brush with egg wash. If desired, cut out leaves or other decorations from the pastry scraps and glue them on with egg wash; brush the decorations with egg wash too.

5. Bake the beef tenderloin for 30 minutes and then cover loosely with foil to prevent the pastry from getting too dark. Continue baking until an instant-read thermometer inserted in the center of the meat registers 120° for rare. Transfer the beef tenderloin to a cutting board and let rest for 5 minutes.

6. Meanwhile, melt 2 tablespoons of the butter in the skillet used to brown the meat. Add the leek, the carrot and the shallot and cook over moderately high heat, stirring occasionally, until they are lightly browned, about 3 minutes. Season the mixture with salt and

Beef Tenderloin and Mushrooms in Golden Puff Pastry, with green beans.

pepper. Add ⅔ cup of the Pinot Noir and simmer, scraping up the brown bits, until reduced by half, about 5 minutes. Add the remaining 1 cup of Pinot Noir and the ruby port and simmer over moderate heat until reduced by half again, about 7 minutes.

7. Cut the remaining 6 tablespoons of butter into small pieces. Pour the sauce through a fine sieve into a small saucepan. Set the saucepan over low heat and gradually whisk in the remaining butter. Season the sauce with salt and pepper. Carve the beef into thin slices and serve hot; pass the sauce separately. —*Marie-Andrée Nauleau*

NOTE Rice paper becomes translucent and pleasantly chewy after being moistened with water. It is available at Asian groceries and some supermarkets.

Honey Grilled Steaks

6 SERVINGS

- 1 bunch scallions, minced
- 2 tablespoons minced fresh ginger
- 1 tablespoon minced garlic
- ¾ cup soy sauce
- ¼ cup mushroom soy sauce (see Note)
- ¼ cup rice vinegar
- ¼ cup fresh lime juice
- 3 tablespoons honey
- 1 tablespoon sugar

Salt and freshly ground pepper
- ¼ cup plus 2 tablespoons canola oil
- 2 tablespoons Asian sesame oil

Six ¾-inch-thick rib-eye steaks (about ¾ pound each)

1. In a large jar with a tight-fitting lid, combine the scallions, ginger, garlic, soy sauce, mushroom soy sauce, rice vinegar, lime juice, honey and sugar. Season with salt and pepper and shake well. Add the canola oil and sesame oil and shake again. Arrange the steaks in a glass or stainless steel baking dish large enough to hold them in a single layer. Pour the marinade over the steaks and let stand at room temperature for at least 30 minutes or up to 1 hour.

2. Light a grill or preheat the broiler. Cook the steaks about 4 minutes per side for medium rare. Let stand a few minutes before serving. —*Lisa Ahier*

NOTE Mushroom soy sauce is available from Asian markets and specialty food shops.

MAKE AHEAD The marinade can be refrigerated for up to 3 days.

WINE The touch of honey in the marinade suggests a plummy, deep-flavored California Merlot, such as the 1997 Echelon or the 1996 St. Francis.

Black Pepper–Crusted Roast Beef

6 SERVINGS

A variety of rich, meaty cuts, including loin, prime rib and top round roast, can stand up to this intense crust.

- 6 garlic cloves, 4 minced and 2 thinly sliced
- 2 tablespoons olive oil
- 2 tablespoons soy sauce
- 1½ tablespoons kosher salt
- 2 tablespoons cracked black peppercorns
- 1 teaspoon finely chopped rosemary

One 3½-pound boneless rib-eye beef roast

1. In a blender, combine the minced garlic with the oil, soy sauce, kosher salt, peppercorns and rosemary; process to a paste. Make fifteen 1-inch-deep cuts all over the roast and insert a thin slice of garlic in each cut. Set on a rack in a roasting pan; rub all over with the paste. Let sit at room temperature for 2 hours.

2. Preheat the oven to 500°. Roast the meat for about 10 minutes, or until the crust begins to brown. Reduce the oven temperature to 350° and cook for about 1¼ hours longer, or until an instant-read thermometer inserted in the thickest part registers 125° for medium rare.

3. Transfer the roast to a carving board and let it rest, uncovered, for 10 minutes. Carve the roast into ½-inch-thick slices. —*Wilder Fulford*

SERVE WITH Roasted shallots and mixed baby vegetables, such as potatoes, beets and carrots.

WINE Peppery and garlicky, this dish requires a similarly meaty California Syrah with some spice of its own, such as the 1997 Qupé or the 1995 Preston Vineyard Select.

Coriander-Crusted Standing Rib Roast

12 SERVINGS

- ⅓ cup coriander seeds
- 2½ tablespoons kosher salt
- 1½ tablespoons cracked black peppercorns
- 3 tablespoons extra-virgin olive oil

Finely grated zest of 1 orange

---

menu

Basil Blini with Salmon Caviar (p. 21)

Porcini and Black Olive Canapés (p. 19)

NONVINTAGE DEUTZ BRUT CHAMPAGNE

Salad of Mixed Greens with Mushroom Vinaigrette (p. 64)

Grouper Chowder (p. 97)

1996 CHATEAU CARBONNIEUX GRAVES BLANC

Coriander-Crusted Standing Rib Roast

Tomato and Goat Cheese Gratin (p. 29)

Winter Vegetable Ragout with Madiera (p. 284)

Kale and Bacon Bread Pudding (p. 270)

1995 DUCKHORN HOWELL MOUNTAIN MERLOT

Cinnamon Lace Cookies (p. 352)

Cranberry-Pear Tartlets with Cranberry Ice Cream (p. 344)

1997 GEORGES DUBOEUF MUSCAT DE BEAUMES-DE-VENISE

Coriander-Crusted Standing Rib Roast, with Kale and Bacon Bread Pudding (p. 270) and Winter Vegetable Ragout with Madeira (p. 284).

Grilled Steaks with, CLOCKWISE FROM TOP LEFT, Beet and Green Bean Salad (p. 53), Tomato and Sweet Onion Salad (p. 68), Crisp Celery Fans (p. 273) and Tomato Salsa (p. 319).

One 7-pound beef rib roast,
    at room temperature

½ cup fresh orange juice

1. Preheat the oven to 375°. In a spice grinder or mortar, coarsely grind the coriander with the kosher salt and peppercorns. Transfer the spice mixture to a bowl and stir in the olive oil and orange zest to make a paste. Spread the spice paste all over the roast and set it, fat side up, on a rack in a large roasting pan. Pour the orange juice into the pan.

2. Roast the meat for 25 minutes; lower the oven temperature to 325° and roast for about 2 hours and 20 minutes longer, or until an instant-read thermometer inserted in the center of the roast registers 125° for rare to medium rare. Transfer the roast to a carving board, cover loosely with foil and let rest for at least 15 minutes before carving into ½-inch-thick slices. —*Tim McKee*

MAKE AHEAD The recipe can be prepared through Step 1 up to 4 hours ahead; let stand at room temperature.

WINE The roast demands a full-flavored red with some velvety tannins to check the fattiness of the meat. It's a job for a grand California Merlot, such as the 1995 Duckhorn Howell Mountain or the 1995 Sterling Three Palms.

Grilled Steaks

6 SERVINGS

Six 1½-to-2-inch-thick boneless strip steaks (about 1½ pounds each)

Coarse sea salt

Freshly ground pepper

Light a charcoal grill or preheat a gas grill. Season the steaks with sea salt and pepper. Grill over moderate heat, turning once, until medium rare, about 9 minutes per side. Serve the steaks at once. —*Ruth Van Waerebeek-Gonzalez*

Herbed Hanger Steak

2 SERVINGS

Hanger steak, recently discovered by restaurant chefs, has always been a favorite butcher's cut in the United States; it's also hugely popular in France, where it's known as *onglet*.

One 1-pound hanger steak, about 1 inch thick, trimmed (see Note)

3 **tablespoons olive oil**

1 **tablespoon thyme leaves**

Salt and freshly ground pepper

2 **large shallots, thinly sliced**

1. Rub the steak with 2 tablespoons of the olive oil and coat with the thyme. Season with salt and pepper.

2. In a large cast-iron skillet, heat the remaining 1 tablespoon of olive oil until shimmering. Add the meat and pan-fry over moderately high heat until browned

Herbed Hanger Steak

and crusty, about 4 minutes per side for medium rare. Transfer the steak to a cutting board and let stand for 5 minutes.

3. Add the shallots to the skillet; cook over moderately high heat, stirring occasionally, until softened and browned, about 3 minutes.

4. Thickly slice the steak across the grain and arrange on plates. Spoon the sautéed shallots on top of the steak and serve immediately. —*Marcia Kiesel*

NOTE If the steak has a membrane that runs down the middle, remove it by cutting on either side of the membrane, dividing the steak into 2 long strips.

Argentine Barbecue with Salsa Criolla

8 SERVINGS

One of the most traditional Argentine barbecues is *asado de tira,* a cut of beef ribs, which is served with tomato salsa. To approximate the tender Argentine cut, use skirt steak. If cooking the meat in a grill pan, lightly oil the pan first.

- 2 medium tomatoes, finely chopped
- 1 medium onion, finely chopped
- 1 red or yellow bell pepper, finely chopped
- ½ green bell pepper, finely chopped
- 1 garlic clove, minced
- 2 tablespoons olive oil
- ¼ cup chopped cilantro

Salt and freshly ground black pepper

- 4 pounds skirt steak

1. Light a grill or preheat a grill pan. In a glass or stainless steel bowl, combine the tomatoes with the onion, bell peppers, garlic, olive oil and cilantro. Season with salt and black pepper.

2. Season the skirt steak with salt and black pepper. Grill over moderately high heat for about 3 minutes per side, or until lightly charred and medium rare. Transfer the steak to a cutting board to rest for 5 minutes. Thinly slice the steak on the diagonal and pass the salsa separately. —*Pablo Massey*

WINE The 1996 Catena Cabernet Sauvignon Agrelo Vineyards has the vibrant fruit of a New World Cabernet, but the structure and ageability of a Bordeaux. The tannins in this wine are beefy, just like a good Argentine *asado.*

Argentine Barbecue with Salsa Criolla

---

menu

Roasted Vegetable Bruschetta (p. 16)

1997 CATENA MALBEC
LUNLUNTA VINEYARD

———

**Butternut Squash Gnocchi
with Sage Butter (p. 125)**

1997 CATENA ALTA CHARDONNAY
LUCA VINEYARD

———

**Argentine Barbecue with
Salsa Criolla**

1996 CATENA CABERNET SAUVIGNON
AGRELO VINEYARDS

———

**Grilled Polenta with Mushrooms
and Toasted Pumpkin Seeds (p. 312)**

1997 CATENA ALTA MALBEC
ANGELICA VINEYARDS

———

Lemony Rice Pudding (p. 381)

Goin's Grilled Steak with Tomato Bread Salad

4 SERVINGS

Suzanne Goin is chef at Lucques in Los Angeles. She advises to always cut steak against the grain. A skirt steak's grain can curve, so turn the meat as you slice. Cut the cherry tomatoes in half for extra juiciness. Her tender steak needs to marinate overnight, so plan accordingly.

- 6 garlic cloves, mashed
- ¼ cup plus 3 tablespoons extra-virgin olive oil
- 1 teaspoon coarsely cracked black pepper
- 2 skirt steaks (about 14 ounces each), halved crosswise with the grain
- 8 thyme sprigs
- 2 tablespoons crumbled Roquefort cheese, at room temperature
- 2 tablespoons unsalted butter, softened
- 2 tablespoons balsamic vinegar
- 1 teaspoon fresh lemon juice

Sea salt and freshly ground pepper
- 2 cups crustless torn sourdough bread pieces (about 1 inch)
- 1 pound heirloom tomatoes, some sliced and some cut into wedges
- 2 cups mixed cherry tomatoes
- ½ cup thinly sliced red onion
- ¼ cup Niçoise olives, pitted
- 1 bunch arugula, stemmed
- ¼ cup tiny green and purple basil leaves

1. In a bowl, combine the garlic with 1 tablespoon of the olive oil and the cracked pepper. Spread the paste on the skirt steaks, top with the thyme and stack the steaks on top of each other. Transfer the steaks to a plate and refrigerate overnight. Bring to room temperature before grilling.

2. In a small bowl, mash the Roquefort with the butter until smooth.

3. In a small glass or stainless steel bowl, combine the balsamic vinegar, the lemon juice and ¼ teaspoon sea salt and let stand until the salt is dissolved. Whisk in ¼ cup of the olive oil and season the vinaigrette with freshly ground pepper.

4. Preheat the oven to 350°. Toss the pieces of sourdough bread with the remaining 2 tablespoons of olive oil and arrange them on a baking sheet. Toast the bread pieces for about 15 minutes, or until they are golden and just crisp. Let the bread cool.

5. Light a grill or heat a grill pan. Scrape the marinade off the skirt steaks and season the steaks with sea salt. Grill the steaks over moderately high heat until seared and crusty, about 3 minutes per side for medium rare. Transfer the steaks to a cutting board and let rest for 5 minutes.

6. In a glass or stainless steel bowl, toss the toasted bread pieces with the heirloom tomatoes, the cherry tomatoes, the red onion, the Niçoise olives and the vinaigrette. Gently toss in the arugula and the basil leaves and season the salad with sea salt. Transfer the salad to large plates.

7. Thinly slice the grilled skirt steaks across the grain and arrange the slices alongside the salads. Place a spoonful of the Roquefort butter on top and serve immediately. —*Suzanne Goin*

MAKE AHEAD The steak, Roquefort butter and vinaigrette can be prepared through Step 3 and refrigerated overnight; let return to room temperature before proceeding.

WINE Garlic, thyme, tomatoes and Roquefort butter add savoriness to this steak; a rich Cabernet Sauvignon will do the same. Consider the 1995 Carmenet Moon Mountain Reserve from California or the 1997 Wolf Blass Yellow Label from Australia.

Korean Grilled Beef with Scallion Salad

6 SERVINGS

Variations on this Korean dish, called *bul kogi,* are available throughout Australia. It's usually served with condiments, such as kimchi—the spicy cabbage that is sold at Asian markets. Let guests prepare their own *bul kogi* packages by dabbing a bit of chili paste on the lettuce and wrapping it around the meat and scallion salad.

RIGHT: **Korean Grilled Beef with Scallion Salad.**
TOP: **Goin's Grilled Steak with Tomato Bread Salad.**

wines for thai food

Identify key flavors in a Thai dish and then pick a wine to match.

Sharp and spicy If there's lots of ginger (as in Stir-Fried Ginger Beef, below right), go for beer. Microbrew ales are particularly good.

Spicy and aromatic If there are chiles and a generous amount of fresh herbs (as in Spicy Shrimp with Basil, p. 154), try a fresh, young white Bordeaux.

Sweet and tangy If there's sugar and lots of lime (as in Thai Chicken and Jicama Salad, p. 169), look for a white with plenty of acidity, like a New Zealand Sauvignon Blanc.

Sweet and pungent If the primary flavors are sugar or molasses and fish sauce (as in Asian Chicken Casserole, p. 164), choose an off-dry Gewürztraminer from Washington State or California.

Stir-Fried Ginger Beef

1 tablespoon sesame seeds

3 tablespoons plus 2 teaspoons sake

3 tablespoons soy sauce

3 tablespoons peeled and minced fresh ginger

1 tablespoon minced garlic

9 scallions—3 minced and 6 cut into 2-inch matchsticks

¼ cup plus 1½ teaspoons canola or other mild vegetable oil

2½ teaspoons sugar

Cayenne pepper

1½ pounds lean sirloin steak, thinly sliced across the grain into long strips

½ teaspoon Asian sesame oil

1 head leaf lettuce, leaves separated

Asian chili paste

1. In a small skillet, toast the sesame seeds over moderate heat until lightly browned, about 3 minutes. Let cool.

2. In a large glass baking dish, combine 3 tablespoons of the sake with the soy sauce, ginger, garlic, minced scallions, 2 teaspoons of the sesame seeds, 1½ teaspoons each of the canola oil and sugar and a pinch of cayenne. Add the meat and turn to coat. Let marinate at room temperature for 20 minutes.

3. Heat a large, heavy skillet. Add 2 tablespoons of the canola oil and swirl to coat. Add about one fourth of the meat at a time in a single layer and cook over high heat until browned and crisp around the edges, about 2 minutes per side; transfer to a large platter. Repeat with the remaining meat, adding more oil as needed.

4. In a medium bowl, combine the remaining 2 teaspoons of sake with the sesame oil, a pinch of cayenne and the remaining 1 teaspoon toasted sesame seeds and 1 teaspoon sugar. Add the scallion matchsticks.

5. Arrange the lettuce leaves on the platter alongside the grilled meat and top with the scallion salad. Serve the chili paste on the side. —*John Ash*

SERVE WITH Steamed rice.

WINE The assertive dressing adds kick to this grilled beef dish, making a full-bodied Down Under Cabernet Sauvignon a solid choice. Two terrific ones are the 1997 Rosemount Show Reserve and the 1995 Moss Wood.

Stir-Fried Ginger Beef

4 SERVINGS 🌼

Bean paste adds pungency to this luscious Thai beef recipe. The paste is available at Asian markets and specialty food stores.

¼ cup minced fresh ginger, plus 1 tablespoon finely julienned

1 teaspoon all-purpose flour

3 tablespoons vegetable oil

1 pound lean top sirloin steak, sliced across the grain ¼ inch thick

1½ tablespoons minced garlic

1½ tablespoons soy sauce

1 tablespoon bean paste (see Note)

1 teaspoon sugar

2 fresh red Thai or serrano chiles, seeded and thinly sliced

¼ cup cilantro leaves

1. Soak all of the ginger in a small bowl of warm water for 5 minutes. Drain and pat dry. Return the ginger to the bowl and toss with the flour.

2. Heat the oil in a large nonstick skillet. Add half the meat in a single layer and cook over high heat until browned on both sides, about 3 minutes. Using a slotted spoon, transfer to a platter. Return the skillet to high heat. Add the garlic; cook until fragrant, about 30 seconds. Add the remaining meat in a single layer and cook until browned, about 3 more minutes. Return all the meat to the skillet. Add the soy sauce, bean paste, sugar, chiles and ginger; stir-fry for 1 minute. Stir in the cilantro, transfer to a bowl and serve. —*Su-Mei Yu*

NOTE Bean paste is available from Asian markets and specialty food shops.

SERVE WITH Steamed jasmine rice.

Lean, Mean Chili

12 SERVINGS

1 cup (6 ounces) coarsely chopped sun-dried tomatoes

3½ cups boiling water

3 tablespoons vegetable oil

6 pounds lean sirloin, cut into 1-inch cubes

Salt and freshly ground black pepper

10 scallions, sliced crosswise

6 large garlic cloves, coarsely chopped

3 large onions, diced

2 red bell peppers, diced

1 green bell pepper, diced

¼ cup mild pure chile powder, such as ancho

¼ cup medium-hot pure chile powder, such as pasilla

One 28-ounce can crushed tomatoes

1 large chipotle chile

Lime wedges, for serving

Lean, Mean Chili, with White Rice with Black Beans and Winter Squash (p. 304).

1. In a medium heatproof bowl, cover the sun-dried tomatoes with the boiling water and let them soak until softened, about 20 minutes. Using a slotted spoon, transfer the sun-dried tomatoes to a food processor and puree. Reserve the soaking liquid.

2. In a large enameled cast-iron casserole, heat the vegetable oil. Season the sirloin cubes with salt and freshly ground black pepper. Working in batches, brown the sirloin cubes on all sides in the vegetable oil over high heat and then transfer the browned meat to a large plate.

3. Add 6 of the scallions, the garlic, the onions, half of the red bell peppers and all of the green bell pepper to the casserole. Cook the vegetables over moderate heat, stirring often, until they are softened, about 10 minutes. Add the chile powders and cook, stirring, until fragrant, about 4 minutes. Add the sun-dried tomato puree and the reserved soaking liquid, the browned meat, the crushed tomatoes and the chipotle chile and stir well.

4. Bring the chili to a simmer, cover partially and cook over low heat, stirring occasionally, until richly flavored, about 2

Beef and Olive Empanadas

hours. Season with salt and black pepper. Transfer to a serving bowl; discard the chipotle. Garnish with the remaining scallions and red bell pepper and the lime wedges. Serve hot. —*Marcia Kiesel*

MAKE AHEAD The chili can be refrigerated for up to 2 days.

ONE SERVING Calories 432 kcal, Total Fat 14.6 gm, Saturated Fat 4 gm

WINE Look for a hearty, spicy California Zinfandel—such as the 1996 Ridge Sonoma Station or the 1995 Grgich Hills—to stand up to the heat and the smokiness of this intense and tomatoey chili.

Beef and Olive Empanadas

6 SERVINGS

In Argentina there's a saying that the oven should be hot enough for the empanadas to finish baking by the time the cook recites the Lord's Prayer. Every region has its preferred empanada filling; this one, with onion, olive, egg and beef, is typical of the Mendoza region.

DOUGH

2 cups (about ¾ pound) lard or vegetable shortening
2 cups water
⅓ cup kosher salt
5½ cups all-purpose flour

FILLING

2 Idaho potatoes
3 tablespoons vegetable oil
2 pounds beef sirloin, cut into ½-inch dice
Salt and freshly ground black pepper
1 tablespoon unsalted butter
3 small onions, thinly sliced
2 tablespoons mild pure chili powder, such as ancho
1 tablespoon crushed red pepper
1 teaspoon ground cumin
½ cup water
4 scallions, thinly sliced
1 cup (about 6 ounces) black olives, such as Calamata, pitted and coarsely chopped
3 hard-cooked eggs, chopped
Hot sauce (optional)

I. MAKE THE DOUGH: In a saucepan, combine the shortening, the water and the kosher salt and simmer over moderately high heat until the shortening melts and the salt dissolves. Sift the all-purpose flour into a large bowl, make a well in the center of the flour and then pour in the shortening mixture. Stir until a dough forms; it will be soft and oily. Pat the dough into a 12-inch square and cover. Refrigerate the dough until it is firm, about 1 hour.

2. MAKE THE FILLING: In a saucepan, cover the potatoes with water and boil over moderately high heat until tender, about 20 minutes. Drain and let cool. Peel the potatoes and cut into ½-inch dice.

3. In a large skillet, heat 1 tablespoon of the vegetable oil. Add one third of the sirloin and cook over high heat without stirring until well browned on the bottom, about 3 minutes. Stir and cook until the beef is browned all over, about 3 minutes longer. Season the beef with salt and black pepper and transfer to a plate. Repeat with the remaining beef, adding 1 more tablespoon of vegetable oil before browning the last batch.

4. In the skillet, melt the butter in the remaining 1 tablespoon of oil. Add the onions and cook over low heat until softened, about 10 minutes. Add the chili powder, crushed red pepper and cumin and cook over moderate heat, stirring, until fragrant, about 3 minutes. Add the water and simmer until slightly reduced, about 3 minutes. Stir in the scallions, sirloin and any accumulated juices. Transfer the filling to a bowl and let cool. Fold in the cooked potatoes, olives and eggs and season with salt and black pepper.

5. Preheat the oven to 500°. Cut the dough in half and then cut each half into 9 equal pieces. Shape each piece into a ball. On a lightly floured surface, roll each ball out to a 7-inch round. Moisten the outer edge of 1 round. Scoop a rounded ⅓ cup of filling on one half of the round and fold the other side over the filling. Press the edge down firmly and then fold it over onto itself at ½-inch intervals to seal. Transfer the empanada to a baking sheet. Repeat with the remaining dough and filling and then arrange the empanadas on 2 or 3 baking sheets.

6. Bake the empanadas about 25 minutes, or until browned. Serve the empanadas hot or at room temperature, with hot sauce. —*Francis Mallmann*

MAKE AHEAD The empanadas can be refrigerated overnight or frozen for up to 2 weeks; rewarm in a 350° oven.

WINE These spicy, salty, olive-rich turnovers need only a flavorful Argentinean red, such as the 1996 Catena Malbec or the 1995 Catena Alta Cabernet Sauvignon.

Beef with Crushed Peppercorns

4 SERVINGS

The Christian community in southern India is fond of goat and beef curries, often prepared using vinegar as a tenderizer. In this popular dish, the meat is boiled before it is fried, which seems to make it especially succulent.

1¾ pounds well-marbled beef sirloin or boneless lamb shoulder, cut into ½-inch cubes

⅔ cup water

1 tablespoon plus 1 teaspoon coriander

1½ teaspoons salt

1½ teaspoons white vinegar

¼ teaspoon turmeric

¼ teaspoon cayenne pepper

¼ teaspoon coarsely crushed fennel seeds

⅛ teaspoon cinnamon

⅛ teaspoon ground cloves

⅛ teaspoon ground cardamom

¼ cup coconut oil or vegetable oil

2 medium onions, thinly sliced

2 garlic cloves, minced

2 teaspoons minced fresh ginger

2 teaspoons coarsely crushed black peppercorns

1. In a medium saucepan, combine the meat with the water, coriander, salt, white vinegar, turmeric, cayenne, fennel seeds, cinnamon, cloves and cardamom. Bring to a boil and then reduce the heat to low and simmer until the meat is just cooked through, about 5 minutes. Drain the meat, reserving the cooking liquid.

2. In a large skillet, heat the oil. Add the onions and cook over moderately high heat, stirring occasionally, until lightly browned, about 8 minutes. Add the garlic, ginger and black peppercorns and cook, stirring, for 1 minute. Stir in the meat. Add the reserved liquid, a few tablespoons at a time, and stir constantly over moderate heat until the meat is coated with the sauce, about 5 minutes. The curry should be moist, not runny or dry. Serve hot. —*Maya Kaimal*

SERVE WITH Pappadams (p. 12) and steamed rice.

WINE The spiciness of this dish narrows the choice of an accompanying red wine to one with a similar assertiveness: California Zinfandel. Try the 1996 Pedroncelli Mother Clone or the 1996 Cline.

Beef with Crushed Peppercorns

Gorgonzola Cheeseburgers with Pancetta

4 SERVINGS

Handle the meat as little as possible when making burgers: a few pats with wet hands is all that's necessary to shape the patties.

1½ pounds ground sirloin or chuck

Salt and freshly ground pepper

8 thin slices pancetta

Four ¼-inch-thick slices Gorgonzola cheese (4 ounces)

4 hamburger buns or kaiser rolls, split

2 tablespoons unsalted butter, melted

Paper-thin sweet onion slices, tomato slices, and romaine lettuce leaves

1. Light a grill. Shape the meat into 4 patties and season on both sides with salt and pepper. Wrap each hamburger with 2 slices of pancetta.

2. Grill the hamburgers over a medium-hot fire for about 4 minutes, or until

Gorgonzola Cheeseburgers with Pancetta

they are nicely browned on the bottom. Flip the hamburgers and top with the Gorgonzola cheese. Grill the cheeseburgers for about 4 minutes longer, or until the burgers are nicely browned and cooked through.

3. Meanwhile, brush the cut sides of the buns with the butter and grill them, cut side down, until lightly toasted.

4. Set the cheeseburgers on the bun bottoms and top with the onion, tomato and lettuce. Serve the cheeseburgers at once. —*Steven Raichlen*

BEER Beer is all that's needed between bites of this rich Gorgonzola-topped burger—a flavorful brew, such as Catamount Gold, would be ideal.

Aromatic Wine-Braised Beef

8 SERVINGS

The restaurant Jamin, in Paris, is the source for this dish. When you prepare it, you will be rewarded with an extraordinarily fragrant and inviting kitchen. The beef is equally delicious whether prepared with white wine or red.

- 2 tablespoons unsalted butter
- 2 tablespoons olive oil
- 5 pounds beef chuck steak with bone, cut into 8 portions

Sea salt and freshly ground pepper

- 2 bottles (750 ml each) red or dry white wine
- 24 shallots, quartered
- 4 carrots, quartered
- 2 large onions, quartered
- 1 large bunch of fresh parsley and several fresh bay leaves, tied together with string
- 2 whole star anise
- 1 teaspoon whole black peppercorns

I. Preheat the oven to 200°. In a large enameled cast-iron casserole, melt the butter in the olive oil. Add the meat in batches and brown it over moderate heat, about 5 minutes per side. Transfer the meat as it's browned to a platter and immediately season it generously with sea salt and pepper.

2. Add ½ cup of the wine to the casserole; use a metal spatula to scrape up any brown bits from the bottom. Return the meat to the casserole. Add the shallots, carrots, onions, herb bundle, star anise, peppercorns and remaining wine. Cover with a sheet of buttered wax paper and a lid. Bring the wine to a boil.

3. Transfer the casserole to the oven and braise the beef for about 3 hours, or until very tender. Remove from the oven and transfer the meat to a platter. Strain the cooking juices, pressing on the solids; discard the solids.

4. Rinse out the casserole. Return the cooking juices to it; skim off the fat and simmer over moderately high heat until reduced by about one third, about 10 minutes. Return the meat to the casserole and cook until heated through, about 10 minutes. Season with salt and pepper. Serve with the cooking juices in rimmed plates. —*Benoît Guichard*

MAKE AHEAD The recipe can be prepared through Step 3 and refrigerated for up to 2 days.

SERVE WITH Macaroni Gratin (p. 114) and Carrots with Cumin (p. 271).

WINE Drink the same wine you'd use for braising the beef, an inexpensive Syrah, such as a French Vin de Pays d'Oc Syrah, or an Australian Shiraz, or the red favored at Jamin, Château la Bastide Faugères Réserve. For a white, consider a French Muscadet de Sèvre et Maine or a California Pinot Blanc.

Yankee Pot Roast

8 SERVINGS

Grandma's Country Restaurant is where families in Albany, New York, eat when they want the kind of food that Mom would make if only she had the time. Try Grandma's ultratender pot roast spiked with hot sauce when you feel deeply deserving of a good meal.

One 35-ounce can whole Italian plum tomatoes, with their juices
- ¼ cup vegetable oil

One 3¾-pound boneless chuck roast

Salt and freshly ground pepper
- 6 tablespoons unsalted butter
- 3 medium onions, coarsely chopped
- 6 large carrots, thickly sliced
- 3 medium celery ribs, thickly sliced
- 3 large garlic cloves, minced
- ¼ cup plus 2 tablespoons all-purpose flour
- 2 cups canned beef broth diluted with 2 cups water
- ¼ cup soy sauce
- 1 tablespoon Asian chili sauce

Pinch of sugar
- 1 pound medium red new potatoes, quartered

I. Preheat the oven to 350°. In a blender or food processor, puree the Italian plum tomatoes with their juices until almost smooth.

2. Heat the vegetable oil in a large enameled cast-iron casserole. Season the chuck roast generously with salt and freshly ground pepper and add it to the casserole. Brown the roast over moderate heat until it is crusty all over, 10 to 12 minutes. Transfer to a platter.

3. Melt the butter in the casserole. Add the onions, carrots and celery and cook over moderate heat, stirring, until the vegetables are barely softened, about 5 minutes. Add the garlic and cook until fragrant, about 2 minutes. Sprinkle in the flour and cook, stirring, until it is incorporated, about 1 minute. Gradually stir in the diluted beef broth. Add the pureed tomatoes, the soy sauce, the Asian chili sauce and the sugar and bring to a simmer.

4. Put the roast and any accumulated juices back in the casserole. Cover the casserole and cook the roast in the oven for 2 hours, turning it halfway through. Add the quartered red new potatoes, cover and cook for about 30 minutes longer or until both the roast and the potatoes are fork-tender but not falling apart.

5. Transfer the roast to a cutting board and cover it loosely with foil. Using a slotted spoon, transfer the vegetables to a large deep platter, cover and keep warm. Thickly slice the meat across the grain and arrange on the platter. Return the casserole to high heat and boil the sauce, skimming frequently, until thickened and reduced to about 5 cups. Season with salt and pepper, pour it over the meat and vegetables and serve. —*Grandma's Country Restaurant*

MAKE AHEAD The pot roast can be refrigerated for up to 4 days. Slice the meat before rewarming it with the sauce and vegetables.

WINE To complement the richness of the meat and the sweet acidity of the tomatoes and soy, as well as to balance the heat of the chili sauce, the wine must offer lush, ripe fruit with low tannin and little, if any, obvious new oak. Try the 1996 Foris Rogue Valley Cabernet blend from Oregon or the 1996 Rosenblum Annette's Reserve Zinfandel from California.

Beef and Veal Stew in Pumpkins
6 SERVINGS

Called *carbonada* in its native Argentina, this shredded meat stew flavored with scallions and pancetta is served in large pumpkins. In season, add peaches to the mix. If you can't find pumpkins, use acorn squash instead.

- 2 meaty pieces of veal shank (1 pound each)
- 2 pounds of beef brisket, cut across the grain into 2 pieces
- 6 cups chicken stock or canned low-sodium broth
- 2 bay leaves
- 2 parsley sprigs
- 2 thyme sprigs

Salt and freshly ground black pepper

Two 5-pound pumpkins, or 3 large acorn squash

- 2 tablespoons unsalted butter
- ½ cup milk
- 2 tablespoons olive oil
- 4 ounces thinly sliced pancetta, coarsely chopped

- 2 scallions, thinly sliced
- 3 ears of corn, shucked and cut into 1½-inch rounds
- 3 medium onions, thinly sliced
- 1 red bell pepper, cut into ½-inch dice
- 1 teaspoon crushed red pepper

1. In a large saucepan, cover the veal and beef with the stock. Add the bay leaves, parsley and thyme, season lightly with salt and black pepper and bring to a boil over moderate heat. Reduce the heat to low, cover partially and simmer until the meats are very tender, about 2 hours for the veal, 3½ hours for the beef. As the meats are done, transfer them to a bowl and let cool slightly. Discard the bones and gristle. Cut the meats into 1-inch pieces. Strain the cooking liquid into a bowl; you should have about 2 cups.

2. Preheat the oven to 350°. Cut the tops off the pumpkins and reserve. Scrape out the seeds and season the insides with salt and black pepper. Add 1 tablespoon of butter and ¼ cup of milk to each pumpkin, cover with the top and set on a rimmed baking sheet. Bake for about 1¼ hours, or until the pumpkins are just tender. Cover with foil and keep warm on the baking sheet. Alternatively, halve the acorn squash lengthwise and scrape out the seeds. Season the squash with salt and black pepper and evenly divide the butter and milk among the squash halves. Transfer the squash to a large baking dish and roast, cut side up, for about 30 minutes, or until tender; keep them warm.

3. In a large skillet, heat 1 tablespoon of the olive oil. Add the pancetta and cook over low heat, stirring often, until crisp, about 5 minutes. Stir in the scallions and transfer the mixture to a plate.

4. In a medium saucepan of boiling water, cook the corn until tender, about 5 minutes; drain.

5. In a large saucepan, heat the remaining 1 tablespoon of olive oil. Add the onions and red bell pepper and cook

over low heat until softened, about 10 minutes. Add the crushed red pepper and cook, stirring, for 1 minute. Add the meats and their cooking liquid, the pancetta mixture and corn and simmer until heated through, about 4 minutes. Season with salt and black pepper.

6. Spoon the stew into the pumpkins or squash. Cover the pumpkins with the tops, or cover the squash with foil; bake until heated through, about 20 minutes for the pumpkins and 10 for the squash. Stir the stew to scoop up the pumpkin and bring it to the table in the pumpkin shells, then spoon the stew into bowls. Alternatively, serve each guest a stew-filled squash half. —*Francis Mallmann*

WINE Try a soft, round Chilean Merlot, such as the 1996 Caliterra or the 1995 Cousiño-Macul, with this meaty stew.

Brisket of Beef
10 SERVINGS

Brisket has great flavor but needs to be tenderized by slow cooking in liquid in a covered pot.

- 4 large onions, halved lengthwise and thinly sliced crosswise
- 6 garlic cloves, finely chopped

Kosher salt

- 2 teaspoons vegetable oil

Freshly ground pepper

One 5-pound brisket, trimmed

- 1 cup tomato juice
- 1 cup water
- 2 bay leaves

1. Preheat the oven to 325°. Spread the onions in a roasting pan that will hold the meat snugly.

2. On a work surface, mince the garlic with 1 teaspoon of kosher salt to make a paste. Transfer to a small bowl and stir in the oil and ½ teaspoon of pepper. Rub this paste all over the brisket. Set the brisket, fat side up, on the onions. Pour the tomato juice and water around the meat and add the bay leaves.

3. Cover the pan tightly with foil, transfer to the oven and braise the meat 3 to 4 hours, or until very tender. Uncover

Beef and Veal Stew in Pumpkins

the pan; bake for 30 minutes longer, or until the top is lightly browned and the cooking liquid has thickened slightly.

4. Transfer the meat to a carving board and discard the bay leaves. Strain the cooking liquid, reserving the onions. Skim the fat from the surface of the cooking liquid and discard. In a food processor, puree the cooking liquid with half of the onions. Transfer to a medium saucepan, season with kosher salt and pepper and keep warm over low heat.

5. In a saucepan, reheat the remaining onions with some of the sauce and season with kosher salt and pepper. Carve the meat across the grain into thin slices and transfer to a large serving dish. Pour the hot sauce over the meat and serve at once, passing the onions separately. —*Susan Shapiro Jaslove*

MAKE AHEAD The brisket can be prepared through Step 3 and refrigerated in the sauce for up to 2 days. Defat and reheat gently before proceeding.

WINE This dish needs an equally beefy red wine. Try the 1996 Barons Edmond and Benjamin de Rothschild Bordeaux from France or the 1995 Baron Herzog Cabernet Sauvignon from California.

Braised Short Ribs with Dried Cherries

Pot-au-Feu
8 SERVINGS

- 6 quarts water
- 6 pounds beef short ribs, cut into 2-inch pieces
- 1 onion stuck with 4 cloves
- 2 tablespoons tomato paste
- 3 thyme sprigs
- 10 whole peppercorns

Kosher salt

- 1 small green cabbage (2 pounds), quartered lengthwise and cored
- 8 leeks, white and light green only
- 2 celery ribs, halved crosswise
- 8 carrots, halved crosswise
- 2 large turnips, peeled and quartered
- 8 large boiling potatoes, peeled and cut in half

Dijon mustard, cornichons and freshly ground pepper, for serving

1. Boil the water in a large pot. Add the beef and return to a boil; skim. Add the onion, tomato paste, thyme and peppercorns. Season with salt and simmer over low heat for 3 hours, skimming.

2. Cook the cabbage in boiling salted water for 5 minutes; drain. Tie the leeks and celery into a bundle with string. Add the cabbage, the leek and celery bundle, the carrots and the turnips to the beef and simmer over moderately low heat for 30 minutes.

3. Cook the potatoes in boiling salted water until tender, about 20 minutes; drain. Add the potatoes to the beef and cook until the vegetables and the meat are tender, about 20 minutes longer.

4. Skim the broth. Remove the leek bundle from the pot and discard the string. Spoon the meat and vegetables into soup plates, ladle a little of the broth over them and serve. Pass the mustard, cornichons, salt and pepper separately. —*Josette Riondato*

WINE The 1995 Château Loudenne Médoc has the youthful flavors of Merlot plus the tannic structure and body to match the boiled beef.

Braised Short Ribs with Dried Cherries
4 SERVINGS

- 2 tablespoons olive oil

Sixteen 2-inch-long pieces of beef short ribs (about 5 pounds)

Salt and freshly ground pepper

- 1½ cups red wine
- ¼ cup all-purpose flour
- 1 quart water
- 8 garlic cloves
- 8 large shallots
- 1 cup (¼ pound) dried sour cherries

1. Heat the oil in a large enameled cast-iron casserole or Dutch oven. Season the ribs with salt and pepper. When the oil is almost smoking, add half of the ribs and brown on all sides over moderately high heat, about 10 minutes. Transfer the ribs to a plate and repeat with the remaining ribs.

2. Pour off the oil from the casserole. Add the wine and boil over high heat until reduced to ¼ cup, about 15 minutes. Stir in the flour to make a paste. Gradually whisk in the water until smooth. Return the ribs to the casserole with any accumulated juices, add the garlic and shallots and bring to a simmer. Add 1 teaspoon of salt, cover partially and simmer the ribs over low heat for 2½ hours.

3. Add the cherries to the casserole and continue simmering until the meat is very tender, about 30 minutes longer. Using a slotted spoon, transfer the ribs, garlic, shallots and cherries to a plate. Skim the cooking liquid to remove the fat and then simmer the sauce over moderate heat to concentrate the flavor, about 5 minutes. Skim again. Return the ribs, vegetables and cherries to the casserole, season with salt and pepper and serve. —*Stephen Kalt*

MAKE AHEAD The braised short ribs can be refrigerated for up to 2 days.

WINE The concentrated beefy flavors in this dish point to a big, luscious wine, such as a peppery red Rhône or a California Syrah or Cabernet.

Pot-au-Feu

Red Flannel Hash

6 SERVINGS

The addition of corned beef makes this New England favorite outstanding. You can peel the potatoes or leave them unpeeled.

1½ pounds all-purpose potatoes
2 medium beets (about ½ pound)
1 pound corned beef, finely diced
1 medium onion, finely chopped
1 teaspoon mild pure chile powder, preferably ancho
Salt and freshly ground pepper
6 tablespoons unsalted butter
6 large eggs

1. In a medium saucepan, cover the potatoes with water and boil until just tender, about 20 minutes. Drain and let cool slightly. Finely chop the potatoes.

2. In another saucepan, cover the beets with water and boil until tender, about 20 minutes. Drain and let cool slightly. Peel and finely chop the beets.

3. In a large bowl, toss the potatoes and the beets with the corned beef, the onion and the chile powder; season with salt and pepper.

4. In a large cast-iron skillet, melt the butter until foamy. Add the hash and cook over moderate heat without stirring until golden and crusty on the bottom, about 10 minutes. Using the back of a large spoon, make 6 evenly spaced pockets in the hash; crack an egg into each. Cover and cook until the eggs are just set, about 5 minutes. Serve immediately. —*Jonathan King and Jim Stott*

Corned Beef Pot-au-Feu

6 SERVINGS

The provincial French pot-au-feu (literally, "pot-on-the-fire") usually means boiled beef accompanied by an array of vegetables. French home cooks often build the dish around short ribs of beef, which are wonderfully moist, flavorful and fatty. This lightened twist on the classic uses supermarket corned beef; look for a piece that does not have a layer of fat down the middle.

Corned Beef Pot-au-Feu

3 small leeks, white and tender green parts only
One 2-pound piece of corned beef, rinsed
10 cups cold water
1 pound medium red potatoes
1 head of Savoy cabbage (1 pound), tough outer leaves discarded, head cut into 6 wedges
4 white turnips, peeled and quartered
2 medium onions, cut into thirds
2 large carrots, cut into thirds
2 kohlrabi, peeled and cut into thirds
2 bay leaves
½ teaspoon dried thyme

1. Split the leeks lengthwise to within 2 inches of the root ends; soak in warm water at least 30 minutes to remove the grit. Lift out of the water and cut the leeks into thirds crosswise.

2. In a large pot, cover the corned beef with the water and bring to a boil, skimming off any foam that rises to the surface. Reduce the heat to low, cover and cook, skimming occasionally, until the meat is tender, about 2¼ hours.

3. Add all the vegetables and herbs and cook over low heat until the vegetables are just tender, about 30 minutes.

4. Transfer the corned beef to a cutting board and thinly slice it against the grain. Arrange the corned beef and the vegetables in warmed soup plates. Spoon some of the broth on top and serve hot. —*Jacques Pépin*

ONE SERVING Calories 468 kcal, Total Fat 23.1 gm, Saturated Fat 7.2 gm

WINE The salty and earthy flavors of this dish call for a light red wine or a big white wine—ideally, an all-embracing oak-aged California Chardonnay. Look for the 1996 Beringer or the 1996 Swanson Estate.

Lamb Chops with Olive Salad

4 SERVINGS

If making this recipe for eight, double everything except the rosemary. You'll need only a half tablespoon more fresh rosemary, or a half teaspoon dried.

SALAD

- 6 ripe plum tomatoes, coarsely chopped
- ½ cup coarsely chopped red onion
- ½ cup (about 3 ounces) Calamata or other black olives, pitted and coarsely chopped
- ½ cup crumbled feta cheese
- 2 tablespoons minced mint
- 2 tablespoons olive oil
- 2 tablespoons fresh lemon juice

Salt and freshly ground pepper

LAMB

- 1 tablespoon minced rosemary, or 1 teaspoon dried, crumbled
- 2 tablespoons fresh lemon juice
- 2 tablespoons olive oil
- 2 garlic cloves, minced

Eight 4- to 5-ounce lamb rib chops (1¼ inches thick)

Salt and freshly ground pepper

1. MAKE THE SALAD: In a glass or stainless steel bowl, combine the tomatoes, onion, olives, feta and mint. Add the oil and lemon juice and toss to combine. Season with salt and pepper.

2. PREPARE THE LAMB: Preheat the broiler. In a glass or stainless steel bowl, combine the rosemary, lemon juice, olive oil and garlic. Rub the mixture on both sides of the lamb chops and season with salt and pepper.

3. Arrange the lamb chops on the rack of a broiling pan. Broil about 2 inches from the heat for 3 to 4 minutes per side for medium rare. Transfer the lamb chops to a platter, spoon the salad alongside and serve. —*Howard Miller*

WINE A full-flavored Rhône or Rhône-style red, like the 1997 Foppiano Petite Sirah from California or the 1997 Chave St-Joseph Offerus, would be perfect.

Chile-Rubbed Lamb Chops with Pumpkin Seed Sauce

4 SERVINGS

A single serrano chile gives the tangy pumpkin seed sauce a mild, pleasant heat. If you'd like more spice, add another serrano; you can also use a spicier chile powder to coat the lamb. Leg of lamb steaks are a good alternative to chops. Cook them for about five minutes per side on the stove; they won't need to roast in the oven.

- ½ cup loosely packed cilantro leaves
- ¼ cup loosely packed mint leaves
- 1 small shallot, coarsely chopped
- 1½ tablespoons raw pumpkin seeds
- 1 serrano chile, coarsely chopped
- 2 tablespoons water
- 1 tablespoon fresh lime juice
- 3 tablespoons peanut oil

Salt

- 2 tablespoons mild pure chile powder, such as chimayo
- 2 teaspoons ground cumin
- 1 teaspoon dried oregano

Four ½-pound lamb loin chops

1. Preheat the oven to 350°. In a blender or food processor, puree the cilantro, mint, shallot, pumpkin seeds, serrano, water, lime juice, 2 tablespoons of the oil and ¼ teaspoon salt until smooth.

2. On a plate, combine the chile powder with the cumin, oregano and ½ teaspoon salt. Rub all over the lamb chops.

3. Heat the remaining 1 tablespoon of the oil in a large ovenproof skillet. Add the lamb chops and cook over moderately high heat until browned, about 3 minutes per side. Transfer the lamb chops to the oven and bake for about 12 minutes for medium-rare meat. Transfer the chops to large plates and serve with the sauce. —*Jan Newberry*

WINE Spicy lamb chops call for a spicy red. Look for California Syrah-Shiraz bottlings, such as the 1995 Rabbit Ridge Syrah or the 1996 Simi Shiraz.

Lamb Loins with Mustard Crumbs

4 SERVINGS

The lamb loin includes the tenderloin and is often called the saddle. The more expensive rib roast is also wonderful with the mustard crumbs.

- 8 tablespoons unsalted butter, 5 tablespoons melted
- 2 whole boneless lamb loins (about 1 pound each)

Salt and freshly ground pepper

About ¼ cup all-purpose flour, for dredging

- ¼ cup plus 2 tablespoons Dijon mustard
- 1 cup coarse dry bread crumbs
- 2 tablespoons coarsely chopped flat-leaf parsley
- 2 teaspoons minced garlic
- 1 teaspoon minced shallot
- 2 teaspoons finely chopped oregano
- 2 teaspoons finely chopped basil
- 2 teaspoons freshly grated Parmesan cheese

1. Preheat the oven to 450°. Melt 3 tablespoons of butter in a large ovenproof skillet. Season the lamb loins with salt and pepper and dredge in the flour. Add the lamb to the skillet and cook over moderately high heat, turning, until browned all over, about 6 minutes. Let

Lamb Loins with Mustard Crumbs

the lamb cool slightly and then pat dry and brush with the mustard.

2. On a plate, mix the bread crumbs with the parsley, garlic, shallot, oregano, basil, Parmesan and the melted butter. Roll the lamb in the crumb mixture, pressing it into the meat.

3. Return the lamb to the skillet and roast for about 15 minutes for medium-rare meat. Transfer to a work surface, cover loosely with foil and let stand for 5 minutes. Slice the lamb loins ⅓ inch thick and serve. *—George Gebhardt*

SERVE WITH Grilled asparagus.

WINE There's no reason to stray here from the traditional pairing, red Bordeaux. The crust adds a tangy note to the richness of the lamb, so young, vigorous bottlings, with their cleansing tannins, will make the best match. Consider the 1995 Château Cantemerle or the 1995 Château Talbot.

Port-Marinated Rack of Lamb

4 SERVINGS ❋

- ¼ cup plus 1 tablespoon extra-virgin olive oil
- ¼ cup ruby port
- ¼ cup red wine vinegar
- ¼ cup fresh lemon juice
- ¼ cup whole-grain mustard
- 1½ tablespoons finely chopped rosemary
- 1½ tablespoons coarsely cracked black peppercorns
- 1 tablespoon minced garlic
- 1 tablespoon minced shallots

Two 8-rib racks of lamb, chine bones removed, racks frenched (see Note)

Kosher salt and freshly ground pepper

1. In a large glass baking dish, combine ¼ cup of the oil with the port, red wine vinegar, lemon juice, mustard, rosemary, peppercorns, garlic and shallots. Add the lamb; turn to coat. Let stand at room temperature for 40 minutes.

2. Meanwhile, light a grill or preheat the oven to 375°. Drain the lamb and scrape off the marinade. Rub the racks with the remaining 1 tablespoon of olive oil and season with kosher salt and pepper. Grill over a medium-hot fire for 10 to 15 minutes, turning often, until an instant-read thermometer registers 130° for medium rare. Alternatively, heat a large, ovenproof skillet and sear the lamb over moderately high heat until browned on both sides, 5 to 6 minutes total. Transfer the skillet to the oven and roast the lamb for 12 minutes for medium rare.

3. Transfer the rack of lamb to a cutting board and let rest for 5 minutes. Cut the lamb between the bones into chops, arrange 4 of the chops on each plate and serve. *—Todd Slossberg*

NOTE Ask your butcher to french, or clean and scrape, the bones for you.

WINE Lamb calls for a hearty red wine. Try a full-bodied, spicy California Zinfandel, such as the 1996 Ravenswood Monte Rosso or the 1996 Niebaum-Coppola Edizione Pennino.

Rack of Lamb with Roasted Tomato Jus

8 SERVINGS

Two 8-rib racks of lamb, chine bones removed, racks frenched (see Note)

Salt and freshly ground pepper

- ¼ cup extra-virgin olive oil
- 8 roasted garlic cloves (from Roasted Tomatoes and Garlic, p. 326)
- 2 tablespoons unsalted butter, softened
- 2 thyme sprigs
- 1 cup rich veal stock or demiglace (see Note)
- 20 roasted tomato halves (from Roasted Tomatoes and Garlic, p. 326), 4 finely chopped

1. Preheat the oven to 350°. Season the lamb racks with salt and pepper. In a large ovenproof skillet, heat 1 tablespoon of the olive oil until shimmering. Add 1 of the lamb racks and cook over moderately high heat until browned all over, about 10 minutes. Transfer the lamb to a platter and brown the other rack. Return both of the lamb racks to the skillet with the ribs pointing up. Rub each rack with 3 of the garlic cloves and ½ tablespoon of the butter and tuck the thyme sprigs underneath. Roast the lamb 10 minutes for medium rare, or until an instant-read thermometer inserted in the center of the meat registers 130°. Transfer the lamb to a cutting board, cover loosely and let stand for 10 minutes before slicing.

2. Meanwhile, pour off the fat in the skillet; discard the thyme sprigs. Set the skillet over high heat. Add the rich veal stock and simmer, scraping up any brown bits on the bottom. Mash the remaining 2 garlic cloves and add them to the skillet with the chopped roasted tomatoes; cook until slightly thickened, about 5 minutes. Reduce the heat to low and whisk in the remaining 3 tablespoons of olive oil and 1 tablespoon of butter. Season with salt and pepper and keep warm.

3. Cut the rack of lamb into double chops between the ribs and serve the lamb with the tomato jus and roasted tomatoes. *—Tom Colicchio*

---

menu

Artichokes Braised in Olive Oil and White Wine (p. 276)

1994 ALBERT BOXLER GRAND CRU SOMMERBERG RIESLING

———

Rack of Lamb with Roasted Tomato Jus

Potato Gratin (p. 298)

Garlic Flans (p. 286)

1991 QUERCIABELLA CAMARTINA

———

Wedding Cake with Dots and Daisies (p. 336)

1997 LA MORANDINA MOSCATO D'ASTI

NOTE Ask your butcher to french, or clean and scrape, the bones for you. A rich veal stock is available at specialty food shops, and a duck and veal demiglace can be ordered from D'Artagnan (800-327-8246).

Siegel's Lamb Chops with Fava Beans and Potato Gnocchi

4 SERVINGS ♛

Ron Siegel, chef at Charles Nob Hill in San Francisco, says, "Don't depend on a thermometer to know when meat is ready. Poke it. If it feels like mush, it's rare. If a little blood comes out, it's medium rare. If it feels like a baseball bat, it's well done and you're in trouble."

- ¾ cup (about ½ ounce) dried morels
- 1 cup boiling water
- One 8-rib rack of lamb, chine bone removed, rack frenched and cut into double chops, scraps reserved (see Note)
- 1 cup rich veal stock or demiglace (see Note)
- Salt and freshly ground pepper
- 2 pounds fresh fava beans, shelled
- Potato Gnocchi (recipe follows)
- 1 tablespoon extra-virgin olive oil
- 4 tablespoons unsalted butter
- 1 teaspoon thyme leaves

1. In a small bowl, cover the morels with the boiling water; let soak until softened, about 15 minutes. Drain the morels, reserving the liquid. Slice the morels ½ inch thick, discarding the stems. Pour the soaking liquid into a bowl, leaving behind any grit.

2. In a saucepan, cook the lamb scraps over moderately high heat, stirring often, until browned all over. Add the veal stock and cook over moderate heat until reduced to ½ cup, about 20 minutes. Strain, add ½ cup of the morel soaking liquid and cook until the sauce is reduced to ½ cup. Season the sauce with salt and pepper.

3. In a large pot of boiling, salted water, cook the fava beans for 2 minutes. Using a slotted spoon, transfer the fava beans to a plate. Let the fava beans cool and then peel them.

4. Return the water to a boil and add the gnocchi. Stir gently twice and let the gnocchi rise to the surface. Cook for about 1 minute; the gnocchi should be puffed and cooked through. Drain and transfer to an oiled plate.

5. Preheat the oven to 400°. In an ovenproof skillet, heat the oil until shimmering. Season the lamb with salt and pepper and cook, fatty side down, until browned and crusty, about 5 minutes. Turn the chops, transfer the skillet to the oven and roast for 10 minutes for medium rare. Let rest for 5 minutes on a cutting board.

6. Melt ½ tablespoon of the butter in a large nonstick skillet. Add the morels and the fava beans and cook over moderately high heat until warmed through, about 3 minutes. Add to the lamb sauce; swirl in 1½ tablespoons of the butter.

7. In the skillet, melt the remaining 2 tablespoons of butter over moderately high heat until golden. Add the gnocchi and thyme leaves, season with salt and pepper and cook, tossing, until lightly golden.

8. Spoon the gnocchi onto 4 plates and add the morels and the fava beans. Slice the lamb between the bones and

Siegel's Lamb Chops with Fava Beans and Potato Gnocchi

arrange 2 chops on each plate. Drizzle any remaining sauce around the lamb chops and serve. —*Ron Siegel*

NOTE Have your butcher french, or clean and scrape, the lamb bones. Ask for the trimmings and save them for the decadent sauce for the lamb. A rich veal stock is available at specialty food shops, and a duck and veal demiglace can be ordered from D'Artagnan (800-327-8246).

POTATO GNOCCHI

MAKES ABOUT 6 DOZEN

- 2 baking potatoes (about ½ pound each)
- ¾ teaspoon salt
- ⅛ teaspoon freshly ground pepper
- 2 large egg yolks
- 1 cup all-purpose flour, plus more for dusting

1. Preheat the oven to 400°. Bake the potatoes for about 1 hour, or until tender. Halve the potatoes and scoop out the centers. Press the potato flesh through a fine sieve or a ricer into a large bowl. Season with the salt and pepper and let cool slightly. Make a well in the center, add the egg yolks and stir until combined. Stir in ½ cup of the flour. Turn the dough out onto a work surface and gently knead in the remaining ½ cup of flour, until the dough is smooth and no longer sticky. Wrap the dough in plastic and let stand at room temperature for 15 minutes.

2. Divide the dough into quarters and roll each piece into a ½-inch-thick rope. Cut the ropes into 1-inch lengths and dust with flour. To shape the gnocchi, hold a fork in one hand, tines pointing slightly downward, and use the thumb of your other hand to press the pieces of dough lightly across the back of the fork, rolling downward around your thumb to make an indentation around the outside. —*R. S.*

MAKE AHEAD The gnocchi can be refrigerated overnight on a wax-paper-lined baking sheet.

Rosemary-Scented Lamb and Vegetables

4 SERVINGS

If you can't find fava beans to make this colorful dish, use a half pound of snowpeas or lima beans.

- 1 pound fava beans, shelled
- 8 thin asparagus, cut into 2-inch lengths
- 1½ cups small cauliflower florets
- 6 tablespoons unsalted butter
- 1 tablespoon vegetable oil
- 1¾ pounds trimmed boneless loin of baby lamb or leg of lamb, cut into 1½-inch cubes

Fine sea salt

Piment d'Espelette or mildly hot paprika (see Note)

- ½ pound pearl onions, peeled and scored on the bottom (see Note)
- 1 pound chanterelle mushrooms, quartered if large
- 2 medium tomatoes—peeled, seeded and cut into ½-inch dice
- 1 tablespoon coarsely chopped rosemary, plus leaves for garnish

1. In a saucepan of boiling salted water, blanch the fava beans for 1 minute. Drain and rinse in cold water. Peel the favas. In another saucepan of boiling salted water, cook the asparagus and then the cauliflower until just tender, about 3 minutes each. Drain, rinse in cold water and drain on paper towels.

2. In a large nonstick skillet, melt 3 tablespoons of the butter in the oil. Add the lamb in batches, season with sea salt and *piment d'Espelette* and cook over moderately high heat until browned outside but still pink in the center, about 4 minutes per batch; transfer the lamb to a platter.

3. Add the pearl onions to the skillet and add enough water to cover by half. Bring to a boil over high heat. Reduce the heat to moderately high; cook, stirring and shaking the pan often, until the water has evaporated and the onions are tender and slightly caramelized, 10 to 15 minutes.

menu

Chilled English Pea Soup with Extra-Virgin Olive Oil (p. 82)

1993 TAITTINGER COMTES DE CHAMPAGNE BLANC DE BLANCS

Seared Tuna Salad with Creamy Mustard Sauce (p. 37)

1995 TAITTINGER BRUT MILLESIME

Rosemary-Scented Lamb and Vegetables

1997 DOMAINE CARNEROS PINOT NOIR

Caramelized Peaches with Honey and Raspberries (p. 364)

NONVINTAGE TAITTINGER PRESTIGE CUVEE ROSE

4. Melt the remaining 3 tablespoons of butter in a large nonstick skillet over moderate heat. Add the chanterelles, season with sea salt and cook, stirring often, until lightly browned, about 3 minutes. Add the favas, asparagus, cauliflower, onions, mushrooms and tomatoes along with the lamb and chopped rosemary and season with sea salt and *piment d'Espelette*. Bring to a simmer; stir until heated through. Spoon onto plates, garnish with rosemary leaves and serve. —*Philippe Renard*

NOTE *Piment d'Espelette,* a crushed red pepper from France's Basque region, is available by mail from Igo Foods (888-IGO-9966). To peel the onions easily, blanch in boiling water 1 minute.

MAKE AHEAD The recipe can be made through Step 1 and refrigerated for up to 1 day.

WINE Medium body and richness make Pinot Noir a classic complement to any lamb dish. The ripe fruit in the 1997 Domaine Carneros Pinot Noir also pairs well with the vibrant flavors of the vegetables and rosemary.

Lamb Biryani

12 SERVINGS

In India, where rice is an exalted grain, the *biryani* is an exalted rice dish. It's typically served at weddings and festivals—anywhere there's a need to feed many people lavishly. In this version, the baked rice-and-lamb casserole is decorated with a golden wheel of saffron-infused milk and served with raisins, almonds and hard-cooked eggs. Leave the cinnamon stick in or remove it. In India it's generally left in but, of course, not eaten.

½ cup plus 2 tablespoons vegetable oil
3 large Spanish onions—1 thinly sliced into rings, 2 coarsely chopped
5 pounds trimmed boneless leg of lamb, cut into 2-inch pieces
Salt and freshly ground black pepper
3 tablespoons *garam masala*
1 teaspoon cumin seeds
1 cinnamon stick, broken in half
¼ cup minced peeled fresh ginger
6 large garlic cloves, minced
1 teaspoon turmeric
1 teaspoon cayenne pepper
1¼ teaspoons saffron threads
6 cups chicken stock or canned low-sodium broth
1 cup chopped cilantro, plus 1 cup small cilantro sprigs
1 cup (5 ounces) golden raisins
½ cup milk
1 cup (6 ounces) whole blanched almonds
6 cups (2¼ pounds) basmati rice
1 cup plain whole-milk yogurt at room temperature, whisked
6 hard-cooked eggs, halved lengthwise

1. In a large enameled cast-iron casserole, heat ½ cup of the oil. Cook half of the onion rings at a time over moderate heat, stirring occasionally, until deeply browned, about 5 minutes. Using a slotted spoon, transfer the browned onions to paper towels to drain.

2. Add the pieces of lamb to the casserole in batches, season with salt and freshly ground black pepper and brown well on all sides. Transfer the lamb to a large plate.

3. Discard the oil in the casserole and add 1 tablespoon of fresh oil. Add the chopped onions and cook over moderate heat, stirring often, until softened but not browned, about 8 minutes. Add the *garam masala,* cumin seeds and cinnamon and cook, stirring occasionally, until fragrant, about 4 minutes.

4. Return the lamb and any accumulated juices to the casserole, add the ginger, garlic, turmeric, cayenne and ¼ teaspoon of the saffron and cook, stirring often, until fragrant, about 5 minutes. Add the chicken stock and the chopped cilantro and bring to a boil. Cover partially and simmer over low heat, stirring occasionally, until the meat is tender and the sauce is flavorful, about 1½ hours.

5. Meanwhile, in a small skillet, heat the remaining 1 tablespoon of oil. Add the raisins and cook over moderately high heat until browned on 1 side, about 3 minutes. Transfer the raisins to a plate to cool. In a small saucepan, bring the milk to a bare simmer. Remove the pan from the heat and crumble the remaining 1 teaspoon of saffron threads into the milk. Let steep for up to 2 hours.

6. Preheat the oven to 375°. Put the almonds on a rimmed baking sheet and bake for about 8 minutes, or until toasted. In a large pot of boiling water, cook the rice for 5 minutes, stirring occasionally. Drain in a colander.

7. Stir the yogurt into the lamb and season with salt and black pepper. Carefully mound the blanched rice over the lamb. Using a wooden spoon handle, make a hole in the center of the rice, moving the handle in a circle to widen the hole to about 1 inch. Spoon the saffron milk over the rice in a spokelike pattern. Cover the casserole and bake the rice for 40 minutes. Remove from the oven and let the *biryani* stand, covered, for 5 minutes.

8. Arrange the browned onion rings, almonds, raisins, cilantro sprigs and eggs in separate bowls or arrange on a platter. Serve the *biryani* from the casserole and pass the accompaniments at the table. —*Marcia Kiesel*

BEER The best choice for the complex flavors of this dish is a beer that will refresh the palate and quickly send you back for more *biryani*. Kingfisher, from India, is a perfect, if obvious, choice.

Roasted Lamb with Potatoes and Rosemary Chimichurri

8 SERVINGS

If you're a year-round griller, you can grill the lamb instead of roasting it. The potent, garlic-accented *chimichurri,* the ubiquitous Argentinean accompaniment to grilled or roasted meat, is excellent with the charred lamb and buttery fried potatoes.

1 cup extra-virgin olive oil
½ cup rosemary leaves, finely chopped
1 head of garlic, minced
Finely grated zest of 1 lemon
2 tablespoons fresh lemon juice
½ teaspoon crushed red pepper
Kosher salt
One 5½-pound boneless leg of lamb, butterflied
Freshly ground black pepper
1 stick (4 ounces) unsalted butter
5 large Idaho potatoes, peeled and sliced ¼ inch thick

1. In a glass or stainless steel bowl, combine the olive oil, rosemary, garlic, lemon zest, lemon juice, crushed red pepper and 1 tablespoon kosher salt. Let the *chimichurri* stand at room temperature for at least 20 minutes.

2. Preheat the oven to 500°. Season the leg of lamb with salt and freshly ground black pepper and brush the lamb on both sides with ⅔ cup of the *chimichurri*. Set the lamb, fat side up,

Roasted Lamb with Potatoes and Rosemary Chimichurri

on a large rimmed baking sheet and roast in the upper third of the oven for about 25 minutes, or until an instant-read thermometer inserted in the thickest part of the meat registers 130° for medium rare. Transfer the lamb to a cutting board, cover with foil and let rest for 10 minutes.

3. Meanwhile, divide the butter between 2 large skillets, preferably cast iron. Add one quarter of the potatoes to each skillet and cook over low heat until browned on the bottom, about 15 minutes. Turn the slices with tongs and fry until browned on the other side, about 5 minutes longer. Transfer the potatoes to a rack set over a baking sheet, season with kosher salt and keep warm on the back of the stove. Repeat with the remaining potatoes.

4. Thickly slice the lamb. Arrange the potatoes on a plate, top with the lamb slices and spoon the *chimichurri* over it all. —*Francis Mallmann*

MAKE AHEAD The *chimichurri* is best made 1 to 2 days ahead and refrigerated. Let it return to room temperature before serving.

WINE A Cabernet Sauvignon will echo the rosemary and match the gaminess of the lamb. Try a Chilean bottling—the 1996 Casa Lapostolle Cuvée Alexandre or the 1996 Los Vascos Reserve.

Spiced-Braised Leg of Lamb

8 SERVINGS

What goes better with lamb than vibrant spices, such as coriander, cumin and curry? The leg of lamb is braised ever so slowly with a little stock in the oven until it is very tender.

- 4 garlic cloves, minced
- 1 tablespoon plus 1 teaspoon thyme leaves
- 1 tablespoon cumin seeds
- 2 teaspoons finely chopped rosemary
- 2 teaspoons curry powder
- 2 teaspoons fine sea salt
- 1½ teaspoons ground cumin
- 1 teaspoon ground coriander
- 1 teaspoon coriander seeds
- 1 teaspoon coarsely ground white pepper

One 5-pound half leg of lamb, preferably from the hip section
- ¼ cup extra-virgin olive oil
- 2 cups chicken stock or canned low-sodium broth

I. Preheat the oven to 250°. In a small bowl, combine the minced garlic with the thyme leaves, cumin seeds, rosemary, curry powder, sea salt, ground cumin and coriander, coriander seeds and white pepper. Cut 16 slits, each about 1 inch long by 1 inch deep and spaced 1 inch apart, in the leg of lamb. Rub the spice mixture all over the leg of lamb, working it into the slits. Set aside any of the spice mixture that does not adhere to the lamb.

2. In a medium flameproof casserole, heat the extra-virgin olive oil. Add the leg of lamb and lightly brown it on all sides over moderate heat, about 2 minutes per side. Add the chicken stock and any remaining spice mixture. Cover with a sheet of buttered wax paper and a lid. Braise the leg of lamb in the oven for 3 hours, or until it is very tender. Check the leg of lamb from time to time and baste as necessary to prevent it from drying out.

3. Transfer the braised leg of lamb to a carving board. Strain the cooking juices through a fine sieve and skim the fat. Transfer the cooking juices to a gravy boat. Thickly slice the lamb and serve with the juices. —*Eric Lecerf*

SERVE WITH Braised seasonal mixed vegetables, such as carrots, leeks, shallots and potatoes.

WINE With all of these spices, you need a bold red wine, such as Philippe and Michele Laurent's velvety Domaine Gramenon Côtes-du-Rhône.

Braised Lamb Shanks with Tangerine Gremolata

8 SERVINGS

Braising the lamb shanks for hours in a mixture of red wine and tomatoes gives them a tangy flavor. This recipe is from *Sharing the Vineyard Table* (Ten Speed Press) by Carolyn Wente and Kimball Jones.

8 meaty 1-pound lamb shanks, trimmed

Kosher salt and freshly ground pepper

2 tablespoons olive oil

2 small carrots, coarsely chopped

1 medium onion, coarsely chopped

1 bottle (750 ml) red wine

Two 28-ounce cans Italian peeled tomatoes with their juice

4 cups chicken stock or canned low-sodium broth

2 large heads of garlic, cloves peeled, 2 minced

4 bay leaves

2 cinnamon sticks

8 flat-leaf parsley sprigs, plus 1 tablespoon minced parsley

1 tablespoon finely grated tangerine or orange zest

1. Preheat the oven to 325°. Season the lamb generously with kosher salt and pepper. Heat the oil in a large enameled cast-iron casserole. Working in batches, brown the lamb thoroughly over moderately high heat, turning often, about 3 minutes per side; transfer to a large bowl.

2. Pour off any fat from the casserole. Add the carrots and onion; cook over moderately high heat, stirring occasionally, until browned, about 5 minutes. Add the wine and boil for 5 minutes, using a wooden spatula to scrape up the brown bits from the bottom of the casserole.

3. Return the lamb to the casserole. Add the tomatoes, chicken stock, the whole garlic cloves, the bay leaves and the cinnamon. Tie the parsley sprigs with string and add them to the casserole. Bring to a boil and skim. Cover and cook in the preheated oven for 1½ to 2 hours, or until the lamb is very tender. Remove the casserole from the oven.

4. Transfer the lamb shanks to a large bowl and cover with foil. Pick out and discard the cinnamon sticks, bay leaves and parsley sprigs. Let the cooking liquid stand for 5 minutes and then skim off the fat. Working in batches, puree the cooking liquid and the vegetables in a blender. Strain the sauce back into the casserole through a coarse sieve. Boil the sauce until reduced by half, stirring frequently, about 30 minutes. Season

---

menu

Sesame Crisps with Seared Sea Scallops (p. 21)

Mussels with Lemon-Fennel Butter (p. 36)

1996 WENTE ESTATE GROWN CHARDONNAY

———

Braised Lamb Shanks with Tangerine Gremolata

Butternut Squash Polenta (p. 314)

1996 WENTE RELIZ CREEK RESERVE PINOT NOIR

———

Apple Tarts with Candied Ginger (p. 347)

Late Harvest Riesling Ice Cream (p. 384)

1995 WENTE LATE HARVEST RIESLING

Braised Lamb Shanks with Tangerine Gremolata and roasted parsnips

with kosher salt and pepper and return the lamb shanks to the sauce.

5. Bring the lamb shanks to a simmer. In a small bowl, combine the minced garlic with the minced parsley and the tangerine zest. Set a lamb shank on each plate. Spoon the sauce over the meat, sprinkle with the *gremolata* and serve. —*Kimball Jones*

MAKE AHEAD The lamb shanks can be prepared through Step 3 and refrigerated for up to 2 days.

SERVE WITH Roasted parsnips and carrots or other root vegetables.

WINE The 1996 Wente Reliz Creek Reserve Pinot Noir, with its spicy oak, raspberry overtones and solid tannins, is a good match for the earthy and full-flavored lamb.

Lamb Shanks with Vegetable Tagine

4 SERVINGS

It's not unusual to find dried fruits in North African tagines. This contemporary recipe also includes a seared banana sprinkled with sugar.

LAMB SHANKS

¼ cup olive oil

4 meaty 1-pound lamb shanks

Salt and freshly ground pepper

1 large onion, finely chopped

5 garlic cloves, crushed

½ cup (3 ounces) mixed dried fruits, such as raisins, dried currants and chopped dried apricots

2 tablespoons all-purpose flour

1 cup red wine

1 quart chicken stock or canned low-sodium broth

1 cinnamon stick

TAGINE

3 tablespoons olive oil

1 red bell pepper, cut into ½-inch dice

1 small onion, cut into ½-inch dice

1 medium zucchini, cut into ½-inch dice

½ small eggplant, cut into ½-inch dice

1 cup dried currants

1 garlic clove, chopped

1 teaspoon cinnamon

1 tablespoon unsalted butter

1 large banana, cut into ½-inch dice

1 teaspoon sugar

Salt

I. PREPARE THE LAMB SHANKS: Preheat the oven to 400°. Heat the olive oil in a large enameled cast-iron casserole or Dutch oven. Season the lamb shanks with salt and pepper and brown them in the casserole over moderate heat, about 10 minutes. Transfer the shanks to a plate.

2. Add the onion and garlic to the casserole and cook over low heat until very soft, about 20 minutes. Stir in the dried fruits and flour and cook for 1 minute. Add the wine to the casserole and simmer over moderate heat until almost evaporated, about 5 minutes.

3. Return the lamb shanks to the casserole and add the stock, cinnamon stick and enough water to barely cover the shanks. Season with salt and pepper and bring to a boil. Cover with foil, transfer to the oven and cook the shanks for about 1½ hours, or until the meat is very tender. Remove the casserole from the oven; leave the oven on.

4. Transfer the shanks to a plate and strain the cooking liquid. Skim off as much fat as possible. Return the cooking liquid to the casserole and simmer until reduced by half, about 5 minutes. Keep the shanks warm in the sauce.

5. MAKE THE TAGINE: Heat ½ tablespoon of the oil in a medium skillet. Add the red bell pepper and cook over moderate heat, stirring, until softened, 4 to 5 minutes; transfer to a small baking dish. Repeat with the onion and then with the zucchini, adding ½ tablespoon of oil to the skillet for each vegetable; add the onion and zucchini to the baking dish as they are done.

6. In the same skillet, heat 1 tablespoon of olive oil. Add the eggplant and cook, stirring occasionally, for 2 minutes. Add

the currants, garlic and ½ teaspoon of the cinnamon and cook until the eggplant is tender, about 10 minutes; transfer to the baking dish.

7. In the same skillet, melt the butter in the remaining ½ tablespoon of olive oil. Add the banana and sprinkle with the sugar and the remaining ½ teaspoon cinnamon. Cook over moderately high heat until lightly browned, about 2 minutes. Transfer to the baking dish and season with salt.

8. Cover the vegetable tagine with foil and bake in the oven for 20 minutes. Set a lamb shank on each plate, mound the vegetable tagine alongside the lamb and serve. Pass the lamb sauce separately. —*Stephen Kalt*

MAKE AHEAD The braised lamb shanks can be prepared through Step 3 and refrigerated for up to 2 days.

WINE To match the strong flavor of the lamb, look for a big, tannic, palate-cleansing wine, such as a Valpolicella from Italy or a red from Priorato, Spain.

Lamb Osso Buco with Tapenade

4 SERVINGS

Have your butcher cut the lamb shanks into thirds.

LAMB

¾ cup extra-virgin olive oil

6 garlic cloves, crushed

6 thyme sprigs

1 rosemary sprig, leaves only

4 meaty lamb shanks (6 pounds total), cut crosswise into thirds

Salt and freshly ground pepper

1 medium onion, coarsely chopped

1 small fennel bulb—trimmed, halved lengthwise, cored and coarsely chopped

1 small carrot, finely chopped

1½ cups dry white wine

3 flat-leaf parsley sprigs

Strips of zest from ½ lemon

1 bay leaf

3 cups lamb stock or beef stock, or 1½ cups canned beef broth mixed with 1½ cups water

TAPENADE

- 1 anchovy fillet, mashed
- 1 garlic clove, halved
- ¼ cup extra-virgin olive oil
- ½ cup (about 4 ounces) Niçoise olives, pitted and chopped
- 1 tablespoon fresh lemon juice
- 1 tablespoon chopped flat-leaf parsley
- 1 teaspoon capers, rinsed

SHELL BEANS

- 1 tablespoon extra-virgin olive oil
- 2 tablespoons minced shallots
- 1 teaspoon minced garlic
- 1 teaspoon thyme leaves
- 2 cups (about 10 ounces) fresh shelled or frozen beans, such as black-eyed peas or cranberry beans
- 2 cups water
- ½ teaspoon salt

I. PREPARE THE LAMB: In a large bowl, combine ½ cup of the olive oil with the garlic, thyme and rosemary. Add the lamb and turn to coat. Let stand at room temperature for 2 to 3 hours, turning occasionally, or refrigerate overnight.

2. Preheat the oven to 325°. Scrape off the marinade; season the lamb with salt and pepper. Heat the remaining ¼ cup oil in a large enameled cast-iron casserole until shimmering. Working in 2 batches, sear the lamb over moderate heat until well browned all over, 8 to 10 minutes per batch. Transfer to a platter.

3. Add the onion, fennel and carrot to the casserole and cook over low heat, stirring, until lightly browned, about 6 minutes. Add the wine, parsley, lemon zest and bay leaf and boil until reduced by half, about 6 minutes. Return the lamb to the casserole, add the stock and bring to a boil. Cover and braise in the oven for 2½ to 3 hours, or until the meat is almost falling off the bones; turn the lamb twice during cooking.

4. Using a slotted spoon, transfer the lamb to a platter. Strain the cooking liquid, pressing the vegetables through

the strainer. Skim off the fat and season with salt and pepper. Return the meat and the sauce to the casserole and keep warm.

5. MAKE THE TAPENADE: Meanwhile, in a mortar, crush the anchovy and garlic to a paste. Alternatively, mash the anchovy and garlic with the side of a large knife. Stir in the olive oil, olives, lemon juice, parsley and capers.

6. PREPARE THE BEANS: Heat the olive oil in a medium saucepan. Add the shallots, garlic and thyme and cook over moderate heat until softened. Stir in the beans, add the water and salt and cook over low heat until tender, about 20 minutes.

7. Drain the beans and spoon them into bowls. Spoon the lamb stew over the beans and then top with the tapenade and serve. —*Suzanne Goin*

MAKE AHEAD The recipe can be prepared through Step 5 and refrigerated overnight. Reheat the lamb in its sauce. Let the tapenade return to room temperature.

Anatolian Purslane, Lamb and Lentil Stew

4 SERVINGS

This dish is a specialty of Anatolia, Turkey. Make it in late summer when bulky bunches of purslane are available. The chickpeas and black-eyed peas need to soak overnight, so you'll need to plan accordingly.

- ½ **cup dried black-eyed peas, soaked overnight and drained**
- ⅓ **cup dried chickpeas, soaked overnight and drained**
- ¾ **cup mini brown lentils, picked over and rinsed (see box, right)**
- ¼ **cup olive oil**

About 4½ **cups water**

- 5 **ounces boneless lamb shoulder, cut into ½-inch dice**
- 1 **medium onion, finely chopped**
- 2 **teaspoons tomato paste**
- 2 **teaspoons Turkish red pepper paste (see box, right)**

Anatolian Purslane, Lamb and Lentil Stew

turkish pantry

The following ingredients are staples in Anatolian households. They are available at Middle Eastern groceries or by mail order from Kalustyan's (212-685-3451).

Turkish mini brown lentils are smaller than our common lentils. They have a distinctive flavor and hold their shape during cooking. Any mini lentils can be used in their place—Indian whole masoor dhal, Spanish Pardina lentils or mini brown Egyptian or Ethiopian varieties.

Turkish red pepper flakes are coarsely textured and mildly hot. They can be dark in color and intensely aromatic or bright red with an almost berrylike flavor.

Turkish red pepper paste is hot and vibrantly flavored. It's made with seeded and chopped hot and sweet peppers that are tossed with salt and spread out in large shallow pans to dry under a hot sun for a week. Look for the Selin or Melis brands.

- 1½ **pounds purslane, thick stems discarded and leaves coarsely shredded (see Note)**
- ½ **cup coarse bulgur**
- 2 **tablespoons minced garlic**
- 3 **tablespoons fresh lemon juice**

Salt

1 tablespoon dried spearmint,
  leaves crushed to a fine powder
¼ teaspoon Turkish red pepper
  flakes (see box, previous page)
¼ teaspoon freshly ground black
  pepper

Trimmed scallions and lemon wedges,
  for serving

1. Rinse the black-eyed peas and chick-peas. Pour them into separate medium saucepans and cover with several inches of water. Cover and cook over moderate heat until tender, about 20 minutes for the black-eyed peas and 1 hour for the chickpeas. Drain the black-eyed peas and discard the liquid. Drain the chickpeas; reserve ⅓ cup of the cooking liquid.

2. Meanwhile, in a medium saucepan, combine the lentils with 4 cups of the water, cover partially and cook over moderate heat until tender, about 40 minutes. Drain; reserve 2 cups of the lentil cooking liquid.

3. In a large, enameled cast-iron casserole, heat 2 tablespoons of the olive oil. Add the lamb and cook over moderate heat, stirring occasionally, until browned, about 5 minutes. Stir in the onion, cover and cook until softened but not browned, about 2 minutes. Add the tomato paste, red pepper paste and ½ cup of water and bring to a simmer. Cover and cook, stirring once or twice, until the mixture begins to caramelize, about 20 minutes.

4. Add the purslane, bulgur and the reserved chickpea and lentil cooking liquids to the casserole. Cover and cook for 10 minutes. Add the chickpeas, black-eyed peas, lentils, garlic and enough water to barely cover. Cover and simmer for 5 minutes. Remove from the heat, stir in the lemon juice and season with salt.

5. In a small skillet, heat the remaining 2 tablespoons olive oil. Add the spearmint, red pepper flakes and ¼ teaspoon freshly ground black pepper. When the olive oil begins to sizzle, give it a stir and

drizzle it over the stew. Stir once and let stand for 30 minutes. Serve the stew at room temperature, or let cool, refrigerate and serve chilled the following day. Pass the scallions and lemon at the table. —*Paula Wolfert*

NOTE Purslane is available from farmers' markets and specialty food shops.

Spicy Lamb Stew with Green Olives

6 SERVINGS

Australian lamb is famous worldwide, but olives, which were brought to Australia by early Mediterranean immigrants, are a less well-known national ingredient.

¼ cup olive oil
3 pounds boneless lamb shoulder,
  trimmed and cut into 2-inch
  pieces

Salt and freshly ground black
  pepper

2 medium onions, coarsely
  chopped
4 garlic cloves, thinly sliced
4 anchovy fillets, minced
1 teaspoon coriander seeds,
  coarsely ground
½ teaspoon cumin seeds,
  coarsely ground
½ teaspoon crushed red pepper
3 cups lamb stock, or 1½ cups
  canned low-sodium beef broth
  mixed with 1½ cups water
1¼ cups dry white wine
1 teaspoon dried oregano
¾ pound (2 cups) cracked green or
  Calamata olives, pitted and
  halved
½ cup coarsely chopped parsley
½ cup coarsely chopped cilantro
1 teaspoon red wine vinegar

Fragrant Orange Rice (p. 306)

1. Heat 2 tablespoons of the olive oil in a large, enameled cast-iron casserole. Add half of the lamb in a single layer, season with salt and black pepper and cook over moderately high heat until browned all over, 8 to 10 minutes;

transfer the lamb to a platter. Repeat with the remaining olive oil and lamb.

2. Pour off all but 2 tablespoons of the fat in the casserole. Add the onions, garlic, anchovies, coriander and cumin seeds and crushed red pepper and cook over moderate heat, stirring, until the onions are lightly browned, about 5 minutes. Return the lamb to the casserole and add the stock, wine and oregano. Cover partially and simmer over low heat until the meat is tender, about 1 hour and 45 minutes.

3. Using a slotted spoon, transfer the lamb to a platter. Boil the liquid in the casserole over high heat until it is reduced by one fourth, about 20 minutes. Skim the fat from the surface of the sauce. Return the lamb to the casserole and stir in the olives, parsley, cilantro and red wine vinegar. Season the stew with salt and black pepper and serve with the rice. —*John Ash*

MAKE AHEAD The stew can be made through Step 2 and refrigerated for up to 2 days. Reheat before proceeding.

WINE Match this spicy, meaty stew with a full-throttle, peppery Australian Shiraz, such as the 1996 Tim Adams Shiraz or the 1996 Penfolds Koonunga Hill Shiraz-Cabernet.

Kibbe

8 SERVINGS

The seasoned bulgur and lamb paste that is truly Lebanon's national dish exists in dozens of forms. Most typically, it is served as part of the meze spread as *kibbe nayyeh,* a sort of Lebanese steak tartare of raw lamb, drizzled with olive oil. The same paste, layered with a meat and pine nut filling and baked in the oven becomes *kibbe bi saniyeh* (kibbe in a tray). But the most spectacular presentation—the one that tests the skills of traditional cooks—involves shaping the kibbe mixture into thin-walled torpedoes, stuffing them with the aforementioned filling and deep-frying them.

FILLING

- 1½ tablespoons unsalted butter
- 1½ tablespoons extra-virgin olive oil
- ⅓ cup (2 ounces) pine nuts
- 1½ cups chopped onions
- ½ pound lean ground lamb
- 1 teaspoon allspice
- ½ teaspoon cinnamon

Pinch of cumin

Salt and freshly ground pepper

- 1 teaspoon pomegranate molasses, more if desired (see Note)
- ½ teaspoon ground sumac, more if desired (see Note)

KIBBE

- 1 pound yellow onions (about 4 medium), coarsely chopped
- 1 teaspoon salt
- ½ teaspoon freshly ground black pepper
- ½ teaspoon allspice
- ½ teaspoon cinnamon
- ½ teaspoon cumin

Pinch of cayenne pepper

- 1 pound very lean ground lamb
- 1 cup fine bulgur

Vegetable oil, for frying

Eggplant-Yogurt Sauce (recipe follows)

I. MAKE THE FILLING: In a medium skillet, melt the butter in the olive oil over moderate heat. Add the pine nuts and cook, stirring constantly, until golden. Transfer the nuts to a plate.

2. Add the onions to the skillet; cook, stirring, until softened but not browned. Add the lamb and cook, stirring to break it up, until no trace of pink remains. Remove from the heat; stir in the toasted pine nuts and the allspice, cinnamon and cumin. Season with salt and pepper. Stir in the 1 teaspoon pomegranate molasses and ½ teaspoon sumac. Taste and add the remaining pomegranate molasses and sumac if desired.

3. MAKE THE KIBBE: In a food processor, pulse the onions until finely chopped; add the salt, black pepper, allspice, cinnamon, cumin and cayenne and process until minced. Distribute the ground lamb over the onions and pulse to mix. Transfer the mixture to a large bowl.

4. Put the bulgur in a large bowl and stir in enough water to cover. When the wheat dust and chaff rise to the surface, pour off the water. Rinse the bulgur 3 or 4 more times, until the water is clear. Cover the bulgur with fresh water and let it soak for 20 minutes. Drain the bulgur, squeeze it dry and add it to the lamb mixture. Using wet hands, knead the kibbe as you would bread dough, wetting your hands frequently to prevent sticking. The texture of the kibbe should resemble light biscuit dough. Refrigerate until well chilled.

5. FOR FRIED KIBBE: Moisten your hands and roll about ¼ cup of the kibbe into a football shape. Using your index finger, poke a hole in 1 end of the football and gently work your finger into the kibbe until you have a 3-inch-long torpedo-shaped shell with ⅓-inch-thick walls. Cradling the kibbe in one hand so that the walls don't collapse, spoon about 1 tablespoon of the filling into the cavity. Pinch the end to seal, patting the kibbe into a 3-by-1½-inch torpedo. Set the kibbe on a baking sheet lined with plastic wrap. Repeat with the remaining kibbe and filling.

6. In a medium saucepan, heat 2 inches of oil to 350°. Fry the kibbe, 5 at a time, until browned, about 3 minutes. Drain on a rack lined with paper towels. Serve with the Eggplant-Yogurt Sauce.

7. FOR BAKED KIBBE: Pat half of the kibbe mixture into a generously buttered 10-inch round cake pan in an even layer. Spread the lamb filling evenly on top and cover with the remaining kibbe mixture, pressing into a smooth, even layer. Score a decorative pattern on top; brush with 2 tablespoons butter melted in 1 tablespoon olive oil. Bake at 375° for 30 minutes and then broil to brown the top. Let stand for 20 minutes before serving with the Eggplant-Yogurt Sauce. —*Nancy Harmon Jenkins*

NOTE Sumac is a spice widely prized in the Middle East for its dark red color and tangy flavor. Both sumac and pomegranate molasses are available from specialty food stores and spice shops.

MAKE AHEAD Kibbe can be prepared ahead and reheated in a 400° oven for about 10 minutes, or until warmed through and crisp outside.

EGGPLANT-YOGURT SAUCE
MAKES ABOUT 3 CUPS

One medium eggplant, peeled and sliced ½ inch thick

- ¼ cup extra-virgin olive oil
- 2 cups plain whole milk yogurt
- ½ garlic clove, minced

Salt

Preheat the oven to 375°. Brush the eggplant slices on both sides with the oil and arrange on a lightly oiled rimmed baking sheet. Bake for about 30 minutes, or until very soft and lightly browned. Let the eggplant cool slightly and then transfer the slices to a cutting board and chop coarsely. In a medium bowl, combine the eggplant with the yogurt and garlic and season with salt. Serve at room temperature. —*N. H. J.*

Kibbe

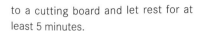

Seared Buffalo Salad

2 SERVINGS

The strip steak is one of the firmest cuts of buffalo. Together with crisp spicy radishes and silky cellophane noodles, it makes a delicious meal. Cutting the noodles is easiest if you use scissors.

- 1 ounce cellophane noodles, cut into 4-inch lengths

One 8-ounce buffalo strip steak

Salt and freshly ground pepper

- 3½ tablespoons olive oil
- 2 tablespoons sherry vinegar
- ½ pound radishes, cut into matchsticks
- 2 large scallions, cut lengthwise into 2-inch-long strips

1. In a medium bowl, cover the cellophane noodles with warm water and let stand until pliable, about 20 minutes; drain. Bring a medium saucepan of water to a boil and add the noodles. Cook, stirring, until al dente, about 1 minute. Drain the noodles in a colander, lifting them every few minutes to dry them.

2. Season the buffalo with salt and pepper. Heat ½ tablespoon of the olive oil in a small skillet. Add the buffalo steak and cook over moderately high heat until well browned and rare in the center, about 3 minutes per side. Transfer

Seared Buffalo Salad

to a cutting board and let rest for at least 5 minutes.

3. In a small glass or stainless steel bowl, combine the remaining 3 tablespoons of oil with the sherry vinegar and ¼ teaspoon each salt and pepper.

4. Thinly slice the buffalo steak crosswise across the grain. Stack the slices; cut the meat lengthwise into thin strips. In a glass or stainless steel bowl, toss the strips with the radishes, scallions and noodles. Add the dressing and toss again. Serve at once. —*Marcia Kiesel*

Buffalo Steaks with Chile-Garlic Oil

4 SERVINGS

You can use any extra chile-garlic oil on toast, in stir-fries or on grilled chicken, fish or pork. The flavor of the oil improves as it stands.

- ½ cup plus 1 tablespoon vegetable oil
- 8 large garlic cloves, thinly sliced
- 1 tablespoon crushed red pepper, preferably Aleppo or Korean

Salt

- 4 buffalo strip steaks (about ½ pound each), about 1 inch thick

Freshly ground black pepper

1. In a small saucepan, warm ½ cup of the oil over moderate heat. Add the garlic and crushed red pepper and simmer over low heat until the garlic turns pale gold, about 5 minutes. Pour the flavored oil into a heatproof bowl or jar and season with salt.

2. Season the buffalo steaks with salt and black pepper. In a large cast-iron skillet, heat the remaining 1 tablespoon of oil just until smoking. Add the steaks and cook over moderately high heat until browned, crusty and rare, about 3 minutes per side. Transfer the steaks to a cutting board and let rest for 5 minutes.

3. Thickly slice the steaks crosswise across the grain and arrange on plates. Drizzle the chile-garlic oil over the meat and serve. —*Marcia Kiesel*

SERVE WITH Steak fries.

Cured Buffalo Sirloin Roast with Mushroom Jus

8 SERVINGS

Lean buffalo sirloin roast should be cooked rare so it stays tender; the mushroom jus helps keep the meat moist. The curing also helps keep the roast juicy; allow time for it to refrigerate overnight. Rewarm any leftovers in what's left of the jus and serve the slices on kaiser rolls.

- 6 cups water
- 6 large garlic cloves, crushed
- 2 tablespoons kosher salt
- 2 tablespoons sugar
- 1 tablespoon allspice berries
- 4 bay leaves

One 4½-pound buffalo sirloin roast

Salt and freshly ground pepper

- 3 tablespoons vegetable oil

Mushroom Jus (recipe follows)

1. In a large saucepan, combine the water, garlic cloves, kosher salt, sugar, allspice berries and bay leaves. Bring to a boil, cook for 2 minutes and then let the brine cool to room temperature. In a very large bowl, cover the buffalo sirloin roast with the brine and refrigerate overnight.

2. Preheat the oven to 325°. Pat the buffalo sirloin roast dry with paper towels. Season the roast with salt and pepper. In a large skillet, heat the vegetable oil until it is almost smoking. Add the buffalo roast, widest side down, and brown over high heat, about 4 minutes. Continue cooking, turning, until the buffalo roast is browned all over, about 10 more minutes. Transfer the buffalo roast to a large roasting pan and cook it for about 1½ hours, or until an instant-read thermometer registers 120° for very rare. Let the buffalo roast rest for 20 minutes.

3. Cut the buffalo roast in half across the grain and then thinly slice each of the halves of the roast across the grain. Arrange the slices of buffalo roast on plates and serve them with the Mushroom Jus. —*Marcia Kiesel*

Buffalo Steaks with Chile-Garlic Oil

buying buffalo

Because the buffalo industry is small, the meat is often hard to find at supermarkets. Some mail-order sources: **Georgetown Farm** (888-EAT-LEAN; www.eatlean.com) Great for ribs and steaks; also offers such pioneers' favorites as liver and tongue.

Heartland Buffalo (800-277-0125; www.heartlandbuffalo.com) Hot dogs are their one and only product.

M & S Meats & Sausage (800-454-3414; www.vtown.com/msmeats) Distributor for White's Wholesale Meats. Carries steaks, roasts, salami, breakfast sausages, pepperoni and jerky.

U.S. Bison (800-618-0613) Owned by Ted Turner. Sells steaks, hot dogs and meat ravioli.

MUSHROOM JUS
MAKES ABOUT 4 CUPS

- 1 ounce dried shiitake mushrooms
- 4 cups hot water
- 1 tablespoon olive oil
- ¼ cup soy sauce
- 2 large garlic cloves, crushed
- Salt and freshly ground pepper

1. Put the shiitake mushrooms in a bowl and add the hot water. Cover and let the mushrooms stand until softened, about 20 minutes. Using a slotted spoon, remove the mushrooms from the water and cut off and discard the stems. Swish the mushrooms in the soaking water to loosen any grit. Finely chop the mushrooms; reserve the soaking liquid.

2. Heat the olive oil in a saucepan. Add the mushrooms and cook over high heat until they are starting to brown, about 3 minutes. Add 2 tablespoons of the soy sauce and the garlic and cook over high heat until the soy sauce evaporates and the mushrooms brown, about 5 minutes. Pour in the reserved mushroom soaking liquid, stopping when you reach the grit at the bottom, and the remaining 2 tablespoons of soy sauce and stir well. Cover and simmer over low heat until the mushrooms are tender, about 5 minutes. Season the jus with salt and pepper. —*M. K.*

MAKE AHEAD The Mushroom Jus can be refrigerated overnight. Rewarm before serving.

Buffalo Ribs with Tomato Glaze
4 SERVINGS

Savory buffalo ribs are less fatty than their pork counterparts but rich enough to be luscious.

- 2 racks of buffalo spare ribs (about 6 pounds total)
- Salt and freshly ground black pepper
- 8 large garlic cloves, 4 coarsely chopped and 4 minced
- 1 cup dry vermouth
- ¼ cup plus 2 tablespoons cider vinegar
- 1 tablespoon tomato paste
- 1½ teaspoons crushed red pepper

1. Preheat the oven to 325°. Set the buffalo spare ribs in a large roasting pan, meaty side up. Season the spare ribs with salt and freshly ground black pepper and then sprinkle them with the chopped garlic. Pour the dry vermouth over the ribs. Cover the ribs with foil and bake for 2 hours.

2. Meanwhile, in a small glass or stainless steel bowl, combine the minced garlic with the cider vinegar, the tomato paste, the crushed red pepper, 1 teaspoon of salt and ½ teaspoon of black pepper.

3. Raise the oven temperature to 400°. Scrape the garlic off the buffalo spare ribs and discard the liquid in the pan. Set the ribs on a rack in the roasting pan, meaty side up, and spread one quarter of the vinegar glaze on top. Bake in the upper third of the oven for 1 hour and 20 minutes, brushing the ribs every 20 minutes with more glaze; the ribs should be tender and deeply glazed. Let stand for 5 minutes before cutting down in between the ribs and serving. —*Marcia Kiesel*

Buffalo Burgers with Raisin-Garlic Mayonnaise
4 SERVINGS

Ground buffalo has an intense meaty but not gamy flavor. The meat is so lean, it's best to cook the burgers rare.

- ½ cup mayonnaise
- 2 tablespoons chopped raisins
- 2 garlic cloves, minced
- 1 tablespoon minced flat-leaf parsley
- Salt and freshly ground pepper
- ¼ cup pine nuts
- 2 pounds ground buffalo
- 1 tablespoon soy sauce
- 1 tablespoon vegetable oil
- 4 hamburger buns, toasted
- Romaine lettuce leaves, for serving

1. In a small bowl, combine the mayonnaise, raisins, garlic and parsley. Season with salt and pepper.

2. Heat a large cast-iron skillet. Add the pine nuts and cook over low heat, stirring a few times, until well browned, about 5 minutes; let cool. In a large bowl, gently mix the ground buffalo with the pine nuts. Pat into 4 burgers. Rub each burger with some of the soy sauce and season with salt and pepper.

3. In the skillet, heat the oil just until smoking. Add the burgers; cook over high heat until browned, crusty and rare, about 2 minutes per side. Serve on the buns with lettuce and the raisin-garlic mayonnaise. —*Marcia Kiesel*

MAKE AHEAD The mayonnaise can be refrigerated for up to 2 days.

Navajo Fry Bread with Chili
8 SERVINGS

The bread can be kept in a warm oven while you finish frying the rest of the batch, but it's best served hot out of the pan, with meaty chili spooned on top.

CHILI

- 1 large ancho chile
- 3 cups boiling water
- ¼ cup dried porcini mushrooms
- 3 tablespoons olive oil
- 2 pounds ground buffalo or beef chuck

Salt and freshly ground black pepper

2 large onions, coarsely chopped

4 large garlic cloves, minced

2 tablespoons pure chile powder

2 tablespoons tomato paste mixed
with ¼ cup water

1 cup chicken stock or canned
low-sodium broth

FRY BREAD

4 cups all-purpose flour

½ cup cornmeal

1 tablespoon plus 1 teaspoon
baking powder

1¼ teaspoons salt

2⅔ cups water

Vegetable oil, for frying

I. MAKE THE CHILI: In a heatproof bowl, cover the ancho with 2 cups of the boiling water. Put the porcini in a small heatproof bowl and cover with the remaining 1 cup of boiling water. Let both soak until softened, about 20 minutes. Remove the ancho from the soaking liquid and discard the stem and seeds. Reserve the soaking liquid. Finely chop the chile. Rub the porcini to remove any grit and finely chop them; reserve the porcini soaking liquid.

2. In a large enameled cast-iron casserole, heat 2 tablespoons of the olive oil until almost smoking. Add half of the ground buffalo in an even layer and season with salt and pepper. Sear the meat over high heat for 3 minutes without stirring; leave the meat in large pieces. Gently stir the meat and continue to brown it for 2 minutes more. Using a slotted spoon, transfer the meat to a plate; brown the remaining meat.

3. Heat the remaining 1 tablespoon of olive oil in the casserole. Add the onions and cook over low heat until softened, about 10 minutes. Add the garlic and cook, stirring, until fragrant, about 2 minutes. Add the chile powder and cook, stirring, for 4 minutes. Add the tomato paste mixture, the stock and the chopped ancho and porcini. Add the ancho and porcini soaking liquids, stopping when you reach any grit at the bottom. Season with a large pinch of salt and simmer over moderately low heat until the sauce reduces by a third, about 10 minutes. Gently stir in the meat and any accumulated juices and season with salt and pepper. Rewarm just before serving.

4. MAKE THE FRY BREAD: Sift together the flour, cornmeal, baking powder and salt. With a wooden spoon, stir in the water until just blended.

5. In a 2-quart saucepan, heat 2 inches of oil to 350°. Brush a ½-cup measuring cup with oil and have 2 wooden spoons ready. Scoop a ½-cup portion of the batter into the hot oil and then use the 2 spoons to carefully spread the batter out to a 6- to 7-inch disk. Fry the bread until golden brown and cooked through, about 2 minutes per side; lower the heat if the oil becomes too hot. Drain on paper towels and transfer to a dinner plate. Top with the chili and serve at once. Repeat to make 7 more fry breads and serve with the remaining chili. —*Marcia Kiesel*

MAKE AHEAD The chili can be refrigerated for up to 3 days; reheat gently. The fry bread batter can stand at room temperature for up to 30 minutes.

Buffalo Corn Dogs

MAKES 10 CORN DOGS

2 cups yellow or white cornmeal

2 cups all-purpose flour

2 tablespoons sugar

2 teaspoons baking powder

1 teaspoon salt

2 large eggs

½ cup buttermilk

1 jalapeño, seeded and minced

4 tablespoons unsalted butter,
melted

10 buffalo hot dogs, scored lightly
on 2 sides

Vegetable oil, for frying

Smoky barbecue sauce, for serving

I. In a large bowl, stir together the cornmeal, flour, sugar, baking powder and salt. In a small bowl, combine the eggs, buttermilk and jalapeño. Using a wooden spoon, blend the egg mixture and butter into the dry ingredients, stirring just until thoroughly combined.

2. At the short end of a long sheet of wax paper, shape ⅓ cup of the cornmeal mixture into a 4-by-6-inch rectangle. Set a buffalo hot dog in the center of the cornmeal mixture and lift the wax paper up and over the hot dog to enclose it in cornmeal. Pull the wax paper around the hot dog and press to coat the meat completely with the cornmeal, rolling until evenly coated. Remove the wax paper and set the corn dog on a large plate. Repeat with the remaining cornmeal mixture and buffalo hot dogs.

3. In a saucepan, heat 2 inches of oil until shimmering. Fry the corn dogs 1 at a time over moderate heat, turning once, until golden, about 3 minutes per side. Serve the corn dogs hot with barbecue sauce. —*Marcia Kiesel*

chapter 10

breads pizzas
sandwiches tortillas

263

257

266

253

Focaccia

MAKES ONE 14-BY-10-INCH
FOCACCIA

This focaccia is soft, tender, cakey and about an inch and a half thick.

- 1 envelope active dry yeast
- ½ cup warm water
- 2 tablespoons extra-virgin olive oil, plus more for brushing
- ½ cup water, at room temperature
- 3½ cups all-purpose flour
- 1 teaspoon sugar
- ½ teaspoon salt
- ⅓ cup cool water

Kosher salt, for sprinkling

1. In a small bowl, sprinkle the yeast over the warm water and let the mixture stand until foamy, 5 to 8 minutes. Stir in the 2 tablespoons of olive oil and the room temperature water.

2. In a large bowl, combine the flour with the sugar and salt. Make a well in the center and pour in the yeast mixture. Using a wooden spoon, stir slowly to incorporate the dry ingredients into the well. When roughly half of the flour has been incorporated, add the cool water. When the dough becomes too thick to stir, use your hands to fold it from the side of the bowl toward the center and then flatten it down, repeating the motion until a ball forms.

3. On a lightly floured work surface, knead the dough until smooth and elastic, about 5 minutes. Transfer the dough to a bowl and cover with plastic wrap. Let rise at warm room temperature until doubled in bulk, about 1 hour. Knead the dough for 3 minutes and then let it rest again until relaxed, about 1 hour.

4. Preheat the oven to 400°. Lightly oil a large rimmed baking sheet. On a lightly floured work surface, roll the dough into a 14-by-10-inch rectangle. Transfer the dough to the baking sheet, cover with a towel and let rise until doubled in bulk, about 30 minutes.

5. Using your fingertips, dimple the dough, making indentations all over the surface. Brush the dough with olive oil, sprinkle with kosher salt and bake for 30 to 35 minutes, or until golden brown. Remove from the oven and drizzle with additional olive oil if desired. Transfer the focaccia to a wire rack to cool slightly and then cut into slices or squares and serve. —*Lori De Mori*

MAKE AHEAD The focaccia can be made through Step 3 and refrigerated overnight. Bring the dough to room temperature before rolling out.

Walnut-Lavender Bread

MAKES 2 LOAVES

If you want a stronger walnut flavor in this light, soft bread, toast the nuts and then let them cool before adding them to the dough, which gets a long slow rise of up to 24 hours.

- 1½ cups water, at room temperature
- 1 package active dry yeast (not rapid rise)
- 3 cups unbleached bread flour
- 1½ tablespoons honey
- 1 tablespoon coarsely chopped fresh lavender buds, or
- ¾ tablespoon dried lavender
- 2 teaspoons salt
- 1 cup (3 ounces) walnut halves or pieces

1. Pour the water into a food processor and sprinkle the yeast on top. Add the flour, honey, lavender and salt and process for 1 minute. Add the walnuts and pulse just until they're evenly incorporated into the dough. Scrape the side and bottom of the bowl as needed with a rubber spatula. The dough should be very soft and sticky. Transfer the dough to a bowl, cover and let rise in the refrigerator for at least 12 and up to 24 hours.

2. On a lightly floured work surface, pat the dough into a 10-inch square. Fold it in half, pat it out a little and then fold it in half in the other direction so that you end up with a 6-inch square. Cut the dough in half.

3. Stretch out each piece of dough to a 9-by-4-inch oval; it will look like the sole of a very big shoe. Transfer the loaves to a lightly floured baking sheet. Cover with a dish towel and let rise at room temperature until doubled in bulk, 1½ to 2 hours.

4. Preheat the oven to 375°. Bake the loaves on the middle shelf for 30 to 35 minutes, or until browned. Cool the loaves completely on a rack before slicing. —*Jerry Traunfeld*

Sticky Buns with Toasted Almonds

MAKES 10 STICKY BUNS
DOUGH

- 1 cup whole milk
- 1 envelope active dry yeast
- 3 cups all-purpose flour
- ¼ cup granulated sugar

Finely grated zest of 1 orange

- 1½ teaspoons salt
- 1 large egg yolk
- 2 tablespoons unsalted butter, at room temperature
- 1 teaspoon pure vanilla extract

TOPPING AND FILLING

- 2 sticks (½ pound) unsalted butter
- ¾ cup light brown sugar
- ½ cup pure maple syrup
- 1½ tablespoons cinnamon
- 1 large egg beaten with
- 2 tablespoons milk or cream
- ½ cup granulated sugar
- ½ cup natural almonds

1. MAKE THE DOUGH: In a small saucepan, heat ½ cup of the milk to 110°. In a bowl, mix the yeast with the warm milk; let stand for 5 minutes.

2. In the bowl of a standing electric mixer fitted with a dough hook, combine the flour with the sugar, orange zest and salt. On low speed, mix in the yeast mixture, egg yolk, butter and vanilla. Add the remaining ½ cup of milk and knead the dough at medium speed until smooth and silky, about 5 minutes. Cover and refrigerate for 1 hour.

3. MAKE THE TOPPING AND FILLING: Lightly grease a 9-by-13-inch baking dish and line the bottom with parchment or wax paper. In a medium

Sticky Buns with Toasted Almonds, LEFT, and Mom's Banana-Apple Bread (p. 256).

saucepan, combine the butter with the brown sugar, maple syrup and ½ tablespoon of the cinnamon. Bring to a boil, stirring, until the butter is melted and the sugar is dissolved. Pour the syrup into the baking pan.

4. On a lightly floured surface, roll out the dough to a 12-by-16-inch rectangle, with a long edge facing you. Lightly brush the egg wash over the dough. Combine the granulated sugar with the remaining 1 tablespoon cinnamon and

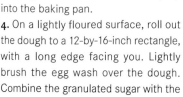

sprinkle the mixture heavily all over the dough, leaving a 1-inch border at the bottom. Starting at the top edge, roll up the dough jelly-roll style and pinch the bottom edge to seal.

5. Cut the roll into 10 even slices and arrange the slices, cut side down, in the syrup. Cover the pan with plastic wrap and let the dough rise in a warm, draft-free place until doubled in bulk and soft to the touch, 1 to 2 hours.

6. Preheat the oven to 350°. Put the almonds on a baking sheet and roast until fragrant and golden, 8 to 9 minutes. Let the almonds cool and then coarsely chop them.

7. Bake the buns for 40 minutes, or until the dough is a deep golden brown and the syrup is bubbling. Let cool slightly and then use tongs to transfer the buns, 1 at a time, to a serving dish. Spoon any remaining syrup over the buns; sprinkle with the almonds. Serve warm. —*Melissa Murphy Hagenbart*

MAKE AHEAD The sticky buns can be prepared through Step 5 and refrigerated overnight. Let the dough return to room temperature before baking.

Bakewell Cream Biscuits

MAKES 1 DOZEN BISCUITS

Bakewell Cream, the traditional New England leavening agent, makes these biscuits rise high. The unusual baking method ensures that the biscuits don't overcook, even if you leave them in the oven too long.

  4 cups all-purpose flour
  1 tablespoon plus 1 teaspoon
      Bakewell Cream (see Note)
  2 teaspoons baking soda
  1 teaspoon salt
  ½ cup cold vegetable shortening
1¾ cups buttermilk

ı. Preheat the oven to 475°. In a large bowl, whisk the flour with the Bakewell Cream, baking soda and salt. Using a

pastry blender or 2 knives, cut in the shortening until the mixture resembles small peas. Add the buttermilk and stir with a fork until a dough forms.

2. Turn the dough out onto a lightly floured work surface and knead 3 or 4 times. Roll out the dough ¾ inch thick. Using a 2-inch-round biscuit cutter or glass, cut out 12 biscuits. Transfer the biscuits to a baking sheet and bake in the bottom third of the oven for 5 minutes. Turn off the heat and let the biscuits sit in the hot oven, without opening the door, for about 10 minutes longer, or until golden and cooked through. Transfer to a basket and serve immediately. —*Jonathan King and Jim Stott*

NOTE Bakewell Cream can be ordered from Apple Ledge Company (207-989-5576). Or substitute 2 teaspoons of baking powder for the Bakewell Cream and baking soda in the recipe.

Rosemary Biscuits with Sausage and Cheese

MAKES 8 BISCUITS

Mustard is a particularly good accompaniment for these biscuits. They can also be served unstuffed.

  2 cups all-purpose flour
  2 teaspoons baking powder
  ¾ teaspoon salt
  ¼ teaspoon baking soda
  4 tablespoons cold unsalted butter,
      cut into small pieces, plus melted
      butter for brushing
  ½ cup (about 2 ounces) grated
      extra-sharp Cheddar cheese
  1 tablespoon chopped rosemary
  ¾ cup cold milk
  ⅓ pound Maytag blue cheese, sliced
  1 pound duck or lamb sausage,
      grilled and sliced ½ inch thick

ı. In a food processor, combine the flour, baking powder, salt and baking soda and process until blended. Add the cold butter, the Cheddar and the

LEFT: Rosemary Biscuits with Sausage and Cheese.
TOP: Bakewell Cream Biscuits.

rosemary and pulse until the mixture resembles coarse meal. Gradually pulse in the milk until the dough just comes together. Turn the dough out onto a lightly floured work surface and knead gently. Shape the dough into a flat disk. Wrap the disk in plastic and refrigerate until the dough is firm, about 1 hour.

2. Preheat the oven to 375°. On a lightly floured surface, roll out the dough ⅓ inch thick. Using a 3-inch biscuit cutter, cut out 8 biscuits. Transfer the biscuits to a baking sheet, brush with melted butter and bake for about 20 minutes, or until golden. Slice the biscuits in half, fill with the blue cheese and sausages and serve. —*John Currence*

Spiced Buttermilk Scones with Marmalade

MAKES 1 DOZEN SCONES

- 3 cups all-purpose flour
- ⅓ cup sugar
- 2½ teaspoons baking powder
- ¾ teaspoon salt
- ½ teaspoon baking soda
- ½ teaspoon ground ginger
- Scant ¼ teaspoon ground cloves
- 1½ sticks (6 ounces) cold unsalted butter, cut into ½-inch pieces, plus 2 tablespoons softened butter
- 1 cup buttermilk
- ½ cup orange marmalade

1. Preheat the oven to 425°. Line a large rimmed baking sheet with parchment paper. In a large bowl, whisk together the all-purpose flour, sugar, baking powder, salt, baking soda, ginger and cloves. Using a pastry blender or 2 knives, cut in the cold butter until the mixture resembles small peas. Stir in the buttermilk. Turn the dough out onto a lightly floured surface and knead just until it holds together; don't overwork it. Divide the dough into 4 pieces and roll each piece into a 7-inch round.

2. In a bowl, combine the softened butter with half of the marmalade and spread half on each of 2 dough rounds,

Sour Cherry Scones and Ginger-Marmalade Cream

to within ½ inch of the edges. Set the remaining 2 dough rounds on top and press the edges together to seal. Strain the remaining marmalade and brush it over the rounds. Cut each round into 6 wedges; arrange on the prepared baking sheet. Bake in the lower third of the oven for 20 to 25 minutes, or until golden on both top and bottom and cooked through. —*Jonathan King and Jim Stott*

Sour Cherry Scones and Ginger-Marmalade Cream

MAKES 8 SCONES

SCONES

- ½ cup dried sour cherries
- 2 cups all-purpose flour
- ¼ cup sugar
- 2 teaspoons baking powder
- ½ teaspoon ground cardamom
- ½ teaspoon salt
- 1 cup heavy cream
- 1 tablespoon unsalted butter, melted

CREAM

- 1 cup heavy cream
- 2 tablespoons confectioners' sugar
- ¼ cup ginger marmalade, at room temperature

1. MAKE THE SCONES: Preheat the oven to 425°. Soak the dried sour cherries in hot water until plump, about 10 minutes. In a large bowl, whisk the flour with the sugar, baking powder, cardamom and salt. Drain the cherries and pat dry. Add the cherries to the dry ingredients along with the cream and stir until the dough is evenly moistened. Gather the dough into a ball and gently knead it 4 or 5 times.

2. On a lightly floured surface, roll or pat the dough into a ¾-inch-thick round. Using a 2½-inch biscuit cutter, cut out 8 rounds. Transfer the rounds to a baking sheet and brush the tops with the melted butter. Bake for about 20 minutes, or until the scones are lightly browned and cooked through.

3. MAKE THE CREAM: In a medium bowl, whip the heavy cream with the confectioners' sugar until soft peaks form. Transfer the whipped cream to a serving bowl and spoon the ginger marmalade on top.

4. Split the hot scones and serve them at once with the ginger marmalade cream. —*Rori Spinelli*

Wild Rice Muffins

Wild Rice Muffins

MAKES 1 DOZEN MUFFINS

Serve these savory muffins on their own or as an unorthodox counterpoint to poultry or meat with a fruity sauce.

- ¾ **cup wild rice**
- ½ **cup (about 2 ounces) hazelnuts**
- 1 **stick (4 ounces) unsalted butter, melted**
- 2 **large eggs, lightly beaten**
- 3 **tablespoons sugar**
- 1 **onion, finely chopped**
- 1 **cup all-purpose flour**
- 1 **teaspoon baking powder**
- 1 **teaspoon kosher salt**

1. In a medium saucepan, cover the wild rice with 1 inch of water. Cover the saucepan and simmer the wild rice over moderately low heat until tender, about 20 minutes. Drain and let cool.

2. Preheat the oven to 400°. Butter a 12-cup muffin pan. In a pie plate, toast the hazelnuts in the oven for about 10 minutes, or until the skins blister. Transfer the nuts to a kitchen towel and rub off the skins. Finely chop the nuts. Raise the oven temperature to 425°.

3. In a medium bowl, beat the butter with the eggs and the sugar. Stir in the cooked wild rice, the onion and the hazelnuts until combined.

4. In another medium bowl, sift together the flour, baking powder and kosher salt. Stir the dry ingredients into the wild rice mixture just until incorporated.

5. Fill the muffin cups two thirds of the way with the batter and bake for about 20 minutes, or until the muffins are golden brown. Let the muffins cool in the pan for 2 minutes and then unmold and transfer to a rack to cool completely. —*Kerry Sear*

MAKE AHEAD The muffins can be frozen for up to 1 month.

Peppered Ginger Spice Muffins with Orange Maple Butter

MAKES 1 DOZEN MUFFINS

Ginger muffins have a more sophisticated flavor than gingerbread—and a spicier kick.

- 2 **cups all-purpose flour**
- 1¼ **teaspoons baking soda**
- ¼ **teaspoon salt**
- 1 **tablespoon ground ginger**
- 1 **teaspoon cinnamon**
- ½ **teaspoon cloves**
- ½ **teaspoon freshly ground black pepper**
- ½ **teaspoon ground cardamom**
- ¼ **teaspoon dry mustard**
- ¼ **teaspoon freshly ground white pepper**
- ¼ **teaspoon cayenne pepper**
- ¼ **cup finely grated peeled fresh ginger (from a 6-inch piece)**
- 2 **large eggs**
- ½ **cup dark brown sugar**
- ¼ **cup granulated sugar**
- ½ **cup unsulphured molasses**

Peppered Ginger Spice Muffins with Orange Maple Butter

⅓ cup vegetable oil
⅔ cup hot strong coffee
Confectioners' sugar, for dusting
Orange Maple Butter (recipe follows)

I. Preheat the oven to 350°. Line a 12-cup muffin pan with paper liners. In a medium bowl, mix together the flour, baking soda, salt, ground ginger, cinnamon, cloves, black pepper, cardamom, dry mustard, white pepper and cayenne. Stir in the fresh ginger.

2. In a large bowl, with a handheld mixer, beat the eggs with the brown and granulated sugars on medium speed until thick and light, about 4 minutes. Add the molasses and oil; beat until smooth. On low speed, beat in the dry ingredients in 2 batches, alternating with the coffee.

3. Spoon the batter into the muffin cups until they are three-fourths full and bake for about 25 minutes, or until a skewer inserted in the centers of the muffins comes out clean. Let cool completely in the pan before unmolding. Dust with confectioners' sugar and serve with the butter. —*Melissa Murphy Hagenbart*

MAKE AHEAD The muffin batter can be prepared 1 day ahead and refrigerated overnight.

ORANGE MAPLE BUTTER
MAKES ½ CUP

1 stick (4 ounces) unsalted butter, softened
1 tablespoon pure maple syrup
2 teaspoons finely grated orange zest
Pinch of salt

In a medium bowl, using a handheld mixer, beat the butter, pure maple syrup, orange zest and salt together on medium speed until light and fluffy. Transfer the butter to a small bowl and serve. —*M. M. H.*

MAKE AHEAD The butter can be refrigerated for up to 1 week. Bring to room temperature before serving.

Country Corn Bread
MAKES ONE 9-BY-13-INCH CORN BREAD

2 cups all-purpose flour
2 cups yellow cornmeal
¼ cup sugar
1 tablespoon salt
1 tablespoon baking powder
½ teaspoon baking soda
2 large eggs, lightly beaten
2½ cups buttermilk
1 stick (4 ounces) unsalted butter, melted

I. Preheat the oven to 350°. Butter a 9-by-13-inch baking dish. In a bowl, combine the flour, cornmeal, sugar, salt, baking powder and baking soda. In another bowl, combine the eggs and buttermilk and add to the dry ingredients. Add the butter and stir just until moistened.

2. Pour the batter into the prepared baking dish and bake for about 40 minutes, or until the corn bread is golden and a toothpick inserted in the center comes out clean. Let the corn bread cool in the baking dish for 10 minutes and then turn it out onto a wire rack to cool completely. —*Robert Del Grande*

MAKE AHEAD The corn bread can be wrapped in plastic and frozen for 1 week or refrigerated for up to 2 days.

Country Corn Bread Stuffing
8 TO 12 SERVINGS

Use Country Corn Bread as the base for a poblano-spiked stuffing that's a great accompaniment for Mole-Inspired Roasted Turkey (p. 190).

Country Corn Bread (left) • 4 medium poblano chiles • 4 tablespoons unsalted butter • 2 small onions, finely chopped • 2 medium celery ribs, finely chopped • 2 medium carrots, finely chopped • 2 tablespoons minced garlic • 1 pound coarsely ground country sausage meat or breakfast sausage without casings • 1 tablespoon dried oregano, crumbled • 2 teaspoons salt • 1 teaspoon freshly ground pepper • 1 cup turkey or chicken stock or canned low-sodium broth

I. Butter a 9-by-13-inch baking dish. Break the corn bread into 1-inch pieces, spread the pieces on a baking sheet and let dry slightly, for at least 4 hours or overnight.

2. Meanwhile, roast the chiles over a gas flame or under the broiler, turning until charred all over. Transfer to a bowl, cover with plastic wrap and let steam for 15 minutes. Peel, core and seed and cut into ½-inch pieces.

3. In a large skillet, melt the butter until foaming. Add the onions, celery, carrots and garlic; cook over moderately high heat, stirring, until softened, 8 to 10 minutes. Add the sausage, breaking it up; cook until no pink remains, about 10 minutes. Stir in the oregano, salt, pepper and roasted chiles and transfer to a large bowl. Mix in the corn bread and then stir in the stock. Spread the stuffing in the prepared baking dish.

4. Preheat the oven to 350°. Cover the stuffing with foil; bake for about 30 minutes, or until heated through. Uncover and bake for 15 to 20 minutes, or until the top is crisp and golden. Serve hot. —*Robert Del Grande*

Mom's Banana-Apple Bread

MAKES ONE 9-INCH LOAF

- 1   stick plus 2 tablespoons (5 ounces) unsalted butter, at room temperature
- 2   tablespoons dark brown sugar
- 2   Granny Smith apples—peeled, cored and cut into ½-inch dice
- 1   teaspoon cinnamon
- 1½ teaspoons pure vanilla extract
- 2   cups all-purpose flour
- 1   teaspoon baking soda
- ½   teaspoon salt
- ¼   teaspoon ground cloves
- ¼   teaspoon freshly grated nutmeg
- 1   cup granulated sugar
- 2   large eggs
- 2   very ripe bananas, mashed (1 cup)
- ¼   cup fresh orange juice

1. In a large skillet, melt 2 tablespoons of the butter with the dark brown sugar. Add the diced apples and cook over moderately high heat, stirring, until tender and golden, 4 to 5 minutes. Add ½ teaspoon of the cinnamon and ½ teaspoon of the vanilla extract and transfer the apples to a plate.

2. Preheat the oven to 350°. Grease and flour a 9-by-5-by-4 ½ inch loaf pan. In a medium bowl, stir together the flour, baking soda, salt, cloves, grated nutmeg and the remaining ½ teaspoon cinnamon.

3. In a large bowl, using a handheld electric mixer, beat the remaining stick of butter with the granulated sugar on medium speed until light and fluffy. Add the eggs, one at a time, and mix until smooth. Add the bananas, orange juice and the remaining 1 teaspoon of vanilla extract and beat until smooth. Add the dry ingredients and beat on low speed until smooth. Using a rubber spatula, fold in the apples.

4. Scrape the batter into the prepared loaf pan and smooth the surface. Bake the banana-apple bread for 1 hour and 20 minutes, or until a toothpick inserted in the center of the loaf comes out clean; cover loosely with foil if the loaf becomes too dark. Let the bread cool in the pan for 10 minutes before turning the loaf out onto a rack to cool completely. —*Melissa Murphy Hagenbart*

MAKE AHEAD The banana-apple bread can be wrapped in plastic and refrigerated for up to 3 days.

Maine Blueberry Pancakes

MAKES ABOUT 16 PANCAKES

If you can find them, wild Maine blueberries add a refreshing tartness to the pancakes, and so do huckleberries.

- 2   cups all-purpose flour
- 2   tablespoons sugar
- 1   teaspoon baking powder
- 1   teaspoon baking soda
- 1¾ cups plus 2 tablespoons buttermilk
- 2   large eggs, at room temperature
- 3   tablespoons unsalted butter, melted, plus more for cooking and serving
- 2   cups fresh or frozen blueberries

Pure maple syrup, for serving

1. In a medium bowl, whisk together the flour, sugar, baking powder and baking soda. In another bowl, whisk the buttermilk with the eggs and melted butter. Add the buttermilk mixture to the dry ingredients and stir just until incorporated. Fold in the blueberries; be careful not to crush them or the batter will turn purple.

2. Heat a cast-iron griddle or skillet over moderately high heat and brush lightly with butter. Spoon rounded ¼ cupfuls of the pancake batter onto the griddle, spreading each one out slightly. Cook the blueberry pancakes until the bottoms of the pancakes are browned, the tops are slightly set and small bubbles appear, about 3 minutes. Flip the blueberry pancakes and cook until golden, about 1 minute. Serve the blueberry pancakes hot off the griddle with butter and pure maple syrup. Continue making pancakes with the remaining batter. —*Jonathan King and Jim Stott*

Pizza with Roasted Peppers and Manchego Cheese

MAKES FOUR 9-INCH PIZZAS

Cooking pizza on the grill takes just a few minutes. Have all your toppings assembled before you begin to grill the crusts. Unless your grill is huge, you'll only be able to cook one pizza at a time.

DOUGH

- 1   package active dry yeast
- 1   cup warm water
- 1   teaspoon sugar
- 3   cups all-purpose flour
- ⅓   cup whole wheat flour
- 2   teaspoons kosher salt
- 1   tablespoon extra-virgin olive oil

TOPPINGS

- 2   red bell peppers

About ½ cup olive oil

- 4   ounces (1½ cups) Manchego cheese, shredded
- 2   large tomatoes, coarsely chopped
- 2   garlic cloves, minced
- 2   tablespoons drained capers

Salt and freshly ground black pepper

1. **MAKE THE DOUGH:** In a small bowl, combine the yeast with the warm water and sugar. Let stand until foamy, about 5 minutes. In the bowl of a food processor, combine both flours with the kosher salt and process to blend. Add the oil and the yeast mixture and process until the dough comes together.

2. On a lightly floured work surface, knead the dough until smooth and elastic. Put in a large oiled bowl and turn to coat. Cover and let rise until doubled in bulk, about 1 hour. Punch down and cut in quarters; shape into 6-inch disks.

3. Generously oil 2 large rimmed baking sheets and transfer 2 of the disks to each sheet; lightly brush the dough with olive oil. Let rest for 30 minutes.

4. **PREPARE THE TOPPINGS:** Light a charcoal grill. Roast the peppers over a hot fire until charred all over. Transfer to a bowl, cover with plastic wrap and let steam for 10 minutes. Peel the peppers; discard the stems, seeds and cores. Cut the peppers into thin strips.

5. Rake three fourths of the coals to one side of the grill, leaving a thin layer of coals on the other side. Working on the baking sheet, pat and stretch 1 dough disk to form a 9-inch round. Lift the dough up by the edge and drape onto the grate over the hot part of the grill. Grill the dough until nicely toasted on the bottom, about 1 minute. Rotate 45 degrees; cook for an additional minute. **6.** Flip the crust over onto the cooler part of the grill and brush with olive oil. Sprinkle one quarter of the cheese over the crust and top with one quarter of the red bell peppers, tomatoes, garlic and capers. Move the pizza back to the hot area of the grill to melt the cheese. Cook until the bottom of the crust is lightly charred, about 2 minutes; if it starts to burn, move it to the cooler side. Sprinkle with salt and black pepper and serve immediately. Repeat with the remaining dough and toppings to make 3 more pizzas. —*Steven Raichlen*
WINE The rich cheese on this pizza says red wine; the tomatoes narrow the choice to one with matching acidity. Best bet? A fruity, tart California Sangiovese, such as the 1996 Atlas Peak or the 1996 Shafer Firebreak.

Chickpea Flour Pizza with Tomato and Parmesan

MAKES ONE 12-INCH PIZZA
Called *socca* in Nice and *farinata* in Genoa, this workingman's morning snack is traditionally baked in brick ovens in pizza pans. The version below calls for using a skillet on the stovetop, and then moving the pizza to the broiler.

- 2/3 **cup chickpea flour (see Note)**
- 1/3 **teaspoon salt**
- 1 **cup water**
- 1/2 **teaspoon finely chopped rosemary**
- 3 **tablespoons extra-virgin olive oil**
- 2 **tablespoons chopped tomato**
- 1 **tablespoon finely chopped onion**
- 3 **tablespoons freshly grated Parmesan cheese**
- 1/4 **teaspoon freshly ground pepper**

1. Preheat the broiler. Sift the flour with the salt into a medium bowl. Slowly add 1/4 cup of the water, whisking constantly to form a paste. Beat with a wooden spoon until smooth. Whisk in the remaining 3/4 cup water. Let stand at room temperature 30 minutes; stir in the rosemary. **2.** Heat 1 tablespoon of the oil in a 12-inch nonstick ovenproof skillet. Stir the batter once. Pour it into the skillet; drizzle the remaining 2 tablespoons oil on top. Cook over moderately high heat until the bottom is golden and crisp and the top is almost set, 2 to 3 minutes. Burst any large air bubbles with the tip of a knife.

3. Sprinkle the tomato, onion, Parmesan and pepper over the top of the pizza; place the skillet under the broiler. Cook until golden and crisp, 4 to 5 minutes. Slide onto a work surface, cut in wedges and serve hot. —*Madhur Jaffrey*
NOTE Chickpea flour is available at Indian and Middle Eastern markets, at health-food stores and by mail from Kalustyan's (212-685-3451).
WINE Among many white wine possibilities, consider the 1997 Château Bonnet Entre-Deux-Mers from France or the 1997 Carmenet Old Vines Colombard from California.

Chickpea Flour Pizza with Tomato and Parmesan

Pizza with Smoked Salmon, Crème Fraîche and Caviar

Pizza with Smoked Salmon, Crème Fraîche and Caviar

MAKES FOUR 8-INCH PIZZAS

- 2 **tablespoons chopped chives**
- **Pizza Dough (recipe follows)**
- ¼ **cup extra-virgin olive oil**
- 6 **tablespoons crème fraîche**
- ½ **pound thinly sliced smoked salmon**
- 6 **tablespoons (3 ounces) black or golden caviar**

1. Preheat the oven to 500°. Set a pizza stone in the oven for 30 minutes.
2. Knead ½ teaspoon of the chives into each of the four balls of pizza dough. On a lightly floured work surface, roll each ball of pizza dough into an 8-inch round. Brush each round with 1 tablespoon of the olive oil, leaving a 1-inch unbrushed rim. Transfer the rounds to a lightly floured baker's peel or the back of a flat cookie sheet dusted with flour. Slide the rounds of pizza dough onto the hot pizza stone and bake for 8 to 10 minutes, or until golden brown.
3. Spread the pizza crusts evenly with the crème fraîche; top with the sliced smoked salmon. Place a heaping tablespoon of caviar in the center of each pizza, garnish with the remaining chives and serve immediately. —*Wolfgang Puck*
W I N E A simple, crisp Sauvignon Blanc is all that's needed to complement these upscale pizzas. The 1997 Michel Lynch from Bordeaux and the 1998 Mulderbosch from South Africa are both good choices.

PIZZA DOUGH

MAKES ENOUGH DOUGH
FOR FOUR 8-INCH PIZZA CRUSTS

- ¾ **cup cool water**
- 2 **tablespoons olive oil**
- 1 **tablespoon honey**
- 1 **teaspoon salt**
- 1 **envelope active dry yeast**
- ¼ **cup warm water**
- **About 3 cups all-purpose flour**

1. In a small bowl, combine the cool water with the olive oil, honey and salt. In another small bowl, dissolve the yeast in the warm water and set aside in a warm place for 10 minutes.
2. Pulse the 3 cups of all-purpose flour in a food processor. With the machine on, slowly add the honey mixture. Pour in the dissolved yeast and then process until the pizza dough forms a ball. If the pizza dough is tacky, add a little more of the flour.
3. On a lightly floured surface, knead the pizza dough until it is smooth. Transfer the pizza dough to a buttered bowl, cover it with plastic wrap and let rest for 30 minutes.
4. Divide the pizza dough into 4 pieces and then roll each of the pieces into a smooth, tight ball. Transfer the pizza-dough balls to a baking sheet, cover them with a damp towel and refrigerate until chilled, or for up to 4 hours. Bring the pizza dough to room temperature before baking. —*W. P.*

Pizza Rustica

MAKES ONE 9-INCH PIZZA

With its savory filling and sweet pastry, this peasant dish highlights the best ingredients from Italy's Amalfi Coast: ricotta, from rich cow's milk; salami, which every farmer prepares himself; and basil, a staple of the family garden.

DOUGH

- 2¼ **cups all-purpose flour**
- ¼ **cup plus 2 tablespoons sugar**
- 2 **large eggs**
- 2 **large egg yolks**
- ¼ **cup extra-virgin olive oil**

FILLING

- ½ **pound ricotta cheese**
- ½ **pound (about 2 cups) mozzarella cheese, grated**
- ⅓ **cup freshly grated Parmigiano-Reggiano cheese**
- 5 **ounces spicy salami, cut into ⅓-inch dice**

3 large egg yolks

½ cup coarsely chopped basil

½ teaspoon salt

1 large egg white, beaten with
  1 teaspoon water, for glazing

1. MAKE THE DOUGH: Pour the flour onto a work surface. Make a well in the center. Add the sugar, eggs, egg yolks and olive oil to the well; blend together with a fork. Gradually incorporate the flour into the well until a dough forms. Gently knead the dough until smooth. Cover with plastic wrap. Refrigerate 1 hour or overnight.

2. Roll out two thirds of the dough between 2 sheets of parchment or wax paper to a 14-inch round about ⅛ inch thick. Transfer the pastry to a 9-inch springform pan; it should reach about two thirds of the way up the side of the pan. Roll out the remaining third of the dough between 2 sheets of parchment to a 9-inch round about ⅛ inch thick. Refrigerate the dough until chilled.

3. MAKE THE FILLING: Preheat the oven to 350°. In a bowl, combine the ricotta, mozzarella, Parmigiano-Reggiano, salami and egg yolks. Stir in the basil and salt. Spread the filling evenly in the pastry-lined pan. Brush the rim of the dough with some of the egg glaze and set the dough round on top; press the edge down firmly to seal and brush the top evenly with more egg glaze.

4. Set the springform pan on a baking sheet and bake in the center of the oven for about 1 hour, or until the crust is golden. Remove the pan from the oven and let the pizza cool on a rack for 15 minutes.

5. Remove the side of the springform pan and let the pizza cool completely. Using a metal spatula, carefully transfer the pizza to a plate. Cut the pizza into wedges and serve it warm or at room temperature. —*Alfonso Iaccarino*

MAKE AHEAD The baked pizza can be refrigerated overnight. Rewarm in a 350° oven for about 30 minutes before cutting into wedges and serving.

Roasted Chicken and Leek Pizza

MAKES ONE 14-INCH PIZZA

Store-bought rotisserie chicken, with its juicy meat, makes a great topping for a fast pizza.

1 tablespoon unsalted butter

3 large leeks, white and tender green portions only, sliced crosswise ¼ inch thick and separated into rings

2 cups shredded skinless roasted chicken (from 2 legs)

½ pound (2 cups) Fontina cheese, shredded

⅓ cup spicy oil-cured olives, pitted and coarsely chopped

Salt and freshly ground pepper

1 pound pizza dough, at room temperature

1 teaspoon extra-virgin olive oil

1. Preheat the oven to 500°. Preheat a pizza stone, or generously oil a large baking sheet. Melt the butter in a large skillet. Add the leeks and cook over moderate heat until they are just softened but still bright green, about 5 minutes. Transfer the leeks to a bowl and let cool. Stir in the chicken, half of the Fontina and the olives and season with salt and pepper.

2. On a lightly floured surface, roll or stretch the pizza dough to a rough 14-inch round. Transfer the round of pizza dough to a floured pizza peel or rimless cookie sheet, or to the oiled baking

Pizza Rustica

sheet. Spread the chicken and leek mixture on the pizza dough, leaving a 1-inch border of dough. Brush the border with the olive oil. Sprinkle the remaining Fontina over the top of the pizza and season with pepper.

3. Slide the pizza onto the hot pizza stone, if using, and bake for about 10 minutes on the pizza stone or 16 minutes on the oiled baking sheet, until the crust is golden and the Fontina is bubbling. Transfer the chicken and leek pizza to a rack and let cool slightly before serving. —*Grace Parisi*

WINE The pungent leeks on this pizza point to a crisp California Sauvignon Blanc. Try the 1997 Quivira or the 1997 Mill Creek.

Pizza with Marinated Tomatoes and Capicola

MAKES ONE 14-INCH PIZZA
Capicola is a spicy, tender Italian ham that is similar to prosciutto.

One 28-ounce can Italian peeled tomatoes—drained, tomatoes quartered lengthwise, seeded and patted dry
2 tablespoons plus 1 teaspoon extra-virgin olive oil
1 teaspoon minced garlic
½ teaspoon dried oregano, crumbled
¼ teaspoon crushed red pepper
1 pound pizza dough, at room temperature
5 ounces mild goat cheese
2 ounces thinly sliced capicola

Pizza with Marinated Tomatoes and Capicola

I. Preheat the oven to 500°. Preheat a pizza stone, or generously oil a large baking sheet. In a small bowl, combine the tomatoes with 2 tablespoons of the olive oil and the garlic, oregano and crushed red pepper. Let stand for 15 minutes.

2. On a lightly floured surface, roll or stretch the dough to a rough 14-inch round. Transfer the dough to a floured pizza peel or rimless cookie sheet, or to the oiled baking sheet.

3. Arrange the tomatoes on the pizza in slightly overlapping concentric circles, leaving a 1-inch border of dough. Brush the border with the remaining 1 teaspoon of olive oil. Crumble the goat cheese over the tomatoes, spoon any remaining marinade on top and then arrange the capicola in concentric circles over all.

4. Slide the pizza onto the hot stone, if using, and bake for about 10 minutes on the stone or 16 minutes on the baking sheet, until the crust is golden and the capicola is sizzling. Transfer the pizza to a rack and let cool slightly before serving. —*Grace Parisi*

WINE The tomatoes and ham on this pizza call for a straightforward California red, such as the 1997 Preston Faux or 1997 Qupé Syrah.

Pizza with Asparagus and Smoked Ham

MAKES ONE 14-INCH PIZZA
Some hams and cheeses are saltier than others, so be sure to taste them before seasoning the asparagus.

1 tablespoon plus 1 teaspoon extra-virgin olive oil
1 pound medium asparagus—peeled, trimmed to 5-inch lengths and halved lengthwise
½ pound smoked ham, sliced ¼ inch thick and cut into 2-inch-long matchsticks
3 small scallions, sliced

Salt and freshly ground pepper

¼ pound (1 cup) mild provolone or Fontina cheese, shredded

1 pound pizza dough, at room temperature

2 tablespoons freshly grated Asiago, Parmesan or sharp provolone cheese

1. Preheat the oven to 500°. Preheat a pizza stone, or generously oil a large baking sheet. Heat 1 tablespoon of the olive oil in a large skillet. Add the asparagus and cook over high heat, stirring occasionally, until lightly browned, about 5 minutes; transfer to a bowl.

pizza 101

For great quick pizza, use frozen dough and follow these tips.

Thaw the frozen pizza dough. Let the dough defrost in the refrigerator overnight, or let it stand at room temperature for three to five hours. To defrost in a microwave oven, heat for one-minute intervals at 20 percent power until the dough is soft, four to five minutes total. If the dough feels hot, turn down the setting.

Preheat a pizza stone. Set a stone directly on the oven floor or on the lowest oven rack. Allow at least 30 minutes for the stone to fully preheat.

Work the dough. If the dough pulls back after you roll or stretch it, let it relax, uncovered, for about 10 minutes and then try again. Check that the dough isn't sticking to the pizza peel before you add the toppings. Gently shake the peel or baking sheet back and forth. If the dough sticks, lift it up and sprinkle a bit more flour underneath.

Bake the pizza. Allow up to 10 minutes of extra baking time for pizza cooked on a baking sheet instead of a pizza stone. Reheat cold or soggy pizza directly on the rack of a preheated 350° oven until the top is bubbling and the crust is crisp.

Add the ham and scallions to the asparagus and season with salt and pepper. Let cool slightly. Add half of the shredded cheese.

2. On a lightly floured surface, roll or stretch the dough to a rough 14-inch round. Transfer the dough to a floured pizza peel or rimless cookie sheet, or to the oiled baking sheet. Top the pizza with the asparagus mixture, leaving a 1-inch border of dough. Brush the border with the remaining 1 teaspoon oil. Scatter the grated cheese and the remaining shredded cheese on top.

3. Slide the pizza onto the hot stone, if using. Bake for about 10 minutes on the stone, 16 minutes on the baking sheet, until the crust is golden and the cheese bubbling. Transfer to a rack and let cool slightly before serving. —*Grace Parisi*

WINE A clean, light white, such as the 1997 Torres Viña Sol from Spain or the 1997 Domaine de la Jalousie Sauvignon from France, is a refreshing choice.

Pizza with Swiss Chard and Bacon

MAKES ONE 14-INCH PIZZA

Dandelion greens, broccoli rabe, escarole and even baby beet greens all make great alternatives to the Swiss chard in this recipe. If you use broccoli rabe, peel the stems, blanch the broccoli rabe in boiling water for four minutes and drain well before tossing it with the other ingredients.

½ pound sliced bacon

1½ pounds Swiss chard, stems and tough ribs removed, leaves cut into ½-inch-wide ribbons (4 cups)

Pizza with Swiss Chard and Bacon

½ pound (2 cups) Fontina or mild provolone cheese, shredded

Salt and freshly ground pepper

1 pound pizza dough, at room temperature

1 teaspoon extra-virgin olive oil

I. Preheat the oven to 500°. Preheat a pizza stone or generously oil a large baking sheet. In a large skillet, cook the bacon over high heat until browned and most of the fat is rendered, about 6 minutes. Drain on paper towels and let cool. Break into 1-inch pieces.

2. Pour off all but 1 tablespoon of the bacon fat from the skillet and heat until shimmering. In a large heatproof bowl, toss the Swiss chard with the hot fat. Add the bacon and half of the cheese. Season with salt and pepper; toss well.

3. On a lightly floured surface, roll the dough to a rough 14-inch round. Transfer to a floured pizza peel or rimless cookie sheet, or to the oiled baking sheet. Spoon the Swiss chard topping over the pizza, leaving a 1-inch border of dough. Brush the border with the oil; scatter the remaining cheese on top.

4. Slide the pizza onto the hot stone, if using, and bake for about 10 minutes on the stone or 16 on the baking sheet, until the crust is golden and the cheese is bubbling. Transfer to a rack and let cool slightly before serving. —*Grace Parisi*

WINE Try a dry white, such as the 1997 California Fumé Blanc from Robert Mondavi or Dry Creek.

White Pizza with Sweet Italian Sausage

MAKES ONE 14-INCH PIZZA

Don't use fresh mozzarella and ricotta for this pizza—surprisingly, the pie tastes best when made with commercial mozzarella and ricotta.

2 teaspoons extra-virgin olive oil

¾ pound sweet Italian sausages (about 4), meat removed from the casings

½ pound (2 cups) mozzarella, shredded

1 cup (½ pound) whole-milk ricotta

1½ tablespoons finely chopped flat-leaf parsley

1½ tablespoons snipped chives

Salt and freshly ground pepper

1 pound pizza dough, at room temperature

2 tablespoons freshly grated Parmesan or Asiago cheese

I. Preheat the oven to 500°. Preheat a pizza stone, or generously oil a large baking sheet. Heat 1 teaspoon of the olive oil in a large skillet. Slightly flatten the sausage meat, add it to the skillet and cook over moderately high heat until browned and cooked through, 5 to 6 minutes. Using a slotted spoon, transfer the sausage meat to paper towels and crumble it into ½-inch pieces. Let cool slightly and then transfer to a bowl and toss with half of the mozzarella.

2. In a bowl, combine the ricotta with 1 tablespoon each of the parsley and chives and season with salt and pepper. On a lightly floured surface, roll or stretch the dough to a rough 14-inch round. Transfer the dough to a floured pizza peel or flat cookie sheet, or to the oiled baking sheet. Dollop the ricotta mixture all over the pizza, leaving a 1-inch border of dough. Brush the border with the remaining 1 teaspoon of olive oil. Using the back of the spoon, spread the ricotta out to the border in an even layer. Scatter the sausage mixture over the ricotta and top with the remaining mozzarella and the Parmesan.

3. Slide the pizza onto the hot stone, if using, and bake for about 10 minutes on the stone or 16 minutes on the baking sheet, until the crust is golden and the cheese is bubbling. Transfer to a rack and let it cool slightly. Sprinkle with the remaining ½ tablespoon each of parsley and chives and serve. —*Grace Parisi*

WINE The 1997 Ruffino Fonte al Sole, an appealing red wine from Tuscany, is soft and accessible yet has enough acidity to stand up to the combination of rich cheese and sweet sausage.

Grilled Vegetable Muffulettas

MAKES 8 SANDWICHES

Muffulettas, a New Orleans specialty, are serious sandwiches piled high with Italian meats and cheese. In this vegetarian version, grilled vegetables take the place of the meat. Refrigerate any remaining pesto for your next sandwich.

¼ cup plus 2 tablespoons walnuts

½ cup oil-packed sun-dried tomatoes, drained

¼ cup freshly grated Parmesan cheese

½ cup (tightly packed) basil leaves

1 tablespoon minced garlic

2 tablespoons extra-virgin olive oil, plus more for brushing

Salt and freshly ground black pepper

2 medium red bell peppers

2 medium zucchini, sliced lengthwise ¼ inch thick

1 small eggplant, sliced crosswise ¼ inch thick

1 large baguette, halved lengthwise

20 small spinach leaves, washed and dried

½ pound sliced Provolone cheese

I. Preheat the oven to 350°. Toast the walnuts for about 7 minutes, or until golden; let cool. In a food processor, combine the sun-dried tomatoes, Parmesan, basil, garlic and walnuts and pulse until finely chopped. Add the 2 tablespoons of olive oil and process until smooth. Season the pesto with salt and black pepper.

2. Light a grill or preheat the broiler. Brush the red bell peppers, zucchini and eggplant with olive oil, season the zucchini and eggplant with salt and black pepper and grill over a medium-hot fire or broil for 12 to 15 minutes, turning, until lightly charred all over and very tender. Transfer the red bell peppers to a bowl, cover with plastic wrap and let cool. Peel, core and seed the peppers and cut into quarters.

3. Slice open the baguette and discard the center, leaving a scant ½ inch of bread all around. Spread a thin layer of

LEFT: **Grilled Vegetable Muffulettas.**
ABOVE: **Spanish Omelet Sandwiches.**

pesto on both sides of the baguette and arrange half of the spinach on the bottom. Top with half of the cheese and vegetables and then repeat with the remaining ingredients. Cut the muffuletta in half. Tightly wrap the halves in plastic and let stand at room temperature for 4 hours or refrigerate overnight. Cut each sandwich into 4 pieces and serve. —*Martha McGinnis*

Spanish Omelet Sandwiches

MAKES 4 SANDWICHES

Rubbing the cut bread with tomato, as the Spaniards do, adds great flavor. If you prefer, you can simply tear the ham into large pieces instead of chopping it.

- 8 large eggs, lightly beaten
- 4 ounces thinly sliced Serrano ham or prosciutto, finely chopped

Salt and freshly ground pepper

- 3 tablespoons extra-virgin olive oil, plus more if necessary
- 4 long Italian rolls, halved, or 1 large baguette, cut into four pieces and each halved lengthwise
- 1 large tomato, halved

1. In a medium bowl, beat the eggs with the ham. Season with salt and plenty of pepper. In a large nonstick skillet, heat the 3 tablespoons oil over high heat until shimmering. Pour in the egg mixture, evenly distributing the ham. Using a spatula, lift the cooked edges, tilting the pan so the uncooked eggs seep underneath. If the omelet sticks, drizzle a little more oil around the edge. Lower the heat to moderate; cook until the omelet is golden on the bottom and the top is almost completely set, 2 to 3 minutes. Fold in thirds and slide onto a platter.

2. Rub the cut sides of the rolls with the cut sides of the tomato. Cut the omelet into quarters and tuck it into the 4 rolls. Serve warm or at room temperature. —*Teresa Barrenechea*

MAKE AHEAD The omelet sandwiches can be kept at room temperature for 4 hours.

Crab Salad on Brioche

MAKES 8 OPEN-FACED SANDWICHES

To take these on a picnic, just top each with another slice of brioche.

- ¼ cup crème fraîche
- 2 teaspoons red wine vinegar
- 1 teaspoon sherry vinegar
- 2 teaspoons finely chopped cilantro
- 2 teaspoons finely chopped chervil

Salt and freshly ground black pepper

- 1 pound lump crabmeat, picked over
- ½ European cucumber—peeled, halved, seeded and finely chopped
- ¼ cup finely diced red bell pepper
- 1 bunch watercress, tough stems discarded, dried well
- 8 thick slices brioche

Crab Salad on Brioche

In a bowl, combine the crème fraîche, red wine vinegar, sherry vinegar, cilantro, chervil and a large pinch of salt and black pepper. Fold in the crabmeat, cucumber and red bell pepper. Mound the crab salad and watercress on the brioche and serve. —*Craig Shelton*

Shrimp and Avocado Sandwiches with Spiced Kirbys

MAKES 2 SANDWICHES

- 12 medium (about 5 ounces) shrimp, shelled and deveined
- 2 kaiser rolls, halved
- Dijon mustard
- 4 Spiced Kirby Pickles (p. 324), very thinly sliced lengthwise
- 1 ripe avocado, cut into thin lengthwise slices
- 1 large tomato, thinly sliced
- Salt and freshly ground pepper
- ¼ cup finely shredded basil leaves
- Hot pepper sauce

1. In a small saucepan of boiling water, cook the shrimp until they are bright pink and just opaque throughout, about 1 minute. Drain and halve the shrimp lengthwise.
2. Spread the kaiser rolls with Dijon mustard. Arrange half the Spiced Kirby Pickles on the bottom half of each roll. Layer the avocado and tomato slices on

top, seasoning both with salt and pepper. Arrange half the shrimp and basil on each sandwich and add a dash of hot sauce. Cover with the top halves of the rolls, cut the sandwiches in half and serve. —*Marcia Kiesel*

Curried Duck and Mango Sandwiches

MAKES 4 SANDWICHES

Make your way to a Chinese market to buy a succulent cooked Peking duck for these sweet-and-spicy sandwiches. Alternatively, substitute four sautéed duck breast halves.

- 1 tablespoon unsweetened coconut milk
- 1 teaspoon honey
- 1 teaspoon minced fresh ginger
- 1 teaspoon fresh lime juice
- ¼ teaspoon Thai red curry paste
- Salt
- 1 whole Peking duck, skin removed, meat sliced
- 4 scallions, white and tender green parts, thinly sliced
- 1 large ripe mango, cut into ¾-inch dice
- 1 ripe Bartlett or Anjou pear, peeled and cut into ¾-inch dice
- 8 slices raisin-walnut bread

In a bowl, combine the coconut milk, honey, ginger, lime juice and curry paste. Season with salt. Add the sliced duck and scallions and mix well. Fold in the mango and pear just until combined. Spoon the salad onto 4 slices of the bread, top with the remaining slices and serve. —*Craig Shelton*

MAKE AHEAD The duck salad can be refrigerated for up to 4 hours. Fold in the fruit and assemble the sandwiches just before serving.

WINE A ripe, fat California Chardonnay, such as the 1997 Cambria Katherine's Vineyard or 1997 Sonoma-Cutrer Russian River Ranches, would echo the richness of the roasted duck and sweet fruit and soften the bite of the scallions and curry paste.

Steak, Tomato and Arugula Sandwiches

MAKES 4 SANDWICHES

- 1 large shallot, minced
- 2 teaspoons red wine vinegar
- One 1½-pound boneless sirloin steak, about 1¼ inches thick
- 3 tablespoons extra-virgin olive oil
- Kosher salt and freshly ground pepper
- Eight ½-inch-thick slices country bread
- 1 garlic clove, peeled
- 2 ripe tomatoes, thinly sliced
- 1 bunch of arugula, large stems trimmed
- 8 anchovy fillets

1. Light a grill or preheat the broiler and position a rack 8 inches from the heat. In a small bowl, combine the shallot and the red wine vinegar. Lightly rub the boneless sirloin steak with some of the extra-virgin olive oil. Sprinkle the steak generously with kosher salt and pepper and let stand for 10 minutes.
2. Grill or broil the steak, turning once, for 12 to 13 minutes for medium-rare meat. Transfer the steak to a cutting board. Let the steak rest for 5 minutes and then thinly slice the meat.
3. Brush the slices of country bread on both sides with the remaining extra-virgin olive oil and grill or broil until the slices are golden on both sides. Rub one side of each toast with the garlic clove and set 4 of the slices, garlic side up, on a work surface. Arrange the tomato slices on the toast and season with kosher salt and pepper. Spoon the shallot vinegar over the tomato slices and top with the arugula, the steak and the anchovies. Cover with the remaining pieces of toast and cut the sandwiches in half. Serve the sandwiches immediately. —*Seen Lippert*

WINE Pair these steak sandwiches with a soft, super-fruity red wine, such as an Australian Shiraz. The 1998 Hermitage Road or the 1996 Taltarni would work best.

Steak, Tomato and Arugula Sandwiches

tortilla primer

In Mexico, corn tortillas are the staff of life. They're served everywhere—at elegant restaurants, at makeshift stands and at home.

Serving plain tortillas To warm corn tortillas, wrap a stack of up to 12 tortillas in a clean kitchen towel. Place on a steamer rack set over one inch of boiling water in a large pot and cover; when you see steam, wait for one minute and then remove the tortillas from the pot, still wrapped in the towel. Let stand for up to 15 minutes before serving.

Filling tortillas Tortillas can be folded around any number of impromptu fillings—shredded chicken or roast pork, barbecued beef or lamb, scrambled eggs, sautéed vegetables or squash blossoms. When tortillas are filled and folded or rolled, they're called tacos. When filled tortillas (whether they contain cheese or not) are cooked on a griddle, they become quesadillas. You can use leftovers or maybe just a good melting cheese like Cheddar or Jack and a little hot sauce or cilantro. Warm the tortillas on a hot griddle and serve them right away, like pancakes.

Soft Tacos with Potato and Green Chile Filling

MAKES 10 SOFT TACOS

Two 6-ounce boiling potatoes
5 poblano chiles
1 tablespoon vegetable oil
1 medium onion, chopped
Salt
Ten 6-inch corn tortillas

1. In a medium saucepan, cook the potatoes in salted water until tender but slightly undercooked, about 20 minutes. Drain; let cool under running water and then peel. Cut into ½-inch dice.
2. Roast the poblano chiles directly over a gas flame or under a broiler as close to the heat as possible, turning, until charred all over. Transfer to a bowl, cover with plastic wrap and let steam for at least 5 minutes. Using a thin knife, scrape the skins off the chiles. Remove and discard the cores, seeds and ribs. Cut the chiles crosswise into ¼-inch strips.
3. Heat the oil in a large nonstick skillet. Add the onion, cover and cook over moderate heat, stirring occasionally, until slightly softened, about 5 minutes. Uncover and cook, stirring, until beginning to brown. Add the potatoes; cook, stirring occasionally, until golden, about 15 minutes. Stir in the chiles and cook until warmed through. Season with salt.
4. Meanwhile, heat a cast-iron skillet or griddle over moderate heat. When it is hot, add the tortillas, 1 at a time, and cook until dry on the bottom, about 1 minute. Turn the tortilla and cook until slightly puffed and golden spots appear on the bottom. Spoon the potato and chile filling onto the tortillas, fold or roll up and eat at once. —*Sally Schneider*
ONE TACO Calories 118 kcal, Total Fat 2.1 gm, Saturated Fat .3 gm

Huevos Rancheros

4 SERVINGS

Huevos rancheros are a very popular breakfast dish on the Texas–Mexico border. You can scramble the eggs rather than frying them, if you prefer, or top them with sliced black olives or avocados.

SALSA

3 unpeeled large garlic cloves
5 ripe plum tomatoes
1 large sweet onion, such as Texas 1015 or Vidalia, sliced ½ inch thick
1 canned chipotle chile in *adobo* sauce, stemmed and minced

¼ cup chopped cilantro

Salt

ENCHILADAS AND EGGS

¼ cup plus 2 tablespoons
vegetable oil

Eight 6-inch corn tortillas

1½ cups (about 6 ounces) shredded
sharp Cheddar cheese

8 large eggs

I. MAKE THE SALSA: Heat a large cast-iron skillet. Add the garlic cloves and cook over moderate heat until they are slightly softened and just beginning to blacken all over, about 5 minutes. Add the tomatoes and onion to the skillet and cook until they are slightly softened and charred all over, about 7 minutes longer. Peel the garlic cloves and transfer the garlic, tomatoes and onion to a food processor; add the chipotle and the cilantro and pulse until the salsa is still slightly chunky.

2. Reheat the skillet. Add the salsa and cook over moderately high heat, stirring often, until it is slightly thickened, 3 to 4 minutes. Season the salsa with salt and keep warm.

3. MAKE THE ENCHILADAS: Preheat the oven to 350°. Heat ¼ cup of the vegetable oil in a large skillet until shimmering. Using tongs, dip both sides of a tortilla into the hot oil and cook just until softened, about 10 seconds; let any excess oil drip back into the pan. Drain the tortilla on paper towels and then set it on a work surface. Repeat with the remaining tortillas. Spoon 1½ tablespoons of the shredded Cheddar cheese onto each of the tortillas and then loosely roll the tortillas up and arrange them side by side in a 9-by-13-inch baking dish. Sprinkle the enchiladas with the remaining ¾ cup of shredded Cheddar cheese and bake them for about 10 minutes, or until the enchiladas are warmed through and the cheese is melted.

4. Heat the remaining 2 tablespoons of vegetable oil in a nonstick skillet. Fry the eggs sunny-side up for 3 to 4 minutes. Arrange 2 of the enchiladas on each plate and then top them with some of the warm salsa and 2 of the fried eggs. —*Lisa Ahier*

Corn and Zucchini Enchiladas with Chile Sauce

4 SERVINGS

If you can't find spicy brick red de árbol chiles, use dried Thai or Chinese chiles instead.

1 pound tomatillos, husks removed

1 large unpeeled garlic clove, plus
1 peeled and minced

2 dried de árbol chiles, stemmed

2 tablespoons water

1 teaspoon salt

¼ cup vegetable oil

Huevos Rancheros

1 onion, finely chopped

1 teaspoon dried oregano

1 zucchini, cut into ½-inch chunks

1 cup thawed frozen corn kernels

Eight 6-inch corn tortillas

1 cup (about 3½ ounces) grated Monterey Jack cheese

1. Preheat the oven to 400°. Heat a grill pan or a large cast-iron skillet. Grill the tomatillos and the unpeeled garlic clove over moderately high heat, turning often, until the tomatillos and the garlic are soft and blackened in spots, 8 to 10 minutes. Add the dé arbol chiles to the grill and toast just until they are lightly charred, about 3 minutes. Transfer the tomatillos, garlic clove and chiles to a plate and let them cool slightly. Coarsely chop the chiles.

2. Remove the papery skin from the grilled garlic clove. Transfer the garlic clove to a blender, add the grilled tomatillos and dé arbol chiles, the water and ½ teaspoon of the salt and blend to a coarse sauce.

3. In a large skillet, heat 1 tablespoon of the vegetable oil. Add the onion, the minced garlic, the oregano and the remaining ½ teaspoon salt and cook over moderately high heat until the onion has softened, about 5 minutes. Add the zucchini and cook, stirring, until softened, about 5 minutes longer. Stir in the corn kernels and cook just until heated through, about 1 minute.

4. Pour half of the tomatillo sauce into a 9-by-13-inch baking dish. In a medium skillet, heat the remaining 3 tablespoons of vegetable oil over moderately high heat. Using tongs and working with 1 tortilla at a time, dip both sides of each tortilla briefly in the hot oil just until the tortilla softens; let any excess oil drip back into the pan. Lay the tortillas on a work surface and then spoon about 2½ tablespoons of the zucchini filling across the center of each; sprinkle each one with 1 tablespoon of the grated Monterey Jack cheese. Roll up the tortillas and transfer them to the baking dish.

5. Pour the remaining tomatillo sauce over the enchiladas and sprinkle with the remaining Monterey Jack cheese. Cover the dish with foil and bake the enchiladas for about 10 minutes, or until they are heated through. Serve immediately. —*Katharine Kagel*

BEER Beer is the best choice with these tart and cheesy enchiladas. Stick with the southwestern theme and serve Santa Fe Pale Ale.

chapter 11
vegetables

274

275

293

294

Braised Endives

4 SERVINGS

If you have your grill going, you can braise the endives in a roasting pan or in two skillets set over a low fire.

1 cup water
¼ cup sugar
2 tablespoons fresh lemon juice
Olive oil, for brushing
8 Belgian endives, halved lengthwise
Salt and freshly ground pepper
4 tablespoons unsalted butter, cut into small pieces

I. Preheat the oven to 400°. In a small saucepan, combine the water and the sugar and bring to a simmer to dissolve the sugar, stirring occasionally. Remove from the heat; stir in the lemon juice.

2. Brush a large flameproof roasting pan with olive oil and arrange the endives in the pan, cut side up. Pour the sugar syrup over the endives and season with salt and pepper. Dot the endives with the butter. Cover the roasting pan with foil and bake for about 30 minutes, or until the endives are tender when pierced with a knife. Discard the foil. Set the pan on 2 burners and simmer over moderate heat until the liquid begins to caramelize, about 10 minutes. Serve hot. —*Raphael Lunetta*

Stir-Fried Baby Bok Choy and Shiitake Mushrooms

8 SERVINGS

Serving mushrooms whole, according to Asian tradition, is a sign of wealth. For a more pronounced mushroom flavor, replace the fresh shiitake mushrooms with a quarter pound of dried shiitakes that have been soaked in hot water until tender and then drained and stemmed.

2 teaspoons vegetable oil
1 teaspoon sesame oil
1 large garlic clove, minced
1 pound small shiitake mushrooms, stemmed
2 pounds baby bok choy

1 tablespoon Asian fish sauce
Kosher salt and freshly ground pepper
3 Thai chiles—halved, seeded and julienned

Heat the vegetable oil and sesame oil in a wok. Add the garlic and stir-fry over high heat until golden, about 5 seconds. Add the shiitakes and stir-fry for 5 minutes. Add the bok choy and stir-fry until just wilted, about 5 minutes longer. Add the fish sauce and season with kosher salt and pepper; stir-fry for 1 minute. Transfer to a platter, top with the chiles and serve. —*Corinne Trang*

Sautéed Baby Greens and Prosciutto

4 SERVINGS

Prosciutto makes these wilted greens versatile enough to be served as a salad with melon or as a sandwich filling with fresh ricotta and crusty bread.

8 slices (about 6 ounces) prosciutto
2 tablespoons extra-virgin olive oil
½ pound tender young greens, such as arugula, *tatsoi,* dandelion or mesclun
Kosher salt and freshly ground pepper
2 tablespoons fresh lemon juice

Arrange the prosciutto on 4 plates. In a large skillet, heat 1 tablespoon of the olive oil until shimmering. Add the greens and a generous pinch each of kosher salt and pepper and cook over moderate heat, tossing, until barely wilted, about 1 minute. Add the lemon juice, toss and then mound the greens alongside the prosciutto. Drizzle with the remaining 1 tablespoon of olive oil, season with pepper and serve. —*Seen Lippert*

Kale and Bacon Bread Pudding

12 SERVINGS

This earthy, kale-studded variation on traditional bread stuffing should be made with baguettes that are at least two inches in diameter.

½ pound sliced bacon, cut crosswise into ½-inch strips
1 large onion, finely chopped

3 celery ribs, finely chopped
6 garlic cloves, minced
2½ pounds kale, stems and tough ribs discarded, leaves coarsely chopped
1½ baguettes, cut into ¾-inch dice (about 12 cups)
4 large eggs, lightly beaten
2 cups milk
2 cups heavy cream or half-and-half
1 cup chicken stock or canned low-sodium chicken broth
1 tablespoon salt
¾ teaspoon freshly ground pepper

I. In a large deep skillet, cook the bacon over moderately high heat, stirring occasionally, until it is crisp, 6 to 8 minutes. Transfer the bacon to paper towels to drain.

2. Pour off all but 2 tablespoons of the bacon fat from the skillet. Add the onion and celery and cook over moderate heat, stirring, until softened, about 6 minutes. Add the garlic and cook until fragrant, about 2 minutes. Add the kale, a handful at a time, and cook, stirring, until completely wilted and just tender, 4 to 5 minutes. Transfer the kale to a large bowl and then toss with the diced baguette.

3. Preheat the oven to 350°. Butter a 3-quart baking dish. In a large bowl, whisk the eggs with the milk, cream, chicken stock, salt and pepper. Pour the custard over the bread and kale, add the bacon and toss well. Transfer the bread pudding to the prepared baking dish. Press plastic wrap directly on the bread and let stand at room temperature until the custard is absorbed, about 1 hour. Remove the plastic wrap.

4. Bake the bread pudding for about 1 hour, or until the custard is set and the top is golden and crisp. Let stand for 20 minutes before serving. —*Tim McKee*

MAKE AHEAD The recipe can be prepared through Step 3 and refrigerated overnight. The baked bread pudding can stand at room temperature for 3 hours. Rewarm before serving.

Green Beans with Sea Salt

8 SERVINGS

- 2 pounds thin green beans or haricots verts
- 1 tablespoon extra-virgin olive oil

Coarse sea salt

Bring a large pot of salted water to a boil. Add the green beans and cook until crisp-tender, about 5 minutes. Drain, shake dry and return the beans to the pot. Toss the beans with the olive oil and sea salt. Transfer to a platter and serve. —*Robert Del Grande*

Fava Beans with Aged Sheep's Milk Cheese

4 SERVINGS

Once blanched, fava beans need only the barest embellishment: a fine, buttery extra-virgin olive oil and thin shavings of aged sheep's milk cheese. Parmigiano-Reggiano, an aged Pecorino Toscano or a Spanish Manchego are also delicious with the beans.

- 3 pounds (about 4 cups) fava beans, shelled

Salt and freshly ground pepper

- 4 teaspoons extra-virgin olive oil
- 2 ounces aged sheep's milk cheese, thinly shaved (1 loosely packed cup)

1. Bring a large saucepan of water to a boil. Add the fava beans and cook just until tender, 2 to 4 minutes. Drain the fava beans and cool them under running water. Peel and discard the outer skins of the beans.

2. Put the fava beans in 4 shallow soup plates and season them lightly with salt and pepper. Drizzle each portion of fava beans with 1 teaspoon of the olive oil, garnish with the cheese shavings and serve. —*Sally Schneider*

MAKE AHEAD The cooked fava beans can be refrigerated overnight. Bring the beans to room temperature before garnishing.

ONE SERVING Calories 174 kcal, Total Fat 9.3 gm, Saturated Fat 3.8 gm

Stir-Fried Pea Shoots and Shiitakes with Shrimp

4 SERVINGS

Pea shoots, or pea leaves, taste like sweet peas but look like leafy greens. They are available at some supermarkets and at Chinese markets and farmers' markets. In this dish, they're topped with a sauce that contains lightly beaten egg whites for body.

- 3 cups chicken stock or canned low-sodium broth
- ¼ cup canola or other mild vegetable oil
- 3 quarter-size slices of fresh ginger, lightly smashed
- 2 large garlic cloves, smashed
- ½ pound medium shrimp, shelled and deveined

Salt

- ¼ pound shiitake mushrooms, stemmed, caps thinly sliced
- 1 pound tender young pea shoots, thick stems discarded
- 1 tablespoon cornstarch
- 3 tablespoons rice wine
- 2 teaspoons Asian sesame oil

Few drops of hot chili oil

- 2 large egg whites, lightly beaten

1. In a medium saucepan, boil the chicken stock over high heat until reduced to 1½ cups, about 20 minutes. Let the stock cool.

2. Heat a large wok. Add the canola oil and swirl to coat. Add the smashed ginger and garlic and stir-fry over high heat until they are deep golden, 2 to 3 minutes. Remove and discard the ginger and garlic.

3. Add the shrimp to the wok and season with salt. Cook over high heat, turning once, until lightly browned, 2 to 3 minutes. Using a slotted spoon, transfer the shrimp to a bowl. Add the shiitake mushrooms to the wok and stir-fry until lightly browned, about 2 minutes. Add the pea shoots, season with salt and stir-fry until just wilted, about 3 minutes. Transfer the pea shoots and shiitake mushrooms to a bowl.

4. Stir the cornstarch into the stock. Return the wok to high heat and add the stock mixture, the rice wine, the Asian sesame oil and the chili oil. Stir until the sauce thickens and becomes glossy, about 5 minutes. Stir the cooked shrimp into the sauce and season with salt. Add the egg whites and cook without stirring until just beginning to set, about 10 seconds. Stir gently so the egg whites form shreds and then simmer for 30 seconds. Pour the shrimp and the sauce over the pea shoots and shiitake mushrooms and serve the stir-fry immediately. —*John Ash*

WINE Try a crisp, fruity-ripe, aromatic, light white, such as a Riesling, with this delicate dish. Consider New Zealand bottles, such as the 1997 Allan Scott or the 1997 Villa Maria Private Bin.

Carrots with Cumin

8 SERVINGS

The secret to these beautifully seasoned carrots is orange juice, which adds a note of fruity acidity to the carrots as they cook.

- 1 teaspoon cumin seeds
- 2 tablespoons extra-virgin olive oil
- 2 pounds carrots, sliced on the diagonal ½ inch thick

Sea salt

- ½ cup fresh orange juice

1. Set a small skillet over moderate heat for 2 minutes. Add the cumin seeds and toast, shaking the pan constantly, until the seeds darken slightly and are fragrant, about 1 minute. Immediately transfer the toasted seeds to a plate to cool completely. In a spice mill or mortar, grind half of the toasted cumin seeds to a fine powder. Add the ground cumin seeds to the whole cumin seeds and set aside.

2. In a large skillet, warm the olive oil over moderately high heat. Add the carrots, stir to coat with oil and then reduce the heat to low and season lightly with sea salt. Add the orange juice, cover

Carrots with Cumin, with Aromatic Wine-Braised Beef (p. 227) and Macaroni Gratin (p. 114).

and cook, stirring often, until just tender, about 15 minutes. Add the cumin mixture, season with salt and cook, uncovered, until the carrots are lightly caramelized, about 15 minutes. Serve warm. —*Benoît Guichard*

MAKE AHEAD The cooked Carrots with Cumin can be refrigerated for up to 1 day. Reheat gently before serving.

Carrot Pudding

8 SERVINGS

If you're serving this with the Marinated Pork Roast with Prunes and Apricots (p. 204), the pudding can be baked in the oven along with the roast once the temperature has been turned down to 400°. Set it on the bottom shelf.

- 1½ pounds carrots, cut into 2-inch lengths
- 4 large eggs, separated
- ¼ cup plus 2 tablespoons freshly grated Parmesan cheese
- 1 tablespoon unsalted butter
- 1 tablespoon all-purpose flour
- ½ teaspoon salt
- ¼ teaspoon freshly ground pepper
- Freshly grated nutmeg
- ¼ cup heavy cream
- 1 tablespoon chopped chives

1. Preheat the oven to 400°. Butter a 2-quart soufflé dish. Cook the carrots in boiling salted water until they are tender, about 30 minutes; drain well. Puree the carrots in a food processor and then scrape the puree into a bowl. Let cool slightly and then stir in the egg yolks, ¼ cup of the Parmesan cheese, the butter, flour, salt, freshly ground pepper and a few gratings of nutmeg.

2. In a stainless steel bowl, beat the egg whites until they hold soft peaks. Using a rubber spatula, stir one third of the egg whites into the carrot mixture and then fold in the remaining egg whites in 2 batches; scrape the mixture into the prepared dish.

3. Set the soufflé dish in a baking pan and pour enough hot water into the pan to reach halfway up the side of the dish. Bake for about 30 minutes, or until the carrot pudding is set. Remove from the oven and let stand for 5 minutes.

4. Meanwhile, in a small saucepan, simmer the heavy cream over low heat until it is slightly thickened, about 3 minutes. Stir in the remaining 2 tablespoons of Parmesan cheese and remove the pan from the heat.

5. Run a sharp knife around the side of the pudding and invert it onto a round serving plate. Pour the Parmesan cream over the top and sprinkle with the chives. Cut the pudding into wedges and serve. —*Maria José Cabral and Emília Augusta Magalháes*

Crisp Celery Fans

6 SERVINGS

- 6 large celery ribs, peeled and cut into 2-inch lengths
- ¼ cup fresh lemon juice
- 2 tablespoons vegetable oil
- 1 tablespoon chopped cilantro
- Salt

1. Make 4 lengthwise slits from one end to halfway down each piece of celery to make a fan. Put the celery in a large bowl and cover with ice water. Refrigerate for 1 to 4 hours.

2. Drain the celery and pat dry. In a bowl, toss the celery with the lemon juice, oil and cilantro. Season with salt; serve. —*Ruth Van Waerebeek-Gonzalez*

Provençal Braised Celery Hearts

4 SERVINGS

This is adapted from a favorite old cookbook, André Marty's *Fourmiguetto: Souvenirs, Contes et Recettes du Languedoc*. The celery is delicious with grilled or roasted poultry or meat.

- 1 lemon, halved
- 1½ pounds celery hearts with leaves, cut into 1½-inch lengths

- 1 tablespoon extra-virgin olive oil
- 1 tablespoon all-purpose flour
- 3 scallions, white and tender green parts, thinly sliced crosswise
- ⅓ cup (2 ounces) minced pancetta
- 1 tablespoon tomato paste
- ½ teaspoon crushed garlic
- Salt and freshly ground pepper

1. Squeeze the lemon into a large bowl of water. Add the celery and let soak at room temperature for 1 hour.

2. Heat the olive oil in a large heavy saucepan. Stir in the flour and the scallions. Add the pancetta, the tomato paste and the garlic and stir until the mixture sizzles and sticks to the pan, about 2 minutes.

3. Drain the celery (but do not dry it) and add it to the pan. Moisten a sheet of parchment paper that is slightly larger than the pan. Crumple it and spread it directly on the celery. Tightly cover the pan and cook over low heat, stirring occasionally, until the celery is tender, about 40 minutes. Check the pan after 15 minutes and add 1 to 2 tablespoons of water if the celery looks dry. Season the celery with salt and pepper and serve warm. —*Paula Wolfert*

Carrot Pudding, with Marinated Pork Roast with Prunes and Apricots (p. 204).

Roasted Asparagus with Sage and Lemon Butter

White Asparagus with Brown Butter

4 FIRST-COURSE SERVINGS ♛

20 white asparagus (about 1¼ pounds), trimmed and peeled

3 tablespoons unsalted butter

½ pound chanterelle or hedgehog mushrooms, coarsely chopped

Salt and freshly ground pepper

2 shallots, thinly sliced crosswise and separated into rings

1 teaspoon coarsely chopped thyme

1½ tablespoons fresh lemon juice

1 tablespoon finely chopped flat-leaf parsley, plus 1 tablespoon whole leaves

I. Bring a large saucepan of salted water to a boil. Add the asparagus and cook until tender, 4 to 5 minutes. Drain and pat dry.

2. Melt the butter in a large skillet and cook until just beginning to brown. Add the mushrooms, season with salt and pepper and cook over moderately high heat, stirring often, until just tender, about 8 minutes. Add the shallots and thyme and cook, stirring, until softened, about 2 minutes longer. Add the asparagus and cook, tossing, until warmed through. Add the lemon juice, the chopped parsley and the whole parsley leaves and season with salt and pepper. Arrange the asparagus on 4 plates and serve. —*Suzanne Goin*

Roasted Asparagus with Sage and Lemon Butter

6 SERVINGS

2 pounds thin asparagus, ends trimmed

2 teaspoons olive oil

Salt

4 tablespoons unsalted butter

30 sage leaves

3 tablespoons fresh lemon juice

Shredded zest of ½ lemon

Parmigiano-Reggiano cheese, for shaving

I. Preheat the oven to 450°. Toss the asparagus with the olive oil and ½ teaspoon of salt. Spread the asparagus spears on a baking sheet and roast in the oven for about 5 minutes, or until the spears are just tender when pierced with a knife.

2. In a small skillet, melt the butter over moderately low heat. Add the sage leaves and cook, stirring often, until the butter is lightly browned, about 2 minutes. Stir in the lemon juice and ¼ teaspoon of salt.

3. Transfer the asparagus to a warmed platter and spoon the sage-lemon butter on top. Garnish with the lemon zest, top with shavings of Parmigiano-Reggiano and serve. —*Jerry Traunfeld*

Baked Artichokes with Fennel

4 SERVINGS ♛

When shopping for artichokes, choose those that are firm and fresh with tightly closed leaves.

4 artichokes (½ pound each)

½ lemon

¼ cup plus 3 tablespoons extra-virgin olive oil

2 medium fennel bulbs—trimmed, halved lengthwise, cored and finely chopped

1 large red onion, finely chopped

4 garlic cloves, thinly sliced lengthwise

1 teaspoon thyme leaves

Salt and freshly ground pepper

Baked Artichokes with Fennel

2 tablespoons finely chopped
flat-leaf parsley, plus ½ cup
leaves

½ cup coarse fresh bread crumbs

½ teaspoon fresh lemon juice

1. Using a sharp knife, trim the artichoke stems to 1 inch and cut off 1 inch from the tops. Using kitchen shears, trim ½ inch from the leaves. Halve the artichokes lengthwise and, using a melon baller or spoon, scoop out the small spiky leaves and hairy chokes; leave a few layers of leaves. Rub the cut parts of the artichokes with the halved lemon and set them, cut side down, in a large steamer basket. Steam the artichokes over boiling water until the hearts are tender, about 10 minutes.

2. In a large deep skillet, heat ¼ cup of the olive oil until shimmering. Add the fennel and the onion and cook over moderately high heat, stirring, until the vegetables are translucent, about 5 minutes. Add the garlic and thyme, season with salt and freshly ground pepper and cook until the vegetables are just beginning to brown, about 4 minutes longer. Remove from the heat, let the vegetables cool slightly and then stir in the chopped parsley.

3. Preheat the oven to 375°. Toss the bread crumbs with 1 tablespoon of the olive oil and spread the crumbs on a baking sheet. Toast for about 3 minutes, or until golden. Transfer the bread crumbs to a plate. Raise the oven temperature to 450°.

4. Heat 1 tablespoon of the olive oil in a very large skillet. Pat the cooked artichokes dry and add them to the skillet, cut side down. Cook over moderate heat until deep golden, about 4 minutes. Arrange the artichokes, cut side up, in a large baking dish and fill them with the fennel mixture. Sprinkle the artichokes with the toasted bread crumbs and bake for about 15 minutes, or until heated through.

5. Arrange 2 artichoke halves on each of 4 plates. In a glass or stainless steel bowl, toss the parsley leaves with the remaining 1 tablespoon of olive oil and the fresh lemon juice and season with salt and freshly ground pepper. Top the artichokes with the parsley mixture and serve. —*Suzanne Goin*

MAKE AHEAD The recipe can be prepared through Step 2 and refrigerated overnight.

WINE Artichokes make wines taste sweeter, so stick to a white—the effect is less noticeable. This rich, aromatic dish points to a full-bodied Chardonnay. Look for fruity California bottles like the 1997 Fetzer Bonterra (from organically grown grapes) or the 1997 Clos du Bois Alexander Valley Selection.

Artichokes Braised in Olive Oil and White Wine

Artichokes Braised in Olive Oil and White Wine

8 SERVINGS

Here's a way to be sure that the vegetarians at your table have something hearty to eat, even if they skip the main dish. These braised artichokes, with lots of baby vegetables, are just the thing. Feel free to add additional cooked vegetables, such as Portobello mushrooms, radishes and cucumbers.

1 lemon, halved

8 large artichokes

⅓ cup extra-virgin olive oil

2 medium leeks, white and tender green, quartered lengthwise and cut into 2-inch lengths

2 celery ribs, peeled and thinly sliced

1 large onion, halved and thinly sliced

1 large carrot, cut into ¼-inch dice

4 garlic cloves, thinly sliced

4 thyme sprigs

4 tarragon sprigs

2 bay leaves

Salt and freshly ground pepper

2 cups dry white wine

2 cups water

½ pound fresh peas, shelled (½ cup)

8 pencil-thin asparagus

1 small fennel bulb—halved lengthwise, cored and thinly sliced crosswise

2 ounces haricots verts

4 small tomatoes—halved, seeded and finely diced

½ cup mixed herbs, such as parsley and chervil leaves and coarsely chopped chives and basil

1. Squeeze the lemon juice into a large bowl of water. Working with 1 artichoke at a time, snap off the outer leaves and trim off all but ½ inch of the stem. Using a sharp knife, cut off the remaining leaves at the top of the heart and peel the base and stem. Using a spoon or a melon baller, scoop out the furry choke. Add the artichoke to the lemon water.

2. In a large, deep skillet, heat the olive oil. Add the leeks, celery, onion and carrot and cook over low heat, stirring often, until softened but not browned, about 20 minutes. Add the garlic and cook until fragrant, about 1 minute.

3. Drain the artichokes and add them to the skillet in a single layer. Tuck the thyme, tarragon and bay leaves in between the artichokes and season with salt and pepper. Add the wine and water; cover partially and braise over moderately low heat until tender, about 40 minutes. Discard the herbs.

4. Meanwhile, blanch the peas, asparagus, fennel and haricots verts separately in boiling salted water until crisp-tender, 5 minutes for the peas and fennel

and 3 to 4 minutes for the asparagus and haricots verts. Using a slotted spoon, transfer the vegetables to paper towels to drain after they are cooked.

5. Mound the peas, asparagus, fennel and haricots verts in soup plates and add some of the braised vegetables and liquid. Season with salt and pepper. Set an artichoke on top and fill with diced tomato. Scatter the mixed herbs over the top and serve warm. —*Tom Colicchio*

MAKE AHEAD The vegetables can be prepared through Step 3 and refrigerated for up to 1 day. Reheat before proceeding.

Extra-Virgin Olive Oil and Artichokes

4 SERVINGS

You can, if you like, use baby artichokes instead of larger ones; simply trim the leaf tips, break off the stems and cut them in half before cooking. The cooking time will be shorter.

1 lemon, halved

4 large artichokes

¼ cup extra-virgin olive oil, preferably Spanish

¼ cup dry white wine

½ cup water

4 garlic cloves, coarsely chopped

Salt

2 teaspoons fresh lemon juice

1. Squeeze the juice from the lemon into a bowl of water. Working with 1 artichoke at a time, break off the stem and snap off the dark outer leaves. Using a serrated knife, cut off the remaining leaves at the top of the base. Using a small, sharp knife, trim the base. Using a spoon or a melon baller, scoop out the hairy chokes. Rub the artichoke bottom all over with the cut lemon and drop it in the water.

2. In a medium saucepan, combine the olive oil, wine, water and garlic and bring to a simmer. Add the artichoke bottoms and a large pinch of salt and simmer over moderately low heat until tender, about 12 minutes. Let the artichokes cool slightly in the cooking liquid and

then add the lemon juice and season with salt. Serve warm or at room temperature. —*Marcia Kiesel*

MAKE AHEAD The artichokes can be refrigerated overnight. Rewarm gently in the olive oil before serving.

SERVE WITH Toasted peasant bread.

Twice-Cooked Broccoli with Hazelnuts and Garlic

6 SERVINGS

¼ cup hazelnuts

1 large bunch of broccoli, cut into 1½-inch florets

2½ tablespoons hazelnut oil

2 garlic cloves, thinly sliced

¼ teaspoon crushed red pepper

Salt

1. Preheat the oven to 350°. Toast the hazelnuts in a pie pan for about 12 minutes, or until the skins blister. Let cool slightly and then transfer the nuts to a kitchen towel and rub to remove the skins. Coarsely chop the nuts.

2. In a steamer, cook the broccoli until just tender, about 5 minutes.

3. In a large skillet, combine the oil, garlic and hazelnuts. Cook over high heat, stirring, until the garlic is pale golden, about 2 minutes. Add the broccoli and crushed red pepper and toss. Season with salt and cook, stirring occasionally, until tender, 1 to 2 minutes. Serve hot or at room temperature. —*Grace Parisi*

ONE SERVING Calories 125 kcal, Total Fat 9.2 gm, Saturated Fat .7 gm

Broccoli Rabe with Pancetta and Garlic

6 SERVINGS

2 quarts salted water

2 pounds broccoli rabe, cut into 2-inch lengths, thick stems discarded

2 tablespoons extra-virgin olive oil

4 ounces pancetta, sliced ⅛ inch thick and cut into 1-inch matchsticks

4 large garlic cloves, thinly sliced

Salt and freshly ground pepper

1. In a saucepan, bring the salted water to a boil. Add the broccoli rabe and cook until it is crisp-tender, about 5 minutes. Drain the broccoli rabe, shaking off the excess water.

2. Wipe out the saucepan. Add the extra-virgin olive oil and the pancetta matchsticks and cook over moderately low heat, stirring often, until the pancetta is golden, 8 to 10 minutes. Add the garlic to the saucepan and cook, stirring, until golden, about 3 minutes. Add the broccoli rabe, season with salt and freshly ground pepper and cook over moderately high heat until tender, 3 to 4 minutes. Transfer the broccoli rabe to a bowl and serve. —*Michele Scicolone*

Caramelized Brussels Sprouts with Pistachios

10 SERVINGS

- 4 tablespoons unsalted butter
- 4 small red onions, thinly sliced
- ¼ cup plus 2 tablespoons red wine vinegar
- 4 pounds brussels sprouts
- 2 tablespoons sugar
- Salt and freshly ground pepper
- ½ cup lightly salted pistachios, coarsely chopped

1. Melt the butter in a large deep skillet. Add the red onions and 3 tablespoons of the red wine vinegar and cook over moderate heat until the onions begin to brown, 5 to 6 minutes.

2. Meanwhile, steam the brussels sprouts until they are crisp-tender, 4 to 5 minutes. Add the brussels sprouts to the red onions. Stir in the sugar and the remaining 3 tablespoons of red wine vinegar and cook over moderately high heat, tossing, until the brussels sprouts are tender and lightly caramelized, 8 to 10 minutes. Season the caramelized brussels sprouts with salt and pepper. Transfer the brussels sprouts to a bowl, garnish with the chopped pistachios and serve. —*Grace Parisi*

Okra Fritters

6 SERVINGS

You'll find these crisp, sweet cornmeal fritters delectable even if you're not a big okra fan.

- 3 large eggs, lightly beaten
- 1 cup buttermilk
- 1½ cups all-purpose flour
- 1 cup yellow cornmeal
- Salt
- 1 teaspoon freshly ground black pepper
- ½ teaspoon dried thyme
- ½ teaspoon cayenne pepper
- 1 pound okra, trimmed and cut into ½-inch rounds
- ½ cup finely chopped green bell pepper
- ½ cup finely chopped onion
- ½ cup finely chopped celery
- Vegetable oil, for frying
- Hot sauce, for serving

1. In a large bowl, whisk together the lightly beaten eggs and the buttermilk. Stir in the all-purpose flour, the yellow cornmeal, 2 teaspoons of salt, the freshly ground black pepper, the dried thyme and the cayenne pepper. Fold in the okra rounds and the chopped green bell pepper, onion and celery. Let the fritter batter sit at room temperature for 15 minutes.

2. In a large cast-iron skillet, heat ¾ inch of vegetable oil to 360°. Working in batches, add heaping tablespoons of the fritter batter to the hot oil and fry over moderate heat until deep golden all over, 4 to 5 minutes. Transfer the fritters to paper towels to drain and season with salt. Serve immediately with hot sauce. —*Jimmy Kennedy*

Fried Spicy Tomatoes

4 SERVINGS

Even winter tomatoes taste good when sautéed with onions and spices. Once cooked, these sliced tomatoes are soft, but they still hold their shape. If you have two large skillets, you can cook all the tomatoes at one time.

- 2 teaspoons salt
- 1½ teaspoons ground cumin
- 1 teaspoon coarsely crushed black peppercorns
- ½ teaspoon coarsely crushed mustard seeds
- ½ teaspoon sugar
- ¼ teaspoon turmeric
- ¼ teaspoon cayenne pepper
- ¼ cup plus 2 tablespoons vegetable oil
- 12 fresh curry leaves (optional)
- 2 medium onions, thinly sliced
- 2 large garlic cloves, minced
- 2 pounds large tomatoes, cored and sliced crosswise ½ inch thick

1. In a small bowl, combine the salt with the ground cumin, the crushed black peppercorns and mustard seeds, the sugar, the turmeric and the cayenne pepper.

2. In a large skillet, warm 3 tablespoons of the vegetable oil over moderately high heat. Add 6 of the curry leaves, if using, and when they begin to crackle, add half of the sliced onions. Reduce the heat to moderately low and cook, stirring, until the onions are softened but not browned, about 4 minutes. Add half of the minced garlic and cook, stirring, until fragrant, about 2 minutes. Add half of the spice mixture and cook, stirring, for 1 minute.

3. Push the onions to one side of the skillet and add half of the tomato slices to the skillet in a single layer. Cook over moderately high heat until the tomatoes are browned on the bottom, about 1 minute. Turn each slice of tomato and brown the second side. Stir the tomatoes lightly to blend with the onions. Slide the tomatoes and the onions onto a platter and cover them with foil to keep warm. Wipe out the skillet and repeat the process with all of the remaining ingredients. Serve the vegetables hot. —*Maya Kaimal*

Champagne-Tomatillo Fritters

4 SERVINGS

The batter for these fritters forms a light, crisp coating that would also work well with sliced eggplant and zucchini.

- ¾ cup all-purpose flour
- 1 teaspoon table salt
- 1 large egg
- ¼ cup warm water
- ½ cup dry Champagne or sparkling wine
- 2 tablespoons unsalted butter, melted and cooled
- 1 pound large tomatillos—husks removed, tomatillos cored and sliced ¼ inch thick

Kosher salt

Pinch of freshly grated nutmeg

- 4 cups vegetable oil, for frying

1. Sift the flour with the table salt into a large bowl. Make a well in the center. Break the egg into the well, add the water and beat lightly to blend with the egg. Gradually beat in the flour while pouring in the wine and then the butter. Let the fritter batter stand for 1 hour; it should be as thick as pancake batter.

2. In a bowl, mix the tomatillos with a pinch of kosher salt and the nutmeg. Let stand for 15 to 30 minutes.

3. In a large skillet, heat the oil to 375°. Pat the tomatillo slices dry with paper towels. One at a time, dip the tomatillo slices in the batter. Using tongs, add the slices to the oil in a single layer, without crowding the skillet. Fry the tomatillo fritters, turning once, until golden, 1 to 3 minutes total. Drain the fritters on paper towels and keep warm in a low oven. Season with kosher salt and serve as soon as possible. —Jane Sigal

Bob's Eggplant

8 SERVINGS

This is one of artist Robert Rauschenberg's favorite vegetable dishes.

- 4 medium eggplants, sliced crosswise 1½ inches thick

About ¼ cup plus 2 tablespoons canola oil, plus more for brushing

Salt and freshly ground black pepper

- ¾ cup sake
- ¼ cup mirin (sweet rice wine)
- ¼ cup sugar
- 3 tablespoons miso (see Note)

Pinch of cayenne pepper

1. Preheat the oven to 350°. Using a small sharp knife, make ¼-inch-deep crisscrossed slashes in the center of the fleshy part of each slice of eggplant; take care not to cut through the skin so the slices remain intact. Lightly brush the eggplant with oil and season with salt and black pepper.

2. In a large skillet, heat 1 tablespoon of the oil. Add the eggplant slices in batches and cook over moderately high heat until golden brown, about 4 minutes per side; add more oil as needed. Transfer the eggplant to a large rimmed baking sheet and bake for about 20 minutes or until meltingly tender. Remove from the oven. Preheat the broiler.

3. While the eggplant slices roast, combine the sake, mirin, sugar, miso and cayenne in a small saucepan and cook over moderately high heat until reduced by half, about 15 minutes.

4. Generously brush both sides of the eggplant slices with the sake miso glaze. Broil for about 1 minute per side, shifting the pan for even browning; the slices should be sizzling and caramelized. Serve hot or at room temperature. —Hisachika Takahashi

NOTE Miso is available at Asian grocery stores.

MAKE AHEAD The recipe can be prepared through Step 3 and kept at room temperature for up to 6 hours. Don't brush the eggplant with the sake-miso glaze until just before broiling.

Eggplant-Parmesan Timbales

6 SERVINGS

Light and elegant, these timbales of eggplant parmigiana are a three-star take on a very simple dish. Serve them hot from the oven or at room temperature. You'll need six half-cup ramekins.

kitchen wisdom

Tips for cooking with wine:

1. **Cork opened wine (white and red)** and store it in the refrigerator for up to two weeks.

2. **Keep a few extra intact corks** in case one crumbles and can't be reused. Or reuse plastic ones—they're indestructible.

3. **Feel free to mix different kinds of wines** into any dish that you're preparing, as long as they're the same color.

4. **Remember that red wine acts as a food coloring.** Pears and peaches gain a nice rosy blush, but pork, chicken and white-fleshed fish turn a muddy red (something to keep in mind when you're entertaining).

5. **Select pots and pans with nonreactive linings,** such as glass, stainless steel, tin and enamel. Avoid aluminum, unlined copper and cast iron, which turn food dark and give it a metallic taste when an acidic ingredient—such as wine—is in the pot.

- ½ cup extra-virgin olive oil, plus more for brushing
- ¼ cup fresh fine bread crumbs
- 3 pounds tomatoes—peeled, halved, seeded and coarsely chopped
- 2 garlic cloves, smashed
- ½ cup plus 2 tablespoons coarsely chopped basil

Fine sea salt

- 2 Italian eggplants, 1 medium wide and 1 narrow (about ¾ pound each)

Freshly ground pepper

- 6 ounces salted mozzarella, cut into ½-inch dice (about 1⅓ cups)

1. Preheat the oven to 400°. Brush six ½-cup ramekins with olive oil and coat the bottoms and sides with the bread crumbs. Tap out any excess crumbs.

2. Squeeze as much juice from the tomatoes as possible; discard the juice. Heat 2 tablespoons of the olive oil in a large saucepan. Add the garlic and cook over moderate heat until golden,

about 2 minutes; discard the garlic. Add the tomatoes and cook over moderately high heat until reduced to a thick sauce, about 20 minutes. Remove from the heat, add 2 tablespoons of the basil and season with sea salt.

3. Slice the wider eggplant lengthwise into eighteen 6-by-¼-inch-thick strips. Cut the narrow eggplant crosswise into eighteen ¼-inch-thick rounds. Arrange the strips and rounds on a rimmed baking sheet, brush with 6 tablespoons of the olive oil and season with sea salt and pepper. Bake for about 8 minutes, or until tender. As the eggplant is done, transfer the slices to a platter, keeping them intact. Lower the oven temperature to 375°.

4. Line each ramekin with 3 strips of eggplant, allowing the excess to hang over the edges. Add about 1 tablespoon of the tomato sauce, a large pinch of the basil and 1 tablespoon of the mozzarella and cover with an eggplant round. Repeat the layering process 2 more times. Bring the overhanging strips of the eggplant over the filling to enclose it.

5. Arrange the ramekins on a baking sheet and bake for about 25 minutes, or until heated through. Let the timbales

Cheese Grits and Morel Ragout

cool for 10 minutes and then unmold each one onto a small plate. Drizzle the remaining tomato sauce around the timbales, garnish with any remaining basil and serve. —*Alfonso Iaccarino*

MAKE AHEAD The baked timbales can be refrigerated overnight. Rewarm and then unmold before serving.

Morel Sformato
6 SERVINGS

Sformato is the Italian term for a kind of molded custard. It makes a wonderful side dish with roast chicken or veal, or you can serve it as a main dish with a tossed green salad or a tomato salad.

½ cup (½ ounce) dried morels
½ cup boiling water
6 tablespoons unsalted butter
⅓ cup all-purpose flour
1½ cups milk
Salt and freshly ground pepper
1 shallot, minced
½ cup heavy cream
5 large egg yolks
2 tablespoons freshly grated Parmesan cheese

I. Preheat the oven to 375°. Butter a deep 3- to 4-cup glass or ceramic baking dish. In a heatproof bowl, soak the morels in the boiling water until softened, about 20 minutes. Rub them to remove any grit and then remove them with a slotted spoon and cut into 1-inch pieces. Let the soaking liquid stand for 5 minutes so the grit falls to the bottom. Pour off the liquid, leaving any grit behind, and reserve.

2. In a small saucepan, melt 4 tablespoons of the butter over moderate heat. Stir in the flour to make a paste and then whisk in the milk until smooth. Bring to a boil, whisking, and then simmer over low heat, whisking often, until there's no floury taste, about 15 minutes. Season with salt and pepper and then scrape the white sauce into a medium bowl. Press a piece of wax paper directly on the surface of the sauce and set aside.

3. In a small skillet, melt the remaining 2 tablespoons of butter. Add the shallot and cook over low heat until softened but not browned, about 4 minutes. Add the soaked morels, a pinch of salt and the reserved morel soaking liquid and simmer over moderate heat until the liquid is reduced by half, about 3 minutes. Add the cream and simmer over low heat until it is reduced by two thirds, about 5 minutes.

4. Add the morel mixture to the white sauce and season with salt and pepper. Stir in the egg yolks and Parmesan until blended and then scrape the mixture into the prepared baking dish.

5. Set the dish in a small roasting pan and pour enough hot water into the pan to reach halfway up the side of the dish. Transfer the pan to the oven and bake the *sformato* for about 45 minutes, or until just set. Remove the baking dish from the pan and let stand for 5 minutes. Run a knife around the side of the dish and invert the *sformato* onto a serving plate. Cut into wedges and serve at once. —*Marcia Kiesel*

MAKE AHEAD The *sformato* can be prepared through Step 4 and then refrigerated overnight, covered. Bake the chilled *sformato* for an extra 10 to 15 minutes.

WINE A mouth-cleansing red is a wonderful contrast to this rich custard. Try the 1994 Penfolds St. Henri Shiraz from Australia or the 1994 Beaulieu Vineyard Georges de Latour Private Reserve Cabernet Sauvignon from California.

Cheese Grits with Morel Ragout
6 SERVINGS

Although this recipe calls for dried morels, it is a fabulous showcase for fresh morels if available. Buy one pound and replace the soaking liquid in the recipe with chicken or beef stock. The grits must be served as soon as they are done, so prepare the morel ragout first and then reheat it when the grits are ready.

RAGOUT

- 2 cups (2 ounces) dried morels
- 2½ cups boiling water
- 3 slices of bacon
- 2 tablespoons unsalted butter, softened
- 1 large leek, white and tender green parts only, halved lengthwise and thinly sliced crosswise
- 1 garlic clove, minced
- 1 tablespoon all-purpose flour
- 3 scallions, chopped

Salt and freshly ground pepper

GRITS

- 6½ cups water
- 1½ cups stone-ground, whole-grain grits (see Note)

Salt

- ½ cup milk
- 1 tablespoon unsalted butter

Freshly ground pepper

- 1½ cups (4 ounces) grated extra-sharp Cheddar cheese

I. MAKE THE RAGOUT: In a large heatproof bowl, soak the morels in the boiling water until softened, about 25 minutes. Rub the morels to remove any grit and then remove them from the soaking liquid with a slotted spoon. Let the soaking liquid stand for 5 minutes so the grit falls to the bottom. Pour off the liquid, leaving any grit behind, and reserve.

2. In a medium saucepan, cook the bacon over moderate heat until crisp, 8 to 10 minutes. Drain on paper towels, coarsely crumble the bacon and set aside. Drain off all but 1 teaspoon of the bacon fat and add 1 tablespoon of the butter to the saucepan. Add the leek and cook over low heat, stirring often, until softened but not browned, about 8 minutes. Add the soaked morels and garlic to the saucepan and cook over moderate heat, stirring, until fragrant, about 2 minutes. Add the reserved morel soaking liquid, cover and simmer over low heat until the morels are tender, about 10 minutes.

3. Meanwhile, in a small bowl, blend the flour with the remaining 1 tablespoon of butter to make a paste. Uncover the saucepan and add the paste, stirring, until blended. Simmer the ragout over low heat, stirring occasionally, until the sauce has thickened, about 4 minutes. Stir in ⅔ of the chopped scallions. Season with salt and pepper. Remove the pan from the heat.

4. MAKE THE GRITS: In a large saucepan, bring the water to a boil. Add the grits and ½ teaspoon of salt, stir well and bring to a simmer. Whisk the grits and cover. Simmer over low heat, whisking often and vigorously, until the grits are thick, creamy and tender but still slightly chewy, about 1 hour. Stir in the milk and butter and season the grits with salt and pepper. Add the cheese and stir until melted. Serve the grits in individual bowls and spoon the morel ragout on top. Garnish with the remaining chopped scallion and the crumbled bacon. —*Marcia Kiesel*

NOTE Freshly stone-ground grits can be ordered through Hoppin' John's (800-828-4412 or www.hoppinjohns.com).

MAKE AHEAD The recipe can be prepared through Step 3 and refrigerated for up to 2 days. Reheat the morel ragout and season with salt and pepper before serving.

WINE This earthy ragout with creamy grits requires a red with the intensity to contrast the double-barreled richness. Go for a Barbaresco from Italy, such as the 1995 Prunotto or the 1993 Vietti.

Steamed Bean Curd with Chinese Mushrooms

4 SERVINGS

The addition of honey makes these mushrooms slightly sweet.

- 5 large dried Chinese black or shiitake mushrooms (1½ ounces)
- 1 cup boiling water
- ½ cup chicken stock or canned low-sodium broth
- 1 teaspoon white sesame seeds
- 1 teaspoon black sesame seeds
- 1½ tablespoons cornstarch
- 1 tablespoon plus ½ teaspoon dark soy sauce
- 1 tablespoon honey
- 1 pound soft bean curd
- 2 tablespoons thinly sliced scallions
- 10 cilantro leaves

I. In a heatproof bowl, soak the Chinese black or shiitake mushrooms in the boiling water for 30 minutes. Drain and rinse the mushrooms. Cut off and discard the stems.

2. In a small saucepan, bring the chicken stock to a boil and add the soaked mushrooms. Cover partially and simmer over low heat for 20 minutes. Drain the mushrooms and then cut them into ¼-inch dice.

3. In a small skillet, toast the white and black sesame seeds over moderate heat, shaking the pan often, until the white sesame seeds turn a light tan, about 1 minute. Transfer the toasted sesame seeds to a plate to cool.

4. In a small bowl, combine the cornstarch with the dark soy sauce and the honey. In another bowl, mash the soft bean curd with a fork. Add the cornstarch mixture and the diced mushrooms and mix well. Transfer the bean curd mixture to a 4-cup soufflé dish or other deep baking dish and smooth the top. Set the soufflé dish in a steamer and cover with a plate. Steam the bean curd mixture until it has set, about 15 minutes. Sprinkle the steamed bean curd with the toasted sesame seeds, the sliced scallions and the cilantro and serve hot. —*Eileen Yin-Fei Lo*

MAKE AHEAD The recipe can be prepared through Step 3 up to 2 days ahead. Refrigerate the soaked mushrooms and store the toasted sesame seeds at room temperature in an airtight container.

ONE SERVING Calories 138 kcal, Total Fat 4.1 gm, Saturated Fat .2 gm

Mixed Vegetable Stir-Fry

Mixed Vegetable Stir-Fry

4 SERVINGS

6 cups water

One ¼-inch-thick slice of peeled fresh
    ginger, lightly smashed

10 ounces mung bean sprouts

1½ teaspoons peanut oil

½ teaspoon salt

1½ teaspoons minced garlic

2 large carrots, thinly sliced on the
    diagonal

½ European cucumber, peeled,
    halved lengthwise, seeded and
    sliced crosswise ¼ inch thick

½ teaspoon Asian sesame oil

1. In a medium saucepan, bring the
water to a boil with the ginger. Add the
bean sprouts and cook for 5 seconds;
drain and discard the ginger. Rinse the
bean sprouts and drain again.

2. Warm a wok over high heat for 45
seconds. Add the peanut oil and swirl to
coat the wok. Stir in the salt and garlic
and cook for 10 seconds. Add the carrots and stir-fry for 2½ minutes. Add
the cucumber and stir-fry for 1 minute.
Add the bean sprouts and stir-fry for 10
seconds. Turn off the heat and stir in
the sesame oil. Serve the stir-fry at
once. —*Eileen Yin-Fei Lo*

SERVE WITH Steamed rice.

ONE SERVING Calories 60 kcal,
Total Fat 2.5 gm, Saturated Fat 0.5 gm

Braised Fall Vegetables
with Coriander

4 SERVINGS

2 tablespoons olive oil

1 medium onion, halved and thinly
    sliced

2 large garlic cloves, thinly sliced

1 tablespoon crushed coriander
    seeds

2 bay leaves

2 cups dry white wine

2 cups vegetable stock, chicken
    stock or canned low-sodium
    broth

1 teaspoon sugar

Cayenne pepper

1 fennel bulb, trimmed and cut
    lengthwise into eighths

16 baby carrots

Salt

1 zucchini, cut into 2-by-½-inch
    strips

1 red bell pepper, cut into
    2-by-½-inch strips

About 1 tablespoon hazelnut oil

Watercress sprigs, for garnish

1. Heat the olive oil in a large saucepan.
Add the onion and cook over moderate
heat until softened but not browned,
about 5 minutes. Add the garlic and
cook until fragrant, about 1 minute.
Wrap the coriander seeds and bay
leaves in cheesecloth and tie with
kitchen string. Stir the herb bundle into
the saucepan along with the wine, stock,
sugar and a pinch of cayenne and bring
to a boil. Reduce the heat, cover and
simmer gently for 10 minutes.

2. Add the fennel, carrots and a little
salt to the saucepan; simmer over moderate heat until almost tender, about 10
minutes. Add the zucchini and red bell
pepper and simmer until all the vegetables are tender, about 10 minutes. Using

a slotted spoon, transfer the vegetables
to a bowl. Boil the cooking liquid until
flavorful and slightly thickened, about
10 minutes. Discard the herb bundle.

3. Remove the pan from the heat, let
the liquid cool to lukewarm and stir in
the hazelnut oil. Season with salt; add
more cayenne or oil if needed. Pour the
liquid over the vegetables, scatter the
watercress sprigs sparingly over the top
and serve warm or at room temperature. —*Jane Sigal*

Grilled Vegetables with
Provençal Vinaigrette

4 SERVINGS

You can choose the vegetables for this
salad based on what looks best at the
market. Prepare the dressing with
Banyuls vinegar, made from the sweet
fortified French red wine, or use sherry
vinegar instead.

2 artichokes

¾ cup extra-virgin olive oil

2 teaspoons *herbes de Provence*

1 large fennel bulb—halved, cored
    and cut lengthwise into 12
    wedges

Grilled Vegetables with Provençal Vinaigrette

1 large ripe tomato, sliced crosswise ¾ inch thick

1 medium zucchini, sliced ¾ inch thick

2 Portobello mushrooms, stemmed, caps halved

Salt and freshly ground pepper

1 tablespoon vinegar, preferably Banyuls or sherry

1 teaspoon Dijon mustard

1 teaspoon Worcestershire sauce

1. Using a sharp knife, trim the artichoke stems to 1 inch. Using kitchen scissors, trim ½ inch from the outer leaves. Cut the artichokes in half and scoop out the spiky leaves and hairy chokes. Steam the artichokes, cut side down, over boiling water until just tender, 10 to 12 minutes. Transfer to a plate, let cool and pat dry with paper towels.

2. Light a grill, heat a grill pan or preheat the broiler. In a small bowl, combine ½ cup of the oil with the *herbes de Provence* and brush it on the artichokes, fennel, tomato, zucchini and Portobellos. Sprinkle the vegetables with salt and pepper and grill or broil, turning, until tender and lightly charred, about 2 minutes for the tomato, about 8 minutes for the artichokes, about 16 minutes for the fennel and about 25 minutes for the zucchini and mushrooms. Transfer the vegetables to a platter, cover with foil and keep warm.

3. In a bowl, combine the vinegar with the mustard and Worcestershire. Whisk in the remaining ¼ cup of oil and season with salt and pepper. Drizzle the vegetables with the dressing; serve warm or room temperature. —*Craig Shelton*

MAKE AHEAD The grilled vegetables can be refrigerated overnight. The dressed vegetables can be kept at room temperature for up to 3 hours.

SERVE WITH Olive bread.

Grilled Ratatouille

8 SERVINGS

For best results, rake the coals so your grill has hotter and cooler cooking areas.

4 red bell peppers, halved

2 red onions, sliced lengthwise ⅓ inch thick, root end left intact

2 medium yellow squash, sliced lengthwise ⅓ inch thick

2 medium zucchini, sliced lengthwise ⅓ inch thick

24 cherry tomatoes

Olive oil, for brushing

Salt and freshly ground black pepper

About 1 teaspoon dried thyme

Light a grill or preheat the broiler. Arrange the bell peppers, onions, yellow squash and zucchini on a large tray. Thread the cherry tomatoes onto bamboo skewers and add to the tray. Brush the vegetables with olive oil and season with salt, black pepper and thyme. Grill or broil the bell peppers and onions over the cooler part of the grill for about 4 minutes per side, or until tender. Grill or broil the yellow squash and zucchini over the hotter part of the grill for about 2 minutes per side, or until almost tender. Grill the cherry tomatoes over the hotter part for about 1 minute, or until hot. Transfer the vegetables to a platter, toss gently to combine and serve. —*Fred Eric*

Vegetable Kebabs with Greek Marinade

4 SERVINGS

In Greece they use this marinade to spice up lamb, poultry and seafood, but it's also good on vegetable kebabs. Use red wine when marinating red meats, white wine for poultry and seafood. For a special, if untraditional, marinade that works with either, try retsina (a resin-flavored Greek wine).

MARINADE

4 garlic cloves, minced

3 bay leaves

½ cup extra-virgin olive oil

¼ cup dry white wine or retsina

2 tablespoons fresh lemon juice

1 tablespoon chopped oregano

1 teaspoon sea salt

1 teaspoon finely grated lemon zest

½ teaspoon freshly ground pepper

KEBABS

1 large red bell pepper, cut into 1-inch dice

1 medium sweet onion, cut lengthwise into 4 wedges

2 small zucchini, cut into ½-inch-thick rounds

1 pint cherry tomatoes

1 pound boiled small potatoes

1. MAKE THE MARINADE: Stir all of the ingredients together in a bowl.

2. ASSEMBLE THE KEBABS: Light a grill and thread the vegetables onto skewers. Brush generously with the marinade and cook over a medium-hot fire, basting a few times with the additional marinade, until the vegetables are tender and lightly charred, about 4 minutes per side. —*Steven Raichlen*

WINE The herbal flavors of a Washington State Sauvignon Blanc, such as the 1997 Waterbrook or the 1997 Chateau Ste. Michelle, would pair well with the grilled vegetables.

Winter Vegetable Ragout with Madeira

12 SERVINGS

4 large carrots, cut into ¾-inch chunks

1 butternut squash (2½ pounds), peeled and cut into ¾-inch dice

2 medium turnips, peeled and cut into ¾-inch dice

2 medium red onions, cut into 1-inch pieces

¼ cup olive oil

Salt and freshly ground pepper

¾ cup Madeira or Marsala

1 large tomato—peeled, seeded and cut into 1-inch chunks

2 teaspoons thyme leaves

Preheat the oven to 350°. In a large roasting pan, toss the carrots, squash, turnips and onions with the olive oil and season with salt and pepper. Roast the vegetables for about 25 minutes, or until they are beginning to soften but not browned. Add the Madeira and the tomato and cook for about 25 minutes, stirring once, until the Madeira has evaporated and the vegetables are golden. Add the thyme and roast for 20 to 25 minutes longer, stirring occasionally until the vegetables are lightly caramelized. —*Tim McKee*

MAKE AHEAD The baked vegetables can stand at room temperature for up to 6 hours. Rewarm before serving.

West Texas Onion Rings

6 SERVINGS

The key to these addictive onion rings is to use sweet onions, such as the Texas 1015 variety or Walla Wallas from Washington State. Coat the onions just before you fry them. You can use the *adobo* sauce that canned chipotle chiles are packed in, or buy *adobo* sauce on its own. Canned chipotle chiles and *adobo* sauce are now available at most supermarkets.

1½ cups milk or buttermilk
1½ cups all-purpose flour
  2 tablespoons *adobo* sauce
  2 large sweet onions (about
    1 pound each), sliced ¼ inch
    thick and separated into rings
Vegetable oil, for frying
1½ cups yellow cornmeal
  1 tablespoon ground cumin
Salt

1. In a large bowl, whisk the milk with ½ cup of the flour and the *adobo* sauce

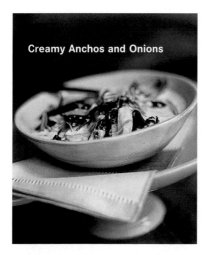

Creamy Anchos and Onions

until smooth. Add the onion rings and toss to moisten with the mixture.

2. In a cast-iron skillet, heat 1 inch of oil to 350°. In a large paper bag, combine the remaining 1 cup of flour with the cornmeal, cumin and ½ tablespoon salt. Working in batches, dredge the onion rings in the cornmeal mixture, shaking off the excess. Transfer the rings to a baking sheet.

3. Working in batches, fry the onion rings in the hot oil until golden brown, 3 to 4 minutes. Using tongs, transfer the onion rings to paper towels to drain. Season the onion rings with salt and serve immediately. —*Lisa Ahier*

Creamy Anchos and Onions

8 TO 10 SERVINGS

Anchos and onions simmered in cream make a sublime accompaniment to Mole-Inspired Roasted Turkey (p. 190). Or you could serve this dish with any type of grilled or roasted meat.

  5 medium ancho chiles, stemmed
    and seeded
  1 tablespoon unsalted butter
  1 pound small white onions,
    trimmed but with the root end
    left intact, halved lengthwise
  4 garlic cloves, coarsely chopped
  1 cup turkey stock (p. 192),
    chicken stock or canned
    low-sodium broth
  2 cups heavy cream
¼ cup tarragon leaves
  1 teaspoon salt
  1 teaspoon fresh lime juice

1. Heat a large cast-iron skillet. Add the ancho chiles and toast over moderate heat, pressing down with a spatula, until the chiles are fragrant and blistered, about 20 seconds per side. Transfer to a plate, let cool and then cut the chiles into ½-inch pieces.

2. Melt the butter in a large skillet. Add the onions and garlic, cover and cook over moderate heat, stirring, until the onions are softened, about 5 minutes. Add the stock and cook until reduced

by half, 6 to 7 minutes. Add the toasted anchos, the heavy cream and the tarragon and cook over moderately low heat until the onions and the anchos are tender and the cream is thickened, about 10 minutes. Add the salt and the lime juice, transfer the mixture to a bowl and serve. —*Robert Del Grande*

MAKE AHEAD The dish can be refrigerated overnight. Rewarm gently before serving, adding a few tablespoons of water if the cream is too thick.

Bread Pudding with Leeks and Garlic

10 SERVINGS

One 1½-pound brioche or
    challah loaf, cut into
    ¾-inch dice
  6 tablespoons unsalted butter,
    4 melted
  3 large leeks, white and tender
    green parts only, sliced ½ inch
    thick
  3 large garlic cloves, thinly
    sliced
Salt and freshly ground pepper
¼ cup dry white wine
¼ cup chopped flat-leaf parsley
  1 teaspoon chopped thyme
  4 eggs, lightly beaten
  2 cups milk
  2 cups heavy cream or
    half-and-half
  1 cup turkey stock (p. 192) or
    canned low-sodium broth
  1 cup coarsely grated Swiss cheese

1. Preheat the oven to 350°. On a rimmed baking sheet, toss the diced brioche with the melted butter and bake for 20 minutes, or until golden and crisp. Let cool.

2. Melt the remaining 2 tablespoons butter in a large skillet. Add the leeks and the garlic and season with salt and pepper. Cover and cook over moderate heat for 5 minutes and then uncover and cook, stirring, until softened, about 5 minutes longer. Add the white wine and cook until evaporated. Remove

Turnips and Turnip Greens with Mustard Butter

Garlic Flans

8 SERVINGS

You will need eight two-ounce ramekins to make this creamy, garlicky side dish.

- 1 cup heavy cream
- 2 large egg yolks
- 1 large egg
- 4 small roasted garlic cloves (from Roasted Tomatoes and Garlic, p. 326), mashed
- ½ teaspoon salt
- ⅛ teaspoon freshly ground white pepper

1. Preheat the oven to 300°. Butter eight 2-ounce ramekins. In a bowl, whisk the cream with the egg yolks, whole egg, garlic, salt and white pepper until smooth. Pour the mixture into the ramekins and set them in a small roasting pan. Carefully pour enough hot water into the roasting pan to reach halfway up the sides of the ramekins.

2. Bake the flans for about 30 minutes, or until set. Transfer the ramekins to a rack and let stand for 10 minutes. Run a knife around the edges, invert the flans onto plates and serve. —*Tom Colicchio*

Turnips and Turnip Greens with Mustard Butter

10 SERVINGS

- 1 stick (4 ounces) unsalted butter, softened
- 2 tablespoons whole-grain Dijon mustard
- 1 tablespoon finely chopped shallots
- 11 garlic cloves, minced

Kosher salt and freshly ground black pepper

- 6 pounds turnip or collard greens, large stems discarded
- 2 tablespoons extra-virgin olive oil
- 2 medium onions, halved and thinly sliced
- 4 oil-packed anchovy fillets, drained and mashed
- 5 pounds medium turnips, peeled and cut into eighths
- 8 piquillo peppers, seeded and cut into ¼-inch strips (see Note)

from the heat and stir in the parsley and thyme; let cool.

3. In a large bowl, whisk the eggs with the milk, heavy cream and stock. Add the leek mixture and season generously with salt and pepper. Stir in the brioche and the Swiss cheese. Transfer the mixture to a 3- to 4-quart buttered baking dish. Cover with plastic and refrigerate overnight. Bring to room temperature before baking.

4. Preheat the oven to 375°. Toss the brioche to make sure it's evenly soaked. Cover with a buttered sheet of foil and bake for 1 hour, or until just set. Remove the foil and bake for 30 minutes longer, or until the top is golden and crisp. —*Grace Parisi*

MAKE AHEAD The bread pudding can be refrigerated overnight. Cover the baking dish with foil. Reheat in a 350° oven; uncover and recrisp under a broiler.

1. In a bowl, blend the butter with the mustard, the shallots and 1 teaspoon of the garlic. Season with kosher salt and black pepper.

2. In a stockpot of boiling water, cook the turnip greens until they are tender, about 10 minutes. Drain and let cool; squeeze the greens dry and coarsely chop them.

3. In a large enameled cast-iron casserole, heat the olive oil. Add 2 tablespoons of the mustard butter and the onions and cook over moderately low heat until softened, about 10 minutes. Add the anchovies and the remaining garlic and cook until the garlic softens. Add the turnip greens and cook, stirring, for 10 minutes.

4. Bring a large pot of salted water to a boil. Add the turnips and cook until tender, about 12 minutes. Drain and return the turnips to the pot; shake over high heat to dry them out. Remove from the heat and stir in 3 tablespoons of the mustard butter. Season with salt and black pepper.

5. Reheat the turnip greens. Stir in the piquillo peppers and 3 tablespoons of the mustard butter. Season with salt and black pepper. Spoon the greens into a warmed bowl. Top with the turnips and serve. —*Marcia Kiesel*

NOTE Wood-roasted piquillo peppers from Spain have an intense sweet-smoky flavor. Two peeled and seeded roasted red bell peppers can be substituted.

Parsnip Fries with Hot Vinegar Dip

8 SERVINGS

You can serve these fries with aged balsamic vinegar, but the hot vinegar dip is a sublime match.

- ½ cup rice vinegar
- 2 tablespoons *tamari* or soy sauce
- 2 teaspoons chili paste
- 3 tablespoons extra-virgin olive oil
- 4 pounds parsnips, peeled and cut into 4-by-⅓-inch sticks
- 2 teaspoons fine sea salt

1. Preheat the oven to 375°. In a small glass or stainless steel bowl, combine the vinegar, *tamari* and chili paste.

2. Spread half of the olive oil on each of 2 large rimmed baking sheets. Add the parsnips; toss to coat thoroughly. Roast the parsnips for about 1 hour, or until tender and browned in spots. Sprinkle with the salt, transfer to a platter and serve with the vinegar dip. —*Anne Disrude*

ONE SERVING Calories 202 kcal, Total Fat 5.8 gm, Saturated Fat 0.9 gm

Cream of Celery Root with Shrimp Butter

10 SERVINGS

- 1 stick (4 ounces) plus 1 tablespoon unsalted butter
- 3 large leeks, white and tender green parts only, halved lengthwise and thinly sliced crosswise
- 2 thyme sprigs, plus 1 teaspoon minced thyme
- ½ cup dry white wine
- 6 cups chicken stock or canned low-sodium broth
- 2½ pounds celery root—quartered, peeled and cut into 2-inch chunks
- ½ pound Yukon Gold potatoes, peeled and cut into 2-inch chunks
- Salt
- ½ cup heavy cream
- 1 tablespoon minced shallots
- ½ pound medium shrimp, shelled and deveined, shells reserved, shrimp halved lengthwise
- Freshly ground pepper
- ¼ cup finely diced Granny Smith or other tart green apple

1. Melt 3 tablespoons of the butter in a large enameled cast-iron casserole. Add the leeks and thyme sprigs and cook over low heat until softened, about 8 minutes. Add the wine and simmer over moderately high heat for 2 minutes. Add the stock, celery root, potatoes and a large pinch of salt and bring to a boil. Cover and simmer over low heat until the celery root and potatoes

are tender, about 45 minutes. Remove the thyme sprigs.

2. Working in batches, puree the celery root mixture in a blender until it is very smooth. Return the celery root puree to the casserole and stir in ¼ cup of the heavy cream.

3. In a medium skillet, melt the remaining 6 tablespoons of butter. Add the shallots and the reserved shrimp shells and cook over low heat, stirring, for 8 minutes. Strain through a coarse strainer, pressing on the shells to extract as much butter as possible; you should have about 2 tablespoons. Keep warm.

4. In a small saucepan, bring the remaining ¼ cup of heavy cream to a simmer. Add the shrimp and a pinch of salt and cook over low heat, stirring, until just cooked through, about 1 minute. Remove from the heat.

5. Reheat the celery root puree and season with salt and pepper. Ladle the puree into warm shallow bowls. Spoon the shrimp and cream into the bowls. Drizzle each serving lightly with the shrimp butter, garnish with the diced apple and minced thyme and serve at once. —*Marcia Kiesel*

MAKE AHEAD The recipe can be prepared through Step 3 up to 2 days ahead and refrigerated. Melt the shrimp butter over low heat before using.

Fried Plantains

4 SERVINGS

Crisp, salty fried plantain slices, or *tostones,* are a ubiquitous side dish at Latin American restaurants.

- Vegetable oil, for frying
- 4 yellow plantains, peeled and sliced diagonally ½ inch thick
- Salt

1. In a large heavy skillet, heat ¼ inch of vegetable oil until shimmering. Add half of the plantains and fry over moderate heat until golden and tender, about 3 minutes per side; lower the heat if necessary and transfer the plantains to paper towels to drain. Season the plantains

Chile-Spiked Grilled Corn
Rolled in Cotija Cheese

with salt. Repeat with the remaining plantains, adding more oil if necessary. Reserve the oil in the skillet.

2. Press the fried plantains between paper towels to flatten them slightly. Heat the reserved oil until shimmering, adding more if necessary to return it to ¼ inch. Add half of the flattened plantains and fry over moderate heat until deep brown and crisp, about 1 minute per side. Season the plantains again with salt and keep warm while you fry the rest. —*Luis Rivera*

Chile-Spiked Grilled Corn Rolled in Cotija Cheese

6 SERVINGS

Use a pure ground chile with some kick to it, such as Mexican *chile piquín,* to counterpoint the sweet grilled corn and creamy coating. If you can't find the chile, use one teaspoon paprika mixed with a half teaspoon cayenne pepper and a half teaspoon salt.

  6 **ears of corn, shucked**
  ¼ **cup mayonnaise**
  ¼ **cup crème fraîche or sour cream**
  ½ **cup (about 2 ounces) freshly grated *cotija* or Pecorino-Romano cheese**

  2 **teaspoons *chile piquín***
Lime wedges, for serving

1. Light a charcoal grill or preheat the oven to 500°. In a large pot of boiling water, cook the corn until crisp-tender, about 3 minutes. Drain well.

2. Grill the corn, turning frequently, until well browned, 10 to 12 minutes. Alternatively, roast the corn on a baking sheet for 10 to 15 minutes, turning the ears occasionally.

3. Meanwhile, in a small bowl, mix the mayonnaise with the crème fraîche.

4. Attach corn holders to each of the ears of corn, or press a bamboo skewer through the centers. Generously brush the mayonnaise mixture all over the ears and sprinkle with the cheese and *chile piquín.* Serve right away, with lime wedges. —*Richard Ampudia*

Creamed Corn

8 TO 10 SERVINGS

  2 **dozen ears of corn, shucked**
  2 **tablespoons unsalted butter**
  1 **medium onion, finely chopped**
  1 **cup heavy cream**
  2 **teaspoons salt**

1. Using a thin knife and working over a bowl, cut the corn kernels from the cobs. Working over another bowl, scrape the cobs with the back of a knife to release the corn milk. In a blender or food processor, puree half of the corn kernels with the corn milk.

2. Melt the butter in a large deep skillet. Add the chopped onion and cook over moderate heat, stirring, until translucent, 4 to 5 minutes. Add the whole corn kernels and cook, stirring, until the corn is crisp-tender, about 10 minutes. Add the corn puree and cook until it is slightly thickened, 8 to 10 minutes. Reduce the heat to low, add the heavy cream and the salt and cook until heated through. Serve the creamed corn warm. —*Robert Del Grande*

MAKE AHEAD The creamed corn can be refrigerated overnight. Rewarm over low heat, stirring constantly.

Roasted Corn and Pepper Maque Choux

8 SERVINGS

No one seems to know the exact definition of the popular Creole side dish *maque choux,* or smothered corn, but it has its roots in the classic Southern recipe for skillet-fried corn.

  8 **ears of corn, shucked**
  3 **tablespoons Asian sesame oil**
Salt and freshly ground black pepper
  ½ **pound sliced bacon, cut into ½-inch pieces**
  1 **large onion, cut into ½-inch dice**
  1 **large red bell pepper, cut into ½-inch dice**
  1 **tablespoon minced garlic**
  1 **cup heavy cream**
  12 **medium scallions, white and tender green parts thinly sliced**

1. Preheat the oven to 425°. Brush the corn with the sesame oil and season with salt and black pepper. Wrap each ear in foil and bake for about 30 minutes, or until tender. Let cool, unwrap the corn and, working over a bowl, cut the kernels from the cobs.

2. In a large enameled cast-iron casserole, cook the bacon over moderately low heat, stirring, until the bacon is lightly crisp and the fat is rendered, about 5 minutes. Transfer the bacon to paper towels to drain. Pour off all but 2 tablespoons of the rendered fat.

3. Add the onion and the red bell pepper to the casserole and cook over moderate heat, stirring, until softened, about 5 minutes. Add the corn kernels, the cooked bacon and the garlic and cook, stirring, for 3 minutes. Add the heavy cream, cover and simmer, stirring occasionally, until the cream thickens and coats the corn, about 8 more minutes. Stir in the sliced scallions and season the *maque choux* with salt and black pepper. Serve hot. —*John Currence*

MAKE AHEAD The *maque choux* can be refrigerated overnight. Reheat and stir in the sliced scallions just before serving.

CLOCKWISE FROM TOP: **Roasted Corn and Pepper Maque Choux, Spicy Pickled Carrots and Asparagus (p. 12) and Red Potato Salad with Mustard Dressing (p. 75).**

ABOVE: **Fresh Bean and Corn Stew with Paprika Oil**. RIGHT: **Spicy Chickpeas**.

Fresh Bean and Corn Stew with Paprika Oil

6 FIRST-COURSE SERVINGS

Chileans love beans and have a vast repertoire of bean recipes, but this one is the national favorite. It's usually served as a first course, but makes a luscious side dish with grilled or roasted meats. Just cut the recipe in half.

STEW

- 4 cups (about 1½ pounds) fresh or frozen shelled beans, such as kidney beans, cranberry beans, black-eyed peas or lima beans
- ¾ pound pumpkin or butternut squash, peeled and cut into ½-inch cubes (2 cups)
- 2 cups chicken stock or canned low-sodium broth
- 2 cups water
- 1½ tablespoons vegetable oil
- 1 large onion, finely chopped
- 1 medium carrot, coarsely grated

Salt and freshly ground pepper

- 6 ears corn, kernels removed, or 3 cups frozen corn (two 10-ounce packages)
- 10 basil leaves, coarsely chopped

PAPRIKA OIL

- ½ cup vegetable oil
- 2 garlic cloves, crushed
- 1 tablespoon paprika

1. MAKE THE STEW: In a large heavy casserole, combine the beans with the pumpkin, chicken stock and water and bring to a boil. Cover and cook over low heat until the beans are barely tender, about 15 minutes, depending on the size and type of bean.

2. Heat the vegetable oil in a medium skillet. Add the onion and carrot and cook over moderate heat, stirring frequently, until lightly browned, about 8 minutes. Season with salt and pepper.

Add this mixture to the beans and simmer for 15 minutes longer.

3. Add 1 cup of the corn kernels to the beans. Puree the rest of the corn in a blender. If the puree is very dry, add a ladle of the bean cooking liquid. Stir the corn puree and basil into the beans and simmer for another 15 minutes, stirring frequently; the corn puree will thicken the stew. If it gets too thick, thin the stew with hot water; it should be slightly runny. Taste and adjust the seasonings.

4. MAKE THE PAPRIKA OIL: Heat the vegetable oil in a small skillet. Add the garlic and cook over moderate heat until golden, about 2 minutes; discard the garlic. Remove the skillet from the heat and then stir in the paprika. Drizzle the stew with the paprika oil and serve hot. —*Ruth Van Waerebeek-Gonzalez*

MAKE AHEAD The stew and paprika oil can be refrigerated separately for up to 2 days. Reheat before serving.

Spicy Chickpeas

4 SERVINGS

Amazingly simple yet delicious, this side dish was created specifically for canned chickpeas.

- 2 tablespoons vegetable oil
- 1 medium onion, finely chopped
- 1 teaspoon ground coriander
- ½ teaspoon ground cumin
- ⅛ teaspoon cayenne pepper
- ⅛ teaspoon turmeric
- One 15½-ounce can chickpeas, rinsed and drained
- ½ teaspoon coarsely ground black peppercorns
- ½ teaspoon salt
- 1 teaspoon fresh lemon juice
- 2 tablespoons chopped cilantro

In a large skillet, heat the oil. Add the onion and cook over moderately high heat, stirring, until lightly browned, about 5 minutes. Add the coriander, cumin, cayenne and turmeric and cook, stirring, about 1 minute. Add the chickpeas, peppercorns and salt and cook over moderate heat until warmed through. Remove from the heat and stir in the lemon juice and cilantro. Transfer to a bowl and serve warm or at room temperature. —*Maya Kaimal*

Beluga Lentil Salad

6 SERVINGS

Tiny black lentils get a Latin flavor from smoky poblanos and chorizo in this "poor man's caviar" salad.

- 1½ cups (¾ pound) beluga lentils
- 4 garlic cloves, 2 smashed and 2 minced
- 1 carrot, halved crosswise
- 1 small yellow onion, halved
- 4 cups water
- 2 large poblano peppers
- ½ chorizo sausage (1½ ounces), casing removed and meat finely diced
- ½ small red onion, cut into slivers
- 2 hard-cooked eggs, coarsely chopped
- 2 tablespoons chopped cilantro, plus cilantro leaves for garnish
- 3 tablespoons fresh lime juice
- 3 tablespoons vegetable oil
- Salt and freshly ground black pepper

1. In a medium saucepan, combine the lentils with the smashed garlic, carrot, yellow onion and water and bring to a boil. Simmer over low heat until the lentils are just tender, about 30 minutes. Drain the lentils and discard the garlic, carrot and onion. Let the lentils cool slightly.

2. Meanwhile, roast the poblano peppers over a gas flame or under a broiler, turning several times, until they are charred all over. Transfer the poblanos to a bowl, cover with plastic wrap and let steam for 15 minutes. Peel, core and seed the poblanos and then chop them finely.

3. In a small skillet, cook the chorizo over high heat, stirring occasionally,

Beluga Lentil Salad

until crisp, about 5 minutes. Drain the chorizo on paper towels.

4. In a large bowl, combine the chorizo, red onion, hard-cooked eggs, the chopped cilantro and the minced garlic. Add the lime juice and oil, season with salt and black pepper and toss to coat. Sprinkle the cilantro leaves over the top and serve. —*Grace Parisi*

MAKE AHEAD The salad components can be prepared through Step 3 and refrigerated separately overnight. Return the lentils to room temperature and rewarm the chorizo before tossing with the remaining ingredients.

Black Bean and Chorizo Stuffed Chiles

4 SERVINGS ✳

New Mexico chiles and Anaheims, their mostly milder relatives, can be either red or green. The red chiles are riper and are often fruitier in flavor. Spicy chorizo sausages are available at supermarkets.

- 8 fresh New Mexico or Anaheim chiles
- 1 tablespoon canola oil
- 1 medium onion, coarsely chopped
- ½ teaspoon dried oregano
- ½ teaspoon salt
- ¼ teaspoon ground cumin
- ½ pound chorizo, coarsely chopped

One 15-ounce can black beans, drained and rinsed

- 2 tablespoons tomato paste
- ¼ cup water

Crème fraîche or sour cream, for serving

1. Preheat the broiler. Broil the chiles for about 5 minutes per side, or until the skin is blistered. Transfer the chiles to a bowl. Cover with a towel and let the chiles cool slightly. Lower the oven temperature to 400°.

2. Heat the oil in a large skillet. Add the onion and cook over moderately high heat until softened, about 5 minutes. Stir in the oregano, salt and cumin. Add the chorizo, black beans, tomato paste

Black Bean and Chorizo Stuffed Chiles

and water, reduce the heat to low and cook until warmed through, about 10 minutes.

3. Peel the chiles, slit them lengthwise and scrape out the seeds. Stuff the chiles with the black bean filling and arrange them in a large baking dish. Bake for 5 to 7 minutes, or until they are heated through. Transfer the chiles to plates, spoon the crème fraîche on top and serve. —*Jan Newberry*

SERVE WITH Corn tortillas.

WINE The intensity of a California Zinfandel can match the heat here. Try the 1996 Kenwood or the 1996 Quivira.

Turlu Turlu

4 MAIN-COURSE SERVINGS

Here's a vegetarian version of the Turkish stew *turlu turlu,* usually made with mutton.

- 1½ pounds zucchini, cut into 4-by-½-inch strips
- 1 pound Asian eggplants, cut into 4-by-½-inch strips

Kosher salt

- 3 carrots, quartered and cut into 2-inch lengths
- 2 green bell peppers, cut into wide strips
- 2 medium Yukon Gold potatoes (¾ pound), peeled and diced
- 1 red onion, sliced ½ inch thick
- 3 tablespoons extra-virgin olive oil
- 1 garlic clove, thinly sliced
- ¼ teaspoon coarsely ground allspice
- 1 teaspoon crushed coriander seeds

Freshly ground black pepper

- 2 cups canned tomato sauce
- ½ cup canned chickpeas, drained
- ½ cup coarsely chopped parsley
- ½ cup coarsely chopped cilantro

1. Preheat the oven to 425°. In each of 2 colanders set in the sink, toss the zucchini and eggplants separately with

1 teaspoon each of kosher salt; let stand for 30 minutes. Rinse under cold water; pat dry with paper towels.

2. In a large roasting pan, toss the eggplants with the carrots, green bell peppers, potatoes, onion, olive oil, garlic, allspice and coriander seeds; season with kosher salt and black pepper. Transfer to the oven and roast for 45 minutes, stirring every 15 minutes. Add the zucchini and roast for 15 minutes. Stir in the tomato sauce and chickpeas and roast for 10 minutes longer to blend the flavors. Stir in the parsley and the cilantro and serve. —*Sam Clark*

Village-Style Carrots and Peas with Tofu

4 MAIN-COURSE SERVINGS

This vegetarian dish from the villages of the Punjab in northwestern India is normally made with *paneer,* but you can take a shortcut and use tofu. Also, this version uses frozen peas. If you'd rather use fresh ones, cook them at the same time as the carrots. If the fresh peas seem especially tender, add them after the carrots have cooked for ten minutes.

- ¼ **cup vegetable oil**
- 1 **medium onion, finely chopped**
- 1 **tablespoon minced fresh ginger**
- 2 **medium tomatoes, finely chopped**
- 2 **teaspoons** *garam masala*
- 2 **teaspoons salt**
- ½ **teaspoon cayenne pepper**
- ¼ **teaspoon turmeric**
- 1 **pound carrots, cut into** ½-**inch dice**
- 1 **pound boiling potatoes, peeled and cut into** ½-**inch dice**
- 1 **cup water**
- ½ **pound firm tofu or Homemade Paneer with Indian Flavors (p. 295), cut into** ½-**inch pieces**
- 1 **cup (5**½ **ounces) frozen baby peas**

I. In a large deep skillet, heat 3 tablespoons of the vegetable oil until shimmering. Add the onion and cook over moderately high heat, stirring occasionally, until lightly browned, about 5 minutes. Add the ginger. Cook, stirring, until fragrant, about 1 minute. Add the tomatoes, *garam masala,* salt, cayenne and turmeric; cook until thickened slightly, about 4 minutes. Add the carrots, potatoes and water and bring to a simmer. Cover and cook over low heat until the vegetables are just tender, about 20 minutes.

2. Meanwhile, heat the remaining 1 tablespoon of oil in a large nonstick skillet until shimmering. Add the tofu; cook over moderately high heat, shaking the pan often, until golden all over, about 5 minutes. Using a slotted spoon, add the tofu to the curried vegetables along with the peas. Cover; cook over low heat until the peas are tender and warmed through, 4 to 5 minutes. Serve hot. —*Madhur Jaffrey*

WINE The mild heat of this curry calls for a simple white wine with just enough aromatic fruitiness to balance the spice. Look for a California Viognier, such as the 1997 Smith & Hook, the 1997 R. H. Phillips EXP or the 1997 Bonterra.

Turlu Turlu

Indian-Style Grilled Vegetables with Paneer

Indian-Style Grilled Vegetables with Paneer

4 MAIN-COURSE SERVINGS

Paneer is the Indian equivalent of farmer cheese. It's easy and quick to make at home, but you can substitute feta cheese, if you prefer.

MARINADE

- 1 tablespoon cumin seeds
- ¼ cup tomato juice
- ¼ cup coarsely chopped cilantro
- 2 tablespoons hot pepper sauce
- 2 tablespoons red wine vinegar
- 2 tablespoons finely chopped fresh ginger
- 1½ tablespoons sugar
- 1 tablespoon minced garlic
- 1 tablespoon Dijon mustard
- 1½ teaspoons salt

VEGETABLES WITH PANEER

- 4 large yellow cherry tomatoes
- 8 large snowpeas
- 8 large shiitake mushrooms, stemmed
- 1 medium zucchini, cut on the diagonal ½ inch thick
- 1 small Spanish onion, quartered lengthwise and layers separated
- 1 red bell pepper, cored and sliced lengthwise into eighths
- 1 green bell pepper, cored and sliced lengthwise into eighths
- 1 large russet potato
- ½ small butternut squash, peeled and cut into 2-inch chunks
- 4 large broccoli florets
- 4 large cauliflower florets

Homemade Paneer with Indian Flavors (recipe follows) or feta cheese, cut into 1½-inch chunks

Salt and freshly ground black pepper

1. MAKE THE MARINADE: In a small skillet, toast the cumin seeds over moderately high heat until fragrant, about 1 minute. Let cool and then coarsely grind in a spice mill or mortar. In a blender, combine the tomato juice with the cilantro, hot pepper sauce, red wine vinegar, ginger, sugar, garlic, mustard, ground cumin and salt. Pulse until smooth. Strain the marinade into a large glass baking dish.

2. PREPARE THE VEGETABLES WITH PANEER: Skewer the cherry tomatoes and add them to the marinade along with the snowpeas, shiitakes, zucchini, onion and bell peppers; toss to coat.

3. Cook the potato in boiling water until just tender, about 20 minutes. Drain and let cool slightly. Peel the potato, quarter it lengthwise and add it to the marinade.

4. Bring a large saucepan of lightly salted water to a boil. Add the butternut squash, broccoli and cauliflower to the water and cook until crisp-tender, 1 to 2 minutes. Transfer to the marinade and toss all of the vegetables until coated. Add the *paneer,* turning it gently to coat. Cover with plastic wrap and refrigerate for 3 hours or overnight.

5. Light a charcoal grill or heat a grill pan. Grill the vegetables over medium-high heat, turning, until they are tender and lightly charred all over, 2 to 3 minutes for the tomatoes and snowpeas; 5 to 7 minutes for the potato, butternut squash, cauliflower, broccoli, mushrooms, onion and zucchini, and 8 to 10 minutes for the bell peppers. Season the vegetables with salt and black pepper. Season the *paneer* with salt and grill, turning, until lightly charred and heated through, 2 to 3 minutes. Serve the vegetables and *paneer* hot or at room temperature. —*Madhur Jaffrey*

HOMEMADE PANEER WITH INDIAN FLAVORS

MAKES ½ POUND

- 1 teaspoon black peppercorns
- ½ teaspoon cumin seeds
- 2 quarts milk
- 3 to 4 tablespoons white vinegar

1. In a small, dry skillet, toast the peppercorns with the cumin seeds over moderate heat until fragrant, about 1 minute. Let cool and then coarsely grind in a spice mill or mortar.

2. Set a large colander in the sink and line with 3 layers of moistened cheesecloth, leaving 2 inches of overhang all around. In a large saucepan, bring the milk to a boil. Reduce the heat to low, immediately add 3 tablespoons of the white vinegar and stir gently; the milk should separate into fluffy curds and watery whey. If not, add another tablespoon of vinegar. Pour the curds into the lined colander and let drain for 10 minutes.

3. Gently stir the ground spices into the curds. Gather up the corners of the cheesecloth and twist the cheese into a tight ball, squeezing out as much liquid as possible. Tie the cheesecloth with string and then transfer it to a work surface with the twisted end of the cloth off to the side. Set a cutting board on the cheese and weigh it down with heavy skillets or large cans. Let the cheese stand until firm and dry, about 5 minutes. Remove the cheesecloth before refrigerating or cutting the cheese. —*M. J.*

MAKE AHEAD The cheese can be wrapped in a damp towel and refrigerated for up to 24 hours.

chapter 12

potatoes grains

312

313

311

303

Buttermilk Mashed Potatoes with Tarragon

4 SERVINGS ✳ ⚘

It's quicker to leave the potatoes un-peeled, but if you like your mashers smooth, you can certainly go ahead and peel them before cooking.

- 4 large Yukon Gold potatoes, scrubbed and cut into large chunks
- 1 cup low-fat (1.5%) buttermilk
- 1 tablespoon snipped chives
- 1 teaspoon finely chopped tarragon

Salt and freshly ground pepper

1. In a large saucepan, cover the pota-toes with water and bring to a boil over high heat. Cook until the potatoes are tender, 10 to 15 minutes.

2. Drain the potatoes, shaking them to remove the excess water. Return the potatoes to the saucepan and mash, adding the buttermilk. Stir in the chives and the tarragon, season the mashed potatoes with salt and pepper and serve. —Sue Chapman

ONE SERVING Calories 208 kcal, Total Fat 1 gm, Saturated Fat .3 gm

Golden Mashed Potatoes with Truffle Butter

10 SERVINGS

- 6½ pounds large Yukon Gold potatoes, peeled and cut into 4-inch chunks

Salt

- 1½ cups warm milk
- 4 tablespoons unsalted butter, at room temperature

Freshly ground pepper

- 6 tablespoons truffle butter, at room temperature (see Note)

1. In a large pot, cover the potato chunks with cold water and bring to a boil. Salt the water generously and boil the potato chunks over moderately high heat until they are very tender, about 20 minutes.

2. Drain the potato chunks in a colan-der. Return the potatoes to the pot and shake the pot over moderately high heat until the potatoes are completely dry, about 1 minute. Remove the pot from the heat.

3. Using a potato masher, crush the po-tatoes in the pot. Add ¾ cup of the warm milk and the butter and season the potatoes with salt and pepper. Con-tinue mashing until the potatoes are smooth. Add the remaining ¾ cup of warm milk and the truffle butter to the potatoes and mash until thoroughly blended. Season the mashed potatoes again with salt and pepper and serve piping hot. —Marcia Kiesel

NOTE Truffle butter is available at specialty food shops or by mail from Urbani USA (800-281-2330).

Potato Gratin

8 SERVINGS

For this rich gratin, russet potatoes are parboiled in heavy cream and then baked in the reduced cream until they are golden brown.

- 3 pounds russet potatoes, peeled and sliced crosswise ¼ inch thick
- 5 cups heavy cream

Salt and freshly ground white pepper

1. Preheat the oven to 250° and butter a 9-by-13-inch baking dish. In a large pot, combine the potato slices and the heavy cream and season with salt and freshly ground white pepper. Bring to a boil and then press a round of parch-ment or wax paper on the potatoes. Simmer over moderately low heat until the potato slices are tender, 15 to 20 minutes.

2. Using a slotted spoon, transfer the potatoes to the prepared baking dish in layers. Season the potatoes with salt and white pepper as you go. Return the pot with the cream to high heat and boil, stirring constantly, until the cream is reduced to 2½ cups, 6 to 7 minutes. Pour the cream over the potatoes while shaking the baking dish.

3. Bake the potato gratin for 1½ hours, or until golden on top. Blot any excess fat and let the gratin stand 15 minutes before cutting. —Tom Colicchio

MAKE AHEAD The gratin can be pre-pared through Step 2 and refrigerated overnight.

Fried Potatoes with Cilantro

6 TO 8 SERVINGS

- 8 large baking potatoes, cut into ½-inch chunks
- 2 tablespoons sea salt
- 1¾ cups extra-virgin olive oil
- 8 garlic cloves, coarsely chopped
- 2 small dried red chiles, broken up
- 1½ cups chopped cilantro

1. In a large colander, toss the potatoes with 1 tablespoon of sea salt; let stand for 5 minutes. Pat the potatoes dry with paper towels.

2. Heat ¾ cup of the extra-virgin olive oil in each of 2 large skillets. Add half of the potatoes to each skillet, spreading them in an even layer. Fry the potatoes over moderately high heat until they are beginning to brown on the bottom, about 10 minutes. Stir and continue cooking until the potatoes are crisp and tender, about 5 minutes; adjust the heat as necessary. With a slotted spoon, transfer the potatoes to a rimmed bak-ing sheet.

3. In a small bowl, mash the garlic with the remaining 1 tablespoon of salt. Wipe out the skillets and add 2 table-spoons of the remaining olive oil to each. Add half of the garlic to each skil-let and cook over moderately low heat, stirring, until fragrant and golden, about 3 minutes. Add half of the chile pieces to each pan and cook for 1 minute. Add half of the cilantro and fried potatoes to each skillet and stir to coat the pota-toes. Cook over moderate heat, stirring, until heated through, about 3 minutes. Transfer to a large platter and serve at once. —Nancy Harmon Jenkins

Fried Potatoes with Cilantro, TOP, and Najwa's Okra Stew (p. 210).

Jonathan's Favorite Home Fries

4 TO 6 SERVINGS

These spicy sautéed potatoes go with just about anything.

- 5 medium red-skinned potatoes (about 1¼ pounds)
- 2 tablespoons unsalted butter
- 2 tablespoons canola oil
- 1 red bell pepper, cut into ¾-inch pieces
- 1 large onion, cut into ¾-inch pieces
- ¼ teaspoon cayenne pepper
- ¼ teaspoon mild pure chile powder
- ¼ teaspoon sweet paprika
- ¼ teaspoon celery seeds

Salt

1. Steam the red-skinned potatoes over boiling water until they are almost cooked through, about 15 minutes. Let the potatoes cool and then cut them into 1-inch chunks.

2. In a large cast-iron skillet, melt the butter in the canola oil until foamy. Add the red bell pepper and the onion. Cook the pepper and onion over moderately high heat until they are just softened, about 5 minutes. Stir in the potato chunks and cook over moderate heat without stirring until they are golden and crusty on the bottom, about 5 minutes. Turn the potatoes and cook, turning occasionally, until they are golden all over, about 15 minutes longer. Stir in the cayenne pepper, the chile powder, the paprika, the celery seeds and a generous pinch of salt and serve immediately. —*Jonathan King*

Chunky Fried Potato Cakes

8 SERVINGS

- 7 large russet potatoes, peeled and halved

Salt

- ½ cup milk
- 3 tablespoons unsalted butter

Vegetable oil, for frying

1. Put the russet potato halves in a large pot of salted water and bring to a boil. Cook over moderately high heat until the potatoes are tender, about 25 minutes. Drain the potatoes, return them to the pot and shake over high heat to dry the potatoes, about 30 seconds. Partially mash the potatoes with a fork, blending in the milk and the butter. Season the mashed potatoes with salt. Let cool slightly and then shape the mashed potatoes into eight 1½-inch-thick patties.

2. In a large skillet, heat ¼ inch of vegetable oil until shimmering. Add 4 of the potato cakes to the skillet; cook over moderate heat until they are browned and crusty, about 4 minutes per side. Transfer the fried potato cakes to a warm oven while you fry the rest. Serve the potato cakes hot. —*Fred Eric*

Crisp Potato-Parsnip Cake

10 SERVINGS

- 4 tablespoons unsalted butter, melted
- 4 pounds medium Yukon Gold potatoes, peeled and sliced crosswise ¼ inch thick
- ½ pound parsnips, peeled and sliced crosswise ¼ inch thick
- ¾ teaspoon minced rosemary

Salt and freshly ground pepper

- 1¼ cups chicken stock or canned low-sodium broth

1. Preheat the oven to 350°. Lightly butter a round 3-quart glass or ceramic baking dish. Line the dish with parchment paper and brush the paper with some of the melted butter.

2. Arrange a single layer of overlapping potato slices and parsnip slices in an attractive pattern in the bottom of the prepared baking dish. Carefully layer ⅓ of the remaining potato slices and parsnip slices on top. Brush the potato and parsnip slices with some of the melted butter, sprinkle with half of the minced rosemary and then season generously with salt and freshly ground pepper. Repeat the layering, ending with parsnip and potato slices and seasoning generously with salt and pepper in between the layers.

3. Pour the chicken stock over the potato and parsnip slices. Cover with a sheet of parchment paper that is slightly larger than the baking dish. Set a heavy ovenproof skillet in the baking dish to weight down the potato-parsnip cake and bake the cake in the middle of the oven for 1 hour and 15 minutes, or until the chicken stock is absorbed and the vegetables are tender.

4. Preheat the broiler. Remove the skillet and the parchment paper and broil the potato-parsnip cake 8 inches from the heat for about 10 minutes, rotating the dish to evenly brown and crisp the vegetables. Let the cake stand for 15 minutes. Cover the baking dish with a flat cookie sheet and, using oven mitts, carefully invert the cake onto the cookie sheet. Remove the baking dish and parchment paper. Brush the potato-parsnip cake with melted butter and season with salt.

5. Broil the potato-parsnip cake 8 inches from the heat for about 12 minutes, rotating the cookie sheet as necessary to evenly brown and crisp the cake. Slide the potato-parsnip cake onto a large platter, cut the cake into wedges and serve. —*Grace Parisi*

MAKE AHEAD The potato-parsnip cake can be prepared through Step 4 and refrigerated for 2 days. Reheat in the oven and then crisp the top under the broiler.

Parmesan Roasted Potatoes

6 SERVINGS

These tiny roasted potatoes with Parmesan crusts are delicious as a side dish or as an hors d'eouvres, served with toothpicks.

- 2 pounds tiny new potatoes
- 2 large eggs, beaten

Salt

- ¾ cup (about 3 ounces) freshly grated Parmesan cheese
- ¼ teaspoon cayenne pepper

Parmesan Roasted Potatoes

1. Preheat the oven to 400° and line a large rimmed baking sheet with foil. Steam the new potatoes over boiling water until they are just tender, 10 to 12 minutes. Transfer the potatoes to a plate to cool slightly.

2. Strain the eggs into a soup plate and season lightly with salt. In another soup plate, combine the grated Parmesan cheese with the cayenne pepper. Working in small batches, coat the steamed new potatoes with the egg, shaking off the excess, and then toss in the Parmesan mixture. Set the Parmesan-coated potatoes on the baking sheet and roast for about 25 minutes, or until the potatoes are golden. Serve the potatoes hot or at room temperature. —*Grace Parisi*

MAKE AHEAD The potatoes can be kept at room temperature for 3 hours.

Crispy Twice-Roasted Potatoes

12 SERVINGS

    4 **pounds small Yukon Gold
       potatoes**
    3 **tablespoons extra-virgin
       olive oil**
Fine sea salt
Coarse salt

1. Preheat the oven to 375°. Pierce the Yukon Gold potatoes and spread them on 2 rimmed baking sheets. Roast

the potatoes for about 1 hour, or until they are very tender.

2. Halve the roasted potatoes and smash them lightly on the baking sheets with the bottom of a glass. Drizzle with the olive oil, sprinkle with fine sea salt and roast for 45 minutes longer, or until browned and crisp, turning once. Serve the potatoes hot, with coarse salt for sprinkling. —*Anne Disrude*

ONE SERVING Calories 224 kcal, Total Fat 5.5 gm, Saturated Fat 0.8 gm

Grilled Potato-Morel Pierogies

6 SERVINGS

Strain the morel soaking liquid in this recipe and save it for adding depth of flavor to soups or stews.

    1 **cup (1 ounce) dried morels**
    1 **cup boiling water**
    2 **cups all-purpose flour**
Salt
    2 **large eggs, beaten with
       ¼ cup water**
  1½ **pounds Idaho potatoes, peeled
       and cut into 2-inch chunks**
    ½ **cup warm milk**
    ¼ **cup sour cream**
    2 **tablespoons freshly grated
       Parmesan cheese**
    1 **tablespoon unsalted butter**
Freshly ground pepper
Vegetable oil, for coating
Celery leaves, for garnish

1. In a heatproof bowl, soak the dried morels in the boiling water until they are softened, about 20 minutes. Rub the morels to loosen any grit and then remove them with a slotted spoon and coarsely chop.

2. In a large bowl, combine the flour with ½ teaspoon of salt. Add the egg mixture and stir until the dough just comes together. Transfer the dough to a lightly floured work surface and knead briefly until soft and smooth. Wrap the dough in plastic and set aside at room temperature for 30 minutes.

3. Meanwhile, cook the potato chunks in a large saucepan of boiling salted

water until they are tender, about 20 minutes; drain. Return the potatoes to the pan and shake over high heat to dry them, about 1 minute. Using a potato masher, mash the potatoes. Mash in the warm milk, the sour cream, the Parmesan cheese and the butter. Stir in the morels and season with salt and pepper. Transfer the potato filling to a bowl and let cool slightly.

4. Cut the dough in half and pat each piece into a disk. On a well-floured work surface, roll out the disks to 9-inch rounds. Cover the rounds of dough with plastic wrap and let them stand for 15 minutes.

5. On a floured work surface, roll out 1 round of dough at a time to a ¹⁄₁₆-inch thickness. Using a 4-inch biscuit cutter, stamp out 9 smaller rounds. Lightly moisten the edge of 1 round and dollop 1 rounded tablespoon of the potato filling on half of it. Pat the filling slightly and then fold the dough over the filling to form a half moon; press the edges to seal. Set aside on a floured platter. Repeat with the rest of the dough rounds and potato filling.

6. Cook half the pierogies at a time in a large pot of boiling salted water until they rise to the surface, about 1 minute. Using a slotted spoon, transfer the pierogies to paper towels and dry. In a large bowl, toss the pierogies with just enough oil to coat.

7. Light a grill or heat a grill pan. Grill the pierogies over a hot fire, turning once, until they are browned, about 3 minutes per side. Alternatively, cook the pierogies in the grill pan over moderately high heat for about 3 minutes per side. Remove the pierogies from the heat. Add the celery leaves and grill until lightly charred, about 1 minute per side. Transfer the pierogies to a platter and garnish with the grilled celery leaves. —*Marcia Kiesel*

MAKE AHEAD The pierogies can be prepared through Step 5 and then frozen for up to 1 month. Boil the frozen

Grilled Potato-Morel Pierogies

pierogies for the same amount of time as indicated for the fresh ones.

WINE The rich, smoky filling in these pierogies makes them perfect foils for a full-flavored Merlot with velvety tannins, like the 1994 Columbia Crest Estate Series from Washington State or the 1995 Meerlust from South Africa.

Whipped Sweet Potatoes with Crispy Shallots

10 SERVINGS ✳

5 pounds medium to large sweet potatoes
1 stick (4 ounces) unsalted butter, at room temperature
½ teaspoon ground cardamom
Salt and freshly ground white pepper
Vegetable oil, for frying
¾ pound shallots, thinly sliced

1. Preheat the oven to 400°. Pierce the sweet potatoes with the tip of a knife and bake them for about 40 minutes, or until the sweet potatoes are tender. Turn the oven down to 250°.

2. Slit the skins and scoop the sweet potatoes into a large bowl. Add the butter and cardamom and beat with an electric mixer at low speed until the sweet potatoes are smooth and fluffy. Season the whipped sweet potatoes with salt and white pepper. Transfer the sweet potatoes to a serving dish and keep in the warm oven.

3. In a large deep skillet, heat 1 inch of vegetable oil until shimmering. Add half of the shallots and fry them over moderate heat, stirring, until they are crisp, 2 to 3 minutes. Using a slotted spoon, transfer the shallots to paper towels. Sprinkle the fried shallots with salt. Repeat with the remaining shallots. Scatter the shallots over the whipped sweet potatoes and serve. —*Grace Parisi*

MAKE AHEAD The recipe can be prepared 1 day ahead. Store the shallots in an airtight container. Rewarm and rewhip the potatoes; recrisp the shallots in the oven if necessary.

Sweet Potato Oven-Fries with Lemon-Mint Gremolata

10 SERVINGS ✳

2 tablespoons finely chopped flat-leaf parsley
1 tablespoon finely chopped spearmint
1 teaspoon finely chopped lemon zest
½ teaspoon finely chopped garlic
3 tablespoons canola oil
5 pounds medium sweet potatoes, each one cut lengthwise into 16 wedges
3 tablespoons extra-virgin olive oil

¼ teaspoon cayenne pepper
Salt

1. Preheat the oven to 450°. On a work surface, combine the parsley, spearmint, lemon zest and garlic and chop together until blended. Transfer the *gremolata* to a bowl; stir in the canola oil.

2. In a large bowl, toss the sweet potatoes with the olive oil and cayenne. Season with salt. Spread the potatoes in a single layer on 2 large rimmed nonstick baking sheets. Roast on the upper and middle racks of the oven for 45 minutes, or until tender and browned in spots; shift the pans halfway through to

Whipped Sweet Potatoes with Crispy Shallots

ensure even cooking. Mound the fries on a platter; pass the *gremolata* separately. —*Grace Parisi*

MAKE AHEAD The oven fries and *gremolata* can be refrigerated overnight. Bring the *gremolata* to room temperature. Spread the fries on the baking sheets in a single layer and reheat in a 450° oven before serving.

Sweet Potatoes with Poblano Chile Rajas

8 SERVINGS

In the Southwest, strips of cooked chiles or bell peppers are called *rajas*. Here, they're used to accent a sweet potato side dish.

- 3 pounds sweet potatoes, peeled and sliced ½ inch thick
- 3 tablespoons unsalted butter, melted
- ¾ teaspoon coarse sea salt
- 6 medium poblano chiles
- 3 small onions, sliced crosswise ½ inch thick, separated into rings
- 1 cup (loosely packed) cilantro leaves
- ⅓ cup crème fraîche or sour cream

1. Preheat the oven to 375°. Generously butter a 3-quart gratin dish. Arrange the sweet potato slices in an overlapping layer in the prepared dish. Brush the potato slices with 1½ tablespoons of the melted butter and sprinkle with the sea salt. Bake for about 40 minutes, or until tender and just beginning to brown.

2. Roast the poblano chiles directly over a gas flame or under the broiler, turning, until charred all over. Transfer the chiles to a bowl, cover with plastic wrap and let steam for 15 minutes. Peel, core and seed the chiles; cut them into ¼-inch strips.

3. Transfer the poblano chiles to a bowl, add the onion rings and toss with the remaining 1½ tablespoons of butter. Scatter the mixture over the sweet potatoes.

4. Reduce the oven temperature to 350° and roast the sweet potatoes for about 35 minutes more, or until the poblanos and the onions are tender and beginning to brown. Scatter the cilantro leaves on top of the sweet potatoes, drizzle with the crème fraîche and serve. —*Robert Del Grande*

MAKE AHEAD The sweet potatoes can be prepared through Step 3 and refrigerated overnight. Let the sweet potatoes return to room temperature before baking.

Pan-Roasted Sweet Potatoes with Fennel

10 SERVINGS

- 4 pounds sweet potatoes, peeled and cut into 1½-inch chunks
- 4 fennel bulbs, halved lengthwise and cut into ¾-inch wedges, some of the feathery tops finely chopped
- ¼ cup extra-virgin olive oil
- 1 tablespoon light brown sugar
- ¼ teaspoon ground mace
- Salt and freshly ground pepper

1. Preheat the oven to 400°. In a bowl, toss the sweet potato chunks and the fennel wedges with the olive oil, brown sugar and mace; season the mixture with salt and pepper.

2. Spread the sweet potatoes and fennel wedges in a large nonstick roasting pan. Roast for about 1 hour, stirring occasionally, until the sweet potatoes and the fennel wedges are tender and caramelized. Transfer the vegetables to a platter, sprinkle with the fennel tops and serve. —*Grace Parisi*

MAKE AHEAD The roasted sweet potatoes and fennel wedges can be refrigerated overnight. Reheat in a 400° oven before serving.

ONE SERVING Calories 211 kcal, Total Fat 6.2 gm, Saturated Fat 1 gm

White Rice with Black Beans and Winter Squash

12 SERVINGS

The black beans need to soak overnight, so plan accordingly. Rinsing the rice before cooking it will keep the grains from sticking together.

- 1½ cups (10 ounces) dried black beans, picked over and rinsed
- 1 small onion, halved
- 1 bay leaf
- 3 quarts plus 3½ cups water
- Salt
- 3 cups long-grain rice
- One 2-pound butternut squash— peeled, seeded and cut into ½-inch dice

1. Put the black beans in a large bowl and add enough water to cover. Let the beans soak overnight. Drain the beans before using.

2. In a large saucepan, combine the black beans with the onion halves, the bay leaf and 12 cups of the water. Bring to a boil and then reduce the heat to low and simmer, stirring occasionally, until tender, about 1 hour. Drain the black beans, transfer them to a bowl and season with salt. Keep covered until ready to use.

3. In a large saucepan, rinse the long-grain rice in several changes of water and then drain. Return the rice to the saucepan, add the remaining 3½ cups of water and bring to a boil. Add 2 teaspoons of salt, stir in the diced butternut squash and return to a rolling boil. Cover, reduce the heat to low and cook without uncovering for 14 minutes. Uncover the saucepan and stir the rice to fluff it. Cover the pan again and let the rice stand off the heat for 5 minutes. Stir in the black beans and serve at once. —*Marcia Kiesel*

ONE SERVING Calories 284 kcal, Total Fat .7 gm, Saturated Fat 0.2 gm

FRONT TO BACK: Country Corn Bread Stuffing (p. 255), Sweet Potatoes with Poblano Chile Rajas and Green Beans with Sea Salt (p. 271).

Fragrant Orange Rice

4 SERVINGS

 1 tablespoon unsalted butter
 1 small onion, finely chopped
 1 cup (7 ounces) basmati rice
 1¼ cups chicken stock or canned
    low-sodium chicken broth
 ½ cup fresh orange juice
 1 tablespoon finely chopped
    golden raisins
 2 teaspoons minced fresh ginger
 1 teaspoon finely grated orange zest
Pinch of salt

Melt the butter in a medium saucepan. Add the onion and cook over moderate heat until softened but not browned, about 4 minutes. Add the rice; cook, stirring constantly, for 3 minutes. Add the stock, orange juice, raisins, ginger, zest and salt and bring to a boil. Cook, covered, over low heat for 18 minutes. Fluff with a fork, cover and let rest for 5 minutes before serving. —*John Ash*

Saffron Rice

8 SERVINGS

 ¼ teaspoon saffron threads
 3 tablespoons boiling water
 4 cups cold water
 2 cups (14 ounces) basmati rice

Persian Pilaf with Lime and Green Beans

1. In a small heatproof bowl, crumble the saffron into the boiling water. In a large saucepan, combine the cold water with the rice; bring to a boil. Cover and cook over low heat until the water is absorbed and the rice is tender, about 17 minutes. Fluff the rice with a fork.

2. Transfer 1 cup of the cooked rice to the bowl of saffron water and stir until yellow. Spoon the white rice into a large shallow bowl, top with the saffron rice and serve at once. —*Rori Spinelli*

Peppercorn Pulao

8 SERVINGS

Crushed black peppercorns give a nice bite to this simple but elegant Indian rice pilaf.

 3 tablespoons vegetable oil
 2 medium onions, thinly sliced
 1½ teaspoons coarsely crushed black
    peppercorns
 ⅛ teaspoon turmeric
 3¼ cups water
 2 cups (14 ounces) basmati rice,
    rinsed well and drained
 1¼ teaspoons salt
 1 tablespoon unsalted butter
 ⅓ cup broken raw cashews
 1 cup frozen peas

1. In a 4-quart enameled cast-iron casserole, heat 2 tablespoons of the oil. Add one of the onions and cook over moderately high heat, stirring occasionally, until the onion is softened but not browned, about 4 minutes. Add the peppercorns and turmeric and cook, stirring, until fragrant, about 1 minute. Add the water, rice and salt and stir well. Bring to a boil and then cover tightly, reduce the heat to low and cook for 15 minutes.

2. Meanwhile, in a large skillet, melt the butter in the remaining 1 tablespoon of oil. Add the cashews to the skillet and cook, stirring constantly, until golden brown, 4 to 5 minutes. Using a slotted spoon, transfer the cashews to paper towels, leaving as much oil behind as possible. Add the remaining onion and

cook over moderate heat, stirring constantly, until the onion turns deep brown, about 8 minutes. Add the browned onion to the cashews.

3. When the rice is cooked, stir in the peas. Cover until the peas have warmed through, about 3 minutes. Turn the rice into a bowl and garnish with the onion and the cashews. Serve the pulao immediately. —*Maya Kaimal*

Persian Pilaf with Lime and Green Beans

6 SERVINGS

This vegetarian pilaf looks like a slightly collapsed cake with a crust of reddish-gold sliced potatoes. Underneath are layers of basmati rice and green beans and tomatoes.

 2 cups (14 ounces) basmati rice
 ¼ cup vegetable oil
 2 large shallots, finely chopped
 ½ pound green beans, cut into
    1-inch lengths
 3 plum tomatoes—peeled, seeded
    and finely chopped
 1 teaspoon tomato paste
 ¾ teaspoon cinnamon
Salt
10¼ cups plus 1 tablespoon water
 1 tablespoon fresh lime juice
 2 tablespoons unsalted butter
 ⅛ teaspoon turmeric
 1 large boiling potato, peeled
    and sliced ⅛ inch thick

1. Soak the basmati rice in a large bowl of lukewarm water for 30 minutes. Drain well.

2. Meanwhile, heat the oil in a medium saucepan until shimmering. Add the shallots and cook over moderately high heat, stirring, until lightly browned, about 4 minutes. Add the green beans and cook, stirring, until the beans are bright green but still crisp, about 4 minutes. Add the tomatoes, tomato paste, ¼ teaspoon of the cinnamon, ¾ teaspoon of salt and 3 tablespoons of water and bring to a simmer. Cover and cook over low heat until the green beans are tender, about 12 minutes. Stir in the lime juice and transfer the green bean mixture to a bowl.

3. In a large pot, combine 10 cups of the water with 1½ tablespoons of salt and bring to a boil. Stir in the rice and return to a boil. Cook the rice until it is barely tender, about 5 minutes. Drain the rice.

4. Melt the butter in a 3-quart nonstick saucepan over low heat. Stir in the remaining 2 tablespoons of water and the turmeric. Arrange the potato slices, slightly overlapping, in the bottom of the saucepan. Spread one third of the rice over the potatoes and top with half of the green bean mixture and ¼ teaspoon of the cinnamon. Repeat the layering, ending with a final layer of rice.

5. Pat the rice to make it compact, cover and cook over moderately high heat for 4 minutes. Reduce the heat to moderately low and cook for 4 minutes. Remove the lid and stretch a kitchen towel over the saucepan, being sure not to let the towel touch the rice. Cover with the lid and then fold the corners of the towel up and away from the heat. Cook the rice cake over very low heat for 30 minutes.

6. Remove the lid and the towel and run a thin bladed spatula around the edge of the saucepan. Set a large plate over the saucepan and carefully invert the rice pilaf onto the plate. Serve immediately. —*Madhur Jaffrey*

Wild Rice with Escarole

10 SERVINGS

- 3 quarts cold water
- 2½ cups (14 ounces) wild rice
- Salt
- ¼ cup dried currants
- ¼ cup hot water
- Two 1½-pound heads escarole, cored, leaves separated
- ¼ cup extra-virgin olive oil
- 4 shallots, thinly sliced
- 2 garlic cloves, minced
- 1 tablespoon fresh lemon juice
- ½ teaspoon finely grated lemon zest
- Freshly ground pepper

1. In a large saucepan, bring the cold water to a boil. Add the wild rice and a large pinch of salt, cover and simmer until tender, about 30 minutes. Drain the rice.

2. In a bowl, soak the currants in the hot water for 10 minutes. Drain.

3. In a pot of boiling salted water, cook the escarole leaves until they are tender, about 4 minutes. Drain and let cool. Squeeze the escarole leaves dry and then coarsely chop them.

4. Heat the olive oil in a large enameled cast-iron casserole. Add the shallots and cook over low heat until softened, about 5 minutes. Add the garlic and cook until fragrant, about 3 minutes. Add the cooked escarole and the soaked currants and cook over moderate heat, stirring, for 2 minutes. Add the wild rice and cook until warmed through. Stir in the lemon juice and the lemon zest and season with salt and freshly ground pepper. Serve hot. —*Marcia Kiesel*

MAKE AHEAD The recipe can be prepared through Step 3 and refrigerated overnight.

ONE SERVING Calories 224 kcal, Total Fat 6.3 gm, Saturated Fat 0.9 gm

Stir-Fried Sushi Rice with Morels, Ham and Asparagus

6 SERVINGS

- 2 cups (½ pound) Japanese sushi-style rice
- 2½ cups water, at room temperature
- 1 cup (1 ounce) dried morels
- 1 cup boiling water
- 1 pound asparagus
- 3 tablespoons unsalted butter
- 2 large shallots, minced
- ¼ pound baked ham, cut into ¼-inch dice (1 cup)
- Salt and freshly ground pepper
- ½ teaspoon Asian sesame oil

1. In a medium saucepan, combine the rice with the room temperature water

ingredients 101

Legumes are plants bearing seeds in pods that split when ripe. Lentils, beans and peas are the dried seeds, or pulses.
Grains are the edible seeds of various plants belonging to the grass family. Wheat, corn, rice and oats are the most familiar grains. Plant researchers debate whether such grains as *farro* are wheat species or just wheatlike grains.
Couscous and *fregola* are commonly mistaken for grains. They are actually grain products, made from coarsely ground durum wheat that has been sprinkled with water and rolled or grated to form grainlike bits that are similar to pasta.
Sources for special legumes, grains and couscous include health food stores and specialty food shops. Items are also available by mail order from Kalustyan's (212-685-3451).

and bring to a boil. Reduce the heat to low, cover and cook the rice for 15 minutes. Remove the pan from the heat and let the rice stand, covered, for 5 minutes. Uncover and fluff the rice. Spread the rice on a large baking sheet and let cool to room temperature.

2. Meanwhile, in a heatproof bowl, soak the morels in the boiling water until they are softened, about 20 minutes. Rub the morels to loosen any grit and then remove them from the soaking liquid with a slotted spoon. Let the soaking liquid stand for 5 minutes so that the grit falls to the bottom. Pour off ½ cup of the soaking liquid, leaving any grit behind, and reserve the liquid.

3. Cook the asparagus in a medium saucepan of boiling salted water until just tender, about 4 minutes. Drain and rinse the asparagus under cold water and then cut the asparagus into ½-inch lengths.

4. In a wok or very large skillet, melt the butter over low heat. Add the shallots and cook, stirring, until softened but not

Stir-Fried Sushi Rice with Morels, Ham and Asparagus

browned, about 4 minutes. Add the soaked morels, the cooked asparagus and the ham and stir-fry for 2 minutes. Add the sushi-style rice and cook over moderate heat, breaking the rice up with a spatula. Add the reserved ½ cup of morel soaking liquid and stir-fry until heated through, about 4 minutes. Season the rice with salt and freshly ground pepper and then stir in the sesame oil. Serve at once. —*Marcia Kiesel*

Risotto with Red Wine and Rosemary

6 SERVINGS

Red wine risotto is traditional in many of Italy's grape-growing regions, particularly in Piedmont, where it is made with the local Barolo. This hearty risotto is delicious on its own or as an accompaniment to roasted meats and game. You can also stir in leftover meats and poultry, braised wild mushrooms or root vegetables. Alan Tardi of Follonico restaurant in New York City adds a handful of tiny Champagne grapes at the last minute for a surprising sweet counterpoint.

About 4¼ cups rich unsalted
    chicken or veal stock or
    canned low-sodium broth
1½ tablespoons unsalted butter
  1 teaspoon extra-virgin olive oil
  2 medium shallots, finely chopped
One 2-inch sprig rosemary, or
    1 teaspoon dried rosemary
  1 bay leaf
1½ cups (10½ ounces) Italian
    rice for risotto, preferably
    Carnaroli or Vialone Nano
    (see box, right)
1½ cups full-bodied red wine, such as
    Italian Barolo or Barbera
  ½ cup (2 ounces) freshly grated
    Parmesan cheese
Salt and freshly ground pepper
Scant ½ cup Champagne grapes
    (optional)

I. In a medium saucepan, bring the stock to a boil over high heat. Lower the heat to maintain a bare simmer.

2. Meanwhile, in a large heavy saucepan, melt 1 tablespoon of the butter in the olive oil over low heat. Add the shallots, rosemary and bay leaf, cover and cook, stirring occasionally, until the shallots are translucent, about 4 minutes. Uncover, increase the heat to moderate and add the rice. Cook, stirring constantly, until the grains look chalky with a white dot in the center of each, 4 to 5 minutes.

3. Add 1 cup of the wine to the saucepan and cook, stirring, until it has been absorbed by the rice. Add the remaining ½ cup of wine and boil, stirring frequently, until absorbed.

4. Stir ½ cup of the stock into the rice and simmer, stirring frequently, until the liquid is almost absorbed. Continue adding stock, ½ cup at a time, as it is absorbed; the risotto is done when the rice is tender yet still firm in the center and the liquid is creamy, 20 to 25 minutes. Discard the bay leaf and rosemary sprig. Stir in the remaining ½ tablespoon of butter and the Parmesan and season the risotto with salt and pepper. Fold in the grapes and serve immediately. —*Sally Schneider*

ONE SERVING Calories 286 kcal, Total Fat 7.5 gm, Saturated Fat 4.1 gm

WINE A Piedmontese wine with woodsy, licorice nuances is a classic match with this dish. Look for a Barbaresco, such as the 1995 Prunotto or the 1995 Ceretto Asij, a Barbera d'Asti, such as the 1997 Michele Chiarlo, or a Barolo, such as the 1995 Ceretto Zonchera.

Creamy Asparagus Risotto

10 SERVINGS

This risotto gets its velvety texture from the asparagus puree that's stirred in before serving.

2½ pounds asparagus, trimmed,
    tips cut off and reserved
Salt
  8 cups chicken stock or canned
    low-sodium broth

rice pantry

Carnaroli The ideal rice for a classic stirred risotto. Its grains are tender yet firm, and they make the liquid luxuriously creamy.

Vialone Nano A chewier, heartier rice, this is the kind Venetians favor for their risottos. The cooked grains won't get mushy even if they stand for a while. Reach for Vialone Nano when making a risotto cake or when using the chef's trick of cooking risotto halfway through and finishing it right before serving. This rice can absorb up to 30 percent more liquid than the other varieties, so plan accordingly.

¼ cup extra-virgin olive oil
  3 medium shallots, minced
  3 garlic cloves, minced
3½ cups (1 pound) Arborio rice
¾ cup dry white wine
  1 tablespoon unsalted butter
¾ cup (3 ounces) freshly grated
    Parmesan cheese
Freshly ground pepper

I. Cook the asparagus tips in a medium saucepan of boiling salted water until they are just tender, about 2 minutes. Using a slotted spoon, transfer the asparagus tips to a colander and rinse them in cold water. Drain the asparagus tips well.

2. Break the asparagus stalks in half. Add the asparagus stalks to the boiling water and cook until they are very tender, about 10 minutes. Reserve ⅓ cup of the cooking water and then drain the asparagus stalks. Puree the asparagus stalks with the reserved cooking water in a food processor. Using a rubber spatula, work the asparagus puree through a coarse sieve; you should have about 2 cups.

3. In a medium saucepan, bring the stock to a simmer. Meanwhile, heat the olive oil in a large, heavy saucepan. Add the shallots and cook over low heat,

stirring frequently with a wooden spoon, until softened but not browned, about 4 minutes. Add the garlic and cook until the shallots are lightly browned, about 2 minutes. Add the rice and stir over moderate heat to coat the grains of rice with the olive oil. Pour in the wine and continue stirring until the wine is almost evaporated, about 2 minutes.

4. Add 1 cup of the hot stock to the rice and stir constantly until it is almost absorbed. Continue adding the stock, 1 cup at a time, stirring constantly until the stock is absorbed before adding more. When the rice is almost tender, after about 15 to 20 minutes, add the asparagus puree. Continue to cook, stirring, until the rice is tender but still firm to the bite, about 4 minutes. Add the asparagus tips to the risotto and stir for 1 minute to heat through.

5. Remove the asparagus risotto from the heat and then stir in the butter and Parmesan cheese. Season the asparagus risotto with salt and pepper and let it stand for 2 minutes. Spoon the asparagus risotto into shallow bowls and serve. —*Lori De Mori*

WINE The 1997 Michele Chiarlo Gavi di Gavi from Piedmont is a delicate, crisp wine that harmonizes beautifully with the fresh flavor of the Creamy Asparagus Risotto.

Creamy Asparagus Risotto

Risotto with Pancetta and Wild Mushrooms

6 SERVINGS

Texture is paramount in this risotto: the salty crunch of the pancetta serves as a palate-pleasing counterpoint to the tenderness of the mushrooms, with the al dente rice marking a midpoint between the two.

> 8 paper-thin slices (about 2 ounces) of pancetta or bacon
> 1 tablespoon extra-virgin olive oil
> 1 pound mixed mushrooms, such as chanterelles, cremini and Portobellos, thickly sliced

Sea salt

> 3 tablespoons unsalted butter
> 1 teaspoon finely chopped parsley or tarragon
> 5 cups chicken stock or canned low-sodium broth
> 1 garlic clove, lightly smashed
> 1 shallot, minced
> 1½ cups Arborio rice
> ½ cup (2 ounces) freshly grated Parmigiano-Reggiano cheese, plus shavings for garnish
> 2 tablespoons heavy cream

Freshly ground white pepper

1. Preheat the broiler. Arrange the pancetta slices on a baking sheet in a single layer and broil for 1 to 2 minutes, or until golden and sizzling. Drain on paper towels and then crumble.

2. In a large nonstick skillet, heat the olive oil. Add the mushrooms, season with sea salt and cook over high heat, stirring, just until the mushrooms exude their juices, 3 to 4 minutes. Transfer the mushrooms and their liquid to a strainer set over a bowl and press lightly on the mushrooms; reserve the liquid. Wipe out the skillet and add 1 tablespoon of the butter. Return the mushrooms to the skillet and cook, stirring, until tender and just beginning to brown, about 3 minutes. Add the parsley, cover and keep warm.

3. In a medium saucepan, combine the stock with the reserved mushroom liquid, bring to a simmer and then keep warm over low heat. In a large, deep nonstick skillet, melt 1 tablespoon of the butter. Add the garlic and cook over moderate heat until fragrant. Add the shallot and cook until softened but not browned, 3 to 4 minutes; discard the garlic. Add the rice; stir until the grains are thoroughly coated with butter.

4. Add 1 cup of the hot stock to the pan and cook, stirring constantly, until the rice has absorbed most of the stock, 1 to 2 minutes. Continue to cook the risotto, adding the stock 1 cup at a time and stirring constantly between additions until it is absorbed. Cook the risotto until it has a creamy, porridgelike consistency, about 20 minutes.

5. Remove the risotto from the heat and stir in the grated Parmigiano-Reggiano, the cream and the remaining 1 tablespoon of butter. Season with salt and white pepper and transfer to warm soup plates. Garnish the risotto with the cooked mushrooms and pancetta and shavings of Parmigiano-Reggiano. Serve immediately. —*Frédéric Anton*

WINE The wild mushrooms in this dish suggest an Italian red, such as a Barolo or Chianti, or a fine Bordeaux, such as a Saint-Estèphe or Pauillac.

Oven-Baked Polenta

6 SERVINGS

Use a well-greased, wide ovenproof saucepan for this fuss-free polenta so that a large quantity of the cornmeal is exposed to the direct heat of the oven. This method coaxes more flavor from the corn by toasting it as it cooks. The resulting polenta is soft and tender, with a lovely sheen. As a guide, for soft polenta, use five parts liquid to one part cornmeal; for firmer polenta, use four parts liquid to one part cornmeal.

> 2 cups medium-coarse or coarse organic stone-ground cornmeal
> 8 or 10 cups cool water
> 2 tablespoons unsalted butter or olive oil

Salt

Risotto with Pancetta and Wild Mushrooms

Preheat the oven to 350°. Butter a heavy 12-inch ovenproof saucepan. Stir together the cornmeal, water, butter and 2 teaspoons of salt in the prepared saucepan. Bake the polenta uncovered for 1 hour and 20 minutes. Stir the polenta, season with salt and bake for 10 minutes longer. Remove from the oven and let the polenta rest for 5 minutes before pouring it into a buttered bowl. —*Paula Wolfert*

Creamy Polenta with Tomato-Corn Ragout

6 SERVINGS

Like pasta, polenta can be a quick main dish any time of the year. If you use nonstick pans, cleanup is fast too.

    8 cups water
Salt
 1½ cups coarse polenta
  ½ cup mascarpone cheese, plus
       more for serving
  ½ cup (2 ounces) freshly grated
       Parmesan cheese
    2 tablespoons unsalted butter
Freshly ground pepper
    1 tablespoon canola oil
    1 cup finely chopped Vidalia onion
 2½ cups fresh corn kernels
       (from 4 ears)
    2 tablespoons finely chopped
       seeded jalapeño
 1½ pounds tomatoes—cored,
       seeded and coarsely chopped
  ¼ cup coarsely chopped basil
  ¼ cup coarsely chopped mint
    6 thyme sprigs, for garnish

1. Bring the water to a boil in a medium nonstick saucepan. Add a pinch of salt and then slowly add the polenta in a steady, thin stream, stirring constantly, to avoid lumps. Cook the polenta over moderately low heat, stirring often, until it is tender and very thick, about 35 minutes. Remove the pan from the heat and stir in ½ cup of the mascarpone cheese, the Parmesan cheese and 1 tablespoon of the butter. Season the polenta with salt and pepper and keep warm.

Creamy Polenta with Tomato-Corn Ragout

2. Meanwhile, melt the remaining 1 tablespoon of butter in the canola oil in a large nonstick skillet. Add the Vidalia onion and cook over moderately high heat until the onion is softened but not browned, about 4 minutes. Add the corn kernels and the jalapeño and cook until the corn is tender, about 5 minutes. Stir in the tomatoes, season with salt and pepper and cook until the tomatoes are just warmed through and some of their juices have been released, about 5 minutes. Stir in the basil and mint.

3. Stir the polenta, add a little hot water if it is too thick and spoon into bowls. Top the polenta with the tomato-corn ragout, garnish with thyme sprigs and serve hot. Pass more of the mascarpone cheese at the table. —*Grace Parisi*

WINE A round, rich Merlot would complement the polenta perfectly and have enough edge to balance the tomato-corn ragout. Consider the 1995 Meerlust from South Africa or the 1996 Silverado from California.

Grilled Polenta with Mushrooms and Toasted Pumpkin Seeds

8 SERVINGS

This polenta makes a great side dish for grilled meat, but it can also stand alone as a first course. Serve roasted heads of garlic alongside.

POLENTA

    6 cups chicken stock or canned
       low-sodium broth
 1¼ cups (6 ounces) polenta
  ¼ cup (1½ ounces) crumbled
       Roquefort cheese
    2 tablespoons unsalted butter
    2 tablespoons coarsely chopped
       parsley
Salt and freshly ground pepper
TOPPING
  ¼ cup raw pumpkin seeds
    2 tablespoons unsalted butter
    2 shallots, sliced
    1 garlic clove, finely chopped
  ½ pound small white mushrooms,
       stems trimmed
  ½ pound fresh morels or cremini
       mushrooms, halved if large

Grilled Polenta with Mushrooms and Toasted Pumpkin Seeds

½ pound chanterelle mushrooms, stems trimmed, halved if large

Salt and freshly ground pepper

1 tablespoon sage leaves

½ cup red wine

½ cup chicken stock or canned low-sodium broth

½ cup heavy cream

1 tablespoon coarsely chopped parsley

2 tablespoons olive oil

I. MAKE THE POLENTA: Butter a 9-by-13-inch baking dish. In a medium saucepan, bring the chicken stock to a boil. Gradually whisk in the polenta until smooth. Cook over moderately low heat, stirring often with a wooden spoon, until the polenta pulls away from the side of the pan, about 15 minutes. Remove from the heat and beat in the Roquefort, butter and parsley. Season with salt and pepper. Pour the polenta into the prepared baking dish and smooth the top. Cover with plastic wrap and refrigerate until firm, at least 2 hours or overnight.

2. MAKE THE TOPPING: In a small skillet, toast the pumpkin seeds over moderate heat until lightly browned, about 4 minutes. Transfer the seeds to a plate to cool completely.

3. Melt the butter in a large enameled cast-iron casserole. Add the shallots and garlic and cook over moderate heat, stirring occasionally, until softened but not browned, about 3 minutes. Add all of the mushrooms and season with salt and pepper. Cook over moderately high heat until the mushroom liquid has evaporated and the mushrooms are lightly browned, about 8 minutes. Add the sage and wine and cook until the liquid has reduced by half, about 2 minutes. Add the chicken stock and simmer for 2 minutes. Add the cream and simmer until slightly thickened, about 2 minutes longer. Season with salt and freshly ground pepper and stir in the parsley. Remove from the heat and keep warm.

4. Preheat the oven to 350°. Cut the polenta crosswise into 8 strips. Heat 1 tablespoon of the olive oil in a large nonstick skillet. Add 4 of the polenta strips and cook over moderate heat until browned on the bottom, about 3 minutes. Using a long spatula, carefully turn the polenta and brown on the other side. Transfer the polenta to a baking sheet and keep warm in the oven while you heat the remaining 1 tablespoon of olive oil and brown the remaining strips. Set a polenta strip on each plate and spoon the cooked mushrooms over the top. Sprinkle with the pumpkin seeds and serve. —*Pablo Massey*

MAKE AHEAD The polenta and topping can be prepared through Step 3 and refrigerated for up to 1 day.

WINE The crunchy, nutty flavors of the earthy polenta melt in with the sweet velvety tannins of the 1997 Catena Alta Malbec Angélica Vineyards.

Butternut Squash Polenta

8 SERVINGS

Adding butternut squash to polenta makes it especially smooth and slightly sweet.

1 small butternut squash (1½ pounds), halved lengthwise

1 tablespoon olive oil

Kosher salt and freshly ground pepper

4 cups water

4 cups milk

½ teaspoon table salt

2 cups fine cornmeal, preferably organic

4 tablespoons unsalted butter

½ cup (2 ounces) freshly grated Parmesan cheese

I. Preheat the oven to 350°. Rub the cut side of the butternut squash halves with the olive oil and season them with kosher salt and pepper. Set the butternut squash halves cut side down on a baking sheet and roast them for 45 minutes, or until they are very tender when pierced. Let the butternut squash

cool and then scoop the flesh into a bowl and mash lightly.

2. Meanwhile, in a large saucepan, combine the water, milk and table salt and bring to a boil. Gradually whisk in the cornmeal and bring to a simmer. Reduce the heat to low and cook, stirring every few minutes, until the cornmeal is smooth, about 30 minutes. Stir in the butter, the Parmesan and the mashed butternut squash. Season the polenta with kosher salt and pepper and serve hot. —*Kimball Jones*

MAKE AHEAD The polenta can be kept warm in a water bath for up to 30 minutes.

Creamed Parsley and Hominy

10 SERVINGS ✳

6 large bunches flat-leaf parsley

Salt

3 tablespoons unsalted butter, 2 melted

1 large sweet onion, cut into 1-inch dice

4 garlic cloves, minced

1 cup chicken stock or canned low-sodium broth

1¾ cups heavy cream

4 ounces country ham, coarsely chopped

Five 15-ounce cans yellow or white hominy, drained

Freshly ground pepper

1 cup coarse fresh bread crumbs

I. Bring a large pot of water to a boil. Hold a bunch of parsley by the stems and, starting at the top of the bunch, coarsely cut the parsley crosswise until you reach the thicker part of the stems. Discard the stems. Repeat with the remaining bunches. Wash the chopped parsley in a large bowl of water and then drain. Add salt to the boiling water; add the parsley and cook until tender, about 4 minutes. Drain well.

2. Preheat the oven to 350°. In a large saucepan, melt 1 tablespoon of the butter. Add the diced onion, cover and cook over low heat until softened, about 8

minutes. Add the garlic, increase the heat to moderate and cook until fragrant, about 3 minutes. Add the stock and simmer until reduced by half, about 8 minutes. Add the cream and ham and simmer for 5 minutes. Stir in the cooked parsley and the hominy, cover and simmer over low heat, stirring occasionally, until warmed through, about 8 minutes. Season with salt and pepper and transfer to a 9-by-13-inch glass baking dish. Cover with foil.

3. Bake the hominy for about 20 minutes, or until bubbling. In a small bowl, toss the bread crumbs with the melted butter. Turn the broiler on. Sprinkle the bread crumbs over the hominy and broil for about 1 minute, or until the crumbs are golden brown. Serve the hominy piping hot. —*Marcia Kiesel*

MAKE AHEAD The recipe can be prepared through Step 2 a day ahead.

Mushroom Orzotto

6 SERVINGS ✻

In the Friuli region of Italy, *orzo,* or barley, is cooked the way rice is cooked for risotto in the rest of the country.

- 3 tablespoons unsalted butter
- 1 tablespoon extra-virgin olive oil
- 1 medium onion, finely chopped
- 1 garlic clove, minced
- 1 pound pearl barley
- ½ pound white mushrooms, trimmed and sliced ¼ inch thick
- 4 ounces shiitake mushrooms, stemmed, caps sliced ¼ inch thick
- 4 ounces oyster mushrooms, sliced ¼ inch thick
- 2 cups beef stock or canned broth
- 3 cups water

Salt and freshly ground pepper

1. In a large heavy saucepan, melt 2 tablespoons of the butter in the olive oil. Add the onion and garlic and cook over moderate heat, stirring occasionally, until softened, about 5 minutes. Raise the heat to high, add the barley and cook, stirring frequently, for 1 minute.

2. Add the white mushrooms, shiitake mushrooms and oyster mushrooms and cook over high heat, stirring occasionally, until softened, about 5 minutes. Stir in the beef stock and water and bring to a simmer. Cover and cook over moderately low heat, stirring from time to time, until the barley is tender, about 25 minutes. Season the orzotto with salt and pepper and cook uncovered until the liquid has evaporated, about 5 minutes. Stir in the remaining 1 tablespoon of butter and serve the orzotto at once. —*Michele Scicolone*

MAKE AHEAD The orzotto can stand at room temperature for up to 2 hours. Rewarm over moderately low heat with a few tablespoons of water.

Quinoa with Caramelized Onions

8 SERVINGS

Quinoa is a South American grain; it was a staple of the ancient Incas. You can find quinoa at specialty food shops.

- 3 tablespoons extra-virgin olive oil
- 1½ pounds onions, thinly sliced

About 2½ cups water

Salt and freshly ground pepper

- 1½ cups quinoa, rinsed and drained (½ pound)

1. Heat 2 tablespoons of the oil in a large skillet. Add the onion; cook over low heat, stirring often, until meltingly soft and deep golden, about 30 minutes. Add a little bit of water as the onions begin to look dry. Season with salt and pepper and transfer to a plate.

2. Heat the remaining 1 tablespoon of olive oil in a large saucepan. Add the quinoa and cook over high heat, stirring, until light golden and fragrant, 3 to 4 minutes. Add 2½ cups of water and ¾ teaspoon of salt and bring to a boil. Cover and cook over low heat until all of the water has been absorbed and the grains are tender, 12 to 15 minutes. Fluff the quinoa with a fork and stir in the cooked onions. Season with salt and pepper. Transfer the quinoa to a bowl and serve at once. —*Grant Achatz*

Farro Tabbouleh Salad

6 SERVINGS

Farro—Italian spelt—gives this tabbouleh a chewy texture, while arugula adds a pleasantly sharp bite. Try this salad with grilled lamb chops.

- ⅔ cup (5 ounces) *farro* (see Note)
- 3 tablespoons fresh lemon juice
- 3 tablespoons extra-virgin olive oil

Salt and freshly ground pepper

- ½ pound tomatoes, coarsely chopped
- 2 large scallions, thinly sliced
- 1 cup parsley leaves
- ⅓ cup mint leaves
- 1 bunch arugula (6 ounces), coarsely chopped

1. In a medium saucepan, cover the *farro* with 2 inches of cold water and bring to a boil. Cook over high heat for 5 minutes. Turn off the heat and let the *farro* stand until plump and al dente, 45 to 60 minutes. Drain the *farro* in a colander, shaking off the excess water. Let stand until cool; shake the colander occasionally to dry the *farro*.

2. In a large glass or stainless steel bowl, whisk the lemon juice with the olive oil and season generously with salt and pepper. Add the cooked *farro,* the tomatoes, scallions, parsley and mint and toss. Season with salt and pepper, gently fold in the arugula and serve. —*Grace Parisi*

NOTE *Farro* is available at specialty food shops.

MAKE AHEAD The *farro* can be prepared through Step 1 and refrigerated for up to 2 days. The finished salad can stand at room temperature for up to 30 minutes before serving.

chapter 13
sauces dips condiments

321

323

Fiery Jalapeño Sauce

MAKES ABOUT ½ CUP ✳

- 2 jalapeños
- 1 unpeeled garlic clove
- 1 bunch cilantro, stems discarded
- ¼ cup water
- 1 tablespoon fresh lime juice

Salt

1. Heat a cast-iron skillet. Add the jalapeños and the unpeeled garlic clove and toast over high heat until they are lightly charred, about 5 minutes. Let the jalapeños and the garlic clove cool slightly and then peel the jalapeños and discard their stems, cores and seeds. Peel the garlic clove.

2. In a blender, combine the toasted jalapeños and garlic clove with the cilantro, water and fresh lime juice and puree. Season the jalapeño sauce with salt. —*Jan Newberry*

SERVE WITH Grilled or broiled skirt steak or chicken, grilled or seared pork chops, nachos or quesadillas.

Caribbean Seasoning Sauce

MAKES ABOUT 2½ CUPS

Try spreading this herb-filled sauce thickly on such fish fillets as salmon or sea bass and letting them marinate for 30 minutes before grilling.

- 4 cups basil leaves
- 1 cup oregano leaves
- ½ cup thyme leaves
- ½ cup snipped chives
- ½ cup red wine vinegar
- 1 large onion, coarsely chopped
- 12 garlic cloves, coarsely chopped
- 3 jalapeños, coarsely chopped
- 1 celery rib, coarsely chopped
- 1½ teaspoons paprika
- 1 teaspoon ground cumin
- ½ teaspoon sugar
- ½ teaspoon turmeric
- ½ teaspoon salt

In a blender or a food processor, pulse the basil, oregano, thyme, snipped chives, red wine vinegar, onion, garlic cloves, jalapeños, celery, paprika, cumin, sugar, turmeric and salt to a coarse paste. —*Madhur Jaffrey*

MAKE AHEAD The sauce can be refrigerated for up to 3 months.

Skordalia

8 SERVINGS ❁

The Greeks traditionally make the unctuous, earthy garlic sauce called *skordalia* by mashing potatoes with lots of olive oil. For a lighter version, mash the potatoes with some of their flavorful cooking water and add a little olive oil at the end. Serve it with sliced beets, huge white beans called *gigantes* and coarse bread, or as a delicious dip for asparagus, tomatoes, peppers and fennel.

- 1½ pounds Yukon Gold potatoes, peeled and cut into 2-inch chunks
- 8 small garlic cloves

Kosher salt

- 5 tablespoons extra-virgin olive oil
- 2 teaspoons fresh lemon juice

Freshly ground pepper

1. In a medium saucepan, combine the potatoes, 4 of the garlic cloves and ½ teaspoon kosher salt. Add enough water to cover by ½ inch and bring to a boil. Reduce the heat, cover and simmer until the potatoes are tender, about 25 minutes.

2. Using a slotted spoon, transfer the potatoes and cooked garlic to a bowl; reserve the cooking liquid. With an electric mixer, beat the potatoes and the cooked garlic at low speed until they are coarsely pureed. Then very gradually beat in about 1 cup of the reserved cooking water, until the potato and garlic puree is smooth.

3. Smash the remaining 4 garlic cloves in a mortar or on a work surface. Sprinkle with ½ teaspoon kosher salt and mash until reduced to a paste. Beat the garlic puree into the potatoes along with 3 tablespoons of the olive oil and the lemon juice; season the mixture with kosher salt and pepper. Garnish

Skordalia, with beets, beans and bread.

with the remaining 2 tablespoons of olive oil. *Skordalia* is best when served within 4 hours, either warm or at room temperature. —*Sally Schneider*

ONE SERVING Calories 141 kcal, Total Fat 8.9 gm, Saturated Fat 1.3 gm

Tomato Salsa

MAKES ABOUT 4 CUPS

Chileans almost always serve this salsa as an accompaniment to grilled meats.

- 4 large garlic cloves
- 1 large jalapeño, seeded and minced
- 1½ teaspoons coarse sea salt
- 5 ripe medium tomatoes (about 1½ pounds)—peeled, seeded and coarsely chopped
- 1 cup finely chopped Vidalia onion
- ½ cup canola oil
- ¼ cup minced cilantro
- 1 to 2 tablespoons red chile sauce

In a large mortar, crush the garlic cloves, the jalapeño and the sea salt to a paste. Alternatively, mince the garlic cloves and jalapeño with the sea salt and then use the flat side of the knife to pound or smash the mixture to a paste. Transfer the paste to a serving bowl and then stir in the tomatoes, onion, canola oil and cilantro. Add red chile sauce to taste. —*Ruth Van Waerebeek-Gonzalez*

MAKE AHEAD The salsa can be refrigerated for up to 2 days.

Tomatillo Salsa

MAKES ABOUT ¾ CUP

This tangy salsa is wonderful with grilled beef, chicken or pork.

- 4 tomatillos, husked
- 2 unpeeled large garlic cloves
- 1 canned chipotle chile in *adobo*
- ½ teaspoon sugar

Salt

Light a grill or heat a medium cast-iron skillet. Grill or sear the tomatillos and garlic cloves over moderate heat until the tomatillos have blackened and the garlic has softened, 7 to 8 minutes for the tomatillos and 12 minutes for the garlic. Peel the garlic cloves and then

transfer them to a food processor. Add the tomatillos, the chipotle chile and the sugar and puree until the salsa is smooth. Season the salsa with salt and serve. —*Lisa Ahier*

MAKE AHEAD The salsa can be refrigerated for 1 day. Let return to room temperature before serving.

Tomatillo-Chile Salsa

MAKES ABOUT 4 CUPS

The salsa's heat makes it wonderful with grilled salmon, tuna or chicken.

- ¾ pound tomatillos, husked
- 4 Anaheim chiles
- 2 jalapeño chiles
- 1 red bell pepper
- 1 yellow bell pepper
- 1 red onion, sliced ½ inch thick
- 1 tablespoon vegetable oil
- ¼ cup fresh lime juice
- 2 tablespoons olive oil

Salt and freshly ground black pepper

Tortilla chips, for serving

1. Light a grill or preheat the broiler. Brush the tomatillos, Anaheim and jalapeño chiles, red and yellow bell peppers and the red onion with the vegetable oil and grill over a medium-hot fire, turning occasionally, until softened and lightly charred all over, about 8 minutes for the tomatillos and 10 to 12 minutes for the chiles, bell peppers and onion. Transfer the chiles and bell peppers to a bowl, cover with plastic wrap and let cool completely. Coarsely chop the tomatillos and onion and transfer to another bowl.

2. Peel, core and seed the bell peppers. Finely chop the jalapeños and coarsely chop the Anaheims and bell peppers. Add the chopped chiles and peppers to the bowl with the tomatillo mixture. Stir in the lime juice and the olive oil and season the salsa with salt and black pepper. Serve the salsa with tortilla chips. —*Martha McGinnis*

MAKE AHEAD The grilled vegetable salsa can be refrigerated in an airtight container for up to 4 days.

Tomatillo-Chile Salsa

Roasted Tomatillo Salsa from Las Mañanitas

MAKES ABOUT 2 CUPS

Mildly spicy salsas made from tomatillos, green chiles, garlic and onions are ubiquitous in Cuernavaca, Mexico, because their tart herbal flavor complements just about everything that is served there. This recipe is based on one from the highly esteemed restaurant Las Mañanitas. Roasting the tomatillos, chiles and garlic mellows their flavor and gives the sauce a subtle smokiness.

- 1 pound tomatillos, husked
- 4 serrano chiles, stemmed
- 2 unpeeled garlic cloves
- 1 small onion—chopped, rinsed under cold water and dried
- ⅓ cup chopped cilantro
- ⅓ cup water
- ¾ teaspoon salt
- ¾ teaspoon sugar

1. Preheat the broiler. In a broiler pan, roast the tomatillos as close to the heat as possible, turning, until they are blackened and beginning to release their juices, about 8 minutes. Transfer the tomatillos to a bowl to cool.

2. Meanwhile, heat a small cast-iron skillet. Add the chiles and garlic cloves

and cook over moderate heat, turning occasionally, until softened and blistered with dark spots, 10 to 15 minutes.

3. Peel the garlic cloves. Coarsely chop them with the chiles and transfer to a blender along with the tomatillos and any accumulated juices. Pulse until coarsely pureed and then transfer to a bowl. Stir in the onion, cilantro, water, salt and sugar and let the tomatillo salsa stand at room temperature for 1 hour before serving. —*Sally Schneider*

MAKE AHEAD The roasted tomatillo salsa can be kept in the refrigerator for up to 2 days.

ONE-QUARTER CUP Calories 23 kcal, Total Fat .3 gm, Saturated Fat 0 gm

Avocado—Black Bean Salsa

MAKES ABOUT 3½ CUPS ✳

One 15-ounce can black beans, drained and rinsed
1 small Hass avocado, finely chopped
6 radishes, finely chopped
6 scallions, finely chopped
⅓ cup fresh lime juice
¼ cup chopped cilantro
¼ cup vegetable oil
2 serrano chiles, minced
½ teaspoon salt, plus more if needed

In a medium bowl, mix the black beans, avocado, radishes, scallions, lime juice, cilantro, vegetable oil, chiles and ½ teaspoon salt until combined. Season with more salt, if desired. —*Jan Newberry*

SERVE WITH Tortilla chips, roasted sea bass or salmon, grilled chicken or pork chops.

Whipped Morel and Prune Butter

MAKES ABOUT ¾ CUP

There are lots of ways to use this rich, smoky and slightly sweet butter: soften it, spread it on slices of bread and toast them in the oven, or top sautéed chicken or duck breasts, pan-fried pork, lamb chops or steak with a round of the butter.

¾ cup (¾ ounce) dried morels
½ cup boiling water
1 tablespoon extra-virgin olive oil
1 shallot, minced
1 stick (4 ounces) unsalted butter, softened
2 pitted prunes, finely chopped
2 teaspoons Madeira
Salt and freshly ground pepper

1. In a heatproof bowl, soak the morels in the boiling water until softened, about 20 minutes. Rub the morels to remove any grit and then lift them out and finely chop.

2. In a small skillet, heat the olive oil. Add the shallot and cook over low heat until softened but not browned, about 4 minutes. Let cool to room temperature.

3. In a medium bowl, using a handheld mixer at medium speed, beat the butter with the morels, shallot, prunes and Madeira until well blended, light and fluffy. Season the butter with salt and pepper. Use at once or scrape the butter into a log shape on plastic wrap and roll it up in the plastic. Refrigerate the butter until ready to use, or freeze for up to 1 month. —*Marcia Kiesel*

Garlicky Spinach Dip

8 SERVINGS

This brilliant green puree takes almost no time to make because it's not cooked. Serve it with sliced focaccia, Belgian endive leaves or both.

¼ cup plus 2 tablespoons extra-virgin olive oil
One ½-inch-thick slice peasant bread, about 6 inches wide
½ pound baby spinach
2 tablespoons fresh lemon juice
1 garlic clove, coarsely chopped
Salt and freshly ground pepper

1. In a bowl, pour 2 tablespoons of the olive oil over the bread. Turn the bread to coat and then let stand until the oil is absorbed. Tear the oil-soaked bread into small pieces.

2. In a food processor, finely chop the spinach. Add the bread, lemon juice

shopping for morels

1. Select fresh morels individually to ensure quality. Smell morels before buying them; they should have a woodsy, earthy fragrance. Choose morels that are very firm and springy to the touch, with no soft spots. Reject any that are dry or moldy. **2. Inspect the honeycombed crevices** of the caps to be sure that they are not infested with worms or insects. **3. Opt for dried morels** when fresh ones are out of season. With their wonderfully intense flavor, they are an excellent alternative. Fragrance is key when choosing dried morels; they should have a deep, smoky, woodsy scent. **4. Buy dried morels that are small;** they tend to be the most delicious. **5. Check the bottoms of bags** of prepackaged dried morels; avoid those with a lot of broken pieces or a powdery residue. **6. Mail-order fresh or dried morels** through Marché aux Delices (888-547-5471); for dried ones only, call Epicurean Specialty (800-500-0065).

and garlic and process until well blended. Add the remaining ¼ cup of olive oil and process to a fine puree. Scrape the puree into a bowl and season with salt and pepper. Serve at room temperature. —*Lori De Mori*

WINE A light, fruity 1995 Plozner Tocai from Friuli is versatile enough to drink alone or to pair with an appetizer like this spinach dip.

Spinach and Serrano Dip

MAKES ABOUT 1 CUP

Serve this spicy, slightly creamy dip with whatever vegetables look best at the market. Try for an assortment that includes raw celery, carrots and radishes, and blanched cauliflower, broccoli, green beans and asparagus.

½ pound fresh spinach, trimmed
¼ cup plus 1 tablespoon olive oil
2 large scallions, coarsely chopped
2 serrano chiles—halved, seeded and coarsely chopped

TOP: **Soft Tacos with Potato and Green Chile Filling** (p. 265).
BOTTOM: **Roasted Tomatillo Salsa from Las Mañanitas.**

¾ cup coarsely chopped cilantro

¼ cup sour cream

2 tablespoons fresh lime juice

Salt and freshly ground pepper

Assorted vegetables, for dipping

1. Set a large skillet over high heat. Add the spinach by the handful and stir to wilt. Cook just until all of the spinach has wilted and then transfer to a colander. Let cool slightly and then squeeze the spinach dry and coarsely chop it.

2. Heat 1 tablespoon of the olive oil in a small skillet. Add the scallions and serranos and cook over moderately high heat until softened, about 2 minutes. Transfer to a blender and add the wilted spinach, cilantro, sour cream, lime juice and the remaining ¼ cup of olive oil. Blend to a smooth puree, scraping down the side occasionally. Transfer the dip to a bowl and season with salt and pepper. Serve chilled or at room temperature with a platter of assorted vegetables. —*Fred Eric*

MAKE AHEAD The dip can be refrigerated for up to 2 days. Season again before serving if necessary.

Creamy Truffled Hazelnut Dip
MAKES ABOUT 2½ CUPS ✳

⅔ cup (about 3 ounces) hazelnuts

1 pound fresh ricotta cheese

½ cup soft goat cheese

1 teaspoon Dijon mustard

About ¼ teaspoon truffle oil

Salt and freshly ground white pepper

1. Preheat the oven to 350°. Spread the hazelnuts in a pie plate and bake for about 12 minutes, or until the nuts are fragrant and the skins blister. Let cool and then transfer the hazelnuts to a kitchen towel and rub to remove the skins. Transfer the hazelnuts to a food processor and pulse until finely ground. Transfer the hazelnuts to a bowl and wipe out the food processor.

2. In the food processor, combine the ricotta, goat cheese, mustard and truffle oil and process until smooth and creamy, scraping down the side of the

bowl. Transfer to a serving bowl and stir in the hazelnuts. Season with salt and white pepper, add a little more truffle oil, if needed, and serve. —*Grace Parisi*

MAKE AHEAD The dip can be refrigerated overnight.

SERVE WITH Pear and apple slices, garlic or black pepper crackers, flatbreads and grissini.

Hummus bi Tahini
MAKES 3 CUPS

Hummus bi Tahini is always part of the Lebanese meze, the appetizer course that sometimes becomes the whole meal. But this creamy puree can also be served simply with crisp pita triangles and cut-up fresh vegetables. Be sure to allow time for the chickpeas to soak. Can you make this with canned chickpeas? Well, yes, if time is a factor, but the flavor won't be nearly so dramatic and interesting.

1 cup (7 ounces) dried chickpeas, picked over and rinsed

½ teaspoon baking soda

½ cup tahini (see Note)

¾ cup fresh lemon juice

2 garlic cloves, coarsely chopped

1 teaspoon salt

1 tablespoon finely chopped flat-leaf parsley

1½ tablespoons extra-virgin olive oil

1. In a medium bowl, cover the dried chickpeas with 1 inch of water and stir in the baking soda. Let soak overnight.

2. Drain and rinse the soaked chickpeas. In a medium saucepan, cover the chickpeas with 1 inch of water and bring to a boil, skimming as necessary. Cook over low heat until the chickpeas are very tender, about 40 minutes. Drain the chickpeas, reserving 1 cup of the cooking liquid.

3. In a food processor, puree all but ¼ cup of the chickpeas until smooth; add some of the reserved cooking liquid if the puree is dry. Add the tahini and lemon juice and process until satiny. Add more of the reserved cooking liquid

until the consistency is that of sour cream. Transfer the hummus to a bowl.

4. Remove the skins from the reserved chickpeas. Mash the garlic with the salt until smooth. Stir the mashed garlic into the hummus and transfer to a shallow bowl. Add the parsley to the olive oil and drizzle it over the hummus. Garnish with the whole peeled chickpeas and serve. —*Nancy Harmon Jenkins*

NOTE Good tahini (sesame paste) has a sweet, nutty flavor without a trace of bitterness. Stir any separated oil back into the tahini before measuring.

MAKE AHEAD The chickpeas can be cooked 1 day ahead and refrigerated.

Jerusalem Artichoke Hummus with Spiced Oil
8 SERVINGS ❀

Tangy Jerusalem artichokes, known as sunchokes, are really a variety of sunflower. Buy ones that are roughly the same size so they'll cook evenly. Drizzle the leftover spiced oil on bean salads, pizza, or roasted vegetables. The oil has to sit overnight, so plan accordingly.

1½ teaspoons fennel seeds

1½ teaspoons coriander seeds

½ teaspoon crushed red pepper

2 teaspoons hot paprika

½ cup extra-virgin olive oil

12 medium pita breads, cut into 8 wedges each

2 pounds Jerusalem artichokes

One 19-ounce can chickpeas, drained and rinsed

2 garlic cloves, smashed

⅓ cup tahini

¼ cup fresh lemon juice

Salt and freshly ground pepper

1 tablespoon coarsely chopped flat-leaf parsley

1. In a small skillet, stir the fennel and coriander seeds over moderate heat until fragrant, about 30 seconds. Add the crushed red pepper and paprika; cook, stirring, for 30 seconds longer.

2. Transfer the spices to a blender. Add the olive oil and blend until almost

CLOCKWISE FROM BOTTOM: **Hummus bi Tahini**, **Tabbouleh** (p. 74), **pita bread**, **Fattoush** (p. 49) and **Falafel** (p. 25).

smooth. Pour the spiced oil into a jar, cover and let stand overnight at room temperature. Strain the oil through cheesecloth and discard the spices.

3. Preheat the oven to 375°. Spread the pitas on 2 large baking sheets and toast them for about 12 minutes, or until they are crisp.

4. Spread the Jerusalem artichokes on a rimmed baking sheet, cover tightly with foil and bake until tender, about 45 minutes to 1¼ hours, depending on their size. Remove the Jerusalem artichokes as they are done and let cool to room temperature. Using a small metal spoon, scoop out and reserve the flesh of the Jerusalem artichokes, discarding the skins.

5. In a food processor, puree the chickpeas and the garlic. Add the Jerusalem artichokes, tahini and lemon juice and process until smooth. Season the hummus with salt and pepper to taste and let stand for at least 2 hours or refrigerate overnight.

6. Spoon the Jerusalem artichoke hummus into a bowl and drizzle with 2 tablespoons of the spiced oil. Garnish the hummus with the parsley and serve with the toasted wedges of pita bread alongside. —*Trey Foshee*

ONE SERVING Calories 436 kcal, Total Fat 11 gm, Saturated Fat 1.4 gm

Mint and Cumin Pickled Carrots

Smoked Trout Brandade

MAKES ABOUT 6 CUPS ✳

1¼ cups extra-virgin olive oil
3 large garlic cloves, thickly sliced
½ cup heavy cream
2 pounds Yukon Gold potatoes
3 smoked trout fillets
   (4 to 5 ounces each), skin
   removed and fish flaked
Salt and freshly ground white pepper
1 tablespoon snipped chives

1. In a skillet, cook 1 cup of the olive oil and the garlic over low heat until the garlic is pale golden and softened, about 7 minutes. Using a slotted spoon, transfer the garlic to a bowl and mash with a fork. Let the garlic oil cool slightly and then add the cream.

2. In a saucepan, cover the potatoes with water and cook until tender, about 30 minutes. Let cool slightly and then peel the potatoes and pass them through a ricer or sieve. Alternatively, whip the potatoes with an electric mixer. Add the mashed garlic and the garlic-oil cream. Stir in the trout and season with salt and white pepper.

3. Preheat the oven to 350°. Spread the brandade in a shallow 1½-quart baking dish. Make shallow depressions in the brandade and spoon the remaining ¼ cup of olive oil into the depressions. Bake for about 15 minutes, or until heated through. Sprinkle with the chives and serve warm. —*Grace Parisi*

SERVE WITH Garlic crackers, flatbreads, grissini and thick potato chips.

Spiced Kirby Pickles

MAKES 2 QUARTS

3 pounds kirby cucumbers, halved
   lengthwise
6 whole cloves
4 bay leaves
2 to 3 dried red chiles
2 teaspoons whole black
   peppercorns
2 tablespoons coriander seeds
2 tablespoons mustard seeds
2 teaspoons fennel seeds

2 teaspoons cumin seeds
2 cups white vinegar, plus more if
   needed
1 cup water
10 garlic cloves, coarsely chopped
2 tablespoons sugar
2 tablespoons kosher salt

1. In one 2-quart heatproof jar or a few smaller jars, pack the kirby cucumbers, cloves, bay leaves, chiles and peppercorns and the coriander, mustard, fennel and cumin seeds.

2. In a small saucepan, combine the vinegar with the water, garlic, sugar and kosher salt. Bring to a boil. Simmer until the sugar and salt dissolve. Ladle the pickling liquid into the jar; if necessary, add more vinegar to cover the cucumbers. Let the pickles cool, cover with a lid and refrigerate until flavorful, about 3 weeks. —*Marcia Kiesel*

Mint and Cumin Pickled Carrots

MAKES 1 QUART

The length of the carrot pickles depends on the size of the jar; cut them to fit. Or use baby carrots with the tops removed.

12 medium carrots, cut into
   ½-inch-wide strips
8 large spearmint sprigs
2 teaspoons cumin seeds
1½ cups white wine vinegar, plus
   more if needed
¼ cup water
6 garlic cloves, coarsely chopped
2½ tablespoons kosher salt
1½ tablespoons sugar

1. In a large saucepan of boiling water, blanch the carrots for 1 minute. Drain, let cool and then pack the carrots into a 1-quart heatproof jar. Add the mint.

2. In a small skillet, toast the cumin seeds over moderate heat, stirring, until fragrant, about 40 seconds. Let cool and then add to the jar. In a saucepan, bring the vinegar, water, garlic, kosher salt and sugar to a boil. Simmer over moderately high heat until the salt and sugar dissolve. Ladle the pickling liquid

a cook's pickle policies

Follow these tips to make beautiful and full-flavored vegetable pickles.

Work with firm vegetables. Get the best-looking ones you can find. Success depends on produce that isn't flawed or flabby.

Use plain white vinegar for vibrant, brightly colored pickles. You can use white wine vinegar for a slightly more refined taste, but the colors will be dull.

Pickle with kosher salt. It won't cloud the liquid the way table salt does.

Take the time to arrange the vegetables vertically in jars according to shape. You'll be able to pack more in, and the filled jars will look nicer. (A chopstick can get into corners that your fingers can't reach.)

LEFT TO RIGHT: Spiced Kirby Pickles, Jamaican Jardinière Pickles (p. 326) and Lemon-Okra Pickles.

into the jar; if necessary, add more vinegar to cover the carrots. Let the pickles cool and then cover with a lid and refrigerate until flavorful, about 3 weeks. —*Marcia Kiesel*

Lemon-Okra Pickles

MAKES 1 QUART

¾ pound medium okra, stems trimmed

Six 3-inch-long strips of lemon zest

6 oregano sprigs

1 dried red chile (optional)

1 cup white wine vinegar, plus more if needed

1 cup water

4 garlic cloves, coarsely chopped

2 tablespoons sugar

1½ tablespoons kosher salt

I. Pack the okra, lemon zest, oregano and chile into a 1-quart heatproof jar.

2. In a small saucepan, combine the vinegar with the water, garlic, sugar and kosher salt and bring to a boil. Simmer over moderately high heat until the sugar and salt dissolve. Ladle the pickling liquid into the jar; if necessary, add more vinegar to cover the okra. Let the

pickles cool. Cover the jar of pickles with a lid and refrigerate until flavorful, about 3 weeks. —*Marcia Kiesel*

Leroy's Spicy Pickled Cabbage

MAKES ABOUT 5 CUPS

Leroy Gain, a farmer in Helvetia, West Virginia, is the source for this recipe. Rather than taking the trouble to stuff banana peppers with cabbage, he found you can shred both the peppers and the cabbage and then pack them together in a light vinegar syrup. The result is a cross between a kraut and a slaw and has a spicy flavor. Salting the peppers draws out any sharpness and leaves a pleasant heat.

⅓ cup plus 1 teaspoon salt

1⅓ cups boiling water

12 banana peppers—halved lengthwise, cored and seeded

1 cup sugar

⅓ cup plus 3 tablespoons white wine vinegar, plus more to taste

1¼ cups plus 3 tablespoons cold water

½ medium cabbage, shredded (about 6 cups)

½ teaspoon slivered lemon zest

I. In a medium heatproof bowl, combine ⅓ cup of the salt with the boiling water and stir until dissolved; let cool. Add the banana peppers to the brine and cover with a plate to keep them submerged. Let the banana peppers stand overnight at room temperature.

2. In a large bowl, combine ½ cup of the sugar with 3 tablespoons of the vinegar, 3 tablespoons of the cold water and ½ teaspoon of the salt. Add the cabbage, toss well and let stand for 45 minutes.

3. Drain the cabbage well. Drain the peppers, discarding the brine. Thinly slice the peppers crosswise.

4. In a large saucepan, combine the remaining 1¼ cups of cold water, ½ cup sugar, ⅓ cup vinegar and ½ teaspoon salt. Boil, stirring constantly, until a syrup forms, about 3 minutes. Add the cabbage and the peppers and cook for 2 minutes. If the pickle seems sweet, add a tablespoon or two of vinegar. Stir in the lemon zest and let cool. Pack the mixture into jars and refrigerate for up to 2 weeks. Serve the pickled cabbage chilled. —*Sally Schneider*

SERVE WITH Bean soups and stews, rich meats, such as duck and goose, and just about any kind of dish that features pork.

ONE-HALF CUP Calories 65 kcal, Total Fat 0.1 gm, Saturated Fat 0 gm

Jamaican Jardinière Pickles

MAKES 2½ QUARTS

Aromatic allspice berries and fiery Scotch bonnet chiles give these pickles their Caribbean edge. To avoid irritation when cutting chiles, wear thin rubber gloves and don't touch your face.

1½ pounds cauliflower, separated into small florets

4 medium carrots, cut into 3-by-½-inch sticks

1 large red bell pepper, cut into ½-inch-thick strips

12 Scotch bonnet or habanero chiles, 6 halved

6 large garlic cloves, peeled

6 large thyme sprigs

One 2-inch piece of ginger, peeled and sliced ¼ inch thick

1 quart white vinegar, plus more if needed

⅓ cup whole allspice berries, 1 tablespoon crushed

1 cup sugar

¼ cup kosher salt

1 tablespoon whole black peppercorns, coarsely crushed

1. In a medium saucepan of boiling water, blanch the cauliflower for 1 minute. Drain and let cool.

2. In one 2½-quart heatproof jar or a few smaller jars, pack the cauliflower, carrots, red bell pepper, chiles, garlic cloves, thyme and ginger, alternating in an attractive pattern.

3. In the saucepan, combine the vinegar, allspice, sugar, kosher salt and peppercorns and bring to a boil. Simmer over moderately high heat until the sugar and salt dissolve. Ladle the pickling liquid into the jar. If necessary, add more vinegar to cover the vegetables. Let the pickles cool and then cover the jar with a lid and refrigerate until the pickles are very flavorful, at least 10 days. —*Marcia Kiesel*

Onion Marmalade

MAKES ABOUT 1 CUP

Thinly sliced onions become almost jam-like when they're cooked in a small amount of butter over very low heat for a long time. Adding a little sugar helps the onions to caramelize, and cooking them further with sherry and balsamic vinegars turns them into a marvelous sweet-and-sour condiment.

1¼ pounds Vidalia or other sweet onions such as Walla Walla or Maui, peeled and halved lengthwise

2 teaspoons unsalted butter

Salt

½ teaspoon sugar

1 tablespoon sherry or Banyuls vinegar

1 teaspoon aged balsamic vinegar

Freshly ground pepper

1. Using a mandoline or a very sharp knife, slice the onions ⅛ inch thick. In a large nonstick skillet, melt the butter

over moderately low heat. Add the onions, sprinkle with ½ teaspoon salt and stir well with a wooden spoon. Cover and cook, stirring once or twice, until the onions have released their liquid, about 15 minutes.

2. Uncover and continue to cook the onions, stirring occasionally, until all of the liquid has evaporated, about 10 minutes. Sprinkle the onions evenly with the sugar and cook, stirring frequently, until they are golden brown, about 10 minutes longer.

3. Increase the heat to moderate and add the sherry vinegar and balsamic vinegar. Stir the onions to dissolve the juices that have caramelized on the bottom of the pan and cook until the vinegars have evaporated, about 3 minutes longer. Season the marmalade with salt and pepper. Let cool slightly and then transfer to a glass jar with a lid. Serve the marmalade warm, at room temperature or cold. —*Sally Schneider*

MAKE AHEAD The marmalade can be refrigerated for up to 1 week.

SERVE WITH Grilled pork chops and steaks, cold meats and poultry or in sandwiches or omelets.

ONE TABLESPOON Calories 18 kcal, Total Fat 0.5 gm, Saturated Fat 0.3 gm

Roasted Tomatoes and Garlic

MAKES 24 TOMATO HALVES AND ABOUT 15 GARLIC CLOVES

12 ripe medium tomatoes, cored and halved crosswise (about 3 pounds)

2 tablespoons extra-virgin olive oil

Salt and freshly ground pepper

1 head garlic, separated into unpeeled cloves (about 15)

4 thyme sprigs

1. Preheat the oven to 350° and line a rimmed baking sheet with parchment paper. Arrange the tomato halves, cut side down, on the baking sheet and drizzle with the olive oil. Season with salt and pepper and scatter the garlic and thyme on top.

2. Roast the tomatoes for about 20 minutes, or until the skins begin to wrinkle. Remove the baking sheet from the oven and carefully pull off the skins. Return the baking sheet to the oven and roast the tomatoes until leathery on the outside but still slightly wet on the underside, about 1½ hours longer. Peel the garlic and discard the skins and the thyme. Serve warm, at room temperature or cold. —*Tom Colicchio*

MAKE AHEAD The tomatoes and garlic can be refrigerated in a glass jar for up to 3 weeks.

Incredibly Rich Lemon Curd

MAKES ABOUT 1½ CUPS

Though more familiar as a filling for pies, lemon curd can also be used as a spread. This do-it-yourself version of the luscious curd sold by Stonewall Kitchen in York, Maine, is perfect with white toast and delectable on Bakewell Cream Biscuits (p. 252).

- 2 sticks (½ pound) unsalted butter, softened
- ½ cup fresh lemon juice, strained
- ½ cup sugar
- 3 large egg yolks

In a medium bowl set over a saucepan of simmering water, melt the butter with the lemon juice and sugar, stirring occasionally, until the sugar is dissolved. Whisk in the egg yolks, 1 at a time, and cook over moderately high heat, whisking constantly, until the curd is very hot to the touch and the consistency of loose sour cream, about 15 minutes. Strain into a bowl; press a piece of plastic wrap directly onto the surface to prevent a skin from forming. Refrigerate before serving. —*Jonathan King and Jim Stott*

MAKE AHEAD The curd can be kept in the refrigerator for up to 1 week.

Cranberry-Walnut Conserve

MAKES ABOUT 6 CUPS

This chunky, tart-sweet condiment epitomizes the splendid cooking of the Mennonites of Lancaster, Pennsylvania.

It's hearty and immensely satisfying with roasted meats or poultry, but it's also tempting straight off the spoon as a sweet snack.

- 1½ cups (6 ounces) walnuts
- 2 large or 3 small organic navel oranges (1¼ pounds), scrubbed
- 1¼ pounds (5 cups) fresh or frozen cranberries
- ⅔ cup wildflower honey
- 1½ cups hot water
- 1¼ cups raisins or dried currants

1. Preheat the oven to 375°. Put the walnuts in a pie pan and toast for about 7 minutes, or until fragrant and golden. Let cool.

2. Using a sharp knife, cut ½-inch from the ends of the oranges to just expose the fruit. Quarter the oranges lengthwise and then slice them crosswise as thinly as possible. Discard any seeds.

3. In a large saucepan, combine the orange slices with 4 cups of the cranberries, the honey and water and bring to a boil over moderate heat. Cook, stirring occasionally, until the cranberries soften and the conserve has thickened slightly, about 15 minutes. Stir in the raisins and the remaining 1 cup of cranberries and cook just until the raisins plump, about 5 minutes longer. Let the mixture cool and then stir in the toasted walnuts. Ladle the compote into clean, dry jars. Cover the jars and refrigerate. —*Sally Schneider*

MAKE AHEAD The conserve can be refrigerated for up to 1 month.

TWO TABLESPOONS Calories 58 kcal, Total Fat 2.2 gm, Saturated Fat .2 gm

Yemenite Haroset

MAKES ABOUT 2 CUPS

Haroset, the traditional seder condiment, is served with matzoh as part of the Passover ritual.

- ¼ cup pomegranate juice (see Note) or sweet kosher red wine
- ¾ cup (4 ounces) coarsely chopped pitted dates
- ¼ cup (2 ounces) raisins

Cranberry-Walnut Conserve

- ½ cup (2 ounces) whole almonds
- ½ cup (2 ounces) walnut pieces
- 2 tablespoons sesame seeds
- 1 large Granny Smith apple— peeled, cored and coarsely chopped
- ¼ teaspoon cinnamon
- 2 large pinches each of freshly ground black pepper, ground cloves, ground cardamom, ground ginger and ground cumin

1. Preheat the oven to 400°. In a small saucepan, warm the pomegranate juice. Add the dates and raisins and let soak until softened, about 10 minutes.

2. Spread the almonds and walnuts on a rimmed baking sheet and bake for 6 to 8 minutes, or until lightly toasted. Transfer to a work surface, let cool and then chop coarsely. Spread the sesame seeds in a pie pan and bake for 1 to 2 minutes, or until lightly browned.

3. Combine all the ingredients in a large bowl; mix well. Serve chilled or at room temperature. —*Susan Shapiro Jaslove*

NOTE Pomegranate juice can be mail-ordered from Kalustyan's (212-685-3451).

MAKE AHEAD The *haroset* can be refrigerated for up to 8 hours.

chapter 14
cakes tarts cookies

339

347

349

Angel Food Cake

MAKES ONE 10-INCH TUBE CAKE

Angel food cake is fat-free, but for those who don't count calories, it's wonderful buttered and toasted until golden. To toast a piece, cut a one-inch wedge and spread one side with softened butter. Place the wedge on a cookie sheet and broil with the door open for about 30 seconds, rotating the pan, until the cake is evenly browned and crisp. It's best when still hot.

1 cup all-purpose flour
1½ cups sugar
2 cups egg whites (from about 20 large eggs)
1½ teaspoons cream of tartar
1 teaspoon pure vanilla extract
¼ teaspoon salt

I. Preheat the oven to 350°. In a bowl, whisk the flour with ¾ cup of the sugar.

2. In a large mixing bowl, using an electric mixer, beat the egg whites on low speed until foamy. Increase the speed to medium and beat for 8 seconds and then add the cream of tartar, vanilla and salt. Increase the speed to high. Hold the remaining ¾ cup of sugar about 6 inches above the bowl and gradually let it flow into the whites in a thin stream. When all the sugar has been incorporated, scrape around the side and bottom of the bowl with a large rubber spatula. Continue beating at high speed until the whites are firm and shiny but not at all dry.

3. With the mixer on low, slowly sift one third of the flour-and-sugar mixture over the whites. Scrape all around the bowl with the spatula. Sift half of the remaining flour mixture over the whites and beat at the lowest speed until blended; repeat with the remaining flour mixture.

4. Using the spatula, scoop the batter into an ungreased 10-inch tube pan. Lightly smooth the top. Bake in the center of the oven for about 40 minutes, or until a tester inserted in the middle comes out completely clean. If any moist crumbs cling to the tester, bake the cake for 5 minutes more and test again.

5. Gently remove the pan from the oven, turn it upside down and let the cake cool completely. If your pan does not have metal legs to raise it up so that air can circulate below the cake, you can suspend it over the neck of a bottle or rest it on top of glasses. When the cake is cool, run a knife around the pan and around the tube to loosen it. Turn the angel food cake out onto a platter and serve. —*Marion Cunningham*

Spiced Angel Food Cake with Butterscotch Glaze

MAKES ONE 10-INCH TUBE CAKE 🌾
CAKE

Vegetable oil spray
1½ cups confectioners' sugar
1 cup cake flour
½ teaspoon freshly grated nutmeg
½ teaspoon cinnamon
½ teaspoon allspice
¼ teaspoon cloves
12 large egg whites, at room temperature
1½ teaspoons cream of tartar
1 cup granulated sugar
2 teaspoons pure vanilla extract
Pinch of salt
GLAZE
4 tablespoons unsalted butter
¼ cup dark brown sugar
¼ cup heavy cream
Pinch of salt
1½ teaspoons pure vanilla extract
1½ cups confectioners' sugar, sifted
FROSTING
¾ cup sugar
¼ cup plus 2 tablespoons water
Scant ¼ teaspoon freshly grated nutmeg
Scant ¼ teaspoon cinnamon
Scant ¼ teaspoon allspice
Scant ⅛ teaspoon cloves
3 large egg whites, at room temperature

I. MAKE THE CAKE: Preheat the oven to 375°. Spray a 10-inch tube pan with vegetable oil spray.

2. In a medium bowl, sift together the confectioners' sugar, flour, nutmeg, cinnamon, allspice and cloves. In a large bowl, using a handheld mixer, beat the egg whites with the cream of tartar at medium speed just until foamy. Gradually beat in the granulated sugar, vanilla and salt; continue beating at high speed until the whites form firm, glossy peaks. Using a large rubber spatula, fold the dry ingredients into the whites, ½ cup at a time, until no streaks of white remain.

3. Spoon the batter into the prepared pan and bake for 35 minutes, or until the cake is golden and a skewer inserted in the center comes out clean. Turn out onto a wire rack. Remove the pan; let cool.

4. MAKE THE GLAZE: In a medium saucepan, combine the butter, brown sugar, cream and salt and bring to a boil, stirring occasionally. Transfer the mixture to a bowl and add the vanilla and confectioners' sugar. Using a handheld mixer, beat the glaze at medium speed until completely smooth and spreadable, about 2 minutes. Evenly spread the glaze over the cake with a metal spatula and set aside at room temperature to harden.

5. MAKE THE FROSTING: In a medium saucepan, combine the sugar with the water, nutmeg, cinnamon, allspice and cloves and bring to a boil without stirring. Continue to boil the spiced syrup until it reaches 248° on a candy thermometer, about 8 minutes.

6. Meanwhile, in a large glass or stainless steel bowl, beat the egg whites until stiff. Working carefully, gradually pour in the hot syrup while beating the whites constantly at medium speed. Increase the speed to high and beat until the frosting is cool, about 4 minutes longer.

7. Transfer the cake to a platter and then cover the cake completely with the frosting. —*Dana Speers*

MAKE AHEAD The cake can stand at room temperature for 5 hours.

ONE SERVING Calories 430 kcal, Total Fat 7 gm, Saturated Fat 4.3 gm

Italian Almond Cake

MAKES ONE 10-INCH CAKE

Just the right ending to an extravagant dinner, this light, flourless cake has a not-too-sweet flavor and a wonderful texture from all the nuts.

- 2 tablespoons matzo meal, plus more for coating
- 2 cups whole blanched almonds
- ½ cup granulated sugar
- 6 large eggs, separated
- ½ cup light brown sugar
- 1 teaspoon vanilla extract
- ¾ teaspoon almond extract
- 1 teaspoon grated lemon zest

Pinch of salt

Confectioners' sugar, for dusting

1. Preheat the oven to 350°. Grease a 10-inch springform pan. Line the bottom of the pan with parchment or wax paper and grease the paper. Evenly coat the bottom and side of the lined pan with matzo meal, tapping out any excess.

2. In a food processor, pulse the almonds with 2 tablespoons of the matzo meal and ¼ cup of the granulated sugar until very finely ground. In a bowl, beat the egg yolks with the brown sugar and the remaining ¼ cup of granulated sugar at high speed until very light and fluffy, about 3 minutes. At low speed, gradually add the ground almond mixture, the vanilla extract, the almond extract and the lemon zest.

3. In a medium bowl, using clean beaters, whip the egg whites with the salt until stiff peaks form. Beat one fourth of the egg whites into the yolk mixture to lighten it and then quickly fold in the remaining egg whites. Scrape the batter into the prepared pan and smooth the surface.

4. Bake the cake for about 45 minutes, or until a toothpick inserted in the center comes out clean. Run a small, sharp knife around the side of the cake, transfer it to a rack and let cool completely in the pan. Remove the side of the springform pan and invert the cooled cake onto a serving plate. Remove the base of the springform pan and then carefully peel off the paper. Sift confectioners' sugar over the almond cake before serving. —*Susan Shapiro Jaslove*

MAKE AHEAD The almond cake, before it has been dusted with confectioners' sugar, can be kept well wrapped in plastic, at room temperature, for up to 2 days.

Almond Cakes with Bananas and Warm Caramel Sauce

MAKES TEN 4-INCH CAKES ✳

You'll need ten four-inch fluted tart pans with removable bottoms for this recipe.

Vegetable oil spray

- ¾ cup whole blanched almonds, finely ground
- ¾ cup plus 2 tablespoons all-purpose flour

Almond Cakes with Bananas and Warm Caramel Sauce

1 stick (4 ounces) unsalted butter, melted

2 tablespoons dark rum

1½ teaspoons pure vanilla extract

1⅓ cups sugar

6 ripe bananas, 2 coarsely chopped

7 large egg whites, at room temperature

⅛ teaspoon salt

Warm Caramel Sauce (recipe follows)

1. Preheat the oven to 350°. Place ten 4-inch fluted tartlet pans with removable bottoms on a baking sheet. Spray the pans with vegetable oil spray.

2. In a medium bowl, combine the almonds, flour, butter, rum, vanilla and ⅔ cup of the sugar. Fold in the chopped bananas.

3. In a large bowl, beat the egg whites with the salt at high speed until frothy. Slowly pour in the remaining ⅔ cup of sugar and beat until stiff peaks form.

4. Using a rubber spatula, fold the beaten whites into the almond batter, 1 cup at a time. Spread the batter evenly in the prepared pans; bake for about 20 minutes, or until golden and firm in the centers. Meanwhile, slice the 4 remaining bananas ¼ inch thick on the diagonal.

5. Unmold the cakes. Set each in the center of a dessert plate; cover with the sliced bananas, pour the sauce on top and serve. —*Dana Speers*

WARM CARAMEL SAUCE

MAKES ABOUT 2 CUPS

1 cup sugar

1 cup hot water

1 stick (4 ounces) unsalted butter, cut into tablespoons

¼ cup rum

3 tablespoons sour cream

In a medium saucepan, bring the sugar and ½ cup of the water to a boil. Cook over moderate heat, without stirring, until a deep amber caramel forms, about 3 minutes. Gradually whisk in the remaining ½ cup of water; it may splatter, so be careful. Stir in the butter, rum and sour cream and serve warm. —*D. S.*

Honey Walnut Cake

Honey Walnut Cake

MAKES ONE 8-INCH CAKE

The tender, nut-rich cakes of France and Italy inspired this recipe. Roasting the walnuts and using a fragrant roasted nut oil intensifies the flavor. Since both honey and rosemary have an affinity for walnuts, they're mixed with the whipped cream that's served with the cake. Assemble all of your ingredients before you start because you'll need to work quickly once the eggs are beaten.

½ teaspoon plus 1 tablespoon roasted walnut oil (see Note)

2 tablespoons fine dry bread crumbs

1¼ cups (5 ounces) walnuts

3 tablespoons all-purpose flour

½ teaspoon baking powder

3 large eggs, separated, at room temperature

½ cup plus 2 tablespoons granulated sugar

¼ teaspoon salt

2 teaspoons pure vanilla extract

½ teaspoon finely grated lemon zest

¼ teaspoon cream of tartar

2 teaspoons confectioners' sugar

Rosemary Whipped Cream (recipe follows)

1. Preheat the oven to 350°. Line an 8-inch round cake pan with a round of parchment or wax paper. Brush the paper and the side of the pan with ½ teaspoon of the walnut oil. Coat the pan evenly with the bread crumbs.

2. Spread the walnuts in a pie pan and roast in the oven for 10 to 12 minutes or until very fragrant. Let cool completely.

3. In a food processor, combine the walnuts with the flour and baking powder and process to a fine powder.

4. In a small bowl, using an electric mixer, beat the egg yolks with ½ cup of the granulated sugar and ⅛ teaspoon of the salt at high speed until the mixture is thick and pale and forms a ribbon when the beaters are lifted, 4 to 5 minutes. Beat in the vanilla extract, the lemon zest and the remaining 1 tablespoon of walnut oil.

5. In a clean, dry bowl, using clean beaters, beat the egg whites with the cream of tartar and the remaining ⅛ teaspoon salt until soft peaks form. Gradually add the remaining 2 tablespoons granulated sugar and beat until stiff peaks form. With a rubber spatula, push the whites to one side of the bowl and pour in the egg yolk mixture; fold together 3 or 4 times. Sprinkle the walnut mixture on top and fold together until the batter is uniform.

6. Scrape the batter into the prepared pan and gently smooth the top. Bake in the middle of the oven for 35 to 40 minutes, or until the cake pulls away from the side of the pan and a knife inserted in the center comes out clean. Let the cake cool on a rack for 15 minutes in the pan, then invert it onto the rack and let cool completely. Sift confectioners' sugar over the top and serve with the whipped cream. —*Sally Schneider*

NOTE Roasted walnut oil is available from specialty food shops.

MAKE AHEAD The cooled cake can be wrapped well in plastic and frozen for up to 1 month. Defrost in the refrigerator without unwrapping.

WINE The honey-scented whipped cream served with this cake would find an enticing echo in a chilled glass of aromatic, grapey Italian Moscato, such as the 1997 Vietti Cascinetta or the 1997 Rivetti La Spinetta.

ROSEMARY WHIPPED CREAM
MAKES 2 CUPS
- ¼ cup wildflower, lime blossom or tupelo honey
- Three 1-inch rosemary sprigs
- 1 cup cold heavy cream

1. Place a medium stainless steel bowl and beaters in the freezer to chill. In a small heavy saucepan, combine the honey and rosemary and bring almost to a simmer over low heat; bruise the rosemary with the back of a spoon. Remove from the heat, cover and set aside until the honey cools to room temperature. Taste the honey as it stands; it should have a pleasant rosemary flavor without being harsh. Discard the rosemary sprigs.

2. Pour the cream into the chilled bowl, add the honey and beat at high speed until soft peaks form. Serve immediately or cover and refrigerate for a few hours. —*S. S.*

Peach Spice Cake with Caramel Sauce

MAKES ONE 9-INCH CAKE
This summery version of upside-down cake is served with a decadent caramel sauce, but the moist peach cake is also nice plain. Removing the peach skin is easiest with a vegetable peeler.

PEACHES
- 2 tablespoons unsalted butter
- ½ cup (packed) dark brown sugar
- 6 ripe freestone peaches—peeled, halved lengthwise and pitted

CAKE
- 1¾ cups cake flour
- 1½ teaspoons baking powder
- ½ teaspoon ground ginger
- ¼ teaspoon cinnamon
- ¼ teaspoon salt
- 1 stick plus 2 tablespoons (5 ounces) unsalted butter, softened
- 1 cup (packed) dark brown sugar
- 1 teaspoon pure vanilla extract
- ¼ teaspoon finely grated lime zest
- 3 large eggs
- ½ cup half-and-half
- Creamy Caramel Sauce (recipe follows)

1. PREPARE THE PEACHES: Preheat the oven to 375°. Butter a 9-inch round cake pan.

2. In a large ovenproof skillet, melt the butter. Stir in the brown sugar over low heat. Arrange the peach halves in the skillet, cut side up. Cover with foil and bake for about 10 minutes, or until the peaches are tender and the sauce is syrupy. Transfer the peach halves to the prepared cake pan, cut side down. They may overlap. Spoon the brown sugar sauce over the peaches and let cool. Lower the oven temperature to 350°.

3. PREPARE THE CAKE: In a medium bowl, sift together the cake flour, baking powder, ginger, cinnamon and salt. In another bowl, using a handheld mixer, beat the butter with the brown sugar until fluffy. Beat in the vanilla and the lime zest. Add the eggs, 1 at a time, beating well after each addition. Fold in half of the dry ingredients. Fold in the half-and-half and then fold in the remaining dry ingredients. Spoon the batter over the peach halves in the cake pan and bake for about 1 hour, or until a tester inserted in the center of the cake comes out clean. Let the cake cool to room temperature and then run a knife around the side and invert the cake onto a plate. Cut the cake into wedges and serve with the Creamy Caramel Sauce. —*Fred Eric*

MAKE AHEAD The unmolded cake can stand at room temperature for up to 2 hours before serving.

Peach Spice Cake with Caramel Sauce

CREAMY CARAMEL SAUCE
MAKES ABOUT 2 CUPS

1½ cups sugar

½ cup water

1¼ cups heavy cream

In a heavy medium saucepan, combine the sugar and water and simmer over high heat without stirring until the sugar dissolves. Stir lightly and lower the heat to moderate. Simmer undisturbed until a deep amber caramel forms, about 10 minutes. Remove from the heat and gently stir in the cream until the sauce is smooth. Let the sauce cool to room temperature. —*F. E.*

MAKE AHEAD The sauce can be refrigerated for up to 3 days. Let return to room temperature before serving.

Apple Spice Cake
MAKES ONE 10-INCH TUBE CAKE

2 cups all-purpose flour

1 teaspoon cinnamon

1 teaspoon freshly grated nutmeg

1 teaspoon ground cloves

½ teaspoon salt

2 sticks (½ pound) unsalted butter, softened

2 cups sugar

4 large eggs

¼ cup Calvados or other brandy

Apple Spice Cake

1 teaspoon baking soda mixed with 1 tablespoon warm water

1 teaspoon pure vanilla extract

3 Red Delicious apples—halved, cored and sliced ½ inch thick

1 cup coarsely chopped pecans

I. Preheat the oven to 350°. Butter and flour a 10-inch tube pan. In a small bowl, combine the flour, cinnamon, nutmeg, cloves and salt.

2. In a bowl, beat the butter until creamy. Beat in the sugar. Add the eggs, 1 at a time, beating after each addition. Add the Calvados, baking soda mixture and vanilla. Stir in the flour mixture, apples and pecans just until incorporated.

3. Scrape the batter into the prepared pan; bake for about 1 hour, or until the cake is deep brown and a toothpick inserted in the center comes out clean. Let cool completely. Turn out onto a plate, cut into wedges and serve. —*Gary Peese*

SERVE WITH Mascarpone cream.

Mace-Spiced Crumb Cake with Bourbon Glaze
MAKES ONE 9-INCH CAKE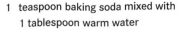

CRUMB TOPPING

1 cup all-purpose flour

¼ cup granulated sugar

¼ cup light brown sugar

½ teaspoon baking powder

Pinch of salt

¼ cup canola oil

CAKE

1 teaspoon unsalted butter

2 cups plus 2 tablespoons cake flour, plus more for dusting

¼ cup low-fat (1.5%) buttermilk

1 teaspoon pure vanilla extract

1 teaspoon baking powder

1 teaspoon baking soda

½ teaspoon salt

¼ teaspoon ground mace

1 cup granulated sugar

½ cup canola oil

2 large eggs

GLAZE

⅓ cup confectioners' sugar

2 teaspoons bourbon

I. MAKE THE CRUMB TOPPING: In a bowl, combine the flour, granulated sugar, brown sugar, baking powder and salt. Add the oil and stir until combined. Using your fingers, pinch the mixture together to form crumbs.

2. MAKE THE CAKE: Preheat the oven to 350°. Grease a 9-inch springform pan with the butter and dust with flour. In a small pitcher, combine the buttermilk and vanilla. In a medium bowl, whisk together the flour, baking powder, baking soda, salt and mace. In a large bowl, beat the sugar and oil for 1 minute. Add the eggs, 1 at a time, beating well after each addition. Beat in the flour mixture at low speed in 3 batches, alternating with the buttermilk mixture, just until the batter is smooth.

3. Scrape the batter into the prepared pan and scatter the crumb topping over it. Bake in the center of the oven for about 1 hour, or until a toothpick inserted in the center comes out clean. Transfer to a rack to cool slightly.

4. MAKE THE GLAZE: In a small bowl, combine the confectioners' sugar with the bourbon; add up to ½ teaspoon of water if the glaze is too stiff. Using a small spoon, drizzle the glaze over the warm cake. Let cool before unmolding. —*Grace Parisi*

MAKE AHEAD The cake can be wrapped in plastic and kept at room temperature for up to 5 days or frozen for up to 1 month.

ONE SERVING Calories 399 kcal, Total Fat 16.7 gm, Saturated Fat 1.7 gm

Blueberry—Sour Cream Coffee Cake
MAKES ONE 10-INCH BUNDT CAKE

Blueberry preserves give this moist cake a pretty swirl and a fruity sweetness.

2 cups all-purpose flour

1 tablespoon baking powder

½ teaspoon salt

2 sticks (½ pound) unsalted butter, softened

1½ cups granulated sugar

Blueberry—Sour Cream Coffee Cake

2 large eggs, at room temperature, lightly beaten

1 cup sour cream

1 tablespoon pure vanilla extract

¾ cup blueberry preserves, plus 1 tablespoon melted preserves

Confectioners' sugar, for dusting

1. Preheat the oven to 350°. Butter and flour a 10-inch Bundt pan. In a medium bowl, whisk together the flour, baking powder and salt. In a large bowl, beat the butter until creamy. Add the granulated sugar and beat until fluffy. Beat in the eggs, sour cream and vanilla. Beat in the dry ingredients just until incorporated.

2. Spread all but ½ cup of the batter into the prepared pan. Using the back of a spoon, make a trough in the batter, all the way around the pan. Mix the ¾ cup of blueberry preserves with the reserved batter; spoon it into the trough.

3. Bake the cake for about 1 hour, or until it begins to pull away from the pan and a skewer inserted in the center comes out clean. Let the cake cool in the pan for 15 minutes. Invert the cake onto a wire rack, remove the pan and let cool completely. Sift confectioners' sugar over the coffee cake, drizzle with the melted blueberry preserves and serve. —*Jonathan King and Jim Stott*

MAKE AHEAD The coffee cake can be stored at room temperature in an airtight container for up to 3 days or frozen for up to 1 month.

Pepper Pound Cake

MAKES ONE 10-INCH BUNDT CAKE

Pepper lends this sweet, rich, moist cake a fine complexity without making it spicy. The cake is best the day it's made.

3 cups all-purpose flour

1 teaspoon baking powder

2 sticks (½ pound) unsalted butter, softened

2½ cups sugar

5 large eggs, separated

2 tablespoons honey

1½ teaspoons freshly ground pepper

½ teaspoon ground ginger

½ teaspoon salt

Finely grated zest of 1 lemon

1 cup buttermilk

1. Preheat the oven to 325°. Butter and flour a 10-inch Bundt pan. Sift the flour with the baking powder into a medium bowl. In a large bowl, using an electric mixer, beat the butter with the sugar at high speed until light and fluffy. Beat in the egg yolks, honey, pepper, ginger, salt and lemon zest. Beat in the sifted dry ingredients alternately with the buttermilk.

2. In a stainless steel bowl, beat the egg whites until they hold firm peaks. Using a spatula, stir one third of the beaten whites into the cake batter until well mixed. Fold in the remaining whites until just blended. Scrape the batter into the prepared pan and bake for about 1 hour and 10 minutes, or until a cake tester inserted in the center comes out clean. Let cool in the pan for 20 minutes and then unmold onto a rack and let cool completely before slicing. —*Maya Kaimal*

Wedding Cake with Dots and Daisies

MAKES ONE 8-INCH LAYER CAKE

This cake is bridal white and very light. The airiness is the result of beating whole warmed eggs with sugar until fluffy.

1 cup cake flour, plus more for dusting

½ cup cornstarch

1½ sticks (6 ounces) unsalted butter

6 large eggs, at room temperature

¾ cup sugar

Finely grated zest of 1 orange

Grand Marnier Syrup (recipe follows)

Grand Marnier Buttercream (recipe follows)

1 pint raspberries

Sugar dots and daisies (see Note)

Satin ribbon (optional)

1. Preheat the oven to 350°. Butter two 8-inch round cake pans; line the bottoms with parchment paper. Butter the paper; dust with flour, tapping out any excess. Sift the flour and cornstarch together twice. Melt the butter and keep warm.

2. In the bowl of a standing mixer, beat the eggs with the sugar and orange zest just until combined. Set the bowl over a saucepan of simmering water and whisk until the eggs are warm. Return the bowl to the standing mixer and beat the egg mixture at medium-high speed until pale and tripled in volume, 3 to 5 minutes.

3. Sift the flour mixture over the egg mixture in 3 batches, folding it in after each addition with a rubber spatula. Gradually pour the warm butter into the batter in a stream at the side of the bowl, folding it in until no streaks appear. Divide the batter between the pans and bake for about 20 minutes, or until the tops are light golden and the cakes spring back when lightly pressed. Let the cakes cool in the pans for 10 minutes and then run a thin blade around the sides and invert onto a wire rack to cool completely.

4. Using a sharp serrated knife, split each cake into 2 layers. Brush the cut sides with the Grand Marnier Syrup. Set 1 layer on a cake plate, cut side up, then spread it with a thin layer of the Grand Marnier Buttercream. Put 1 cup of the buttercream into a pastry bag fitted with a small round tip and pipe a buttercream border ½ inch thick around the edge of the cake layer. Scatter one third of the raspberries inside the border. Spread the cut side of a second cake layer with a thin layer of the buttercream and set it frosted side down on the raspberries. Spread a thin layer of buttercream over the cake and then pipe a border all around. Repeat with the remaining raspberries, buttercream and cake layers. Spread the remaining buttercream around the side and top; refrigerate until firm, about 3 hours or up to 2 days. Let the cake stand at room temperature for 30 minutes and then decorate with the sugar dots and daisies and satin ribbon before serving. —*Claudia Fleming*

NOTE Sugar decorations are available at baking supply stores or by mail from Sweet Celebrations (800-328-6722).

Wedding Cake with Dots and Daisies

GRAND MARNIER SYRUP

MAKES ½ CUP

- 2 tablespoons sugar
- 2 tablespoons water
- 1 tablespoon Grand Marnier

In a small saucepan, heat the sugar and water, stirring, until dissolved. Add the Grand Marnier and let cool; refrigerate for up to 1 week. —C. F.

GRAND MARNIER BUTTERCREAM

MAKES ABOUT 3 CUPS

- 8 large egg whites
- 1 cup sugar
- 1 pound unsalted butter, softened
- 3 tablespoons Grand Marnier

In the bowl of a standing mixer, beat the egg whites with the sugar just until combined. Set the bowl over a saucepan of simmering water and whisk constantly until the mixture is very warm. Return the bowl to the mixer and beat the egg whites at high speed until stiff and glossy, about 5 minutes. Add the butter, 2 or 3 tablespoons at a time, beating at medium-high speed, until glossy and smooth. Add the Grand Marnier to the frosting and beat until incorporated. —C. F.

Devil's Food Cake

MAKES ONE 9-INCH LAYER CAKE

The chocolate cake at The Lark Creek Inn in Larkspur, California, is as soul satisfying as you could wish (even with beets as a surprise ingredient). It's even better than anything Mom used to make. The cake has four layers, so if you have only two nine-inch cake pans, plan to bake the cake layers in two batches.

FROSTING

- 2 pounds bittersweet chocolate, coarsely chopped
- 3 cups heavy cream
- 1 stick (4 ounces) unsalted butter
- ¼ cup sugar

CAKE

- 4 cups all-purpose flour
- 1½ cups unsweetened cocoa powder, preferably Dutch process
- 3½ cups sugar
- 1 tablespoon baking soda
- 1 teaspoon baking powder
- 1½ teaspoons salt
- 3 cups buttermilk
- 6 large eggs
- 1 cup sour cream
- 3 sticks (¾ pound) unsalted butter, melted and cooled
- 3 medium beets (about 1¼ pounds), peeled and grated

1. MAKE THE FROSTING: In a large heatproof bowl set over a large saucepan of simmering water, combine the bittersweet chocolate, cream, butter and sugar. Whisk occasionally until the sugar dissolves and the frosting is smooth. Transfer the frosting to a large bowl, cover and let stand at room temperature until firmed up, about 5 hours, or refrigerate for up to 2 days. Let return to room temperature before frosting the cake.

2. MAKE THE CAKE: Preheat the oven to 350°. Butter four 9-inch cake pans and line the bottoms with parchment paper. In a large bowl, sift together the flour, unsweetened cocoa powder, sugar, baking soda, baking powder and salt. In another bowl, whisk together the buttermilk and eggs. Beat the buttermilk mixture into the dry ingredients until combined. Beat in the sour cream. Add the butter and beets and mix until fully incorporated.

3. Pour the batter into the prepared pans and bake for about 35 minutes, or until a tester inserted in the center of each cake comes out clean. Transfer the cakes to racks and let cool completely in their pans.

4. Invert the cooled cake layers onto a work surface and peel off the parchment paper. Set one layer on a large plate and spread ¼ inch of chocolate frosting on top. Stack and frost the remaining cake layers. Spread the remaining frosting all around the side of the cake. Cut the cake into wedges and serve. —Bradley Ogden

MAKE AHEAD The frosted Devil's Food Cake can be refrigerated overnight, covered. Let return to room temperature before serving.

Molten Chocolate Cakes

MAKES FOUR 3½-INCH CAKES

You will need four six-ounce ramekins to make these cakes.

- 1 stick (4 ounces) unsalted butter
- 6 ounces bittersweet chocolate, preferably Valrhona
- 2 eggs
- 2 egg yolks
- ¼ cup sugar

Pinch of salt

- 2 tablespoons all-purpose flour

1. Preheat the oven to 450°. Butter and lightly flour four 6-ounce ramekins. Tap out the excess flour. Set the ramekins on a baking sheet.

2. In a double boiler, over simmering water, melt the butter with the chocolate. In a medium bowl, beat the eggs with the egg yolks, sugar and salt at high speed until thickened and pale.

3. Whisk the chocolate mixture until smooth. Quickly fold the chocolate mixture into the egg mixture along with the flour. Spoon the cake batter into the prepared ramekins and bake for 12 minutes, or until the sides of the cakes are firm but the centers are soft. Let the cakes cool in the ramekins for 1 minute and then cover each with an inverted dessert plate. Carefully turn each one over, let stand for 10 seconds and then unmold. Serve the cakes immediately. —Jean-Georges Vongerichten

MAKE AHEAD The cake batter can be refrigerated for several hours. Bring the batter to room temperature before baking.

SERVE WITH Vanilla ice cream.

WINE Chocolate is too intense and bitter for many sweet wines, but not port. Try these chocolate cakes with a Ruby Porto, such as the nonvintage Sandeman Founder's Reserve or the nonvintage Fonseca Bin No. 27.

Key Lime Pie

MAKES ONE 9-INCH PIE

Situated on Florida's Sugar Loaf Key and almost hidden by overgrown bushes, the restaurant Mangrove Mama's looks like a shack. The food inside, however, is delicious. The Key Lime Pie's flawlessly creamy yet firm consistency is matched by its perfectly balanced sweet tart flavor.

1¾ cups (about 7 ounces) graham cracker crumbs

1 stick (4 ounces) unsalted butter, melted

¼ teaspoon cinnamon

3 large egg yolks

¼ teaspoon cream of tartar

Two 14-ounce cans sweetened condensed milk

⅔ cup Key lime juice, preferably fresh

I. Preheat the oven to 350°. In a medium bowl, stir together the graham cracker crumbs, butter and cinnamon. Evenly press the crumbs into a 9-inch pie plate. Bake for about 12 minutes, or until firm. Remove the crust from the oven; lower the temperature to 325°.

2. In a large bowl, whisk the egg yolks with the cream of tartar until frothy. Stir in the condensed milk and then whisk in the lime juice until it is fully incorporated.

3. Pour the filling into the crust. Bake for about 15 minutes, or until set. Let cool on a rack; refrigerate until chilled before serving. —Mangrove Mama's

MAKE AHEAD The pie can be refrigerated overnight.

Pear Tart with Almond Cream

MAKES ONE 11-INCH TART

Restaurant Le Miroir d'Argentine in Solalex, Switzerland, is a happy combination of *The Sound of Music* and Chez Panisse, an unkitschy chalet that features fresh local ingredients and fabulous fruit tarts.

PASTRY CREAM

1½ large egg yolks (1½ tablespoons)

2 tablespoons sugar

Molten Chocolate Cakes

1 tablespoon plus 1 teaspoon all-purpose flour

Pinch of salt

½ cup milk

½ teaspoon pure vanilla extract

TART

1 disk Tart Dough (recipe follows)

4 ripe pears, such as Bartlett or Anjou

½ lemon

6 tablespoons (3 ounces) unsalted butter, softened

⅔ cup confectioners' sugar, sifted

⅔ cup (about 3½ ounces) ground almonds

1 tablespoon cornstarch

2 teaspoons white rum

1 egg, lightly beaten

1 tablespoon granulated sugar

I. MAKE THE PASTRY CREAM: In a medium bowl, whisk the egg yolks and sugar until pale and thick. Whisk in the flour, salt and 1 tablespoon milk. In a medium saucepan, bring the remaining milk just to a simmer. Gradually whisk the hot milk into the egg mixture.

2. Scrape the egg mixture into the saucepan and bring to a boil, whisking constantly. Cook for 2 minutes. Scrape into a small bowl and stir in the vanilla. Press a piece of plastic wrap directly onto the surface of the pastry cream and let the cream cool completely.

3. MAKE THE TART: Preheat the oven to 425°. On a lightly floured surface, roll out the dough ⅛ inch thick. Gently ease the dough into an 11-inch fluted tart pan with a removable bottom, preferably not a dark pan. Trim any overhanging dough flush with the rim. Prick the bottom several times with a fork and refrigerate until the dough is firm, about 10 minutes.

4. Line the dough with foil, leaving 2 inches of overhang, and fill the pan with pie weights or dried beans. Bake the tart shell in the middle of the oven for 12 minutes, or until it is barely set and pale golden. Lift out the foil and the pie weights and bake for 5 minutes longer, or until the shell is lightly browned and dry to the touch but not cooked through. Let cool.

5. Peel and halve the pears. Using a melon baller, scoop out the cores. Rub the pears with the cut side of the lemon to prevent discoloration. Thinly slice each pear half crosswise, keeping the halves intact. Using the palm of your hand, press the cut pears slightly to fan them out.

6. In a medium bowl, beat the butter until it is smooth and creamy. Add the confectioners' sugar, almonds, cornstarch, rum and the cooled pastry cream and beat until smooth. Add the egg and beat until blended.

7. Spread the almond cream in the tart shell. Using a long metal spatula, arrange the sliced pears in a radiating pattern over the almond cream, keeping the halves intact. Sprinkle the tart with the granulated sugar and bake until the almond cream is browned and set, the pears are tender and just beginning to brown and the crust is golden, about 40 minutes. —*Le Miroir d'Argentine*

TART DOUGH

MAKES ENOUGH DOUGH FOR TWO 11-INCH TART SHELLS

- 3 **cups all-purpose flour**
- ¼ **teaspoon salt**
- ¼ **cup plus 2 teaspoons chilled solid vegetable shortening**
- 1 **stick plus 6 tablespoons (7 ounces) cold unsalted butter, cut into small pieces**
- ¾ **cup ice water**

1. Combine the flour and salt in a food processor and pulse for a few seconds. Add the shortening and process until completely incorporated. Add the butter and pulse until the mixture resembles small peas. Add the ice water and pulse until the dough is evenly moistened and just begins to hold together.

2. Transfer the dough to a work surface and gather it into a ball. Divide the dough in half and pat each half into a 6-inch disk. Wrap each of the disks in plastic and refrigerate the disks for at least 30 minutes, or freeze for up to 1 month. —*Le Miroir d'Argentine*

Plum and Hazelnut Tart

MAKES ONE 11-INCH TART

At Le Miroir d'Argentine in Solalex, Switzerland, tarts are always on the menu.

- ¾ **cup hazelnuts**
- 1 **disk Tart Dough (recipe above)**
- 1¾ **pounds purple plums or Italian prune plums—halved, pitted and cut into sixths**
- 4 **tablespoons sugar**
- 2 **tablespoons apricot preserves, strained**

1. Preheat the oven to 425°. In a cake pan, toast the hazelnuts for 6 to 8 minutes, or until the nuts are fragrant and their skins blister. Transfer the hot nuts to a kitchen towel and rub them together to remove the skins. Let cool completely. Finely grind the nuts in a food processor.

2. On a lightly floured surface, roll out the dough ⅛ inch thick. Gently ease the dough into an 11-inch fluted tart pan with a removable bottom. Line the dough with

foil, leaving 2 inches of overhang. Fill the foil with pie weights or dried beans and bake for 20 minutes, or until the edges are golden and the bottom is dry. Lift out the foil and weights and bake for 5 minutes longer. Turn the oven down to 375°.

3. Spread the hazelnuts in the tart shell in an even layer. Arrange the plums, skin side down, in concentric circles over the nuts; sprinkle with the sugar. Bake in the middle of the oven for about 35 minutes, or until the plums are tender. Brush the plums with the apricot preserves and let the tart cool slightly before serving. —*Le Miroir d'Argentine*

Peach Tart

MAKES ONE 10-INCH TART

You can also use this recipe to make six individual tartlets. Fresh apricots, plums or nectarines can replace the peaches. The apricots and plums don't need to be peeled, and they can be halved or cut into wedges. If the fruit is on the tart side, add up to a quarter cup more sugar than is called for below.

- ½ **vanilla bean, split lengthwise**
- ¼ **cup granulated sugar**
- 1½ **pounds peaches—peeled, pitted and cut into ¼-inch wedges**
- 1 **tablespoon fresh lemon juice**
- 1 **teaspoon framboise or kirsch**

Flaky Pastry (recipe follows)

- 2 **tablespoons all-purpose flour**
- 1 **teaspoon unsalted butter, cut into thin slices and chilled**
- 2 **teaspoons confectioners' sugar (optional)**

1. Preheat the oven to 400°. In a small bowl, using the back of a table knife, scrape the seeds from the vanilla bean into the granulated sugar and mix well. In a glass or stainless steel bowl, toss the peaches with the lemon juice, framboise and 3 tablespoons of the vanilla sugar.

2. On a lightly floured surface, roll out the pastry to a 14-inch round. Transfer the round to a baking sheet.

3. Combine the flour with the remaining 1 tablespoon of vanilla sugar. Sprinkle

BACK: **Plum and Hazelnut Tart.**
FRONT: **Pear Tart with Almond Cream.**

Peach Tart

the flour-and-sugar mixture evenly over the dough to within 2 inches of the edge. Arrange the peaches over the flour-and-sugar mixture.

4. Fold the edge of the dough over the peaches. Moisten your fingers lightly and gently press the creases together so that they hold their shape. Dot the peaches with the butter.

5. Bake the peach tart in the middle of the oven for about 40 minutes, or until the crust is golden brown, the peaches are tender and the juices are syrupy. Cover the tart with foil halfway through if it is browning too quickly. Let the tart cool for at least 10 minutes; sift confectioners' sugar over the edge of the tart if desired. —*Sally Schneider*

ONE SERVING (SERVES 6) Calories 267 kcal, Total Fat 10.4 gm, Saturated Fat 6.2 gm

FLAKY PASTRY

MAKES ENOUGH DOUGH FOR
ONE 10-INCH TART,
FOUR 4-INCH TARTS OR
6 INDIVIDUAL TARTLETS

- 1 cup bleached flour
- 1 teaspoon sugar
- ¼ teaspoon baking powder
- ¼ teaspoon salt
- 4 tablespoons cold unsalted butter, cut into ½-inch pieces
- 3 tablespoons sour cream

1. In a food processor, combine the flour, sugar, baking powder and salt. Pulse until mixed. Add the butter pieces and pulse until the mixture resembles coarse meal. Chill a work bowl for 15 minutes.

2. Transfer the mixture to the chilled bowl, add the sour cream and process until the mixture resembles coarse sand. Gather the dough into a ball and pat it into a disk. Wrap the disk in plastic and refrigerate for at least 30 minutes before rolling out. —*S. S.*

MAKE AHEAD The dough can be frozen for up to 1 month. Thaw in the refrigerator before using.

Rhubarb Tart

MAKES ONE 10-INCH TART 🌸

Dried strawberries or cherries add sweet, fruity notes that balance the tangy flavor of the rhubarb. Be sure to cut off and discard any leafy portions still attached to the rhubarb; the leaves are poisonous. This recipe can also make six individual tartlets.

- 1¼ pounds rhubarb stalks, cut into 2-inch pieces (4 cups)
- 3 tablespoons all-purpose flour
- 2 tablespoons dried strawberries or cherries, chopped
- 2 teaspoons kirsch or pure vanilla extract
- ¾ cup granulated sugar
  Flaky Pastry (recipe at left)
- 1 teaspoon unsalted butter, cut into thin slices and chilled
- 2 teaspoons confectioners' sugar

1. Preheat the oven to 400°. In a medium bowl, toss the rhubarb with 2 tablespoons of the flour, the strawberries, kirsch and all but 1 tablespoon of the granulated sugar.

2. On a lightly floured surface, roll out the pastry to a 14-inch round. Transfer the round to a baking sheet.

3. Combine the remaining 1 tablespoon each of flour and granulated sugar and sprinkle over the dough to within 2 inches of the edge. Spread the rhubarb evenly over the flour-and-sugar mixture.

4. Fold the edge of the dough over the rhubarb. Moisten your fingers lightly and gently press the creases together so that they hold their shape. Dot the rhubarb with the butter.

5. Bake the tart in the middle of the oven for about 40 minutes, or until the crust is golden brown, the rhubarb is tender and the juices are syrupy. Cover the tart with foil halfway through if it is browning too quickly. Let cool for at least 10 minutes and sift confectioners' sugar over the edge. —*Sally Schneider*

ONE SERVING (SERVES 6) Calories 304 kcal, Total Fat 10.2 gm, Saturated Fat 6.2 gm

Pear-Cranberry Pie with Crumb Topping

MAKES ONE 9-INCH PIE

This recipe is heaven: pears are tossed with cranberries and lightly sweetened. Sweet and spicy gingersnap crumbs top the whole thing off.

- 1 disk Flaky Pie Dough (recipe follows)
- 1 large egg beaten with 1 tablespoon milk or cream

TOPPING

- 1 cup all-purpose flour
- ⅓ cup granulated sugar
- ⅓ cup (packed) light brown sugar
- 12 Gingersnaps (p. 353), crushed (see Note)
- ⅛ teaspoon ground ginger
- ⅛ teaspoon salt
- 1 stick (4 ounces) unsalted butter, melted and cooled

FILLING

- 2 pounds (about 5) ripe Anjou pears—peeled, halved, cored and sliced ¼ inch thick
- 1½ cups fresh cranberries
- 2 tablespoons fresh lemon juice
- 1 teaspoon finely grated lemon zest
- ½ teaspoon pure vanilla extract
- ¾ cup sugar
- 2 tablespoons cornstarch

1. On a lightly floured surface, roll out the dough to a 12-inch round and fit it into a 9-inch glass pie plate. Trim the overhang to 1 inch, fold under and crimp decoratively. Brush the rim with the egg wash and refrigerate until chilled.

2. MAKE THE TOPPING: In a medium bowl, stir together the flour, granulated sugar, brown sugar, gingersnap crumbs, ginger and salt. Stir in the butter until large crumbs form.

3. MAKE THE FILLING: Preheat the oven to 350°. In a large glass or stainless steel bowl, toss the pears with the cranberries, lemon juice and zest and vanilla. In a small bowl, toss the sugar with the cornstarch; stir the sugar into the fruit.

4. Pour the fruit into the chilled pie shell. Pour the crumb topping onto the

Pear-Cranberry Pie with Crumb Topping

pie, carefully spreading it to the edge to cover the filling completely. Set the pie on a foil-lined baking sheet and bake on the bottom rack of the oven for 1½ hours, or until the crust is golden and the filling is bubbling; cover the pie loosely with foil if the top is browning too quickly. Let the pie cool before slicing. —*Melissa Murphy Hagenbart*

NOTE If you aren't planning on making gingersnaps from scratch, use 4 ounces of spicy store-bought cookies instead.

FLAKY PIE DOUGH

MAKES ENOUGH DOUGH FOR TWO 9-INCH SINGLE CRUST PIES

2 ¾ cups all-purpose flour

1½ teaspoons salt

½ teaspoon finely grated lemon zest

¼ teaspoon cinnamon

6 tablespoons cold unsalted butter, cut into small pieces

¾ cup solid vegetable shortening, cut into small pieces and chilled

5 to 6 tablespoons ice water

In a food processor, combine the flour, salt, lemon zest and cinnamon. Add the butter and shortening and pulse until the butter is the size of small peas. Transfer the mixture to a large bowl. Add 5 tablespoons of ice water and stir with a fork until the dough comes together; add more water if necessary. Divide the dough in half and pat each piece into a 6-inch disk. Wrap the disks in plastic and refrigerate 1 of them for at least 1 hour before rolling out. Put the second disk of dough in a sturdy resealable plastic bag or wrap it again in foil and freeze for later use. Thaw the dough without unwrapping it. —*M. M. H.*

Cranberry-Pear Tartlets with Cranberry Ice Cream

12 SERVINGS

You will need one dozen four-inch fluted tartlet pans with removable bottoms to make this recipe.

ICE CREAM AND COMPOTE

2 pounds fresh or frozen cranberries

3 cups water

3 ¾ cups sugar

1½ cups heavy cream

1½ cups golden raisins

¾ cup dried currants

1 vanilla bean, split lengthwise

1 cinnamon stick, cracked

10 firm but ripe pears, such as Bartlett or Anjou—peeled, cored and thinly sliced

PASTRY

3 ¾ cups all-purpose flour

3 tablespoons sugar

1½ teaspoons salt

3 sticks (¾ pound) unsalted butter, cut into small pieces and chilled

⅓ cup ice water

Mint sprigs, for garnish

I. MAKE THE ICE CREAM AND COMPOTE: In a large saucepan, combine 5 cups of the cranberries with the water and 1¾ cups of the sugar and bring to a boil, stirring to dissolve the sugar. Cook over moderate heat until the cranberries split, 4 to 5 minutes.

Pour the cranberries into a colander set over a bowl without pressing on the solids; reserve the cranberry syrup.

2. In a blender, chop the cooked cranberries with ½ cup of the sugar. With the machine on, pour in 1 cup of the reserved cranberry syrup and puree until smooth. Strain in a fine sieve and refrigerate until chilled.

3. Combine the cream with the cold cranberry sauce and freeze in an ice cream maker according to the manufacturer's instructions. Transfer the ice cream to an airtight container; freeze until firm, at least 2 hours.

4. In a saucepan, combine the remaining 1½ cups of sugar with 3 tablespoons of the cranberry syrup and stir until the sugar is moist and pink. Cook the sugar over moderate heat, brushing down the side of the pan with a wet brush, until a light amber caramel forms, about 8 minutes. Remove from the heat and add ½ cup of the cranberry syrup, gently swirling until blended.

5. Add the remaining 3 cups of cranberries to the caramel sauce and cook over moderate heat, gently pressing the cranberries against the side of the pan, until slightly softened, about 5 minutes. Stir in the raisins and currants and transfer the compote to a large bowl.

6. In a saucepan, combine the remaining cranberry syrup with the vanilla bean and cinnamon stick and bring to a boil. Add the pears, cover and cook over moderately high heat, stirring, until tender, 10 to 12 minutes. Let cool slightly and then strain. Discard the vanilla and cinnamon. Stir the pears into the compote. Reserve 1 cup of the pear cooking liquid for serving. (You can reserve the remaining cooking liquid for poaching fruit later.)

7. MAKE THE PASTRY: In a food processor, combine the flour, sugar and salt and pulse to blend. Add the butter and pulse until the mixture is the size of peas. Add the ice water and process just until the dough comes together. Transfer the dough to a lightly floured

Cranberry-Pear Tartlets with Cranberry Ice Cream

work surface and knead it several times. Shape the dough into a 3-inch-wide log. Wrap it in plastic and refrigerate until chilled, at least 1 hour.

8. Unwrap the dough and cut it into 12 rounds. Working with 1 at a time, roll each piece of dough out to a 6-inch round. Transfer the rounds to 4-by-1-inch fluted tartlet pans with removable bottoms, pressing the dough into the corners. Trim the edges and prick the bottoms several times with a fork. Refrigerate the shells until chilled.

9. Preheat the oven to 400°. Line the tartlet shells with foil and fill the foil with pie weights or dried beans. Bake for about 10 minutes. Carefully remove the shells from the oven and remove the foil and weights. Bake the shells for about 20 minutes longer or until golden. Let cool completely on a wire rack.

10. Unmold the shells and set on small plates. Fill with the compote. Spoon a scoop of the cranberry ice cream next to each tartlet and spoon the reserved poaching liquid alongside. Garnish with mint sprigs and serve. —*Tim McKee*

MAKE AHEAD The dessert can be made through Step 9 up to 2 days ahead. Freeze the ice cream. Refrigerate the compote. Keep the shells in an airtight container at room temperature; recrisp in a 325° oven and let the compote return to room temperature before using.

WINE If there's room for a dessert wine, serve a Muscat de Beaumes-de-Venise from France, such as the 1997 Georges Duboeuf.

Cranberry-Walnut Tart

MAKES ONE 10-INCH TART

PASTRY

1 2/3 **cups all-purpose flour**
2 1/2 **teaspoons sugar**
1/4 **teaspoon salt**
1/4 **teaspoon cinnamon**
7 **tablespoons cold unsalted butter, cut into small pieces**
1 **large egg yolk**
1/4 **cup ice water**

FILLING

12 **ounces cranberries**
1/2 **cup plus 1 tablespoon light brown sugar**
1/2 **cup plus 1 tablespoon granulated sugar**
Finely grated zest of 1 orange
Finely grated zest of 1 lemon
1/2 **cup fresh orange juice**
1/8 **teaspoon cinnamon**
4 **tablespoons plus 1 teaspoon unsalted butter**
1/2 **cup coarsely chopped walnuts**
Vanilla ice cream, for serving

1. MAKE THE PASTRY: In a food processor, combine the flour, sugar, salt and cinnamon and pulse. Add the butter and pulse just until the mixture resembles coarse meal. Transfer the mixture to a bowl. Whisk the egg yolk with the ice water and add to the bowl; stir until an evenly moistened dough forms. Transfer the dough to a lightly floured surface and knead it several times. Pat the dough into a 6-inch disk, wrap it in plastic and refrigerate for at least 30 minutes.

2. MAKE THE FILLING: In a medium saucepan, combine the cranberries with the brown and granulated sugars, the citrus zests, orange juice and cinnamon and bring to a boil. Lower the heat and simmer, stirring, until thickened, 8 to 10 minutes. Stir in the butter and transfer to a bowl to cool. Stir in the walnuts.

3. Preheat the oven to 375°. Butter a 10-inch fluted tart pan with a removable bottom. On a lightly floured surface, roll out the dough to a 12-inch round about 1/8 inch thick. Transfer the dough to the tart pan and fit it into the side. Trim off the overhang. Prick the bottom of the tart shell all over and refrigerate until chilled.

4. Line the pastry with foil and fill with pie weights or dried beans. Bake the tart shell for 30 minutes, or until lightly golden around the edge. Carefully remove the foil with the weights and bake the shell for 5 minutes longer, or until dry on the bottom. Let the shell cool slightly.

5. Spread the cranberry filling evenly in the tart shell and bake for about 25 minutes, or until the edge of the pastry is golden. Let the tart cool on a rack before unmolding. Serve the tart warm or at room temperature, with vanilla ice cream. —*Dana Speers*

MAKE AHEAD The baked tart can be refrigerated overnight; rewarm in a 350° oven for 15 minutes before serving.

Tarte Tatin

MAKES ONE 9-INCH TART

3/4 **cup sugar**
1 **stick plus 2 tablespoons (5 ounces) unsalted butter, cut into thin slices**
1 **teaspoon pure vanilla extract**
5 **pounds apples, such as Golden Delicious, Fuji, Jonagold or Northern Spy—peeled, halved and cored**
Classic Flaky Pastry (recipe follows)
Crème fraîche or whipped cream, for serving

1. Spread the sugar evenly in the bottom of a 9-inch cast-iron skillet. Scatter the butter over the sugar and drizzle with the vanilla. Arrange the apple halves on their sides in the skillet in 2 concentric circles with all of the apples facing the same direction. Pack the apples closely together. Place 1 apple half in the center to fill the empty space.

2. Set the skillet over moderately low heat and cook the apples until the surrounding syrup becomes a thick, golden brown, 45 minutes to 1 hour. Baste the apples regularly with a bulb baster. The liquid should remain at a gentle bubble.

3. Preheat the oven to 425°. Set the skillet on a baking sheet and bake the apples for 15 minutes. Remove from the oven. Set the pastry on top of the apples and carefully push the edge of the pastry down inside the pan. Return the skillet to the oven and bake for 25 to 30 minutes, or until the pastry is golden and the juices are bubbling over.

4. Remove the tart from the oven and immediately invert a platter with a lip over the skillet. Quickly and carefully invert the tart onto the platter so that the apples are on top. If any apples stick to the skillet, set them back into the tart. Serve the tart warm or at room temperature, with dollops of crème fraîche. —*Benoît Guichard*

WINE An apple tart calls out for a sweet white, such as a honeyed and unctuous German Auslese.

CLASSIC FLAKY PASTRY

MAKES ONE 11½-INCH PASTRY ROUND

- 1 cup unbleached all-purpose flour
- ⅛ teaspoon fine sea salt
- 1 stick (4 ounces) cold unsalted butter, cut into cubes
- 3 tablespoons ice water

I. Blend the flour with the salt in a food processor. Add the butter and process until well blended, about 8 seconds. Add the water and process just until the water has been absorbed and the mixture looks like wet sand. Transfer the pastry to a work surface and knead lightly until it comes together. Pat the dough into a disk, wrap in plastic and refrigerate until firm, about 1 hour.

2. On a lightly floured surface, roll the pastry into an 11½-inch round. Drape the dough over a rolling pin and then open it out on a baking sheet lined with plastic wrap. Refrigerate until ready to use. —*B. G.*

MAKE AHEAD The pastry disk can be wrapped and frozen for up to 1 month.

Glazed Apple Tart

MAKES ONE 12-BY-10-INCH TART

- ½ pound all-butter puff pastry
- 2 tablespoons unsalted butter, melted
- 2 large Granny Smith apples— peeled, halved, cored and sliced lengthwise ¼ inch thick
- 2 tablespoons sugar

I. Preheat the oven to 400°. Line a baking sheet with parchment paper. On a lightly floured work surface, roll out the puff pastry to a 12-by-10-inch rectangle about ⅛ inch thick. Transfer the pastry to the baking sheet and brush with 1 tablespoon of the butter.

2. Arrange the apple slices on the pastry in 3 neat lengthwise rows, overlapping the slices slightly and leaving a ½-inch border all around. Brush the apples with the remaining 1 tablespoon of butter and sprinkle with 1 tablespoon of the sugar. Bake the tart on the bottom rack of the oven for about 30 minutes, or until the pastry is cooked through and nicely browned. Remove the tart from the oven and preheat the broiler.

3. Sprinkle the apples with the remaining 1 tablespoon of sugar. Broil for about 30 seconds, or until the apples start to brown on top; rotate the pan as necessary. Cut the tart into 6 large squares and serve hot. —*Francis Mallmann*

Apple Tarts with Candied Ginger

MAKES EIGHT 5½-INCH TARTS

- 2 pounds all-butter puff pastry, thawed overnight in the refrigerator if frozen
- 4 medium Granny Smith or Golden Delicious apples— peeled, halved, cored and thinly sliced
- ¼ cup sugar

Cinnamon, for dusting

Late Harvest Riesling Ice Cream (p. 384)

- 1½ tablespoons finely chopped candied ginger

I. Preheat the oven to 425°. On a lightly floured surface, roll out the puff pastry ¼ inch thick. Using a pan lid as a guide, cut out eight 5½-inch rounds. Prick the pastry rounds with a fork. Transfer the rounds to 2 parchment-lined baking sheets.

2. Arrange the apple slices on the pastry rounds, overlapping slightly. Sprinkle

Tarte Tatin

Apple Tarts with Candied Ginger, with Late Harvest Riesling Ice Cream (p. 384).

Apple-Pecan Crumb Pie

each of the tarts with ½ tablespoon of the sugar and bake on the bottom shelf of the oven for about 30 minutes, or until the tarts are golden brown. Remove the baking sheets from the oven and transfer each of the tarts to an individual plate. Sprinkle the tarts with cinnamon and top each with a scoop of Late Harvest Riesling Ice Cream. Garnish with the chopped candied ginger and serve. —*Kimball Jones*

Apple-Pecan Crumb Pie

MAKES ONE 9-INCH PIE

You would never guess from the modest faces of the citizens having lunch at Peoples Restaurant in New Holland, Pennsylvania, that they are eating the food of angels. This blue plate special café serves fine versions of the simple specialties for which Amish country is known, but it's the melt-in-your-mouth pies—the shoofly and especially the apple crumb—that suggest the people of Lancaster County are getting their recipes direct from heaven.

CRUST

- 1 cup all-purpose flour
- ¼ teaspoon salt
- ½ cup cold vegetable shortening
- ¼ cup ice water

TOPPING AND FILLING

- ¼ cup light brown sugar
- ½ cup all-purpose flour
- 5 tablespoons unsalted butter, softened
- 2 pounds baking apples, such as Rome or Cortland—peeled, cored and cut into 2-inch chunks
- ¾ cup granulated sugar
- ½ teaspoon cinnamon
- ½ teaspoon salt
- 2 tablespoons unsalted butter, melted
- ¼ cup warm water mixed with 1 tablespoon cornstarch
- ⅓ cup coarsely chopped pecans

1. MAKE THE CRUST: In a large bowl, combine the flour and salt. Using a pastry blender or 2 knives, cut in the shortening until the mixture resembles coarse meal. Add the water and gently mix to form a dough. Pat the dough into a disk and wrap in plastic. Refrigerate until very firm, about 1 hour.

2. Preheat the oven to 375°. On a lightly floured surface, roll out the dough to an 11-inch round. Transfer it to a 9-inch glass pie pan and trim the overhanging dough to ½ inch. Fold the dough under, crimp the edge decoratively and refrigerate until firm.

3. MAKE THE TOPPING AND FILLING: In a bowl, using your fingers, rub the brown sugar into the flour until blended. Work in the softened butter until the mixture is crumbly.

4. In a large bowl, toss the apples with the granulated sugar, cinnamon and salt. Add the butter and then the cornstarch mixture and stir well. Spoon the apple filling into the chilled pie shell. Sprinkle the crumb topping over the apple filling and then sprinkle the pecans on top.

5. Bake the pie for about 50 minutes, or until it is browned on top and bubbling around the edges. Transfer the pie to a rack and let it cool slightly. Serve warm. —*Peoples Restaurant*

MAKE AHEAD The recipe can be prepared through Step 3 and refrigerated for up to 2 days.

SERVE WITH Vanilla ice cream.

Deep Dish Pecan Pie

MAKES TWO 9-INCH PIES

If you'd prefer regular pies rather than deep dish, roll out the dough to 12-inch rounds and bake in standard 10-inch pie plates.

PASTRY

- 3⅓ cups all-purpose flour, plus more for dusting
- 1½ teaspoons sugar
- ½ teaspoon salt
- 2 sticks plus 5 tablespoons (⅔ pound) cold unsalted butter, cut into ½-inch pieces
- ½ cup ice water

FILLING

- 3 cups (about 10 ounces) pecan halves
- 8 large eggs, at room temperature
- 4 large egg yolks, at room temperature
- 2 tablespoons pure vanilla extract
- ½ teaspoon salt
- 2 cups light brown sugar
- 4 tablespoons unsalted butter, melted
- 3 cups light corn syrup

1. MAKE THE PASTRY: In a food processor, pulse the flour with the sugar and salt. Add the butter and pulse until the mixture resembles coarse meal. Transfer to a bowl and stir in the ice water. Knead the dough 2 or 3 times; divide in half and pat each half into a 6-inch disk. Wrap the disks of dough separately in plastic and refrigerate them for 1 hour.

2. On a lightly floured surface, roll out 1 pastry to an 11-inch round. Fit the pastry into a deep 9-inch pie plate. Trim the overhang to ½ inch, fold the edge under and crimp decoratively; refrigerate. Repeat with the remaining disk.

3. MAKE THE FILLING: Preheat the oven to 375°. Line the bottom of the oven with foil in case of spills. Divide the pecans evenly between the pie shells. In a large bowl, combine the eggs, egg yolks, vanilla and salt. Whisk in the brown sugar and butter until smooth. Whisk in the corn syrup. Pour the filling over the pecans, pressing them down with a spoon to coat them with the syrup. Bake the pies in the center of the oven for 15 minutes.

4. Lower the oven temperature to 300° and bake the pies for about 1 hour, or until the crusts are golden and the filling is puffed and beginning to crack around the edges; it should still be slightly jiggly. Let the pies cool on a rack and then serve. —*Robert Del Grande*

MAKE AHEAD The pie pastry can be frozen for up to 1 week. The pecan pies can be refrigerated overnight.

Deep Dish Pecan Pie

Cinnamon Lace Cookies

Pine Nut Meringues

MAKES ABOUT 3 DOZEN ✳

These pine nut studded meringues are crisp on the outside and airy inside; for chewier cookies, undercook the meringues slightly.

2 large egg whites
Small pinch of salt
¾ cup plus 2 tablespoons sugar
¼ teaspoon pure vanilla extract
Scant ¼ teaspoon pure almond extract
1½ cups (about 6 ounces) almond meal or finely ground blanched almonds
2¼ cups (¾ pound) pine nuts

1. Preheat the oven to 375° and line several baking sheets with parchment or wax paper. In a large bowl, beat the egg whites with the salt on high speed until firm peaks form. Add the sugar, 2 tablespoons at a time, beating for 2 seconds between additions; beat until glossy and stiff. Add the vanilla and almond extracts and then fold in the almond meal.

2. Spread the pine nuts on a pie plate. Coat slightly rounded teaspoons of the meringue with the pine nuts. Arrange the pine nut coated meringues on the baking sheets about 1 inch apart and bake in batches for 15 to 18 minutes, or until golden. Slide the paper with the meringues onto wire racks and let the meringues cool completely. Remove the pine nut meringues from the paper and serve. —*Anthony Roselli*

Cinnamon Lace Cookies

MAKES 4 TO 6 DOZEN COOKIES

So fragile are these delicate, chocolate-edged cookies that some of them may break as they're removed from the cookie sheet.

1 stick (4 ounces) unsalted butter
⅔ cup sugar
⅓ cup light corn syrup
2 tablespoons heavy cream
⅔ cup all-purpose flour
1¼ teaspoons cinnamon
4 ounces semisweet chocolate, chopped

1. In a medium saucepan, combine the butter with the sugar, the light corn syrup and the heavy cream and bring just to a boil, stirring often. Remove the saucepan from the heat. Add the flour and the cinnamon to the butter mixture and beat until smooth. Transfer the cookie batter to a bowl and refrigerate until chilled.

2. Preheat the oven to 325°. Line 2 baking sheets with parchment paper. Scoop six ½-teaspoon-size mounds of batter onto each of the prepared baking sheets, leaving plenty of room for the cookies to spread. Bake for about 8 minutes, or until lacy and golden. Let the cookies cool on the baking sheet just until they are firm and then transfer them to a rack to cool. Wipe off the parchment paper and repeat with the remaining batter, chilling the batter between batches.

3. Melt the chopped semisweet chocolate in a heatproof bowl set over a pan of simmering water, stirring until the chocolate is smooth. Roll the edges of the cinnamon cookies in the melted chocolate and then set the cookies on wax paper until the chocolate is hardened. —*Tim McKee*

MAKE AHEAD The cookies can be stacked between sheets of wax paper and then frozen in an airtight container for 1 week.

Snickerdoodles

MAKES 32 COOKIES

Snickerdoodles, nonsensically named cookies that originated in 19th-century New England, are always made with cinnamon, but this version mixes the cinnamon with sugar to make a delectable coating. If you prefer to mix the dough by hand, the cookies will be a little denser.

2 sticks (½ pound) unsalted butter, softened
1½ cups plus 2 tablespoons sugar
2 large eggs, lightly beaten
2¾ cups all-purpose flour
2 teaspoons cream of tartar
1 teaspoon baking soda
¼ teaspoon salt
2 teaspoons cinnamon

1. In the bowl of a standing mixer fitted with a paddle attachment, beat the butter with 1½ cups of the sugar until the mixture is light and fluffy. Beat the eggs into the butter mixture. Add the flour, cream of tartar, baking soda and salt and beat at low speed until a smooth dough forms. Cover the cookie dough with plastic wrap and then refrigerate until the dough is firm, about 1 hour or overnight.

2. Preheat the oven to 350°. In a small bowl, mix the remaining 2 tablespoons of the sugar with the cinnamon. Scoop the cookie dough into tablespoon-size balls and roll the balls in the cinnamon sugar to coat. Arrange the balls 2 inches apart on cookie sheets and bake for about 20 minutes, or until the cookies are golden on the bottom. Leave the cookies on the cookie sheets for 2 minutes and then transfer them to a rack to cool. —*John Currence*

Chocolate Chip Macaroons

MAKES ABOUT 4 DOZEN MACAROONS

1¼ cups (about 5 ounces) pecan
  halves
Two 7-ounce bags sweetened
  shredded coconut
1¼ cups (about ½ pound) semisweet
  mini chocolate chips
⅓ cup plus 1 tablespoon
  all-purpose flour
⅛ teaspoon salt
One 14-ounce can sweetened
  condensed milk
2½ teaspoons pure vanilla extract

1. Preheat the oven to 350°. Lightly butter 2 large baking sheets. Toast the pecan halves in a pie plate for about 8 minutes, or until they are fragrant. Transfer the toasted pecans to a plate to cool and then chop them. Leave the oven on.
2. In a large bowl, combine the shredded coconut with the semisweet mini chocolate chips, the flour, the salt and the chopped toasted pecans. Add the sweetened condensed milk and the vanilla extract and stir until evenly moistened. Mound level tablespoons of the macaroon batter on the prepared baking sheets and bake for about 20 minutes, or until the cookies are lightly golden but still moist inside. Let the macaroons cool to room temperature before serving. —*Martha McGinnis*

MAKE AHEAD The macaroons can be stored in an airtight container at room temperature for up to 3 days.

Gingersnaps

MAKES 5½ DOZEN COOKIES
Using fresh spices makes all the difference in these buttery ginger crisps. If you've had spices for a year, it's time to replace them.

2¼ cups all-purpose flour
2 teaspoons ground ginger
1 teaspoon cinnamon
½ teaspoon allspice
¼ teaspoon freshly ground
  white pepper
2 teaspoons baking soda
½ teaspoon salt
2 sticks (½ pound) unsalted
  butter, softened
½ cup granulated sugar
½ cup light brown sugar
1 large egg
⅓ cup unsulphured molasses

1. In a medium bowl, stir together the flour, ginger, cinnamon, allspice, freshly ground white pepper, baking soda and salt.
2. In a large bowl, using a handheld electric mixer, beat the butter until smooth. Add the granulated sugar and light brown sugar and beat until light and fluffy. Beat the egg and molasses into the butter mixture. Add the dry ingredients and beat on low speed until blended. Form the gingersnap dough into a 10-inch disk, wrap the disk in plastic and refrigerate until firm.
3. Preheat the oven to 350°. Line several cookie sheets with parchment or wax paper. Roll tablespoons of the gingersnap dough into 1-inch balls and then arrange the balls about 2 inches apart on the prepared cookie sheets. Bake the gingersnaps on the upper and middle racks of the oven for about 15 minutes, or until they are browned and set; shift the cookie sheets halfway through baking. Let the gingersnaps cool completely on the baking sheets before serving. —*Melissa Murphy Hagenbart*

MAKE AHEAD The gingersnaps can be stored in an airtight container for up to 1 week or frozen for up to 1 month.

Pistachio Linzer Thumbprints

MAKES ABOUT 5 DOZEN COOKIES
A takeoff on the Austrian Linzertorte, these festive cookies use roasted pistachios rather than the usual hazelnuts to flavor the dough.

2 cups (10 ounces) unsalted
  pistachios
2 cups all-purpose flour
½ cup plus 1 tablespoon granulated
  sugar
1 teaspoon baking powder
1 teaspoon cinnamon
¼ teaspoon salt
2 sticks (½ pound) cold
  unsalted butter, cut into
  ½-inch cubes
2 large eggs, separated
1 teaspoon pure vanilla extract
1 tablespoon finely grated lemon
  zest
⅔ cup seedless raspberry jam
Confectioners' sugar, for dusting

1. Preheat the oven to 350°. Spread the pistachios on a rimmed baking sheet; bake in the oven for about 5 minutes, or until toasted. Let the pistachios cool.
2. In a food processor, grind 1 cup of the roasted pistachios until they are coarsely chopped; transfer to a plate.
3. Add the remaining 1 cup of roasted pistachios to the food processor along with ½ cup of the flour and pulse until the pistachios are finely ground. Add the remaining 1½ cups of flour along with the granulated sugar, baking powder, cinnamon and salt and pulse until combined. Add the butter and pulse until the mixture resembles a coarse meal. Add the egg yolks, vanilla and lemon zest and pulse until the dough begins to come together. Transfer the cookie dough to a bowl and refrigerate until firm.
4. Line 2 baking sheets with parchment or wax paper. In a medium bowl, beat the egg whites until they are frothy. Roll scant tablespoons of the cookie dough into 1-inch balls. Dip the balls in the beaten egg whites and then roll them in the chopped pistachios. Arrange the cookies 2 inches apart on the prepared baking sheets. With a floured finger, make an indentation in the center of each of the cookies. Chill the cookies until they are firm.
5. Using a small spoon or a pastry bag fitted with a ¼-inch tip, fill each of the cookies with ½ teaspoon of the raspberry jam. Bake the cookies in the lower half of the oven for about 25 minutes or

Pistachio Linzer Thumbprints

until they are golden; shift the pans halfway through baking. Cool the cookies on the baking sheets.

6. Sift confectioners' sugar over the cookies. Using a moistened finger or a soft brush, tap the center of each of the cookies so the jam shines through the sugar. —*Melissa Murphy Hagenbart*

MAKE AHEAD The Pistachio Linzer Thumbprints can be stored in an airtight container for 1 week.

Raspberry-Almond Bars
MAKES 4 DOZEN BARS

Margarine makes the crumbly crust of these bar cookies especially crisp. Serve the bars as dessert or an afternoon snack.

- 1 stick (4 ounces) unsalted butter, softened, plus 3 tablespoons melted
- 1 stick (4 ounces) margarine, softened
- 1½ cups all-purpose flour
- 1 cup confectioners' sugar
- ¾ cup seedless raspberry jam
- 3 cups (about ¾ pound) sliced natural almonds
- ½ cup light brown sugar
- ½ cup granulated sugar
- 2 large eggs, lightly beaten
- 1 teaspoon pure vanilla extract
- 1 teaspoon pure almond extract

I. Preheat the oven to 350°. Lightly butter a 9-by-13-inch baking pan. In a standing mixer, beat the softened butter with the margarine until the mixture is smooth. Add the flour and the confectioners' sugar and beat on low speed until combined. Pat the dough evenly into the bottom of the prepared baking pan and bake in the middle of the oven for about 30 minutes, or until golden. Let cool slightly and then spread with the raspberry jam. Leave the oven on.

2. Toast the almonds for 7 to 8 minutes, or until they are golden and fragrant. Let the almonds cool.

3. In a medium bowl, whisk the brown sugar and granulated sugar with the melted butter, the eggs, vanilla extract and almond extract until smooth, then fold in the toasted almonds. Spread the almond topping over the raspberry jam in an even layer. Bake for about 25 minutes, or until the topping is set and golden. Let cool completely in the pan. Using a sharp knife, cut into 48 bars and serve. —*Martha McGinnis*

MAKE AHEAD The baked bar cookies can be wrapped in plastic and refrigerated for up to 1 week.

Sundance Mountain Bars
MAKES 16 BARS

These fruity snack bars feature seven-grain cereal, wheat bran flakes and barley syrup, all of which are available at health food stores.

- ⅔ cup (about 4 ounces) dried black Mission figs, finely chopped
- ⅔ cup (about 4 ounces) dried apricots, finely chopped
- 1 quart unsweetened apple juice
- 1 cup stone-ground seven-grain cereal
- ⅔ cup wheat germ
- ⅓ cup wheat bran flakes
- 3 tablespoons barley malt syrup
- 1 tablespoon honey
- 1 tablespoon finely ground espresso beans (optional)
- 1 tablespoon powdered skim milk

I. In a medium saucepan, combine the figs and apricots with 1 cup of the apple juice and cook over moderately low heat until the dried fruits are softened and plump, about 15 minutes. Drain the fruit, discarding the cooking liquid.

2. In a medium saucepan, combine the seven-grain cereal with the remaining 3 cups of apple juice and cook over moderate heat until the cereal is tender and has absorbed the apple juice, about 15 minutes. Stir in the wheat germ, wheat bran flakes, barley malt syrup, honey, ground espresso, powdered milk and the cooked dried fruits. Cover and let the fruit and cereal mixture stand for at least 4 hours or overnight.

3. Preheat the oven to 325°. Line a 9-by-13-inch rimmed baking sheet or baking pan with plastic wrap. Spread the bar mixture in the baking sheet or pan in an even layer, pressing the mixture out to the edges and the corners. Set a cutting board on top and invert the bar mixture onto the cutting board; remove the plastic wrap. Cut the mixture lengthwise into 4 long strips and then cut the strips crosswise to make 16 bars. Transfer the bars to a cookie sheet lined with parchment paper and bake for about 25 minutes, or until the tops of the bars are dry. Turn the bars and bake for about 25 minutes longer, or until dry. Let the bars cool before serving. —*Trey Foshee*

MAKE AHEAD The Sundance Mountain Bars can be refrigerated for up to 1 week.

ONE SERVING Calories 139 kcal, Total Fat 3.5 gm, Saturated Fat .1 gm.

Nell's Espresso Brownies
MAKES 16 BROWNIES

You can use Newman's Own Organics espresso sweet dark chocolate bars for these intense brownies, or you can add one tablespoon of very finely ground espresso beans to plain bittersweet chocolate.

- 6 ounces espresso-flavored sweet dark chocolate, coarsely chopped
- 1½ sticks (6 ounces) unsalted butter
- 2 tablespoons unsweetened cocoa powder
- 2 large eggs
- 1 cup sugar
- 2 teaspoons pure vanilla extract
- 1 cup all-purpose flour
- Scant ¼ teaspoon salt

I. Preheat the oven to 350°. Lightly butter a 9-inch square baking pan. Melt the dark chocolate and butter in a heatproof bowl that has been set over a saucepan with 1 inch of simmering

Peanut Squares

Nell's Espresso Brownies

water. Remove the chocolate mixture from the heat, stir in the cocoa powder and let cool.

2. In a large bowl, beat the eggs at medium speed for 1 minute. Add the sugar and beat until the mixture is pale yellow, about 2 minutes. Fold in the melted chocolate mixture and the vanilla extract. Sift the flour over the batter, add the salt and fold in just until combined. Spread the brownie batter evenly in the prepared baking pan.

3. Bake the brownies for about 45 minutes, or until a toothpick inserted in the center comes out clean. Let the brownies cool before cutting them into squares. —*Nell Newman*

Peanut Squares

MAKES 25 SQUARES

Neither cookie nor candy, these are truly a melt-in-your-mouth confection, satisfying enough to have for dessert with strong coffee.

1½ **cups unsalted dry roasted peanuts**
1 **cup confectioners' sugar**
2 **teaspoons pure vanilla extract**
¼ **teaspoon peanut oil**

1. In a food processor, pulse the peanuts until they are finely chopped. Add the sugar and process until the mixture resembles coarse sand. With the food processor on, dribble in the vanilla extract. When the peanut mixture resembles very fine, moist sand, it is ready.

2. Brush an 8-inch-square baking pan with the oil. Press the peanut mixture into the baking pan as compactly as possible. Smooth the top as well as you can by pressing down hard with your fingers or a flat-bottomed glass. Make 4 evenly spaced parallel cuts in each direction to form 25 peanut squares; they will be quite fragile. Remove the peanut squares carefully with a small spatula and serve them at room temperature. —*Sally Schneider*

MAKE AHEAD The peanut squares can be refrigerated in an airtight tin between sheets of wax paper for several weeks.

ONE SQUARE Calories 72 kcal, Total Fat 4.4 gm, Saturated Fat .6 gm

chapter 15
fruit desserts

364

368

Lemon-Rosemary Sorbet

1. Preheat the oven to 450°. Butter a 13-by-9-inch baking pan. Line the bottom of the baking pan with wax paper and then butter the paper. Dampen a clean kitchen towel and sprinkle it generously with sugar. Using a sharp knife, peel the oranges, removing all of the bitter white pith, and then thinly slice the oranges crosswise.

2. In a large bowl, combine the eggs with the 1 cup sugar, the orange juice and the orange zest. Using a handheld mixer, beat on high speed until the mixture is pale and thick, about 1 minute. Scrape the mixture into the prepared baking pan and bake for about 5 minutes, or until the dessert is puffed and browned on top.

3. Remove the dessert from the oven; let it stand for 2 minutes. Run a sharp knife around the edge of the dessert and invert it onto the sugared kitchen towel. Peel off the wax paper from the bottom of the dessert. Lift half of the towel up to fold the dessert in half and then cut the dessert crosswise into 8 slices. Garnish with the orange slices and mint leaves and serve. —*Maria José Cabral and Emília Augusta Magalhães*

Sour Cherries in Grappa

MAKES 4 CUPS

Keep these cherries on hand to serve chilled in stemmed glasses as an impromptu dessert. You can also spoon the cherries over vanilla ice cream and sip the infused grappa from a glass.

  2 **cups fruity full-bodied red wine, such as Barbera d'Asti**
  1 **cup water**
  ¼ **cup plus 2 tablespoons sugar**
  1 **vanilla bean, split lengthwise, seeds scraped**
  2 **cups (½ pound) unsulphured dried sour cherries**
  1 **cup grappa**

1. In a medium stainless steel saucepan, combine the red wine with the water, the sugar and the vanilla bean and scraped seeds and bring to a boil

Lemon-Rosemary Sorbet

MAKES ABOUT 3 CUPS

  2 **cups water**
  1 **cup sugar**
  2 **rosemary sprigs**
  ½ **cup fresh lemon juice**

In a saucepan, bring the water, sugar and rosemary to a boil. Cover and simmer over low heat for 5 minutes. Discard the rosemary and let the syrup cool to room temperature. Add the lemon juice and refrigerate until chilled. Transfer to an ice-cream maker and freeze according to the manufacturer's directions. —*John Currence*

MAKE AHEAD The sorbet can be kept in the freezer for up to 2 days.

Orange Delicia

8 SERVINGS

Somewhere between a custard and a soufflé, this is a lovely dessert.

  1 **cup sugar, plus more for sprinkling**
  2 **oranges (optional)**
  6 **large eggs, at room temperature**
  ⅓ **cup fresh orange juice**
  1 **tablespoon finely grated orange zest**
Mint leaves, for garnish

Orange Delicia

Sour Cherries in Grappa

over high heat. Remove from the heat; add the dried sour cherries, cover and let stand until the cherries are plumped, about 5 minutes. Uncover and let cool completely.

2. Spoon the cherries and their liquid into a clean jar along with the vanilla bean and then pour the grappa on top. Cover and let stand at room temperature for at least 1 week to let the flavors deepen. —*Sally Schneider*

MAKE AHEAD The macerated cherries will keep indefinitely in a tightly sealed jar.

ONE-QUARTER CUP Calories 108 kcal, Total Fat 0 gm, Saturated Fat 0 gm

Cherry Turnovers

MAKES 10 TURNOVERS

3 **pounds Bing cherries, pitted**
¾ **cup granulated sugar**
¼ **cup fresh lemon juice**
¼ **cup plus 1 tablespoon cornstarch**
½ **cup water**
½ **teaspoon pure vanilla extract**
2 **pounds frozen puff pastry, preferably all butter, thawed but chilled**

1 **large egg, lightly beaten**
¼ **cup turbinado sugar**

1. In a saucepan, cook the cherries over low heat, stirring, until they soften and most of their liquid has been exuded, about 10 minutes. Drain the cherries in a fine sieve, pressing lightly to extract as much juice as possible; reserve the cherries separately. There should be about 2 cups of juice; if necessary, add ¼ cup of hot water. Return the juice to the pan, add the granulated sugar and lemon juice and bring to a boil.

2. Meanwhile, in a small bowl, stir the cornstarch into the ½ cup water until dissolved. Add the cornstarch mixture to the cherry juice, stirring constantly. Add the cooked cherries, bring to a boil and cook until very thick, 2 to 3 minutes. Stir in the vanilla, transfer the cherry mixture to a bowl and refrigerate until chilled.

3. On a lightly floured work surface, roll out the pastry ⅛ inch thick. Using a 7-inch saucer or bowl, cut out 10 rounds; if necessary, stack the scraps, reroll them and cut out more rounds. Refrigerate the pastry rounds until firm.

4. Preheat the oven to 375°. Line a large baking sheet with parchment paper or foil. Working with 1 pastry round at a time, brush the edge of the round with the egg. Spoon a scant ½ cup of the filling in the center of the round and fold the dough over to make a half moon. Press the edges to seal and crimp the seam with a fork. Transfer the turnover to the baking sheet. Continue to brush, fill and shape the remaining turnovers. Reserve the remaining egg. Refrigerate the turnovers until firm, about 10 minutes.

5. Cut three 1-inch-long slashes on each turnover. Brush the tops with the egg and sprinkle with the turbinado sugar. Bake the turnovers for about 35 minutes, or until the pastry is golden and the filling is bubbling. Transfer the turnovers to a wire rack to cool before serving. —*Martha McGinnis*

MAKE AHEAD The baked cherry turnovers can stand overnight at room temperature. Recrisp the turnovers in a 325° oven.

Peaches with Vanilla—Red Wine Syrup and Ice Cream

6 SERVINGS ✳

The cassia buds in the syrup are the dried, unopened flowers from trees that produce cinnamon from their bark. They have a peppery flavor and are available in specialty food stores or by mail order. A crushed cinnamon stick is an acceptable substitute. If your peaches don't taste especially sweet, sprinkle the wedges with a tablespoon or two of sugar; assemble the dessert, spooning the juices over the peaches.

1 **bottle (750 ml) rich red wine, such as Chianti or Barbera**
1 **cup sugar**
1 **vanilla bean, split lengthwise**
¼ **teaspoon black peppercorns, coarsely crushed**
½ **teaspoon allspice berries, coarsely crushed**
8 **cassia buds, or one 4-inch cinnamon stick, crushed**
Pinch of salt
¼ **teaspoon pure vanilla extract**
1 **pint vanilla ice cream**
3 **ripe peaches, peeled and cut into 8 wedges each**

1. In a medium saucepan, combine the red wine, sugar, vanilla bean, black peppercorns, allspice berries, cassia buds and salt. Bring to a boil over high heat and cook, stirring once or twice, until reduced to 1 cup, about 25 minutes. Remove the syrup from the heat and stir in the vanilla extract. Strain and let cool to room temperature; if the syrup is too thick, stir in a few tablespoons of cold water.

2. Scoop the ice cream into individual bowls and top with the peach wedges. Drizzle each of the desserts with a few tablespoons of the wine syrup and serve. —*Lynne Rossetto Kasper*

Cherry Turnovers

Rum Babas with Peaches

12 SERVINGS

Lemon verbena is added to the typical rum syrup that permeates these babas. The herb adds a refreshing note that enhances the peaches' flavor as well.

BABAS

¼ cup lukewarm milk (105° to 115°)

1 tablespoon active dry yeast

1¾ cups all-purpose flour

6 tablespoons unsalted butter, softened, plus more for the molds

3 large eggs

1 tablespoon sugar

Pinch of salt

¼ cup water

SYRUP

1 cup water

½ cup sugar

1 sprig lemon verbena, crushed, or two 3-inch-long strips lemon zest

1 cup dark rum

6 ripe peaches, cut into ¼-inch wedges

I. MAKE THE BABAS: In a bowl, stir the milk, yeast and ⅓ cup flour with a fork until smooth. Set aside until small bubbles appear, about 10 minutes.

2. Butter six ½-cup baba molds or muffin tins. In the bowl of a standing mixer fitted with a whisk, combine the eggs, sugar, salt and remaining flour. Add the softened butter; beat on medium speed 10 minutes. Add the yeast mixture and water and beat for 1 minute. With a rubber spatula, scrape the dough from the whisk and scrape the side of the bowl. With moistened hands, fill the molds two thirds full with dough. Set in a warm place; let rise until the dough just reaches the rims, about 20 minutes.

3. Preheat the oven to 350° and bake the babas for about 15 minutes, or until puffed and golden brown. Remove from the oven and immediately turn out onto a wire rack to cool completely.

4. MAKE THE SYRUP: In a small saucepan, combine the water and sugar. Bring to a boil over moderately high heat and cook until the sugar is dissolved. Transfer the syrup to a heatproof bowl and add the lemon verbena and rum. Let cool to room temperature.

5. Arrange the babas in a large, shallow dish; pour the syrup on top. Baste, turning occasionally, until the babas have absorbed as much syrup as possible without falling apart, about 25 minutes. Remove the babas from the syrup.

6. Cut each of the babas in half lengthwise and place on dessert plates. Surround the babas with peach wedges and serve. —*Alfonso Iaccarino*

MAKE AHEAD The recipe can be prepared through Step 4 up to 1 day ahead; let the babas and syrup stand separately at room temperature.

SERVE WITH Lightly sweetened whipped cream.

Rum Babas with Peaches

Caramelized Peaches with Honey and Raspberries

4 SERVINGS

Since the peaches in this updated version of peach Melba are left whole and unpitted, you can choose a tasty cling variety. They are caramelized in a delicious blend of honey and butter.

Caramelized Peaches with Honey and Raspberries

Peach and Berry Crumble

4 large peaches (1¾ pounds)
6 cups water
1¾ cups granulated sugar
¾ pint raspberries
2 tablespoons confectioners' sugar
1 teaspoon fresh lemon juice
½ teaspoon pure vanilla extract
¼ cup plus 2 tablespoons honey
4 tablespoons unsalted butter
4 scoops vanilla ice cream
4 mint sprigs

1. Blanch the peaches in boiling water for 1 to 2 minutes. Remove from the heat and transfer the peaches to a plate to cool. Meanwhile, in a medium saucepan, combine the water and granulated sugar and bring to a boil, stirring until the sugar dissolves. Peel the peaches and add them to the hot sugar syrup. Let them cool completely in the syrup, turning them once or twice.

2. In a mini-processor, puree ½ cup of the raspberries with the confectioners' sugar, lemon juice and vanilla. Strain the puree into a small bowl and refrigerate until needed.

3. In a large nonstick skillet, combine the honey and butter and cook over moderately high heat, stirring occasionally, until smooth, about 5 minutes. Add the peaches and turn until coated.

Transfer the peaches to dishes and set a scoop of vanilla ice cream next to each. Spoon some of the raspberry puree over the peaches and ice cream. Garnish with the remaining raspberries and the mint sprigs and serve immediately. —*Philippe Renard*

MAKE AHEAD The recipe can be made through Step 2 and refrigerated for up to 1 day.

WINE Nonvintage Taittinger Prestige Cuvée Rosé. The fruity flavors of this pink Champagne match both the raspberries and the caramelized peaches.

Peach and Berry Crumble

4 SERVINGS ❋

¼ cup plus 2 tablespoons light brown sugar
¼ cup all-purpose flour
¼ cup rolled oats
¼ teaspoon cinnamon
Pinch of salt
2 tablespoons unsalted butter, cut into pieces
¼ cup broken pecan halves
4 large freestone peaches
2 tablespoons fresh lemon juice
1 tablespoon cornstarch
¼ teaspoon finely grated fresh ginger
1 cup mixed fresh berries

1. Preheat the oven to 400°. Bring a medium saucepan of water to a boil. In a medium bowl, combine the ¼ cup brown sugar with the flour, oats, cinnamon and salt. Using your fingers or a pastry blender, work in the butter until the mixture resembles peas. Stir in the pecans.

2. Using a small sharp knife, make a shallow X in the bottom of each peach. Add the peaches to the boiling water and blanch for about 30 seconds; remove and refresh with cold water. Peel, pit and slice the peaches.

3. In a large bowl, toss the peaches with the lemon juice, the cornstarch, the ginger and the remaining 2 tablespoons of brown sugar. Fold in half of the berries

and then spoon the fruit into a 1-quart baking dish. Sprinkle the crumbs over the fruit, top with the remaining berries and bake the crumble for about 30 minutes, or until bubbling and the top is golden. —*Todd Slossberg*

MAKE AHEAD The crumble can be baked up to 6 hours ahead and reheated before serving.

SERVE WITH Vanilla ice cream or whipped cream.

Rhubarb and Berry Compote with Mint

4 TO 6 SERVINGS

Strawberries, blackberries and blueberries are all delicious with rhubarb, and the darker colors look striking in the compote. There are two things to be careful about when you're working with rhubarb (which, by the way, is technically a vegetable, not a fruit). Always cut off and discard the leaves, which are poisonous. And do be sure to wash the stalks thoroughly, though you don't need to peel them.

1 cup red wine, such as Beaujolais or Syrah
1 cup cranberry juice
1 jar (12 ounces) strawberry jam
¼ cup sugar
2 pounds rhubarb, leaves discarded, stalks cut into 1-inch pieces
1 small bunch of peppermint, tied together, plus additional sprigs for garnish
2 cups (12 ounces) blackberries, blueberries or small strawberries
Sour cream, for serving

1. In a large saucepan, combine the wine with the cranberry juice, jam and sugar and bring to a boil over high heat, stirring occasionally. Lower the heat and simmer until the mixture is reduced to 1¼ cups, about 15 minutes. Add the rhubarb and the bunch of mint. Cook over moderate heat without stirring until the rhubarb is tender, 7 to 8 minutes. Discard the mint.

2. Transfer the rhubarb to a large heatproof bowl and fold in the berries. Let cool and then cover and refrigerate the compote until chilled. Spoon the compote into parfait glasses or shallow soup plates and garnish each serving with a dollop of sour cream and a mint sprig. —*Jacques Pépin*

SERVE WITH Biscotti, butter cookies or slices of brioche or pound cake.

Fresh Figs and Plums in Manzanilla

4 SERVINGS

Manzanilla is a very dry pale sherry, used here as the basis of a syrup in which the figs and the plums are macerated.

- 1 cup manzanilla or other dry sherry
- 3 tablespoons sugar
- 2 imported bay leaves
- ½ teaspoon minced lemon zest
- 8 fresh black figs, stemmed and quartered
- 6 plums, pitted and quartered
- ¼ cup crème fraîche

In a medium saucepan, cook the sherry with the sugar, bay leaves and lemon zest over moderately high heat, stirring, just until the sugar dissolves. Transfer the mixture to a large bowl and let cool. Add the figs and plums and let stand for 15 minutes, tossing occasionally. Discard the bay leaves. Serve the sherried fruit in shallow bowls topped with a dollop of crème fraîche. —*Seen Lippert*

SERVE WITH Biscotti.

Figs with Honey and Champagne

6 SERVINGS

The ancient Romans gave their friends New Year's offerings of dried figs and dates in honey with a branch of bay leaves. Not only does this dessert incorporate many of those traditional good luck ingredients (figs, honey, bay leaves), it's also an indulgent sweet for a cold winter day.

- 1 pound dried Calimyrna figs
- 1 cup warm water
- 1½ cups dry sparkling wine
- 1 tablespoon honey
- 2 teaspoons sugar
- 3 long strips lemon zest
- 3 bay leaves
- ½ teaspoon fennel seeds, lightly toasted

I. In a medium saucepan, combine the figs and water and let stand for 1 hour. Add the sparkling wine, honey, sugar, lemon zest and bay leaves and bring to a boil. Reduce the heat to low and simmer the figs until they are softened, about 20 minutes.

2. With a slotted spoon, transfer the softened figs to a bowl and then boil the cooking liquid until it is syrupy, 6 to 8

Rhubarb and Berry Compote with Mint

Wine-Poached Pears with Prunes and Citrus

minutes. Remove the strips of lemon zest and the bay leaves from the syrup and pour the syrup over the figs. Sprinkle the figs with the fennel seeds and serve warm. —*Erica De Mane*

WINE Italians match the sweetness of their desserts with light, and slightly sweet, Muscat-based wines to add a grace note to the finale of the meal. For this dessert, try a Moscato d'Asti, such as the 1997 Vietti Cascinetta or the 1996 Bera.

Wine-Poached Pears with Prunes and Citrus

8 SERVINGS

This recipe for poached pears is nothing if not flexible. You can use white wine or red, add prunes or not. If your pears aren't perfectly ripe, you can still use them here, but you may need to cook them longer than specified.

- 8 pears
- 1 bottle (750 ml) white or red wine
- ¾ cup sugar
- 20 pitted prunes
- 1 orange, sliced into rounds
- 1 lemon, sliced into rounds
- 1 tablespoon unsalted butter

Pinch of cinnamon

1. Peel the pears, leaving on some lengthwise strips of skin to make an attractive pattern. In a saucepan small enough to hold the pears snugly, combine the white or red wine and the sugar and simmer over high heat until the sugar is dissolved. Add the pears, prunes, orange slices, lemon slices, butter and cinnamon. Set a large heat-proof plate directly on the pears to keep them submerged in the liquid and bring to a boil. Reduce the heat to low and simmer, turning the pears once, until they are tender when pierced, about 20 minutes.

2. Using a slotted spoon, transfer the pears and the prunes to a large shallow dish. Discard the orange slices and the lemon slices and simmer the poaching liquid until it is reduced to a thick syrup, about 15 minutes. Pour the syrup over the poached pears and prunes and serve the dessert warm or at room temperature. —*Josette Riondato*

MAKE AHEAD The pears and prunes can be refrigerated in their syrup for up to 2 days.

WINE Château Loudenne Blanc, which develops a honeyed character as it ages, could go happily with the poached pears. Try the 1995 or, if you can find it, the 1990.

Maple Baked Pears

4 SERVINGS ✳ ॐ

There's just enough butter here to give the luscious maple syrup glaze a bit of richness.

- 2 ripe but firm Bartlett pears
- ½ lemon
- 1 tablespoon unsalted butter
- 2 tablespoons packed dark brown sugar
- 2 tablespoons maple syrup
- ½ teaspoon pure vanilla extract

1. Preheat the oven to 375°. Peel the pears and cut them in half lengthwise. Using a melon baller or a teaspoon, scoop out the cores of the pears. Rub the pear halves with the cut lemon to prevent browning.

2. Melt the unsalted butter in an oven-proof skillet just large enough to hold the pears in a single layer. Add the dark brown sugar and the maple syrup and cook over moderately low heat, stirring, until the brown sugar is dissolved. Add the pear halves and turn them several times to coat them with the syrup. Arrange the pear halves, cut side down, in a single layer and bake for about 30 minutes, basting occasionally with pan juices, until the pears are just softened and golden.

3. Transfer the pear halves to a platter and keep them warm. If necessary, add a little water to the skillet to thin the syrup. Remove the skillet from the heat and stir in the vanilla extract. Pour the syrup over the pear halves and serve the baked pears warm or at room temperature. —*Jan Newberry*

ONE SERVING Calories 128 kcal, Total Fat 3.2 gm, Saturated Fat 1.8 gm

Banana Pudding

6 SERVINGS

This recipe is based on the childhood classic that's printed on the side of the Nilla wafer box.

- ½ cup granulated sugar
- 4 large egg yolks
- 3 tablespoons all-purpose flour
- 2 cups milk
- 4 tablespoons unsalted butter
- 1 tablespoon pure vanilla extract
- 36 vanilla wafer cookies
- 4 large firm-ripe bananas, cut into ½-inch slices
- ½ cup heavy cream
- 1 tablespoon confectioners' sugar

1. In a medium bowl, whisk the granulated sugar and the egg yolks until they are pale in color and thick. Whisk in the all-purpose flour and 2 tablespoons of the milk. In a medium saucepan, heat the remaining milk and the unsalted butter until steaming. Whisk the hot milk into the egg mixture. Return the mixture to the saucepan and bring to a boil over moderate heat, stirring constantly. Cook, stirring, for 2 minutes. Transfer the custard to a bowl and then stir in the vanilla.

2. Arrange one third of the vanilla wafer cookies in the bottom of an 8-cup soufflé dish. Top the vanilla wafers with one third each of the banana slices and the custard. Continue to layer the ingredients, ending with a layer of the custard, and then chill.

3. Beat the heavy cream with the confectioners' sugar until firm. Spoon the whipped cream over the layered vanilla wafers, banana slices and custard and serve. —*Jimmy Kennedy*

Cool Pineapple and Kiwi Dessert

Cool Pineapple and Kiwi Dessert

8 SERVINGS

Plan to make this light and intensely fruity molded dessert a day ahead since it needs to set up overnight.

Two 20-ounce cans crushed pineapple in unsweetened pineapple juice

1 **cup warm water**

3 **packets unflavored powdered gelatin**

1 **cup heavy cream**

1 **cup sugar**

3 **long strips of lemon zest, removed with a vegetable peeler**

2 **tablespoons fresh lemon juice**

4 **kiwis, peeled and thinly sliced crosswise**

1. In a blender, puree the crushed pineapple with its juice in 2 batches. Using a rubber spatula, press the pineapple puree through a strainer. Discard the solids.

2. In a small bowl, combine the warm water with the unflavored powdered gelatin and allow to stand until the gelatin has softened, about 10 minutes.

3. Line the bottom of a 2-inch deep, 9-inch round cake pan with a round of wax paper. In a medium saucepan, combine the pineapple puree with the heavy cream, sugar, lemon zest, lemon juice and softened gelatin. Cook over moderate heat, stirring occasionally, until bubbles appear around the edge, about 12 minutes. Remove the lemon zest. Pour the mixture into the prepared pan and refrigerate overnight.

4. Run a knife around the inside of the pan and unmold the dessert onto a large platter. Remove the wax paper. Decorate with the kiwi slices and serve cut in wedges. —*Pilar Huguet*

ONE SERVING Calories 319 kcal, Total Fat 11.27 gm, Saturated Fat 6.9 gm

Mango Freeze

8 SERVINGS

This deceptively simple dessert offers all of the pleasures of ice cream without having to fuss with making a custard and using an ice-cream machine. Just freeze cut-up mangoes with a little syrup and dessert is ready.

6 **large ripe but firm mangoes**

¼ **cup plus 2 tablespoons sugar**

3 **tablespoons fresh lemon juice**

½ **cup crème fraîche**

1. Using a sharp vegetable peeler, peel half of a mango. Holding the fruit by its unpeeled half, cut ½-inch-thick lengthwise slices down to the pit. Then cut crosswise against the pit to release the slices. Repeat with the other half of the mango and then repeat with the remaining mangoes. Cut the slices into ½-inch dice; transfer to a medium bowl.

2. In a small saucepan, combine the sugar with the lemon juice and cook over low heat, stirring, until dissolved. Let the syrup cool and then pour over the mango dice and toss well. Transfer the mangoes to a shallow baking dish lined with plastic wrap. Cover with plastic wrap and freeze until the mangoes are semifrozen, 3 to 4 hours. If the mangoes are frozen solid, let them stand in the refrigerator until slightly thawed. Scoop the frozen mangoes into individual bowls and drizzle with the crème fraîche. —*Hisachika Takahashi*

MAKE AHEAD The mangoes can be frozen for up to 5 days.

Mango Freeze

chapter 16

other desserts

375

381

Silky Wine Meringue

Silky Wine Meringue

6 SERVINGS

Natural barriers such as the Atacama Desert, the Andes Mountains and the Pacific Ocean isolated Chile from the rest of the world for many centuries, allowing old traditions to survive. For instance, dishes that gained and lost popularity in Europe still appear on Chilean tables. This elegant, old-fashioned dessert is a perfect example. The meringue is customarily served with a custard sauce made with the leftover egg yolks, but a raspberry puree would make a colorful accompaniment.

1 cup red or white wine
1 cup sugar
3 large egg whites, at room temperature
Pinch of cream of tartar
¼ cup coarsely chopped walnuts (optional)
Mint leaves, for garnish
Vanilla Custard Sauce (recipe follows)

1. In a small saucepan, combine the wine and sugar and bring to a boil, stirring with a wooden spoon. Simmer over moderate heat until a candy thermometer registers 248°, about 15 minutes.
2. In a heatproof mixing bowl, using a handheld mixer, beat the egg whites with the cream of tartar at moderate speed until soft peaks form. Then, beating constantly at high speed, slowly pour the hot wine syrup into the egg whites. Continue beating until the egg whites are stiff and glossy.
3. Spoon the meringue into a serving bowl or decorative wineglasses. Sprinkle with the chopped walnuts, garnish with mint and serve. Pass the sauce separately. —Ruth Van Waerebeek-Gonzalez

VANILLA CUSTARD SAUCE

MAKES 1⅓ CUPS

1 cup milk
½ cup heavy cream
1 teaspoon pure vanilla extract
3 large egg yolks
½ cup sugar

1. In a small saucepan, heat the milk and cream with the vanilla. In a large bowl, whisk the egg yolks with the sugar until light and foamy, about 3 minutes. Whisking constantly, pour the milk mixture into the egg yolks in a thin stream.
2. Return the custard to the saucepan and cook over moderately low heat, whisking constantly, until thickened, about 5 minutes; do not let the custard boil or it will curdle. Immediately scrape the sauce into a clean bowl and whisk constantly to cool slightly. Set aside to cool completely. Refrigerate until ready to use. —R. V. W.

Mango and Blueberry Pavlovas

6 SERVINGS

Pavlova is Australia's classic dessert. It's a bit tricky to cook since it needs a short period of high heat to crisp the exterior and a longer period at lower heat so the interior is set but still chewy. Don't make meringues on humid days; the results will almost surely be soggy.

4 large egg whites, at room temperature
1 cup superfine sugar, plus more for sprinkling
1 tablespoon fresh lemon juice
2 teaspoons cornstarch

Mango and Blueberry Pavlovas

1 teaspoon pure vanilla extract
1 large ripe mango—peeled, fruit cut off the pit and thinly sliced
1 cup blueberries
1 cup heavy cream
Confectioners' sugar, for dusting

1. Preheat the oven to 325°. Line a large baking sheet with parchment paper or foil. In a large bowl, beat the egg whites at medium speed until soft peaks form. Beat in the superfine sugar, 1 tablespoon at a time; continue beating until the meringue is thick, glossy and stiff. Quickly beat in 2 teaspoons of the lemon juice, the cornstarch and the vanilla. Spoon 6 evenly spaced mounds of meringue on the parchment-lined sheet. Using the tip of the spoon, make a well in each meringue.

2. Bake the meringues for 5 minutes, or until slightly dry and set. Reduce the temperature to 225°. Bake for 1 hour. Turn off the oven; leave the meringues in the oven for 1 hour with the door closed. They should be perfectly white and crisp on the outside, chewy inside.

3. Toss the mango slices and blueberries with the remaining 1 teaspoon lemon juice and sprinkle with superfine sugar if desired. Set the meringues on dessert plates. Whip the heavy cream and spoon onto the meringues. Top with the mango slices and blueberries, sift confectioners' sugar over the tops and serve at once. —*John Ash*

MAKE AHEAD The meringues can be stored in an airtight container for up to 3 days, if the weather is not humid.

The Knickerbocker Kick

6 SERVINGS

2 envelopes unflavored powdered gelatin
½ cup cold water
1 cup boiling water
¾ cup sugar
1⅔ cups Marsala or sherry
⅓ cup fresh lemon juice
Sweetened whipped cream, for serving

In a large heatproof bowl, sprinkle the unflavored gelatin over the cold water and let stand until softened, about 5 minutes. Add the boiling water and the sugar; stir until completely dissolved. Stir in the Marsala and the lemon juice and let the gelatin cool to room temperature. Refrigerate the gelatin until firm, at least 4 hours or preferably overnight. Use a dinner fork to scramble the gelatin. Spoon the gelatin into wineglasses, top each serving of gelatin with a dollop of sweetened whipped cream and serve. —*Nancy Knickerbocker*

Maria Estrella Rabat's Soufflé

6 SERVINGS

Delicate and low in fat, this egg dessert, flavored with Grand Marnier, is easy to prepare. Unlike a traditional soufflé, in which the egg yolk mixture is folded into the beaten whites and spooned into a deep soufflé dish, in this recipe the egg whites are spread in the bottom of a shallow baking dish and then partially covered with the egg yolk mixture. The resulting soufflé looks something like a fried egg. It does need to be made at the last moment, and—watch out—if the oven temperature is too hot, the soufflé will turn into an omelet!

4 large eggs at room temperature, separated
Pinch of cream of tartar
½ cup plus 2 tablespoons confectioners' sugar
3 tablespoons Grand Marnier or other orange liqueur

Individual Vanilla Custards

1. Preheat the oven to 300°. Butter a 9-by-13-inch glass baking dish. In a clean bowl, beat the egg whites with the cream of tartar until the whites begin to stiffen. Add ¼ cup plus 2 tablespoons of the confectioners' sugar and continue beating until the whites hold stiff peaks and become glossy.

2. In a separate bowl, whisk the egg yolks with the remaining ¼ cup of confectioners' sugar until light and foamy, about 3 minutes. Stir in the Grand Marnier and set aside.

3. Gently spread the egg whites in the prepared baking dish. Pour the yolk mixture over the whites, leaving a 1-inch border all around. Bake in the oven 7 to 10 minutes, or until the whites and yolks are just set. Serve the soufflé at once. —*Ruth Van Waerebeek-Gonzalez*

Individual Vanilla Custards

8 SERVINGS

For this simple, sublime dessert, called *petits pots de crème* in French, you will need eight half-cup ramekins—unless you're lucky enough to have porcelain pots designed specifically for this dish.

3⅓ **cups milk**
3 **vanilla beans, split lengthwise**
8 **large egg yolks**
⅔ **cup sugar**

1. Preheat the oven to 325°. In a medium saucepan, combine the milk and vanilla beans and bring to a bare simmer over high heat. Remove the pan from the heat, cover and let the mixture steep for 15 minutes.

2. In a heatproof medium bowl, whisk the egg yolks with the sugar until thick. Bring the milk back to a simmer and whisk it into the yolks in a thin stream. Strain the custard through a fine sieve set over a bowl. Let stand for 2 to 3 minutes and then skim off the foam.

3. Set eight ½-cup ramekins in a large baking pan and fill the ramekins three quarters full with the custard. Pour enough hot water into the baking pan to reach about halfway up the sides of the

ramekins. Cover the baking pan loosely with foil; bake for 30 to 35 minutes, or until the custard is just set at the edge but still trembling in the center.

4. Remove the baking pan from the oven. Carefully lift the ramekins out of the pan and let the custards cool at room temperature. Cover loosely and refrigerate, for at least 2 hours or up to 2 days. Serve the custards well chilled in the ramekins. —*Eric Lecerf*

WINE Any good, sweet regional French wine would be fine here. Try a Loupiac, a Ste-Croix-du-Mont, a Monbazillac or, of course, a Sauternes.

Mexican Chocolate Pots de Crème

10 SERVINGS

The French make charming little porcelain pots especially for *pots de crème*. But half-cup ramekins, espresso cups or custard cups will do just as fine. You'll need eight.

3 **cups milk**
⅓ **cup (packed) light brown sugar**
2 **cinnamon sticks, cracked**
9 **large egg yolks**
⅓ **cup granulated sugar**
1½ **teaspoons pure vanilla extract**
1 **pound plus 2 ounces bittersweet chocolate, melted and cooled (see Note)**
Lightly sweetened whipped cream and ground cinnamon, for serving

1. In a medium saucepan, combine the milk, brown sugar and cinnamon sticks and bring just to a boil. Remove from the heat, cover the saucepan and let the milk infuse for 20 minutes.

2. In a large bowl, whisk the egg yolks with the granulated sugar and vanilla until pale. Whisk in the melted chocolate until smooth and glossy, about 1 minute; the mixture will be quite thick. Remove the cinnamon sticks from the warm milk and discard. Gradually add the warm milk to the chocolate mixture, whisking constantly, until smooth and creamy. Strain the custard through a

Mexican Chocolate Pots de Crème

fine sieve and refrigerate until it is well chilled, at least 4 hours or overnight.

3. Preheat the oven to 300°. Place a kitchen towel in the bottom of a large roasting pan. Arrange ten ½-cup ramekins in the roasting pan. Stir the chocolate custard until smooth and divide it among the ramekins. Pour enough hot water into the roasting pan to reach halfway up the sides of the ramekins.

4. Cover the roasting pan with foil and bake the custards for 35 to 40 minutes, or until just set around the edges but still slightly jiggly in the centers. Carefully remove the ramekins from the pan; let cool to room temperature. Refrigerate until chilled, at least 3 hours. Garnish each custard with a small dollop of whipped cream and a little sprinkle of cinnamon. —*Robert Del Grande*

NOTE The best way to melt chocolate is in the microwave. Chop the chocolate and melt in a microwave-safe bowl on high power about 3 minutes, stirring after each minute. Alternatively, melt in the top of a double boiler over barely simmering water, stirring frequently.

MAKE AHEAD The *pots de crème* can be covered with plastic wrap and refrigerated for up to 2 days.

Le Cirque's Crème Brûlée

8 SERVINGS

You'll need eight shallow four-and-a-half-inch crème brûlée dishes to make this recipe. Or you can substitute deeper three-quarter cup ramekins, but you'll need to adjust the cooking time for these (see Note).

- 4 cups heavy cream
- 1 vanilla bean, split lengthwise

Pinch of salt

- 8 egg yolks
- ¾ cup plus 2 tablespoons granulated sugar
- 16 teaspoons turbinado sugar, for glazing (see Note)

1. Preheat the oven to 300°. In a medium saucepan, cook the heavy cream with the vanilla bean and salt over moderate heat until the surface begins to shimmer.

2. In a large heatproof bowl, blend the egg yolks and the granulated sugar with a wooden spoon and then slowly add the hot cream mixture, stirring gently. Strain the custard into a large measuring cup and skim off any bubbles.

3. Arrange 8 shallow 4½-inch-wide ramekins in a roasting pan (see Note). Slowly pour the custard into the ramekins, filling them almost to the top. Set the roasting pan in the center of the oven and carefully pour in enough hot water to reach halfway up the sides of the ramekins. Cover the pan loosely with foil and bake for about 1 hour, or until the custards are firm at the edges, but still a bit wobbly in the center.

4. Transfer the ramekins to a wire rack to cool completely. Cover and refrigerate until the custard is cold, at least 3 hours or up to 2 days.

5. Preheat the broiler. Set the ramekins on a baking sheet. Blot the surfaces of the custards to remove any condensation. Using a small sieve, sift 2 teaspoons of the turbinado sugar over each custard in a thin, even layer. Broil the custards as close to the heat as possible until the turbinado sugar is

evenly caramelized, 30 seconds to 2 minutes. Let the custards cool slightly and then serve. —*Egidiana Maccioni*

NOTE If using the deeper ¾-cup ramekins, bake the custards for about 20 minutes longer and reduce the sugar topping to 1 teaspoon per custard.

Mascarpone Custards with Summer Berries

8 SERVINGS

These lovely, creamy custards are based on a traditional *zabaglione*. You will need eight three-and-a-half-inch ramekins for this recipe.

- 8 large egg yolks
- 1 cup sugar
- ¼ cup plus 2 tablespoons sweet Marsala
- 1½ cups brewed espresso, cooled
- 4 dozen 1½-inch Italian amaretti cookies (see Note)
- 2 cups (1 pound) mascarpone, at room temperature
- 2 cups mixed fresh berries, such as blueberries, blackberries and raspberries

1. In a large stainless steel bowl, beat the egg yolks with the sugar until slightly thickened, about 2 minutes. Set the bowl over a medium saucepan of simmering water. Gradually whisk in the Marsala and whisk constantly until the mixture triples in volume, about 8 minutes. Remove the bowl from the pan; continue whisking for another minute.

2. Pour the espresso into a shallow bowl. Dip the amaretti cookies in the espresso one by one and use them to line the bottoms of eight 3½-inch ramekins; use any broken amaretti cookies to fill the spaces.

3. In a medium bowl, beat the mascarpone with a rubber spatula until it is creamy. Add the Marsala custard and fold together until smooth. Spoon the mixture into the ramekins and refrigerate until firm, about 2 hours. Garnish the mascarpone custards with the berries and serve. —*Lori De Mori*

NOTE Amaretti are sweet, crumbly cookies that are perfect for serving with creamy desserts or coffee. They are available in Italian groceries and by mail order from Salumeria Italiana (800-400-5916). The charming tins in which amaretti are often sold are worth holding onto for storing homemade cookies.

MAKE AHEAD The mascarpone custards can be refrigerated, covered, for up to 2 days. Serve chilled.

WINE The perfumed sweetness of the 1993 Bonny Doon Muscat Canelli nicely complements the slightly tart berries and creamy custard.

Ricotta Caramel Custards

8 SERVINGS

Here's an innovative custard that tastes like a caramel-glazed ricotta cheesecake. It must be refrigerated overnight, and you'll need eight half-cup ramekins.

- 1¼ cups sugar
- ¼ cup water
- 2 pounds fresh whole milk ricotta
- 1 large egg
- 2 large egg yolks
- ⅓ cup heavy cream
- 1 tablespoon light rum
- 1 teaspoon pure vanilla extract
- 1 teaspoon orange flower water (see Note)
- 2 teaspoons finely grated orange zest

1. Preheat the oven to 375° and position a rack in the middle of the oven.

2. In a medium saucepan, combine 1 cup of the sugar with the water and bring to a boil over moderately high heat. Stir with a wooden spoon to dissolve the sugar. Using a wet pastry brush, wash down any sugar crystals from the side of the pan. Continue to boil the sugar syrup, without stirring, until a golden amber caramel forms, 6 to 8 minutes.

3. Remove the saucepan from the heat; dip the bottom of the pan in a bowl of cool water to stop the cooking. Immediately pour the hot caramel into eight

Mascarpone Custards with Summer Berries

½-cup ramekins; swirl to evenly coat the bottoms of the ramekins with caramel. Set the ramekins in a roasting pan.

4. In a food processor, combine the ricotta with the whole egg, egg yolks, heavy cream, light rum, vanilla, orange flower water, orange zest and the remaining ¼ cup sugar; process until smooth and pour the mixture into the ramekins. Put the roasting pan in the oven and pour enough hot water into the roasting pan to reach halfway up the sides of the ramekins.

5. Bake the ricotta custards for about 45 minutes or until they are golden brown on top and set around the edges but still slightly soft in the center. Transfer the ramekins to a rack and let cool. Cover the ricotta custards and refrigerate them overnight.

6. To unmold the custards, run a small knife around each one, place a dessert plate on top of the ramekin and invert, giving the ramekin a little shake. If the custard sticks, briefly dip the bottom of the ramekin in hot water and invert again. —*Erica De Mane*

NOTE Orange flower water, a flavoring distilled from orange blossoms, is available at specialty food shops and Middle Eastern markets.

Cheesecake Flan

Cheesecake Flan

6 SERVINGS

New York–style cheesecake was the inspiration for this recipe. Six one-cup ramekins are needed to make it.

- ¾ cup sugar
- 1 teaspoon fresh lemon juice
- ¾ cup plus 2 tablespoons (7 ounces) softened cream cheese
- ¾ cup plus 2 tablespoons sweetened condensed milk
- ½ cup plus 2 tablespoons evaporated milk
- ½ cup plus 2 tablespoons half-and-half
- 3 large eggs
- ½ teaspoon pure vanilla extract
- Boiling water
- Whipped cream and fresh berries, for serving (optional)

1. Preheat the oven to 275°. In a small, heavy saucepan, combine the sugar and the fresh lemon juice and cook over moderately low heat until an amber caramel forms, 6 to 8 minutes. Immediately pour the hot caramel into six 1-cup ramekins, swirling them to coat the bottoms. Set the ramekins in a small roasting pan.

2. In a blender, combine the softened cream cheese with the condensed and evaporated milks, half-and-half, eggs and vanilla and blend on medium speed until smooth. Refrigerate the custard for 10 minutes, skim off the foam and then pour the custard into the prepared ramekins.

3. Put the roasting pan in the oven and add enough boiling water to reach halfway up the sides of the ramekins. Bake the flans for about 1½ hours or until they are set and a toothpick inserted in the centers of the flans comes out almost clean. Remove the ramekins from the water bath, let cool and then refrigerate the flans for at least 6 hours or overnight before serving.

4. To unmold each of the flans, set the bottom of the ramekin in a pan of hot water for about 1 minute. Run a thin blade around the edge of the flan and cover with a plate. Invert the plate and shake once or twice; the flan should release easily. Serve with whipped cream and berries. —*Richard Ampudia*

Mocha Panna Cotta with Cherry Coulis

10 SERVINGS

You will need ten half-cup ramekins to make the panna cotta.

PANNA COTTA

- 2 tablespoons unsalted butter, melted
- 2 envelopes unflavored gelatin
- ½ cup milk
- 5½ cups heavy cream, preferably not ultrapasteurized
- 1 cup sugar
- 2 teaspoons unsweetened cocoa powder
- 1 tablespoon plus 1 teaspoon instant espresso powder
- ⅛ teaspoon freshly grated nutmeg
- 1½ tablespoons finely chopped semisweet chocolate, plus chocolate shavings for garnish

CHERRY COULIS

- 1¼ cups (6 ounces) frozen sweet cherries
- 1 cup jarred pitted sour cherries packed in juice
- ¼ cup sugar
- 1 tablespoon fresh lemon juice
- Pinch of freshly grated nutmeg
- 2 tablespoons water

1. MAKE THE PANNA COTTA: Brush ten ½-cup ramekins with the melted butter and transfer to a large roasting pan. In a small bowl, whisk the gelatin into the milk and let stand until softened, about 5 minutes.

2. In a medium saucepan, combine the heavy cream with the sugar and bring just to a boil over moderate heat. Remove from the heat; whisk in the cocoa, espresso powder and nutmeg. Whisk in the gelatin mixture until completely

ABOVE: **Orange-Scented Clafoutis.**
LEFT: **Cherry Coulis for the Mocha Panna Cotta.**

melted. Add the chopped chocolate and stir until melted. Strain the mixture into a large bowl and let it cool to room temperature.

3. Pour the panna cotta mixture into the ramekins and refrigerate until firm, at least 4 hours or overnight.

4. MAKE THE CHERRY COULIS: Combine all of the ingredients in a saucepan and simmer over moderate heat for 6 minutes. Transfer the sauce to a blender and puree. Strain and refrigerate.

5. To unmold each panna cotta, set the bottom of the ramekin in a pan of hot water for 30 seconds. Run a thin blade around each panna cotta and invert it onto a dessert plate. Lift off the ramekin. Spoon the cherry coulis around each panna cotta, garnish with chocolate shavings and serve. —*Dana Speers*

Orange-Scented Clafoutis

8 SERVINGS

This recipe is unique because it separates during baking into a dense clafoutis bottom and an airy soufflé topping.

- 4 large eggs, separated
- ½ cup granulated sugar
- ¾ cup all-purpose flour
- 1½ cups milk, at room temperature
- 2 teaspoons finely grated orange zest
- ⅛ teaspoon orange flower water (optional)
- 2 tablespoons orange liqueur, rum or Cognac

1. Preheat the oven to 350°. Butter a 9-inch round cake pan. In a medium bowl, beat the egg yolks with the sugar until pale. Add the flour and mix well and then gradually whisk in the milk, orange zest, orange flower water and orange liqueur.

2. In a large stainless steel bowl, beat the egg whites with clean beaters until stiff but not dry. Fold the whites into the yolk mixture; pour the batter into the prepared pan. Bake for about 30 minutes, or until golden brown. Remove from the oven and let cool slightly. Cut into wedges and serve warm or at room temperature. —*Josette Riondato*

NOTE Orange flower water is available at specialty food shops and Middle Eastern markets.

Lemony Rice Pudding

8 SERVINGS

Pinch of salt
- 1 cup (6 ounces) long-grain rice
- 2 cups heavy cream
- 2 cups milk
- ½ cup plus 2 tablespoons sugar

Three 3-inch strips of lemon zest
- 1 cinnamon stick
- 1 teaspoon pure vanilla extract
- 2 large egg yolks
- 1 tablespoon unsalted butter

Cinnamon or unsweetened cocoa powder, for sprinkling

1. Bring a medium saucepan of water to a boil. Add the salt and rice and cook over moderately high heat, stirring occasionally, until the rice is barely tender, about 10 minutes. Pour the rice into a colander to drain it.

2. In the same saucepan used to boil the rice, combine the cream, milk and sugar and bring to a boil. Stir in the rice, lemon zest, cinnamon stick and vanilla and simmer over low heat, stirring often, until the rice is tender and the mixture is thick, about 45 minutes. Remove and discard the cinnamon stick and the lemon zest.

3. In a small bowl, beat the egg yolks with ½ cup of the hot rice. Remove the rice pudding from the heat and stir in

the yolk mixture. Scrape the pudding into a large heatproof bowl and blend in the butter. Let cool to room temperature, stirring often. Sprinkle with cinnamon and serve at room temperature or chilled. —*Pablo Massey*

MAKE AHEAD The rice pudding can be refrigerated overnight.

Pumpkin Bread Pudding with Caramel Rum Raisin Sauce

8 TO 10 SERVINGS

Buttery brioche soaked in a pumpkin crème brûlée base and then baked with a cinnamon sugar topping and served with a decadent caramel sauce—this pudding is an excellent alternative to pumpkin pie. The sauce recipe makes more than you'll need, but the leftovers are great to have on hand for turning ice cream and pear or apple pies into spectacular desserts.

- 2 cups milk
- 1½ cups heavy cream
- 3 cinnamon sticks, crushed
- One 2-inch piece of fresh peeled ginger, coarsely chopped
- 1 vanilla bean, split lengthwise
- 6 whole cloves
- 1 loaf of brioche (¾ pound), cut into 1-inch cubes
- 4 large eggs
- 3 large egg yolks
- ½ cup canned unsweetened pumpkin puree
- ½ teaspoon salt
- ½ cup plus 3 tablespoons sugar
- 2 teaspoons cinnamon
- Caramel Rum Raisin Sauce (recipe follows), for serving

1. In a medium saucepan, combine the milk and cream. Add the cinnamon, ginger, vanilla bean and cloves. Cook over moderate heat until just steaming; do not let it boil. Remove the saucepan from the heat, cover and let stand until the milk is fragrant, about 30 minutes.

ABOVE: **Lemony Rice Pudding.**
LEFT: **Pumpkin Bread Pudding with Caramel Rum Raisin Sauce.**

2. Preheat the oven to 375°. Lightly butter a 9-by-13-inch glass or ceramic baking dish. On a rimmed baking sheet, toast the cubed brioche in the oven for about 8 minutes, or until dry and golden. Spread the brioche cubes in an even layer in the prepared baking dish.

3. Rewarm the spiced milk over moderate heat until steaming and then strain it into a heatproof medium bowl.

4. Meanwhile, in another medium bowl, combine the eggs, the egg yolks, the pumpkin puree and the salt and whisk until blended and smooth. Whisk in ½ cup of the sugar. Gradually whisk 1 cup of the hot milk into the pumpkin mixture and then whisk the mixture back into the remaining milk.

5. Pour the pumpkin custard evenly over the brioche and cover with plastic wrap. Let stand until the brioche has absorbed the custard, about 30 minutes. Discard the plastic wrap.

6. In a small bowl, combine the remaining 3 tablespoons of sugar with the cinnamon and sprinkle over the bread pudding. Set the baking dish in a large roasting pan and add enough hot water to the pan to reach halfway up the side of the baking dish.

7. Bake the bread pudding, uncovered, about 45 minutes, or until puffed and set. Let cool slightly, spoon into bowls and serve warm, with the sauce drizzled on top. —*Melissa Murphy Hagenbart*

MAKE AHEAD The baked pudding can be refrigerated overnight. Cover with foil and rewarm in a 325° oven for 15 to 20 minutes before serving.

CARAMEL RUM RAISIN SAUCE

MAKES ABOUT 3 CUPS

- ¾ cup dark rum
- 1 cup raisins
- 3 cups sugar
- ½ cup water
- 1 cup heavy cream

Toasted Panettone with Orange Mascarpone Cream

Chocolate-Chestnut Semifreddo Pops with Candied Cranberries

8 SERVINGS

Tangy ruby-red cranberries offer the perfect counterpoint to these rich frozen mousse pops. The *semifreddo* mixture can also be frozen in a seven-cup loaf pan lined with wax paper and then sliced before serving.

- 3 large egg yolks
- ½ cup superfine sugar
- 1 cup (10 ounces) canned sweetened chestnut puree
- ¼ cup unsweetened cocoa powder
- 1 teaspoon pure vanilla extract

Pinch of salt

- 2½ cups heavy cream
- ¾ cup granulated sugar
- ¼ cup water
- 1 cup fresh cranberries
- 8 cigar cookies
- 1 cup minced roasted chestnuts (optional)

I. In a large bowl, beat the egg yolks with the superfine sugar at high speed until pale and thick, about 5 minutes. Add the chestnut puree, cocoa powder, vanilla and salt and beat at medium speed until smooth. In another bowl, whip the cream to soft peaks. Beat one third of the whipped cream into the chestnut mixture and then fold in the remaining whipped cream.

2. Spoon the chestnut mixture into eight 6-ounce paper cups. Tap the cups gently to release any air pockets and then freeze until the *semifreddo* is firm, at least 6 hours.

3. In a small saucepan, combine the granulated sugar and the water and stir over moderate heat until the sugar dissolves. Add half of the cranberries to the syrup and cook until they're barely soft, about 1 minute. Using a slotted spoon, transfer the cranberries to a plate. Add the remaining cranberries to the syrup and cook over low heat until the cranberries are completely broken down, about 5 minutes. Transfer the cranberry sauce to a bowl to cool. Add

I. In a small saucepan, warm the rum with the raisins. Remove from the heat and let soak for 20 minutes.

2. In a heavy medium saucepan, combine the sugar and water and cook over moderate heat until a deep amber caramel forms. Remove the pan from the heat. Slowly and carefully add a little of the heavy cream to stop the cooking. Add the remaining heavy cream and stir in the raisins and rum. Serve the sauce warm. —*M. M. H.*

MAKE AHEAD The sauce can be refrigerated for 1 week. Reheat gently, stirring occasionally, before serving.

Toasted Panettone with Orange Mascarpone Cream

6 SERVINGS ❈

To make the best chocolate shavings, bring the chocolate to room temperature. Use a sturdy, swivel-headed peeler to create the curls, pressing firmly against the chocolate.

- 1 cup (8 ounces) mascarpone
- ½ teaspoon finely grated orange zest
- 3 tablespoons fresh orange juice
- 1 tablespoon orange liqueur
- 1 tablespoon confectioners' sugar
- 6 thick slices best-quality panettone

Bittersweet chocolate shavings, for garnish

I. In a small bowl, whisk the mascarpone until smooth. Add the orange zest and orange juice along with the orange liqueur and confectioners' sugar and whisk until smooth.

2. Preheat the oven to 350°. Arrange the panettone on a cookie sheet and bake for about 10 minutes, until golden and heated through, turning once. Transfer the slices to dessert plates and spoon the mascarpone cream on top. Sprinkle with the chocolate shavings and serve. —*Michele Scicolone*

MAKE AHEAD The mascarpone cream can be refrigerated for 4 hours.

WINE Asti has a wonderful orange-flower aroma that complements the mascarpone cream. Try the 1998 Cascinetta Moscato d'Asti or the 1998 Fontanafredda Asti Spumante.

the whole cranberries to the cranberry sauce and then refrigerate until the cranberry sauce is chilled.

4. Peel the paper cup off each *semifreddo* and set on a platter. Let soften slightly in the refrigerator, 20 to 30 minutes. Gently ease a cigar cookie into the center of each and roll the *semifreddo* pops in the minced roasted chestnuts if desired. Transfer the *semifreddo* pops to dessert plates, drizzle them with the cranberry sauce and serve immediately. —*Grant Achatz*

MAKE AHEAD The *semifreddo* pops can be prepared through Step 3 three days ahead.

Frozen Chocolate Soufflés with Warm Berry Compote

10 SERVINGS
You will need ten ramekins that are two and a half inches in diameter for this recipe.

1½ pounds imported semisweet chocolate, finely chopped
1 quart heavy cream
⅓ cup raspberry liqueur
4 large eggs
8 large egg yolks
⅔ cup granulated sugar

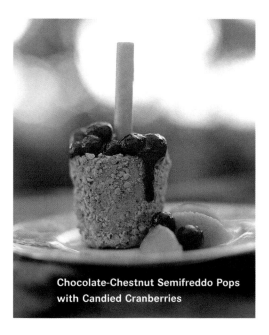

Chocolate-Chestnut Semifreddo Pops with Candied Cranberries

¼ teaspoon pure vanilla extract
Confectioners' sugar, for dusting
Warm Berry Compote (recipe follows)

1. Put 10 ramekins that are 2½ inches in diameter on a baking sheet. Cut 10 six-inch-long sheets of foil and fold each sheet so it is 3 inches wide. Wrap the foil collars around the ramekins with 1 edge flush with the baking sheet; tape the foil collars to secure them. The foil collars should extend 2 to 2½ inches beyond the ramekins. Freeze the ramekins on the baking sheet.

2. Put the chopped chocolate in a large stainless steel bowl. Bring 1¼ cups of the heavy cream to a boil and then pour it over the chocolate; stir until the chocolate is melted. Stir in the raspberry liqueur and let cool.

3. Meanwhile, in another stainless steel bowl, combine the eggs, egg yolks, granulated sugar and vanilla. Set the bowl over a pan of simmering water and beat the mixture at medium speed until it is thick and hot to the touch, about 8 minutes. Remove the bowl from the heat and beat the mixture until it is cooled.

4. Beat the remaining 2¾ cups of heavy cream until it holds soft peaks. Using a rubber spatula, fold the cooled egg mixture into the chocolate mixture and then fold in the whipped cream until no streaks remain. Spoon the mousse into the chilled ramekins and tap the ramekins gently to release any air bubbles. Freeze the chocolate soufflés until they are firm, at least 3 hours or overnight.

5. Remove the foil collars from the ramekins. Dust the soufflés with confectioners' sugar and set the ramekins on oval plates. Serve the Warm Berry Compote on the side. —*Dana Speers*

MAKE AHEAD If the chocolate soufflés were frozen overnight, remove the foil collars and then set the soufflés in the refrigerator for 30 minutes before serving.

WARM BERRY COMPOTE

MAKES 3 CUPS
2 pints fresh raspberries
1 vanilla bean, split lengthwise
½ cup sugar
¼ cup raspberry liqueur
6 tablespoons water
4 teaspoons fresh lemon juice

In a medium saucepan, combine half of the raspberries with the vanilla bean, sugar, raspberry liqueur and water. Simmer for 4 minutes and then remove the vanilla bean. Transfer the berry sauce to a blender and puree. Strain the sauce into a clean saucepan and return to a simmer. Put the remaining raspberries in a heatproof glass bowl and pour the hot sauce on top. Stir in the lemon juice and refrigerate for up to 2 days. Rewarm before serving. —*D. S.*

Late Harvest Riesling Ice Cream

MAKES 5 CUPS
A mere one-quarter cup of wine gives the very rich ice cream a lovely flavor.

2 cups heavy cream
8 large egg yolks
¾ cup plus 2 tablespoons sugar
½ cup milk
¼ cup Late Harvest Riesling or other dessert wine

1. In a medium saucepan, heat the heavy cream until bubbles appear around the edge. Beat the egg yolks with the sugar until smooth. Gradually beat the hot heavy cream into the egg yolks. Return the mixture to the saucepan and cook over moderate heat, stirring constantly, until the custard is thick enough to coat a spoon, about 5 minutes; do not let the custard boil or it will curdle. Strain the custard into a bowl set in a larger bowl of ice water. Stir the milk into the custard and let cool completely, stirring occasionally.

2. Freeze the custard in an ice-cream maker according to the manufacturer's instructions. When the custard is frozen but still soft, add the wine and continue churning until the ice cream is firm.

Transfer the Riesling ice cream to a chilled container and freeze for 1 to 2 hours. —*Kimball Jones*

MAKE AHEAD The ice cream can be frozen for up to 2 days.

WINE Finally! A wine that goes with ice cream (it's also *in* the ice cream). The appealing apricot notes of the 1995 Wente Late Harvest Riesling are balanced by a brisk and cleansing acidity.

Alice B. Toklas's Honey Ice Cream

MAKES ABOUT 1 QUART

This ice cream, adapted from one in the 1954 classic *The Alice B. Toklas Cookbook*, is a sublime combination of honey, pistachios and roasted almonds.

- 2 cups milk
- 1 cup heavy cream
- 6 large egg yolks
- ½ cup plus 1 tablespoon orange blossom or lime blossom honey
- 1 tablespoon sugar
- 1½ teaspoons orange flower water (see Note)
- ½ cup shelled unsalted pistachios
- ⅓ cup blanched whole almonds

1. In a medium saucepan, combine the milk with ½ cup of the cream and bring to a boil over moderately low heat.

2. In a medium bowl, whisk the egg yolks to break them up. Gradually whisk half of the hot milk into the yolks and then pour the mixture into the saucepan and whisk constantly over low heat until the custard is thick enough to coat the back of a spoon; do not let it boil.

3. Strain the custard through a fine sieve into a medium bowl. Whisk in the honey and sugar until completely dissolved and then whisk in the remaining ½ cup cream and the orange flower water. Cover and refrigerate the custard for at least 4 hours or preferably 24 hours to allow the flavor to develop.

4. Preheat the oven to 350°. Spread the pistachios and the almonds in separate pie plates and roast until the pistachios are fragrant but not browned, about 5 minutes. Roast the almonds for 10 minutes, or until golden brown and fragrant, and then turn off the oven and leave the almonds in to dry for 20 minutes longer. Transfer the pistachios and almonds to a plate to cool and chop them coarsely.

5. Freeze the custard in an ice-cream machine according to the manufacturer's instructions. Add the chopped pistachios and almonds when the ice cream is almost set. —*Sally Schneider*

NOTE Orange flower water, a flavoring distilled from orange blossoms, is available at specialty food shops and Middle Eastern markets.

Coconut and Fresh Mint Ice Cream

MAKES ABOUT 1 QUART

- 3 cups unsweetened coconut milk
- 1 cup plus 2 tablespoons half-and-half
- Pinch of salt
- ¾ cup sugar
- 4 large egg yolks
- 1½ tablespoons tapioca starch (see Note)
- ¾ cup shredded unsweetened dried coconut
- ½ cup finely chopped mint, plus leaves for garnish

1. In a heavy medium saucepan, combine the coconut milk with 1 cup of the half-and-half and the salt and bring to a simmer. In a bowl, whisk the sugar with the egg yolks until thick and pale. Gradually add 1 cup of the coconut milk mixture, whisking vigorously; whisk in the remaining coconut milk mixture in a steady stream. Pour the mixture back into the saucepan and cook over low heat, whisking constantly, until thickened, about 5 minutes; do not let it boil or the eggs will curdle.

2. In a bowl, stir the tapioca starch with the remaining 2 tablespoons of half-and-half until smooth and then whisk the mixture into the custard along with the dried coconut. Simmer until thick enough to coat the back of a spoon, about 2 minutes. Transfer the custard to a heatproof bowl, let cool to room temperature and refrigerate until chilled.

3. Pour the custard into an ice-cream maker and freeze according to the manufacturer's instructions. Add the chopped mint halfway through to ensure even distribution. Transfer the ice cream to an airtight container and freeze until ready to serve, up to 2 days. Scoop into bowls, garnish with mint leaves and serve. —*Corinne Trang*

NOTE Make tapioca starch by grinding instant tapioca in a spice mill until powdery. The starch keeps homemade ice cream from melting too quickly.

Cornets à la Crème

MAKES ABOUT 20 CONES

After a hike in the Swiss Alps, a homemade pastry wafer filled with whipped cream at Restaurant Le Miroir d'Argentine in Solalex is a sweet reward. A pizzelle iron, similar to a waffle iron, is used to make the thin, intricately patterned cookie cones. To make these treats at home, you'll need a pizzelle iron that is at least five inches in diameter.

- 2⅓ cups heavy cream
- 1 cup all-purpose flour
- ½ cup plus 1 tablespoon granulated sugar
- ⅓ cup milk
- 1 large egg, lightly beaten
- 1 tablespoon fresh lemon juice
- 1 teaspoon finely grated lemon zest
- 4½ tablespoons unsalted butter, melted and cooled
- 2 tablespoons confectioners' sugar
- 2 teaspoons pure vanilla extract

1. In a medium bowl, combine ⅓ cup of the cream with the flour, granulated sugar, milk, egg, lemon juice, lemon zest and 2½ tablespoons of the butter. Beat until the batter is smooth.

2. Preheat a pizzelle iron over moderately low heat. Lightly brush the iron with some of the remaining butter and place a heaping tablespoon of the batter in the center. Close the iron and

Cornets à la Crème

squeeze the handles for a few seconds. Release the pressure and cook for about 30 seconds, or until the wafer comes away from one side of the iron. If using a manual iron, flip it and cook the wafer on the other side until golden, 20 to 30 seconds longer.

3. Using a knife tip, lift the edge of the wafer away from the iron; carefully peel the wafer off the iron and roll it around a large pastry tip or cannoli mold to form a cone. Repeat to form the remaining cones, buttering the pizzelle iron and adjusting the heat under it as necessary.

4. In a large bowl, whip the remaining 2 cups of heavy cream with the confectioners' sugar and the vanilla. Spoon or pipe the cream into the cones and serve. —*Le Miroir d'Argentine*

Crisp Crêpes Filled with Caramel

6 SERVINGS

Called *tableton* in Argentina, this supersweet dessert consists of layers of crunchy pastry rounds and a rich caramel filling made by simply boiling milk and sugar until thickened and golden.

    4 large egg yolks
    ½ cup dessert wine, such as Marsala
    2 cups all-purpose flour
    1 quart milk
    2 cups granulated sugar
    1 vanilla bean, split lengthwise
    2 tablespoons confectioners' sugar

1. In a large bowl, whisk the egg yolks with the dessert wine. Stir in the flour. When the dough becomes too stiff to stir, transfer it to a floured work surface and knead in any remaining flour until smooth. Cover the dough with plastic wrap and refrigerate until it is firm, about 2 hours.

2. In a saucepan, combine the milk, granulated sugar and vanilla bean. Bring to a boil and simmer over moderate heat, stirring occasionally, until golden brown and reduced to 2 cups, about 1 hour. Transfer to a bowl; discard the vanilla bean. Let the caramel stand, stirring often, until cooled.

3. Preheat the oven to 400°. Cut the dough into 8 equal pieces and shape each piece into a ball; cover the balls with a kitchen towel. On a lightly floured surface, roll out one of the balls to a rough 8-inch round and transfer to a baking sheet; repeat with another ball. Bake the crêpes for about 10 minutes, or until they are browned and crisp. Transfer the crêpes to a plate. Roll out and bake the remaining balls.

4. Place a crêpe on a cake plate. Using a metal spatula, spread a scant ¼ cup of caramel over the crêpe and then set another crêpe on top. Repeat with the remaining caramel and crêpes; don't glaze the last crêpe. Sift the confectioners' sugar on top of the crêpes. Using a serrated knife, gently saw the stack of crêpes into 6 wedges and serve. —*Francis Mallmann*

MAKE AHEAD The crêpes can be kept in an airtight container for 1 day; you can refrigerate the caramel, but be sure to let it return to room temperature before using.

Almond Maple Granola

MAKES 8 CUPS

This is a breakfast staple at FOOD & WINE; almost everyone on the staff has asked for the recipe. Plain yogurt and maple syrup are lovely accompaniments.

    4 cups mixed organic whole
       grain flakes, such as oat,
       kamut, barley and wheat
       (see Note)
    1 cup sliced natural almonds
    2 tablespoons cold unsalted butter,
       cut into 6 pieces
    ¼ cup all-purpose flour
    2 tablespoons sugar
Pinch of salt
    ⅓ cup pure maple syrup
    1 teaspoon pure vanilla extract
    ½ teaspoon pure almond extract
    ½ cup golden raisins
    ½ cup dried cranberries

1. Preheat the oven to 350°. Combine the whole grain flakes with the almonds

Crisp Crêpes Filled with Caramel

on a large rimmed baking sheet. Spread in an even layer and toast for about 10 minutes, stirring once, until light golden. Transfer the toasted grain mixture to a large bowl. Leave the oven on. Coat the warm baking sheet with 1 of the pieces of butter.

2. In a mini processor, combine the remaining 5 pieces of butter with the flour, sugar and salt and pulse until the mixture resembles coarse crumbs. Or, pinch the ingredients together with your fingers. Add the crumbs to the grain mixture and toss. In a small pitcher, combine the maple syrup with the vanilla and almond extracts. Pour over the grain mixture and stir until the grains are evenly moistened.

3. Spread the granola on the buttered baking sheet in an even layer. Toast the granola for 12 to 14 minutes, stirring once, until it is golden and dry. Let the granola cool completely and then stir in the golden raisins and the dried cranberries. —*Grace Parisi*

NOTE Organic whole grain flakes are available at health food stores.

MAKE AHEAD The Almond Maple Granola can be kept in an airtight container for up to 2 weeks or frozen for 2 months.

ONE-HALF CUP Calories 186 kcal, Total Fat 6.2 gm, Saturated Fat 1.4 gm

chapter 17
beverages

397

399

391

394

Hibiscus Tea

MAKES ABOUT 2 QUARTS

Maroon-colored dried hibiscus flowers from Jamaica are available at Caribbean and Mexican groceries. They make a fragrant and intense ruby-red drink that Mexicans serve very sweet.

4   ounces dried hibiscus flowers
2½ quarts cold water
1½ to 2 cups sugar
Crushed ice and orange slices,
   for serving

In a large saucepan, combine the hibiscus flowers and water and bring to a boil. Simmer over moderate heat for 30 minutes. Strain, let cool and then stir in the sugar until it dissolves. Refrigerate until very cold. Serve over ice and garnish with orange slices. —*Richard Ampudia*

Ginger-Lemon Tea

8 SERVINGS

2   quarts water
2   cups fresh lemon juice
1   cup honey
One 3-inch piece fresh ginger,
   peeled and thinly sliced

Combine all of the ingredients in a large saucepan. Bring to a simmer over moderate heat, stirring to dissolve the honey. Remove from the heat. Let the tea steep for 1 hour; strain. Serve hot or cold. —*Trey Foshee*

ONE SERVING Calories 105 kcal, Total Fat 0 gm, Saturated Fat 0 gm

Ginger-Honey Drink with Fresh Herbs

8 SERVINGS

In this soothing drink, the crushed lavender is both pretty and aromatic.

¾   cup wildflower honey
Six 4-inch lavender or rosemary
   sprigs, plus more for garnish
1   pound fresh ginger, peeled and
   cut into 1-inch pieces
Ice cubes, lime wedges and sparkling
   or still water, for serving

I. In a saucepan, combine the honey and lavender; bring to a boil. Turn off the heat, cover and let steep for 1 hour.

2. Line a sieve with several layers of dampened cheesecloth and set it over a medium bowl. In a food processor, finely chop the ginger and then puree for 1 minute. Transfer the ginger puree to the cheesecloth and wring out the juice into the bowl; discard the pulp. Add the lavender honey to the ginger juice.

3. For each drink, fill a tall glass with ice. Add 2 to 3 tablespoons of the ginger syrup and the juice from a lime wedge. Top with water, garnish with a

ABOVE LEFT: Hibiscus Tea. LEFT: Rose Geranium and Blueberry Infusion with Garden-Pea Blossoms.

lightly crushed lavender sprig and serve. —*Anne Disrude*

ONE SERVING Calories 99 kcal, Total Fat 0 gm, Saturated Fat 0 gm

Rose Geranium and Blueberry Infusion with Garden-Pea Blossoms

MAKES ABOUT 2½ QUARTS

Still water infused with fresh herbs and other aromatics is a refreshing alternative to wine. Adding edible flowers to the pitcher turns it into a lovely centerpiece. Be sure to use garden-pea, *not* sweet-pea, blossoms.

2½ quarts water

A large handful of rose geranium leaves, lightly bruised

⅓ cup blueberries

A small handful of garden-pea blossoms

Ice

Pour the water into a large pitcher. Add the leaves, berries and blossoms. Let steep for at least 1 hour. The longer the infusion stands, the more flavorful it will be. Serve over ice. —*Anne Disrude*

VARIATIONS Some other wonderful combinations include lemon verbena and sliced nectarines; strawberries, thyme and sliced lemons or lemon peel; peppermint and sliced fresh ginger; rosemary and orange peel; and kaffir lime leaves and black peppermint.

Cucumber-Lovage Cooler

8 SERVINGS

2 large European cucumbers, peeled and cut into 1-inch chunks

16 large lovage leaves or large dill sprigs

2 teaspoons fresh lemon juice

¾ teaspoon salt

Ice, sparkling water, freshly ground pepper and orange zest or celery sticks, for serving

I. In a food processor, finely chop the cucumbers and lovage leaves and then

puree for 1 minute. Line a sieve with several layers of dampened cheesecloth and set it over a medium bowl. Transfer the puree to the cheesecloth, gather up the edges and wring the juice into the bowl; discard the pulp. Add the lemon juice and salt.

2. For each cooler, fill a glass with ice and add ⅓ cup of the cucumber juice. Add some water and pepper. Garnish each cooler with orange zest or celery and serve. —*Anne Disrude*

ONE SERVING Calories 6 kcal, Total Fat 0 gm, Saturated Fat 0 gm

Spicy Pineapple Cocktail

8 SERVINGS

This easy three-ingredient blend is surprisingly complex in flavor.

1 golden pineapple—peeled, cored and cut into 1-inch chunks

8 large mint sprigs, plus more for garnish

½ hot chile, seeded and chopped

Ice and sparkling water, for serving

I. In a food processor, finely chop the pineapple with the 8 mint sprigs and the chile; puree 1 minute. Line a sieve with several layers of dampened cheesecloth and set over a medium bowl. Transfer the puree to the cheesecloth. Wring the juice into the bowl; discard the pulp.

2. For each drink, fill a tall glass with ice and add ¼ cup of the juice. Add some sparkling water, garnish with a crushed mint sprig and serve. —*Anne Disrude*

ONE SERVING Calories 33 kcal, Total Fat 0 gm, Saturated Fat 0 gm

Spicy Pineapple Cocktail, with Parsnip Fries with Hot Vinegar Dip (p. 287).

Watermelon-Fennel Cocktail

8 SERVINGS

    5 pounds watermelon, rind removed,
       flesh cut into 1-inch chunks
2 ½ teaspoons finely ground fennel
       seeds
Ice, sparkling water, lemon wedges
    and tarragon sprigs, for serving

fruit-syrup drinks

For each drink, pour about a half inch
of syrup into a tall glass, add ice and
fill the glass with water or seltzer.

Sour Cherry Syrup

MAKES ABOUT 3 QUARTS

6 ½ pounds fresh sour cherries,
stemmed and pitted, or 4 ½ pounds
pitted, unsweetened frozen sour cherries • Scant 11 cups sugar • 5 ½ cups
water • ¾ cup fresh lime juice

Working in batches, puree the cherries in a blender. Pass the juice
through a fine sieve, pressing hard on
the solids to extract as much juice as
possible. In a large saucepan, combine the cherry juice, sugar, water
and lime juice. Bring to a boil, stirring
constantly, until the sugar dissolves.
Cook over moderate heat for 10 minutes, skimming off the foam that
rises to the top with a slotted spoon.
Reduce the heat to moderately low
and simmer, stirring and skimming
occasionally, until syrupy, about 1
hour. Strain into jars. —Madhur Jaffrey

Lime and Ginger Syrup

MAKES ABOUT 1 ½ QUARTS

6 cups sugar • 2 cups water • One 3-
inch piece of fresh ginger, peeled and
thinly sliced • 1 ½ cups fresh lime juice

In a large saucepan, combine the sugar, water and ginger. Bring to a boil,
stirring until the sugar dissolves. Simmer over low heat, stirring occasionally, for 15 minutes longer. Stir in the
lime juice. Simmer until syrupy, about
15 minutes. Strain into jars. —M. J.

1. In a food processor, puree the watermelon for 1 minute. Line a sieve with
several layers of dampened cheesecloth
and set the sieve over a medium bowl.
Transfer the watermelon puree to the
cheesecloth and wring out the juice into
the bowl; discard the pulp. Add the fennel to the watermelon juice.

2. For each cocktail, fill a tall glass with
ice. Add ½ cup of the watermelon-fen-
nel juice, some sparkling water, a lemon wedge and a crushed tarragon sprig
and serve. —Anne Disrude

ONE SERVING Calories 50 kcal,
Total Fat 0.7 gm, Saturated Fat 0 gm

Blackberry Limeade

MAKES ABOUT 2 QUARTS

    3 cups fresh blackberries
    7 cups cold water
    1 cup sugar
    1 cup fresh lime juice
Ice, for serving

1. In a blender, puree the blackberries
with 1 cup of the cold water. Strain the
puree through a fine sieve. In a small
saucepan, combine the sugar with 1
cup of the cold water and bring to a
boil. Simmer until the syrup is reduced
to 1 cup, about 15 minutes; let cool.

2. In a pitcher, combine the blackberry
puree with the sugar syrup, the fresh
lime juice and the remaining 5 cups of
cold water and refrigerate until chilled.
Serve the limeade in tall glasses over
ice. —Martha McGinnis

Masala Chai

MAKES ABOUT 4 CUPS

This warming beverage is easy to prepare by steeping spices in hot water
and milk before adding black tea. It's
not as milky as the *chai* often sold at
American coffee bars; to make it richer,
add more milk and sugar to taste.

    4 whole cloves
    2 cardamom pods
    1 cinnamon stick, broken into pieces
    3 cups water
  ¼ teaspoon ground ginger

  ⅛ teaspoon freshly ground
       black pepper
  ½ cup milk
    2 tablespoons sugar
    2 tablespoons black tea, such as
       Darjeeling or Orange Pekoe

1. In a mortar, crush the cloves, cardamom pods and cinnamon. Transfer the
crushed spices to a small saucepan,
add the water, ginger and pepper and
bring to a boil. Remove the pan from the
heat, cover and let steep for 5 minutes.

2. Add the milk and sugar to the pan
and bring to a boil. Remove from the
heat and add the tea. Cover and let
steep for 3 minutes. Stir the *chai*, then
strain it into a warmed teapot or directly into teacups. —Maya Kaimal

Jet-Lag Smoothie

2 SERVINGS

This jet-lag buster combines protein-
rich yogurt, high-carbohydrate fruit and
lots of ice.

    1 cup sliced strawberries
    1 cup sliced bananas
    1 cup fresh tangerine or orange
       juice
    1 cup crushed ice
  ½ cup plain nonfat yogurt
    1 tablespoon honey

In a blender, combine all the ingredients. Blend on high speed until smooth
and frothy. —Grace Parisi

Litchi Champagne Cocktail

8 SERVINGS

A variation on the Kir Royale, this exotic aperitif combines sweet Asian litchis
and their syrup (instead of black currant
liqueur) with dry French Champagne. A
bottle of another sparkling wine is an
acceptable and less-expensive alternative to Champagne.

One 11-ounce can litchis, chilled
    1 bottle brut Champagne, chilled

Drop a litchi into each of 8 Champagne
flutes; add 2 tablespoons of the syrup
from the can to each. Fill the flutes with
Champagne and serve. —Corinne Trang

Masala Chai

ABOVE: **White Wine and Sparkling Cider Sangria.**
RIGHT: **San Moritz Martini.**

White Wine and Sparkling Cider Sangria

MAKES ABOUT 1½ QUARTS

- 1 bottle dry white wine, such as Vinho Verde or Pinot Grigio
- 1 cup fresh orange juice

Juice of 2 limes

Orange and lime slices

- 10 strawberries, thickly sliced (optional)
- 1½ cups sparkling sweet cider

Ice

In a large glass pitcher, combine the wine, orange juice, lime juice, orange and lime slices and strawberries, if using, and set aside to macerate for 15 minutes. Just before serving, add the sparkling cider and ice. Stir well; serve at once. —*Steven Raichlen*

Red October

1 SERVING

- 1 cup crushed ice
- 2 ounces vodka, preferably raspberry

- ½ ounce raspberry liqueur

Champagne

Raspberries, for garnish

In a cocktail shaker, combine the ice, the vodka and the raspberry liqueur and shake vigorously. Strain into a chilled glass. Add a splash of Champagne, garnish with raspberries and serve. —*Bryan Evans*

San Moritz Martini

1 SERVING

- 1 cup crushed ice
- 3 ounces black currant vodka
- 1 ounce Champagne

Clear crème de menthe

Pomegranate seeds, for garnish

In a cocktail shaker, combine the ice and the black currant vodka and shake vigorously. Strain into a chilled glass. Add the Champagne, a splash of crème de menthe and the pomegranate seeds and serve. —*F&W*

The Big Apple Martini

1 SERVING

- 1 cup crushed ice
- 3 ounces vodka
- ½ ounce applejack brandy

Calvados

Lady apple, for garnish

In a pitcher, combine the ice, vodka and brandy and stir. Strain the mixture into a chilled glass. Add a splash of Calvados, garnish with the Lady apple and serve. —*Clementine, New York City*

Clementini

1 SERVING

- 1 cup crushed ice
- 3 ounces orange vodka
- ½ ounce orange liqueur
- 1 ounce fresh clementine juice

In a cocktail shaker, combine all of the ingredients and shake vigorously. Strain the cocktail into a chilled glass and serve. —*Clementine, New York City*

The Big Apple Martini

Swingalicious

Swingalicious

1 SERVING

- 1 cup crushed ice
- 1 ounce fresh lemon juice
- ¾ ounce fresh clementine juice
- ½ ounce orange liqueur
- ½ ounce simple syrup (see Note)
- ¼ ounce raspberry liqueur
- 2 ounces vodka

Maraschino cherry, for garnish

In a cocktail shaker, combine the ice, lemon juice, clementine juice, orange liqueur, simple syrup, raspberry liqueur and vodka and shake vigorously. Strain the mixture into a chilled glass. Garnish the cocktail with a maraschino cherry and serve. —*Clementine, New York City*

NOTE To make simple syrup, combine equal amounts of sugar and water in a saucepan. Cook over moderately low heat, stirring, until the sugar dissolves.

Mexican Gin and Tonic

1 SERVING

Mexican bartenders make a different version of the gin and tonic than their counterparts north of the border. Their secret: they use lime as an ingredient, not just a garnish.

Ice

- ¼ cup gin
- 1 tablespoon fresh lime juice

Tonic and lime slice, for serving

Fill a highball glass with ice. Add the gin and lime juice. Top off the glass with tonic and stir gently. Garnish with a lime slice. —*Pete Wells*

Tom Collins

1 SERVING

The Tom Collins never tasted the same after the invention of sour mix. But there's no reason to take this supposed shortcut; mixing the drink from scratch is really very simple.

- 2 tablespoons fresh lemon juice
- 1¾ teaspoons superfine sugar

Ice

- ¼ cup gin

Club soda and lemon slice, for serving

Pour the fresh lemon juice into a collins glass. Add the superfine sugar and stir briskly to dissolve. Fill the collins glass with ice and then add the gin. Top off the cocktail with some club soda and stir. Garnish the cocktail with a slice of lemon. —*Pete Wells*

Singapore Sling

1 SERVING

Probably no mixed drink has been as mistreated as this one. As Dale De-Groff, mixologist of Blackbird Restaurant in New York City, says, "The only thing most bartenders know about the Singapore Sling is that it's supposed to be red." This version is an adaptation of

Mexican Gin and Tonic

rules for mixing

While vodka simply disappears into a drink, gin, which has a more assertive flavor, is a little trickier to blend. When a combination is successful, though, it attains a level of complexity that's impossible with vodka. Some guidelines for home bartenders:

Try aromatic mixers The botanicals in gin make it a natural match for aromatized wines (vermouth, Lillet), bitter spirits (Campari) and concentrated bitters (Angostura, Peychaud's or orange bitters).

Use fresh citrus juices Most gins are flavored with orange and lemon peel; for that reason they work well in cocktails that contain sweetened citrus juice.

Chill the drink thoroughly The best way to compare brands of gin is to taste them at room temperature, but mixed gin drinks should be icy cold. Use plenty of ice and chilled club soda or tonic (keep bottles in the refrigerator) and, if using a shaker, shake it until it is almost too cold to hold.

the original recipe from Raffles Hotel in Singapore.

Ice

6	tablespoons pineapple juice
2	tablespoons gin
2	tablespoons fresh lime juice
1	tablespoon Cherry Heering
1	tablespoon grenadine
½	tablespoon Benedictine

Triple Sec

Angostura bitters

Fill a shaker with ice. Add the pineapple juice, gin, lime juice, Cherry Heering, grenadine, Benedictine, a dash of Triple Sec and 3 dashes of Angostura bitters. Shake for 1 minute and strain over ice into a tall glass. —*Pete Wells*

French 75

1 SERVING

Gin and Champagne? *Mais oui*. Named for an artillery gun used in World War I, the French 75 has a surprisingly clean taste and an explosive effect.

Ice

1	tablespoon gin
1	tablespoon Cointreau
1	tablespoon fresh lemon juice
½	cup Champagne or sparkling wine

Put a handful of ice cubes in a shaker and add the gin, Cointreau and lemon juice. Shake and strain into a Champagne flute. Add the Champagne and stir gently. —*Pete Wells*

Ramos Gin Fizz

1 SERVING

Few drinks provide a smoother landing after a bumpy night than this New Orleans hangover remedy. Be careful not to slip when pouring the orange flower water; too much spoils the drink.

Ice

1	tablespoon superfine sugar
3	drops orange flower water
1	tablespoon fresh lime juice
2	tablespoons fresh lemon juice
3	tablespoons gin
1	egg white

| 3 | tablespoons half-and-half |
| 2 | tablespoons club soda |

Put a handful of ice cubes in a shaker and add, in order, the sugar, orange flower water, lime juice, lemon juice, gin, egg white, half-and-half and club soda. Shake long and hard, until the half-and-half and egg white are frothy and the sound of the ice is muffled. Strain into a large glass. —*Pete Wells*

Dry Martini

1 SERVING

The adjective *dry* applies to the type of vermouth; it doesn't mean that you do not use vermouth at all. Unfortunately, many bartenders do just that, believing that vermouth makes the drink too per-fumey. In truth, it softens and comple-ments the gin. A martini without ver-mouth isn't a martini. It's just cold gin.

Ice

| 6 | tablespoons gin |
| 1 | teaspoon dry vermouth |

One 1-inch piece of lemon zest

Fill a shaker with ice. Pour in the gin and dry vermouth. Stir for 1 minute. Strain into a chilled martini glass. Gently twist the lemon zest over the drink and drop it in. —*Pete Wells*

Valencia

1 SERVING

This elegant variation on the martini simply substitutes sherry for vermouth.

Ice

| 6 | tablespoons gin |
| 1 | tablespoon fino sherry |

Strip of orange zest

Fill a shaker with ice. Pour in the gin and sherry. Stir for 1 minute. Strain into a chilled martini glass. Gently twist the strip of orange zest over the drink and drop it in. —*Pete Wells*

Southside

1 SERVING

According to legend, this cocktail was invented at New York's '21' Club. It has been almost completely forgotten, but

Hot Potato

it's an easy summer cocktail that can impress even the most jaded drinker.

Ice

¼	cup gin
2	tablespoons fresh lemon juice
1½	teaspoons superfine sugar

2 fresh mint sprigs

Fill a shaker with ice. Add the gin, fresh lemon juice, superfine sugar and one mint sprig. Shake vigorously for 1 min-ute. Strain into a chilled martini glass and garnish the cocktail with the re-maining mint sprig. —*Pete Wells*

Aviation

1 SERVING

A jazz-age standard, the Aviation has made a bit of a comeback recently after being featured on a number of cocktail Web sites. Maraschino liqueur, which is indispensable, can often be found in liquor stores in Italian neighborhoods.

Ice

¼	cup gin
2	tablespoons fresh lemon juice
1	tablespoon Maraschino liqueur

Fill a shaker with ice. Add the gin, lemon juice and Maraschino liqueur. Shake vigorously for one minute. Strain into a chilled martini glass.—*Pete Wells*

Hot Potato

1 SERVING

- 1 cup crushed ice
- 2 ounces vodka
- 2 ounces pepper vodka

Pequín chiles, for garnish

In a cocktail shaker, combine the crushed ice, vodka and pepper vodka and shake vigorously. Strain into a chilled glass. Garnish with pequín chiles and serve. —*Bryan Evans*

Tequila with Sangrita

6 SERVINGS

One of the great pleasures of traveling in Mexico is the opportunity to sample different tequilas. Really good tequilas are very smooth, with complex flavors that range from earthy to almost floral. Fine unusual tequilas include Herradura, El Tesoro and Chinaco. Look for those labeled *añejo,* which means aged. For a new way to enjoy a good tequila, try sipping it straight up from a small narrow glass, followed with a second identical glass of sangrita, a spicy mixture of tomato, orange and lime juices and grenadine.

- ⅔ cup tomato juice
- ½ cup fresh orange juice
- ¼ cup fresh lime juice
- 2 teaspoons grenadine
- ½ teaspoon chipotle adobo or hot sauce
- ½ teaspoon Maggi seasoning or Worcestershire sauce

Pinch of salt

Fine tequila

Lime wedges, for serving

I. In a small pitcher, combine the tomato juice, orange juice and lime juice with the grenadine, adobo sauce, Maggi seasoning and salt. Cover the pitcher and refrigerate until the sangrita is thoroughly chilled.

2. To serve, pour the cold sangrita into six 2- to 3-ounce glasses. Pour 1 ounce of tequila into each of 6 glasses of the same size. Serve 1 glass of each to each guest, along with lime wedges, which

City Grocery Mojitos

can be squeezed into the sangrita or sucked between sips. —*Sally Schneider*

ONE SERVING Calories 111 kcal, Total Fat .1 gm, Saturated Fat 0 gm

City Grocery Mojitos

8 SERVINGS

- 1 large bunch of spearmint, plus 8 additional sprigs for garnish
- ¾ cup sugar
- 1 lime, rinsed and quartered, plus ⅓ cup fresh lime juice
- 1 cup club soda, plus more for serving
- 2 cups dark rum

Ice cubes

In a bowl, using a wooden spoon, crush the large bunch of spearmint with the sugar and lime quarters until the sugar starts to dissolve and tastes like mint. Add 1 cup of the club soda and stir until the sugar dissolves completely. Strain the mixture through a coarse sieve into a pitcher and then stir in the lime juice and rum. Fill 8 tall glasses with ice and add a mint sprig to each, lightly crushing the mint sprig with your hands. Pour the rum mixture over the ice, top each glass with club soda and serve. —*John Currence*

MAKE AHEAD The strained *mojito* mixture can be refrigerated overnight.

guide to special recipes

The recipes marked with symbols throughout the book are listed here so that you can quickly locate all the dishes of a particular type.

Quick

175

78

292

357

Health-Conscious

recipe guide

25

390

♕ Best New Chefs

91

index

Page numbers in **boldface** indicate photographs

index

index

index

index

index

index

index

index

index

contributors

Grant Achatz is the sous-chef at The French Laundry Restaurant in Yountville, California.

Lisa Ahier is the chef at Cibolo Creek Ranch in the southwestern Texas town of Shafter.

Richard Ampudia is an owner of Café Habana in New York City.

Frédéric Anton is the chef at the restaurant Pré Catelan in the Bois de Boulogne of Paris.

John Ash is the culinary director of Fetzer Vineyards.

Didier Banyols oversees the restaurants La Grand Vigne and La Table du Lavoir, both at Les Sources de Caudalíe, a wine spa in the Bordeaux region of France.

Ben Barker is the chef at Magnolia Grill in Durham, North Carolina. His book *Not Afraid of Flavor: Recipes from Magnolia Grill,* co-written with his wife, Karen, will be published in late 2000 by the University of North Carolina Press.

Teresa Barrenechea is the chef and owner of the Basque restaurant Marichu in New York City.

John Besh was named one of FOOD & WINE's Best New Chefs in 1999. He is the chef at the restaurant Artesia in Abita Springs, Louisiana.

Daniel Boulud is the chef and owner of Daniel and Café Boulud, both in New York City. He is the author of *Daniel Boulud's Café Boulud Cookbook* (Scribner) and *Cooking with Daniel Boulud* (Random House).

Terrance Brennan is the chef and owner of the restaurant Picholine in New York City.

Giuliano Bugialli, teacher and author of many cookbooks, most recently wrote *Bugialli's Italy* (William Morrow), one of FOOD & WINE's Best Cookbooks of 1998.

Maria José Cabral and **Emília Augusta Magalháes** cook at the Quinta da Aveleda estate, the largest winery in Portugal's Vinho Verde region.

Patrick Callarec is the chef and co-owner of the restaurant Chez Paul in Lahaina, Maui.

Anna Teresa Callen is a cooking teacher and the author of four cookbooks, including *Food and Memories of Abruzzo: Italy's Pastoral Land* (Macmillan).

Sue Chapman is the executive chef at The Lodge at Skylonda, on the San Francisco peninsula.

Sam and **Sam Clark,** a husband and wife team, are the chefs and owners of the London restaurant Moro. They are currently writing *The Moro Cookbook,* due out in 2001 from Ebury Press.

Tom Colicchio is the chef at Gramercy Tavern in New York City.

Marion Cunningham has written seven cookbooks, the latest of which is *Learning to Cook with Marion Cunningham* (Knopf).

John Currence is the chef and owner of the restaurant City Grocery in Oxford, Mississippi.

Erica De Mane is the author of *Pasta Improvvisata* (Scribner).

Lori De Mori is the coauthor of *Italy Anywhere*, a collection of recipes and stories to be published in the fall of 2000 by Viking/Penguin.

Robert Del Grande co-owns the restaurant Taco Milagro in Houston and a growing southwestern restaurant chain called Cafe Express.

Rocco DiSpirito was named one of FOOD & WINE's Best New Chefs in 1999. He is the chef at the restaurant Union Pacific in New York City.

Anne Disrude lives in Jersey City, New Jersey, and works as a food stylist for photographers.

Binh Duong is the chef and owner of the restaurant Truc Orient Express in Hartford, Connecticut, and a coauthor of *Simple Art of Vietnamese Cooking* (Simon & Schuster).

Fred Eric is the chef and owner of the restaurants Vida and Fred 62, both in L.A.'s Los Feliz neighborhood.

Bryan Evans is the general manager of New York City's Cibar, a cigar-friendly watering hole with upscale bar food.

Bob Farrish is a sales manager for DuPont Automotive in Troy, Michigan, and an excellent home cook.

Claudia Fleming is the pastry chef at Gramercy Tavern in New York City.

Trey Foshee was named one of FOOD & WINE's Best New Chefs in 1998. He is the executive chef at the restaurant George's at the Cove in La Jolla, California.

Wilder Fulford is an investment banker and enthusiastic home cook.

George Gebhardt owns a greenhouse in Southampton, Massachusetts, and is an amateur chef.

Suzanne Goin was named one of FOOD & WINE's Best New Chefs in 1999. She is the chef at the restaurant Lucques in Los Angeles.

Edwin Goto is the executive chef at The Manele Bay Hotel in Lanai, Hawaii.

Benoît Guichard is the owner and executive chef at the renowned Paris restaurant Jamin.

Melissa Murphy Hagenbart is the chef and co-owner of Sweet Melissa Pâtisserie in Brooklyn, New York.

Pilar Huguet is matriarch of the winemaking Huguet family, famous for its Champagne-class *cava* from Spain's Catalonia.

Alfonso Iaccarino is the chef and owner of the restaurant Don Alfonso 1890 in the town of Sant'Agata sui Due Golfi, one of only three restaurants in Italy awarded all three *Michelin* stars.

Madhur Jaffrey, the author of 12 cookbooks, is a chef, food consultant and teacher—as well as an actress. Her most recent work is *Madhur Jaffrey's World Vegetarian* (Clarkson Potter).

Susan Shapiro Jaslove is a food writer, recipe developer and cooking instructor based in Warren, New Jersey.

Nancy Harmon Jenkins lives much of the year in Cortona, Italy. Her latest cookbook, *Flavors of Tuscany* (Broadway Books), was one of FOOD & WINE's Best Cookbooks of 1998. She is currently working on a book about key Mediterranean ingredients.

Kimball Jones is the executive chef at Wente Vineyards in Livermore, California, and the coauthor, with Carolyn Wente, of *Sharing the Vineyard Table* (Ten Speed Press).

Barbara Kafka is the author of eight cookbooks, most recently, *Soup: A Way of Life* (Artisan), one of FOOD & WINE's Best Cookbooks of 1998.

Katharine Kagel is the chef at Cafe Pasqual in Santa Fe, New Mexico.

Paul Kahan was named one of FOOD & WINE's Best New Chefs in 1999. He is the chef at the restaurant Blackbird in Chicago.

Maya Kaimal, author of *Curried Favors* (Abbeville), is currently at work on a second cookbook, called *Savoring the Spice Coast of India: Fresh Flavors from Kerala,* to be published in the spring of 2000 by HarperCollins.

Stephen Kalt is the chef and owner of the restaurants Spartina and Spazzia in New York City.

Lynne Rossetto Kasper hosts the public radio show *The Splendid Table with Lynne Rossetto Kasper.* Her newest book is *The Italian Country Table* (Scribner).

Diana Kennedy, author of seven cookbooks, most recently wrote *My Mexico* (Clarkson Potter), one of FOOD & WINE's Best Cookbooks of 1998.

Jimmy Kennedy is the chef and co-owner of the restaurant River Run in Plainfield, Vermont.

Marcia Kiesel is the test kitchen supervisor at FOOD & WINE and a coauthor of *Simple Art of Vietnamese Cooking* (Simon & Schuster).

Jonathan King and **Jim Stott** are the team behind Stonewall Kitchen, which produces jams, mustards and vinegars in York, Maine.

Nancy Knickerbocker, mother of the San Francisco–based food writer and cooking teacher Peggy Knickerbocker, was an adventuresome home cook and entertainer.

Eric Lecerf is the executive chef of the restaurant L'Astor in Paris.

Seen Lippert, after ten years of cooking at Berkeley's renowned Chez Panisse, is currently scouting New York City locations for her own restaurant.

Eileen Yin-Fei Lo has written eight cookbooks. Her latest, *The Chinese Kitchen* (William Morrow), recounts the history and lore of Chinese cuisine, as well as memories of cooking with her grandmother.

contributors

Michael Locascio is an insurance salesman and former student at Peter Kump's New York Cooking School.

Raphael Lunetta is the executive chef at the restaurant Jiraffe in Santa Monica, California.

Egidiana Maccioni is the wife and partner of Sirio Maccioni, owner of four restaurants: Le Cirque in both New York City and Las Vegas and Circo in the same cities.

Deborah Madison is the author of five cookbooks, all published by Broadway Books, including *Vegetarian Cooking for Everyone* and the forthcoming *This Can't be Tofu!*

Francis Mallmann is the force behind three restaurants in South America: Patagonia Sur in Buenos Aires; 1884 Francis Mallmann in the Escorihuela Winery in Mendoza; and Los Negros on the coast of Uruguay.

Pablo Massey is the chef and owner of two restaurants in Buenos Aires, both called Massey.

George Mavrothalassitis is the chef and owner of the restaurant Chef Mavro in Honolulu.

James Mazzio, formerly chef at 15 Degrees in Boulder, Colorado, was named one of FOOD & WINE's Best New Chefs in 1999.

James McDevitt was named one of FOOD & WINE's Best New Chefs in 1999. He is the chef at the restaurant Hapa in Scottsdale, Arizona.

Martha McGinnis works as a personal chef in Traverse City, Michigan.

Tim McKee, one of FOOD & WINE's Best New Chefs in 1997, is the chef and owner of the restaurant La Belle Vie in Stillwater, Minnesota.

Howard Miller is the perishables director at Central Market Westgate in Austin, Texas.

Larry Mufson is the managing partner of an architectural design firm in New York City and an avid cook.

Marie-Andrée Nauleau, along with her mother and sister, runs the Domaines Mugneret-Gibourg & Georges Mugneret wine estate in the Vosne-Romanée region of Burgundy.

Jan Newberry, a cookbook editor and food writer, lives in Oakland, California.

Nell Newman, sustainable agriculture advocate, cofounded Newman's Own Organics. Like her father's company, Newman's Own, all after-tax profits go to charity.

Bradley Ogden is the chef and co-owner of The Lark Creek Restaurant Group, which has locations in Larkspur, California, and surrounding cities.

Philippe Padovani is the chef and owner at Padovani's Bistro & Wine Bar in Honolulu.

Grace Parisi, recipe developer and tester at FOOD & WINE, is also the author of *Summer/Winter Pasta* (William Morrow).

Gary Peese is a partner in a nursery and landscape-design firm in Austin, Texas, and has studied at cooking schools in Mexico, New York and Paris.

Jacques Pépin, master chef, TV personality, food columnist, cooking teacher and contributing editor to FOOD & WINE, is the author of numerous books and the cohost, with Julia Child, of the television show *Julia and Jacques: Cooking at Home* on PBS.

Wolfgang Puck owns six restaurants, including Spago and Chinois in Los Angeles, and a chain of pizza cafés.

Steven Raichlen is a syndicated columnist and the author of several cookbooks. Upcoming are *High-Flavor, Low-Fat Jewish Cooking,* to be published by Viking, and *Barbecue Sauces, Rubs, and Marinades,* from Workman.

Dale Reitzer was named one of FOOD & WINE's Best New Chefs in 1999. He is the chef at the restaurant Acacia in Richmond, Virginia.

Philippe Renard is the chef of the hotel Lutétia in Paris.

Josette Riondato has been the cook for 34 years at the Château Loudenne, a vineyard estate in Bordeaux.

Eric Ripert is the co-owner and executive chef of Le Bernardin in New York City. He is the coauthor of *Le Bernardin Cookbook: Four Star Simplicity* (Doubleday), one of FOOD & WINE's Best Cookbooks of 1998.

Luis Rivera is a sous-chef at Jimmy's Bronx Café in New York City.

Anthony Roselli is the executive chef at Orso in Los Angeles.

Steve Rosen was named one of FOOD & WINE's Best New Chefs in 1999. He is the chef at the restaurant Salts in Cambridge, Massachusetts.

Sally Schneider, a contributing editor at FOOD & WINE Magazine, is currently writing *A New Way to Cook,* to be published by Simon & Schuster.

Michele Scicolone authored *Savoring Italy* (Time-Life Books) and coauthored *Pizza Any Way You Slice It!* (Broadway Books).

Kerry Sear is the chef and owner of the restaurant Cascadia in Seattle.

David Selex is the head chef at the London restaurant The Sugar Club.

Craig Shelton is chef and owner of The Ryland Inn in Whitehouse, New Jersey.

Ron Siegel was named one of FOOD & WINE's Best New Chefs in 1999. He is the chef at Charles Nob Hill in San Francisco.

Jane Sigal is a senior editor at FOOD & WINE and the author of *Backroad Bistros, Farmhouse Fare* (Doubleday) and *Normandy Gastronomique* (Abbeville).

Todd Slossberg is the chef at the historic Hotel Jerome in Aspen, Colorado.

Dana Speers was assistant pastry chef at Lespinasse in New York City for three years before becoming assistant editor at FOOD & WINE Books.

Rori Spinelli is a professional cook and a photography food stylist based in New York City.

Mark Strausman, author of *The Campagna Table* (William Morrow), is the chef and owner of the restaurant Campagna in New York City and the chef of Fred's at Barneys New York. He'll open a new restaurant, Chinghalle, in 2000.

Göran Streng is the executive chef at the Hawaii Prince Hotel in Oahu, Hawaii.

Hisachika Takahashi, a painter and a curator for the artist Robert Rauschenberg, is an accomplished home cook.

Corinne Trang is the author of *Authentic Vietnamese Cooking—Food from a Family Table* (Simon & Schuster).

Jerry Traunfeld, chef at The Herbfarm Restaurant in Washington State, is the author of *The Herbfarm Cookbook,* due in bookstores in March, 2000 from Scribner.

Charlie Trotter is the owner and executive chef of Charlie Trotter's Restaurant in Chicago. His most recent cookbook is *The Kitchen Sessions by Charlie Trotter* (Ten Speed Press), honored as one of FOOD & WINE's Best Cookbooks of 1998.

Ming Tsai is the chef and owner of the restaurant Blue Ginger in Wellesley, Massachusetts.

Ruth Van Waerebeek-Gonzalez, Belgian by birth and Chilean by marriage, is a cookbook author. Her most recent book is *The Chilean Kitchen* (HPBooks).

Marc Vetri was named one of FOOD & WINE's Best New Chefs in 1999. He is the chef and owner of the restaurant Vetri in Philadelphia.

Jean-Georges Vongerichten, chef and co-owner of the New York City restaurants Jo Jo, Mercer Kitchen, Jean Georges and Vong, is also the coauthor of *Jean-Georges: Cooking at Home with a Four-Star Chef* (Broadway Books), named one of FOOD & WINE's Best Cookbooks of 1998.

Pete Wells is an associate editor at FOOD & WINE Magazine.

Paula Wolfert is the author of six cookbooks, most recently *Mediterranean Grains and Greens* (HarperCollins), honored by FOOD & WINE as the Best Cookbook of 1998. She is currently at work on *Mediterranean Cooking—Slow and Easy.*

Alan Wong, the chef and owner of Alan Wong's Restaurant in Honolulu, is the author of *New Wave Luau* (Ten Speed Press).

Su-Mei Yu is the chef and owner of the San Diego restaurant Saffron. Her book *Cracking the Coconut: Classic Thai Home Cooking* will be published by William Morrow in August, 2000.

Special thanks to the following restaurants for their contributions to this book:
Auberge de l'Onde, St. Saphorin, Switzerland
Clementine, New York City
Dahlia Lounge, Seattle
Grandma's Country Restaurant, Albany, New York
J. Sheekey, London
Jacques-Imo's, New Orleans
Mangrove Mama's, Sugar Loaf Key, Florida
Le Miroir d'Argentine, Solalex, Switzerland
Peoples Restaurant, New Holland, Pennsylvania
Restaurant l'Ermitage, Clarens, Switzerland
Woodside Restaurant, Los Angeles

photo credits

Melanie Acevedo: 64 (right), 98, 217, 345, 352; Sang An: 110, 189; Quentin Bacon: 12, 27 (right), 41, 43, 44 (left), 50 (left), 69, 76, 103 (right), 105, 122, 129 (right), 148, 151, 154, 158, 160 (right), 161 (right), 164, 166, 170, 178, 186, 191, 196 (right), 197 (left), 200, 204, 206, 222, 232, 233, 252 (top), 258, 265, 268 (left), 275, 285, 292, 305, 310, 328 (right), 334, 335, 339, 351, 377, 379; Fernando Bengoechea: 5 (bottom right), 19, 42, 94, 96, 128 (left), 133, 197 (right), 201, 218, 290, 374; Bill Bettencourt: 141, 367; Monica Buck: 5 (bottom left), 80 (left), 101, 117 (top), 140 (top), 160 (left), 162 (right), 171, 183, 205, 230, 251, 255, 288, 344, 354, 373 (left and right), 380, 382 (bottom), 390 (top); Beatriz Da Costa: front cover, 40, 50 (right), 51, 52, 53, 71, 79, 99, 106 (left), 126, 147, 153, 168, 213 (left), 241, 243, 254, 260, 261, 291, 299, 316 (left and right), 321, 323, 327, 356, 362; Reed Davis: 66, 90, 104, 129 (left), 155, 156, 176, 179, 196 (left), 211, 244, 245, 249 (left), 252 (bottom), 253, 282, 289, 358 (left), 360, 384, 388 (right), 399; Francois Dischinger: 57, 167, 333; Miki Duisterhof: 142, 224, 229, 238, 341, 386, 387; Jim Franco: 137, 157, 165; Matthew Hranek: 26 (left), 33, 95, 371; Grace Huang: 78 (right), 366; David Loftus: 5 (top left), 10 (right), 20, 25, 30, 56, 63, 91, 132, 134, 215, 273, 358 (right), 361, 370; Maura McEvoy: back cover—top left, 26 (right), 35, 48, 62, 65, 81 (right), 87, 93, 102 (left and right), 108, 111, 115, 117 (bottom), 118, 124, 135, 144, 181, 214, 221 (top), 235, 276, 280, 302, 308, 329 (left), 332, 337, 348; James Merrill: 38, 83, 365; Minh & Wass: 272, 297 (right), 311, 328 (left), 347, 376; Amy Neunsinger: back cover—bottom right, 6, 8, 21 (bottom), 44 (right), 47, 175, 208, 212 (left), 226, 239, 349, 394 (left); Daniel Proctor: 146, 357; Maria Robledo: 317 (right), 318, 342, 389 (right), 390 (bottom), 391; Kieran Scott: 16 (top), 125, 220, 296 (left), 313; Zubin Shroff: 13, 172, 212 (right), 225, 248 (left), 257, 269 (right), 290 (right), 294, 306, 393; Evan Sklar: 16 (bottom), 46 (left), 80 (right), 84, 85, 209, 223, 317 (left), 324, 325, 383, 388 (left), 397; Martyn Thompson: 173, 266; Petrina Tinslay: 46 (right), 45 (left), 54, 59, 61, 64 (left), 73, 82, 120, 130, 145, 213 (right), 221 (bottom), 231, 249 (right), 269 (left), 293, 359 (left), 368, 372 (left), 375, 381 (right); Luca Trovato: 45 (right), 58, 78 (right), 106 (right), 140 (bottom), 259, 359 (right), 364; Simon Watson: 14, 23, 60, 203, 248 (right), 263 (left and right), 264, 283, 301, 319, 363, 389 (left), 394 (right), 395, 396, 398; Jonelle Weaver: 2, 10 (left), 11 (left), 15, 18, 21 (top), 22, 32, 37, 103 (left), 113, 114, 116, 161 (left), 180, 198, 268 (right), 274; Anna Williams: 11 (right), 17, 27 (left), 34, 36, 81 (left), 89, 109, 128 (right), 149, 162 (left), 187, 193, 219, 286, 296 (right), 297 (left), 303, 312, 329 (right), 331, 372 (right), 381 (left).

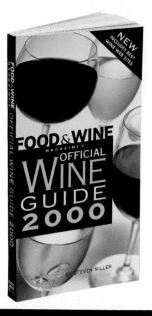